The Handbook of Industrial Innovation

The Handbook of
Industrial Innovation

Edited by

Mark Dodgson
Professor and Director
Managing Business in Asia Program
Australian National University

and

Roy Rothwell
Professor at the Science Policy Research Unit
University of Sussex

Edward Elgar
Cheltenham, UK • Brookfield, US

Published by
Edward Elgar Publishing Limited
8 Lansdown Place
Cheltenham
Glos GL50 2HU
UK

Edward Elgar Publishing Company
Old Post House
Brookfield
Vermont 05036
US

Reprinted 1996
Paperback edition 1996

British Library Cataloguing in Publication Data

The Handbook of Industrial Innovation
I. Dodgson, Mark II. Rothwell, Roy
338.064

Library of Congress Cataloguing in Publication Data

The handbook of industrial innovation / edited by Mark Dodgson and Roy Rothwell.
       p. cm.
    Includes index.
    1. Technological innovations–Handbooks, manuals, etc.
I. Dodgson, Mark, 1957-   . II. Rothwell, Roy.
HC79.T4H353 1994
658.5'14–dc20   94-16371
                                                          CIP

ISBN 1 85278 655 8 (cased)
ISBN 1 85898 445 9 (paperback)

Printed and bound in Great Britain by Hartnolls Ltd., Bodmin, Cornwall

Contents

PART 3: KEY ISSUES AFFECTING INNOVATION

PART 4: THE STRATEGIC MANAGEMENT OF INNOVATION

PART 5: FUTURE CHALLENGES OF INNOVATION IN A GLOBAL
          PERSPECTIVE

Contributors

John Bessant originally trained as a chemical engineer and received his PhD in 1978 based on research on innovation management within the chemical industry. Following this he spent four years as a Research Fellow in the Technology Policy Unit at Aston University before moving to the University of Brighton. In 1988 he was appointed Professor of Technology Management and he is currently Head of the Centre for Research in Innovation Management. His research and consultancy activities centre on issues in the adoption and implementation of advanced manufacturing technology (AMT) and this work has included extensive policy analysis and evaluation of UK programmes. Research sponsors include the UK Department of Trade and Industry, the EC, the United Nations, the World Bank, the OECD and the International Labour Office. Consultancy clients include Glaxo, Mölnlycke, Pilkington, Ericsson, Blue Circle, Shell and BP. He is author of six books and over forty articles on the theme of managing technology, the latest published in 1991 (*Managing Advanced Manufacturing Technology: the Challenge of the Fifth Wave*, NCC-Blackwell, Oxford). In addition he has written for various trade and technical journals and for a number of broadcast media, and has lectured widely in the UK and overseas. At the university he is responsible for a joint MSc programme with the University of Sussex in the 'Management of Technology', which operates in conjunction with a consortium of industrial sponsors including IBM, Philips, Ericsson, Cadbury-Schweppes, BAA, Coca Cola, Hewlett-Packard and ICI.

Bo Carlsson, a native of Sweden, obtained his BA in Economics from Harvard College in 1968 and his PhD in Economics from Stanford University in 1972. From 1972 to 1984 he was a research associate and for five years Deputy Director of the Industrial Institute for Economic and Social Research (IUI) in Stockholm. Since 1984 he has been the William E. Umstattd Professor of Industrial Economics at Case Western Reserve University in Cleveland, Ohio. From 1984 to 1987 he was also Chairman of the Department of Economics. He has had visiting appointments at the Massachusetts Institute of Technology, the University of Paris and Chalmers University of Technology. He has published several books and numerous articles in industrial economics, long-term industrial development, energy economics, and industrial policy. His current research interests include flexibility and competitiveness in manufacturing industries, small business economics, and the nature and role of technological systems in industrial growth. Since 1987 he has been the director of the research project 'Sweden's Technological Systems and Future Development Potential', involving three leading research institutes in Sweden. He has served on several government commissions in Sweden and has been a consultant to the World Bank and to private industry. From 1984 to 1986 he was President of the European Association for Research in Industrial Economics.

Alan Cawson is Professor of Politics at the University of Sussex, and during 1993 Visiting Research Fellow at the Graduate School of Policy Science, Saitama, Japan. He has been researching the consumer electronics industry since 1985, and directed a major ESRC-funded project on government-industry relations which was published by the Clarendon Press in 1990 as *Hostile Brothers: Competition and Closure in the European Electronics Industry.* He is at present researching a book on the innovation process in high definition television, comparing developments in Europe, Japan and the United States.

Philip Cooke is Professor of Regional Development and Director of the Centre for Advanced Studies in the Social Sciences at the University of Wales, Cardiff. His primary research interests are regional innovation studies, institutional networks, and the management of technopoles. His most recent research project was the ESRC-funded study 'Regional Innovation in Europe' (with Kevin Morgan), an in-depth comparative analysis of the innovation systems of Baden-Württemberg and Wales. In 1992 he published *Towards Global Localisation* (UCL Press, 1992), a comparative study of the computing and telecommunications industries in France and the UK conducted jointly with researchers from IFRESI in Lille. Other books include *Back to the Future* (Unwin Hyman, 1990), *Localities* (Unwin Hyman, 1989) and *Theories of Planning and Spatial Development* (Hutchinson, 1983).

Rod Coombs graduated in physics and worked for two years in a biophysics research laboratory before obtaining his PhD in the Economics of Technical Change. He has researched extensively in the areas of technology management, long waves, strategic use of information technology and R&D management. He is currently Professor of Technology Management at the Manchester School of Management in the University of Manchester Institute of Science and Technology (UMIST), where he is Director of CROMTEC (Centre for Research on Organisations, Management and Technical Change) and involved in the teaching of strategic management of technology. He also works on these issues with a group of senior R&D managers through the Technology Strategy Forum, a club founded by CROMTEC.

Mark Dodgson is Professor of Management at the Australian National University. Previously at the Technical Change Centre, London, and the Science Policy Research Unit at the University of Sussex, his research and teaching activities cover broad areas of technology strategy, policy and transfer. The author of numerous books and articles, his recent research has concentrated on technological collaboration and the question of how organizations learn about technology and innovation. He has a continuing research interest in the role of small and medium-sized firms in innovation, and the particular problems and opportunities they face in the management of technology. At the ANU, he is involved in starting the world's first MBA focusing entirely on 'Managing Business in Asia'. His research and teaching currently focus on the approaches to corporate strategy and to technology and innovation management by firms throughout Asia. He lectures at universities and business schools throughout Asia, Europe and Latin America, and has acted as a consultant to numerous firms and government departments in Europe and Asia.

Gerard Fairtlough studied natural sciences at the University of Cambridge and in 1953 joined the Royal Dutch/Shell Group of companies, where he worked for twenty-five years. His final position, which he held for five years, was as Managing Director of Shell Chemicals UK Ltd. In 1978 he joined the newly formed National Enterprise Board (NEB) as a divisional director. During his period with the NEB he, with others, developed the ideas which led to the creation in 1980 of the biotechnology company Celltech, and became its Chief Executive. He continued in this post until his retirement in 1990. From 1984 to 1992 he was Chairman of the Coverdale Organisation plc, a management consultancy in the behavioural field. He has also been a council member of the UK's Science and Engineering Research Council and a Visiting Fellow at the Open University. He is now Chairman of Therexsys Limited, a director of Cantab Pharmaceuticals plc, a member of the Global Business Network, based in Emeryville, California, which works in the field of corporate strategy, a member of the Advisory Panel of the Science Policy Research Unit and a specialist advisor to the House of Commons Select Committee on Science and Technology.

Martin Fransman is Director of the Institute for Japanese–European Technology Studies and Reader in the Department of Economics, University of Edinburgh. In 1992 he was NTT Visiting Professor in the Research Center for Advanced Science and Technology, University of Tokyo. His work on Japan includes *The Market and Beyond* (Cambridge University Press, 1990), which won the Masayoshi Ohira Memorial Prize in 1991. His current research is on the theory of the firm and innovation, on advanced technical and organizational change in Japanese and Western companies, and on the Japanese Innovation System.

Chris Freeman was born in 1921 and educated at the London School of Economics. After service in the Manchester Regiment he graduated and worked in market research before starting as a researcher at the National Institute of Economic and Social Research (NIESR) in the 1950s. At the NIESR he began to work on the economics of technical change, on the measurement of the inputs and output of the R&D systems, and on a series of studies on technical innovation in industry in various countries in synthetic materials, electronic capital goods and chemical process plant. In 1965 he moved to the University of Sussex to start the Science Policy Research Unit (SPRU). He retired as Director in 1981 and since then has continued to work part-time in SPRU and for the Maastricht Economic Research Institute on Innovation and Technology (MERIT) at the University of Limburg in the Netherlands. Research work has included participation in projects for the OECD on technical change and economic performance, leading to such recent publications as *Technology and the Wealth of Nations* and *The Economics of Hope*.

David M. Gann has a degree in Building Construction and Management and a masters degree in Science, Technology and Industrialisation with a doctorate in Science and Technology Policy. He is Research Fellow at the Science Policy Research Unit, University of Sussex, where he has been researching the innovation process in the production of the built environment for a number of years. His recent research includes a study of the conversion of unused offices into flats, and the development of intelligent building technologies in Europe, the US and Japan. Research projects include work on technical change and efficiency in the production of the built environment, and new technology and future housing demand. He was Academic Adviser on DTI Expert Missions to Japan in 1992 and 1993 to assess the development of new technology in construction. He is also a Director of IPRA Ltd (Innovation Policy Research Associates), a consultancy practice providing strategic advice on technological and organisational change, skills and training in the construction and engineering industries. IPRA has recently carried out studies of construction R&D and innovation for the Department of the Environment and for the Construction Industry Council.

Ove Granstrand was appointed Professor of Industrial Management and Economics at Chalmers University of Technology, Göteborg, Sweden, in 1986. In addition to degrees in business economics, mathematics, engineering and operations research, he obtained his PhD in Industrial Management and Economics in 1979. His research interests include technology strategies, internationalization and diversification of technology, intellectual property matters, innovation research, multi-technology corporations, Japanese technology management, technology policy and the history of technology. He is the author of *Technology, Management and Markets* (Pinter, 1982), co-editor of *Technology Management and International Business: Internationalization of R&D and Technology* (John Wiley and Sons, 1992), co-editor of *The Race to European Eminence* (Elsevier, 1994) and editor of *Economics of Technology* (Elsevier, 1994). He has also published widely in various journals.

Andrew Graves is the MIT Professor of Automotive Management and European Director of the Massachusetts Institute of Technology International Motor Vehicle Programme (IMVP) at the School of Management, University of Bath. He was previously a development engineer and team manager in international motor racing. His current research focuses on R&D and technology issues affecting the automobile industry, such as new forms of lean manufacturing organization, the use of human resources, best practice in manufacturing and relationships with component suppliers. He has contributed to a number of books and journals on the IMVP, which aims to bring together experts from all the relevant technical specialities and countries into a single research team. He was formerly at the Science Policy Research Unit, University of Sussex.

Mike Hobday is a Senior Fellow at the Science Policy Research Unit (SPRU), the University of Sussex. He is an economist with extensive industrial experience, having worked for the US corporation, Texas Instruments, for ten years. His DPhil (later a book) concerned the Brazilian telecommunications industry. Since joining SPRU in 1984 he has conducted research on the evaluation of government information technology programmes and the global semiconductor and telecommunications industries. His current research (funded by the Economic and Social Research Council) is concerned with how East Asia (especially South Korea, Taiwan, Singapore and Hong Kong) caught up technologically to become international competitors in electronics. He has acted as consultant to the Brazilian and Venezuelan governments, the House of Commons, the EC, DTI, OECD, UNIDO, NEDO and UNCTAD and several other organizations.

Don Lamberton is Visiting Fellow, Research School of Social Sciences, Australian National University. He was formerly Professor of Economics at the University of Queensland (1972–89) and Case Western Reserve University (1969–72). He is general editor of *Prometheus*, co-editor of *Information Economics and Policy* and a member of the editorial boards of *Telecommunications Policy, Human Systems Management, Economics of Innovation and New Technology, Intelligent Environments* and *Futures Research Quarterly*. His books (authored, edited, co-authored or co-edited) include *The Theory of Profit* (Blackwell, 1965), *Science Technology and* *the Australian Economy* (Tudor Press, 1972), *Economics of Information and Knowledge* (Penguin, 1971), *The Information Revolution* (American Academy of Political and Social Science, 1974), *Economic Effects of the Australian Patent System* (Australian Government Publishing Service, 1982), *Communication Economics and Development* (Pergamon, 1982), *The Trouble with Technology* (Pinter, 1983), *New Office Technology* (Australian Government Publishing Service, 1985) and *The Cost of Thinking* (Ablex, 1988).

F. Lissoni graduated at Bocconi University, Milan, in 1990 with a thesis on the diffusion of innovation in the printing industry. He is now a PhD student at the University of Manchester and a research assistant at the Centre for the Study of Internationalization Processes (CESPRI), Bocconi University. His main interests are in the fields of industrial organization and the economics of technical change. Current research work deals with innovation creation and diffusion, and applications to regional perspectives. His most recent publications include studies on technological policies and performance in the UK and the West Midlands in the 1980s (in *Sistemi Innovativi Regionali a Confronto* edited by Franco Malerba in 1993).

Dale Littler graduated from the University of Manchester and undertook research at the Manchester Business School on various facets of technological innovation. He later moved to Liverpool University Business School as a Lecturer in Marketing before moving to UMIST, where he is Professor of Marketing at the Manchester School of Management. His current research interests focus on strategic marketing, the use and marketing of IT products and consumer purchasing of technologically innovative products. He has written extensively and published several books, including *Marketing and Product Development* and *Technological Development*.

Gordon MacKerron is a Senior Fellow in the Energy Policy Programme, Science Policy Research Unit at the University of Sussex. He is an economist and has specialized for over a decade in the economic and policy issues in the electricity sector, with a particular concentration on nuclear power questions. His recent work in this area has included invited evidence to the House of Commons Select Committee on the costs of nuclear power in Britain, and assessment of nuclear decommissioning policies in Britain and Europe. In addition to producing a wide range of academic and other publications, he has made frequent radio and TV appearances, and has advised numerous institutions in the energy field. These include the National Audit Office, the European Court of Auditors, DG XVII (Energy) of the European Commission, the European Parliament (through its

Scientific and Technological Options Assessment initiative) and the Office of Electricity Regulation. He was Specialist Adviser to the House of Commons Trade and Industry Select Committee in its inquiry into the proposed coal-pit closures and the future of energy policy in 1992–93.

Robin Mansell is Reader in Communication and Information Technology Policy, and Head of the Centre for Information and Communication Technologies, Science Policy Research Unit (SPRU) at the University of Sussex. She has degrees in Social Psychology (BA Manitoba 1974, MSc London 1976) and in Communication Policy (MA 1980, PhD 1984 Simon Fraser, Canada). Before joining SPRU in 1988, she was with the OECD Information, Computers and Communication Policy Division in Paris. She has worked as an academic and consultant in Canada, the US and Europe on issues of international communication policy and regulation. She is the author of many scholarly articles and reports on issues of technical and institutional change in the field, including *The New Telecommunications: A Political Economy of Network Evolution*, Sage, 1993.

Jane Marceau is Professor of Public Policy at the Australian National University in Canberra. She has taught at the Universities of Essex and Paris X (Nanterre) as well as INSEAD and the Manchester Business School. When living in Paris in the 1970s she worked with the research group on education and society headed by Professor Pierre Bourdieu. From 1978 to 1980 as a Project Officer at the OECD she ran a multi-country project on education and local development. A sociologist long interested in business élites, in more recent years she has worked on the organization of small industrial enterprises which she has studied in both Australia and France, and has developed an interest in technological change, industrial policy and economic development. She has published numerous books and papers in different fields over the last decades and recently edited, and was a major contributor to, *Reworking the World: Organisations, Technologies and Cultures in Comparative Perspective* (de Gruyter, 1992). She is currently working with a group of Europeans on the 'complexes' approach to industrial policy for small industrial countries, a project which will culminate in a book to be published by Routledge in 1995.

Roderick Martin has been Professor of Organizational Behaviour and Director of the Glasgow University Business School since 1992. Prior to that he held posts at Oxford and Imperial College, London, where from 1984 to 1988 he was Professor of Industrial Sociology and Director of the Industrial Sociology Unit. He has published several books and papers on industrial relations and new technology, including *New Technology and Industrial Relations in Fleet Street* (Oxford University Press, 1981). His most recent book is *Bargaining Power* (Oxford University Press, 1992). His current research includes the comparative study of the organization of R&D in the UK and Bulgaria, focusing on mechanical engineering and the food, drink and tobacco industries. He has been involved in management education in Eastern Europe since 1988, mainly in Bulgaria; has lectured and presented conference papers to both academic and non-academic audiences in many parts of the world on issues related to research management, and has taught widely, mainly at graduate and post-experience level.

J. S. Metcalfe has been Professor of Economics at the University of Manchester since 1980 and is currently Dean of the Faculty of Economic and Social Studies, having previously held a senior lectureship at the University of Liverpool. He is a Director of Policy Research in Engineering Science and Technology (PREST), a research group at the University of Manchester, advising on questions of science and technology policy and strategy in Whitehall, Brussels and British industry. Between 1985 and 1987 he was a member of the Advisory Council on Applied Research and Development, and between 1987 and 1989 he was a member of the Advisory Council on Science and Technology (ACOST). In 1993 he was reappointed to ACOST. He is President of the Manchester Statistical Society and has published a number of books and articles on various economic topics, in particular on the subjects of innovation and the management of technology. He is a frequent adviser to the Department of Trade and Industry and in 1991 was appointed a member of the Monopolies and Mergers Commission. He has held a number of visiting appointments in overseas universities, most recently during 1992 when he held a three months visiting fellowship at the International Centre for Economic Research, Turin, Italy.

Ian Miles is an Associate Director of PREST (Programme of Policy Research on Engineering, Science and Technology) at the University of Manchester, where he has been since January 1991. He obtained a BSc in Psychology and was a researcher at SPRU (Science Policy Research Unit), University of Sussex from 1972 till 1990. He has published many papers and several books, including *The Poverty of Prediction* (Saxon House, 1975); *Social Indicators for Human Development* (Pinter, 1985); *Home Informatics* (Pinter, 1988); *Mapping and Measuring the Information Economy* (British Library, 1990); and with J I Gershuny, *The New Service Economy* (Pinter, 1983); with S Cole, *Worlds Apart* (Harvester Press, 1984); with H Rush, K Turner and J Bessant, *Information Horizons* (Edward Elgar, 1988); with G Thomas, *Telematics in Transition* (Longmans, 1989); with J C Ferraz and H J Rush, *Development, Technology and Flexibility* (Routledge, 1992).

Kevin Morgan is Professor in the Department of City and Regional Planning, University of Wales, Cardiff. His main research interests are in the fields of technological innovation and regional development. He is currently completing a research project on new models of corporate and regional development in Europe. In addition to other writings he is the co-author of *Microcircuits of Capital: Sunrise Industry and Uneven Development* (Polity Press, 1988).

Keith Pavitt is Professor of Science and Technology Policy at the University of Sussex. He studied engineering, industrial management and economics at Cambridge and Harvard, and then worked at the Organization for Economic Cooperation and Development (OECD) in Paris. During his twenty years at the Science Policy Research Unit he has published widely on the management of technology, and science and technology policy. His central research interests are the nature and measurement of technology, and the reasons why countries, companies and sectors differ in their rates and directions of technical change. He advises numerous national and international bodies on policies for technical change. He has been a Visiting Lecturer at Princeton University, Visiting Professor at the Universities of Strasbourg (Louis Pasteur), Padua, Nice and Paris-Dauphine, and Visiting Scholar at Stanford University. He is a main editor of *Research Policy*.

Roy Rothwell, one of SPRU's six professors, has been leading research in the area of management of technology and has been Director of the Unit's MSc Programme in Technology and Innovation Management. He has been a member of the Department of Trade and Industry's Technology Transfer Services Advisory Committee and a Specialist Adviser to the House of Lords Select Committee on Science and Technology, and is currently a Visiting Professor at the Design Centre, Bilbão; Scuola Superiore Santa Ana, Pisa; University of Girona; and the European Institute for Technology Management, Florence. He has acted as Expert Consultant to the OECD in the areas of venture capital, regulatory impacts on industry and regional development policies; to UNCTAD in the areas of innovation policy evaluation and comparative national innovation policies; and to the European Commission on regional technology infrastructures, growth problems of high technology SMEs and early stage innovation support services for small firms. He is an Assessor for the Portuguese and Irish STRIDE Programmes (European Commission); and is an OECD Referee for Portugal's Science and Technology Policy. Co-author of five books and co-editor of three, he has also published over two hundred assorted articles and has spoken at conferences throughout Europe and Scandinavia and in the US, Canada, Venezuela, Bulgaria and China. He is on the editorial boards of four academic journals and is an Associate Editor of the *British Journal of Management*.

Mari Sako graduated in Philosophy, Politics and Economics from the University of Oxford, subsequently training in economics at the London School of Economics (LSE) and the John Hopkins University, USA. She worked as a research associate at the Technical Change Centre and at the Centre for Japanese and Comparative Industrial Research, Imperial College, London, before joining the Industrial Relations Department at the LSE in 1987. Research interests and areas of expertise include inter-firm relations, vocational education and training, and industrial relations. She is the author of *Prices, Quality and Trust: Inter-firm Relations in Britain and Japan* (Cambridge University Press, 1992), and *How the Japanese Learn to Work* (with Ronald P Dore) (Routledge, 1989).

Margaret Sharp is a Senior Fellow at the Science Policy Research Unit (SPRU), University of Sussex, and Associate Director of the ESRC-funded Centre for Science, Technology, Energy and Environmental Policy at the Unit. An economist by training, she worked in the Civil Service and at the London School of Economics before going to Sussex in 1981. She has written extensively on industrial policies and new technologies and co-edited the SPRU twenty-fifth anniversary volume *Technology and the Future of Europe* (Pinter 1991). Her interest in the chemical industry has grown from her work in biotechnology, and her current research focuses on the impact of biotechnology on the strategy and organization of Europe's large chemical and pharmaceutical companies.

Brian Shaw graduated from the London School of Economics and Political Science in 1960 with a BSc Honours degree. He then joined the Union Discount Company, the largest 'bill brokers' in the City, as a trainee 'bill broker'. The chance to join a small manufacturing business was then taken up and he joined Walter Coles and Co as the general manager. In 1964 he qualified as an Associate of the Chartered Secretaries and Administrators (ACIS) and became the Company Secretary and a Director of Walter Coles and Co. In 1969 he joined the Polytechnic of Central London (PCL) Management School (now the University of Westminster) to teach economics and marketing. In 1975 he gained his MSc (Administrative Science) from City University and in 1976 the Harvard International Teacher's Diploma from the London Business School. In 1983 PCL set up the MBA and he taught Business Policy, Corporate Strategy and Management of Innovation and directed this programme for five years until he joined Oxford Polytechnic (now Oxford Brookes University) as Reader in Business in 1988. Meanwhile he gained his DPhil from the Science Policy Research Unit at the University of Sussex in 1986. In 1989 he led the design team for the MBA that was set up at Oxford Brookes University. He was a member of the CNAA Register of Specialist Advisers in Business Management. Since 1986 he has presented many papers at international conferences and published journal articles and book chapters on the management of innovation.

Sören Sjölander is Professor of Innovation Engineering and Management at Chalmers University of Technology and heads the Department of Innovation Engineering and Management and its Innovation Centre, the Chalmers organization for innovation and entrepreneurship of firms. He is the founding Executive Director of Champs (Chalmers Advanced Management Programmes), an executive development organization running development programmes for industrial executives in Europe, Asia and the US. He obtained his PhD in Industrial Management and Economics from Chalmers in 1985 and holds an MSc in Mechanical Engineering from the same school. His research interests include innovation and entrepreneurship in small technology-based firms, technology management and business strategy as well as innovation policy. He has published a number of books and articles on these subjects.

Jim Skea is Professorial Fellow and Leader of the Programme on Environmental Policy and Regulation at the Science Policy Research Unit at the University of Sussex. He was previously a Visiting Assistant Professor at the Department of Engineering and Public Policy, Carnegie-Mellon University, Pittsburgh. His main research interests are energy and environmental issues and the interactions between environmental regulation and technical change more generally. He has taken a particular interest in the development of the acid rain issue in Europe and has co-authored a book on the subject, *Acid Politics* (Belhaven Press). More recently he has been involved in the climate change issue. One of his current projects, with support from the European Commission, examines the development of the Community's proposed carbon/energy tax. He is a convening lead author for the second assessment of the Intergovernmental Panel on Climate Change and has recently carried out work for the OECD on the communication and monitoring of national plans under the Framework Convention on Climate Change.

Edward Steinmueller is Professor of Economics of Technical Change at the Maastricht Economic Research Institute on Innovation and Technology (MERIT) and the Faculty of Economics, University of Limburg, The Netherlands. His professional areas of study are the economics of technological change and industrial organization. His published work examines the formation of markets, management of R&D, development of inter-firm agreements, and international competition in the electronics industry. His research examines issues of pricing, adoption of new products, cost reduction through learning, science and technology policy, and international competition. He is currently examining factors affecting the generation and use of information products and services, including the use of new information technology technologies as well as international differences in capital formation, research organization, and product strategy in the electronics industry. He has been active in policy advisory roles to agencies of the US government (including the General Accounting Office, the Office of Technology Assessment and the Congressional Budget Office). He is also an economics consultant in the fields of antitrust and intellectual property, a member of the American Economics Association, and a managing editor of the new journal *Economics of Innovation and New Technology*.

Andrew Tylecote studied Philosophy, Politics and Economics (and sociology) at Oxford and went on to postgraduate work in economics at Sussex and Oxford. He has been Visiting Fellow at the Science Policy Research Unit at the University of Sussex, and at the Industrial Relations Research Unit at the University of Warwick, as well as Hallsworth Fellow at the University of Manchester. He is now Senior Lecturer in Strategic and Technology Management at the University of Sheffield Management School where he is a Director of its Centre for Research on Innovation and Technological Change (CRITEC). He is Treasurer of the European Association for Evolutionary Political Economy. He is the author of *The Causes of the Present Inflation* (Macmillan, 1981), and *The Long Wave in the World Economy: The Present Crisis in Historical Perspective* (Routledge, 1992) and has published articles on labour economics, economic history, growth and development economics, and the economics and management of innovation. Having recently finished a major SERC-funded study of performance pressures and innovation in British manufacturing, he is working with various collaborators in Europe and Japan to make it international. He is currently working on a book for Routledge on short-termism and innovation.

C. A. Voss is BT Professor of Total Quality Management at the London Business School. He was formerly Professor of Manufacturing Strategy at the University of Warwick and worked in production in the steel industry. He has a BSc (Eng) from Imperial College and an MSc and PhD in Business from the London Business School. He has researched and taught for many years in the field of manufacturing strategy, service and quality management, technology management and Japanese manufacturing methods. His recent work has included manufacturing strategy, total quality management, the application of service quality in manufacturing, technology implementation and concurrent engineering. His books include *Just-in-Time Manufacturing, Managing Advanced Manufacturing Technology* and *Operations Management in Service Industries and the*

Public Sector. He is chairman of the European Operations Management Association, and acts as an adviser to many companies.

William Walker is Senior Fellow and Director of Research in SPRU. He has written widely on military industries and on the control of military technology, particularly in the nuclear field. In 1993 he co-authored (with Philip Gummett) *Nationalism, Internationalism and the European Defence Market* and (with David Albright and Frans Berkhout) *World Inventory of Plutonium and Highly Enriched Uranium,* the former published by the Western European Union's Institute of Security Studies, the latter by Oxford University Press on behalf of the Stockholm International Peace Research Institute (SIPRI). Since 1989 he has been the leader of a substantial project on Europe's and Japan's plutonium policies.

Malcolm Warner is Professor and Fellow of Wolfson College, Cambridge, and faculty member of the Judge Institute of Management Studies, University of Cambridge. He has written extensively on new technology and training. His most recent book (1992) is (with Adrian Campbell) *New Technology, Skills and Management,* Routledge, London.

Thomas G. Whiston is a Senior Fellow and Director of Studies of the MSc in Technology and Innovation Management at the Science Policy Research Unit, University of Sussex. His main areas of research relate to global forecasting and related policy analysis, higher education policy, and the influence of technical change upon organizational structures. He has published several texts and approximately 150 articles, policy studies and monographs related to these areas. He has been a senior consultant to most UK research councils and several international agencies, such as SERC, ESRC, AFRC, SPSG, UNESCO, IIEP and OECD. During 1992/93 he was co-leader of a large EC programme entitled 'Global Perspective 2010: Tasks for Science and Technology', a programme involving about forty international researchers. The results have been published in twenty-three volumes.

Preface

Industrial innovation profoundly affects us all. It provides the basis for national wealth, corporate profitability and a focus for human creativity and endeavour. It enhances the quality of our lives through improved health, communications and living environment, and can liberate us from monotonous and dangerous work. At the same time, industrial innovation has given us machines of mass destruction, numerous ecological disasters, and the means for accentuating already broad international differences in economic development. Understanding the nature, determinants and consequences of industrial innovation is therefore crucial for our understanding of the world.

We are assisted in the task of studying industrial innovation by the rapidly growing body of research into it. Scholars from a number of disciplines have increasingly taken industrial innovation, in its many guises, as the focus of their studies. This book brings together a very wide range of theoretical and empirical insights from these studies. The approach we took was to select what we saw as the major issues of industrial innovation and to invite leading academics in the field to write about what they believed to be the most important theoretical considerations, and empirical and practical findings.

The range of analyses presented reflects the huge variety in the circumstances in which innovation occurs, the processes that make it manifest, and its economic and social outcomes. The studies reveal how understanding the complexity of industrial innovation requires insights from a variety of perspectives, and consideration at the level of the economy, the sector, the region, the technology and the firm. By pulling together in one volume diverse and interdisciplinary bodies of research, the aim is to provide a source-book for all students of industrial innovation.

Rather than including a limited number of long chapters we chose to cover more ground by asking for many short pieces encompassing more issues. This put a lot of pressure on our contributors who were asked to discuss large bodies of literature, much of which they had authored, in 3000 to 4000 words. They responded admirably. In addition to the concise syntheses provided, we also present chapters which introduce valuable new empirical information and conceptual thinking. Authors were encouraged to submit select bibliographies on what they consider to be the key texts on the subject. This will provide an invaluable guide to further reading.

It is obviously impossible to cover the entire huge range of industrial innovation in one volume. We have been selective, and others might have made different choices. Based on our experiences of researching and teaching industrial innovation, we believe that the issues we have chosen are all centrally relevant to students of this increasingly important subject.

The book is structured as follows:

Part 1: The Nature, Sources and Outcomes of Industrial Innovation

The aims of this section are to introduce a number of ways of conceptualizing industrial innovation, to outline some of the key factors affecting its realization, and to analyze its outcomes for economic growth. The first three chapters provide a number of different levels of analysis of the form and process of innovation, all of which emphasize the interrelated or systemic nature of innovation. Marceau describes, from a broad conceptual perspective, a number of 'analytical lenses' on innovation at a macro level, including 'chains', 'clusters' and 'complexes'. Carlsson analyzes what he calls 'technology systems', delineating the major characteristics of the interrelated system of innovation in a number of different technologies. Cooke and Morgan provide a regional perspective on innovation and argue the spatial significance of 'the creative milieu'. Rothwell's chapter focuses on innovation at the level of the firm, describing strategies and success and failure factors in innovation and the movement towards what he calls the 'Fifth Generation Innovation Process'.

The following two chapters introduce some issues around the multiplicity of sources of innovation, something which is examined in greater detail in later sections. Steinmueller analyzes the important role that science plays in industrial innovation. Fransman then describes the Japanese system of innovation, one denoted not only by its success, but also by its past comparative lack of scientific efforts. He emphasizes the importance of processes, institutions and forms of organization in Japan.

The outcomes of industrial innovation are analyzed by Freeman in his historical theoretical review and analysis of the relationship between innovation and growth at the level of the firm and the economy. The way in which industrial policies supporting innovation can actively encourage economic development is described by Hobday in his chapter on the 'East Asian Tigers', the area of the world presently enjoying the most vigorous economic growth. This section concludes with a review from an economist's perspective, by Lissoni and Metcalfe, of the centrally important question of the diffusion of technology.

Part 2: Sectoral and Industrial Studies of Innovation

This section of the book analyzes innovation in a variety of industries and technologies, and highlights the considerable differences between them.

Cawson analyzes innovation in consumer electronics and examines the importance of standards and the integration of different technologies and firms through strategic alliances. Hobday critically examines the popular 'Silicon Valley' model of innovation in semiconductors. Sharp describes innovation in the much more heterogeneous and more mature chemical and pharmaceutical industry. MacKerron examines innovation in the energy sector with a particular focus on electricity generation. Walker discusses military technology, its impact, proliferation and regulation. Gann analyzes innovation in construction, a traditional but important and innovative industry. Graves discusses the major issues of innovation confronting the automobile industry. Mansell looks at innovation facilitated by new telecommunications technologies, and Miles examines the broad issues of innovation in services.

The chapters presented in this section highlight diversity in the sources of innovation: differences in, for example, the role of basic science, government procurement, the inputs of suppliers and users, the importance of technological collaboration and the significance of small firms. They also clearly reveal the integrated nature of innovation, showing the interdependence of numerous actors in the innovation process.

Part 3: Key Issues Affecting Innovation

In this section some of the major issues influencing innovation are examined. Tylecote analyzes the impact of different financial systems on industrial innovation, separating what he calls 'bank-based' and 'stock exchange-based' systems. The following three chapters develop a key aspect of innovation – inter-firm relationships – discussed in sectoral studies. Sako discusses the importance of the nature of supplier relationships, and the question of 'trust' between them in encouraging innovation. Shaw describes the significance of close links between the suppliers and users of innovation, and Dodgson examines the role of collaboration between firms in the development of technology. Littler then considers the role of marketing in shaping innovation. Lamberton analyzes the relationship between innovation and intellectual property rights. Rothwell and Dodgson consider the role of small and medium-sized firms in industrial innovation. The last three chapters in this section consider the major organizational and personnel issues affecting innovation within the firm. Fairtlough analyzes the crucial question of organization for innovation. Martin discusses the relationship between industrial relations and innovation, and Warner describes the importance of training.

Part 4: The Strategic Management of Innovation

One of the major constraints to successful product and process innovation is its strategic management. This section examines the issues in a variety of ways. Pavitt considers the key characteristics of the innovative firm. Granstrand and Sjölander look at some of the major issues of technology transfer within firms, and corporate integration. Coombs examines the changing strategies that firms have adopted to their R&D functions. Bessant examines manufacturing strategies, and Voss examines the implementation of manufacturing innovations. These contributions combine to provide a broad review of the major strategic challenges facing companies in industrial innovation, and valuable insights into how successful companies have overcome them.

Part 5: Future Challenges of Innovation in a Global Perspective

The problems and challenges of the processes and management of innovation are discussed throughout the book. The adverse consequences of innovation are also discussed, particularly in the chapters on military technology and energy. This section concludes the book with two chapters highlighting the problems and responsibilities of industrial innovation. Skea examines the relationship between innovation and the environment, and Whiston considers innovation into the 21st century. Both of these provide a sobering view of the extensive challenges remaining for industrial innovation.

We would like to record our thanks to all the contributors to the book, and to Chris Freeman and Edward Elgar for the idea of producing it. The book was written when both editors were at SPRU and particular thanks are extended to Lorraine Fowlie and Melna Charin in SPRU for their hard work, excellent production skills and much-tried patience. We are also very grateful to Lynn Frances whose freelance skills saw the book through to completion.

Mark Dodgson
Roy Rothwell

PART 1

The Nature, Sources and Outcomes of Industrial
Innovation

1. Clusters, Chains and Complexes: Three Approaches to Innovation with a Public Policy Perspective

Jane Marceau

Introduction

Models of economic growth and development are central to much analysis of economic activity. The last century has seen a number of such models elaborated by economists of diverse persuasions, from Schumpeter and the neo-Schumpeterians to the neo-classical approaches which dominated many western industrial policies in the 1980s and the 'new growth theorists'. Over the last two decades in particular a focus on the critical role played by innovation in all aspects of the productive process has emerged. Analyses which give innovation a central place in successful competition by firms, industries and nations also give greater room to a broader range of factors than do models of the neo-classical kind. These analyses include the organizational form of the productive entities concerned and pay attention to firm strategies, especially in the field of R&D, to government policies and public institutions, to research organizations and to the users of the goods and services produced in the economy (see, for example, Lundvall, 1992).

The new literature has come increasingly to examine not only intra-firm innovation processes but also inter-firm linkages and the structures of the public and private sector context within which innovation flourishes or can be persuaded to flourish. While the distinction between 'internal' (to the firm) and 'external' factors turns out to be largely artificial when seen from some perspectives (notably, for example, when considering the inter-firm collaboration which often occurs in the period of pre-competitive research), the 'boundaries' of the organizations and systems concerned and the links between them may need to be elucidated so that the efficacy of innovation models can be judged, and the potential of public policy encouragement to innovation assessed.

In trying to evaluate the innovative potential of a firm, an industry, a region or a nation and the public policies which may be appropriate to encourage it, no single perspective seems to be a sufficient guide. Rather a series of different analytical lenses gives a better overall picture. Each 'lens' both highlights particular characteristics of a given firm, group of firms or industry's activities and considers the particular relationships between local firms and institutions in what has come to be called a 'national system of innovation' (see, for example, Nelson, 1992; Lundvall, 1992). (See also Carlsson's 'technology systems' approach described in chapter 2). Each highlights the role of different players and different relationships, thus indicating a variety of possible 'ways in' for governments interested in promoting innovation.

This chapter presents three possible sets of lenses useful to describe and evaluate the innovation processes operating in a given country. These are based on the analysis of *clusters, chains of production* and *complexes.* Some variants of these approaches, such as that focusing on industrial districts, are also mentioned. Some of the approaches are economic in orientation and derive from the work of Schumpeter and the neo-Schumpeterians. Others take a more clearly sociological or political and organizational approach (e.g. Weiss, 1988; Kristensen, 1991). Some are attempts to learn from growth stimulants and patterns in the past (in particular this applies to the 'clusters' approach as it appears in the work of Michael Porter) and may also look at individual business strategy while others are rather analytical tools which seek to uncover relationships between actors and institutions which are usually not detected by more traditional approaches. This is particularly the case of the 'complexes' approach discussed last in this chapter. Together these views are essential complements to those provided by the analysis of the overarching 'business' recipes' developed in a country over time (Whitley, 1992). 'Business recipes' include financial, educational and public policy-making structures and are more or less amenable to public policy action and to those elicited by a focus on national systems of innovation.

Clusters

In recent years much more attention than previously has been paid by analysts of economic growth and development to the *clustering* of innovative activities so often apparent. This clustering, first recognized by Schumpeter, has been interpreted in different ways. Sometimes the focus is on the generation of groups of highly inter-related products where, for example, each develops from and/or contributes to the development of others. As Debresson (1989), for example, has pointed out in discussion of the Canadian snowmobile development, much of the dynamic effect of innovation may come through this clustering rather than through the intrinsic value of a single innovation.

The reasons for this clustering are in part technical and in part organizational. While admitting Schumpeter's recognition that innovation does not require invention but is essentially a new way of combining existing elements, Debresson concludes nonetheless that the opening up of new technological frontiers does affect the rate and directions of opportunities for innovation. Innovations in economic terms (involving exceptional profits), he believes, usually arise from the interaction of paradigmatic discontinuities in technology, from technical systems of complements and from cumulative learning processes. The cumulative nature of technical knowhow encourages economies of scope through the transferability of learning benefits which enable shareable inputs to new products, notably at plant level.

At an organizational level, the innovation process usually involves interaction between the user (innovator) and one or more suppliers (producers): this interaction involves transaction costs but these reduce dramatically with time and a longer-term productive relationship may produce further innovations, as the Japanese productive model has indicated, thus again increasing clustering. This clustering may cross industry lines and in some areas has been successfully fostered by government (Debresson gives the example of the French *Train Grande Vitesse*). This approach thus focuses attention on innovation through the development of inter-related products, each building on the others.

A broader analysis of clusters in the national innovation process is provided by Porter (1990). The question Porter wishes to answer is why only certain countries generate many companies which become successful international competitors in one or more industries.

The analytical lens used by Porter brings into focus the individual company and its place in the structure of a particular cluster of firms in the same industry. Competitive pressure and the associated continuous innovation provide the dynamic of the advantage which companies in this virtuous circle derive. In this analysis, then, it is companies, and the relationships of competition and collaboration between companies in a similar market segment, which are the key to the competitive advantage not just of one leading firm but also of all or most of the firms in the area. The unit of analysis is thus the industry, but Porter points out that most successful national industries comprise groups of firms, not isolated participants, and that most leading international competitors are in the same city or region.

Basing his analysis on ten cases in each of ten countries, Porter suggests that the competitive advantage of these continuously innovating firms in each area derives from their position within a national configuration of four sets of factors which he conceptualizes as a 'diamond'. At the core of explaining national advantage in an industry, he believes, must be the role of the home nation in stimulating competitive improvement and innovation. While firms which achieve economies of scale, technological leads and differentiated products achieve trade success, the ability to gain these advantages is not a cause but an effect: the real question is *which firms* from *which nations* will reap the benefits since only some do so and some nations excel more than others.

The answer to this question, Porter suggests, is a function of the four sets of conditions in the diamond. These are:

1. Factor conditions – the nation's position in factors of production such as skilled labour, capital stock, knowledge resources or infrastructure.
2. Demand conditions – the nature of *home* demand in particular for a product or service.
3. Related and supporting industries – the presence of suitable suppliers and related industries that are also internationally competitive.
4. Firm strategy, structure and rivalry – the conditions governing how companies are created, organized and managed and the nature (intensity) of domestic rivalry.

As a system these elements create the context for firms' birth and growth. According to Porter, nations ultimately succeed in particular industries because their home environment is the most dynamic and the most challenging, stimulating firms to upgrade and widen their advantages over time. Crucially, the different elements of the diamond constitute a mutually reinforcing system so that the effect of one determinant is contingent on the state of the others.

Porter's analysis focuses essentially on firms and their context but says little about two central elements of that environment. These are technological change, and particularly technological paradigm shifts, and the role of government. Major technological changes and what he calls 'pure inventions' are included in the 'chance' category which contains other elements such as war and major shifts in foreign demand. Government is said to have the role principally of influencing the four determinants through policies toward capital formation, education, standards creation and procurement.

When all the elements of the 'diamond' are functioning satisfactorily the outcome is not one but a cluster of successful firms operating within and between given industries. These firms are mutually supporting. As Porter says,

> Benefits flow forward, backward and horizontally. Aggressive rivalry in one industry tends to spread to others in the cluster, through the exercise of bargaining power, spin-offs and related diversification. Entry from other industries within the cluster spurs upgrading by stimulating diversity in R&D approaches... . Information flows freely and innovations diffuse rapidly through the conduits of suppliers or customers... . Interconnections within the cluster ... lead to new ways of competing and entirely new opportunities. (1990:151)

Porter's analysis only incidentally mentions the likely geographic propinquity of the successful clusters and says little about the size of the firm involved. This stands in sharp contrast to the notion of 'industrial district' first developed by Marshall (1920) and since much analysed by writers rediscovering the industrial districts of Italy, Germany, Japan and Denmark (see Morgan's chapter in this volume).

The analyses made of these industrial districts focus on similar elements of competition to those outlined by Porter. In particular, they emphasize skilled and flexible labour and the stimulation of constant competition from other suppliers to the same market acting as a spur to technological innovation. They also, however, emphasize more the importance of *collaboration* between firms rather than the *competition*, albeit balanced by linkages of different kinds, that is at the forefront of Porter's analysis. In both cases geographical propinquity is an important element of the system, this propinquity encouraging both information flows and collaboration and the innovation necessary to compete successfully with dynamic neighbouring firms. Firms in industrial districts are aided by government policies both at the infrastructural level (e.g. provision of excellent technical education in Denmark) and at the taxation level (special regimes for artisans and firms with specified number of workers, as in Italy). Together these factors have encouraged the growth of firms by subdivision and division on an amoeba-like basis rather than the growth of hierarchical ventures.

Chains

The images of pathways to successful innovation and growth provided by these analyses all focus on the notion of 'cluster' or groupings of firms in the same industry and produce images which are 'weblike'.

Another and contrasting image is that provided by analysis of a productive structure and its innovative capacity in terms of 'chains' of production. This view sees the economic structure as made up of chains of interlinked companies which cut across the traditional boundaries of primary, secondary and tertiary activities and link companies in each of these areas together through their contribution to the final product. Each chain appears as a kind of 'rib' where companies primarily link to those ahead and behind them in the productive process. This lens highlights the forward and backward linkages and can do so both for an industry and for a particular major product within it. This lens is perhaps most useful in the analysis of activity in the automotive or aerospace industries where the sector has several key core firms which assemble complex products and through them can 'lead' the development activities of the whole chain through the relationships they generate. Similarly, in such industries large supplier firms also lead segments of the chain.

The lead company does not have to be a manufacturer, however. Senker's

(1988) work on supermarkets in the UK and Greig's (1990 and 1992) work on the clothing sector in Australia indicate clearly that technological and organizational innovation can be pushed through the whole chain by major retailers who force their manufacturing suppliers to upgrade their quality and manufacturing methods.

Governments anxious to find the most effective points of entry to productive systems which they believe to be in need of such upgrading can use the chain of production analysis to find the weak points in the chain, to encourage the filling of gaps which are hindering the development of the whole chain or to put pressure on the lead firms to stimulate the desired changes further down the line. Once a series of companies in an industry changes to just-in-time or total quality management methods reciprocal change in supplier firms is very likely to follow and lead to the upgrading not only of the whole chain but also of at least parts of related chains to which key suppliers are linked through their other markets.

Complexes

This approach has been particularly developed by van Tulder and a group of colleagues from some of the small industrial countries of Europe and from Australia. As so far developed the approach is particularly appropriate for these countries as it contains concern for a strong welfare element as part of the analytical framework, thus playing on these countries' characteristic strengths. It also recognizes the very considerable importance of public rather than private sector research in many small countries and the existence of only a relatively few key players in any area.

It is also important as an analytical tool for use in devising public industry policies because small industrial countries face a particular set of problems with the globalization of production in certain key industries and the dominance of large firms from large countries in crucial sectors of the international economic arena. Such countries have small populations and thus small home markets, especially for more specialized products, small amounts of money available for R&D, little international market power (they are price-and product-takers) and only limited margins for manoeuvre in public policy action. They are, moreover, being 'squeezed' by a series of developments in the international economy (Freeman and Lundvall, 1988) despite the development power of some of their industry blocs.

These factors together mean that small industrial countries tend to do badly in the 'restructuring races' underway in the world economy. The overall international restructuring race, according to van Tulder, involves countries in competing in seven 'sub-races'. These are:

1. A subsidy race for older as well as new complexes: matching other countries becomes the ultimate rationale.

2. A deregulation race or a 'race to the bottom', implying as little government regulation as possible.
3. An internationalization race which suggests to firms that they should move more and more into world markets, especially those of Japan, the US and Europe, and that governments should facilitate this move as much as possible.
4. An emulation race in core technologies in which all countries aim at being a player in the production of the same core or generic technologies (micro-electronics, biotechnology and new materials).
5. A race to find strategic cooperation partners with the implication that firms which do not form such cooperative relationships run the risk either of being taken over or becoming uncompetitive in strategic industrial and technological areas.
6. A race to attract foreign direct investment.
7. A neo-protectionist race; seen in the creation of trade blocs such as the single European market, the North American Free Trade Area and in the growing number of bilateral trade negotiations (Glatz and van Tulder, 1989:27).

The development of policies which have most chances of enabling small countries to maximize their chances of success – or at least to avoid peripheralization – in the international restructuring race, van Tulder and Glatz suggest, requires yet another and a different set of analytical lenses from those of clusters, industrial districts, chains of production or the 'development block' approach of Dahmén (1982 and 1988).

The approach proposed is that of focusing on *complexes* of activities. These complexes are conceptualized as formalized or informal networks of cooperation between four major groups of actors. These are:

- producers (firms);
- public sector research organizations;
- users (consumers, usually other firms);
- regulators (governments of all levels).

Analyzing the functioning of selected complexes or potential complexes involves examining the ways in which these actors interact in given national entities. Successful complexes are those where each actor or set of actors is working to the full extent possible with all the others. It is this productive interaction which constitutes the 'development power' (to use Dahmén's 1988 phrase) of the complex.

Not all actors in any complex have equal power to affect outcomes and each complex is conceived as a bargaining arena in which players are in hierarchies of dependence and in which there may be gaps, created perhaps by the outside investment decisions of foreign firms. Since the bargaining arenas are essentially national (national authorities, public research organizations, etc.) gaps of this kind are serious impediments to the potential development power of the field.

Any national economy, large or small, contains different kinds of complexes. Some are old-established but declining and in need of renovation through technological advancement (although even these may continue to be cash cows for a period); some are in core fields, such as telecommunications, and can be the basis for others; some are welfare-related and relatively assured of continued high levels of public expenditure which can be used for development purposes; others are in emerging sectors and pose special challenges because they are at the leading edge of both private sector and government policy and there are few models elsewhere to guide investment.

Examples of established, declining but potentially recoverable complexes include traditional agriculture (products such as wool, meat or milk) and some other welfare-related complexes, notably the health complex, where hospitals may coordinate a wide range of activities from medical research to high-tech furniture. Emerging complexes may, for example, involve some core technologies such as new materials or be generated by new regulations such as those concerning the conservation of the environment (e.g. sustainable energy or organic foods).

The 'complexes' set of lenses has three major advantages over the other perspectives outlined in this paper as both an analytical approach to the discussion of innovation and as a basis for public policy development. The first is that it contains a specific role for government authorities which may act directly to assist the complex rather than being reduced to providing general infrastructure.

The second is that it indicates the central importance of public R&D facilities, especially in small countries which have few R&D dollars. Analysis of well-functioning complexes indicates successful ways in which such scarce funds can be used and suggests the importance of targeting in government policies aimed at encouraging the innovation increasingly necessary for economic development.

Thirdly, and in particular, the approach allows the analyst to pinpoint weaknesses in the complex much more clearly and to devise policies for plugging gaps. Thus, for example, it may be possible to boost the productivity and local economic development power of a complex where considerable public funds are concerned, such as health, but which at present may be seen as a 'disorganized' or 'malfunctioning' one because the different actors are not maximizing productive interactions and not focusing public resources to encourage innovation. As with chains of production, such complexes usually have to have a lead organization, such as a hospital, which can provide the links if they are to encourage innovation across a broad range of activities.

Conclusion

Finding the right structures for innovation and putting them together in a national system which maximizes the innovative capacity of a country requires the analyst to view an economy with a variety of different lenses. Each approach outlined in this chapter provides a partial view and brings to prominence certain aspects of the economic and socio-political structures concerned. The complexity not only of national economic systems but also the multifaceted ways in which the key players in national economies, including public authorities, relate to the international environment (restructuring race) and the seven 'sub-races' outlined by van Tulder and Glatz make it clear that no single approach is sufficient. None can analyze every aspect of the economy but each adds vital data on the organizational dynamics of the productive system and its transformation, and each is a necessary supplement to the cruder neo-classical views of industrial competitiveness at both national and international levels. In a properly functioning and effective national system of innovation analysis, using any of these lenses should indicate particularly effective linkages between players in both public and private sectors, at a firm and organizational level and across crucial industry sectors.

Bibliography

Dahmén, E. (1988) '"Development Blocks" in Industrial Economics', *Scandinavian Economic History Review and Economy and History*, Vol. xxxvi, No. 1, pp. 3–14.

Debresson, C. (1989) 'Breeding Innovation Clusters: A Source of Dynamic Development', *World Development*, Vol. 17, No. 1, pp. 1–16.

Freeman, C. and B.-A. Lundvall (eds) (1988) *Small Countries Facing the Technological Revolution*, Pinter Publishers, London.

Glatz, H. and van Tulder, R. (1989) *Ways Out of the International Restructuring Race?* Project proposal, Annex B, University of Amsterdam, Amsterdam.

Greig, A. (1990) 'Technological Change and Innovation in the Clothing Industry: The Role of Retailing', *Labour and Industry* 3 (2&3), June/October.

Greig, A. (1992) 'Rhetoric and Reality in the Clothing Industry: The Case of Post-Fordism', *The Australian and New Zealand Journal of Sociology*, Vol. 28, No. 1.

Kristensen, P. (1991) 'When Labour Defines Business Recipes – The Danish Metal Working Industry Cut Off From Corporate Control and Co-operation of Local Networks', paper for the 10th EGOS Colloquium 'Societal Change between Market and Organisation', Vienna, July 15–17, 1991.

Lundvall, B.-A. (ed.) (1992) *National Systems of Innovation*, Pinter Publishers, London.

Marceau, J. (1992) *Reworking the World: Organisations, Technologies and Cultures in Comparative Perspective*, Walter de Gruyter, Berlin and New York.

Marshall, A. (1920) *Principles of Economics*, Macmillan, London.

Nelson, R. (ed.) (1992) *National Systems of Innovation*, Oxford University Press, New York.

Porter, M. (1990) *The Competitive Advantage of Nations*, Macmillan, London.

Senghaas, D. (1985) *The European Experience: A Historical Critique of Development Theory*, Berg, Leamington Spa/Dover, New Hampshire.

Senker, J. (1988) *A Taste for Innovation: British Supermarkets' Influence on Food Manufacturers*, Horton Publishing, Bradford.

van Tulder, R. (ed.) (1988) *Small Industrial Countries and Economic and Technological Development*, SICRA and NOTA, Amsterdam.

Weiss, L. (1988) *Creating Capitalism: The State and Small Business since 1945*, Blackwell, Oxford.

Whitley, R. (ed.) (1992) *The Social Foundations of Enterprise: Europe in Comparative Perspective*, Sage, London.

2. Technological Systems and Economic Performance

Bo Carlsson

Introduction

Even though it is commonly accepted that technological change is one of the primary forces generating economic growth, the causal linkages between innovation and economic growth are still not well understood. This is due in large measure to the fact that in conventional neo-classical (comparative static) analysis, technological change is treated as an exogenous factor. In order to understand the relationship between technological change and economic growth more fully, we need to take an approach in which technological change is at least to some extent endogenized.

If one were to build a theory in which technological change is endogenous, it would seem useful to start with the observation that macroeconomic growth is the aggregate result of lots of microeconomic changes, some of which involve the use of new technology. Therefore, an important requirement of a theory that tries to endogenize technological change is that it must recognize the *variety* of products, processes, economic agents, institutions, etc. which exists in the economy; this, in turn, requires a disaggregated rather than an aggregated approach. Secondly, it must recognize the interdependence among these various entities, i.e., it must deal with *systems* rather than individual units.[1] Thirdly, it must be *dynamic*, i.e. it must recognize economic growth as a continuous process in which technologies and institutions co-evolve over time rather than as an end result at a moment in time.

The purpose of this essay is to explore the concept and dimensions of *technological systems*, to illustrate their key characteristics based on a few case studies, and to show that they are useful building blocks and units of analysis for both theory and policy dealing with economic growth.

The paper is organized as follows: We begin by defining technological systems and describing the ways in which they are both similar to and different from the concept of national systems of innovation. We then explore the key features of technological systems, based on a Swedish study of factory automation, electronics and computers, pharmaceuticals, and powder technology. This is followed by a discussion of the policy issues raised, first from the perspective of the firm and then from a public policy perspective. The concluding section summarizes the argument and suggests some ideas for further research.

From National Systems of Innovation to Technological Systems

A significant step toward recognition of the importance of systems in the analysis of economic growth was taken by Freeman (1987), Lundvall (1988), and others, who suggested the concept of a national system of innovation. A national system of innovation may be defined as a 'set of distinct institutions which jointly and individually contribute to the development and diffusion of new technologies and which provides the framework within which governments form and implement policies to influence the innovation process' (Metcalfe, 1992, p. 82).[2]

Technological systems are similar to national systems of innovation. They have been defined as 'network(s) of agents interacting in each specific technology area under a particular institutional infrastructure for the purpose of generating, diffusing, and utilizing technology' (Carlsson and Stankiewicz, 1991, p. 111).

While the basic concepts are obviously very similar (particularly with regard to the systems aspects), technological systems differ from national systems of innovation in several important dimensions, each of which has to do with certain aspects of variety. First of all, technological systems are defined by technology rather than national boundaries. They are not necessarily bounded by national borders, although they are certainly influenced by cultural, linguistic and other circumstances which facilitate or impede contacts among units within the system. Indeed, an important dimension in which technological systems may differ from each other is the degree to which they are international in character.

Secondly, technological systems vary in character and extent from one technology area to another within any given country. For example, the number and characteristics of actors and their interdependence, the institutional infrastructure, the geographic concentration and the degree of internationalization vary among technology areas. A country may be strong in one technology area and weak in another. Thus, Japan appears to be extremely strong in mechatronics but not in other manufacturing industries such as chemicals and drugs, nor in distribution and other service industries (Imai and Yamazaki, 1992).

A third difference between technological systems and national systems of innovation is the degree of emphasis on diffusion and utilization as distinct from creation of new technology. As a result, technological systems tend to place more emphasis on the microeconomic (as distinct from macro-oriented public policy) aspects of technology diffusion and utilization. The creation of new technology pushes out the production possibility frontier or opportunity set. But it cannot be simply assumed that just because a technology exists, it is also known and used effectively. Unless the expanded opportunity set is converted into economic activity, i.e. unless it results in entrepreneurial activity, it has no economic impact.

This is where the concept of economic competence comes in. We have defined economic competence as the ability to identify, expand and exploit business opportunities (Carlsson and Eliasson, 1991).

Economic or business competence has four main components:

1. *Selective* (strategic) capability: the ability to make innovative choices of markets, products, technologies and overall organizational structure; to engage in entrepreneurial activity; and especially to select key personnel and acquire key resources, including new competence. This aspect has been amply illustrated in recent years as many companies have struggled to define their corporate identities and strategies as distinct from their competitive strategies in each individual business unit (Porter, 1991);
2. *Organizational* (integrative, coordinating) capability, i.e. the ability to organize the business units in such a way that there is greater value in the corporate entity as a whole than in the sum of the individual parts;
3. *Technical* (functional) ability relating to the various functions within the firm, such as production, marketing, engineering, research and development, as well as product-specific capabilities. These are the areas of activity in which firms can compare themselves to their peers or leading competitors;
4. *Learning* ability, or the shaping of a corporate culture which encourages continual change in response to changes in the environment.

Economic competence must be present in sufficient quantity and quality on the part of all relevant economic agents, users as well as suppliers, government agents, etc. in order for the technological system to function well. If the users are not competent to demand or use new technology – or alternatively, if the suppliers are not able or willing to supply it – even a major technical breakthrough has no practical value or may even have negative value if competitors are quicker to take advantage of it.

Dimensions of Technological Systems

The dimensions of technological systems have been explored in a Swedish study.[3] The technological systems studied are those supporting factory automation, electronics and computer technology, pharmaceuticals (especially biotechnology) and powder technology.

Table 2.1 Dimensions and characteristics of technological systems

	Factory automation	Electronics	Pharma-ceuticals	Powder technology
Present development phase	Mature	Rapid dev.	Rapid dev.	Heterogeneous
Future potential	+	+++	+++	++
Buyer competence	+++	++	+++	+
Buyer–supplier collaboration	++	++	+++	+
Supplier competence	++	++	++	++
Industrial R&D	+++	+	+++	++
Academic infrastructure	+	+	+++	++
Government policy	+	+	++	++
Bridging institutions	+++	+	+++	++
Holes/weaknesses	-	- -		-
Compensating mechanisms	++	+	+++	+++

These four case studies have led to the identification of ten dimensions which may be used to describe technological systems. These dimensions are listed in Table 2.1. For each technological system, the number of pluses and minuses indicates the relative strength in each dimension; this (somewhat subjective) rating will be commented upon in the next section.

Most of the dimensions in Table 2.1 are self-explanatory. The *future potential* of a technological system is largely dependent on where basic underlying technologies are currently located in their life cycle, i.e. their present development phase. *Bridging institutions* refer to arrangements and/or organizations which establish and maintain interaction among various actors in the system.

For example, in the area of factory automation a private research institute (IVF), owned jointly by the National Board for Industrial and Technical Development (a government agency) and Mekanförbundet (the engineering industry association), has played such a role.[4] One of its functions is to scan the world for new technology (this scanning is often aided and complemented by the scanning activities of Swedish multinational firms), evaluate it and rapidly disseminate information on it through the network of which it is a part, thus fostering a high level of technical awareness at all levels of Swedish industry which is central to explaining the rapid diffusion of technology. In addition, bridging institutions such as this help to accumulate and integrate the results of innovative activities, which otherwise tend to be highly firm-specific, and make them useful and available to other firms as well.

The role of these organizations is not only to disseminate knowhow but also to provide a *compensating mechanism* for *weaknesses* and lack of domestic capability ('holes') within other parts of the technological system. In some technological systems such weaknesses appear in the form of absence of domestic suppliers of key technologies, lack of buyer competence, lack of research capability in the relevant part of the academic system, etc. In Sweden, a particularly important compensating mechanism is the global monitoring and diffusion of technology via multinational firms. This reflects both the relatively small size of the country and the large role played by Sweden-based multinationals in the economy.

Characteristics of Technological Systems: Results of Four Swedish Case Studies

Due to space limitations it is impossible here to discuss the key characteristics of each technological system.[5] Only a brief summary of the principal findings is presented.

There are several important features which all of these technological systems have in common. First, our study indicates that it may not be sufficient for sustainable economic growth to have only one or a few competent actors in a given system. There has to be a *variety of actors*, each with *specific* (sometimes unique) *competence*. They must also act together, in *clusters or networks*. Given the risk taking necessarily involved in new activities, having a supportive network reduces the risk of any given venture by providing timely information: early identification and quick feedback increase the possibilities of taking corrective action whenever necessary.

Second, the crucial role of *competent buyers* is illustrated in each of the investigated systems. These buyers are often industrial firms but may also be government agencies. *Close collaboration*, often on a continuing and long-term basis, *between buyers and suppliers* seems to be highly beneficial, if not essential.

Third, in spite of the trend toward increased internationalization of all kinds of economic and technical activity, our study suggests that strong *local or domestic technological systems continue to be important*, even in small countries, and even though their links to systems in other countries may also be important, particularly via multinational firms. For example, the factory automation case study shows that while leading users may not be directly dependent on local or domestic suppliers of automation technology, the majority of less advanced users are still highly dependent on competent domestic suppliers (Carlsson and Jacobsson, 1991). Without such suppliers of technology, the leading users may find themselves without domestic suppliers of parts and components, making their continued domestic production less competitive and increasing the attractiveness of moving production elsewhere, thus further weakening the domestic industrial base.

While there are thus some key features which these four technological systems have in common, there are also dimensions in which they differ from each other. First, they differ with respect to future development potential (depending partly on the particular stage of development of the underlying technology in each case) and the extent to which market opportunities have been exploited through the creation of strong networks, infrastructure, and competence on the part of various economic agents.

Secondly, they vary with respect to where within the system new knowledge is being generated. In mechanical engineering, technological change appears to be relatively slow, 'routinized', and codified, meaning both that new technical developments occur to a relatively great extent in universities and that they then become relatively easily accessible to users. In the area of pharmaceuticals, the knowledge base is expanding much faster; technological change tends to take place outside the universities or in joint ventures between pharmaceutical firms and universities. In electronics, the knowledge base is expanding even more rapidly, with the result that academia rarely has the competence to offer advanced knowledge. Instead, universities primarily play the role of supplying basic engineering training, while most research and development takes place in business firms. Frontier knowledge is typically tacit, since receiver competence is typically lacking (Eliasson, 1989).

In the area of factory automation, which is relatively mature technically, the future potential for generating new economic growth is limited in spite of a high user competence and a well-functioning network. Nevertheless, if the now mature technology is diffused widely to new user groups, it may increase the competitiveness and therefore the growth potential of existing industries. An important question is whether the existing compensating mechanisms in the system are strong enough to make up for the holes which are beginning to emerge on the supplier side; several key domestic machine tool suppliers are currently facing bankruptcy.

In the pharmaceutical area, a high level of competence of both users and suppliers and a relatively extensive network, in combination with continued rapid technological change, mean that the future development potential is extraordinarily great. The possibilities of taking advantage of the market opportunities seem to be good, even though there are some doubts as to whether viable new firms can be created both in the pharmaceutical industry and in neighbouring areas of application of biotechnology. The historical record of firm formation is not strong in either of these areas in Sweden.

In the electronics area, the pace of technological change is also very high and the future potential great. The competence level of users and suppliers is very high but spotty; the question is whether the existing competence has sufficient coverage or critical mass to enable the networks to function well. The infrastructure here is not extensive.

Finally, as regards powder technology, the competence level is high, particularly among suppliers on the powder metallurgy side. In ceramics, by contrast, the infrastructure is relatively extensive, especially in the universities, but the industrial competence is still fairly undeveloped. It is therefore difficult to judge the future potential for the technology area as a whole.

As a result of the differences just mentioned, the role of the infrastructure varies from one case to another. In Sweden, the academic part of the infrastructure seems to play a crucial role in pharmaceuticals and powder ceramics, while it does not play a leading role in relatively well-established technology areas such as factory automation and powder metallurgy; it may actually have formed an impediment in the electronics and computer technology area. The rest of the infrastructure (research institutes, branch organizations, government agencies, etc.) also plays varying roles, ranging from highly significant (in the form of bridging institutions) in the factory automation area to a very modest role in the pharmaceutical area.

Policy Issues

In view of these results, and particularly in recognition of the diversity among sectors and technologies, what are the policy issues that arise for both business and public policy? Given the need for variety, networking, and co-evolution of technology and institutional environment, what are the problems which the market alone cannot solve? In other words, what is the proper role, if any, of public policy? Let us first turn to the implications for corporate policy and then examine the issues that remain for public policy.

Implications for management

Business activity results from the exploitation of business opportunities. Through competent management it is possible to identify, expand and exploit business opportunities. Certainly it is advantageous for both the firm and the country if the general management competence is high. But there are also some specific competence aspects which relate to technological systems. These have to do with *absorptive capacity*.[6] By establishing close working relationships with each other, buyers and suppliers can learn from one another. By networking with other units (other firms, research institutes, academic institutions, etc.) they can increase the connectivity of the system, thus helping both themselves and others in the system.

Our study has shown the importance of bridging institutions which can establish links between otherwise disconnected actors within the system, particularly between academic research (whether at home or abroad) on the one hand and users and suppliers on the other. While such institutions do not necessarily have to conduct original research themselves, they can help in early identification of new technologies, increasing awareness, providing testing facilities and training programs, thereby significantly speeding up the diffusion process. Heavy involvement by private industry in such institutions is necessary for success, and there is no reason why the initiative should not come from the private side.

Another finding is that the academic system may sometimes be slow in responding to the challenges offered by new technologies, not only as far as scientific research is concerned but also in providing appropriately trained people in sufficient quantities. One of the reasons for such a slow reaction may be the failure of private industry to articulate the needs in a timely fashion.[7]

The uncertainty (unpredictability) pertaining to innovation means that success can seldom be assured, but it can be enhanced through experimentation with a variety of approaches. This is as true at the business unit level as at the national level. But trying a variety of approaches may involve several areas of competence, and the increasing complexity of technological change often necessitates broadening the competence base. In a study of major corporations in the United States, Japan, and Sweden, Granstrand et al. (1990) have shown that there is indeed a tendency for these corporations to diversify their technology base (as distinct from the products they derive from it) by increasing the number of engineers outside the fields constituting the traditional technology base within each corporation. In Sweden, this was found to be true for twelve of fifteen industries studied, and particularly in pharmaceuticals, computers and business machines, telecommunication equipment, and instruments (ibid., pp. 78-9). The technology diversification appears to be stronger in Japanese than in American and Swedish firms.

There are two main advantages of a broader technology base: (1) it makes it less likely that the firm will be caught by surprise when new developments occur, particularly in the form of basic technology shifts, such as from mechanics to electronics (mechatronics) or from chemistry to biotechnology; and (2) it enables the firm to take better advantage of unexpected results of its own R&D (serendipity).

In summary, then, private businesses can make their contribution to strengthening the technological system of which they are a part, while at the same time enhancing the chances of their own success, by increasing their economic competence in all areas (strategic, organizational, technical, and learning), by increasing their R&D efforts, by initiating and building new bridging institutions while strengthening existing ones, by articulating the requirements to which the academic sector can respond, and by broadening their technology base.

Public policy issues
Keeping in mind the three criteria mentioned earlier (variety, systems features and dynamics), what can public policy do to enhance the functioning of the market system?

The very diversity of technological systems means that any government intervention, if required at all, needs to be targeted to the specific problems in each technology area. This implies that both the means and the magnitude of intervention will vary from one area to another. Thus, in the Swedish cases studied, government policy has played a fairly limited role overall. In factory automation it has primarily involved basic engineering education (though not much research) and creating bridging institutions; in electronics, government agencies (especially those for military procurement, telecommunications, electric power and railroads) have played the role of competent buyer in selected areas; in the pharmaceutical industry the main contribution has been medical research in the academic sector; and in powder technology, government policy has played a role primarily in strengthening research and education.

The system-building tasks involve creation of critical mass, formation of clusters/development blocs,[8] enhancing the connectedness of various entities within the system, initiating and/or facilitating bridging institutions, and strengthening mechanisms to avoid and/or compensate for weak or absent capabilities. As indicated above, most of these tasks can be performed by private industry. In some cases, however, the government can play a crucial role, e.g. as a competent buyer, and thereby provide both the impetus and the resources for system building.

The unpredictability of evolutionary processes implies that there is a need for experimentation and thus for simultaneous pursuit of a plurality and variety of approaches. One of the primary constraints here is financial: it is extremely difficult to obtain finance for risky ventures. While there is no substitute for high growth and profitability resulting in reinvestment of retained earnings, the government may be able to provide an institutional arrangement suitable for experimentation and for creating multiple sources of finance. Another important task for government policy may be to encourage increasing the absorptive capacity.

Conclusion

This study has tried to demonstrate that by examining technological systems as opposed to merely studying their constituent parts (users and suppliers, R&D infrastructure, etc.), it is possible to discover the sources of new technologies, to analyze the diffusion and utilization of new technology and the conditions (especially the institutional arrangements) under which these processes take place, and therefore to gain insight into the relationship between technological change and economic growth. For these reasons, technological systems are suitable building blocks in theories which try to endogenize technological change. They are useful units of analysis in gauging the growth prospects of an economy over the medium term.

Technological systems are also useful units of analysis for public policy. Enhancing the functioning of the market system by strengthening existing technological systems and facilitating the creation of new ones ought to be among the main goals of government technology policy. The emphasis ought to be on creating well-functioning *systems* rather than promoting particular firms, industries, or technical solutions; on creating a variety of approaches and institutions rather than selecting individual projects; on facilitating networking rather than supporting individual actors; and on competence building throughout the system (i.e. diffusion and utilization) as opposed to merely promoting the creation of new technology.

Finally, it hardly needs saying that this study represents only the beginning, not the end, of a research agenda. While the results of the present study are suggestive, they also indicate the desirability of studying more technology areas in order to get a better understanding of the characteristics of technological systems, how they get started, and why certain systems succeed while others fail. The origins of technological systems also need to be studied: do they simply evolve, or can they be created? If so, how? Who should design them? What about declining industries – how do technological systems adjust in such cases, and do public policies help or hinder? Clearly, international comparisons within specific areas of technology could shed light upon many of these issues.

Notes

1. 'System' here refers to a set of interconnected institutions, where 'institutions' may refer to both organizations (e.g. firms, government agencies and universities) and rules of the game (laws, customs, policies, etc.). The distinction between organizations and rules of the game is due to Pelikan (1988).

2. The most comprehensive studies to date on national systems of innovation are probably those reported by Nelson (1993) and Lundvall (1992).

3. The project, 'Sweden's Technological Systems and Future Development Potential', was initiated and funded by the National Board for Industrial and Technical Development (NUTEK, formerly STU), with additional funding from the Swedish Council for Planning and Coordination of Research (FRN). A summary of the preliminary findings is presented in Carlsson (1992). A complete list of reports from the project may be obtained from the author.

4. IVF was set up in 1964 to conduct scanning, monitoring, adaptation and diffusion of production technology in the engineering industry, as well as contract research and testing for individual firms. All of these organizations are cross-represented on numerous committees and task forces, where small as well as large firms also take part. Academic institutions are represented, primarily in NUTEK and IVF. Thus, IVF and NUTEK provide links between academia and business, while Mekanförbundet bridges the gap between government and industry.

5. The four cases were originally selected for the following reasons: Factory automation is a

broad area of technology where Sweden is very strong internationally. It has a long history in Sweden and can therefore be expected to exhibit all the characteristics of a fully developed technological system. Electronics and computers is an even broader technical area involving some of the same actors as factory automation but where the Swedish capability is limited and the technological system much less developed. Pharmaceuticals were selected because they represent an entirely different type of technology. Initially, the primary focus was on biotechnology, but it was soon discovered that there is almost no use of biotechnology in Sweden outside the pharmaceutical industry. Powder technology, finally, was selected because it represents a much more embryonic field, offering possibilities of observing an emerging technological system.

6.   As originally described by Cohen and Levinthal (1989 and 1990), there are two outputs of the research and development efforts of firms: innovations and increased absorptive capacity. The latter refers to the knowledge which firms obtain through their R&D which enables them to identify important new ideas or innovations, to exploit them for their own benefit, and to learn from the experience of others (spillover effects).

7.   In the absence of research on the subject, it is not clear whether the slow response of the academic system to new technologies is a characteristic peculiar to the highly centralized academic system in Sweden or whether it is a more general phenomenon.

8.   The concept of development bloc has been defined by Dahmén (1950, 1989) as a set of interdependent economic agents (often users and suppliers) interacting with each other to bring about new techniques and products.

Bibliography

Carlsson, B. (1992) 'Technological Systems and Economic Development Potential: Four Swedish Case Studies', paper presented to the International J.A. Schumpeter Society Conference, Kyoto, Japan, 19–22 August.

Carlsson, B. and Eliasson, G. (1991) 'The Nature and Importance of Economic Competence', working paper, Case Western Reserve University and IUI.

Carlsson, B. and Jacobsson, S. (1991) 'What Makes the Automation Industry Strategic?', *Economics of Innovation and New Technology*, No. 1, pp. 257–69.

Carlsson, B. and Stankiewicz, R. (1991) 'On the Nature, Function, and Composition of Technological Systems', *Journal of Evolutionary Economics*, Vol. 1, No. 2, pp. 93–118.

Cohen, W. and Levinthal, D. (1989) 'Innovation and Learning: The Two Faces of R&D', *The Economic Journal*, Vol. 99, No. 397, pp. 569–96.

Cohen, W. and Levinthal, D. (1990) 'Absorptive Capacity: A New Perspective on Learning and Innovation', *Administrative Science Quarterly*, No. 35, pp. 128–52.

Dahmén, E. (1950) *Svensk industriell företagarverksamhet* (Swedish Industrial Entrepreneurial Activity), Industriens Utredningsinstitut, Stockholm.

Dahmén, E. (1989) '"Development Blocks" in Industrial Economics' in Carlsson, B. (ed.), *Industrial Dynamics: Technological, Organizational, and Structural Changes in Industries and Firms*, Kluwer Academic Publishers, Boston and Dordrecht.

Eliasson, G. (1989) 'The Dynamics of Supply and Economic Growth – How Industrial Knowledge Accumulation Drives a Path-Dependent Economic Process' in Carlsson, B. (ed.), *Industrial Dynamics: Technological, Organizational, and Structural Changes in Industries and Firms*, Kluwer Academic Publishers, Boston and Dordrecht.

Eliasson, G. (1991) 'Modeling the Experimentally Organized Economy', *Journal of Economic Behavior and Organization*, Vol. 16, Nos 1–2, pp. 153–82.

Freeman, C. (1987) 'National Systems of Innovation: the Case of Japan' in *Technology Policy and Economic Performance: Lessons from Japan*, Pinter Publishers, London.

Granstrand, O., Oskarsson, C., Sjöberg, N. and Sjölander, S. (1990) 'Business Strategies for New Technologies' in Deiaco, E., Hörnell, E. and Vickery, G. (eds), *Technology and Investment: Crucial Issues for the 1990s*, Pinter Publishers, London.

Imai, K-I. and Yamazaki, A. (1992) 'Dynamics of the Japanese Industrial System from a Schumpeterian Perspective', paper presented to the International J.A. Schumpeter Society Conference, Kyoto, Japan, 19–22 August.

Lundvall, B-Å. (1988) 'Innovation as an Interactive Process: From User-Producer Interaction to the National System of Innovation' in Dosi, G. et al. (eds), *Technical Change and Economic Theory*, Pinter Publishers, London.

Lundvall, B-Å. (1992) *National Systems of Innovation – Toward a Theory of Innovation and Interactive Learning*, Pinter Publishers, London.

Metcalfe, J.S. (1992) 'The Economic Foundations of Technology Policy: Equilibrium and Evolutionary Perspectives', mimeo (first draft), University of Manchester, November.

Nelson, R. (1993) *National Innovation Systems: A Comparative Analysis*, Oxford University Press, New York and Oxford.

Pelikan, P. (1988) 'Can the Innovation System of Capitalism Be Outperformed?' in Dosi, G. et al. (eds), *Technical Change and Economic Theory*, Pinter Publishers, London.

Porter, M. (1991) 'From Competitive Advantage to Corporate Strategy' in Harvard Business Review, *Michael E. Porter on Competition and Strategy*, Harvard Business Review Paperback No. 90079.

3. The Creative Milieu: A Regional Perspective on Innovation

Philip Cooke and Kevin Morgan

Introduction

The spatial dimension of innovation has received so little attention in the conventional economics literature that one could be forgiven for thinking that corporate activity is organized on the head of a pin. In this conventional scenario firms tend to be contextualized in terms of industries, sectors and markets, the implication being that location is of little or no real significance in assessing their innovative capacity. Indeed, with the advent of digital communication technologies, which offer firms hitherto unavailable opportunities to reduce the 'tyranny of distance' by giving them a 'global reach', it might be thought that locational considerations are less important than ever, with one location being much the same as another.

In contrast to this spatially insensitive approach a growing corpus of research over the past decade has begun to establish the significance of the *spatial* context of industrial innovation. Among other things this research has highlighted the salience of such concepts as 'territorial production systems', 'industrial districts', 'innovative milieux' and 'regional innovation networks' (Brusco, 1990; Beccatini, 1990; Sabel, 1989; Scott, 1988; Camagni, 1991; Maillat and Vasserot, 1988; Cooke and Morgan, 1990). What triggered this new focus on the spatial dimension of innovation was the recognition that a great deal of innovative activity appeared to be taking place in the form of local or regional agglomerations, latter-day equivalents of the specialized industrial districts (like Sheffield and Manchester) which so impressed Alfred Marshall in the early part of the 20th century. The most notable examples of such regional agglomerations are Silicon Valley in California, Route 128 in Greater Boston, Baden-Württemberg in Southern Germany, Emilia-Romagna in Northern Italy to name but a few.

The origins and dynamics of these regional agglomerations vary from one region to another, so much so that there is no single explanation for this phenomenon. However, in some of the European regions, for example, it is clear that localized buyer–supplier networks, together with robust institutional support mechanisms at the local level, have played a major role in promoting regionalized patterns of innovative activity. Conventional economic theory might say that these regions have benefited from having *low* transaction costs and *high* external economies, both of which contribute to what Marshall called the 'industrial atmosphere' of a centre of specialized industry.

More recent attempts to explain these regional agglomerations argue that the spatial form of development has actually been a major factor in explaining the innovative success of firms in these regions. There are two ways this is said to occur. First, it is claimed that a localized pattern of development actually facilitates a 'collective learning process', such that information, knowledge and best practice are rapidly diffused throughout the local milieu, raising the creative capacity of both firms and institutions. Second, a localized production system helps to reduce the 'elements of dynamic uncertainty': this also facilitates local innovation because it allows for a better understanding of the possible outcomes of a firm's decisions (Camagni, 1991).

These remarks underline the point that innovation is first and foremost a collective social endeavour, a collaborative process in which the firm, especially the small firm, depends on the expertise of a wider social constituency than is often imagined (workforce, suppliers, customers, technical institutes, training bodies, etc.). In the regional agglomerations that we focus upon in this chapter it is clear that firms have benefited from not having to shoulder the entire costs and burdens of innovation. These costs and burdens have been spread throughout the region, in the shape of buyer–supplier networks, technology transfer agencies, trade associations and training consortia, etc. These intermediary forms of *self*-organization, which inhabit the middle ground between 'states' and 'markets', are especially important in regions dominated by small- and medium-sized enterprises (SMEs) because, generally speaking, such firms tend to be handicapped by being both small and lonely.

Although they are often portrayed as being able to look after themselves so far as innovation is concerned, multinational firms are not as impervious to location as is sometimes thought. The past decade has been a chastening time for large firms which thought that size conferred sufficient protection against the vagaries of the innovation process. The list of the humbled giants – IBM, GM, Philips and so forth – testifies to the fact that size alone guarantees nothing. As we shall see, the operating units of multinationals are becoming more and more interested in their local environment: the trend towards decentralization means that these operating units are encouraged to exploit new sources of expertise.

Three Kinds of Innovative Milieu

The research literature on innovative milieux covers a wide range of examples. Summarizing in a very broad-brush way, three kinds of milieu can be identified. First, the directed (or *dirigiste*) model, typically found in France and, to some extent, in Japan with growing evidence of support for the basic concept of *Technopolis* in, for example, Italy (at Bari) and even Britain, as will be shown. Second, the local or 'grassroots' approach, typical of Japan before the arrival of the technopole concept in the form of the *kohsetsushi* or municipal technology centres, but typical also of the latter-day *industrial districts* of southern Europe and even, in more advanced and marketized form, in the silicon landscapes of California. Third, a newer form of milieu than either, and containing some elements in common with both, is the *network* paradigm, found classically in northern continental Europe, especially Scandinavia, the Netherlands and Germany – paradigmatically in Baden-Württemberg – and now beginning to be emulated elsewhere. To repeat, this is broad brushwork, there are many hybrids, but in what follows some flavour can be given of each type of milieu, its strengths and weaknesses, and an assessment can be offered.

Dirigiste Approaches

Classically French in origin, modelled on Perroux' (1950) concept of the 'growth pole', the earliest and perhaps most successful was implanted by the French state (in collaboration with local and municipal *animateurs*) at Meylan near Grenoble, Rhône-Alpes. This Zone for Innovation, Technical and Scientific Achievements (ZIRST) consists of colleges, research institutes, large enterprises (LEs), small and medium enterprises (SMEs) and flexible financial systems. As Colletis (1993) notes, significant economic growth has occurred, though whether due to or in spite of ZIRST is unclear; indeed he hints that technopoles may have strengthened the French innovation 'crisis' because of a lack of synergy rather than proving a model of excellence.

This mood is present, also, in a report by the LATAPSES group from Sophia Antipolis in the south of France, location of one of France's larger technopoles (Charbit et al., 1991). Their conclusion is that innovative cross-fertilization is poor in French technopoles in general because local interaction between players is inadequate. In the Scientific City of Villeneuve d'Ascq near Lille in northern France this very problem has been recognized as a serious drawback to the development of the 'synergetic surplus' there too (Kamann, 1991). A special intermediary agency – the Regional Centre for Industrial Systems (CRGI) – was set up locally in 1989 to facilitate intra-technopole interaction between firms and with the innovation infrastructure (Cooke, 1993).

Thus the *technopole* concept, usually associated with a French *dirigiste* tradition, is becoming increasingly detached from centralist determination even in France. However, much the more interesting large-scale local and regional innovation projects are being developed in Germany. There, learning about the failures of old-style technopoles has led to a wave of relatively large-scale innovation initiatives, for example Ulm Science City, the AGIT partnership at Aachen or GIB at Berlin, where institutional linkage to firms, established or new, is designed into the innovation system at the outset. Not only is public–private partnership cemented in the formal constitution of such ventures but, for example in Aachen, start-up firms only continue to receive rental subsidies when graduating from the laboratory atmosphere of the science park to the production atmosphere of the technology park, if they sign an agreement with a local 'godfather' firm. Godfathers advise start-ups on business practice, keep them well-networked locally, and are intended to enable economic benefits to be retained in the locality.

It is this kind of 'technopole' thinking that now carries more weight and has influenced work on establishing two of them in the less than innovation-rich UK region of Wales. The Snowdonia technopole, promoting biotechnology in particular, is designed as a network of largely pre-existing institutions and recent start-ups. The South Wales technopole, funded by EC-SPRINT and the Welsh Development Agency, is also to be structured as a network, albeit on a regional scale and on a wider industrial spectrum. Interestingly, there is some '*dirigisme*' in these examples but it emanates from the regional and EC levels, is relatively light in touch, and dependent on public–private partnership rather than state initiative.

Grassroots Approaches

Where *dirigisme* is absent, a 'soft infrastructure' of innovation support may emerge from the efforts of local, grassroots organization, perhaps municipal, perhaps private, possibly both. One instance of an essentially local, civic model of technology transfer is Japan's *kohsetsushi*, a system of 169 small-business technology centres funded by the prefectures in which they are situated, and by MITI and the Japan Small Business Corporation. MITI typically provides informal 'guidance', but the centres date from the 1920s and are by no means the creatures of either.

In some of the 'industrial districts' of northern Italy, notably in Emilia-Romagna and Tuscany, different models of local support for innovation by SMEs can be found (Cooke and Morgan, 1991a; Bianchi and Giordani, 1993). In the former case, a remarkably cohesive regional and local political culture, rooted in decentralist socialism, led mono-industrial towns such as Carpi (clothing), Sassuolo (ceramics) and Modena (mechanical engineering) to seek mechanisms to help secure a competitive edge for innovative SMEs. Local artisans' associations, local politicians and Chambers of Commerce worked together and secured support from regional government to discover funding (sometimes from the EC) which helped establish innovative business service centres. One such, the Textile Information Centre

(CITER), was partly responsible for producing a new CAD-CAM fashion design system. This enabled Carpi firms both to escape reductions in market share occasioned by cheaper imitators, because it radically enhanced time economies, and to move up-market into the fashion-design industry.

In Tuscany, by contrast, such efforts in a comparable, albeit larger, clothing district named Prato were fundamentally the responsibility of the local clothing trade-association. This was because the regional and city (Florence) governments were out of sympathy with what their more hardline Communist regimes considered archaic small-firm entrepreneurship. Initiatives which accessed EC funding have often focused, not always successfully, on raising the usage of informatics and telematics in the sub-contracting processes which have been so significant in enabling these SME systems to out-perform larger competitors in the past (Mazzonis, 1991).

The key point about such grassroot methods of innovation support, especially but not exclusively in the Italian case, is that they have outlived their usefulness. It was a minor miracle that CITER could come up with an innovative CAD-CAM system and only possible because of help (at less than cost) from ENEA, the National Energy Agency, located at nearby Bologna. Such arrangements now belong to the past in Italy. The future belongs with university–industry interactions, needed to help develop the new wave of innovations that might help a reorganizing industry to compete in the future. Until 1992 Italian law disallowed what practically everywhere else is considered unexceptional, namely university–industry research collaboration; now the law has been changed and such collaborations can take place.

We might, briefly, compare these experiences with the ostensibly quite different case of Californian high-technology industries which, nevertheless, are increasingly bracketed with the Italian cases as a generic type of neo-Marshallian industrial district founded on the capacity to engage in 'flexible specialization' (Marshall, 1927; Piore and Sabel, 1984; Scott, 1988). On the surface *sui generis* instances of free enterprise, these SME dynamos were nonetheless fundamentally dependent upon NASA and Department of Defense procurement, unable to resist acquisition by Japanese corporations without federal government intervention and, in the semiconductor industry, came to see the benefits of formal collaboration in R&D through Sematech.

The Network Paradigm

The regional system of innovation which many regions would most like to emulate is that of Baden-Württemberg in Germany. This *Land*, created only in 1952, has consistently been one of the Federal Republic's top economic performers in the past two decades. Its strength in innovation is built on 'redundancy' (Herrigel, 1989) in that many different institutions support it, including large and small enterprises, and one or two could be lost without the whole system suffering unduly. But because innovation is so well-embedded institutionally, scarcely any firm, however small, in need of innovation services, need be unable to access them locally.

There is a hierarchy of innovation institutions just as there is a business hierarchy. The institutional hierarchy has, at the apex, the 13 Max Planck Institutes, the primary mission of which is fundamental research, though increasingly augmented in limited ways by commercial technology transfer. Next come the nine universities, many of which are among Germany's leading centres of scientific and technological research (e.g. Heidelberg, Stuttgart, Freiburg and Karlsruhe). Then follow the more applied research institutions such as the 14 Fraunhofer Institutes and the 64 other public non-university centres, ranging from international, through FRG, to industrial cooperative, institutes. Most of this upper and middle part of the hierarchy deals with government and larger-scale industry. At the smaller end of the industrial hierarchy, the main actors are the technology transfer arms of Baden-Württemberg's 13 Chambers of Industry and Commerce, private consultants (who will also contract to large firms) and, unique to the *Land*, the Steinbeis Foundation. The last-named is a network of over 100 technology transfer centres, mostly based in Baden-Württemberg's 39 *Fachhochschulen* (polytechnics) for the services of which SMEs make a contract with the transfer centre, 7 per cent of the value of which goes to the Foundation. Thus, the Steinbeis Foundation is 95 per cent self-funding (Cooke and Morgan, 1990).

This is clearly a rich and well-provided innovation system which acts as such. There are complementarities between institutions as well as competition. This mirrors the industrial scene where much of the dominant engineering industry is vertically disintegrated but functionally highly integrated. There are over 800 main suppliers to the automotive industry, most of whom supply the final assemblers such as Mercedes-Benz, Audi and Porsche or larger systems-assemblers such as Bosch or ZF. Equally, in electronics, with its even larger workforce (266,000 cf. 237,000 in automotives in 1989) a multitude of SMEs supplies giants such as SEL-Alcatel, Sony, IBM and Hewlett-Packard. SEL alone had, in Baden-Württemberg, 3,200 suppliers in 1990 with a purchasing value of DM 530 million. The key point here is that a great deal of innovative activity takes place between suppliers and customers in the region. Many customers have moved towards 'simultaneous engineering' which places new innovation burdens on SMEs (Morgan, Cooke and Price, 1992).

Herein lies the present crisis of the Baden-Württemberg 'network paradigm'. As more expensive and skills-intensive R&D is put out to SMEs they find they have neither the experience nor the knowledge necessary to comply. In 1992, the *Land* government commissioned A.D. Little to come up with recommendations. These, now policy, are to encourage collaborative research on the part of SMEs, stimulated with an incentives package and with precious knowhow protected by the involvement as 'honest-broker' of a Fraunhofer Institute (Cooke, Morgan and Price, 1993).

How replicable is the Baden-Württemberg innovation system elsewhere? The short answer is not at all, because for it to work there has to be a dense set of inter-institutional and inter-firm networks which come with sustained economic success and its associated prosperity. Few regions have thirty-nine polytechnics that can act as the basis for a Steinbeis system, for example. Nevertheless, lessons can be learnt and applied as appropriate. One of these is that 'networking' can fruitfully be practised. A second is that, as in the French or Italian cases, collaborative solutions are often necessary to enable firms to continue innovating the better to compete. The third is that public–private partnership is more robust than state or market approaches to innovation.

Conclusions

In brief, we have shown that the *spatial* dimension, in the form of the *innovation milieu* is an essential part of the innovation infrastructure of the successful economic region. This is becoming more and more the case as the traditional, stand-alone corporation of yore finds leaner and smaller competitors running rings around it. The worldwide increase in putting-out or sub-contracting supply to SMEs is one response, and regions that have the 'soft infrastructure' of innovative firms and institutions are best-placed to embed, for example, inward investors. But this embeddedness (Granovetter, 1985) may not be enough if firms expect market-forces to resolve problems of competitiveness. A collaborative ethic is seen to be in the ascendant, not only between firms seeking to enhance innovative potential, but between the public and private spheres as well. Tying much of this together is a sometimes barely comprehended *modus operandi* referred to as 'networking'. Innovation is increasingly a collaborative, learning process. The evidence we have advanced suggests innovation is strongest where the networks linking the 'soft infrastructure' of institutional support for business are most robust.

Bibliography

Becattini, G. (1990) 'The Marshallian Industrial District as a Socio-Economic Notion', in Pyke, F., Becattini, G. and Sengenberger, W. (eds) *Industrial Districts and Inter-firm Co-operation in Italy*, International Institute for Labour Studies, Geneva, pp. 37–51.

Bianchi, P. and Giordani, M. (1993) 'Innovation Policy at the Local and National Level: The Case of Emilia-Romagna', *European Planning Studies*, Vol. 1, pp. 25–42.

Brusco, S. (1990) 'The Idea of the Industrial District: Its Genesis', op. cit. pp. 10–19.

Camagni, R. (ed.) (1991) *Innovation Networks: Spatial Perspectives*, Belhaven Press, London.

Charbit, C., Gaffard, J., Longhi, C., Perrin, J., Quere, M. and Ravix, J. (1991) *Coherence and Diversity of Systems of Innovation: The Study of Local Systems of Innovation in Europe*, LATAPSES, Valbonne.

Colletis, G. (1993) 'An Analysis of Technological Potential and Regional Development Processes in Rhône-Alpes', *European Planning Studies*, 1, pp. 169–180.

Cooke, P. (1993) 'Regional Innovation Systems: An Evaluation of Six European Cases', in Getimis, P. and Kafkalas, G. (eds) *Urban and Regional Development in the New Europe*, Topos, Athens, pp. 133–54.

Cooke, P. and Morgan, K. (1990) 'Industry, Training and Technology Transfer: the Baden-Württemberg System in Perspective', *Regional Industrial Research Report No.6*, UWCC, Cardiff.

Cooke, P. and Morgan, K. (1991a) 'The Intelligent Region: Industrial and Institutional Innovation in Emilia-Romagna', *Regional Industrial Research Report No. 7*, UWCC, Cardiff.

Cooke, P. and Morgan, K. (1991b) 'The Network Paradigm: New Departures in Corporate and Regional Development', *Regional Industrial Research Report No. 8*, UWCC, Cardiff.

Cooke, P., Morgan, K. and Price, A. (1993) 'The Future of the *Mittelstand*: Collaboration versus Competition', *Regional Industrial Research Report No. 13*, UWCC, Cardiff.

Granovetter, M. (1985) 'Economic Action and Social Structure: The Problem of Embeddedness', *American Journal of Sociology*, 91, pp. 481–510.

Herrigel, G. (1989) 'Industrial Order and the Politics of Industrial Change: Mechanical Engineering', in Katzenstein, P. (ed.) *Industry and Politics in West Germany*, Cornell University Press, Ithaca, pp. 185–220.

Kamann, D. (1991) 'The Distribution of Dominance in Networks and its Spatial Implications', in Bergman, E., Maier, G. and Tödtling, F. (eds) *Regions Reconsidered: Economic Networks, Innovation and Local Development in Industrial Countries*, Mansell, London, pp. 35–58.

Maillat, D. and Vasserot, J. (1988) 'Economic and Territorial Conditions for Indigenous Revival in Europe's Industrial Regions', in Aydalot, P. and Keeble, D. (eds) *High Technology Industry and Innovative Environments*, Routledge, London, pp. 163–83.

Marshall, A. (1927) *Industry and Trade*, Macmillan, London.

Mazzonis, D. (1991) 'Small Firm Networking, Co-operation and Innovation in Italy', in Kuklinski, A. (ed.) *Transformation of Science in Poland*, State Committee for Scientific Research, Warsaw, pp. 270–83.

Morgan, K., Cooke, P. and Price, A. (1992) 'The Challenge of Lean Production in German Industry', *Regional Industrial Research Report No. 12*, UWCC, Cardiff.

Perroux, F. (1950) 'Economic Space, Theory and Applications', *Quarterly Journal of Economics*, 64, pp. 89–104.

Piore, M. and Sabel, C. (1984) *The Second Industrial Divide*, Basic Books, New York.

Sabel, C. (1989) 'Flexible Specialisation and the Re-emergence of Regional Economies', in Hirst, P. and Zeitlin, J. (eds) *Reversing Industrial Decline?*, Berg, Oxford, pp. 17–70.

Scott, A. (1988) *New Industrial Spaces*, Pion, London.

4. Industrial Innovation: Success, Strategy, Trends

Roy Rothwell

Introduction

Whilst for many years technological change was regarded by economists as merely a component of the residual factor in economic growth equations, today few would doubt its importance as a factor in economic progress, industrial change and international competitiveness (G. Dosi et al., 1988). Since the second half of the 1960s when researchers began to look inside the black box of the innovating company (Rosenberg, 1982) a great deal has been learned about the process through which technological change is brought to economic fruition, that is, the industrial innovation process. Below a brief summary is given of the aggregate results of studies of successful innovation and of changing perceptions of, and practice in, the process of innovation.

Success Factors

From the many studies of industrial innovation, including studies of success, studies of failure and comparisons between success and failure, the following success factors can be derived (Rothwell, 1992a):

1. The establishment of good internal and external communication; effective linkages with external sources of scientific and technological knowhow; a willingness to take on external ideas.
2. Treating innovation as a corporate-wide task: effective functional integration; involving all departments in the project from its earliest stages; ability to design for 'makeability'.
3. Implementing careful planning and project control procedures: committing resources to up-front screening of new projects; regular appraisal of projects.
4. Efficiency in development work and high quality production: implementing effective quality control procedures; taking advantage of up-to-date production equipment.

5. Strong market orientation: emphasis on satisfying user-needs; efficient customer linkages; where possible, involving potential users in the development process.
6. Providing a good technical service to customers, including customer training where appropriate; efficient spares supply.
7. The presence of certain key individuals: effective product champions and technological gatekeepers.
8. High quality of management: dynamic, open-minded managers; ability to attract and retain talented managers and researchers; a commitment to the development of human capital.

In addition to these project execution-type success factors Cooper (1980) has highlighted, amongst others, three additional kinds of variable important for success. These are:

- The nature of the product: specifically its uniqueness/superiority and the economic benefit it confers upon the customer.
- The nature of the market: intensity of market need, market growth rate and market size.
- The achievement of technical and production synergies between the new product and existing products.

The latter point emphasizes the importance to success of cumulative knowhow. In other words innovation is best seen in the context of the firm's unique techno/market trajectory and as a process of accumulation of associated specific capabilities and distinctive competences. (Maidique and Zirger, 1985; Dodgson, 1991; Prahalad and Hamel, 1990). Figure 4.1 shows innovation as a process of knowhow accumulation and illustrates the importance of both internal and external learning (Rothwell, 1992a).

The eight success factors listed above define success in terms of what firms do during innovation. To these we can add a set of higher level (strategic) factors that, essentially, are pre-conditions for sustained innovation to take place. These are (Rothwell, 1992a):

1. Top management commitment to, and visible support for, innovation. This is especially important in the case of radical innovations that might encounter internal and external opposition.
2. Long-term strategy in which innovation plays a key role (technology strategy). This enables firms to plan for inter-project technical, production and marketing synergies (planned learning).
3. Long-term commitment to major projects, based not on the sole criterion of short-term return on investment, but on considerations of future market penetration and growth (importance of 'patient money').

INTERNAL LEARNING

- R,D&D – learning by developing
- learning by testing
- learning by making – production learning
- learning by failing
- learning by using in vertically integrated companies
- cross-project learning

EXTERNAL OR JOINT INTERNAL/EXTERNAL LEARNING

- learning from/with suppliers
- learning from/with lead users
- learning through horizontal partnerships
- learning from/with the S&T infrastructure
- learning from the literature
- learning from competitors' actions

- learning through reverse engineering
- learning from acquisitions or new personnel
- learning through customer-based prototype trials
- learning through servicing/fault finding

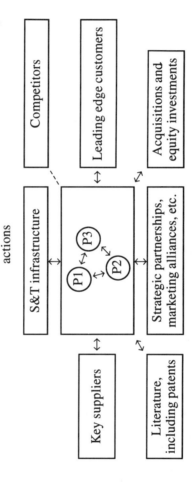

Figure 4.1 *Innovation as a process of know-how accumulation*

35

4. Corporate flexibility and responsiveness to change. This is essential especially in enabling the firm to adapt to the requirements of radical innovation. 'Organic' organizations are more amenable to these requirements than are their 'mechanistic' counterparts (Burns and Stalker, 1961).
5. Top management acceptance of risk and an associated need for sensible termination criteria.
6. Creation of an innovation-accepting, entrepreneurship-accommodating culture. Without this the firm will dampen the activities, or lose altogether, its most valuable asset – dynamic, entrepreneurial individuals.

In general, the project execution and corporate level success factors (summarized in Table 4.1) are common to all sectors, although their rank order of importance can vary between sectors (Rothwell et al., 1974).

In addition, successful innovators generally outperform failures across the board. Success is a matter of competence in all functions and of balance and coordination between them (Cooper and Kleinschmidt, 1988). Finally,

Table 4.1 Success factors

PROJECT EXECUTION FACTORS

– Good internal and external communication: accessing external knowhow
– Treating innovation as a corporate-wide task: effective inter-functional coordination: good balance of functions
– Implementing careful planning and project control procedures: high quality up-front analysis
– Efficiency in development work and high quality production
– Strong marketing orientation: emphasis on satisfying user needs: development emphasis on creating user value
– Providing a good technical service to customers: effective user education
– Effective product champions and technological gatekeepers
– High quality, open-minded management: commitment to the development of human capital
– Attaining cross-project synergies and inter-project learning

CORPORATE LEVEL FACTORS

– Top management commitment and visible support for innovation
– Long-term corporate strategy with associated technology strategy
– Long-term commitment to major projects (patient money)
– Corporate flexibility and responsiveness to change
– Top management acceptance of risk
– Innovation-accepting, entrepreneurship-accommodating culture.

Source: Rothwell, R.(1992a).

success is 'people centred' and, while formal techniques can enhance the performance of dynamic, gifted and entrepreneurial managers, they can do little to raise the performance of innovatory management lacking these qualities.

Innovation and Strategy

Corporate strategy has many targets to address (Figure 4.2) and its formulation and implementation is a complex and interactive process. All the strategy targets are influenced by or have implications for industrial innovation. Until the work of Cooper (1984), however, surprisingly little attention was paid to the relationship between corporate strategy and innovation success. Cooper showed that strategies associated with high innovatory performance were characterized by the following 'dimensions':

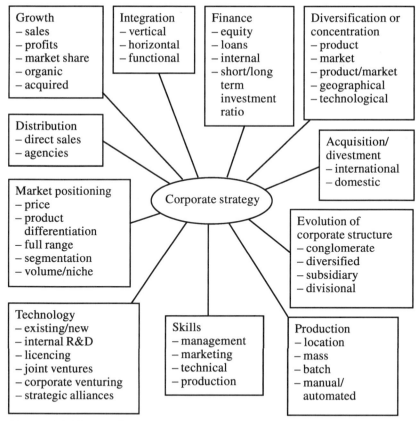

Figure 4.2 Targets for corporate strategy
Source: Rothwell, R. (1992a).

- An aggressive technological orientation: having a strong R&D orientation and being proactive in acquiring new technologies.
- A venturesome, offensive innovation programme that is viewed as a leading edge of corporate strategy.
- A market-oriented programme, featuring strong user linkages and a significant effort directed towards identifying user needs coupled to a proactive search for new product ideas.
- The development of products with marked differential advantages which meet customer requirements better than competitive products and had a marked impact on customers.
- The employment of sophisticated technologies that have a high degree of synergy with the firm's technological and production resource base.
- A relatively diverse new product programme yielding products and end uses not necessarily closely related to each other, but in potentially large, high need, growth markets.

The author concluded: 'What we witness is not a single strategy, but a packet of strategies that differentiated these high performers from the rest of the firms. A marriage of technological prowess, a strong marketing orientation, the search for a differentiated advantage, and a willingness to accept risk appears to be the key to a high performance programme' (Cooper, 1984).

Despite there being no single corporate strategy element uniquely associated with successful innovation, nevertheless at different times during the post-World War II era specific elements have been at the strategic forefront in Western companies. This evolution in 'dominant' strategy elements is outlined in Table 4.2, along with a brief description of the associated major impacting features of the external environment. Taken together this suggests that the dominant elements in corporate strategies at a given time are to a significant extent contingent on exogenous factors although, as Ansoff (1984) points out, firms are also important actors in influencing the environment in which they operate.

Amongst the dominant corporate strategy themes that have come to the fore during the late 1980s – early 1990s are:

- inter-firm collaboration (networking strategy);
- technological accumulation (technology strategy);
- integrated product and manufacturing strategies (design for manufacturability);
- flexibility (organizational, managerial, product, manufacturing);
- product quality/performance (differentiation strategy);
- the environment (environmental strategy); and
- speed-to-market (time-based strategy).

Table 4.2 Corporate strategy evolution

PERIOD 1:   **1950s–MID 1960s**

Period characterized by postwar recovery, the growth of new technology-based sectors and the technology-led regeneration of existing sectors. Introduction and rapid diffusion of major new product ranges. Demand exceeds production capacity. Corporate strategic emphasis on R&D and on manufacturing build-up.

PERIOD 2:   **MID 1960s–EARLY 1970s**

Period of general prosperity; emphasis on corporate growth, both organic and acquired. Growing level of corporate diversification. Conglomerates formed through acquisition and merger. Capacity and demand more or less in balance. During the latter part of the period, intensifying competition. Growing strategic emphasis on marketing.

PERIOD 3:   **MID 1970s–EARLY 1980s**

Period of high inflation and demand saturation (crisis of 'stagnation'). Supply capacity exceeds demand. Strategies of consolidation and rationalization with emphasis on scale and experience curve benefits. Some de-diversification. Growing strategic concern with accountancy and financing issues (cost focus).

PERIOD 4:   **EARLY 1980s–1990**

Initial period of economic recovery followed by recession. Finance-led merger and acquisition boom giving way to concentration on core businesses and core technologies. Growing awareness of the strategic importance of emerging generic technologies with increased strategic emphasis on technological accumulation (technology strategy). Growing emphasis on manufacturing (manufacturing strategy). Growth in strategic alliances, strategic acquisitions and internationalization in ownership and production. Global strategies. Technology fusion.

Major impact of new technologies. High rates of technological change. Intense competition. Rapid product cycles with growing strategic emphasis on time-based strategies. Increased intra-firm and inter-firm integration (networking). Integrated technology and manufacturing strategies. Emphasis on flexibility and product diversity and quality. Continued emphasis on technological accumulation. Environmental issues of growing strategic concern.

The above suggests that today strategy is highly complex with a broad combination of central strategic themes. This is a response to the complex and turbulent nature of the external competitive, technological and economic environment facing companies. To some extent technological innovation is seen as a means by which firms can attempt to adapt to the requirements of this difficult and uncertain environment: on the other hand rapid rates of technological change, associated shorter product cycles and the increased blurring of long-established industrial boundaries (technology fusion) (Kodama, 1992) are themselves a part of the difficulty.

Towards the Fifth Generation Innovation Process

Not only have dominant corporate strategy elements changed during the past forty or so years, but the dominant perceived model of innovation, and to a great extent the practice of innovation, have changed also. These changes are mapped below in the form of five generations of innovation process.

First generation: technology-push
From about 1950 to the second half of the 1960s the dominant model of innovation was the so-called technology-push model shown in Figure 4.3. This was a simple linear model that assumed a stepwise progression from scientific discovery through applied research to technological development and production activities in firms, leading to a stream of new products into the marketplace. The marketplace was seen simply as a sink for receiving the fruits of R&D. A fundamental assumption of this model was that 'more R&D in' equalled 'more innovation out'.

Second generation: need-pull
During the latter part of the 1960s, a period of intensifying competition, studies of actual innovation processes began to place considerably more emphasis on the role of the marketplace in innovation. This led to the emergence of the linear need-pull (or market-pull) model of innovation shown in Figure 4.4, in which innovations were deemed to arise as the result of perceived and sometimes clearly articulated customer needs. In this case the marketplace was seen as the source of ideas for directing R&D, and the R&D department had a largely reactive role to play.

Third generation: coupling model
During the 1970s a spate of detailed and systematic empirical studies showed the linear technology-push and need-pull models of innovation to be oversimplified, extreme and atypical examples of a more general process of *coupling* between science, technology and the marketplace (Myers and Marquis, 1969; Rothwell, 1976; Cooper, 1980). Evidence in favour of this view was summarized by Mowery and Rosenberg (1978) and few today would argue with their case for a more balanced approach between technology supply and market needs.

A still highly simplified, but nevertheless more representative model of the innovation process is given in Figure 4.5. This is the so-called interactive or coupling model which, according to Rothwell and Zegveld (1985), can be regarded as:

> . . . a logically sequential, though not necessarily continuous, process that can be divided into a series of functionally distinct but interacting and interdependent stages.

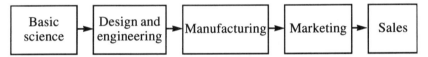

Figure 4.3 Technology push (first generation) (1950s – mid 1960s)

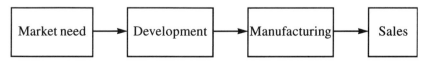

Figure 4.4 Market pull (second generation) (late 1960s – early 1970s)

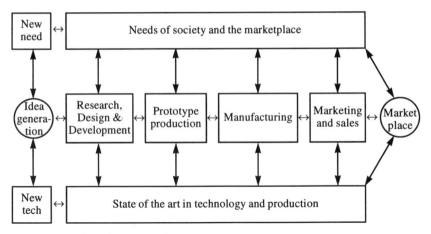

Figure 4.5 'Coupling' model (third generation) (mid 1970s – early 1980s)
Source: Rothwell, R. (1993), 'Systems Integration and Networking: Towards the Fifth Generation Innovation Process', Chaire Hydro-Quebec Conference en Gestion de la Technologie, University of Montreal, Quebec, 28 May (SPRU, University of Sussex, Brighton, UK – mimeo).

The overall pattern of the innovation process can be thought of as a complex net of communication paths, both intra-organisational and extra-organisational, linking together the various in-house functions and linking the firm to the broader scientific and technological community and to the marketplace. In other words the process of innovation represents the confluence of technological capabilities and market needs within the framework of the innovating firm (Rothwell and Zegveld, 1985, p. 50).

Fourth generation: integrated model
Whilst the third generation innovation process contains feedback loops it essentially remains *sequential*, albeit with some inter-functional interaction and coordination. The first truly *parallel* models of innovation emerged following studies of innovation process in the automobile and electronics sectors in Japan. Here there is total or a very high level of functional overlap during innovation. An example of the 4G innovation process is presented in Figure 4.6, taken from the work of Graves (1987), in the Japanese automobile industry. A core feature of this so-called 'rugby team' approach (Imai, Nonaka and Takeuchi, 1985) is not just its parallelism, but also the high level of functional *integration* during concurrent activity.

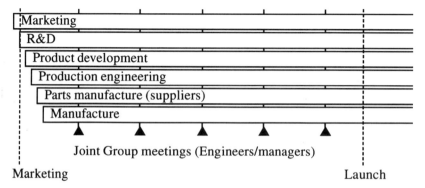

Figure 4.6 Example of the integrated (fourth generation) innovation process (mid-1980s–1990s) – new product development process in Nissan

Source: Graves, 1987.

Note: This representation of 4G focuses essentially on the two primary *internal* features of the process, i.e. its *parallel* and *integrated* nature. Around this in practice is the web of external interactions represented in the 3G process (Figure 4.3).

Fifth generation: systems integration and networking (SIN) (taken from Rothwell, 1992a)
An important feature of product development as practised in Japan is the apparent speed and cost advantages it provides Japanese innovators over their innovating counterparts in the West. For example several authors have, in seeking Japanese/US comparisons, shown that Japanese companies develop products faster and at lower cost in sectors as diverse as marine transmissions (Stalk and Hout, 1990) automobiles (Clark and Fujimoto, 1989) and machinery and instruments (Mansfield, 1988). In other words, cross-functional (parallel) development and more effective overall integration, with their inherently greater potential for higher real-time

information processing efficiency, can yield a speedier and more efficient product development process. Since one of the dominant corporate strategy elements during the 1980s has been development speed (time-based strategy), this has provided Japanese firms with a strong competitive edge.

Achieving increased development speed might, of course, carry with it additional costs; doubling development resources, for example, would almost certainly reduce development time considerably. According to Graves (1987) compressing development time by 1 per cent can increase costs by 1–2 per cent. Gupta and Wileman (1990) propose a 'U'-shaped time/cost curve and, quoting from the work of Mansfield (1988), suggest that Japanese firms are willing to devote considerably more resources to compressing development cycles if the long-term benefits (e.g. greater customer value) justify the short-term expense. Even when being first is not of overriding importance, the ability to be fast or timely might confer advantage to the firm. The ability to control product development speed can be seen as an important corporate core competence.

One interpretation of the comparative US/Japanese time and cost data is that the Japanese firms were operating near the bottom of the 'U' whilst US firms were too far to the right along their particular industry time/cost curve (there will be strong sectoral specificities). There is, however, little or no indication that Japanese firms are faster but more expensive than their US counterparts at product development. It seems reasonable to suggest – and there is strong evidence from the automobile sector in support of this contention (Graves, 1991) – that the US and Japanese firms were operating along different 'U'-curves; that US firms were operating along a third generation (3G) innovation curve whilst Japanese firms were operating along a fourth generation (4G) curve (Figure 4.5).

There is considerable evidence to show that innovation today has become significantly more of a *networking process*. During the 1980s the number of horizontal strategic alliances and collaborative R&D consortia have increased dramatically (Contractor and Lorange, 1988; Hagedoorn, 1990; Dodgson, 1993; Haklisch, Fusfeld and Levinson, 1986), vertical relationships, especially at the supplier interface, have become more intimate and strategic in nature (Maier, 1988; Lamming, 1992) and innovative SMEs are forging a variety of external relationships with both large and small firms (Rothwell, 1989; 1991). At the same time, pressures to become a *fast innovator* increased and, as we have seen, the Japanese have succeeded in being both fast and efficient innovators. Leading edge innovators today are moving towards a third and even more efficient time/cost curve (Figure 4.7) that is determined by the 5G innovation process – which is one of *systems integration and networking* (SIN) – in which, centrally, the use of a sophisticated electronic toolkit (elements of which are described in the following section) is enhancing the speed and efficiency of product development across the whole system of innovation (in-house functions,

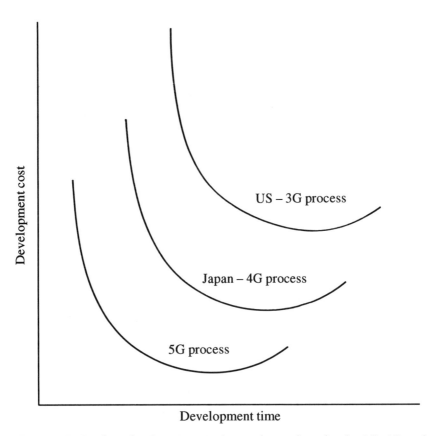

Figure 4.7 Product development time/cost relationships for the 3G, 4G and
5G innovation process

Source: Rothwell, R. (1993), 'Systems Integration and Networking: Towards the Fifth
Generation Innovation Process', Chaire Hydro-Quebec Conference en Gestion de la
Technologie, University of Montreal, Quebec, 28 May (SPRU, University of Sussex,
Brighton, UK – mimeo).

suppliers, customers, collaborators). *5G essentially is a development of 4G*
in which the technology of technological change is itself changing.

A wide variety of managerial, organizational and technological factors
have been identified which contribute to enhanced speed and/or efficiency
of innovation. Many are well established in the innovation literature; a few
are more recent in origin. The most significant of these factors are dealt
with briefly below:

(i)   *Time-based strategy*
Given the scope of activities that needs to be addressed in order appreciably to accelerate product development, it is unlikely that significant gains could be achieved unless the issue was tackled on a broad front. This means that being a fast innovator must be at the forefront of corporate strategy.

(ii)   *Top management commitment and support*
Visible top management commitment and support is important in achieving faster product development speed (McDonough and Barczac, 1991). Moreover, top management should be involved in the development process from the very beginning since, where late involvement occurs, this often results in design changes that are highly costly (Sommerlatte, 1992).

(iii) *Adequate preparation: mobilizing commitment and resources*
This comprises what Ansoff (1992) terms building platforms for change. It involves careful project evaluation, analysis and planning and, centrally, gaining commitment, understanding and support from the corporate entity and staff who will be involved in the project.

(iv)   *Efficiency at indirect development activities*
Activities such as project control, project administration and coordination can account for up to 50 per cent of total project development time (Sommerlatte, 1992). Clearly, actions that render these activities more efficient have potential for significantly reducing development times and costs.

(v)   *Adopting a horizontal management style with increased decision-making at lower levels*
The greater empowerment of managers at lower levels reduces the number of approvals required, and the reduction in hierarchy reduces approval delays (Dumaine, 1989).

(vi)   *Committed and empowered product champions and project leaders*
Empowered product champions and project leaders can play an important role in achieving both successful and faster new product development (Graves, 1991).

(vii) *High quality initial product specification*
Not surprisingly, when the initial definition of product requirements is flawed, it results in unplanned changes during product development and can be a major factor in delay (Gupta and Wileman, 1990). It will also add significantly to development costs.

(viii) *Use of integrated (cross-functional) teams during development and prototyping*
Where parallel activities take place outside the framework of the fully integrated team, then continuous inter-functional interaction

(information integration) is essential throughout the periods of functional overlap (Clark and Fujimoto, 1991).

(ix)   *Commitment to across-the-board quality control*

A company clearly can speed up product development if it is willing to cut corners in the process, but in doing so it is likely to incur high downstream costs and delays when it is faced with remedial re-design activity. According to Hewlett-Packard (1988), total quality control in product development is an essential feature in raising overall product development efficiency, including reduced cycle times.

(x)   *Incremental development strategy*

There is evidence to suggest that one reason Japanese manufacturers achieve relatively rapid product cycles is that they aim for smaller technological steps between successive models (Clark and Fujimoto, 1989). Over-emphasis on 'cheap and easy' incremental changes does, however, carry the danger that more radical changes with high long-term profit potential can be rejected or ignored (Crawford, 1992).

(xi)   *Adopting a 'carry-over' strategy*

This refers to the utilization of significant elements of earlier models in the most recent designs. Examples are the use in the new Airbus A330 and A340 aircraft of existing wide-body fuselage cross-sections and the A310 tail fin, and the use in the top of the range Toyota Lexus of a modified version of the floor plan of the well established and successful Camray.

(xii)   *Product design combining the old with the new*

This relates to factor (xi) but refers to the use of major elements of existing designs as the basis for creating new product types, rather than new models of existing types. A good example of this was the use by Black and Decker of existing drill components to help create their highly successful hot air (heat gun) paint stripper.

(xiii) *Designed-in flexibility*

This refers to the creation of designs that contain inherent flexibility or technological slack such that they can be subsequently stretched into a design family of significant variants (Rothwell and Gardiner, 1988). With those so-called 'robust designs' (they are robust with respect to changing customer requirements and market segmentation), the cost of the original design might be high, but the subsequent costs of creating new family members often over a period of many years, are relatively modest. A good example of a robust design is the Boeing 747.

(xiv)   *Economy in technology*

The economy in technology concept relates, in a sense, to the robust design principle. There are two aspects to this strategy: the first is the aim to apply a particular basic technological capability/understanding across the widest possible range of products; the second is to design core sub-assemblies that can be used across an extended range of products.

(xv) *Close linkages with primary suppliers*
Close and early linkages with suppliers can reduce development costs and increase development speed. This has long been a feature of product development in Japan, where suppliers can be an integral part of the development process, and today it appears increasingly to be occurring in Europe and the USA with the emergence of true supplier/manufacturer partnerships (Lamming, 1992).

(xvi) *Up-to-date component database*
Creating a comprehensive, up-to-date database on new component and material characteristics and availability and the status of preferred suppliers, can facilitate design start-up and reduce the overall design cycle.

(xvii) *Involving leading-edge users*
Users who are technologically strong and innovation-demanding can assist in increasing development speed and reducing development costs especially if, as in the case of partnering suppliers, they become actively involved in product development. Perhaps the most obvious example of this is when the user is also the inventor of the new product and has created a rough prototype for own use before transferring the design to the manufacturer (von Hippel, 1988; Rothwell, 1986).

(xviii) *Accessing external knowhow*
Gold (1987) argues that the use of external R&D can speed up new product development, as can buying or licensing-in existing technology. Mansfield (1988) found, across a range of industries, that both the time and the cost of product development for products that were based mainly on existing ,external technology were less than for those relying mainly on in-house development, and that the effects were particularly strong in Japan. In cases of technology fusion, external alliances should, on the face of it, help to reduce both the time and the cost of developing radical new products.

(xix) *Use of computers for efficient intra-firm communication and data sharing*
Not surprisingly, efficient information flows contribute to efficient product development. Increasingly, computer-based systems are being used to enhance intra-firm information efficiency. For example, during the second half of the 1980s, Black and Decker succeeded in increasing the number of new product introductions while simultaneously reducing product lead times, a process in which computerized linkages played a key role. Stalk and Hout

(1990) argue that 'by reorganising the design staffs and developing a computer-aided design system that links the company worldwide, B&D has been able to halve its design cycle'.

(xx)   *Use of linked CAD systems along the production filière*

Not only are electronic (CAD) linkages important *within* firms, but they are also a powerful tool for closer integration *between* firms at the supplier/manufacturer and the manufacturer/customer interfaces. For example, electronic manufacturer/supplier design linkages are becoming an increasingly common feature in the design of application-specific semiconductors (ASICs) and are also taking place in plastic injection mould manufacturing, and linkages right across the filière are developing in the aeroengine sector.

(xxi)   *Use of fast prototyping techniques*

One of the advantages of the use of information technology in product design is that the 3D-CAD images thus generated can, using a variety of techniques, be rapidly transferred into physical prototypes (Kruth, 1991; Juster, 1992).

(xxii) *Use of simulation modelling*

Replacing physical prototyping by simulation modelling can significantly enhance overall development efficiency. This approach increasingly is being utilized in industries as diverse as automobiles, pharmaceuticals, aeroengines, mould manufacturing and electronics. Simulation does not obviate the need for physical prototyping completely, since to omit this practice entirely would in most cases be too risky. Simulation does, however, considerably reduce the number of required physical prototypes built.

(xxiii) *Creating technology demonstrators*

In fields for which the various critical parameters and operating relationships are well understood, simulation modelling can be relatively straightforward (e.g. in electronic circuit design). In other areas, however, basic data have to be generated as inputs to simulation models, and this can have implications for the balance of expenditure between basic and more downstream technological activity, with a shift towards the more basic end of the spectrum. Technology demonstrators have to be created as a crucial input to simulation models.

(xxiv) *Use of expert systems as a design aid*

The use of computer-based product design and simulation techniques enables innovators to embark on electronics-based heuristics and, in some cases, to develop expert systems. For example, in Japan, Canon have developed OPTEX, an expert system for TV camera lens design. As an example of its effectiveness, OPTEX reduced one design task from six person months (four people working for one and a half months) to half a person month (one person working for two weeks) (Feigenbaum, McCorduck and Nii, 1988).

Not all the above factors will apply equally in the case of radical innovations, successive generations of existing products and product improvements. All will contribute equally to enhancing development speed and improving development efficiency, and between them they more or less encompass the main features of the 5G innovation process, which is outlined in Table 4.3.

Table 4.3: The fifth generation innovation process: Systems Integration and Networking (SIN)

Underlying strategy elements

- Time-based strategy (faster, more efficient product development)
- Development focus on quality and other non-price factors
- Emphasis on corporate flexibility and responsiveness
- Customer focus at the forefront of strategy
- Strategic integration with primary suppliers
- Strategies for horizontal technological collaboration
- Electronic data processing strategies
- Policy of total quality control

Primary enabling features

- Greater overall organizational and systems integration:
  - parallel and integrated (cross-functional) development process
  - early supplier involvement in product development
  - involvement of leading-edge users in product development
  - establishing horizontal technological collaboration where appropriate

- Flatter, more flexible organizational structures for rapid and effective decision-making:
  - greater empowerment of managers at lower levels
  - empowered product champions/project leaders.

- Fully developed internal data bases:
  - effective data sharing systems
  - product development metrics, computer-based heuristics, expert systems
  - electronically assisted product development using 3D-CAD systems and simulation modelling
  - linked CAD/CAE systems to enhance product development flexibility and product manufacturability

- Effective external data links:
  - co-development with suppliers using linked CAD systems
  - use of CAD at the customer interface
  - effective data links with R&D collaborators

Source: Rothwell, R. (1992b).

Summary

There is a wide range of factors associated with successful innovation which appear to be common to all sectors of manufacturing, albeit with different weightings in different sectors. Success is multi-factored and is inextricably linked to the qualities and abilities of those involved in managing the process.

Strategies associated with successfully innovative firms similarly are multi-dimensional emphasizing the importance of both technological and marketing factors. Despite the multi-faceted and highly interactive nature of corporate strategy, at different periods during the past forty years or so one or several strategy elements have dominated, influenced by conditions prevailing in the external environment and by the availability of various tools and techniques to managers and innovators.

During the same period perceptions of and practice in innovation have changed, and this was mapped above in terms of five generations of the innovation process. This sequential model should not be taken to imply successive, across-the-board substitution of one process for the next; today all types of process exist in one form or another. In the first case some firms encounter difficulties in unlearning one process type and shifting to a more appropriate model.

Secondly, there will be differences between the science-based sectors and assembly-type sectors. In the former, the process will be internalized to a greater extent with limited input variety and will, at least in its early stages, be largely sequential (perhaps 3G with limited functional overlap); in the latter the best-practice process will lie somewhere between 4G and the forward-looking 5G and will involve a great variety of inputs and of actors; that is, 5G involves *networks of innovators*.

One of the main differences between 4G and 5G is the use by the latter of a sophisticated electronic toolkit to aid design and development activities. This includes simulation modelling, computer-based heuristics and inter-firm and intra-firm co-development using linked CAD and CAD-CAE systems. Development speed and efficiency gains derive largely from the inherently greater information processing efficiency of 5G across the innovation network, in which electronic-based communications complement and enhance the informal (face-to-face) information exchanges characteristic of 4G. 5G is essentially a *lean innovation* process.

Attaining 5G will not be a frictionless or costless process. Entry costs include not only equipment purchases and training, but more importantly learning costs across the complete system of innovation. Whatever the entry costs, however, it seems likely that it is those companies that succeed in mastering the essential features of 5G today that will be the leading-edge innovators of tomorrow.

Bibliography

Ansoff, H.I. (1984) *Implanting Strategic Management*, Prentice Hall, Englewood Cliffs N.J.

Ansoff, H.I. (1992) 'Managing Discontinuous Strategic Change', in Ansoff, H.I.; Biseman, A. and Storm, P.M. (eds.), *Understanding and Managing Strategic Change*, North-Holland Publishing Company, Amsterdam.

Burns, T. and Stalker, G. (1961) *The Management of Innovation*, Tavistock, London.

Clark, K.B. and Fujimoto, T. (1989) 'Lead Time in Automobile Product Development: Exploring the Japanese Advantage', *Journal of Engineering and Technology Management*, Vol. 6, pp. 25–58.

Clark, K.B. and Fujimoto, T. (1991) *Product Development Performance*, JBS Press, Boston, MA.

Contractor, F.J. and Lorange, P. (1988) *Cooperative Strategies in International Business*, Lexington Books, Lexington, MA.

Cooper, R.G. (1980) 'Project New Prod: Factors in New Product Success', *European Journal of Marketing*, Vol. 14, No. 5–6, pp. 277–92.

Cooper, R.G. (1984) 'The Strategy-Performance Link in New Product Development', *R&D Management*, Vol. 14, No. 4, pp. 247–59.

Cooper, R.G. and Kleinschmidt, E.J. (1988) 'Resource Allocation in New Product Success and Failure', *Industrial Marketing Management*, Vol. 17, No. 3, pp. 249–62.

Crawford, C.M. (1992) 'The Hidden Costs of Accelerated Product Development', *Journal of Product Innovation Management*, Vol. 9, pp. 188–99.

Dodgson, M. (1991) 'Technology Learning, Technology Strategy and Competitive Pressures', *British Journal of Management*, Vol. 2, pp. 133–49.

Dodgson, M. (1993) *Technological Collaboration in Industry*, Routledge, London.

Dosi, G., Freeman, C., Nelson, R., Silverberg, G. and Soete, L. (1988) *Technical Change and Economic Theory*, Pinter, London.

Dumaine, B. (1989) 'How Managers Can Succeed Through Speed', *Fortune*, February 13.

Feigenbaum, E., McCorduck, P. and Nii, H.P. (1988) *The Rise of the Expert Company*, Macmillan, London.

Gold, B. (1987) 'Approaches to Accelerating New Product Development', *Journal of Product Innovation Management*, Vol. 4, pp. 81–8.

Graves, A. (1987) 'Comparative Trends in Automotive Research and Development', DRC Discussion Paper No. 54, SPRU, University of Sussex, Brighton, UK.

Graves, A. (1991) *International Competitiveness and Technology Development in the World Automobile Industry*, DPhil thesis, Science Policy Research Unit, University of Sussex, Brighton, UK.

Graves, S.B. (1989), 'Why Costs Increase When Projects Accelerate, *Research Technology Management*, March–April, pp.16–18.

Gupta, A.K. and Wileman, D.L. (1990) 'Accelerating the Development of Technology-Based New Products', *California Management Review*, Vol. 32, No. 2, Winter, pp. 24–44.

Hagedoorn, J. (1990) 'Organizational Needs of Inter-Firm Cooperation and Technology Transfer', *Technovation*, Vol. 10, No. 1, pp. 17–30.

Haklisch, C.S., Fusfeld, H.I. and Levinson, A.D. (1986) *Trends in Collective Industrial Research*, Centre for Science and Technology Policy, Graduate School of Business Administration, New York University (Reference 20).

Hewlett-Packard (1988) 'Hewlett-Packard and Engineering Productivity', Design Center, Hewlett-Packard, Palo Alto, USA (May).

Imai, K., Nonaka, I. and Takeuchi, H. (1985) 'Managing the New Product Development', in Clark, K. and Hayes, R. (eds), *The Uneasy Alliance*, H.B.S Press, Boston.

Juster, N.P. (1992) 'A Summary of Rapid Prototyping Processes', CARP, Department of Mechanical Engineering, Leeds University, Leeds, UK.

Kodama, F. (1992) 'Technology Fusion and the New R&D', *Harvard Business Review*, July–August, pp. 70–8.

Kruth, J.P. (1991) 'Material Increase Manufacturing by Rapid Prototyping Techniques', *Annals of the CIRP*, Vol. 40, No. 2, pp. 603–14.

Lamming, R. (1992) *Supplier Strategies in the Automotive Components Industry: Development Towards Lean Production*, D.Phil thesis, SPRU, University of Sussex, Brighton, UK.

Maidique, M.A. and Zirger, B.J. (1985) 'The New Product Learning Cycle', *Research Policy*, Vol. 14, December pp. 299–313.

Maier, H. (1988) 'Partnerships between Small and Large Firms: Current Trends and Prospects', Conference on Partnerships between Small and Large Firms, EC, Brussels, 13–14 June.

Mansfield, E. (1988) 'The Speed and Cost of Industrial Innovation in Japan and the United States: External vs. Internal Technology', *Management Science*, Vol. 34, No. 19, pp.1157–68.

McDonough, E.F. and Barczac, G. (1991) 'Speeding Up New Product Development: The Effects of Leadership Style and Source of Technology', *Journal of Product Innovation Management*, Vol. 8, pp. 203–11.

Mowery, D.C. and Rosenberg, N. (1978) 'The Influence of Market Demand upon Innovation', *Research Policy*, Vol. 8, April.

Myers, S. and Marquis, D.G. (1969) *Successful Industrial Innovation*, National Science Foundation, Washington DC.

Prahalad, C.K. and Hamel, G. (1990) 'The Core Competence of the Corporation', *Harvard Business Review*, May–June, pp. 79–91.

Rosenberg, N. (1982) *Inside the Black Box*, Cambridge University Press, Cambridge.

Rothwell, R. (1976) *Innovation in Textile Machinery: Some Significant Factors in Success and Failure*, SPRU Occasional Paper Series, No. 2, June, University of Sussex, Brighton, UK.

Rothwell, R. (1986) 'Innovation and Re-Innovation: A Role for the User', *Journal of Marketing Management*, Vol. 2, No. 2, pp. 109–23.

Rothwell, R. (1989) 'SMFs, Inter-Firm Relationships and Technological Change', *Entrepreneurship and Regional Development*, Vol. 1, pp. 275–91.

Rothwell, R. (1991) 'External Networking and Innovation in Small and Medium-Sized Manufacturing Firms in Europe,' *Technovation*, Vol. 11, No. 2, pp. 93–112.

Rothwell, R. (1992a) 'Successful Industrial Innovation: Critical Factors for the 1990s', *R&D Management*, Vol. 22, No. 3, pp. 221–39.

Rothwell, R. (1992b) 'Issues in User-Producer Relations: Role of Government', presented to 6 Countries Programme Conference on User-Producer Relations in the Innovation Process, Dipoli Conference Centre, Espoo, Finland, 26–27 November, mimeo, SPRU, University of Sussex. To be published in Gold, B. (ed.) Special Annual Issue of the *International Journal of Technology Management*, 1993.

Rothwell, R. (1993) 'Systems Integration and Networking: The Fifth Generation Innovation Process', presented at Chaire Hydro-Quebec Conference en Gestion de la Technologie, Université de Québec à Montréal, 28 May (mimeo, SPRU, University of Sussex).

Rothwell, R. and Zegveld, W. (1985) *Reindustrialization and Technology*, Longman, Harlow.

Rothwell, R. and Gardiner, P. (1988) 'The Strategic Management of Re-Innovation", *R&D Management*, Vol. 18, No. 2, April.

Rothwell, R. et al. (1974) 'SAPPHO Updated: Project SAPPHO Phase II", *Research Policy*, Vol. 3, No. 3, pp. 258–91.

Sommerlatte, T. (1992) 'Raising Technology Development Productivity', in *Enterprise, Innovation and 1992*, TII, Luxembourg.

Stalk, G. Jr., and Hout, T.M. (1990) 'Competing Against Time', *Research Technology Management*, March–April, pp. 19–24.

von Hippel, E. (1988) *The Sources of Innovation*, Oxford University Press.

5. Basic Research and Industrial Innovation

W. Edward Steinmueller

Traditional understanding of the connection between basic research and industrial innovation is based on a 'linear model' of knowledge production and transfer. In that model, basic research produces a flow of theories and findings that are refined through applied research, tested in the 'development' process, and finally commercialized as industrial innovations. The linear model is a framework for categorizing the processes of knowledge creation according to their commercial aims. When research is conducted with little or no regard to commercial applications it is 'basic research'. When commercially useful methods are the subject of examination, the activity is called 'applied research'. When specific products or processes are being designed and tested, the process is called 'development'. The linear model is also a theory of knowledge production. Each level in the linear model produces outputs that are transferred to the next level as inputs. For example, basic research outputs, its theories and findings, are inputs to applied research. In keeping with the sequential nature of the model, the flow is unidirectional; 'later' stages do not provide inputs for earlier stages. Finally, the linear model is a theory of epistemology. It characterizes the transfer of knowledge as involving refinement and adaptation from universal principles to particular instances, from comprehensive theory to specific applications. The linear model is the foundation of present methods for collecting statistical information on research activities, for organizing economic research on the social benefits of scientific research, and for explaining the role of science in industrial innovation. Nonetheless, there is growing criticism of the linear model. As a framework for categorizing the processes of knowledge creation, the linear model diverts attention from the economic and social determinants of scientific research activity (Dasgupta and David, 1992; Merton, 1973). As a theory of knowledge production, the linear model ignores the role of technology in shaping the aims, methods, and productivity of science and neglects the non-scientific origins of many technological developments (Kline and Rosenberg, 1986; Rosenberg, 1974, 1976, 1982; Basalla, 1988). As epistemology, the linear model creates distinctions that closer examinations of scientific and technological activity fail to confirm (Galison, 1987; Narin and Noma, 1985).

The shortcomings of the linear model, to be described in more detail below, should not disqualify it as a useful heuristic for examining the relation between basic research and industrial innovation. Indeed, many of the economic studies and policy discussions described below rely heavily upon this framework. Moreover, alternative theories are at an early stage of development and have often been developed to dispute specific claims of the linear model. Thus, the method employed here is to identify several critical themes that are equally useful for assessing current and suggesting new approaches for understanding the relation between basic research and industrial innovation. First, we will examine the construction of the current linear framework and how it relies on the particularities of relatively recent experience and intermingles assumptions about incentives, institutions, and epistemology. Second, we will consider how, as a research heuristic, the current theory has focused attention on the transmission of knowledge while diverting attention from the interdependencies and social determinants of science and technology. Third, we will explore some of the opportunities for theoretical and empirical understanding that are offered by adopting a 'network of knowledge creating activities' view of the relations between basic research and industrial innovation.

The ideas that science plays an originating role in industrial innovation and transmits utilitarian knowledge to society are not new, but they have become widely shared only in the second half of this century. The experience with the scientific community in World War II was pivotal in establishing the widespread belief that science could make major contributions to industry. Among the most striking and influential pronouncements of the potential contribution of science to public welfare was Vannevar Bush's *Science – The Endless Frontier*.[1] Bush summarizes this report to President Franklin Roosevelt with the comment:

> The pioneer spirit is still vigorous within this Nation. Science offers a largely unexplored hinterland for the pioneer who has the tools for his task. The rewards of such exploration both for the Nation and the individual are great. Scientific progress is one essential key to our security as a nation, to our better health, to more jobs, to a higher standard of living, and to our cultural progress.

Equating scientific progress with virtually all the desiderata of social welfare provided a rationale for public interest and a model for future appeals of the scientific community to the public purse. By 1967, the United Kingdom's Council for Scientific Policy was willing to make the direct statement that 'basic research provides most of the original discoveries from which all other progress flows'.[2]

If scientific knowledge is desirable for the public welfare, how might its production be assured? The answer was contained in the accompanying

'Report of the Committee on Science and the Public Welfare'.[3] It proposed that scientific research be divided into three categories of which two, pure research and applied research and development, are of interest here.[4] According to the appendix: 'Pure research is research without specific practical ends. It results in general knowledge and understanding of nature and its laws'. By contrast, applied research involves activities in which the 'objective can often be definitely mapped out beforehand' and 'are of a definitely practical or commercial value'. While these statements suggest an epistemological differentiation among categories of knowledge, an economic distinction immediately follows. In the case of pure science, results 'have for centuries been immediately consigned to the public domain and no valid precedent exists for restricting the advantages of knowledge of this sort to any individual, corporation, State, or Nation' and 'governments dedicated to the public welfare, therefore, have a responsibility for encouraging and supporting the production of new knowledge on the broadest possible basis'. Thus, the institutions and social norms of science were implicitly used to define basic research knowledge. By contrast, the practical and commercial value of applied research and development means that 'the very heavy expenses of such work are, therefore, undertaken by private organizations only in the hope of ultimately recovering the funds invested'. This division of labor created a potential lacuna – what would prevent industry from funding basic research? – which the report promptly closed.

> But it is important to emphasize that there is a perverse law governing research: Under the pressure for immediate results, and unless deliberate policies are set up to guard against this, *applied research invariably drives out pure*. The moral is clear: It is pure research which deserves and requires special protection and specially assured support.

In paraphrasing Gresham's Law in this way, the report charged the government with responsibility for maintaining the independence of the scientific establishment and deflected attention from deeper investigations of how that establishment operates or is related to industrial technology.

In the United States, the implementation of science policy has involved substantial and growing national government funding of basic research in government laboratories, universities and, to a lesser extent, in business (see Mowery and Rosenberg, 1989). In time, economists recognized and incorporated this worldview as their own (Nelson, 1959; Arrow, 1962), admitting the inadequacy of the market in delivering the socially optimal level of research. Nelson and Arrow greatly improved on Bush's evocation of a Gresham's Law relating basic and applied research by describing scientific knowledge as a public good where private investment will be socially inadequate. Correspondingly, the appropriability of knowledge derived from applied research encourages socially adequate private investment (Mowery, 1983a). To make this distinction, Nelson and Arrow had to assume that the marginal costs of duplicating the information content of scientific knowledge were very low, making exclusion and appropriation impossible.[5] Once articulated in this form, scientific knowledge could be viewed as an exogenous gift to the economy's productive capabilities and the storehouse of results for subsequent economic exploitation as economic growth induced a higher level and a greater variety of demands.[6]

The dissent to the portrayal of science as an exogenous influence first developed among scholars of the history and sociology of science. Historians have long argued that science is a social construct, arising from the particularities of social history, the cultural inheritance of its participants, and the functions assigned science by society. As Bernal (1939) observed, the 19th century scientist deliberately distanced himself from the industrial application of discovery, a self-removal that Bernal saw as a 'sign of the scientist aping the don and the gentleman'.[7] More recently, many historians have focused on the social, philosophical, and technological interdependencies underlying the historical record of scientific progress (see Galison, 1987; Gooding, Pinch and Schaffer 1989). For our purposes, the significance of these studies is that they cast suspicions on the separability of the activities performed by scientists from external social and technological influences. This suspicion is reinforced by sociologists of science who, in examining the scientific research process, have discovered a wealth of social processes governing the flow of information, the determination of research agendas, and the creation of values with specific scientific communities (e.g. Merton, 1973; Latour and Woolgar, 1979; Barnes and Edge, 1982; Callon, Law and Rip, 1986; Latour, 1987). Collectively, these studies indicate that there are social risks in neglecting the study of scientific institutions and relying exclusively on the self-governance of science, but they do not provide a clear agenda for reform or restructuring existing institutions and policies.

If, in fact, there are reverse flows of causation that shape the development of science, then science may still be the pursuit of knowledge 'without practical ends' but with very definite means and constraints that shape scientific activity (Rosenberg, 1974, 1982). In particular, the directions and outcomes of basic research may depend upon the formation and operation of networks for communicating information (Arrow, 1969; von Hippel, 1988; Freeman, 1991; Bijker, Hughes and Pinch, 1987), the development of technologies that facilitate scientific advances in particular disciplines (Rosenberg, 1992), and the recruitment of participants for large scientific research teams or assemblage of research communities (Galison and Hevly, 1992). These sorts of interactions have often been apparent in detailed case studies of innovation (see Jewkes, Sawers and Stillerman, 1969; Langrish, Gibbons, Evans and Jevons, 1972).

Economists have also undertaken explicit examinations of the incentives within the institutions of science. Dasgupta and David (1992) and David

(1991) have proposed an explicit behavioral theory of scientific institutions and of the relation between science and technology that offers explanatory hypotheses about the allocation of resources within basic research, the role of basic research in training technologists, and the incentives governing individual effort and productivity in the sciences. Finally, several policy-oriented studies have identified inadequacies in the decision-making processes governing science policy (see for example Weiner, 1972; Mowery, 1983a; Noll and Cohen, 1991; Shapley and Roy, 1985). At present, historian and social scientist critiques of the role of science in the linear model encourage closer examinations of the institutions of science and the formation of science policy.

We now turn to the operational hypothesis or research heuristic suggested by the view that science contributes knowledge for application. Under this hypothesis, social investments in science increase social welfare and, if such returns are traced, we will be able to account for the return on scientific investment. This method of assessing the economic returns on research investment was pioneered by Griliches (1958). Griliches estimated that social returns of 700 per cent had been realized in the period 1933–55 from the $2 million in public and private investments on the development of hybrid corn from 1910–55. Much or all of this research investment was, however, not 'pure' or basic.[8] Nonetheless, there was a clear justification for public support of hybrid corn research because seed companies were able to appropriate only a portion of the social benefit from the improved strains and it was implausible that the users of this technology (farmers) would finance its creation. This larger conception of the public goods nature of research encouraged other studies of agricultural innovation including poultry research (Peterson, 1967), the creation of the tomato harvester (Schmitz and Seckler, 1970), and an examination of results from several agricultural sectors (Evenson, Waggoner and Ruttan, 1979). All of these studies of public investment in agricultural research indicate very high social rates of return. The latter study concludes that 'a beneficial system of public research continues to be undervalued. Despite annual returns of the order of fifty per cent, which an economist would call clear evidence of underinvestment, investment remains static'.

The measurement of the social returns from research investment pioneered by Griliches has produced a large literature which consistently finds high returns to such investments. The social welfare increases from specific lines of medical research has been examined (see Weisbrod, 1971; Mushkin, 1979), the productivity increases from company-financed basic research in petroleum and chemical firms activities is the subject of Mansfield (1980), and the effect of both government and company-financed basic and applied research is estimated by Link (1981). Sectoral studies of productivity improvements from research investments include Griliches (1986) and Lichtenberg and Siegel (1991). Both of these studies, as well as

Griliches (1980), find that private investments in basic research appear to garner unusually high *private* rates of return. Mansfield's (1991) study of the returns from academic research is a promising line of investigation for extending the empirical results on social returns from research investment. Mansfield selected a random sample of seventy-six major American firms from seven manufacturing industries, polling each firm's top R&D executives about the proportion of the firm's new products and processes commercialized in 1975–85 that could not have been developed (without substantial delay) in the absence of academic research carried out within fifteen years of the first introduction of the innovation. Mansfield also asked the respondents to estimate the 1985 sales of these new products and the cost savings from these new processes. Extrapolating the results from this survey to the total academic research investment and the total returns from new products and processes, Mansfield computes a social rate of return of 28 per cent when user benefits are included. The consistently high returns found in these studies are perplexing given the arguments about the incentives for private underinvestment advanced by Nelson and Arrow. One possible explanation, other than mis-estimation or economic irrationality, is that although firms make investments based on estimates of their direct returns from such investments, the actual returns they receive are higher as the result of spillovers or positive externalities from other firms' investments.

Methodologically, the advances in the above studies over Griliches (1958) involve including the productivity impacts of research investment (Mansfield, 1980; Griliches, 1980) and estimation of research capital stocks as described in Griliches (1979), a paper that also makes the important point that output measurement is worst for the most research-intensive industries. In addition, several novel possibilities have been explored for examining the 'transmission related' benefits from scientific research. Scientific research projects may accelerate the introduction of commercial products (Byatt and Cohen, 1969), a methodology that has been employed to estimate the social benefits of government investment in satellite telecommunications (Teubal and Steinmueller, 1982). The development of scientific knowledge may affect the 'options value' of explorations in applied areas, reducing the expected returns from some lines of applied research (with concomitant savings in avoided costs) or increasing the real returns in other areas (Evenson and Kislev, 1975; David, Mowery and Steinmueller, 1992). Finally, the application of scientific knowledge creates greater variety among available products, a source of large potential social welfare gains. In a pioneering methodological and empirical study, Trajtenberg (1990) traces such gains for the case of Computer Tomography scanners for medical imaging.

While economists have been able to measure significant social welfare gains for specific firms and industrial sectors from aggregate company or public research expenditures, the effort to trace the returns from specific government research efforts (other than in medicine and agriculture) has been less successful. The low point was the effort of the Department of Defense to compute returns from defence research expenditures. Despite the enormous size of these investments, Project Hindsight was unable to compute a positive rate of return and the project's report rejected 'the possibility that any simple or linear relationship exists between cost of research and value received' (Office of the Director of Defense Research and Engineering, 1969). Similar problems were uncovered when the National Science Foundation sought to trace the basic research contributions underlying four major industrial innovations (National Science Foundation, 1969). At one extreme, one might conclude from these results that agricultural and medical research were the only sectors of the US economy that benefited from public research investment. Alternatively, a more plausible interpretation is that the effects of scientific knowledge and, specifically, the enabling characteristics of that knowledge for industrial innovation, are far more difficult to trace because of the long lead times before application and the size of complementary inputs whose costs attenuate any measured effect of scientific inputs (Mowery and Rosenberg, 1989; David, Mowery and Steinmueller, 1992; Pavitt, 1993). Whether significant returns to public basic research investments in specific projects can be measured or predicted with significant accuracy to guide research investments remains an open empirical and conceptual question (see Office of Technology Assessment, 1986).

Our final theme involves adopting the hypothesis that basic research is inextricably woven into the economic and technological fabric of society rather than being the exogenous transmitter of knowledge. Adopting this hypothesis greatly complicates the assignment of causation, but offers several promising directions for research. The appropriate metaphor for incorporating basic research into a more comprehensive theory is that basic research activities are some of the nodes of a larger network of knowledge creation and that private basic research investments are 'a ticket of admission' to this network (Rosenberg, 1990).[9] In addition to the cost of admission, a number of other useful economic ideas accompany the network conception; network externalities may increase the value of being connected as the network adds participants, network centralization may eliminate duplicative research but also suppresses variety in the research outcomes available for commercial exploitation, and complementary investments in identifying useful connections and establishing methods of distributing information may yield significant returns. It is a short step to employing these concepts to re-examine specialized studies on the organization of research networks (Gibbons and Johnston, 1974) and basic research enterprises (Fujimura, 1987, 1988). Further, if knowledge is generated and distributed within networks, government and firms must make increasingly complex choices about specialization, cooperation, and competition – it will prove increasingly difficult to rely exclusively on the public disclosure of scientific knowledge as a foundation for national growth and prosperity (Nelson, 1993; Patel and Pavitt, 1991; Teece, 1986). It will also be necessary to rethink how to analyze the serendipitous outcomes of scientific research and how to more effectively deploy such outcomes in industrial innovation (see Conroe and Dripps, 1976; Jewkes, Sawers and Stillerman, 1969).

Perhaps the most exciting opportunity available from the view that basic research is part of a larger network is the possibility of identifying the rates and directions of technical change by examining several of the activities that are complementary to scientific research. First, the flows of patents, citations and product announcements are complements to both scientific investigation and commercial activities. While efforts to examine the impact of basic research by tracing its research outputs to these flows have been less than satisfactory, the flows have proven useful in identifying areas of intense technological activity in which scientific activities may be quantitatively linked (Carpenter, 1983; Irvine and Martin, 1983, 1985; Griliches, 1984; Pavitt, 1984; Pavitt and Patel, 1992; Averch, 1987; Narin and Noma, 1985; Narin and Olivastro, 1992).[10] Second, at the level of the firm, the costs of receiving information are significant, requiring complementary investments to absorb and utilize information flows (Cohen and Levinthal, 1989; Rosenberg, 1990). Developing theories about the complementary investments firms undertake to utilize knowledge from external sources will require more detailed information on the organization and conduct of industrial research laboratory activities (see Mowery, 1983b; Hounshell and Smith, 1988; Pruitt and Smith, 1986; Graham and Pruitt, 1990). Finally, the scientific research process generates economically important outputs other than published findings and theories. Examples of such by-products of scientific research are the training of individuals and the development of instrumentation that are complements in the conduct of future scientific and industrial research (Dasgupta and David, 1992; David, Mowery and Steinmueller, 1992). Examination of activities that are complements to the conduct of scientific research are a means of illuminating how the structure of scientific knowledge is evolving over time and how this evolution interacts with the technology and institutions of scientific research.

The linear model connecting basic research to industrial innovation appears to be on the wane. Its assumptions about the isolation of scientific activities from social influences, the unidirectional transfer of knowledge from science to technology, and the unique character of scientific knowledge are inconsistent with empirical studies of the conduct and institutions of science. Examinations of industrial innovation have revealed a much more complex pattern of knowledge creation, transfer and utilization than suggested by the linear model. Despite the decline of the linear model, it has been a useful point of departure and heuristic guide for research. New approaches, such as the network model, offer a more complex view and a more diversified research agenda for examining the interaction between scientific research and industrial innovation.

Notes

1. United States Office of Scientific Research and Development (1945).
2. United Kingdom Council for Scientific Policy (1967), para. 45.
3. The report, an appendix of United States Office of Scientific Research and Development (1945), was prepared under the chairmanship of Isaiah Bowman, President of Johns Hopkins University.
4. The other category was called 'background research', the activities of data collection, determination of physical constants, and the establishment of standards 'for hormones, drugs, and X-ray therapy'. The report notes that such research is conducted by scientists in all types of research organizations, but that the federal government, and federal laboratories in particular, are likely to have particular advantages in conducting such research.
5. From a social welfare perspective, charging the marginal cost of distributing scientific knowledge would bankrupt the producer (Mowery 1983a). In later work, both Arrow and Nelson devoted considerable attention to the costs of transmitting and receiving information. See Arrow (1969) and Nelson and Winter (1982).
6. These applications will be immediately recognizable to economists as the enormous literature on economic growth arising from Solow's (1960) application of the aggregate production function approach to technical change and the demand induced application of scientific knowledge described by Schmookler (1966). Romer (1986) rekindled an earlier debate (*Economic Journal*, 1930) about increasing returns by accepting the possibility that increasing returns allow multiple equilibria and rejecting the exogeneity of technical change. Rosenberg (1974) criticizes Schmookler's proposition that scientific and technical knowledge is an unlimited storehouse of potential applications by arguing that the supply of technical opportunities independently shapes the rate and direction of technical change.
7. Bernal (1939), p. 96.
8. As Nelson (1959) notes, hybrid corn was the outgrowth of the research of George Harrison Shull whose work was aimed at establishing reproducible results in plant genetics rather than improvement of crop strains.
9. The network conception is somewhat broader than the earlier 'chain link' theory which depicts basic research as the terminus of feedback loops from applied research, development, and marketing activities (Kline and Rosenberg, 1986).
10. Irvine and Martin's (1983), (1985) studies were particularly controversial because they used citation analysis as a measure of scientific productivity. This 'evaluative' use of citations was criticized by Krige and Pestre (1985), Moed and van Raan (1985), Bud (1985) and Collins (1985), to which Martin and Irvine (1985) offers a reply.

Bibliography

Arrow, K. (1962) 'Economic Welfare and the Allocation of Resources for Invention', *The Rate and Direction of Inventive Activity*, Princeton University Press.

Arrow, K. (1969) 'Classificatory Notes on the Production and Transmission of Technical Knowledge', *American Economic Review*, pp. 29–35.

Averch, H. (1987) 'Measuring the Cost-Efficiency of Basic Research Investment', *Journal of Policy Analysis and Management*, Vol. 6, No. 3, pp. 342–61.

Barnes, B. and Edge, D. (eds) (1982) *Science in Context: Readings in the Sociology of Science*, MIT Press, Cambridge, Massachusetts.

Basalla, G. (1988) *The Evolution of Technology*, Cambridge University Press.

Bernal, J. (1939) *The Social Function of Science*, MIT Press, Cambridge, Massachusetts.

Bijker, W., Hughes, T. and Pinch, T. (1987) *Constructing Networks and Systems, Case Studies and Concepts in the Sociology and History of Science*, MIT Press, Cambridge, Massachusetts.

Bud, R. (1985) 'A Case of the Disappearing Caveat: A Critique of Irvine and Martin's Methodology', *Social Studies of Science*, Vol. 15, pp. 548–53.

Byatt, I. and Cohen, A. (1969) *An Attempt to Quantify the Economic Benefits of Scientific Research*, Department of Education and Science, Science Policy Studies No. 4, HMSO, London.

Callon, M., Law, J. and Rip, A. (eds) (1986) *Mapping the Dynamics of Science and Technology*, Macmillan, New York.

Carpenter, M. (1983) *Patent Citations as Indicators of Scientific and Technological Linkages*, Computer Horizons Inc., N.J.

Cohen, W. and Levinthal, D. (1989) 'Innovation and Learning: The Two Faces of R&D', *Economic Journal*, Vol. 99, pp. 569–96.

Collins, H. (1985) 'The Possibilities of Science Policy', *Social Studies of Science*, Vol. 15, pp. 554–58.

Conroe, J. and Dripps, R. (1976) 'Scientific Basis for the Support of Biomedical Science', *Science*, Vol. 192, No. 4235, April 9, pp. 105–11.

Dasgupta, P. and David, P. (1992) 'Toward a New Economics of Science', Center for Economic Policy Research Publication No. 320, Stanford University, October.

David, P. (1991) 'Reputation and Agency in the Historical Emergence of the Institutions of Open Science', Center for Economic Policy Research Publication No. 261, Stanford University, April.

David, P., Mowery, D. and Steinmueller, W. (1992) 'Analysing the Economic Payoffs from Basic Research', *Economics of Innovation and New Technology*, Vol. 2, pp. 73–90.

Economic Journal (1930) 'Increasing Returns and the Representative Firm: A Symposium', *Economics Journal*, Vol. 40, March 30.

Evenson, R. and Kislev, Y. (1975) *Agricultural Research and Productivity*, Yale University Press, New Haven.

Evenson, R., Waggoner, P. and Ruttan, V. (1979) 'Economic Benefits from Research: An Example from Agriculture', *Science*, Vol. 205, September 14, pp. 1101–7.

Freeman, C. (1991) 'Networks of Innovators: A Synthesis of Research Issues', *Research Policy*, Vol. 20, No. 5.

Fujimura, J. (1987) 'Constructing "Do-Able" Problems in Cancer Research: Articulating Alignment', *Social Studies of Science*, Vol. 17, pp. 257–93.

Fujimura, J. (1988) 'Molecular Biological Bandwagon in Cancer Research: Where Social Worlds Meet', *Social Problems*, Vol. 35, pp. 261–83.

Galison, P. (1987) *How Experiments End*, University of Chicago Press.

Galison, P. and Hevly, B. (1992) *Big Science: The Growth of Large-Scale Research*, Stanford University Press.

Gibbons, M. and Johnston, R. (1974) 'The Roles of Science in Technological Innovation', *Research Policy*, Vol. 3, pp. 220–42.

Gooding, D., Pinch, T. and Schaffer, S. (eds) (1989) *The Uses of Experiment*, Cambridge

University Press.

Graham, M. and Pruitt, B. (1990) *R&D for Industry: A Century of Technical Innovation at Alcoa*, Cambridge University Press.

Griliches, Z. (1958) 'Research Costs and Social Returns: Hybrid Corn and Related Innovations', *Journal of Political Economy*, October, pp. 419–31.

Griliches, Z. (1979) 'Issues in Assessing the Contribution of Research and Development to Productivity Growth', *Bell Journal of Economics*, Vol. 10, No. 1, Spring, pp. 92–116.

Griliches, Z. (1980) 'Returns to Research and Development in the Private Sector' in Kendrick, J. and Vaccara, B. (eds) *New Developments in Productivity Measurement*, NBER Studies in Income and Wealth No. 44, University of Chicago Press, pp. 419–54.

Griliches, Z. (ed.) (1984) *R&D, Patents, and Productivity*, University of Chicago Press.

Griliches, Z. (1986) 'Productivity, R&D, and Basic Research at the Firm Level in the 1970s', *American Economic Review*, Vol. 76, No. 1, pp. 143–54.

Hounshell, D. and Smith, J. (1988) *Science and Corporate Strategy: Dupont R&D, 1902–1980*, Cambridge University Press.

Irvine, J. and Martin, B. (1983) 'Assessing Basic Research: The Case of the Isaac Newton Telescope', *Social Studies of Science*, Vol. 13, pp. 49–86.

Irvine, J. and Martin, B. (1985) 'Quantitative Science Policy Research', Paper presented to the Task Force on Science Policy of the Committee on Science and Technology, US House of Representatives.

Jewkes, J., Sawers, D. and Stillerman, R. (1969) *The Sources of Invention*, W.W. Norton, New York, 2nd edition.

Kline, S. and Rosenberg, N. (1986) 'An Overview of Innovation' in Landau, R. and Rosenberg, N.(eds) *The Positive Sum Strategy*, National Academy Press, Washington, D.C., pp. 275–305.

Krige, J. and Pestre, D. (1985) 'A Critique of Irvine and Martin's Methodology for Evaluating Big Science', *Social Studies of Science*, Vol. 15, pp. 525–39.

Langrish, J., Gibbons, M., Evans, W. and Jevons, F. (1972) *Wealth from Knowledge: A Study of Innovation in Industry*, Halsted Press Division, John Wiley & Sons, New York.

Latour, B. (1987) *Science in Action*, Harvard University Press.

Latour, B. and Woolgar, S. (1979) *Laboratory Life*, Sage, London.

Lichtenburg, F. and Siegel, D. (1991) 'The Impact of R&D Investment on Productivity – New Evidence Using Linked R&D-LRD Data', *Economic Inquiry*, Vol. 29, April, pp. 203–28.

Link, A. (1981) 'Basic Research and Productivity Increase in Manufacturing: Additional Evidence', *American Economic Review*, Vol. 71, No. 5, pp. 1111–2.

Mansfield, E. (1980) 'Basic Research and Productivity Increase in Manufacturing', *American Economics Review*, Vol. 70, No. 5, December, pp. 863–73.

Mansfield, E. (1991) 'Academic Research and Industrial Innovation', *Research Policy*, Vol. 20, pp. 1–12.

Martin, B. and Irvine, J. (1985) 'Evaluating the Evaluators: A Reply to Our Critics', *Social Studies of Science*, Vol. 15, pp. 558–75.

Merton, R. (1973) *The Sociology of Science: Theoretical and Empirical Investigations*, University of Chicago Press.

Moed, H. and van Raan, A. (1985) 'Critical Remarks on Irvine and Martin's Methodology of Evaluating Scientific Performance', *Social Studies of Science*, Vol. 15, pp. 539–47.

Mowery, D. (1983a) 'Economic Theory and Government Technology Policy', *Policy Sciences*, Winter, pp. 27–43.

Mowery, D. (1983b) 'The Relationship between Contractual and Intrafirm Forms of

Industrial Research in American Manufacturing, 1900–1940', *Explorations in Economic History*, October, pp. 351–74.

Mowery, D. and Rosenberg, N. (1989) *Technology and the Pursuit of Economic Growth*, Cambridge University Press.

Mushkin, S. (1979) *Biomedical Research: Costs and Benefits*, Ballinger, Cambridge, Massachusetts.

Narin, F. and Noma, F. (1985) 'Is Technology Becoming Science?', *Scientometrics*, Vol. 7, pp. 369–81.

Narin, F. and Olivastro, D. (1992) 'Status Report – Linkage Between Technology and Science', *Research Policy*, Vol. 21, pp. 237–49.

National Science Foundation (1969) *Technology in Retrospect and Critical Events in Science (TRACES)* Washington, DC.

Nelson, R. (1959) 'The Simple Economics of Basic Scientific Research', *Journal of Political Economy*, June, pp. 297–306.

Nelson, R. (ed.) (1993) *National Systems of Innovation*, Oxford University Press.

Nelson, R. and Winter, S. (1982) *An Evolutionary Theory of Economic Change*, Harvard University Press.

Noll, R. and Cohen, L. (eds) (1991) *The Technology Pork Barrel*, The Brookings Institution, Washington, DC.

Office of the Director of Defense Research and Engineering (1969) *Project Hindsight: Final Report*, Washington, DC.

Office of Technology Assessment (1986) *Research as an Investment: Can We Measure the Returns?*, Washington, DC.

Patel, P. and Pavitt, K. (1991) 'Large Firms in the Production of the World's Technology: An Important Case of Non-Globalisation', *Journal of International Business Studies*, Vol. 22, pp. 1–21.

Pavitt, K. (1984) 'Sectoral Patterns of Technical Change: Towards a Taxonomy and a Theory', *Research Policy*, Vol. 13, pp. 343–73.

Pavitt, K. (1993) 'What do Firms Learn from Basic Research?' in Foray, D. and Freeman, C. (eds) *Technology and the Wealth of Nations: The Dynamics of Constructed Advantage*, Pinter Publishers, London.

Pavitt, K. and Patel, P. (1992) 'Contemporary Patterns of Technological Change: The Widespread (and Neglected) Importance of Improvements in Mechanical Technologies', draft, Center for Economic Policy Research, Stanford University, The Role of Technology in Economics: A Conference in Honor of Nathan Rosenberg, forthcoming *Research Policy*, 1994.

Peterson, W. (1967) 'Return to Poultry Research in the United States', *Journal of Farm Economics*, Vol. 49, No. 3, August, pp. 656–69.

Pruitt, B. and Smith, G. (1986) 'The Corporate Management of Innovation: Alcoa Research, Aircraft Alloys, and the Problem of Stress-Corrosion Cracking' in Rosenbloom, R. (ed.) *Technological Innovation, Management and Policy*, Vol. 3, JAI Press Inc., Greenwich, Connecticut and London.

Romer, P. (1986) 'Increasing Returns and Long-Run Growth', *Journal of Political Economy*, October.

Rosenberg, N. (1974) 'Science, Innovation, and Economic Growth', *The Economic Journal*, Vol. 84, pp. 333ff, reprinted in Rosenberg (1976).

Rosenberg, N. (1976) *Perspectives on Technology*, Cambridge University Press.

Rosenberg, N. (1982) *Inside the Black Box: Technology and Economics*, Cambridge University Press, especially Chapter 7, 'How Exogenous is Science?'.

Rosenberg, N. (1990) 'Why do Firms do Basic Research (With their Own Money)?',

Research Policy, Vol. 19, pp. 165–74.

Rosenberg, N. (1992) 'Scientific Instrumentation and University Research', *Research Policy*, Vol. 21, pp. 381–90.

Schmitz, A. and Seckler, D. (1970) 'Mechanized Agriculture and Social Welfare: The Case of the Tomato Harvester', *American Journal of Agricultural Economics*, Vol. 52, No. 4, November, pp. 559–77.

Schmookler, J. (1966) *Invention and Economic Growth*, Harvard University Press.

Shapley, D. and Roy, R. (1985) *Lost at the Frontier: U.S. Science and Technology Policy Adrift*, ISI Press, Philadelphia, Pennsylvania.

Solow, R. (1960) 'Investment and Technical Progress' in Arrow, K., Karbin, S. and Suppes, P. (eds), *Mathematical Methods in the Social Sciences 1959*, Stanford University Press reprinted in Stiglitz, J. and Uzawa, H. (eds) *Readings in the Modern Theory of Economic Growth*, MIT Press, 1969.

Teece, D. (1986) 'Profiting from Technological Innovation: Implications for Integration, Collaboration, Licensing, and Public Policy', *Research Policy*, pp. 285–305.

Teubal, M. and Steinmueller, W. (1982) 'Government Policy, Innovation, and Economic Growth: Lessons from a Study of Satellite Telecommunications', *Research Policy*, Vol. 11, pp. 271–87.

Trajtenberg, M. (1990) *Economic Analysis of Product Innovation: The CT Scanners*, Harvard University Press, Cambridge.

United Kingdom Council for Scientific Policy (1967) *Second Report on Science Policy*, Cmnd 3420, HMSO, London.

United States Office of Scientific Research and Development (1945) *Science: The Endless Frontier: A Report to the President on a Program for Postwar Scientific Research*, US National Science Foundation, Washington, DC (reprint, 1960).

von Hippel, E. (1988) *The Sources of Innovation*, Oxford University Press.

Weiner, S. (1972) 'Research Allocation in Basic Research and Organizational Design', *Public Policy*, Vol. 20, No. 2, Spring, pp. 227–55.

Weisbrod, B. (1971) 'Costs and Benefits of Medical Research: A Case Study of Poliomyelitis', *Journal of Political Economics*, Vol. 79, May–June, pp. 527–44.

6.   The Japanese Innovation System: How Does it Work?

Martin Fransman

Introduction

It is now widely accepted that innovation drives competition at both the corporate and national levels and that in order to survive in a market-interdependent world, it is essential to become and remain competitive. This paper is concerned with the innovation process in Japan and with the major factors that influence it. The following questions are examined: To what extent is innovation and the competitiveness that follows from it the result of the activities of the private sector in Japan? What role is played by the Japanese government and its various ministries? How great is the contribution of Japanese universities to the innovation process?

The examination of these questions hinges on the notion of the Japanese Innovation System (JIS). JIS is a complex system comprising processes, institutions, and forms of organization. These include the market process, intra- and inter-corporate organization, government regulation and intervention, and university teaching and research. As with any complex system, the analysis of JIS involves a simplification, an abstraction of some of the major factors which influence the system and its behaviour and performance. The present paper accordingly will examine some of the major features of JIS without delving into the complexities that would require more space than is available here.

Before proceeding with the analysis, however, a word of caution is necessary. Like the proverbial elephant, JIS can be all things to all people. For example, those who see market forces as the motor of capitalism see in JIS cut-throat competition between Japanese companies and a government which spends a relatively small proportion of national income while ensuring that its interventions are exclusively of a market-conforming kind. On the other hand, those who believe in the virtues of government intervention see in JIS a strong state which is oriented to the development of the nation's economy and which is prepared to put considerable pressure on Japanese companies to move in the directions which the government feels are desirable. The result has been a vigorous debate between the proponents of these two views (or versions of them) on the effects of industrial policy in Japan which shows little sign of abating.

What Role do Japanese Companies Play in the Innovation Process?

One measure of the role of private industry in Japan in the innovation process is its contribution to total expenditure on R&D. According to this measure private industry contributes about 76 per cent to the total, while government contributes about 18 per cent and universities about 5 per cent. From the point of view of competitiveness, however, this considerably underestimates the role of Japanese companies since much innovation which has an important positive effect on competitiveness is of an incremental kind and takes place on the factory floor (sometimes referred to as 'blue collar R&D') and therefore is not recorded in R&D statistics. (The absolute size of the R&D expenditures of the major Japanese companies is worth emphasizing. Put into perspective, the R&D expenditures of the top five Japanese R&D spenders – Hitachi, Toyota, Matsushita, NEC and Fujitsu – are as great (in terms of purchasing power parity) as the total R&D expenditure of the entire private sector in Britain.)

It may accordingly be concluded that the bulk of expenditure on innovation is undertaken by the private sector in and for this sector. This is particularly true with respect to the 'downstream' portion of R&D, that is the applied research and development portion where the Japanese government and its various organs have little influence. In the following section more will be said about the role of the Japanese government in the innovation process.

Since innovation in JIS is largely the responsibility of Japanese companies, it is necessary to say a little more regarding the factors that influence the innovation process in these companies. Before doing so, however, another *caveat* is necessary. As Porter (1992) has emphasized, while Japan has produced some sectors that have been outstandingly successful in terms of international competitiveness, this by no means applies to all or even most sectors of the Japanese economy. Thus, while consumer electronics, machine tools, motor cars, and memory semiconductors are included in the outstandingly successful sectors, microprocessors, complex telecommunications equipment, chemicals, and pharmaceuticals must be excluded. To stamp all Japanese companies and sectors with the 'success stamp' would be to miss an essential part of the Japanese story.

In most sectors, however – including microprocessors, complex telecommunications equipment, chemicals and pharmaceuticals – *Japanese companies tend to be committed and patient innovators.* This commitment and patience is attributable to a number of interrelated factors. One of these factors is the generally intense competition that Japanese companies face in both the domestic and international markets. Competition through innovation is a common response on the part of Japanese companies to this competitive pressure. The Japanese market, however, does not only provide a source of pressure which motivates innovation. It also provides users of products and processes who are extremely sophisticated and demanding with regard to what they are willing to accept and who generally have alternative sources of supply if a supplier is unwilling or unable to comply with their demands. This demanding environment also generates feedback for companies and gives them the opportunity to learn how to improve their products and processes, in addition to creating the pressure for innovative change.

But why, in those cases where Japanese companies have been internationally successful, have they managed at times to out-innovate their Western rivals? Surely these Western rivals also exist in the same intensely competitive domestic and international markets and therefore should be similarly motivated to innovate like their Japanese counterparts?

One factor which has at times assisted Japanese companies is their possession of what may be referred to as 'committed shareholders'. Committed shareholders may be defined as those who will remain loyal to the company in which they hold shares by retaining their shares in that company even in the face of expected share price differentials which would leave them better off in the short run if they were to sell their shares and switch to another company.

Why do these shareholders choose to 'stay and fight rather than switch'? The reason is that, unlike pension fund managers who are attempting to maximize the short-run value of their portfolios and who therefore have an arm's length relationship with the companies in which they hold shares, committed shareholders usually have close business relationships with these companies. Committed shareholders, for instance, are often banks or other financial institutions which deal with the company, or major customers or suppliers who buy from or sell to it. They therefore have a longer-term stake in the health of the company. Their commitment has removed many (though by no means all) of the pressures that Western companies face when short-term profitability does not meet with the expectations of arm's length shareholders, pressures that frequently impede the process of innovation (see the chapter by Tylecote).

Japanese companies have also been helped in their attempts to innovate by organizational practices that have evolved over time in their companies. One of the key determinants behind these practices has been the institution of life-time employment for most white and blue collar workers in larger firms. More accurately, *the assumption of 'no exit'* has had a number of extremely important consequences which have influenced organizational practices which, in turn, have been conducive to innovation. (The difference between the assumption of continuing employment in the same organization or life-time employment on the one hand and the assumption of no exit on the other hand must be stressed. While Western firms such as IBM until recently offered life-time employment, this did *not* mean that their employees operated on the assumption of no exit. The functioning of labour markets in Western countries typically means that employees, particularly those with sought-after skills, do have the option of exit through employment by another organization.)

The no-exit assumption has facilitated innovation in Japanese companies in a number of ways. Firstly, this assumption has given Japanese companies a strong incentive to train their employees since, by ensuring that these employees do not leave, it has allowed them to reap the returns from investment in training. Secondly, the no-exit assumption has encouraged the companies to provide more general and flexible skills since these allow employees, who have been provided with long-term employment, to be more easily redeployable in different parts of the company. Redeployment may be necessary when a company faces a downturn in some of its business areas. Thirdly, the possession of more general and flexible skills on the part of the workforce has facilitated the widespread practice of job rotation within the company. One major benefit of this practice has been more efficient flows of information within the company which has allowed more effective coordination across corporate functional and other boundaries. This has encouraged innovation in activities such as new product development, the interfacing of R&D, production, and marketing, and just-in-time and quality control activities which depend on information flows and cross-functional coordination.

The no-exit assumption has also benefited the innovativeness and competitiveness of many Japanese companies in another more indirect way. By requiring companies to provide not only continuing jobs for its employees but also opportunities for promotion and other incentives, the no-exit assumption has made it more difficult for Japanese companies to engage in merger and acquisition activities. In turn, this has encouraged Japanese companies to 'stick to their knitting' and concentrate on those activities where they have already acquired distinctive competences, a tendency that has been further encouraged by the engineering background of many Japanese corporate leaders who are often keener than their Western counterparts with financial backgrounds to keep to areas which they know and understand. This has often meant that Japanese companies have been able to focus their limited attention on areas where they have established distinctive competences and have deepened these competences while some of their Western rivals, lured by the hope of financial gain through merger, acquisition, or competence-unrelated diversification, have had their attention diverted to other concerns. The result has been that over time some Western companies have not been able to keep up with the innovation of their more focused Japanese competitors.

These are some of the factors which have generated an innovative dynamic in some Japanese sectors which has resulted in strong international competitiveness and rapid growth in sales and market share both in Japan and abroad. But what role is to be attributed to the Japanese government in accounting for the innovative performance of Japanese companies?

How has the Japanese Government Influenced the Innovation Process?

One measure of the influence of government on the national innovation process is its share of total expenditure on R&D. According to this measure the Japanese government plays a significantly smaller role than its Western counterparts. Figures around 1990 show that the Japanese government was responsible for 18 per cent of total R&D. This compared with about 50 per cent in France, 45 per cent in the United States, and 35 per cent in West Germany. The figure for the United Kingdom was 37 per cent.

What is the significance of the figure for Japan? The first point to make, underscoring that made in the last section on the role of Japanese companies, is that private Japanese companies undertake 76 per cent of R&D in Japan, a significantly higher proportion than in the other industrialized Western countries. Since a greater proportion of R&D is undertaken in companies in Japan which are 'closer' to the point of production and marketing, it follows that a larger proportion of R&D is commercially targeted. (It is worth noting, however, that the Japanese government and the ministries responsible for science and technology expenditure are committed to increasing government's share of total R&D and raising it to a proportional level more commensurate with that of the other Western industrialized countries.)

Secondly, it is necessary to get the relatively low figure of 18 per cent into perspective. It would be wrong to conclude from this figure that the Japanese government has had a negligible influence on the innovation process. This is so for a number of reasons. To begin with, as will be reiterated in the following section on the role of universities, the Japanese government has had a major impact on the process of innovation through its education and training activities which have supplied Japanese companies with a high-quality, literate, numerate, and cooperative work force. This work force, with its high level of general skills, has then been further enhanced by the corporate organizational practices referred to in the last section which have facilitated the development of competitive distinctive competences. Furthermore, although the Japanese government has had a negligible impact on the 'downstream' part of R&D – namely, applied research and development which constitutes some 90 per cent of total R&D – its influence on the 'upstream' part has been significantly greater. This upstream part relates to basic research and, extremely important in Japan, what may be referred to as 'oriented basic' research. In these areas the

Japanese government has directly and indirectly had a greater impact, largely as a result of the degree of uncertainty in this kind of research and the reduced incentive that companies accordingly have to engage in such research.

What impact have Japanese ministries had on innovation and competitiveness? While in answer to this question much Western policy and academic analysis has focused on the role of the Ministry of International Trade and Industry (MITI), it is necessary not to ignore the distinctive role of some of the other ministries. One example is the Ministry of Posts and Telecommunications which is currently, independently of MITI, playing an extremely important role in shaping the whole of the Japanese telecommunications sector in the post-liberalization era. Another example is the role of the Science and Technology Agency and the Ministries of Health and Welfare and Agriculture, Forestry and Fisheries which, together with MITI and the Ministry of Education, Science and Culture, have exerted influence in the area of biotechnology.

Having said this, some concentration on MITI's role is justifiable in view of the influence which this ministry has had, and continues to have although in changing ways, on the largest parts of the Japanese manufacturing and distribution sectors. Historically, MITI's influential role has derived from Japan's position as a late-coming industrializing country with a strong state committed to the development process. Until the late 1960s MITI's power vis-à-vis the companies which fell within its sphere stemmed largely from its control of foreign exchange allocations and its ability to influence the extension of credit to the sectors and companies which it prioritized. Through the exercising of this power MITI was able to influence the allocation of resources within Japan, although analysts continue to debate the extent to which this influence benefited the Japanese economy.

Most analysts now recognize, however, that since the 1960s MITI's influence has changed considerably. There are several reasons for this. Firstly, from the late 1960s MITI lost most of its direct influence over foreign exchange and credit. Secondly, Japanese companies grew in size and strength and their increasing globalization gave them access to international capital markets thus reducing their dependence on the government for finance. Thirdly, as they grew Japanese companies also began allocating larger absolute and often proportional amounts to R&D and as a result came to depend less and less on government research institutes which formerly played a significant role in transferring advanced technologies to these companies.

In terms of total expenditure on science and technology, however, MITI's role is dwarfed by that of the Ministry of Education, Science and Culture and the Science and Technology Agency which spend 46 per cent and 26 per cent respectively of total government expenditure on science and technology compared with MITI's mere 12 per cent. In view of these figures, is it justifiable to argue, as usually is argued, that MITI has a greater influence on the innovation process in Japan than these other ministries?

In the view of the present writer, MITI's relatively great influence derives largely from its central nodal position in a vast and complex information network that criss-crosses not only Japan but also the world. This information network provides MITI's decision-makers with outstandingly high-quality information over a broad range in the areas of science, technology, industry, and trade. On the basis of the information which it possesses MITI is able to make maximum impact, not only with the direct resources which it commands, but also with the influence that it wields through indirect contacts and connections. The close links that MITI has forged over the years with the Japanese companies in the sectors of manufacturing and distribution that are under its influence reinforce both the information flows which the ministry receives and the influence which it exerts. This information network, it is worth noting, was developed originally as a useful resource to help MITI in its efforts to enable Japanese industry to catch up with the more advanced Western countries. While the costs of collecting, storing, analyzing, and recalling information were and are substantial, MITI as an organization became committed to these costs in view of the policy-making benefits which it derived from the information collected. While other ministries also have their own information networks, and while there are important cross-connections between the networks of the different ministries, these are not as extensive as MITI's. The Ministry of Finance, for example, relates closely to the private sector financial institutions, the Ministry of Health and Welfare to the pharmaceuticals companies, the Ministry of Construction to the construction companies, the Ministry of Agriculture, Forestry and Fisheries to the agriculture and food processing sectors, etc.

How is MITI's information network constructed? MITI's internal organizational structure consists of a matrix of vertical units, which correspond to the main industrial sectors in the economy, and horizontal units which deal with issues that cut across the various sectors. Examples are the vertical Machinery and Information Industries Bureau which deals with areas such as computer hardware and software and electronics and the horizontal Industrial Policy Bureau which has responsibility for questions of overall industrial policy. Regular rotation of senior MITI staff between the various units, while sacrificing some of the benefits of specialization, helps to improve knowledge and information flows within the ministry. MITI also has a number of formally-constituted Advisory Councils the membership of which includes company representatives and academics and which constitute important channels of information flow. Equally important are the informal networks that exist between MITI officials and the corporate and academic sectors which provide similar information. Furthermore, industry associations, often set up originally with MITI's assistance and staffed by

MITI personnel, such as the Electronics Industry Association of Japan, serve as subnodes which collect and process information at industry level and form an important link between that industry and the corresponding units in MITI. Abroad, the well-staffed Japan External Trade Research Organisation (JETRO) provides information about markets and technologies in other countries. It is common for MITI officials to be seconded to JETRO offices abroad in order to accumulate international experience. (Ironically – in view of Japan's large trade surplus – JETRO, originally established to aid Japan's export drive, now assists the attempts of foreign organizations to export to Japan.)

But this account of MITI's role in a vast information network raises further questions. Why do Japanese companies continue to cooperate so closely with MITI? Do they need the information that MITI has at its disposal or would they be better off going their own way?

These questions are difficult and within the large companies which have close relationships with MITI contradictory answers are given. Nevertheless, a number of considerations which would probably be fairly widely accepted have a bearing on these questions. To begin with, it is accepted by the companies themselves that government (in this case MITI) must do for private industry what needs to be done and what industry cannot do for itself. One important example is the resolution of international trade conflicts. As the study of cartels shows, it is extremely difficult for autonomous players to coordinate their actions so as to act in their collective self-interest for the simple reason that, while an incentive often exists for individual players to break ranks in the hope of increasing individual gain, this can be to the detriment of the collective interest. Relating this to Japan's international trade conflict, an individual semiconductor or motor car company has an incentive to increase its exports when its counterparts in the industry are voluntarily restricting theirs in order to reduce trade conflict. Another example is environmental protection where MITI is playing an expanding role. Here, too, the incentives facing private firms may not be compatible with the socially desired outcome, thus justifying involvement by MITI. It is widely acknowledged in Japan that MITI's intervention is necessary in these situations in the interests of all the companies concerned as well as in the national Japanese interest. In these cases the information that MITI has at its disposal is an invaluable aid in both policy-making and implementation.

Secondly, and more closely related to innovation, MITI is able to play an extremely constructive role in facilitating cooperative research between competing companies that, in the absence of MITI's interventions, would be less likely to cooperate. Here the information at MITI's disposal has been invaluable in facilitating the choice of research projects in strategic technology areas that will increase the competitive strength of Japanese companies, in selecting appropriate companies to participate in the cooperative research, and in securing the right kind of participation from these companies. Examples include the Fifth Generation Computer Project, its successor the Real World Computer Project that is still in its formative stage, and the Protein Engineering Research Institute which MITI established through the Japan Key Technology Center which it controls together with the Ministry of Posts and Telecommunications. The role that MITI has played in cooperative research has been analyzed in detail (Fransman, 1990).

Thirdly, the rich information available to MITI's decision-makers has enabled the ministry to complement the 'bounded vision' of private companies which tend to have good information in the areas in which they are involved but which are often unable to perceive the importance of emerging new technologies and markets in hitherto unrelated areas. On the basis of its broad detailed information MITI has been able to identify new technology areas with important commercial potential which have not received the attention they deserve in Japan and take steps to encourage companies to develop more actively these technologies and related markets. Recent examples include biotechnology and new materials where MITI has played an extremely important (though not very costly) role in facilitating entry by a large number of Japanese companies. (For further elaboration on the concept of bounded vision and for a study of Japanese biotechnology see the references below.)

This discussion on MITI and information provides an answer to the question as to how MITI is able to exert significant influence on the innovation process while accounting for only a relatively small proportion of the Japanese government's expenditure on science and technology. Drawing on work by Chihiro Watanabe, one of MITI's leading younger theorists, it may be concluded that for the reasons analyzed in this section MITI has been able to 'induce' innovation in Japanese companies on the basis of relatively modest financial sums. The information network which MITI orchestrates has been a crucial resource facilitating its inducement role.

But how important are Japanese universities in the Japanese Innovation System?

How Important are Japanese Universities?

A common judgment by analysts of Japan is that Japanese universities tend not to measure up to their Western counterparts in terms of research and that most advanced research is found, not in universities, but in the research laboratories of the leading companies. As it stands, this judgment, though with some evidence to support it, obscures the role that Japanese universities play in the innovation system. The aim of this section is to briefly elaborate on this role.

The first point to make is that one of the most important functions played by the universities in the innovation system is to provide graduates with good general levels of education to private companies. These graduates are then given company-specific training as outlined in the first section of this chapter. University professors, with close informal links with numbers of companies, frequently play an important role in helping to allocate their students to places in companies. This allocation mechanism with its tight networks of personal contact and information stands in strong contrast to the more impersonal labour market mechanism which is often used in Western countries.

Secondly, while there is some evidence suggesting that in many areas Japanese universities tend not to be as strong as their Western counterparts in *frontier* research, judgment of the role of Japanese universities based on this evidence overstates the importance of such research for innovation and competitiveness. The reason is simply that what counts immediately for most companies is not frontier research but *intra-frontier* research, and Japanese universities are often an important source of this kind of research for Japanese companies. My own research on Japanese biotechnology, for example, suggests that Japanese universities are a more important source of knowledge for some of the major Japanese biotechnology companies than are other companies and non-Japanese universities. To the extent that this is more generally true, Japanese universities make a more significant direct contribution to the innovation and competitiveness of Japanese companies than is usually acknowledged.

Thirdly, Japanese professors also contribute to the innovation system by acting as 'international antennae' and policy advisers and coordinators in the various advisory and consultative committees that are established both in the private and public sectors. In this way, by passing on their knowledge of international research areas and trends, they sometimes make an important contribution to JIS.

It may be concluded, therefore, that in these ways Japanese universities make an important contribution to innovation and competitiveness in Japan.

Conclusion

In this brief account of the Japanese Innovation System it has been possible to do no more than provide an analysis of some of its main characteristics. While it has been stressed that the 'engine' of the system lies in the Japanese companies and the competitive processes of which they form a part, the important role of both government and universities in encouraging innovation and competitiveness has also been emphasized. Returning finally to the proverbial elephant, while the 'true nature' of the beast may still be subject to debate, a satisfactory analysis of innovation and competitiveness in Japan will have to take account of the Japanese Innovation System as a whole and many, if not all, of the points raised in this paper.

Bibliography

Aoki, M. (1990) 'Towards an Economic Model of the Japanese Firm' *Journal of Economic Literature,* Vol. XXVIII, pp. 1–27.

Arrison, T.S. et al. (1992) *Japan's Growing Technological Capability: Implications for the US Economy,* National Academy Press, Washington DC.

Dore, R. (1987) *Taking Japan Seriously: A Confucian Perspective on Leading Economic Issues,* The Athlone Press, London.

Fransman, M. (1990) *The Market and Beyond, Cooperation and Competition in Information Technology in the Japanese System,* Cambridge University Press, Cambridge.

Fransman, M. (forthcoming) *Visions of the Firm and Japan,* Oxford University Press, Oxford.

Fransman, M. (forthcoming) *The Evolution of the Japanese Information and Communications Industry.*

Fransman, M. and Tanaka, S. (1991) 'The Strengths and Weaknesses of the Japanese Innovation System in Biotechnology', JETS Paper No. 3, Institute for Japanese–European Technology Studies, University of Edinburgh.

Freeman, C. (1987) *Technology Policy and Economic Performance: Lessons from Japan,* Pinter Publishers, London.

Komiya, R. et al. (eds) (1988) *Industrial Policy of Japan,* Academic Press, Tokyo.

Kumon, S. and Rosovsky, H. (eds) (1992), *The Political Economy of Japan, Volume 3: Cultural and Social Dynamics,* Stanford University Press, Stanford.

Odagiri, H. (1992) *Growth Through Competition, Competition Through Growth: Strategic Management and the Economy in Japan,* Clarendon Press, Oxford.

Patrick, H. (ed.) (1986) *Japan's High Technology Industries: Lessons and Limitations of Industrial Policy,* University of Washington Press, Seattle.

Porter, M. (1990) *The Competitive Advantage of Nations,* Macmillan, London.

7. Innovation and Growth

Chris Freeman

Introduction: Marx and Schumpeter

There is actually very little disagreement among economists about the importance of innovations for long-term economic growth. From Adam Smith to Robert Solow via Ricardo, Marx, Marshall, Schumpeter and Keynes there is virtual unanimity that the long-term growth of productivity is intimately related to the introduction and diffusion of technical and organizational innovations. Although, as we shall see, there are certainly difficulties about measuring the precise contribution of technical change (or any other factor) to the growth of industries or countries, no one doubts that innovation is essential to this process. Fagerberg (1987) provides recent strong evidence of this association for twenty-seven countries and many other studies have also shown its importance, albeit with varying techniques and models. Yet only Marx in the 19th century and Schumpeter in the 20th could be said to place innovation at the very centre of their growth theory.

Paradoxically, Karl Marx, although the most powerful and consistent critic of capitalist society, was also its most ardent admirer so far as innovation was concerned. He devoted more attention to innovation than any of the other classical economists and Schumpeter was indebted to him for much of his own analysis (Swedberg, 1991). Marx and Engels recognized already in *The Communist Manifesto* (1848) that capitalism depended for its very existence on a constant drive to introduce both new processes and new products. The competitive process itself drove firms to innovate: 'the bourgeoisie cannot exist without constantly revolutionizing the means of production'. Moreover, new products were the weapons with which capitalism overcame and swept aside all older social and economic formations. Ironically, a hundred years after Marx's death, they were still the weapons with which capitalism swept aside the would-be socialist economies created in his name. Both Marx's followers and Schumpeter (1942) underestimated the continuing innovative vitality of mature capitalist economies.

Schumpeter, of course, did not accept many features of Marx's theory; he did not believe, as Marx did, that profits were a surplus based on exploitation and maintained by the social and political power of the capitalist class as well as by innovations. For Schumpeter profits were defined as arising exclusively from entrepreneurship.

In Schumpeter's theory, the ability and initiative of entrepreneurs, drawing upon the discoveries of scientists and inventors, create entirely new opportunities for investment, growth and employment. The profits made from these innovations are then the decisive impulse for new surges of growth, acting as a signal to swarms of imitators. The fact that one or a few innovators can make exceptionally large profits, which they sometimes do, does not of course mean that all the imitators necessarily do so. Nobody else made such profits from nylon as Du Pont, or from main-frame computers as IBM; indeed, many would-be imitators made losses. This is an essential part of the Schumpeterian analysis. The present difficulties of IBM and some other computer firms fit well within his theory. When the bandwagon starts rolling some people fall off, profits are gradually 'competed away' until recession sets in, and the whole process may be followed by depression before high growth starts again with a new wave of technical innovation and organizational and social change.

Whereas in the Keynesian growth theory the emphasis is on the management of demand, and in neo-classical theory on removing market imperfections and price flexibility, with Schumpeter it is on autonomous investment, embodying new technical innovation which is the basis of economic development. In such a framework economic growth must be viewed primarily as a process of reallocation of resources between industries and firms. That process necessarily leads to structural changes and disequilibrium if only because of the uneven rate of technical change between different industries. Economic growth is not merely accompanied by fast-growing new industries and the expansion of such industries; it primarily *depends* on that expansion.

Schumpeter justified on three grounds his view that growth based on technical innovation was more like a series of explosions than a gentle and incessant transformation. First, he argued that innovations are not at any time distributed randomly over the whole economic system, but tend to be concentrated in certain key sectors and their surroundings, and that consequently they are by nature lopsided and disharmonious.

Secondly, he argued that the diffusion process is also inherently an uneven one because first a few and then many firms follow in the wake of successful pioneers. Kuznets (1930) had already emphasized the cyclical pattern underlying the growth of new industries. Product life-cycle theory and international trade theory have since confirmed many of these insights: a normal life-cycle would comprise a hesitant start, then take-off and fast growth and subsequent saturation or maturation, followed by slower growth, decline or stagnation – a typical sigmoid pattern.

There is, of course, enormous variety but inevitably for any new product, as new capacity is expanded, at some point (varying with the product in question) growth will begin to slow down. Market saturation and the tendency for technical advance to approach limits (Wolf's Law), as well as the competitive effects of swarming and changing costs of inputs, all tend to reduce the level of profitability and with it the attractions of further investment. Exceptionally, this process of maturation may take only a few years, but more typically it will take several decades and sometimes even longer. Schumpeter maintained that these characteristics of innovation imply that the disturbances engendered could be sufficient to disrupt the existing system and enforce a cyclical pattern of growth.

Hardly anyone would deny the first of Schumpeter's propositions: it is confirmed by a great deal of empirical observation and research as well as everyday commonsense. The differences between rates of growth in different branches of production are well-known and obvious, as is the fact that some industries decline while others grow rapidly. Moreover, it is now universally agreed that these structural changes are related to the flow of technical innovations. The most R&D-intensive industries are by and large the fastest growing. Most of them did not exist at all before this century. In industries such as electronics, aerospace, drugs, scientific instruments, synthetic materials, it is fairly clear that extremely high growth rates were closely related to clusters of technical innovations.

However, as Kuznets (1940) pointed out, whether or not the very rapid growth of new leading sectors of the economy and new technologies offers a plausible explanation of long-term cycles in economic development depends crucially on whether some of these innovations are so large in their impact as to cause major perturbations in the entire system – as, for example, could plausibly be argued in the case of the railways – or on whether such innovations are bunched together systematically in such a way as to generate exceptional booms and spurts of growth alternating with periods of recession.

The very rapid growth of the world economy in the 1950s and 1960s, followed by the slow-down in the 1970s and 1980s and the resurgence of structural unemployment, might reasonably be held to vindicate at least some of Kondratiev's and Schumpeter's ideas about long waves in the growth of capitalism. If the test of a theory in the social sciences is held to be predictive power, then long-wave theories come out better than most others in considering the development of the world economy in the 20th century. Nevertheless, Schumpeter's theory of long waves is still far from gaining general acceptance, whereas most economists would probably now accept many of his other ideas on the role of innovation in competition.

Neo-Schumpeterian Research on Innovation in Firms

Whilst Schumpeter deserves the credit for restoring innovation to a central place in the theory of economic growth, he actually had very little to say about the origin of innovations or about the management of innovations at the micro-level. Ruttan (1959) put it rather strongly when he said:

> Neither in *Business Cycles* nor in Schumpeter's other work is there anything that can be identified as a theory of innovation. The business cycle in Schumpeter's system is a direct consequence of the appearance of clusters of innovations. But no real explanation is provided as to why the clusters possess the particular types of periodicity which Schumpeter identified (Ruttan, 1959).

A more moderate criticism would be that in describing innovation as an act of will rather than an act of intellect, Schumpeter substituted a theory of entrepreneurship for a theory of innovation. Whilst there is certainly an element of truth in Schumpeter's perception of the exceptional difficulties facing many innovators and the exceptional persistence which is often needed to see an innovation through from the invention stage to commercial success, his conceptualization is lacking in depth and, more surprisingly, in historical perspective (Freeman, 1990).

To be fair to Schumpeter, he looked upon his theories as a first approximation and called upon his followers to criticize and develop his ideas by further research. This request has led to considerable response. From the pioneering studies of Mansfield (1968), Mansfield et al. (1971), Nelson (1962a), Nelson, Peck and Kalachek (1967), Rosenberg (1963, 1976) and Scherer (1965), a wave of neo-Schumpeterian research gathered force in the 1970s and 1980s, so that it is no longer possible in the 1990s to speak of innovation as a neglected area of research. Whilst it is difficult to summarize the results of such an enormous literature (see Dosi, 1988; Freeman, 1994 for recent attempts; see also, of course, the other chapters in this book), it is possible to point to some of the main conclusions so far as they affect theories of the growth of firms. Among the most important results are the following:

First of all, the research points strongly to the cumulative aspects of technology, the great importance of incremental as well as radical innovations, the multiple inputs to innovation from diverse sources within and outside the firm and the changes made to innovations by numerous adopters during diffusion, both within and between countries. Schumpeter's emphasis on the original entrepreneurs had tended to overstate the importance of original innovation and understate the role of diffusion in economic growth. It is true that the empirical research does often confirm the importance of individuals variously described as 'product champions' (Schon, 1973), 'business innovators' (Project Sappho), or 'network coordinators', but they are sometimes hard to identify within a more anonymous process in which pygmies play an essential part as well as giants. The fastest growing firms are distinguished by their capacity for a flow of incremental innovations as well as (more rarely) outstanding success with a radical innovation.

Secondly, the emphasis in much neo-Schumpeterian research on firm-specific technological knowledge accumulation (e.g. Teece, 1988; Amendola and Gaffard, 1988; Pavitt, 1986, 1987; Teubal, 1987; Teubal et al., 1991; Gaffard, 1990; Granstrand, 1982; Eliasson, 1990, 1992; Dosi, 1984; Achilladelis, Schwarzkopf and Lines, 1987, 1990) should not be taken to mean that exogenously generated scientific discoveries and advances play no part in technical innovation and growth at firm level. On the contrary, much of the recent empirical work, like the earlier studies of Carter and Williams (1957, 1958, 1959) points to the importance of contacts with the world of science and to the increasing interdependence of science and technology (Nelson, 1962; Freeman, 1974; Price, 1984).

A particularly important point made by Pavitt (1993) in his paper 'What do firms learn from basic research?' is that the contribution made by basic science to industry is mainly indirect, in the form of young recruits with new and valuable skills and knowledge, rather than direct, in the form of published papers, (though these too, of course, can be very useful). The Yale University Survey of 650 US industrial research executives showed that basic scientific skills and techniques in all disciplines were valued more highly and rated as more relevant than academic research results in most industries. The capability to assimilate the results of recent scientific research, whether directly or indirectly is now essential for innovation and growth in many industries.

Thirdly, most recent research on success and failure in innovation (see Rothwell, 1992) and on growth based on that success, has generally confirmed these conclusions whilst also demonstrating the role of corporate strategy and government policy in developing *networking* relationships with external sources of information, knowledge and advice (Dodgson, 1993; Teubal, 1987; Teubal et al., 1991; Coombs, Saviotti and Walsh, 1990; Carlsson and Jacobsson, 1993; Steele, 1991). The new generic technologies diffusing rapidly in the 1970s and 1980s – ICT (information and communication technology), biotechnology, and new materials technology – have been shown in numerous studies to intensify the science-technology interface and to enhance the importance of external networks for innovative success (see, for example, Orsenigo, 1989, 1993; Dodgson, 1991, 1993; Faulkner, 1986, for bio-technology: Lastres, 1992, and Cohendet, 1988, for new materials technology: Nelson, 1962b; Gazis, 1979; Dosi, 1984; Antonelli, 1992; Lundgren, 1991, and Freeman, 1991, for information and communication technology). The intensity of the interaction between science and technology has also been demonstrated in the 'scientometric' literature using citation analysis and similar techniques, notably in the work of the Leiden Science Studies Unit (Narin and Noma, 1985; Narin and Olivastro, 1992; Van Vianen, Moed and Van Raan, 1990).

Fourthly, empirical research (see, for example, Lundvall 1988, 1992) has also shown that another major determinant of innovative success lies in the nature and intensity of the interaction with contemporary and future *users* of an innovation. In the case of incremental innovations especially, but also for radical innovations, this has often been shown to be a decisive factor. It was one of the main findings of the Sappho project (Rothwell et al., 1974) and the Manchester project 'Wealth from Knowledge' (Langrish, Gibbons, Evans and Jevons, 1972). Von Hippel (1978, 1980, 1988) and Slaughter (1993) have shown that users may often take the lead in stimulating and organizing innovation.

Finally, the *integration* of R&D and design activities with production and marketing functions has been repeatedly shown to be essential for innovative success, for shorter lead times and for simultaneous product and process improvement.

The picture which thus emerges from numerous studies of innovation and growth in firms is one of continuous interactive learning (Lundvall, 1992). Firms learn both from their own experience of design, development, production and marketing *and* from a wide variety of external sources at home and abroad – customers, suppliers, contractors (a particularly important aspect of Japanese firm behaviour – see Imai, 1989; Sako, 1992; Dodgson, 1993) and from many other organizations – universities, government laboratories and agencies, consultants, licensors, licensees and others. The precise pattern of external and internal learning networks varies with industry and size of firm, but *all* firms make use of external sources (Foray, 1991, 1993; Kleinknecht and Reijnen, 1992).

From these results it follows that simple statistical correlations between R&D-intensity of firms and their rate of growth could not be expected to be very strong. Success with innovation depends on many other factors as well as R&D – external relationships, training, integration of design, development, production and marketing functions within the firm, general management quality, the selection environment and so forth. In some industries such as clothing and footwear, fashion design, which is hardly measured in R&D statistics, may be more important than technical innovation. Moreover, R&D statistics do not measure organizational innovations at all, although Schumpeter rightly insisted on their importance and recent research has completely vindicated his view.

R&D-intensity varies greatly between *industries*. Nevertheless, in many industries R&D-intensity may often be a surrogate measure which reflects the importance of many of those activities which *do* contribute to innovative success and growth. Empirical research within each industry tends to show that very high R&D intensity *is* positively related to rapid growth, whilst at the opposite extreme lack of any R&D or very low R&D intensity is often associated with stagnation or decline of firms. In between these extremes there is little clear association between the growth of most firms and their R&D intensity. This reflects the enormous variety of circumstances, of modes of learning, of management and entrepreneurial ability and of marketing and technical uncertainties.

When it comes to the growth of *industries* however, there is a much stronger statistical association between their R&D-intensity and their long-term growth rates (Freeman, 1962; Freeman et al., 1982). This reflects the fact that the advance of science and technology is worldwide and presents similar opportunities to many firms. If one firm does not succeed, others may. Moreover, the very success of some firms may deny that success to others. Thus the competitive process leads generally to the predictably rapid growth of the same industries in most countries but *within* those industries to the unpredictable success or failure of firms. Otherwise, anyone could make a fortune on the stock exchange. When it comes to the growth of *national* economies, the problem is even more complex and it is to these problems of macro-economic growth that we now turn. The innovative success of individual firms and their rate of growth depend not only on their own efforts but on the national environment in which they operate.

Uneven Growth Rates of Nations and of the World Economy

As we have seen, classical economists, neo-classical economists, Keynesians and others have all accepted in a general way that technical innovations have been extremely important for economic growth. Until recently, however, relatively few economists followed up this general proposition with more detailed study of the origins and diffusion of these innovations, their contribution to the performance of *national* economies and the role of public policy in promoting innovation; the others relegated innovations to a 'black box' to be opened up by engineers and historians but not by economists.

When it came to formal neo-classical mathematical models of growth the black box took the form of a 'residual factor' (sometimes called the Third Factor) in an aggregate production function. This residual comprised all those awkward hard-to-measure elements other than labour and capital, such as technical and institutional change. From Solow's (1957) original study onwards, most of these formal models showed that the 'residual' apparently accounted for a larger part of the growth than the simple accumulation of capital and growth of the labour force (sometimes as much as 90 per cent of the total).

A considerable effort went into the improvement of growth models in the 1960s and 1970s. One line of development was the attempt to 'disaggregate' the residual into various components of institutional and technical change (Denison, 1962, 1967) and to measure the 'contribution' of each component even to two decimal places. However, none of these efforts succeeded in answering the main point of critics of these models such as Nelson (1973) on the *complementarities* and interdependence of the various factors involved. The *quality* of the labour force and of the capital stock are changing all the time as new skills and technologies are acquired; technical, institutional changes and investment are all interdependent.

The so-called 'new growth theory' (Romer, 1986; Lucas, 1988; Grossman and Helpman, 1991) has attempted to respond to some of these criticisms by recognizing the central role of technical change and incorporating measures of R&D and/or education and training. Whilst this somewhat belated recognition of the central importance of part of the contents of the black box is certainly to be welcomed, most of these models still suffer from some of the same unrealistic assumptions and the same measurement problems as the 'old' growth models. In particular, they take little or no account of organizational innovations and of the interplay between institutional change, technical change and investment (Verspagen, 1992a and 1992b; Fagerberg, 1992).

It may be that future generations of growth modellers will succeed in overcoming the main problems with formal growth models and they are useful in any case for heuristic purposes. In the meantime, however, greater depth of understanding and more insights for policy have emerged from the work of historians such as Landes (1970), Hughes (1982, 1989), Hobsbawm, (1968), Abramovitz (1986) and those economists who have recognized the importance of path-dependence, institutional variety and public policies for industry and technology. Perhaps the main conclusion which emerges from the work of neo-Schumpeterian economists described earlier is that history matters. Both the internal accumulation of knowledge within the firm and the external networks are strongly affected by the national environment and national policies, as well as by worldwide developments in science and technology and international flows of capital, trade and migration.

Whereas the assumptions of neo-classical growth theory would lead one to expect *convergence* in the growth rates of nations, the central historical experience is actually of increasing *divergence* between a few industrialized countries and the under-developed Third World (Dosi et al., 1992). At various times in the last three centuries, particular countries have 'forged ahead' (to use the expression of Abramovitz, 1986), whilst others have fallen far behind. The leaders have been followed by a group of 'catching-up' countries that have sometimes succeeded in overtaking the leaders: Britain overtaking the Netherlands and forging ahead in the 18th century; the United States and Germany overtaking Britain in the 19th and 20th centuries; Japan overtaking the United States in the late 20th century.

It is notable that it was in catching-up countries that the most pro-active policies for innovation and growth were developed. People in countries which had fallen behind could see that the leaders had introduced technologies and developed industries and institutions which barely existed in their own countries and they were concerned to emulate them. Hamilton (1791) in his *Report on Manufactures* already advocated a variety of measures to strengthen manufacturing industry in the United States but it was List (1841) in Germany who was the most systematic advocate of industrial and technology policies designed to strengthen the innovative capabilities of German industry, even though the various German states were at that time still not one united country.

Contemporary economists such as Lundvall (1992) and Nelson (1993) have coined the expression 'national systems of innovation' to describe the complex mixture of institutions and policies which influence the innovative process at micro-level in any particular national economy. List's (1841) book was entitled *The National System of Political Economy* but it might just as well have been called 'The National System of Innovation' since it covered many of those topics such as technology accumulation, transfer of technology, education and training, strategic industries and trade policies which are at the heart of more recent analysis.

List criticized the free trade and *laissez-faire* policies of the classical economists, maintaining that Germany and other countries could only catch up with England if they protected and nurtured their 'infant' industries: hence his advocacy of a strong Customs Union for the German states. The neo-classical economists in their turn attacked protectionism and state intervention as a hindrance to the free movement of goods, ideas, capital and labour, which were in their view the recipe for rapid growth in any economy. This debate finds its contemporary reflection in the analysis of the astonishing post-Second World War growth performance of Japan and more recently of the so-called Asian 'tigers' or 'dragons' (South Korea, Taiwan, Singapore, Hong Kong and now China and others).

Neo-liberal theorists attempt to explain this rapid growth in terms of opening up these countries to foreign investment and to freer trade. Their performance in competitive export markets is particularly underlined. As against this neo-Schumpeterians and other development economists such as Amsden (1989), Wade (1990), Johnson (1982), and Freeman (1987) point to the pro-active policies for education, R&D, technology import and strategic industries pursued with determination over several decades in the 'tigers' as well as in Japan.

Even greater controversy surrounds the cyclical fluctuations in growth rates which have affected these economies as well as the more mature industrialized economies and the less fortunate Third World countries of Latin America and Africa. Whilst it is true that some Asian countries have continued to grow rapidly through the recessions of the 1980s and 1990s, Japan has been deeply affected in 1992–93 and the other Asian countries have also been affected to some degree. The former socialist countries, which experienced some very rapid growth in the 1950s and 1960s, stagnated or collapsed in the 1980s and 1990s, with the major exception of China.

In attempting to explain the high growth boom of the *belle époque* before

1913 or the even greater boom of the 1950s and 1960s, neo-Schumpeterians point to the rapidly growing industries of each epoch but, as we have seen, the critics of Schumpeter's long-wave theory argue that there is no special reason why innovations should conveniently cluster together just before the take-off of a long-wave boom. Mensch (1975) and Kleinknecht (1987, 1990) have suggested as a possible explanation that depressions stimulate radical innovations in the long-wave troughs and they have argued in support of this theory that the empirical evidence demonstrates a clustering of major innovations in the 1830s, 1880s and 1930s. The depressions themselves occur because a group of formerly fast-growing industries have passed their peak and slow down.

As against this, Freeman, Clark and Soete (1982) maintained that clusters of radical innovations could and did appear at any time in the economic cycle based on breakthroughs in science and technology and that strong demand, whether military or civil, was as likely or more likely to stimulate radical innovations as deep depressions. They argued that in any case a radical innovation had hardly any perceptible effect on the macro-economy. Only the widespread *diffusion* of clusters of radical and incremental innovations (new technological systems) could lead to the huge upswings of investment characteristic of long-wave booms. Perez (1983, 1985, 1989) pointed out that the diffusion of new technologies was strongly inhibited by the institutional framework surrounding older, now mature and obsolescent technologies.

She suggested that each wave is characterized by a dominant technological style or 'techno-economic paradigm' which transforms almost all branches of the economy to some extent as well as creating new dynamic industries. Thus her explanation is not just based on a few major innovations occurring in a particular decade, nor yet on a few leading sectors, but on a pervasive technological style embracing a whole constellation of technically and economically interrelated innovations and influencing an entire phase of economic development. These constellations of innovations, including managerial and organizational innovations, do not emerge suddenly just before a new Kondratiev upswing but crystallize over several decades. They rejuvenate old industries at the same time as creating new ones, thus providing a double impetus to a new upswing after appropriate institutional changes have been made.

A number of economists had pointed to the importance of 'technological trajectories' (Nelson and Winter, 1977) and of 'constellations of innovations' (Keirstead, 1948) which are both technically and economically interrelated. Several also extended Kuhn's notion of scientific paradigms to the concept of 'technological paradigms' (Dosi, 1982). Nelson and Winter (1977) suggested that some trajectories could be so powerful and influential that they could be regarded as 'generalised natural trajectories'. Freeman, Clark and Soete (1982) and other economists had stressed the interdependence of technical innovations in 'new technology systems'. Perez, however, goes much further. Her idea of 'techno-economic paradigms' relates not just to a particular branch of industry but to the broad tendencies in the economy as a whole. Her model may be described as a 'meta-paradigm' or a 'pervasive technology' theory.

It is of particular interest for growth theory as it provides a link between national systems of innovation and business cycle theory. Those nations which prove most adept in making institutional innovations which match the emerging new techno-economic paradigm are likely to prove the most successful in growing fast, catching up or forging ahead. Those, on the other hand, which suffer from institutional 'drag' or inertia may experience a prolonged mis-match between their institutions (including management systems at firm level as well as government structures), and the growth potential of new technologies.

From all this it is evident that economic growth, whether at micro- or at macro-level, offers one of the most exciting, challenging and controversial areas in the whole field of innovation research.

Bibliography

Abramowitz, M. (1986) 'Catching Up, Forging Ahead and Falling Behind', *Journal of Economic History*, Vol. 66, pp. 385–406.

Achilladelis, B.G., Schwarzkopf, A. and Lines, M. (1987) 'A Study of Innovation in the Pesticide Industry', *Research Policy*, Vol. 16, No. 2, pp. 175–212.

Achilladelis, B.G., Schwarzkopf, A. and Lines, M. (1990) 'The Dynamics of Technological Innovation: the Case of the Chemical Industry', *Research Policy*, Vol. 19, No. 1, pp. 1–35.

Amendola, M. and Gaffard, J.L. (1988) *The Innovation Choice: An Economic Analysis of the Dynamics of Technology*, Blackwell, Oxford.

Amsden, A. (1989) *Asia's Next Giant: South Korea and Late Industrialisation*, Oxford University Press, New York.

Antonelli, C. (1992) *The Economics of Localised Technological Change: The Evidence from Information and Communication Technologies*, University of Turin, Department of Economics, forthcoming.

Carlsson, B. and Jacobsson, S. (1993) 'Technological Systems and Economic Performance: the Diffusion of Factory Automation in Sweden', Chapter 4 in Foray, D. and Freeman, C. (eds) *Technology and the Wealth of Nations*, Pinter, London.

Carter, C.F. and Williams, B.R. (1957) *Industry and Technical Progress*, Oxford University Press, Oxford.

Carter, C.F. and Williams, B.R. (1958) *Investment in Innovation*, Oxford University Press, Oxford.

Carter, C.F. and Williams, B.R. (1959) 'The Characteristics of Technically Progressive Firms', *Journal of Industrial Economics*, Vol. 7, No. 2, pp. 87–104.

Cohendet, P.M. et al. (1988) *The New Advanced Materials: Economic Dynamics and European Strategy* (English edition edited by M. Ledoux).

Coombs, R., Saviotti, P. and Walsh, V. (1990) *Technological Change and Company*

Strategies, Harcourt Brace, London.

Denison, E.F. (1962) *The Sources of Economic Growth in the United States*, Committee for Economic Development, New York.

Denison, E.F. (1967) *Why Growth Rates Differ: Post-War Experience in Nine Western Countries*, Brookings Institution, Washington DC.

Dodgson, M. (1991) *The Management of Technological Learning: Lessons from a Biotechnology Company*, De Gruyter, Berlin.

Dodgson, M. (1993a) *Technological Collaboration in Industry*, Routledge, London.

Dodgson, M. (1993b) 'Organisational Learning: A Review of Some Literature', *Organisation Studies*, Vol. 14, No. 3, pp. 375–93.

Dosi, G. (1982) 'Technological Paradigms and Technological Trajectories: a Suggested Interpretation of the Determinants and Directions of Technical Change', *Research Policy*, Vol. 11, No. 3, June, pp. 147–62.

Dosi, G. (1984) *Technical Change and Industrial Transformation*, Macmillan, London.

Dosi, G. (1988) 'Sources, Procedures and Microeconomic Effects of Innovation', *Journal of Economic Literature* 36, pp. 1126–71.

Dosi, G., Freeman, C., Nelson, R., Silverberg, G. and Soete, L. (eds) (1988) *Technical Change and Economic Theory*, Pinter, London; Columbia University Press, New York.

Dosi, G. et al. (1992) 'Convergence and Divergence in the Long-Term Growth of Open Economies', paper at MERIT Conference, Maastricht, December.

Eliasson, G. (1990) 'The Firm as a Competent Team', *Journal of Economic Behavior and Organization*, Vol. 13, No. 3.

Eliasson, G. (1992) 'Business Competence, Organizational Learning and Economic Growth: Establishing the Smith–Schumpeter–Wicksell (SSW) Connection', in Scherer, F. and Perlman, M. (eds) *Entrepreneurship, Technological Innovation and Economic Growth*, University of Michigan Press, Ann Arbor.

Fagerberg, J. (1987) 'A Technology Gap Approach to Why Growth Rates Differ', *Research Policy*, Vol. 16, No. 2–4, pp. 87–101.

Fagerberg, J. (1991) 'Innovation, Catching Up and Growth', in *Technology and Productivity: the Challenge for Economic Policy*, OECD, Paris.

Fagerberg, J. (1992) 'Technology and Economic Growth: a Review of the Theoretical and Empirical Literature', NUPI, Paper No. 457, Oslo.

Faulkner, W. (1986) 'Linkage between Academic and Industrial Research: the Case of Biotechnological Research in the Pharmaceutical Industry', DPhil thesis, University of Sussex, Brighton.

Foray, D. (1991) 'The Secrets of Industry are in the Air: Industrial Cooperation and the Organisational Dynamics of the Innovative Firm', *Research Policy*, Vol. 20, No. 5, pp. 393–405.

Foray, D. (1993) 'General Introduction', in Foray, D. and Freeman, C. (eds) *Technology and the Wealth of Nations*, Pinter, London.

Freeman, C. (1962) 'Research and Development: a Comparison between British and American Industry', *National Institute Economic Review*, Vol. 20, pp. 21–39.

Freeman, C. (1974) *The Economics of Industrial Innovation*, first edition Penguin, Harmondsworth; second edition Frances Pinter, London (1982).

Freeman, C. (1987) *Technology Policy and Economic Performance: Lessons from Japan*, Frances Pinter, London.

Freeman, C. (1990) 'Schumpeter's Business Cycles Revisted', in Heertje, A. and Perlman, M. (eds) *Evolving Technology and Market Structure*, University of Michigan Press, Ann Arbor.

Freeman, C. (1991) 'Networks of Innovators: a Synthesis of Research Issues', *Research*

Policy, Vol. 20, No. 5, pp. 499–514.

Freeman, C. (1994) 'The Economics of Technical Change: a critical survey article', *Cambridge Journal of Economics,* Vol. 18, No. 4, October (forthcoming).

Freeman, C., Clark, J. and Soete, L. (1982) *Unemployment and Technical Innovation,* Frances Pinter, London.

Gaffard, J.-L. (1990) *Economie Industrielle de l'Innovation,* Dalloz, Paris.

Gazis, D.L. (1979) 'The Influence of Technology on Science: a Comment on Some Experiences of IBM Research', *Research Policy,* Vol. 8, No. 4, pp. 244–59.

Granstrand, O. (1982) *Technology, Management and Markets,* Frances Pinter, London.

Grossman, G.M. and Helpman, E. (1991), *Innovation and Growth in the Global Economy,* MIT Press, Cambridge (USA).

Hamilton, A. (1791) *Report on the Subject of Manufactures,* Reprinted US GPO (1913), Washington.

Hobsbawm, E. (1968) *Industry and Empire,* Weidenfeld and Nicolson, London.

Hobday, M. (1992) *Foreign Investment, Exports and Technology Development in the Four Dragons,* UN TNC Division, Campinas Conference, Brazil, November.

Hughes, T.P. (1982) *Networks of Power: Electrification in Western Society 1800–1930,* Johns Hopkins University Press, Baltimore, MD.

Hughes, T.P. (1989) *American Genesis,* Viking, New York.

Imai, K. (1989) 'Evolution of Japan's Corporate and Industrial Networks', in Carlsson, B. (ed.) *Industrial Dynamics,* Kluwer Academic Publishers, Boston.

Johnson, C. (1982) *MITI and the Japanese Miracle: the Growth of Industry Policy 1925–1975,* Stanford University Press, Stanford.

Keirstead, B.S. (1948) *The Theory of Economic Change,* Macmillan, Toronto.

Kleinknecht, A. (1987) *Innovation Patterns in Crisis and Prosperity: Schumpeter's Long Cycle Reconsidered,* Macmillan, London.

Kleinknecht, A. (1990) 'Are There Schumpeterian Waves of Innovation?', *Cambridge Journal of Economics,* Vol. 14, No. 1, pp. 81–92.

Kleinknecht, A. and Reijnen, J.O.N. (1992) 'Why do Firms Cooperate on R&D? An Empirical Study', *Research Policy,* Vol. 21, No. 4, pp. 347–60.

Kuznets, S. (1930) *Secular Movements in Production and Prices,* Houghton Mifflir, Boston.

Kuznets, S. (1940) 'Schumpeter's Business Cycles', *American Economic Review,* Vol. 30, No. 2, pp. 257–71.

Landes, M. (1970) *The Unbound Prometheus: Technological and Industrial Development in Western Europe from 1750 to the Present,* Cambridge University Press, Cambridge.

Langrish, J., Gibbons, M., Evans, P. and Jevons, F. (1972), *Wealth from Knowledge,* Macmillan, London.

Lastres, H. (1992) '*Advanced Materials and the Japanese National System of Innovation*', DPhil thesis, University of Sussex, SPRU, Brighton.

List, F. (1841) *The National System of Political Economy,* English translation, Longman (1904).

Lucas, R.E. (1988) 'On the Mechanisms of Economic Development', *Journal of Monetary Economics,* Vol. 22, pp. 3–42.

Lundgren, A. (1991) *Technological Innovation and Industrial Evolution: The Emergence of Industrial Networks,* DPhil dissertation, Stockholm School of Economics.

Lundvall, B-Å. (1988) 'Innovation as an Interactive Process: from User-Producer Interaction to the National System of Innovation', in Dosi, G. et al. (eds) *Technical Change and Economic Theory,* Pinter, London.

Lundvall, B-Å. (ed.) (1992) *National Systems of Innovation,* Pinter, London.

Maddison, A. (1991) *Dynamic Forces in Capitalist Development,* Oxford University Press, New York.

Mansfield, E. (1961) 'Technical Change and the Rate of Imitation', *Econometrica* 29(4), October, pp. 741–66; and NSF *Reviews of Data in R&D.*

Mansfield, E. (1968) *The Economics of Technological Change,* Norton, New York.

Mansfield, E. et al. (1971) *Research and Innovation in the Modern Corporation,* Norton, New York; Macmillan, London.

Marx, K. and Engels, F. (1848), *The Communist Manifesto,* English translation, Karl Marx Selected Works, Vol. 1, Marx–Engels–Lenin Institute, Moscow, 1935.

Mensch, G. (1975) *Das technologische Patt,* Frankfurt: Umschau, English translation, *Technological Stalemate: Innovations Overcome Depression,* Ballinger, New York.

Narin, F. and Noma, E. (1985) 'Is Technology Becoming Science?', *Scientometrics,* Vol. 7, No. 3, pp. 369–81.

Narin, F. and Olivastro, D. (1992) 'Status Report: Linkage Between Technology and Science', *Research Policy.* Vol. 21, pp. 237–51.

Nelson, R.R. (1962a) 'The Link Between Science and Invention: the Case of the Transistor', in NBER, *The Rate and Direction of Inventive Activity,* Princeton University Press.

Nelson, R.R. (ed.) (1962b) *The Rate and Direction of Inventive Activity,* National Bureau of Economic Research, Princeton University Press, Princeton.

Nelson, R.R., Peck, M.J. and Kalachek, E.D. (1967) *Technology, Economic Growth and Public Policy,* Allen and Unwin, London.

Nelson, R.R. (1973) 'Recent Exercises in Growth Accounting: New Understanding or Dead End?', *American Economic Review,* Vol. 63, pp. 462–68.

Nelson, R.R. and Winter, S.G. (1977) 'In Search of a Useful Theory of Innovation', *Research Policy,* Vol. 6, No. 1, pp. 36–76.

Nelson, R.R. (ed.) (1993) *National Innovation Systems,* Oxford University Press, New York.

Orsenigo, L. (1989) *The Emergence of Biotechnology: Institutions and Markets in Industrial Innovation,* Pinter, London.

Orsenigo, L. (1993) 'The Dynamics of Competition in a Science-based Technology: the Case of Biotechnology', Chapter 2 in Foray, D. and Freeman, C. (eds) *Technology and the Wealth of Nations,* Pinter, London.

Pavitt, K. (1984) 'Patterns of Technical Change: Towards a Taxonomy and a Theory', *Research Policy,* Vol. 13, No. 6, pp. 343–73.

Pavitt, K. (1986) 'International Patterns of Technological Accumulation', in Hood, N. (ed.) *Strategies in Global Competition,* Wiley, New York.

Pavitt, K. (1987) 'On the Nature of Technology', Inaugural Lecture, University of Sussex, 23 June.

Pavitt, K. (1993) 'What do Firms Learn from Basic Research?' Chapter 1 in Foray, D. and Freeman, C. (eds) *Technology and the Wealth of Nations,* Pinter, London.

Perez, C. (1983) 'Structural Change and the Assimilation of New Technologies in the Economic and Social System', *Futures,* Vol. 15, No. 5, pp. 357–75.

Perez, C. (1985) 'Microelectronics, Long Waves and the World Structural Change: New Perspectives for Developing Countries', *World Development,* Vol. 13, No. 3, 13 March, pp. 441–63.

Perez, C. (1989) 'Technical Change, Competitive Restructuring and Institutional Reform in Developing Countries', *World Bank Strategic Planning and Review,* Discussion Paper 4, World Bank, Washington DC, December.

Price, D. de S. (1984) 'The Science/Technology Relationship, the Craft of Experimental

Science and Policy for the Improvement of High Technology Innovation', *Research Policy*, Vol. 13, No. 1, February, pp. 3–20.

Romer, P. (1986) 'Increasing Returns and Long-Run Growth', *Journal of Political Economy*, Vol. 94, No. 5, pp. 1002–37.

Rosenberg, N. (1963) 'Technological Change in the Machine Tool Industry', *Journal of Economic History*, Vol. 23.

Rosenberg, N. (1976) *Perspectives on Technology*, Cambridge University Press, Cambridge.

Rothwell, R. (1992) 'Successful industrial innovation: crirical factors for the 1990s', *R&D Management*, Vol. 22, No. 3, pp. 221–39.

Rothwell, R. et al. (1974) 'SAPPHO Updated', *Research Policy*, Vol. 3, No. 5.

Ruttan, V. (1959) 'Usher and Schumpeter on Innovation, Invention and Technological Change', *Quarterly Journal of Economics*, Vol. 73, No. 4, pp. 596–606.

Sako, M. (1992) *Contracts, Prices and Trust: How the Japanese and British Manage Their Subcontracting Relationships*, Oxford University Press, Oxford.

Scherer, F.M. (1965) 'Firm Size, Market Structure, Opportunity and the Output of Patented Inventions', *American Economic Review*, Vol. 55, No. 5, pp. 1097–1123.

Scherer, F.M. (1973) *Industrial Market Structure and Economic Performance*, Rand McNally.

Schon, D.A. (1973) 'Product Champions for Radical New Innovations', *Harvard Business Review*, March–April.

Schumpeter, J.A. (1928) 'The Instability of Capitalism', *Economic Journal*, Vol. 38, pp. 361–86.

Schumpeter, J.A. (1934) *The Theory of Economic Development*, Harvard University Press, Cambridge, (English translation from 1913 German edition).

Schumpeter, J.A. (1939) *Business Cycles: A Theoretical, Historical and Statistical Analysis of the Capitalist Process*, 2 vols, McGraw-Hill, New York.

Schumpeter, J.A. (1942) *Capitalism, Socialism and Democracy*, McGraw-Hill, New York.

Science Policy Research Unit (1972) *Success and Failure in Industrial Innovation*, London Centre for the Study of Industrial Innovation.

Slaughter, S. (1993) 'Innovation and Learning during Implementation: A Comparison of User and Manufacturer Innovation', *Research Policy*, Vol. 22, No. 1, pp. 81–97.

Solow, R. (1957) Technical Change and the Aggregate Production Function, *Review of Economics and Statistics*, Vol. 39, pp. 312–20.

Steele, I. (1991) *Managing Technology: A Strategic View*, McGraw-Hill, New York.

Swedberg, R. (1991) *Joseph A Schumpeter: His Life and Work*, Polity Press (Blackwell), Oxford.

Teece, D.J. (1986) 'Profiting from Technological Innovation: Implications for Integration, Collaboration, Licensing and Public Policy', *Research Policy*, Vol. 15, No. 6, pp. 285–305.

Teece, D.J. (1988) 'The Nature and the Structure of Firms', in Dosi et al. (eds) *Technical Change and Economic Theory*, Pinter, London.

Teubal, M. (1987) *Innovation, Performance, Learning and Government Policy: Selected Essays*, University of Wisconsin Press, Madison.

Teubal, M., Yinnon, T. and Zuscovitch, E. (1991) 'Networks and Market Creation', *Research Policy*, Vol. 20, No. 5, pp. 381–92.

Van Vianen, B.G., Moed, H.F. and Van Raan, A.J.F. (1990) 'An Exploration of the Science Base of Recent Technology', *Research Policy*, Vol. 19, No. 1, pp. 61–81.

Verspagen, B. (1992a) 'Endogenous Innovation in Neo-Classical Growth Models: A

Survey', *Journal of Macro-Economics,* Vol. 14, No. 4, pp. 631–62.

Verspagen, B. (1992b) *Uneven Growth between Interdependent Economies: An Evolutionary View on Technology Gaps, Trade and Growth,* Dissertation 92-10, University of Limburg.

von Hippel, E. (1978) 'A Customer–Active Paradigm for Industrial Product Idea Generation', *Research Policy,* Vol. 7, pp. 240–66.

von Hippel, E. (1980) 'The User's Role in Industrial Innovation', in Burton, D. and Goldhar, J. (eds) *Management of Research and Innovation,* North Holland, Amsterdam.

von Hippel, E. (1988) *The Sources of Innovation,* Oxford University Press, Oxford.

Wade, R. (1990) *Governing the Market: Economic Theory and the Rise of Government in East Asian Industrialisation,* Princeton University Press, New Jersey.

8.   Innovation in East Asia: Diversity and Development

Mike Hobday

Introduction

The economic and technological development of the Asia-Pacific region is undoubtedly one of the most important events in the world economy in the postwar period. For the first time in history, a group of once poor developing countries looks set to catch up with the industrialized countries. Following Japan, the four 'tigers' or newly industrializing countries (NICs) of East Asia (South Korea, Taiwan, Hong Kong and Singapore) have made remarkable strides in terms of economic growth, per capita incomes and technological progress. As a result, if recent forecasts are correct, by the year 2000 the Asia Pacific Rim GNP will exceed that of the EC and equal that of North America.[1]

Some observers attribute the growth of the NICs and other neighbouring East Asian economies (e.g. China, Malaysia, Thailand and Indonesia) mainly to Japan. This view is expressed in the so-called 'flying geese' model of East Asian development. Although Japan is undeniably important, this chapter argues that in some significant respects the flying geese model is deficient. Indeed, there is a great deal of diversity in the development paths of the NICs. The flying geese model underplays the significance of the US economy, both as a market and as a source of technology. The model also fails to give due recognition to independent impulses in the region's development. These include the aggressive indigenous efforts of the four tigers to accumulate technology and to export overseas. The four tigers are already an important source of East Asian trade competitiveness and regional investment. In terms of foreign direct investment (FDI), the four tigers match Japan's outward investment in the less developed economies (or 'second-tier' NICs) of the region.

Following divergent development paths the East Asian tigers are developing their own distinctive innovation systems. With the exception of South Korea, these models are essentially 'Chinese' in character and differ markedly from the Japanese system of innovation described elsewhere in this book.

94

The Flying Geese Model of East Asian Development

The assessment of Asia-Pacific as an integrated economic region began with the flying geese idea, put forward by Professor A. Kaname in the 1930s and then by Professor K. Akamatsu in 1956.[2] This model gives prominence to Japan as the driving economic and technological force. Japan developed first, gaining a strong technological base. Then as wages and other costs rose at home, Japanese production facilities were relocated to the four tigers and other lower cost economies.

The flying geese, it is argued, took off after 1985 with the appreciation of the yen. As Japanese wages increased and the yen appreciated, production technology flowed outwards from Japan, first to the NICs, then to the second-tier ASEAN economies (principally Thailand, Malaysia and Indonesia) and China. Later as wages, costs and technological levels rose in the tigers and their currencies appreciated, they too increased their outward investment into the second-tier NICs and China.

According to Yamashita (1991) the four tigers owe their export achievements largely to Japanese subsidiaries operating from within their economies and/or joint ventures with Japanese companies (pp. 2–3). Japan, so the argument goes, led the economic development of the region through trade, aid and FDI. The NICs imported not only machines, parts and materials but also management styles from Japan.

Overseas Chinese Models of Development

To date, most business-economic analyses of the Pacific Basin have focused on the Japanese economy, Japanese management and Japanese organizational styles.[3] However, cultural, historical and sociological studies of overseas Chinese competitive behaviour (e.g. Mackie, 1992; Redding, 1991; Whitley, 1992) highlight the nature and importance of the overseas Chinese to the economic development of Asia-Pacific.

The populations of Taiwan and Hong Kong are largely made up of ethnic Chinese (21 million and 6 million respectively) and Singapore's population is mainly Chinese. Also, there are large Chinese minorities in Malaysia, Indonesia and Thailand (*The Economist,* 18 July 1992, p. 21). Taiwan and Hong Kong developed largely on the basis of Chinese business systems, connections and investment capital. While these relate to the Japanese economy, they are distinctive in several respects.

Taiwan's economy (like Hong Kong's) is made up of many tiny family-owned businesses. In contrast with the large Japanese conglomerates, these firms operate in a 'Chinese style' often characterized by autocratic management, fast response to changing market niches and overseas family connections. Successful companies have grown fairly large but still remain tiny compared with the Japanese *keiretsu.* Management styles in Taiwan owe as much (or more) to US firms as Japanese firms. Many leading Taiwanese managers worked abroad in US high technology firms and attended US universities. Often, Taiwanese companies retain strong technological links with US corporations in Silicon Valley and elsewhere.

Traditional overseas Chinese businesses rely heavily on personal connections, sometimes called *guanxi*. Connections are strongest within the family. Then comes clan, village and Chinese home province. Today, worldwide *guanxi* enable Chinese businesses to match, for example, consumer demand in the US with production in China and Taiwan. Typically, the patriarch controls the finances from Hong Kong or Taiwan. His 'number-one-son' manages the factory in China, Thailand or Malaysia. Having been to a leading university in the US, 'number-two-son' may well work in California, assessing new computer innovations (*The Economist,* 16 November 1991, p. 8). A large proportion of Hong Kong's recent outward investment has been directed to relatives in the Guangdong province of China in search of cheap labour, as costs have risen at home.

There are many significant differences between the development strategies of the three 'Chinese tigers' (Taiwan, Hong Kong and Singapore) and between the various groups of overseas Chinese to be found in other countries of the region. It is therefore more accurate to speak of overseas Chinese 'models', rather than one single model.

The flying geese model of development fails to do justice to this increasingly autonomous and powerful growth process. Nor does it do sufficient justice to the autonomous efforts of South Korea (discussed below). In fact, most of the literature fails to address the mechanisms of technology acquisition and learning in the non-Japanese countries of the region.[4] As argued below, one of the key features of the NICs' development is their distinctive strategies towards technology.

Economic Performance

Table 8.1 testifies to the rapid growth experienced by the NICs since the 1960s.[5] Hong Kong experienced GNP growth rates of over 8 per cent per annum during the period 1960 to 1988. Likewise, Singapore's growth outstripped that of Japan and other developed countries (albeit from a lower base). South Korea and Taiwan recorded rates of economic growth generally above 8 per cent throughout the 1960s, 1970s and 1980s. In contrast, US growth averaged around 3 per cent, similar to European Economic Community growth (Wade, 1990, p. 34). Japanese growth slowed to around 5 per cent during the 1970s and 1980s while the tigers continued to average 8 per cent to 9 per cent per annum. During the early 1990s the NICs have enjoyed strong, albeit reduced, growth rates despite the world recession.

All the more remarkable was the sustained economic growth achieved during and after the oil crises and world recession of the early 1970s. While other countries, including Japan, decelerated, three of the four NICs actually increased their pace of growth during the 1970s.

Table 8.1 Average annual rates of growth of real GNP (selected years)

Country/group	1960–69	1970–79	1980–88	1988	1991	1992	1993*
Four NICs							
Hong Kong	10.0	9.4	8.0	10.5	3.9	5.2	5.6
South Korea	7.7	9.5	8.7	15.9	8.4	5.5	6.3
Singapore	8.9	9.5	7.0	10.0	6.7	5.6	6.5
Taiwan	9.5	10.2	7.5	9.5	7.0	6.7	n/a
ASEAN-4							
Indonesia	3.4	7.8	5.8	7.5	7.0	5.5	6.0
Malaysia	6.5	8.1	5.3	6.6	8.6	8.5	8.0
Philippines	3.0	6.3	1.6	6.4	0.0	3.3	1.5
Thailand	8.3	7.4	5.6	7.1	7.9	7.5	7.8
Other Asia							
China	2.9	7.5	9.2	10.2	4.6	12.0	10.0
India		3.2	5.6	4.4	3.7	4.0	4.8
OECD (selected)	3.4						
Canada	5.7	4.7	3.1	4.3	-0.2	0.3	2.8
Japan	10.9	5.2	5.3	5.1	3.1	0.9	2.4
United States	4.1	2.8	2.6	3.6	0.4	2.2	2.5

Sources: Data for all economies 1960–1988 (James, 1990 p. 4); Asian economic data for 1991, 1992 and 1993 (*Far Eastern Economic Review,* 19 November 1992, pp. 76-77; 14 January 1993, pp. 56–57). OECD data for 1991 to 1993 (*The Economist,* 21 March 1992, p. 145; 9 May 1992, p. 147; 26 January 1993, p. 139).
Note: * 1992 official estimates.

During the 1980s, two of the main growth exports from Asia-Pacific (including Japan) were electronics and automobiles. Among the tigers, South Korea benefited most from automobile exports. The other tigers succeeded in exporting large volumes of electronics products, including personal computers, disk drives, semiconductors, colour TVs and video cassette recorders. With export progress each of the tigers has developed significant competitive and technological capabilities in at least some areas of advanced electronics.[6]

Table 8.2, from Fukasaku (1991), illustrates changes in the structure of manufactured exports from Japan and the four tigers during the 1980s. The table illustrates the shift away from export categories 1 and 2 (natural resource and labour-intensive exports) to export categories 3 and 4 (human capital and technology intensive items). For example, South Korea's exports of 3 and 4 increased from 43 per cent in 1979 to 57 per cent in 1988. Similar increases occurred in each of the four tigers.

Electronics is now the largest export item for South Korea, Taiwan and Singapore. In Hong Kong, it is the second largest after clothing and textiles. Each country has progressed gradually from labour-intensive tasks such as testing and assembly to production, product design and development, precision engineering and more recently to research and development.[7] Electronics goods and systems produced in the tigers have become increasingly sophisticated.

Singapore is today the world's largest manufacturer of hard disk drives and a major producer of other complex professional and consumer electronics. Much of South Korea's electronics output is produced under licence for Japanese companies. However, leading firms such as Samsung boast world class technological capabilities in semiconductor memory design and fabrication as well as colour TVs, camcorders and compact disk players. In Taiwan electronics accounted for around 18 per cent to 20 per cent of total exports during the 1980s. Taiwan is currently the world's largest producer of printed circuit boards for PCs. It is also a major supplier of colour monitors, PCs, fax machines and calculators. Hong Kong is perhaps the weakest tiger in terms of research and development capabilities. Nevertheless, it has had significant home produced export successes in fax machines, cordless telephones and workstations.

The flying geese proposition that the four tigers owe their export growth to FDI from Japan (or elsewhere) is not supported by the evidence. Indeed, in the early 1970s Hone (1974) showed that the vast majority of East Asia's exports were accounted for by local firms, not multinational corporations of any nationality. For South Korea, Taiwan and Hong Kong, local firms' contribution to exports has increased since Hone's work. Of the four tigers, only Singapore owes its export success to multinational subsidiary production (including US, Japanese and European firms).

Today, the tigers are no longer low wage economies. Wages and other costs have risen substantially in each of the countries. As incomes have risen, labour-intensive production has gradually been relocated to the second-tier NICs and China. As the electronics case shows, the tigers are now internationally competitive producers of complex technology goods, largely from local firms.

During the 1980s the four NICs increasingly imported technology, machinery and components from Japan, exporting finished goods to the US and Europe. As a result, the four countries' foreign trade balances have for most years been positive, but not very large. As far as the flying geese

Table 8.2 *Structure of manufactured exports from Japan and the four tigers (percentages)*

	Japan		Korea		Taiwan		Hong Kong		Singapore	
	1979	1988	1979	1988	1979	1988	1979	1988	1979	1988
1. Natural resource intensive products	2	2	6	2	7	5	1	1	8	5
2. Unskilled labour intensive products	11	6	51	41	51	43	65	51	20	12
3 Technology intensive products	36	50	16	24	26	33	10	24	49	63
4. Human capital intensive products	51	42	27	33	17	20	24	23	23	20
Totals ($ billion)	99	257	13	57	14	59	11	27	7	28

Source: UNSO, Comtrade Database, cited in Fukasaku (1991, Table 3).

model is concerned, Japan is clearly an important source of goods and technology for the tigers. However, as the trade data show, the US economy and indeed the EC were more important than Japan in terms of export market outlets throughout the 1980s (Chaponnière, 1992, p. 73).

An Assessment of the Flying Geese Model

Strengths
In some respects the flying geese model is useful and informative. It draws attention to the increasing importance of Japan in the region. Japan is far ahead of the four tigers in terms of GNP size and economic development. Indeed, Japan is ahead of the US and Europe in many areas including consumer electronic goods, semiconductor memories and automobiles. Japan is an obvious role model for other modern Asian economies. It boasts a substantial technological lead over the four tigers and supplies them with key components, machinery and materials.

Japan assists the regions with FDI, aid, joint ventures, and through the transfer of modern management practices. Studies show that South Korea had modelled its *chaebol* corporations on the Japanese *keiretsu*, although there are significant differences (Amsden, 1989; Whitley, 1992). Today, the *chaebol* are linked to the Japanese *keiretsu* through OEM (original equipment manufacturer) links whereby technologies are transferred and Korean products are sold under Japanese firms' brand names.

Weaknesses
Despite its strengths, the flying geese model has important deficiencies. Some versions overstress the importance of Japanese FDI. Japanese FDI was only a minor source of growth and capital formation in each of the tigers. In the case of Singapore, American multinationals were a larger contributor to growth than Japanese firms. In addition, US and European FDI played an important role in the initiation of local industries (e.g. Philips of Holland and GE of the US). Today, American FDI flows still challenge Japanese investments in Pacific-Asia, although Japan's FDI is the largest single source. A comprehensive model of East Asian development would need to account for the dynamics of competition between Japanese, US and European multinationals and the different roles played by each in the region.

The flying geese idea grossly understates (or ignores) the importance of the US economy as an export market for East Asian goods. Conversely, it understates the weakness of Japan as an importer of goods from the NICs and other East Asian economies. Even Europe is a larger importer of NIC products than Japan. Statistical analysis of trade from Fukasaku (1991, p. 27) shows that the tigers became more closely integrated with North America during the 1980s. Taking the analogy further, the US economy is equivalent to a 'Jumbo' aeroplane flying in front of the flying geese, pulling the entire region along through its imports.

Within the region, the flying geese model fails to address the significance of the overseas Chinese as an additional, distinctive force for development. Overseas Chinese FDI exceeds Japanese outward investment in the region (IEEE 1991, p. 27). The three Chinese tigers did not merely imitate Japan, nor did they depend primarily on Japanese FDI for growth. Chinese firms embody their own distinctive styles of management and industrial structure, based on small- and medium-sized enterprise and Chinese entrepreneurial abilities (Wade, 1990; Redding, 1991). These business competences have been built up over a very long period of time. They certainly pre-date the post-1985 acceleration of Japanese FDI.

The four tigers owe their growth to independent efforts, investments and rapid technological learning linked to a variety of sources, not only Japan. Gee (1991, p. 12) shows that outward FDI from Taiwan to the US exceeded its outward investment to all other countries together during the period 1986–1989, stressing the importance of direct links between the two economies.

Technologically, leading Taiwanese firms have emerged as independent innovators in world markets. Taiwan's First International Computer Inc., the world's largest producer of circuit boards for PCs, conducts joint development projects with leading US firms such as Intel, Texas Instruments, Microsoft and Motorola. Roughly 80 per cent of Japanese Casio calculators are now produced by Cal-Comp of Taiwan (*The Economist*, 1991, p. 25). Although virtually unknown in the West, Cal-Comp is today the world's largest producer of calculators. It has links with Motorola to jointly develop and produce hand-held computers, the size of calculators. Similarly, ACER, Taiwan's leading computer maker, produced the first desktop PC which a user can upgrade by simply replacing the existing microprocessor unit with a new more powerful one. Many Taiwanese have worked in large US firms and returned to Taiwan, 'jumping ship' to form new start-up companies. Indeed, 120 former Bell Labs. employees recently formed the Bell System Alumni Association (*Business Week*, 30 November 1992, p. 68–75).

Leading South Korean firms have also built up strong in-house capabilities in electronics, forming strategic alliances with overseas market leaders to develop new technologies. Samsung developed the first 16 megabit DRAM semiconductor ahead of the Japanese and Americans, according to *Business Week* (30 November 1992, p. 68). Goldstar and Du Pont are cooperating to develop a new type of 'mask' to increase the density of semiconductors. Anam of Korea is the world's largest chip packaging company, with annual sales of more than $1 billion. It works closely with TI, IBM and others to design innovative new packages ahead of demand.

A further difficulty with the flying geese model is the implicit assumption that the second-tier NICs and China will automatically follow on in the same path of growth as the NICs. This is not necessarily so. It will depend primarily on the building of capabilities within each country. The evidence suggests that the tigers were active exploiters of FDI and technological links with the international economy. A more passive approach may be insufficient to enable the second-tier countries to follow on in the path of the tigers. The question remains as to whether the second-tier NICs embody sufficient domestic capabilities to ensure continued dynamism. Some studies suggest that the second-tier NICs have already begun to face growth constraints.[8] Sustained economic development is not an automatic consequence of the growth of Japan and the tigers.

The above factors suggest that the flying geese model needs to be replaced with a broader model of East Asian development which accounts for US and, to a lesser extent, European involvement. Also, it will require a full understanding of the scale, depth and nature of overseas Chinese patterns of development (and South Korean). The rapid incorporation of the special economic zones of mainland China into the Hong Kong–Taiwan nexus of growth suggests that the Chinese model could rival Japan in East Asia in the future.[9] Above all, a new model should identify and account for the distinctive, indigenous factors which enabled the rapid economic and technological development of the four tigers.

Conclusion

The four tigers have contributed substantially to dynamism and growth in the Pacific Basin. From the GNP level of the poorer African economies in the early 1960s, Taiwan and South Korea have become medium-wage, full-employment economies. Singapore and Hong Kong started from higher income levels. They now match Japan in terms of GNP per capita. All four tigers have moved rapidly upwards in the GNP ranking of nations and contribute significantly to trade expansion in the region. FDI by the four tigers into Pacific Asia overtook Japan's in the late-1980s.

There is a variety of development paths among the NICs. South Korea, like Japan, has been relatively closed to foreign investment and depended on a small number of large conglomerates for much of its industrial development. By contrast, the other three tigers have developed 'overseas Chinese' models of industrialization. Singapore's development has relied heavily on direct investment by large foreign transnational firms. Taiwan has depended on locally-owned small- and medium-sized firms. Another contrast lies in development policy. South Korea, Singapore and Taiwan have relied on strong state intervention for development, whereas Hong Kong has pursued a *laissez faire* free market approach.

The four NICs also have common development features. Among these are outward-looking, export-led development strategies and policies which promoted strong competition among firms. Each of the four began with low-cost labour advantages and gradually progressed to higher value-added, high-wage activities. The tigers have all stressed the importance of education, ensuring widespread literacy and an adequate supply of technicians and engineers for industry. Access to the US market was another common factor in the development of the NICs.

The flying geese model fails to account for the indigenous efforts and the divergent strategies of the four tigers. By focusing exclusively on Japan as the lead economy, the flying geese idea ignores the contrasts between Japanese and overseas Chinese innovation systems. The overseas Chinese have historically been a distinctive and separate force for development in the region. In contrast with Japan, overseas Chinese development has been based on small- and medium-sized firms, family loyalty and personal connections. Indigenous technological learning proceeded rapidly among Taiwanese and Hong Kong firms.

Also, by focusing solely on Japan, the flying geese model understated the importance of the US (and Europe) as competing sources of foreign investment, technology and management styles. The US and recently the European economies have been more important than Japan as markets for the tigers' exports. Clearly, there is a case for a new model of Asian-Pacific development, one which accepts the importance of Japan, but also recognizes and explores the other significant factors in the region's development.

Acknowledgement

This chapter draws on STEEP Discussion Paper No. 4, by the author, entitled 'Economic Development of the Four Tigers: An Assessment of the Flying Geese Model of East Asian Progress'. Research support was provided by the UK Economic and Social Research Council (ESRC).

Notes

1. The terms Pacific Rim, Pacific Basin and Asia-Pacific are used interchangeably in this chapter.
2. Sakong (1993, p. 152) describes Kaname's product cycle version of the model, as well as the more recent work by Saburo Okita. Among the more recent studies which propose the flying geese pattern are Yamashita (1991) and Fukasaku (1991).
3. There are some notable exceptions: see for instance the collection of papers edited by Hughes (1988), especially Riedel's. For an historical interpretation see Freeman (1991). Wade (1990) deals mainly with Taiwan, Amsden (1989) with South Korea. *The Economist* (1991) and *IEEE Spectrum* (1991) provide good recent descriptive accounts of Asia-Pacific's technological development.
4. Most of the studies mentioned in note 4 provide little analysis of technological accumulation by the tigers.
5. Riedel (1988, p. 5) presents earlier historical data which show how Hong Kong and Taiwan

began to grow rapidly during the 1950s. Growth in South Korea and Singapore began accelerating in the mid-1960s.

6.   For the case of South Korea see Jun and Kim (1990). For the case of Taiwan see Chaponnière and Fouquin (1989). Also see below.
7.   See Hobday (1992) for an analysis of the technological progress of each of the four tigers in electronics.
8.   Tho and Urata (1991, p. 23) argue that it is not yet clear how much technology has actually been transferred to the second-tier NICs (or absorbed by them).
9.   Already the Southern Chinese economic zones together with Taiwan and Hong Kong represent an economic region with a population of 120 million and a combined GNP in 1991 of approximately $310 billion – equivalent to Brazil (*The Economist,* November 16 1991, p. 18).

Bibliography

Akamatsu, K. (1956) 'A Wild Geese Flying Pattern of Japanese Industrial Development: Machine and Tool Industries', *Hitotsubashi Review,* Vol. 6, No. 5 (in Japanese).

Amsden, A. (1989) *Asia's Next Giant: South Korea and Late Industrialisation,* Oxford University Press, New York.

Chaponnière, J.R. (1992) 'The Newly Industrialising Economies of Asia: International Investment and Transfer of Technology', *STI Review,* No. 9, April, OECD, Paris.

Chaponnière, J.R. and Fouquin, M. (1989) *Technological Change and the Electronics Sector – Perspectives and Policy Options for Taiwan,* Report prepared for OECD Development Centre Project, May, entitled: 'Technological Change and the Electronics Sector – Perspectives and Policy Options for Newly-Industrialising Economies (NIEs)', OECD, Paris.

The Economist, various issues.

Far Eastern Economic Review (1989) 24 August issue.

Freeman, C. (1991) *Catching up in World Growth and World Trade,* chapter for forthcoming book in honour of Alf Maizels, SPRU mimeo, University of Sussex.

Fukasaku, K. (1991) *Economic Regionalisation and Intra-Industry Trade: Pacific Asian Perspectives,* first draft, Benchmark Study, Research Programme on Globalisation and Regionalisation. OECD Development Centre, Paris.

Gee, S. (1991) *Taiwan Enterprises' Challenges and Responses Under World Economic Globalisation and Regionalisation,* Benchmark Study, Research Programme on Globalisation and Regionalisation. OECD Development Centre, Paris.

Hobday, M.G. (1992) *Foreign Investment, Exports and Technology Development in the Four Dragons,* SPRU mimeo, University of Sussex.

Hone, A. (1974) 'Multinational Corporations and Multinational Buying Groups: Their Impact on the Growth of Asia's Exports of Manufactures – Myths and Realities', *World Development,* Vol. 2, No. 2, February, pp. 145–9.

Hughes, H. (1988) *Achieving Industrialisation in East Asia,* Cambridge University Press, Cambridge.

IEEE Spectrum (1991) June, special report, 'AsiaPower'.

James, W. (1990) *Basic Directions and Areas for Cooperation: Structural Issues of the Asia–Pacific Economies,* Asia Pacific Cooperation Forum, Session 2, 21–22 June, Korea Institute for International Economic Policy, Seoul, Korea.

Jun, Y.W. and Kim, S.G. (1990) *The Korean Electronics Industry – Current Status, Perspectives and Policy Options,* report prepared for OECD Development Centre Project, May, entitled: 'Technological Change and the Electronics Sector – Perspectives and Policy Options for Newly-Industrialising Economies (NIEs)', OECD, Paris.

Mackie, J.A.C. (1992) 'Overseas Chinese Entrepreneurship', *Asian–Pacific Economic Literature*, Vol. 6, No. 1, pp. 41–64.

Redding, S.G. (1991) *The Spirit of Chinese Capitalism*, Walter de Greuter, Berlin and New York.

Riedel, J. (1988) 'Economic Development in East Asia: Doing What Comes Naturally?', H. Hughes (ed.) *Achieving Industrialisation in East Asia*, Cambridge University Press, Cambridge.

Sakong, I. (1993) *Korea in the World Economy*, Institute for International Economics, Washington DC.

Tho, T.V. and Urata, S. (1991) *Emerging Technology Transfer Patterns in the Pacific Asia*, paper presented at International Conference entitled: 'The Emerging Technological Trajectory of the Pacific Rim', held at Fletcher School of Law and Diplomacy, Tufts University, 4–6 October.

Wade, R. (1990) *Governing the Market: Economic Theory and the Role of Government in East Asian Industrialisation*, Princeton University Press, Princeton, New Jersey.

Whitley, R. (1992) *Business Systems in East Asia: Firms, Markets and Societies*, Sage, London.

Yamashita, S. (1991) 'Japan's Role as a Regional Technological Integrator in the Pacific Rim', paper presented at the conference on 'The Emerging Technological Trajectory of the Pacific Rim', Tufts University, Medford, MA., 4–6 October.

9. Diffusion of Innovation Ancient and Modern: A Review of the Main Themes

F. Lissoni and J. S. Metcalfe

Introduction

For anyone interested in the connection between technology and economic progress, the diffusion of innovation must be of central concern. Indeed, any economic study which relates economic growth and development to technological change involves implicit or explicit assumptions about the way innovations, once originated in some points of the economic system, spread over the system itself. Schumpeter (1934), for example, identified two complementary driving forces for diffusion, namely selection and imitation. The first one refers to the competition between 'innovative' and 'traditional' firms, the former having introduced the innovation, the latter being linked to old technologies and therefore subject to the progressive erosion of their market shares; in this case diffusion could be ideally measured by the relative market shares of the two kind of firms. The second force refers to the possibility of traditional firms abandoning the old technology in favour of the new one, so that diffusion is better measured by the rate at which adoption (imitation of innovative firms) occurs.

While the perception of the importance of the subject was derived from Schumpeter and other major economists, the analytical tools were borrowed to some extent from other social sciences, where the study of innovation diffusion was already established. In this regard, the economists' contribution was initially an empirical one, and; together with the new tools, a redefinition of the subject occurred which constrained the scope of the research. This was mainly directed to imitation rather than selection, and confined to the confirmation and explanation of the following empirical regularity. For some reason innovations, which are assumed to be advantageous if compared to the existing technology, are not immediately adopted by all potential users; on the contrary, there is always a lapse of time, often considerable, between when the innovation appears on the technological horizon and when it is adopted by the first consistent group of users. Another relatively long period of time follows in which the innovation is gradually adopted by all the relevant agents. From this an S-shaped (sigmoid) 'diffusion path' results.

At the end of the seventies economists had cumulated substantial empirical evidence about the sigmoid shape of diffusion paths,[1] and a related 'stylized fact', namely that diffusion speed differs widely across innovations, industries, and countries or regions. A few key variables had been found to be significant in explaining differences in diffusion speed, chiefly the 'adoption profitability'[2] and the average firm size.

Despite these successes, two main problems emerged. First, the economic meaning of many explanatory variables was unclear. Second, no investigation had really been made on the effects of diffusion, either on market structure or macroeconomic trends. Both the problems called for an unprecedented theoretical research effort, whose ultimate result has been to provide economics with its own set of diffusion theories. The latter have eventually influenced other disciplines, such as geography, which originally were more advanced in this field.

Within modern approaches, scholars are less concerned with the shape of diffusion curves and more concerned with articulating the underlying dynamic mechanisms. Many of the forces which shape the development of a technology depend upon incentives and focusing devices which are contingent on the pattern of diffusion, so that technologies co-evolve with the pattern of economic and social application. Moreover the environment into which any technology is diffused consists of many other technologies which are themselves part of a wider diffusion process. Compatibility, inter-relatedness and co-development are emerging as important themes in modern diffusion research. Furthermore the single innovation is no more seen as the most appropriate unit for diffusion analysis. Rather what is being diffused is often a sequence of innovations within an evolving design configuration which itself develops in response to competing and complementary configurations. A multi-technology approach is therefore called for.

Preliminary Definitions

As in many other research fields, a jargon emerged from the diffusion studies tradition, which is now well established. This section reviews those elements of it which will be used extensively in the remainder of the chapter.

Units of analysis: innovations and technologies
A distinction is usually drawn between product and process innovations.

With respect to new process technologies we think of one industry supplying new technology embodied in a specific capital good and firms in another industry or industries making decisions to whether to install that technology. With respect to new product technologies, we have a similar conception except that the potential buyers are households (Stoneman and Karshenas, 1991).

Such a sharp distinction is useful from the theoretical point of view, in so far as we consider innovations which are precisely defined as new capital goods, new materials or new consumer durables. Problems arise when such definitions are not appropriate. In particular, not every research project dealing with adoption choices can define 'a specific capital good' or 'a new material' as the proper object of study. Wider definitions, related to systems of different machines, inputs and organizational procedures, are often a more relevant empirical issue. Also, joint innovations in production design and manufacturing techniques often occur, especially when radically new technologies are introduced. Finally, more broadly defined innovations, such as 'steam power', 'electricity' and 'microelectronics', imply the contemporaneous diffusion of products, processes, infrastructures and manpower education.

Measurement problems

In standard microeconomic textbooks firms are supposed to adopt a new technology more or less instantaneously, not only in the sense that no diffusion lags exist, but also in the sense that adoption is a one-off decision: firms convert their whole body of hardware and organization in a negligible lapse of time. Intra-firm studies reverse this common theoretical device, by stressing the gradualism which is typical of the adoption process; they measure the speed at which one innovation reaches given diffusion levels within single firms.

At the inter-firm level, the gradualism of internal adoption is often ignored. What is left to be explained is simply why some firms adopt earlier than others, that is why firms do not all adopt at the same date. A useful measure of diffusion turns out to be the number of adopters divided by the number of total 'potential adopters' at a given time, which has been sometimes labelled 'rate of imitation' (Mansfield, 1961; Romeo, 1975). The obvious drawback of this measure is that firms which we call 'adopters' at a given time actually differ in the extent of their commitment to the new technology. Moreover, some of them may subsequently reverse their adoption decision.

Alternative measures rely on the percentage of output attributable to the new technology or on the stock of new capital goods within the observed industry or geographical area. This is labelled by Davies (1979) the '(overall) rate of diffusion': it cancels out information about single firms' adoption speed, but it is more accurate in measuring the diffusion level within an industry or country, since it accounts for either the intra-firm diffusion, the inter-firm imitation, and the selection effects.

Inter-firm studies are the most common, both at the empirical and the theoretical level. Indeed this survey deals only with them.

Adoption and diffusion

Up to now we have referred to terms such as 'diffusion' and 'adoption' without drawing any distinction between them, but in inter-firm studies a distinction must be made. Diffusion studies refer to the aggregate behaviour of the sample of firms, without necessarily relying on an explicit microeconomic modelling of single firms' decision processes. On the contrary, adoption studies focus on the single firm 'adoption lag' with respect to the first adoption in the sample, that is they explain why the single firm decided to adopt at the observed date and not earlier or later.

This distinction hides quite an important methodological issue: is micro-economic (adoption) modelling necessary to understand the macro-phenomenon of diffusion? We will see that neoclassical (equilibrium) economics has answered positively, while evolutionary (disequilibrium) theories have stressed how ordered patterns of diffusion may emerge from apparently irrational individual behaviours.

Early Studies: The Logistic Curve and the Information-Based Explanations of Diffusion

The first studies of innovation diffusion can be attributed to sociologists, geographers, anthropologists and psychologists.[3] Innovations studied in these fields are mainly agricultural and medical, together with advances in education.

Within this framework, it is natural to assume innovations to be clearly superior to current alternatives, that is, it is natural to assume that late adopters would have been better off by adopting earlier: the diffusion study is asked to explain why this did not happen. The basic answer is that those who delay adoption choose to do so because they do not have enough information about the advantages of the new technology.

> In the case of diffusion of technological innovation *what diffuses is information about the innovation itself.* Firms will have very little information, if any at all, about an innovation that has not been widely adopted and will, therefore, associate it with an high degree of risk. As more firms adopt the innovation the information base available to potential adopters increases and the risk associated with the innovation decreases accordingly (Coombs, Saviotti and Walsh, 1987).

Diffusion is seen as a process of imitation, and the explanation of its length is given in terms of communication problems.

The information-innovation is transmitted by personal contact (word-of-mouth), by analogy with the spread of infectious diseases: early models are therefore referred to as 'epidemic' in nature. Diffusion takes place within a given population of N^* potential adopters (defined as a 'saturation level'). The probability of an agent to contract the illness (i.e. the probability to adopt), rises as the number N_t of other 'ill' firms (i.e. adopters) raises. As the number of adopters increases, the number of agents which still have not adopted decreases. It follows that as time passes, two counteracting forces exist: the first one is favourable to diffusion (increase in the number of 'infected' agents, i.e. adopters), while the other is adverse (decrease in the number of agents still not 'ill', i.e. available for adopting). (See Figure 9.1.)

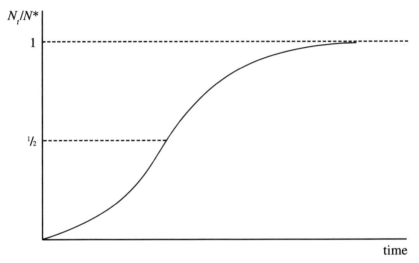

Figure 9.1 The logistic curve as the epidemic diffusion path

The absence of economists from the research field of innovation diffusion until the sixties could be interpreted as a tacit acceptance of the agenda of other disciplines. In particular the latter emphasized the role of psychological or sociological factors in influencing the probability of adoption, and focused on the efficiency of communication networks rather than on the attractiveness of the innovation in explaining diffusion speed.[4] Griliches' (1957) study on the diffusion of hybrid corn in different states of the US and Mansfield's (1961) research on the diffusion of twelve innovations in the US manufacturing industry mark the entry of economists in the research field. Since that beginning, a strong bias has been established towards the study of process innovations, where sociological explanations were perceived as less persuading and the role of the innovation attractiveness (better redefined as 'adoption profitability') more likely to be a key determinant. To demonstrate the role of adoption profitability, both these authors pioneered a two-step econometric procedure which has since dominated the empirical study of diffusion.

The first step consists in collecting and processing data on more than one diffusion path (say *m*): those paths can refer to the same innovation diffused in different markets or industries or different innovations diffused in the same industry. Estimates of β are derived from all the *m* diffusion paths, so that a set of *m* 'diffusion speeds' becomes available for the second step. In the second step, data referring either to each market or industry where the same innovation has been diffused or to each innovation are used as independent variables which explain the diffusion speed.

Both Griliches and Mansfield used the logistic function to fit data in the first step. In the second step, Griliches explained diffusion speed with a linear regression over two variables: the increase in yield per acre allowed by hybrid corn when substituted to traditional seeds, and the average size (field extension) of farm. Both the variables differ from state to state, the first because of the quality of soil, the second for historical–institutional reasons; both can be regarded as a measure of adoption profitability. Mansfield's second step is based on a linear regression as well, where the most significant independent variables are found to be the profitability of installing the new technology (measured with the help of interviews to firms and technical journals) and the required average expenditure, as a percentage of average total assets in the industry.

The debate on this approach followed four main directions, the last two being the main concern of this survey.

Earlier developments were mainly concerned with the second step of the model. Good examples are provided by Mansfield (1968), Swan (1973), Globerman (1975), Romeo (1975, 1977) and, more recently, Norotte and Bensaid (1987): Mansfield's logistic curve is used in the first step, while the second step is enriched with additional independent variables. In particular, attempts to fit 'industry structure' variables were popular, and employed proxies such as the number of firms or the variance of firm size in the industry; the more competitive the industry, the quicker diffusion was expected to be. Results were mixed and, as Romeo (1977) points out, proved not to be very sensitive to the choice of different measures of diffusion. A fertile field of application was that of interregional and international comparisons (Nabseth and Ray, 1974; Ray, 1984; see also the later section on the analysis of diffusion).[5]

A second line of research was originally developed as an empirical one, relating to the choice of better functions than the logistic for the curve-fitting of diffusion paths – although this subsequently revealed much deeper theoretical issues strictly related to the concept of information dissemination. The basic observation is that sigmoid curves can be obtained by a variety of equations, some of them leading to positively skewed diffusion curves which fit data better than the logistic. Most commonly advocated asymmetric curves are the Gompertz (Dixon, 1980; Dinar and

Marom, 1991), the modified exponential (Lekvall and Wahlbin, 1972) and the cumulative Lognormal (Davies, 1979).[6] Lekvall and Wahlbin connect this issue to the description of the information dissemination process. In the epidemic model, information dissemination relies exclusively on an internal information source: agents receive word-of-mouth information from within the population (earlier adopters) and nowhere else. This is indeed a strong assumption, since the innovation producers are very likely to actively promote their products by means of a variety of media which can be consequently regarded as an external source of information. Lekvall and Wahlbin prove that whenever an external information source is present, the diffusion path will be positively skewed.[7] Marketing research has developed this approach much further than economics (Mahajan and Wind, 1986; Mahajan, Muller and Bass, 1990). The distinction between internal and external sources of information will be addressed in the section on the equilibrium approach, in order to criticize the treatment of the information issue implicit in Bayesian learning models.

A third line of research questions the entire two-step procedure, on the ground that the role of adoption profitability is misrepresented. In particular it points out that adoption profitability should be assessed at a microeconomic level, since it is likely to differ from firm to firm according to their individual characteristics. On the contrary, the two-step classical procedure makes use of average measures. Besides, profitability is likely to change in time with the effects of learning processes, appearance of incremental innovations and feedback of diffusion on relative prices.[8] Therefore, the two-step procedure should be regarded as a summary device employed under the constraint of a lack of data.

This position is well expressed by Griliches himself:

> Diffusion research emphasizes the role of time in the transition from one technology of production or consumption to another. If all variables describing individuals ... were observable, one might do without the notion of diffusion and discuss everything within an equilibrium framework. Since much of the interesting data are unobservable, time is brought in to explain at least three distinct sets of forces: 1) the decline over time in the real cost of the technology as the result of learning by doing ... 2) the dying-off of old durable equipment, making room slowly for the new, 3) the spread of information (Griliches, 1980).

By 'equilibrium framework' and 'to do without the notion of diffusion', is meant the possibility of studying the diffusion speed as the aggregation of individual adoption dates, each of them obtained by applying the standard microeconomics of the firm.[9] The past fifteen years have actually seen a great theoretical effort in this direction, which we label as 'the equilibrium approach' and review later.

A fourth class of response relates to the narrowness of Griliches' and Mansfield's research scope. In particular, it is pointed out that the classical approach investigates neither the role of selection nor the effects of innovation diffusion on market structure, firms' relative competitiveness and economic growth. Such a problem becomes clearer as students move from narrowly to broadly defined innovations (see the earlier section on measurement problems). This line of enquiry, which we label as the 'disequilibrium' or 'evolutionary' approach, will be discussed later.

The final section reviews a specific application field, diffusion in space, where economists' contributions have always been relevant, and has recently given some interesting results.

The Equilibrium Approach

Two basic elements characterize the so-called equilibrium approach to diffusion theory.

The first one is the dismissal of information dissemination as the key explanatory variable of innovation diffusion. In the most radical formulations of this approach diffusion takes time not because information is imperfect, but because at its first appearance the innovation itself is not necessarily superior to the existing technology for at least some potential adopters (Probit and game theoretic models). Less radical departure from information-based explanations of diffusion maintain the latter at the centre of the process, but exclude any direct word-of-mouth communication between adopters (Bayesian learning models).

The second basic element is that firms are assumed to behave optimally. Therefore a self-imposed methodological constraint for authors of equilibrium models of diffusion consists in ensuring that at any time all firms for which adoption is profitable have actually adopted. This means that firms which have not done it yet are not 'ill-informed', but are simply waiting for the optimal adoption date to arise.

Probit (threshold) models

The origin of the label 'Probit' can be traced back to Davies (1979), who stressed the logical similarity between consumers' behaviour in front of new durable goods, usually studied with the help of the so-called Probit econometric technique,[10] and firms' adoption decision concerning capital-embodied innovations.

The Probit technique assumes that agents base their consumption decision on the relationship between their own income and a 'critical income': agents buy the good if and only if their income is superior to a certain threshold ('critical income'), which depends either on the price of the good and on agents' own tastes.[11]

Therefore at any time all consumers whose income is greater than the critical income are observed to own the durable. As time passes, consumers who still have not bought it may reverse their decisions either because their

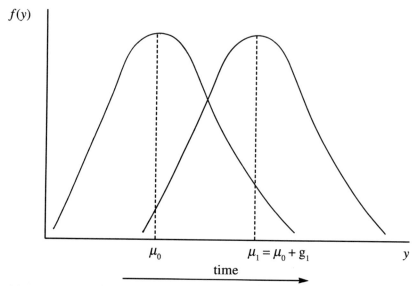

(a)   Income distribution at time $t = 0$ and $t = 1$; constancy of income
variance δ and constant growth of average income μ

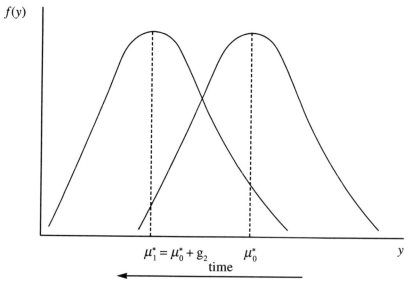

(b)   Critical income distribution at time $t = 0$ and $t = 1$; constancy of
critical income variance δ and constant decline of average critical
income μ^*

Figure 9.2 Probit model mechanism of diffusion (Davies (1979))

income increases or their critical income decreases.

Consequently, a symmetric sigmoid (cumulative normal or lognormal) diffusion path can be obtained by assuming income and critical income are lognormally distributed over the population, and the means of the two distributions respectively grow and decline at a constant rate, with unchanged variances (see Figure 9.2).[12] A simpler way of deriving a sigmoid diffusion path consists in holding income distribution as fixed over time, while reducing the critical threshold to a unique value, which declines at a constant rate (Figure 9.3).[13]

By changing 'consumers' into 'firms', 'income' into 'size', and 'consumer durable' into 'new capital good' the model can be adapted to process innovations. It turns out that bigger firms are the first to adopt, while only a reduction of critical size or a generalized size increase allow smaller firms to reach the adoption conditions. Indeed many empirical studies ensure firm size distribution to be a bell-shaped one, and quite well represented by a lognormal curve.

It should be noted that firm heterogeneity is the only force behind diffusion: the latter is not instantaneous simply because firms are not identical, differing either in size or critical size. The more similar the firms, the faster the diffusion.

Davies' adoption theory was a behaviouralist one, but its Probit approach has been popularized through a neoclassical reformulation, whose roots can be found in David's (1966, 1969) study on the diffusion of mechanical reapers in the US in the last century, to which Davies (1979) himself partially refers.[14] This classic study established the foundations of the equilibrium approach.

The advantage of mechanical reapers over hand techniques consisted mainly in labour savings. We can label the labour requirement per unit of land with a_0 for non-mechanic techniques and a_1 for the mechanical reaper, where $a_0 - a_1 > 0$. Given a general level of wages w, the adoption benefits per unit of land turn out to be equal to $w(a_0-a_1)$: a farm i, whose size (land extension) is S_i, will therefore reap adoption benefits per year which are proportional to its size, that is $S_i w(a_0-a_1)$. Adoption costs are reduced to the price of the innovation, p; given a prevailing interest rate r, it follows that adoption costs per year are given by rp. A key assumption is that the output price is given, which in this case is reasonable since the reaper does not increase the yield, which is constrained by the amount of available land.

These preliminary arguments can be easily assembled to state that the firm will adopt as soon as the adoption benefits compensate adoption costs, that is as soon as the net benefits become positive:

$$S_i w(a_0-a_1) \geq rp$$

from which the critical size S_c can be derived as

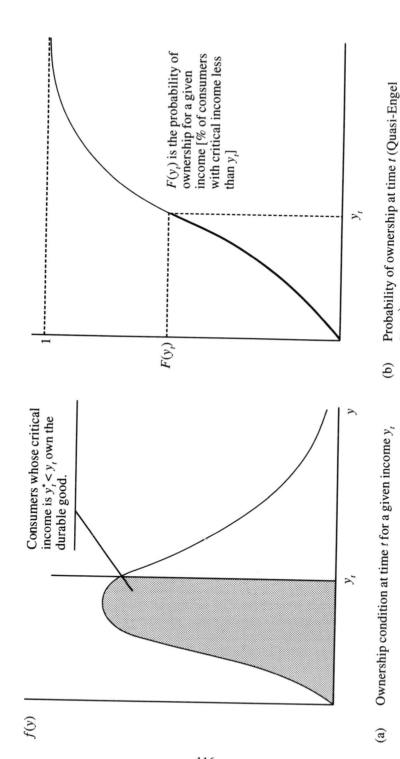

f(y)

Consumers whose critical income is $y_t^* < y_t$ own the durable good.

y_t

y

(a) Ownership condition at time t for a given income y_t

1

$F(y_t)$ is the probability of ownership for a given income [% of consumers with critical income less than y_t]

$F(y_t)$

y_t

(b) Probability of ownership at time t (Quasi-Engel curve)

Figure 9.3 Probit model with fixed critical income (critical size)

$$S_i > \frac{rp}{w\,(a_0 - a_1)} \equiv S_c$$

Notice that in this model uncertainty is absent: firms know the value of the adoption benefits but nevertheless wait before adopting for the simple reason that for many firms such benefits are insufficient. The latter may increase, and the innovation conquer new adopters, only if input prices (w) increase, or the innovation price (p) or the rate of interest (r) decline. Diffusion may also be driven by incremental innovations which improve the performance of the new technology (reduce a_1), although this is not considered by David.

Starting with Stoneman and Ireland (1983), most of the generalizations have focused on the impact of price decline, thus highlighting the role played by the innovation suppliers. Arrow-type learning by doing is assumed to take place on the supply side: as diffusion continues, more pieces of innovation are produced, so that the marginal cost of production declines.[15] When the cost decline is transferred into prices, the latter decline as well, pushing diffusion further. The extent and the speed of diffusion depend on the extent and the speed at which this transfer occurs. Stoneman and Ireland reduce the diffusion problem to an intertemporal price discrimination problem, which suppliers solve by deriving from the equation the demand function for the innovation and by incorporating it in their profit function. Diffusion is shown to be faster the more competitive the supply side.

The equation implies that adopters behave myopically: they do not forecast the innovation price decline and adopt as soon as their reservation price is reached. Ireland and Stoneman (1985, 1986) compare the diffusion paths obtainable under the assumption of adopters' myopia with those derived by assuming perfect foresight.[16] Within this framework, they measure the speed and the welfare effects of different expectation regimes, combined with different supply market structures. Their findings reverse the assumption that a fast diffusion is anyway desirable, which was implicit in epidemic models. Stoneman and David (1986) discuss the implication of these findings for technology policy.

Bayesian learning models

A particular class of models reintroduces lack of information as the main reason for adoption delays while retaining all the features of Probit models, the only difference being that the heterogeneity source is no longer the size, but the attitude of the firm's management toward the innovation.[17] These contributions are usually gathered under the label 'Bayesian learning approach'.

As in the information-based models, the innovation is assumed to be of uncertain value: two possible states for the innovation are assumed, 'good' (adoption would be profitable) or 'bad' (adoption would generate a loss). Firms' managers hold different beliefs, which are reflected in different subjective probability distributions over the two possible states.

At any time t, the managers revise their initial belief, according to the results of experiments which are performed at any time in order to test the innovation.[18] This treatment of information has no relationship to epidemic models: tests are either performed by each firm and kept secret, or carried out and made known by suppliers or independent bodies so that they represent an external source of information. No internal sources are admitted.

On the whole, results from this approach have been quite discouraging: unless tests are public and costless (Jensen, 1979, 1982) nothing guarantees that more optimistic or better informed firms will adopt earlier, i.e. that ordered patterns of diffusion may come out from rational individual choices (McCardle, 1985; Jensen, 1988a,b). These results contrast with those of evolutionary models (see the earlier section on diffusion as a selection process), which on the contrary show that ordered diffusion patterns do not require firms to behave rationally.

The main limitation of the Probit and Bayesian learning can be identified in the narrowness of their definition of 'innovation'. The latter is a single piece of machinery, and its impact on firms' production costs and capacity must be a minor one: in fact, adopters are supposed not to increase their output (capacity constraint) nor to be able to relieve such constraint in the near future (which must mean that the extra profits derived from adoption are insufficient for the purpose).[19]

David and Olsen (1984) and Ireland and Stoneman (1986) show that as soon as the assumption of a given output price is relaxed, firms' strategic behaviour needs to be arbitrarily ruled out by an *ad hoc* hypothesis, otherwise firms which are ranked at the low levels of the critical variables (small firms, 'pessimistic' firms), could be induced to anticipate their adoption dates. Adoption benefits are in fact decreasing: earlier adopters produce some negative externalities, which consist in cutting the output price, so that is anyway better to adopt first.

Game theoretic models: decreasing and increasing returns to adoption

Indeed, the study of the relationship between diffusion and strategic behaviour has been developed as a separate field, whose origins date back to Reinganum's (1981a,b) seminal applications of game theory.[20] A striking characteristic of game theoretic models of adoption is that the existence of strategic behaviour appears to make firm heterogeneity unnecessary for the existence of diffusion paths: under some conditions, identical firms may turn out to adopt at different dates.

Despite some students' claims, it must be stressed that this amounts only to the statement that adoption is sequential: no game theoretic model has really attempted to reconstruct macro-patterns of diffusion, such as those represented by sigmoid curves. Sequential adoption is a precondition for diffusion to exist, but does not tell the whole story.

A key development of game theoretic models consisted in substituting the traditional decreasing returns to adoption with increasing returns. This coincides with substituting the narrow definition of innovation as a single piece of machinery, with the broader description of a new technology as a set of interrelated hardware pieces, software packages and human skills. Problems of compatibility and standardization emerge; the greater the adoption of a new technology, the greater the expected adoption benefits, since the risk of having adopted a non-compatible technology diminishes. Adoption externalities turn out to be positive, and are usually labelled as network externalities. Farrell and Saloner (1986) describe the traditional case of a new technology which displaces an old one, but it is clear that this framework of analysis better applies to the case of two or more new competing technologies. In the first stages of a new technology diffusion, many competing designs and conceptions exist, out of which a dominant one emerges, which replaces the old technology and displaces its contemporary alternatives. Models in this vein are Dybvig and Spatt (1983), Farrell and Saloner (1985, 1988, 1992), Katz and Shapiro (1985, 1986), while a detailed case study is offered by Postrel (1990). This stream of literature addresses the same issues and reaches the same conclusions of the so-called path-dependency models of diffusion (see the later discussion on diffusion as a path-dependent process).

Empirical analysis
Equilibrium models investigate adoption, and derive diffusion from individual adoption dates. Therefore a proper test for their proposition should be carried on by examining individual firms' decisions, rather than aggregate diffusion curves.[21] A very naive way to do so is performing a Probit or Logit analysis, which refers to a given point in time and simply examines which firms in a sample have adopted and which have not. Many studies have employed this technique, a few significant examples being provided by Oster (1982), Gibbs and Edwards (1985), Kelley and Brooks (1991), Dinar and Marom (1991), Franck and Gaussens (1992) and O'Farrell and Oakey (1992).[22] Firm size has been confirmed as a key determinant of adoption, along with firm corporate status and local market conditions (see the later discussion on international and inter-regional comparisons).

A major drawback of Probit and Logit techniques is that they treat adoption as completely detached from diffusion, since neither time nor time-varying variables enters the analysis.

Quite recently a few contributions have appeared (Hannan and McDowell, 1984a, 1987; Waldman, 1985; Levin et al., 1987; Rose and

Joskow, 1990; Stoneman and Karshenas, 1990, 1991), which make use of a more appropriate technique, the so-called 'duration analysis'.[23]

This technique originated in studies of unemployment duration, and the available results for adoption studies are still to be considered very provisional. Roughly speaking, observations refer to individual firms in time (panel data), and the dependent variable is given by the time which the firm has spent waiting before adopting. Therefore it is possible to consider the firm characteristics as changing in time, along with the price of the final output, the price of the innovation and those environmental characteristics which may differ from firm to firm and be time dependent. The diffusion level at each point in time and time itself enter the regression but no agreement exists about the exact relationship between them. Indeed, according to the equilibrium models we have reviewed, diffusion levels determine the price of the innovation and of the final output, so that they may represent either the existence of supply side learning by doing or the influence of strategic behaviour. As for time, Lancaster (1979) has shown that it represents 'unobserved heterogeneity' (related to, for example managerial 'attitude'), while Stoneman and Karshenas try to demonstrate that it also represents the diffusion of information from internal (epidemic) and external sources.

Nevertheless, all these studies confirm heterogeneity as a major explanation of differences in adoption dates. Levin et al. (1987) add the interesting observation that firm heterogeneity seems to be more relevant in the early stages of diffusion, while in the later ones the diffusion level, whatever it means, becomes the major determinant of adoption delays – that is, they show adoption determinants to change over time. This appears to be in line with suggestions coming from the path-dependency theory (see the next section on disequilibrium and evolutionary approaches).

Disequilibrium and Evolutionary Approaches

In this section the theoretical contributions are organized in three groups. The first one is concerned with diffusion as stated in the traditional terms, but under a disequilibrium point of view. The second group stresses the role played by innovation diffusion in shaping the competition between firms and accommodates a multi-technology perspective. The third approach deals with the issues of standardization, technical-interrelatedness and path-dependency.

Diffusion as a disequilibrium process

Metcalfe's (1981), and Cameron and Metcalfe's (1987) models can be usefully portrayed as intermediate ones between the classical model and the disequilibrium view. The innovation is still seen as embodied in a capital good or a new material, and the sigmoid curve is still a key element of analysis; as in many Probit models, the emphasis is upon the simultaneous interaction of demand side and supply side forces in the diffusion process. Nevertheless, elements of disequilibrium are emphasized.

Disequilibrium arises from the assumption of a Schumpeterian dynamic process in which the innovation suppliers earn extra profits by offering a better product than their rivals. Such profits are reinvested in capacity additions, which results in the innovation being supplied in ever-increasing quantities, and at a declining price. Along with this trend another one takes place, which causes the suppliers' production costs to increase over time because of the increasing competition for the necessary inputs. Suppliers' profits are therefore squeezed on the input and the output sides, and ultimately are driven to zero. The diffusion process can therefore be described as the process of gradual erosion of the suppliers' temporary, Schumpeterian profits, that is, as a process which takes place out of equilibrium, and indeed brings the system back to a new equilibrium position.

Diffusion as a selection process
This is the research field which can most rightly be called evolutionary. Its roots can be traced back to Nelson (1968), later developed in Nelson and Winter (1982).

The basic observation is that in equilibrium models, late adopters apparently resist the competition of the early adopters: despite the fact that they rely for a while on an inferior technology they do not go into bankruptcy and have time, sooner or later, to adopt the innovation. This is because the price of their output is not affected by the innovation's diffusion, or, telling the same story in another way, because early adopters are relatively slow in transforming their extra profits into additional capacity, so that imitation has time to take place. That is, selection is too slow to prevent imitation.

In evolutionary models this is not the case. Again this follows from a different definition of technology, which is not just restricted to human artifacts (machinery, materials), but encompasses organizational and cultural elements. The adoption itself of 'simple' innovations (single pieces of machinery, new materials) is not an isolated act, but part of a greater process of change. Indeed, technology adoption cannot be seen as a discrete event fully resumed by the purchase of a single item, but must be portrayed as a wider process during which the firm changes its organization and culture (see Henderson, 1993).

It can almost be said that every firm represents a different technology; at least, different groups of firms share different conceptions of the same technology, and stick to them for a certain period.

Many models (e.g. Nelson and Winter, 1982; Gibbons and Metcalfe, 1986; Metcalfe, 1989) simplify the analysis by assuming that no imitation takes place, so that diffusion is driven exclusively by selection. Firms with the better technologies reinvest their extra profits and increase their market shares; firms with inferior technologies realize losses and either contract (by disinvestment) or exit. A technology diffuses along with the increase of its adopters' market share.

These models can reproduce the observed diffusion patterns, and explain the underlying dynamic changes in the market structure of industries.[24] In particular, they imply that a tendency exists for the relative use of technologies to grow more and more concentrated. Indeed, only the continuous flow of innovations which we observe to take place in industrialized countries is able to restore the necessary technological variety[25] that is to allow new entrants to appear, or incumbents to revive their declining fortunes by adding a new technology to the existing ones.

Similar results are obtained by models which combine selection and (slow) imitation, as in Gibbons and Metcalfe (1986) and Soete and Turner (1984). In these models technologies can be continuously improved by their users. So long as these improvements take place at different rates, the existing advantages of one technology over the others are continuously threatened. Indeed, technologies should be ranked according to their development potentials as well as to their static advantages. Besides, firms may differ in their imitative or innovative capacities, which further complicates the model.

Modelling situations where technological variety co-exists with different imitative/innovative capabilities and different propensities, to invest is clearly difficult. As Nelson and Winter (1982) and Silverberg (1988) point out, it is often impossible to find analytical solutions, and therefore computer simulations remain the only way of portraying diffusion processes. The first simulation models were built by Nelson and Winter (1982) themselves, and still are among the most complex. Others are quoted in Silverberg (1988) and Silverberg (1991). In Silverberg, Dosi and Orsenigo (1988) a set of firms is supposed to exist at the beginning of the process, each firm being characterized by different imitation/innovation capabilities. The innovation being diffused generates public spillovers (productivity gains for adopters and non-adopters) and private productivity gains for adopters; the private and public productivity gains change over time, and the innovation price declines. By changing the parameters of the model, different results can be achieved, but in any case sigmoid diffusion and imitation paths are achieved, while first adopters are shown to be not always better off than 'fast second' imitators. The latter may enjoy a better combination of price decline and productivity gains.

Diffusion as a path-dependent process

So-called models of path dependency deal with multi-technology competition and share some of the conclusions of game theoretic models of network externalities as discussed earlier, in that they assume adoption sequentiality rather than explaining it, and explore its consequences.

Most models are based on sophisticated applications of probability theory, the most popular one being Arthur, Ermoliev and Kaniovski's (1987) Generalized Polya Urn Scheme (see Arthur, 1989a).[26] Polya Urn schemes apply to infinite populations, a feature which makes them suitable for the study of very broadly defined technologies (Cowan, 1987, 1990, 1991, on nuclear reactors;[27] David and Bunn, 1987, on electricity supply systems) or competing standards relative to very widely used technologies (David, 1985, on typewriter keyboards; Puffert, 1988, on railway gauges; Blankart and Knieps, 1991, on telecommunications).

Increasing returns are often seen to emerge over an extended period and to derive not only from short-term network externalities, but also from extensive phenomena of cumulative and localized technical progress, as described in Atkinson and Stiglitz (1969), Stiglitz (1987) and David (1975a).

Heterogeneous agents derive from the adoption of a specific technology 'unconditional' and 'conditional' benefits, the first being irrespective of the number of other adopters, the second being an increasing function of it. Uncertainty derives from the assumption of adoption sequentiality. At every instant *t* only one agent is assumed to adopt, as if agents were randomly extracted from an urn. Uncertainty regards the kind of agents which are going to be extracted: provided that technologies A, B, C, ... compete, the repeated extraction of A-oriented agents at the beginning of the process cause the conditional benefits of adopting A to rise, so that more and more later adopters will choose A, no matter what their unconditional benefits are. Indeed, only one technology will sooner or later end up to dominate the market (technological lock-in). Which one depends on the preferences of the first agents, that is upon the random history of adoption decisions.[28]

Such preferences can therefore represent minor historical accidents which would not be able to exert any influence on the direction of technical process if they occurred today or tomorrow, but are very relevant in the early stages of the diffusion process (path-dependency). Nothing ensures that the best technologies (those with the greatest long-term development potentialities) will diffuse: short-term preferences of influential agents (early adopters) for inferior technologies may cause better alternatives to be prematurely abandoned.

The main task of technology policy turns out to be preventing inferior technologies from becoming dominant (David, 1987). Room for policy exists only at the very beginning of the diffusion process, when government actions (imposition of standards, massive purchases of technology, regulation) can still influence agents' conditional preferences. However, no one can ensure government experts know more about new technologies than private business colleagues. Therefore a trade-off occurs between the need to wait before intervening (in order to gather information) and the need to act before the system locks in. A useful policy could simply consist of supporting some alternatives for a while in order to allow anything which could be possibly 'superior' to fully reveal its long term potentialities.

Empirical evidence on the slowness of imitation

It is clear that a central issue of the selection approach is the relative speed of imitation and selection, together with evidence on the persistence of firm-specific cultural and organizational 'routines'. With this respect Cainarca, Colombo and Mariotti (1989) offer a very valuable piece of evidence, witnessing the pervasiveness of the 'retro-fitting' phenomenon in the diffusion of automation. Retrofitting is defined as the development and integration of stand-alone machines (installed previously or purchased *ex novo*) in new architectures. Its relevance demonstrates that firms are committed to the hardware and knowledge they have cumulated and cannot jump in a short time to new manufacturing practices. On the product innovation side, a similar perspective is developed by Henderson and Clark (1991) and Henderson (1993) by means of the concept of architectural innovations, which refer to product improvements that firms may achieve by redefining the systemic links between established components of their products. In some sense, these findings had been anticipated by Mansfield's (1968) and Romeo's (1977) seminal studies on intra-firm diffusion, which showed the latter to be slow and to follow a sigmoid curve similar to the inter-firm one. Amendola (1990) shows that intra-firm diffusion of new materials in the car industry requires a time-consuming inventive effort by the adopters, since the process of material substitution is made possible only by new product designs.[29]

At a more general level, technology can be seen to differ not only from firm to firm, but from one aggregate of firms to another. Literature on firm cooperation and agreements becomes relevant, as well as all the theoretical and empirical contributions which identify the existence of national systems of innovations or similar geographical entities[30], and spot some regularities in the patterns of diffusion within the latter. Of course one has to ensure that geographical or inter-network differences depend on the organization and culture of the aggregates, rather than on exogenous conditions. The empirical studies which are relevant to these issues are: Lynn (1981), who compares the diffusion of basic oxygen furnaces in Japan and the USA; Arcangeli, Dosi and Moggi (1991), who compare the diffusion of electronic technologies in the US, Japan and Europe (and, within Europe, Italy); Ishitani and Kaya (1989), Mansfield (1989), Tani (1989) and Torii (1989), whose studies mainly relate to automation in Japan and the US. All these authors show that the international differences in the diffusion levels and paths are better explained by the biases in the cumulative experience of each country, rather than by differences in factor endowments; in particular, the cross-industry distribution of new technologies differs widely from one country to another, so that the development of the hardware and the relative culture are channelled through rather firm-specific trajectories. Rosegger (1991) shows that inter-firm agreements have played a remarkable role in the transfer of technical knowhow and organizational procedure from the Japanese car manufacturers to the US ones.

Empirical evidence and reinterpretations of the epidemic approach

Antonelli (1989) suggests that once technology has been redefined as in the evolutionary models, a reconceptualization and a rehabilitation of the epidemic model are due. The word-of-mouth communication process between agents has to be replaced by a wider class of interaction processes, such as vertical and horizontal subcontracting relationships, cooperation, exchange or movement of skilled workers. These processes do not merely support the information dissemination, but create problems of technical and organizational complementarity and standards: the adoption profitability grows together with the number of adopters who can exchange compatible intermediate products, parts and human skills. This argument reinforces the vision of diffusion in geographical units as a process in which the latter can be usefully considered as units of observation, rather than accidental clusters of firm. Antonelli (1989), along with Foray and Grübler (1990), Cainarca, Colombo, Mariotti (1989) and David (1987), supports this view by quoting the recent literature on path-dependency and standardization (see previous sections on game theoretic models and diffusion as a path-dependent process).

This interpretation of diffusion is tailored for broadly defined innovations, like new energy power sources and transport systems. In this respect some compelling evidence has been put forward by students at the International Institute of Applied Systems Analysis (IIASA), which have applied Marchetti and Nakicenovic's (1979) technique for fitting logistic diffusion curves to an impressive number of case studies. Astakhov et al. (1990), Grübler (1991) and Nakicenovic (1991) stress that diffusion has to be seen as either a multivariate and a multiattribute process, which is better understood when more than one innovation is considered (together with the links between innovations) and more than one diffusion measure is used.[31]

Grübler (1991) supports this view by showing how the diffusion paths of many different technologies are related to each other. Two general cases are shown. In the first case, more than two technologies are considered, that is diffusion is not seen as the mere replacement of an old technology by a new one, but as the competition of many technologies, whose dates of appearance do not necessarily differ: diffusion is better seen as linked to the product life cycle theory, each technology knowing a period of incubation, a period of diffusion and a period of displacement, the last corresponding to the take-up of some rival.

In the second case, the technologies which are examined are not competing, but complementary. While in the first case technology means very broad concepts (cars vs. horses and trains, electricity vs. steam power), here more narrowly defined innovations are also considered. For example, the diffusion of cars (measured by the number of cars in circulation) is matched to the diffusion of all those innovations which have contributed to the evolution and success of the car itself, from the different types of engines, to tyres, brakes, body-making techniques and materials or electronic apparatus. These related innovations are not introduced at the same date, so the environment which absorbs each of them differs. In particular, the first innovations to be introduced face a major problem in the relative backwardness of the related technologies or production techniques, so that a major cause of diffusion delay is the need to overcome bottlenecks. Such a problem does not exist for the latest innovations, which are smoothly superimposed onto the well-established new technological regime.[32] The diffusion paths of innovations which are related to major technologies all show a very similar pattern: dates of introduction may differ, but dates of saturation do not, so that all paths converge to saturation level more or less at the same time, the diffusion speed of single innovations being higher the more recent the innovations. An implication is that the most important innovations (i.e. those which originate a cluster of related technologies and further incremental innovations) are slower to diffuse.[33]

The Spatial Analysis of Diffusion

Incorporating some geographical elements in the study of diffusion can have at least three different outcomes, according to the importance given to the spatial element in explaining the observed diffusion patterns. At the minimal level, no link between distinct geographical areas is supposed to be relevant and simple comparisons are performed; at a more complex level, areas are supposed to be linked by communication networks; finally, a further link is recognized in international (inter-regional) trade.

International and inter-regional comparisons
At the simplest level, geography can be seen as a source of cross-section data. The only contribution to understanding spatial patterns consists in the explanation of why diffusion speed differs between the observed geographical areas. No link between these is supposed to exist or to be relevant: different areas are studied as if they were isolated monades.

Many applications either of the classical, equilibrium or evolutionary approaches perform this kind of comparison. The most coherent set of inter-regional studies is offered by a set of contributions on the diffusion of automation and electronics in the British metalworking industry, based on data collected by the Centre for Urban and Regional Development Studies (CURDS) of Newcastle-upon-Tyne.[34] Gibbs and Edwards (1985), Oakey,

Thwaites and Nash (1980), Alderman and Davies (1990), Oakey and O'Farrell (1992) and O'Farrell and Oakey (1992) stress the absence of remarkable differences in the aggregate rates of process innovation diffusion between regions, and the existence of such differences only for the firms' capacity to supply product innovations (microprocessor in products).[35]

Gibbs and Edwards also find that the most significant variables in explaining the adoption speed are the corporate status of the plant,[36] together with its size and R&D expenditure and employees, which again positively influence the probability of adoption. Most British depressed areas host mainly branch plants or small independent firms: this offers an intuitive explanation of the relative backwardness of those areas, and of the fact that such backwardness is particularly relevant when product innovations are considered.

The traditional contribution of geographers

At a more sophisticated level of analysis, one can study the process of transmission of technologies: here we are in the true realm of geography, where concepts related to distance matter. This subject surely influences the 'reduced problem' of comparing the diffusion of the same innovation in different areas. It deals mainly with a number of innovations, and the student is asked to explain why some agents identified by their location in space always adopt later than others. Studies have usually been carried out by comparing regions within a country rather than nations.

Hagerstrand's (1953) and Pred's (1966) seminal studies supported the view of a three-stage spatial diffusion process:

1. The innovation is introduced in some major urban centre;
2. The innovation is both spread in the neighbourhood of the first centres and transmitted to minor centres;
3. The innovation is spread in the neighbourhood of the minor centres and the diffusion process is complete.

Such a three-stage process identifies an ordered spatial pattern of diffusion. A strong resemblance to epidemic models exists, since adoption is assumed to take place only when the potential adopter has accumulated a critical amount of information about the innovation, the information being of an internal form, that is, derived from other users rather than from suppliers or mass media. It follows that the three stages of diffusion are ruled by two main internal information flows: one which follows a hierarchical path from the main centres to the secondary, the other which take place in the neighbourhood of every adoption centre. The two channels are identified by the traffic on a number of communication means, such as roads and telephones. It should be noticed that the three stages can be represented not only by a geographical map (Figure 9.4a), but by an epidemic curve as well (Figure 9.4b).

Unfortunately, both the existence of some spatial order and the empirical relevance of information as a driving force have been seriously questioned by more recent empirical evidence. As Feller (1975) and Brown (1981) recall, geographers' interest in diffusion concerns a wide range of 'innovations': not only new products and processes but also collective goods and, within cultural geography, new ideologies and social habits. Brown (1981) mentions manufacturing innovations (in particular process innovations) as items which less than others follow the hierarchical or neighbourhood paths foreseen by Hagerstrand's and Pred's work. It appears that when innovations have to be adopted by firms, the geographical discipline needs to borrow concepts and measurements from economics (see Alderman and Davies, 1990; Eriksson, 1991; Malecki, 1983).

Brown (1981) is fairly representative of this borrowing process. The author stresses that geographers' emphasis on the communication networks as the key element of diffusion theory needs to be corrected with a consideration of the role of firm heterogeneity (which he calls 'adoption perspective') and suppliers' strategy in providing the necessary complementary infrastructures ('market and infrastructure' perspective). Apart from the case studies mentioned by Brown (1981) himself, some evidence on the fruitfulness of Brown's approach can be also found in Mattingly (1987), Meir (1981) and Sthyr Petersen (1990).

Selection effects: diffusion and location theory

Both the two previously described approaches can be extended to encompass the effects of innovation diffusion. Since innovations affect firms' competitiveness, it may happen that different diffusion speeds result in selective effects. For such effects to exist, regions or nations have to be considered linked at least through the final market that the adopters of the innovation serve; that is, adopters from each area are supposed to sell their products to the same national or international market. Since adoption affects their competitiveness, latecomers can be expelled by the market. If latecomers are not randomly distributed in space but are clustered in specific areas, these areas will be relegated to marginal positions within the industry or the economy being studied. By considering post-adoption effects one makes the diffusion theory overlap location theory (Feller, 1975), and international trade theory.[37]

Such overlapping recalls the possible influence of Marshallian externalities in shaping the geographical distribution of manufacture. Actually, Marshall (1932) considered innovation diffusion within industrial districts as one of the most important externalities contributing to the existence of agglomeration economies. Even if difficult to assess both in empirical enquiries and formal models, such an externality has never ceased to

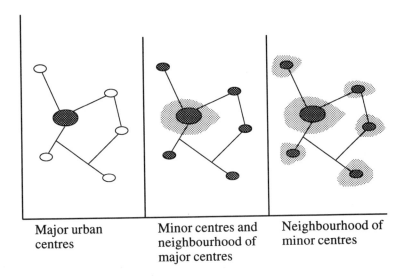

| Major urban centres | Minor centres and neighbourhood of major centres | Neighbourhood of minor centres |

(a)   Hierarchical and neighbourhood paths

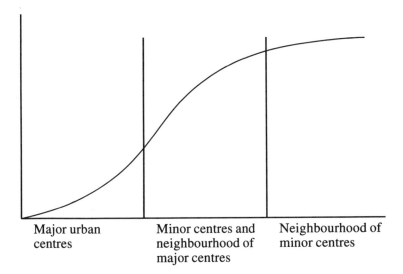

| Major urban centres | Minor centres and neighbourhood of major centres | Neighbourhood of minor centres |

(b)   Spatial diffusion as an epidemic process

Figure 9.4 Geographers' classical model

fascinate economists and economic geographers. Pred's studies on the historical persistence of the north-east manufacturing belt in the US, greatly emphasized the role of 'innovative centres' (Pred, 1966) and indeed are still persuasive (Meyer, 1983). Later, growth pole theory provided some literature in this field (Berry, 1972). More recently, the assessment of the vitality of Italian industrial districts (Becattini, 1989; Brusco, 1986), together with the recognition of the role played by agglomeration of small firms in the birth of the electronic industry (Scott and Kwok, 1989), have boosted a new wave of interest in this field.

This new wave of geographical studies emphasizes the possibility for small firm agglomerations to compete with highly integrated big companies either in mature or high technologies. It is argued that such agglomerations may have some advantages in rapidly diffusing the information concerning innovations. First of all, such advantages should derive from their high reliance on subcontracting: when the intermediate outputs pass through the market (rather than through intra-firm bureaucratic hierarchies, as in big firms) a good deal of information passes with them, together with many incremental innovations, which single firms are pushed to realize in order to enhance their reputation. Secondly, the social life of a localized community helps this information dissemination process by multiplying the information exchange opportunities.

A growing number of articles deal more or less extensively on the subject, ranging from the enthusiastic (see Piore and Sabel, 1984) and the more cautious (Scott, 1986; Storper, 1992), to the highly sceptical (Amin, 1989; Krugman, 1990 and Phelps, 1992).

There remain formidable conceptualization problems which prevent us from a systematic enquiry of the relationship between diffusion of new technologies, agglomeration economies and location. What can ensure that information dissemination is constrained within the neighbourhood of the innovation centre, especially in the well-connected world (see Kamann and Nijkamp (1991))? That is, what can ensure that diffusion requires physical proximity? The answer is both theoretical and empirical, but it is on the empirical side that the elusiveness of the concept is shown to be harder to overcome.

Conclusions

As diffusion theory has developed it has gradually abandoned the single innovation perspective centred on adoption behaviour. A much richer pattern is emerging which distinguishes technology in terms of knowledge and skills as well as discrete artefacts. This development of technologies interacts in complementary and competitive ways and the dual role of supply and demand forces is at the centre of the modern approaches based on equilibrium or evolutionary perspectives. In many ways diffusion is the canonical example to confront Nelson and Winter's (1982) rich theory of economic change. What is clear is that different perspectives coalesce to greatly enrich our understanding.

Notes

1. Some evidence was against the sigmoid shape. See Ray, 1969; Gold, Rosegger and Peirce, 1970; Gold, 1981.
2. The concept of adoption profitability needs to be discussed in great detail, as we do later in the chapter.
3. For a survey on the contribution of these disciplines see Rogers (1962, 1983) and Rogers and Shoemaker (1971); as for the geographers' contribution, see the later section on the spatial analysis of diffusion.
4. Actually, the psychological and informational differences which lead to the sigmoid diffusion path are not very dissimilar from some remarks made by Schumpeter (1934) in order to describe the 'heroic' entrepreneur as an outstanding sociological character:

    > In the first place it is a question of a type of conduct and of a type of person... . Now these aptitudes are presumably distributed in an ethnically homogeneous population just like others, that is the curve of their distribution has a maximum ordinate, deviations on either side of which become rarer the greater they are (Schumpeter, 1934, pp. 81–82, footnote 2).

5. Even if the diffusion curve of the first step is derived from an entirely different theoretical ground (see the section on the equilibrium approach), Davies' (1979) model still leads to a two-step procedure.
6. So long as the forecasting accuracy is the only issue many further refinements are possible even if a cost has to be paid, which Marchetti (1990) defines as the absence of any diffusion theory.
7. Davies (1979) introduces other possible causes of skewness in the diffusion path.
8. None of these events is explicitly modelled by Griliches and Mansfield and the following students, who make use of time-invariant measures of the adoption profitability and other explanatory variables.
9. See Salter (1960) for an early attempt in this direction.
10. For a review of the Probit technique, see Cramer (1986) or Pudney (1989).
11. Independence of tastes, and therefore of individual decision-making, is essential to the model and indeed excludes any possible relationship between Probit and epidemic models. Whatever refinement the former can undergo, their basic assumptions exclude the possibility that early adopters influence non-adopters' evaluation of the innovation which, on the contrary, is the essential feature of epidemic models (cf. Metcalfe (1988) for discussion).
12. For the theorems which ensure that a lognormal or a normal diffusion path can possibly be obtained under the conditions mentioned, Davies (1979) refers to Cramer (1969). As for the assumption of lognormality for the two distributions, they appear to be reasonable for large samples where income and consumers' tastes are randomly distributed.
13. This amounts to saying that all agents have the same tastes, and pay the same price for the consumer durable.
14. Surveys on this approach can be found in Thirtle and Ruttan (1987), Cabe (1991) and Gruber (1992), while for more synthetic overviews the reader is referred to Stoneman and David (1986).
15. To be precise, only Stoneman and Ireland (1983) and David and Olsen (1984) offer models where the learning process is a function of cumulative sales. Ireland and Stoneman (1985, 1986) and the other studies quoted in this section choose an easier way to model the

learning process, choosing time as the independent variable. David and Olsen (1984) develop this approach to define equilibrium diffusion paths.

16. Ireland and Stoneman (1986) also consider other expectations regimes, such as adaptive expectations, but only at a superficial level.

17. For other surveys of these models see Thirtle and Ruttan (1987) and Gruber (1992). See also Stoneman (1980, 1981).

18. These experiments are represented as Bernoulli trials, which are performed at any time t. A positive (negative) outcome suggests the innovation to be good (bad), so that the parameter of the probability distribution of the value of the innovation has to be revised accordingly.

19. Assuming the output price to be independent of the adoption choice is equivalent to assuming the absence of feedbacks from adoption choices to adoption benefits, that is from adoption to its determinants. This was precisely the case of a new consumer durable, where we can imagine consumers' income and tastes to be unaffected by the ownership of a new good, since tastes are given and the good does not enter the production function of its owner's income.

20. The most remarkable applications are Reinganum (1983), Fudenberg and Tirole (1985), Quirmbach (1986), Mariotti (1989), Sadanand (1989) and Jensen (1992). Very good surveys are those by Reinganum (1989) and Gruber (1992).

21. Nevertheless, less complicated models, such as Davies' (1979), suggest that an econometric analysis of sigmoid curves is possible.

22. Tobit analysis is employed for the explanation of intra-firm diffusion rate at a given point in time, with analogous results and limitations of Logit and Probit applications. Again a good example is offered by Franck and Gaussens (1992).

23. See Lancaster (1979), Kiefer (1988), and Cramer's (1986) and Pudney's (1989) textbooks.

24. As Nelson (1968) and Nelson and Winter (1982) make clear, they can also explain income distribution trends.

25. For a practical example of what technological variety means, and a useful classifying methodology for its measurement, see Foray and Grübler (1990).

26. Other approaches have been proposed by Cowan (1987), David (1989) and Vega-Redondo (1990).

27. Cowan does not employ Polya Urn schemes, but the so-called Multi-Arm Bandit schemes, which refer not to adoption by an infinite number of agents, but to the infinite trial of a technology by a single agent (infinite reversible adoption decisions).

28. Arthur (1989b) shows that if upper limits to such increasing returns exist, the growth of the conditional benefits is eventually interrupted, and more than one technology manages to survive.

29. Some evidence which does not fit in this framework is offered by Mansfield (1985), who shows that secrecy rules do not prevent information about work-in-progress innovation to leak from firms and reach their rivals. Similarly, Mansfield et al. (1981) show that patent protection does not prevent imitation for a very long time. But nothing is said either about the time imitators need to transform the acquired information into innovation, or about the distance between the latter and the original project.

30. See Dosi et al. (1988) and Nelson (1993). Malerba (1993) has identified the existence of so-called regional systems of innovation.

31. Besides, considering the diffusion path of single innovations together with the path of the related technologies enhances the accuracy of forecasting of that single diffusion process. A price must be paid, which consists in renouncing to formally sophisticated models or econometric exercises. Therefore the authors referred to support their arguments mainly by offering a large number of empirical examples based on descriptive statistics and diagrams: the strength of their approach is in the accuracy and the amount of data, which are really outstanding.

32. It should be noted that elements of complementarity can also emerge between technologies that are mainly rivals: Grübler recalls that the diffusion of horse-driven carriages led to the construction of a road network which greatly eased the successive diffusion of cars.

33. In the specific case of process technology in the Dutch banking industry, a similar result is

found by Diederen et al. (1991).
34. The same data set has been used by Stoneman and Karshenas (1990 and 1991).
35. Other studies in the same tradition are Rees, Briggs and Oakey (1984) and Thwaites (1982).
36. Dividing plants into national headquarters, regional headquarters, branch plants and single-plant firms, it emerges that a hierarchical order of adoption is the most probable, with single plant firms adopting later than branch plants, and headquarters being the first to adopt.
37. See Metcalfe and Soete (1984) and all the contributions related to the so-called 'technology gap trade theory', a synthesis of which is offered by Krugman (1979).

Bibliography

Alderman, N. and Davies, S. (1990) 'Modelling Regional Patterns of Innovation Diffusion in the UK Metalworking Industry', *Regional Studies*, pp. 513–28.

Amendola, G. (1990) 'The Diffusion of Synthetic Materials in the Automobile Industry: Towards a Major Technological Breakthrough?', *Research Policy*, 19, pp. 485–500.

Amin, A. (1989) 'Flexible Specialization and Small Firms in Italy: Myths and Realities', *Antipode*, No. 21, pp. 13–34.

Antonelli, C. (1986) 'The International Diffusion of New Information Technologies', *Research Policy*, 15, pp. 139–47.

Antonelli, C. (1989) 'The Role of Technological Expectations in a Mixed Model of International Diffusion: The Case of Open-end Spinning Rotors', *Research Policy*, 18, pp. 273–88.

Antonelli, C. (1990) 'Induced Adoption and Externalities in the Regional Diffusion of Information Technology', *Regional Studies*, 24, pp. 31–40.

Antonelli, C., Petit, P. and Tahar, G. (1988) 'Technological Diffusion and Investment Behaviour: The Case of the Textile Industry', paper presented at the Second Congress of the International J.A. Schumpeter Society, Siena (Italy), 23–27 May.

Arai, T. (1989) 'Forecast of Assembling Automation in the Automobile Industry: Technological Progress in Robotics', *Technological Forecasting and Social Change*, 35, pp. 133–48.

Arcangeli, F., Dosi, G. and Moggi, M. (1991) 'Patterns of Diffusion of Electronic Technologies: An International Comparison with Special Reference to the Italian Case', *Research Policy 20*, pp. 515–29.

Arthur, W.B. (1989a) 'Silicon Valley Locational Clusters: When Do Increasing Returns Imply Monopoly?', Santa Fe Institute Working Paper.

Arthur, W.B. (1989b) 'Competing Technologies, Increasing Returns and Lock-in by Historical Events', *Economic Journal*, 99, pp. 116–46.

Arthur, W.B., Ermoliev, Y.M. and Kaniovski, Y. (1987) 'Path-Dependent Processes and the Emergence of Macro-Structure', *European Journal of Operational Research*, 30, pp. 294–303.

Astakhov et al. (1990) 'Technology Diffusion in the Coal Mining Industry of the USSR: An Interim Assessment', *Technological Forecasting and Social Change*, 38, pp. 223–56.

Atkinson, A.B. and Stiglitz, J.E. (1969) 'A New View of Technological Change', *Economic Journal*, 79, pp. 573–78, September.

Ausubel, J.H. (1991) 'Rat-Race Dynamics and Crazy Companies: The Diffusion of Technologies and Social Behaviour', *Technological Forecasting and Social Change*, 39, No. 1–2; republished in Nakicenovic and Grübler (1992).

Balcer, Y. and Lippman, S.A. (1984) 'Technological Expectations and Adoption of

Improved Technology', *Journal of Economic Theory*, 34, pp. 292–318.

Becattini, G. (1989) 'Piccole e medie imprese e distretti industriali nel recente sviluppo italiano', *Note Economiche*.

Berry, B.J.L. (1972) 'Hierarchical Diffusion: The Basis of Developmental Filtering and Spread in a System of Growth', in Hansen N.M. (ed.), *Growth Centers in Regional Economic Development*, The Free Press, New York.

Blankart, C.B. and Knieps, G. (1991) 'Path Dependence, Network Externalities and Standardization', University of Groningen, Institute of Economic Research, research memorandum No. 439.

Brown, L.A. (1981) *Innovation Diffusion: A New Perspective*, Methuen, New York.

Brusco, S. (1986) 'Small Firms and Industrial Districts: the Experience of Italy', in Keeble, D. and Wever, E. (eds), *New Firms and Regional Development*, Croom Helm, London.

Cabe, R. (1991) 'Equilibrium Diffusion of Technological Change through Multiple Processes', *Technological Forecasting and Social Change*, 39, pp. 265–90.

Cainarca, G.C., Colombo, M.G. and Mariotti, S. (1989) 'An Evolutionary Pattern of Innovation Diffusion: The Case of Flexible Automation', Research Policy, 18, pp. 59–86.

Cameron, H.M. and Metcalfe, J.S. (1987) 'On the Economics of Technological Substitution', *Technological Forecasting and Social Change*, 32, pp. 147–62.

Coombs, R., Saviotti, P. and Walsh, V. (1987) *Economics and Technological Change*, Macmillan.

Cowan, R. (1987) 'Backing the Wrong Horse: Sequential Technology Choice Under Increasing Returns', PhD dissertation, Stanford University.

Cowan, R. (1990) 'Nuclear Power Reactors: A Study in Technological Lock-In', *Journal of Economic History*, L, pp. 541–67.

Cowan, R. (1991) 'Tortoises and Hares: Choice among Technologies of Unknown Merit', *Economic Journal*, 101, pp. 801–14.

Cramer, J.S. (1969) *Empirical Econometrics*, North Holland, Amsterdam.

Cramer, J.S. (1986) *The Econometric Applications of Maximum Likelihood Methods*, Cambridge University Press, Cambridge.

Dasgupta, P. and Stoneman, P. (1987) (eds), *Economic Policy and Technology Performance*, Cambridge University Press, Cambridge.

David, P. (1966) 'The Mechanization of Reaping in Ante Bellum Midwest', in Rosovsky, H. (1966); republished in Rosenberg, N. (1971), and in David, P. (1975).

David, P. (1969) 'A Contribution to the Theory of Diffusion', memorandum No. 71, Stanford Center for Research in Economic Growth.

David, P. (1971) 'The Landscape and the Machinery: Technical Interrelatedness, Land Tenure and the Mechanization of the Corn Harvest in Victorian Britain', in McCloskey (1971).

David, P. (1975a), 'Labor Scarcity and the Problem of Technological Practice and Progress in Nineteenth-Century America', in David, P. (1975), ch. 1.

David, P. (1975b) *Technical Choice, Innovation and Economic Growth*, Cambridge University Press, Cambridge.

David, P. (1985) 'Clio and the Economics of QWERTY', *American Economic Review*, Papers and Proceedings.

David, P. (1986) 'Technology Diffusion, Public Policy, and Industrial Competitiveness', in Landau, R. and Rosenberg, N. (eds), *The Positive Sum Strategy: Harnessing Technology for Economic Growth*, National Acamedic Press, Washington.

David, P. (1987) 'Some New Standards for the Economics of Standardization in the Information Age', in Dasgupta and Stoneman (1987).

David, P. (1989) 'A Paradigm for Historical Economics: Path Dependence and Predictability on Dynamic Systems with Local Network Externalities', CEPR paper, Stanford University, March 1989.

David, P. and Bunn, J.A. (1987) 'The Economics of Gateway Technologies and Network Evolution: Lessons from Electricity Supply History', CEPR paper prepared for the 15th Annual Telecommunications Policy Conference, Airlie, Va., 28–29 September.

David, P. and Olsen, T.E. (1984) 'Anticipated Automation: A Rational Expectations Model of Technological Diffusion', CEPR paper, Stanford University, April.

Davies, S. (1979) *The Diffusion of Process Innovations*, Cambridge University Press, Cambridge.

Diederen, P. et al. (1991) 'Diffusion of Process Technology in Dutch Banking', *Technological Forecasting and Social Change*, 39, No. 1–2. Republished in Nakicenovic and Grübler (1992).

Dinar, A. and Marom, D. (1991) 'Rate and Patterns of Computer Adoption and Use in Agricultural Extensions', *Technological Forecasting and Social Change*, 39, pp. 309–18.

Dixon, R. (1980) 'Hybrid Corn Revisited', *Econometrica*, Vol. 48, No. 6, pp. 1451–61, September.

Dosi, G. et al. (1988) *Technical Change and Economic Theory*, Pinter Publishers, London.

Dybvig, P.H. and Spatt, C.S. (1983) 'Adoption Externalities as Public Goods', *Journal of Public Economics*, 20, pp. 231–47.

Eriksson, R.A. (1991) 'The Influence of Economics on Geographical Enquiry', *Progress in Human Geography*, pp. 223–49.

Farrell, J. and Saloner, G. (1985) 'Standardization, Compatibility and Innovation', *Rand Journal of Economics*, Vol. 16, No. 1, pp. 70–83.

Farrell, J. and Saloner, G. (1986) 'Installed Base and Compatibility: Innovation, Product Preannouncements and Predation', *American Economic Review*, 76, pp. 940–55.

Farrell, J. and Saloner, G. (1988) 'Coordination through Committees and Markets', *Rand Journal of Economics*, Vol. 19, No. 2, pp. 235–52.

Farrell, J. and Saloner, G. (1992) 'Converters, Compatibility and the Control of Interfaces', *Journal of Industrial Economics*, XL, No. 1, pp. 9–35.

Feller, I. (1975) 'Invention, Diffusion and Industrial Location', in Collins, L. and Walker, D.F. (eds), *Location Dynamics of Manufacturing Activity*, Wiley, New York.

Fishelson, G. and Rymon, D. (1989) 'Adoption of Agricultural Innovations: The Case of Drip Irrigation of Cotton in Israel', *Technological Forecasting and Social Change*, 35, pp. 375–82.

Fisher, J.C. and Pry, R.H. (1971) 'A Simple Substitution Model for Technological Change', *Technological Forecasting and Social Change*, 2, pp. 75–88.

Foray, D. and Grübler, A. (1990) 'Morphological Analysis and Lock-out of Technologies: Ferrous Casting in France and the FRG', *Research Policy*, 19, pp. 535–50.

Franck, B. and Gaussens, O. (1992) 'L'automatisation des petites et moyennes enterprises: une étude économetrique', *Économie et Prévision*, 1–2, pp. 102–3.

Fudenberg, D. and Tirole, J. (1985) 'Preemption and Rent Equalization in the Adoption of New Technology', *Review of Economic Studies*, LII, pp. 385–401.

Georghiou, L. et al. (1986) *Post Innovative Performance*, Macmillan, London.

Gibbons, M. and Metcalfe, J.S. (1986) 'Technological Variety and the Process of Competition', paper presented at the International Conference on Innovation Diffusion, Venice (Italy), 17–21 March.

Gibbs, D.C. and Edwards, A. (1985) 'The Diffusion of New Production Innovations in

British Industry', in Thwaites, A.T. and Oakey, R.P. (eds), *The Regional Economic Impact of Technological Change*, Frances Pinter, London.

Globerman, S. (1975) 'Technological Diffusion in the Canadian Tool and Die Industry', *Review of Economics and Statistics*, No. 57, pp. 428–34.

Gold, B. (1981) 'Technological Diffusion in Industry: Research Needs and Shortcomings', *Journal of Industrial Economics*, XXIX, pp. 247–69.

Gold, B., Rosegger, G. and Peirce, W.S. (1970) 'Diffusion of Major Technological Innovations in US Iron and Steel Manufacturing', *Journal of Industrial Economics*, XVIII (3), pp. 218–41, July.

Griliches, Z. (1957) 'Research Costs and Social Returns: Hybrid Corn and Related Innovations', *Journal of Political Economy*, October. Republished in Rosenberg (1971).

Griliches, Z. (1960) 'Hybrid Corn and the Economics of Innovations Science', 29 July. Republished in Rosenberg (1971).

Griliches, Z. (1980) 'Hybrid Corn Revisited: A Reply', *Econometrica*, Vol. 48, No. 6, pp. 1451–61, September.

Gruber, H. (1992) 'La teoria dell'adozione delle innovazioni tecnologiche: una rassegna di contributi recenti', *Economia Politica*, anno IX, pp. 123–57.

Grübler, A. (1991) 'Diffusion: Long Term Patterns and Discontinuities', *Technological Forecasting and Social Change*, 39, No. 1–2. Republished in Nakicenovic and Grübler (1992).

Hagerstrand, T. (1953) *Innovation Diffusion as a Spatial Process* English translation 1967, Chicago University Press, Chicago.

Hannan, T.H. and McDowell, J.M. (1984a) 'The Determinants of Technology Adoption: The Case of the Banking Firm', *Rand Journal of Economics*, 15, pp. 328–35.

Hannan, T.H. and McDowell, J.M. (1984b) 'Market Concentration and the Diffusion of New Technology in the Banking Industry', *Review of Economics and Statistics*, 66, pp. 686–91.

Hannan, T.H. and McDowell, J.M. (1987) 'Rival Precedence and the Dynamics of Technology Adoption: an Empirical Analysis', *Economica*, 54, pp. 155–71.

Henderson, R. (1993) 'Underinvestment and Incompetence as Responses to Radical Innovation: Evidence from the Photolithographic Alignment Equipment Industry', *Rand Journal of Economics*, 24, pp. 249–70.

Henderson, R. and Clark, K.B. (1991) 'Architectural Innovation: The Reconfiguration of Existing Product Technologies and the Failure of Established Firms', *Administrative Science Quarterly*, 35, pp. 9–30.

Ireland, N.J. and Stoneman, P. (1985) 'Order Effects, Perfect Foresight and Intertemporal Price Discrimination', *Recherches Économiques de Louvain*, Vol. 51, No. 1, pp. 7–20.

Ireland, N.J. and Stoneman, P. (1986) 'Technological Diffusion, Expectations and Welfare', *Oxford Economic Papers*, No. 38, pp. 283–304.

Ishitani, H. and Kaya, Y. (1989) 'Robotization in Japanese Manufacturing Industries', *Technological Forecasting and Social Change*, 35, pp. 97–131.

Jensen, R. (1979) 'On the Adoption and Diffusion of Innovations Under Uncertainty', Discussion Paper No. 410, Center for Mathematical Studies in Economics and Management Science, North Western University, Evanston.

Jensen, R. (1982) 'Adoption and Diffusion of an Innovation of Uncertain Profitability', *Journal of Economic Theory*, 27, pp. 182–93.

Jensen, R. (1983) 'Innovation Adoption and Diffusion When There Are Competing Technologies', *Journal of Economic Theory*, 29, pp. 161–71.

Jensen, R. (1988a) 'Information Cost and Innovation Adoption Policies', *Management*

Science, 34, pp. 230–39.

Jensen, R. (1988b) 'Information Capacity and Innovation Adoption', *International Journal of Industrial Organization*, 6, pp. 335–50.

Jensen, R. (1992) 'Innovation Adoption and Welfare Under Uncertainty', *Journal of Industrial Economics*, XL, pp. 173–80.

Katz, M.L. and Shapiro, C. (1985) 'Network Externalities, Competition and Compatibility', *American Economic Review*, 75, pp. 424–40.

Katz, M.L. and Shapiro, C. (1986) 'Technology Adoption in the Presence of Network Externalities', *Journal of Political Economy*, 94, pp. 822–41.

Kamann, D.F. and Nijkamp, P. (1991) 'Origins and Diffusion in a Turbulent Environment', *Technological Forecasting and Social Change*, 39, No. 1–2, republished in Nakicenovic and Grübler (1992).

Kelley, M.R. and Brooks, H. (1991) 'External Learning Opportunities and the Diffusion of Process Innovations to Small Firms: The Case of Programmable Automation', *Technological Forecasting and Social Change*, 39, No. 1–2. Republished in Nakicenovic and Grübler (1992).

Kiefer, N.M. (1988) 'Economic Duration Data and Hazard Functions', *Journal of Economic Literature*, XXVI, pp. 646–79.

Krugman, P. (1979) 'A Model of Innovation, Technology Transfer, and the World Distribution of Income', *Journal of Political Economy*, 87, pp. 253–66.

Krugman, P. (1990) *Geography and Trade*, MIT Press – Leuven University Press.

Lancaster, T. (1979) 'Econometric Methods for the Duration of Unemployment', *Econometrica*, 47, pp. 939–56.

Lekvall, P. and Wahlbin, C. (1972) 'A Study of Some Assumptions Underlying Innovation Diffusion, Functions', *Swedish Journal of Economics*, pp. 362–77.

Levin, S.G., Levin, S.L. and Meisel, J.B. (1987) 'A Dynamic Analysis of the Adoption of a New Technology: The Case of Optical Scanners', *Review of Economics and Statistics*, 86, pp. 12–17.

Lynn, L. (1981) 'New Data on the Diffusion of the Basic Oxygen Furnaces in the US and Japan', *Journal of Industrial Economics*, XXX, pp. 123–35.

Mahajan, V., Muller, E. and Bass, F.M. (1990) 'New Product Diffusion Models in Marketing: A Review and Directions for Research', *Journal of Marketing*, Vol. 54, pp. 1–26, January.

Mahajan, V., Muller, E. and Srivastava, R.K. (1990) 'Determination of Adopters Categories by Using Innovation Diffusion Models', *Journal of Marketing Research*, Vol. XXVII, pp. 37–50, February.

Mahajan, V. and Wind, Y. (1986) *Innovation Diffusion of New Product Acceptance*, Ballinger Publishing Company, Cambridge.

Malecki, E.J. (1983) 'Technology and Regional Development: A Survey', *International Regional Science Review*, 8, pp. 89–125.

Malerba, F. (1993) (ed.) *Sistemi Innovativi Regionali a Confronto*, Franco Angeli, Milano.

Mansfield, E. (1961) 'Technical Change and the Rate of Imitation', *Econometrica*, pp. 741–66, October.

Mansfield, E. (1968) *Industrial Research and Technological Innovation*, Norton, New York.

Mansfield, E. (1985) 'How Rapidly Does New Industrial Technology Leak Out?', *Journal of Industrial Economics*, XXXIV, pp. 217–23.

Mansfield, E. (1989) 'The Diffusion of Industrial Robots in Japan and the United States', *Research Policy*, 18, pp. 183–92.

Mansfield, E., Schwartz, M. and Wagner, S. (1981) 'Imitation Costs and Patents: An Empirical Study', *Economic Journal*, 91, pp. 907–18.

Marchetti, C. (1990) 'A Personal Memoir: From Terawatts to Witches: My Life with Logistics at IIASA', *Technological Forecasting and Social Change*, 37, pp. 409–14.

Marchetti, C. and Nakicenovic, N. (1979) 'The Dynamics of Energy Systems and the Logistic Substitution Model', *Research Report*, 13, IIASA, Laxenburg.

Mariotti, M. (1989) 'Being Identical, Behaving Differently: A Theorem on Technological Diffusion', *Economics Letters*, 30, pp. 275–78.

Marshall, A. (1932) *Economics of Industry*, Macmillan, London.

Mattingly, P. (1987) 'Patterns of Horse Devolution and Tractor Diffusion in Illinois, 1920–1982', *Professional Geographer*, 39, pp. 298–309.

McCardle, K. (1985) 'Information Acquisition and the Adoption of New Technology', *Management Science*, 21, pp. 1372–89.

Meir, A. (1981) 'Innovation Diffusion and Regional Economic Development: the Spatial Diffusion of Automobiles in Ohio', *Regional Studies*, 15, pp. 11–25.

Metcalfe, J.S. (1981) 'Impulse and Diffusion in the Study of Technical Change', *Futures*, 13, pp. 347–59, October.

Metcalfe, J.S. (1988) 'The Diffusion of Innovation: An Interpretative Survey', in Dosi, G. et al. (eds) *Technical Change and Economic Theory*, Francis Pinter, London.

Metcalfe, J.S. (1989) 'Evolution and Economic Change', in Silberston, A., *Technology and Economic Progress*, Macmillan, London.

Metcalfe, J.S. and Soete, L. (1984) 'Notes on the Evolution of Technology and International Competition' in Gibbons, M. et al. (eds) *Science and Technology Policy in the 1980s and Beyond*, Longman, London.

Meyer, D.R. (1983) 'Emergence of the American Manufacturing Belt: An Interpretation', *Journal of Historical Geography*, No. 9, pp. 145–74.

Nabseth, L. and Ray, G.F. (1974) *The Diffusion of New Industrial Processes: An International Study*, Cambridge University Press, Cambridge.

Nakicenovic, N. (1991) 'Diffusion of Pervasive Systems: A Case of Transport Infrastructures', *Technological Forecasting and Social Change*, 39, No. 1–2. Republished in Nakicenovic and Grübler (1992).

Nakicenovic, N. and Grübler, A. (eds) (1992) *Diffusion of Technologies and Social Behaviour*, Springer-Verlag, Berlin.

Nelson, R. (1968) 'A "Diffusion" Model of International Productivity Differences in Manufacturing Industry', *American Economic Review*, 58, pp. 1219–48.

Nelson, R. and Winter, S.G. (1982) *An Evolutionary Theory of Economic Change*, Harvard University Press, Cambridge MA.

Nelson, R. (ed.) (1993) *National Innovation Systems: A Comparative Study*, Oxford University Press, New York.

Norotte, M. and Bensaid, J. (1987) 'Comportement d'investissement et diffusion de nouvelles technologies', *Économie et Prévision*, 80, pp. 55–67.

O'Farrell, P.N. and Oakey, R.P. (1992) 'Regional Variations in the Adoption of CNC Machine Tools by Small Engineering Firms: A Multivariate Analysis', *Environment and Planning*, A 24, pp. 887–902.

Oakey, R.P. and O'Farrell, P.N. (1992) 'The Regional Extent of Computer Numerically Controlled (CNC) Machine Tool Adoption and Post Adoption Success in Small British Mechanical Engineering Firms', *Regional Studies*, 26, pp. 163–75.

Oakey, R.P., Thwaites, A.T. and Nash, P.A. (1980) 'The Regional Distribution of Innovating Manufacturing Establishments in Britain', *Regional Studies*, 14, pp. 235–53.

Oster, S. (1982) 'The Diffusion of Innovation Among Steel Firms: The Basic Oxygen Furnace', *Bell Journal of Economics*, 13, pp. 45–56.

Phelps, N.A. (1992) 'External Economies, Agglomeration and Flexible Accumulation', *Transactions of the Institute of British Geographers*, 17, pp. 35–46.

Piore, M. and Sabel, C. (1984) *The Second Industrial Divide*, Basic Books, New York.

Postrel, S.R. (1990) 'Competing Networks and Proprietary Standards: The Case of Quadraphonic Sound', *Journal of Industrial Economics*, XXXIX, pp. 169–85.

Pred, A. (1966) *The Spatial Dynamics of US Urban-Industrial Growth: 1800–1914*, Cambridge University Press, Cambridge.

Pudney, S. (1989) *Modelling Individual Choice: The Econometrics of Corners, Kinks and Holes*, Blackwell, Oxford.

Puffert, D. (1988) 'Network Externalities and Technological Preference in the Selection of Railway Gauges', PhD dissertation, Stanford University.

Quirmbach, H.C. (1986) 'The Diffusion of New Technology and the Market for an Innovation', *Rand Journal of Economics*, 17, pp. 33–47.

Ray, G.F. (1969) 'The Diffusion of New Technology', *National Institute Economic Review*, No. 78, pp. 40–83, May. Reprinted in Nabseth and Ray (1974).

Ray, G.F. (1984) *The Diffusion of Mature Technologies*, Cambridge University Press, Cambridge.

Ray, G.F. (1989) 'Full Circle: The Diffusion of Technology', *Research Policy*, 18, pp. 1–18.

Rees, J., Briggs, R. and Oakey, R. (1984) 'The Adoption of New Technologies in the American Machinery Industry', *Regional Studies*, 18, pp. 489–504.

Reinganum, J. (1981a) 'On the Diffusion of New Technology: A Game Theoretic Approach', *Review of Economic Studies*, XLVIII, pp. 395–405.

Reinganum, J. (1981b) 'Market Structure and the Diffusion of New Technology', *Bell Journal of Economics*, 48, pp. 619–24.

Reinganum, J. (1983) 'Technology Adoption Under Imperfect Information', *Bell Journal of Economics*, 14, pp. 57–69.

Reinganum, J. (1989) 'The Timing of Innovation: Research, Development and Diffusion', in Schmalensee, R. and Willig, R.D. (eds), *Handbook of Industrial Organization*, North Holland, New York.

Rogers, E.M. (1962) *Diffusion of Innovations*, The Free Press, New York.

Rogers, E.M. (1983) *Diffusion of Innovations*, Macmillan, New York (3rd edition).

Rogers, E.M. and Shoemaker, F.F. (1971) *Communications of Innovations: A Cross Cultural Approach*, The Free Press, New York (2nd edition of Rogers, 1962).

Romeo, A.A. (1975) 'Interindustry and Interfirm Differences in the Rate of Diffusion of an Innovation', *Review of Economics and Statistics*, No. 57, pp. 311–19.

Romeo, A.A. (1977) 'The Rate of Imitation of a Capital-Embodied Process Innovation', *Economica*, No. 44, pp. 63–9.

Rose, N.L. and Joskow, P.L. (1990) 'The Diffusion of New Technologies: Evidence from the Electrical Utility Industry, *Rand Journal of Economics*, 21, pp. 354–73.

Rosegger, G. (1991) 'Diffusion through Interfirm Cooperation: A Case Study', *Technological Forecasting and Social Change*, 39, No. 1–2. Republished in Nakicenovic and Grübler (1992).

Rosenberg, N. (1976) 'On Technological Expectations', *Economic Journal*, 86, pp. 523–35.

Rosenberg, N. (ed.) (1971) *The Economics of Technical Change*, Penguin Books, London.

Sadanand, V. (1989) 'Endogenous Diffusion of Technology', *International Journal of Industrial Organization*, 7, pp. 471–87.

Salter, W.E.G. (1960) *Productivity and Technical Change*, Cambridge University Press, Cambridge.

Schumpeter, J.A. (1934) *The Theory of Economic Development*, Harvard University Press, Cambridge, Mass.

Scott, A.J. (1986) 'Industrial Organization and Location: Division of Labour, the Firm and Spatial Process', *Economic Geography*, 62, pp. 215–45.

Scott, A.J. and Kwok, E.C. (1989) 'Interfirm Subcontracting and Locational Agglomeration: A Case Study of the Printed Circuits Industry in Southern California', *Regional Studies*, 23, pp. 405–16.

Silverberg, G. (1988) 'Modelling Economic Dynamics and Technical Change: Mathematical Approaches to Self-Organization and Evolution', in Dosi et al., *Technical Change and Economic Theory*, Frances Pinter, London.

Silverberg, G. (1991) 'Adoption and Diffusion of a Technology as a Collective Evolutionary Process', *Technological Forecasting and Social Change*, 39, No. 1–2. Republished in Nakicenovic and Grübler (1992).

Silverberg, G., Dosi, G. and Orsenigo, L. (1988) 'Innovation, Diversity and Diffusion: A Self-Organization Model', *Economic Journal*, No. 98, pp. 1032–54.

Soete, L. and Turner, R. (1984) 'Technology Diffusion and The Rate of Technological Change', *Economic Journal*, 94, pp. 612–23.

Sthyr Petersen, H. (1990) 'Diffusion of Coal Gas Technology in Denmark 1850–1920', *Technological Forecasting and Social Change*, 38, pp. 37–48.

Stiglitz, J.E. (1987) 'Learning to Learn, Localized Learning and Technological Progress', in Dasgupta, P. and Stoneman, P. (eds) *Economic Policy and Technological Change*, Cambridge University Press, Cambridge.

Stoneman, P. (1980) 'The Rate of Imitation, Learning and Profitability', *Economics Letters*, 6, pp. 179–83.

Stoneman, P. (1981) 'Intrafirm Diffusion, Bayesian Learning and Profitability', *Economic Journal*, 91, pp. 375–88.

Stoneman, P. (1983) *The Economic Analysis of Technological Change*, Oxford University Press, Oxford.

Stoneman, P. (1986) 'Technological Diffusion: The Viewpoint of Economic Theory', *Ricerche Economiche*, 40, pp. 585–606.

Stoneman, P. (1987) 'Some Analytical Observations on Diffusion Policies' in Dasgupta, Stoneman (1987).

Stoneman, P. (1992) 'The Impact of Technological Adoption on Firm Performance: Heterogeneity and Multi-Technology Diffusion Models', mimeo.

Stoneman, P. and Ireland, N.J. (1983) 'The Role of Supply Factors in the Diffusion of New Process Technology', *Economic Journal*, Conference Supplement, pp. 66–78.

Stoneman, P. and David, P. (1986) 'Adoption Subsidies vs. Information Provision as Instruments of Technology Policy', *Economic Journal*, 96, pp. 142–50.

Stoneman, P. and Karshenas, M. (1990) 'Rank, Stock, Order and Epidemic Effects in the Diffusion of New Process Technologies: An Empirical Model', *Warwick Economic Research Papers*, No. 358, April.

Stoneman, P. and Karshenas, M. (1991) 'The Diffusion of New Technology: Extensions to Theory and Evidence', paper prepared for the ESRC Research Initiative on New Technologies and the Firm.

Storper, M. (1992) 'The Limits to Globalization: Technology Districts and International Trade', *Economic Geography*, pp. 60–93.

Swan, P.L. (1973) 'The International Diffusion of an Innovation', *Journal of Industrial Economics*, pp. 61–9, September.

Tani, A. (1989) 'International Comparisons of Industrial Robot Penetration', *Technological Forecasting and Social Change*, 35, pp. 191–210.

Thirtle, C.G. and Ruttan, V.W. (1987) *The Role of Demand and Supply in the Generation and Diffusion of Technical Change*, Harwood Academic Publishers, New York.

Thwaites, A.T. (1982) 'Some Evidence of Regional Variations in the Introduction and Diffusion of Industrial Products and Processes within the British Manufacturing Industry', *Regional Studies*, 15, pp. 371–81.

Torii, Y. (1989) 'Robotization in Korea: Trend and Implications for Industrial Development', *Technological Forecasting and Social Change*, 35, pp. 179–90.

Vega-Redondo, F. (1990) 'Technological Change and Path Dependence: A Co-Evolutionary Model on a Directed Graph', Working Paper 145.90, Universidad Autonoma de Barcelona.

Waldman, D.M. (1985) 'Computation in Duration Models with Heterogeneity', *Journal of Econometrics*, 28, pp. 127–34.

PART 2

Sectoral and Industrial Studies of Innovation

10. Innovation and Consumer Electronics

Alan Cawson

Characteristics of Consumer Electronics Products

Consumer electronics (sometimes called 'brown goods' in contrast to 'white goods' which are domestic electrical appliances) refers to a range of primarily audio-visual products which are purchased mainly by individual consumers for leisure and entertainment purposes. The most important products in terms of market size are televisions and video recorders, and it is towards these products that the most intensive efforts at innovation have been directed in recent years. Many innovative consumer electronics products, such as the tape recorder and video recorder, have been adapted from technologies developed for professional and industrial uses. More recently, however, new technologies developed for consumer applications such as digital audio tape (DAT) recording and high definition television (HDTV) have found important applications in professional and industrial fields, and the differences between consumer and professional products in terms of quality and performance are further eroding with the near-universal trend towards digitalization (see below).

Some of the innovation issues which arise in consumer electronics can be clarified by an analysis of the extent to which the functionality of the products is dependent on additional inputs (such as software or broadcast programmes) or the existence of infrastructure such as telecommunications networks. Product characteristics of this kind will affect the way in which standards are established, and constrain diffusion strategies, for example where the utility of the product is dependent on the number of other users (as in facsimile or electronic mail).

For the purposes of this analysis, four such categories of products can be identified (Cawson, Haddon and Miles, 1993). The first is *stand-alone* products, which are sold as a complete package, and can be used without the further purchase of inputs. Electronic calculators, hand-held games, and electronic watches are examples of products in this category. From the point of view of producers, the innovation issues raised by such products are relatively straightforward judgements about the utility and perceived value of such products. Some stand-alone products, such as music synthesizers and camcorders, can be used to create recordings, and to the extent that consumers are interested in exchanging these or replaying them on other machines, the issue of standardization arises. In such cases, however, the standards used in stand-alone devices (such as Video 8 or VHS, or the MIDI music interface) have been developed for products which are either dependent on software, or developed for connection to other devices.

Software-dependent products are used in conjunction with externally supplied information in a variety of forms, such as music and video recordings, or computer programs. The software is most frequently supplied on storage media, such as tape or disc, where the consumer buys or rents the physical carrier of the information along with the information itself. In some products, such as home computers or games consoles, the software incorporates control functions which allow the user to do more than simply reproduce recordings, permitting interactivity between the user and the product. In this type of product the issue of standards is critical, and it has often been the case that product standardization has emerged from competition between different formats: drums versus discs in early sound reproduction; wire versus tape and later cartridges versus cassettes in sound recording; and most importantly in recent years, competition between video recorder formats. Further, the market prospects for hardware are often determined by the supply of software, so that manufacturers of new software-dependent products, such as compact disc players or video recorders, have had to reach agreements with the music and film industries in order to ensure the availability of software to encourage early purchasers. As the market for these products develops, the value of the market for software tends to overtake the hardware market, as typically consumers spend repeatedly on software rental and purchase, but upgrade hardware products infrequently. Factors such as this lie behind the tendency for leading hardware firms such as Sony and Matsushita to acquire software producers in the music and film industries.

A third type of consumer electronics product can be defined as *broadcast-dependent*, where informational inputs are delivered (broadcast) through point-to-multipoint networks. Television and radio are the most important such products in the consumer electronics industry, reflecting the hold that the consumption of broadcast programmes has over the leisure time of most people in the industrialized countries. Unlike the industries which provide material for the software-dependent products discussed above, television and radio programmes have tended in many countries to have been provided by state monopolies, and governments have been the key actors in determining broadcasting standards. More recently the move towards the deregulation of broadcasting, and the introduction of satellite television, has led to the emergence of private broadcasting organizations, which has made the determination of standards a more complicated process.

Since the advent of colour television in the 1960s, the main innovation in broadcast-dependent products has been the development of the video recorder for time shifting, although just as crucial to the success of the video recorder was its use for watching pre-recorded software, especially films. Digital technology began to be applied to television and radio with teletext and Radio Data Services (RDS) providing additional information to analogue transmission. The next major technological change for this category of products will come with the advent of digital radio and television transmissions, including high definition television.

Finally, some consumer electronics products can be defined as *network-dependent*, in that they depend on the existence of networks, principally the telecommunications network, to provide new forms of interpersonal communication (facsimile, electronic mail, videophone) or new information services (videotext). Often the usefulness of the product depends upon the number of users, so that the diffusion of network-dependent innovations may be dependent on the rapid development of a critical mass of other users. Many of these products (e.g. fax, cellular phones) were initially

Table 10.1 A typology of consumer electronics products

Stand-alone	Software-dependent	Broadcast-dependent	Network-dependent
Electronic watch	Personal/home computer	Television receiver	Citizens Band radio
Hand-held electronic game	Record player	Teletext TV set	Telepoint
Electronic calculator	Tape recorder	Radio receiver	Facsimile
Electronic keyboard	Compact disc player	RDS radio	Cellular phone
Music synthesizer	Videodisc player	Video recorder (VCR)	Electronic mail
Microwave oven	Video recorder (VCR)		Videophone
Camcorder	Games console		Videotext
Electronic still camera	Interactive compact disc player		
	Digital audio recorder		

developed for industrial markets, and then later launched as consumer products when industrial markets began to be saturated, and mass production had reduced prices to within the reach of individual private purchasers.

Table 10.1 is a classification of the most important consumer electronics products according to this typology. The major product markets, and the central products of the major consumer electronics manufacturing firms, fall within the two middle columns.

Characteristics of the Innovation Process

Innovation in consumer electronics has been largely the province of the firm and funded by private investment, with relatively little research and development taking place in the public sector or subsidized by governments. The major exception to this has been in broadcasting technologies, where some significant innovations (such as teletext, NICAM stereo) have taken place in the R&D laboratories of public broadcasters, and where public subsidies have been significant, as in the development of high definition television in Europe and Japan. Until the late 1970s, most of the important innovations had been pioneered by firms in the United States and Europe, with the exception of the transistor radio in the late 1950s, which was the first important Japanese innovation in the industry. The Japanese firms proved to be remarkably inventive in process innovation, and their development of high quality low cost manufacturing technologies involving automated assembly at very large volumes gave Japanese radios, hi-fi systems and televisions an important competitive edge in the 1970s and 1980s (Bowonder and Miyake, 1991; Gregory, 1986).

Japanese firms have been particularly effective at perfecting products which depend on miniaturization and precision engineering, such as the personal stereo (Walkman), video recorder and camcorder (Morita, 1987; Tatsuno, 1990). In most of these cases the innovation process has involved the adaptation and refinement of existing technologies to open up mass markets which the originators of the technologies had not foreseen. For example, the development in Japan of the video recorder for home use deployed technology originated by Ampex in the United States for the professional broadcasting market. The technological challenge was to design a product small enough for the home which could be manufactured at volumes sufficient to reduce prices to a level which would open up the possibility of a mass market (Rosenbloom and Cusumano, 1987; Nayak and Ketteringham, 1986).

A significant factor inhibiting innovation in hardware products has been the resistance of the audio-visual software industry to the marketing of products which might infringe their copyright, especially – as with digital technologies – when it might permit the reproduction of perfect copies of the original recordings. Since the availability of pre-recorded software is critical for the acceptance of software-dependent products, opposition from the software industry cannot be ignored by manufacturers. Negotiations between the two sides have resulted in the addition of copy protection systems into first Digital Audio Tape (DAT) recorders, and subsequently Digital Compact Cassette (DCC) and MiniDisc recorders. Recordable compact disc systems have been marketed as computer peripherals, but their introduction as consumer products has been held back because of fears in the music industry that the (very profitable) market for compact discs would be harmed. The introduction of digital video recorders in the next few years will raise similar fears within the film industry, because, unlike current models, copies made on digital video recorders will be indistinguishable in quality from the original material.

Standardization in Consumer Electronics

Compared to the computer industry, where consumers face a maze of incompatible standards in operating systems, diskette sizes and formats, the consumer electronics industry has been relatively successful in creating standards which allow the free interchangeability of software. From the long-playing record, to the compact cassette tape, to video cassettes, video

Table 10.2 Format battles in consumer electronics

Product	Contenders	Winner
Tape recorders	(1) 8-track cartridge (2) Compact cassette (Philips)	Compact cassette
Video cassette recorders	(1) Betamax (Sony) (2) VHS (JVC) (3) V2000 (Philips)	VHS
Video disc players	(1) LaserDisc (Philips/Pioneer) (2) VHD (JVC) (3) SelectaVision (RCA)	LaserDisc
Interactive multimedia players	Compact Disc-Interactive (Philips/Sony) CDTV (Commodore) Real Multiplayer (Matsushita/3DO)	None as yet
Digital audio recorders	Digital Compact Cassette (Philips/Matsushita) MiniDisc (Sony)	None as yet

discs and the compact disc, consumers have become accustomed to be able to buy software which will work on any machine from any manufacturer. With one exception, such standards have been achieved after bruising format struggles in the marketplace, where firms seek to position their proprietary technologies as the *de facto* standard. Table 10.2 shows the winners and losers in the most recent format battles, including those where the outcome is uncertain at the time of writing.

The one exception so far to the principle that consumer electronics standards emerge by attrition in the marketplace is compact disc. In the early 1980s several companies, including Philips and Sony, were developing rival formats for digital audio discs, and the chances of yet another format battle were high. Philips and Sony had just seen their rival video recorder formats lose out to the VHS system pioneered by JVC, and having both lost a great deal of money, decided to collaborate on a pre-market standard which would be offered for licensing to other manufacturers. Given this alliance between the two leading contenders, the other firms – including JVC's parent company Matsushita – decided to abandon development work on their proprietary formats and adopt the Philips/Sony CD standard. The partnership continued with the agreement on standard for interactive multimedia (CD-I), but in this case it has not dissuaded rivals such as Commodore and Matsushita from launching rival products. Nor has the success of the CD standard cemented a permanent alliance between Philips and Sony; they are currently locked in a struggle to promote as industry standards their own contending digital audio recording technologies DCC and MiniDisc.

Digitalization

The most significant current trend in innovation in the consumer electronics industry is the application of digital technologies – the storage, processing and transmission of information in digital form – to broadcasting and especially television images. Fully digital consumer electronics products – such as compact disc and interactive multimedia players – have been marketed for some time, but the technological basis of the major products of the industry – television receivers and video recorders – has remained largely analogue (although digital text and sound has been added to analogue pictures in teletext and NICAM stereo respectively). The next generation high definition television technology developed in Japan (Hi-Vision) and Europe (HD-MAC) involved a good deal of digital technology, but retained analogue technology for transmission.

The major inhibiting factor in applying digital techniques to television has been the prodigious processing and storage capacities required to handle the television picture, each frame of which requires nearly half a megabyte of capacity, refreshed twenty-five times a second (with the requirements for high definition television roughly four times as great) (Evans, 1992). Faster chips and recent breakthroughs in data compression have now opened up the way for high quality television images to be transmitted in digital form using no more bandwidth than conventional analogue techniques. In the United States three contending digital HDTV systems were involved in a competition run by the Federal Communications Commission to determine a successor standard to the current National Television Systems Committee (NTSC) standard.

The diffusion of digital technologies to broadcast-dependent products is likely to have a profound impact on the consumer electronics industry, since the fully digital television receiver will be technologically similar to a high speed computer workstation, receiving, processing and displaying a stream of digital information either broadcast or sent through cable TV or telecommunications networks. The generic nature of digital technologies has meant that expertise gained by firms in related sectors such as telecommunications and computers can be deployed in broad-casting systems; amongst the contenders in the US competition were American Telephone and Telegraph (AT&T). In addition to display equipment, new digital video recorders and disc players are under development, and once again efforts are being made by the leading firms in the industry to agree standards to avoid another round of format battles.

Networks and Inter-firm Collaboration

Since the 1970s successful innovation in consumer electronics has involved inter-firm collaboration and the development of networks, sometimes (as in the case of HDTV in Europe and Japan) sponsored by governments, but more often negotiated between the firms themselves (Mytelka, 1991). As we have seen, one of the principal reasons for this is the importance of creating standards, so that networks of firms form around competing formats, as with video recorders in the case of the VHS family, the Betamax family and the (rather smaller) V2000 family (Baba and Imai, 1993). A second factor which lies behind the increasing importance of inter-firm collaboration is the extent to which new products or product systems fuse together technologies from related Information Technology sectors (Kodama, 1991). The development of Philips' interactive multimedia technology CD-I required a string of alliances and joint ventures to bring together the requisite hardware and software expertise and a new type of corporate structure to manage the different disciplines involved in bringing together the various media which constitute multimedia: book publishing, video and imaging, audio, and computer programming (Cawson, Morgan, Webber, Holmes and Stevens, 1990). Thirdly, the scale of investment required for major projects such as HDTV would burden the R&D budget of even the largest firms: total spending on HDTV research in Europe and Japan is estimated at over $4 billion.

The case of HDTV suggests that inter-firm collaboration is a necessary but not a sufficient condition for successful innovation, especially in broadcast-dependent technologies where the range of public and private stakeholders is so large. In both Japan and Europe the chosen mode of development was the government-backed R&D consortium which was used in Japan as a means of persuading the manufacturing firms to accept a technology pioneered by the state broadcasting organization, and in Europe in an attempt to persuade private satellite broadcasters to accept a technology pushed by the two leading receiver manufacturers. By contrast, in the United States the government rejected the monopoly R&D consortium approach and invited firms to join a competition where the standard would be set only after the technologies had proved themselves in trials. In this sense the US chose 'pre-collaborative competition' in contrast to the 'pre-competitive collaboration' of the Japanese and European approaches. In the event one of the competitors (General Instruments) made a breakthrough in digital compression technology during the competition, and all contenders then rapidly modified their offerings to fully digital systems. The consequence of the US decision has been to render Japanese and European technologies obsolete even before they have been fully commercialized.

As in Japan and Europe, the actors bidding to be the developers of HDTV in the United States are not single firms, but consortia of firms reflecting the need to fuse together a number of different technologies. One of the teams comprises Philips and Thomson, the European-based multinationals who are the developers of the rival European analogue system HD-MAC. The other two consortia in turn have formed partnerships with Asian consumer electronics firms – principally Toshiba of Japan and Samsung of Korea – in order to harness their expertise in manufacturing consumer electronics products and components.

Conclusions

The case of HDTV illustrates very well the major characteristics of the innovation process in consumer electronics: the crucial importance of standards, and the bitter struggles that lie behind their emergence; the extent to which all consumer electronics products have been fundamentally re-designed to take advantage of digital technology; the tendency for the innovation process to be centred on systems or families rather than discrete products; the trend for competition in the industry to be between coalitions of firms rather than between individual firms; and the extent to which a fusion or convergence is taking place which is eroding the boundaries between consumer electronics and related industries such as computing, telecommunications and professional electronics.

Postscript

In May 1993 the four contenders for the US HDTV standard agreed to form a 'Grand Alliance' (GA) through which their marginally different technologies could be pooled in order to submit a final version to the FCC. The FCC is expected to endorse the GA system as the US HDTV standard in 1995. The commercial prospects for HDTV may be jeopardised, however, by the apparent preference by broadcasters to use digital compression technology to broadcast several channels of standard definition television in the spectrum occupied by a single high definition channel.

Acknowledgement

This chapter is based on research funded by the Economic and Social Research Council, partly done in collaboration with Ian Miles and Leslie Haddon.

Bibliography

Baba, Y. and Imai, K. (1993) 'A Network View of Innovation and Entrepreneurship: The Case of the Evolution of VCR Systems', *International Social Science Journal*, Vol. 45, No. 1, pp. 23–34.

Bowonder, B. and Miyake, T. (1991) 'Industrial Competitiveness: An Analysis of the Japanese Electronics Industry', *Science and Public Policy*, Vol. 18, No. 2, pp. 93–110.

Cawson, A., Morgan, K., Webber, D., Holmes, P. and Stevens, A. (1990) *Hostile Brothers: Competition and Closure in the European Electronics Industry*, Clarendon Press, Oxford.

Cawson, A., Haddon, L. and Miles, I. (1993) 'The Heart of Where the Home Is: The Innovation Process in Consumer Information Technology' in Silverstone, R. and Hirsch, E. (eds) *Consuming Technologies*, Routledge, London.

Evans, B. (1992) *Digital HDTV: The Way Forward*, IBC Technical Services Ltd., London.

Gregory, G. (1986) *The Japanese Electronics Industry*, Chichester, Wiley.

Kodama, F. (1991) *Analyzing Japanese High Technologies: The Techno-Paradigm Shift*, Pinter, London.

Morita, A. (1987) *Made in Japan*, Collins, London.

Mytelka, L.K. (ed.) (1991) *Strategic Partnerships: States, Firms and Multinational Competition*, Pinter, London.

Nayak, P.R. and Ketteringham, J.M. (1986) *Breakthroughs!*, Rawson Associates, New York.

Rosenbloom, R.S. and Cusumano, M.A. (1987) 'Technological Pioneering and Competitive Advantage: The Birth of the VCR Industry', *California Management Review*, Vol. 24, No. 4, pp. 51–76.

Tatsuno, S.M. (1990) *Created in Japan: From Imitators to World Class Innovators*, Harper and Row, New York.

11. Innovation in Semiconductor Technology: The Limits of the Silicon Valley Network Model

Mike Hobday

Introduction

Some network theorists argue that during the 1980s the US witnessed the emergence of a new, flexible, more efficient industrial form (Miles and Snow, 1986; Gilder, 1988). In contrast with Chandler (1990), these studies contend that collaborative, high technology firms are a more modern, more competitive industrial form than the traditional large integrated firm. These views are especially relevant to the US semiconductor (or chip) industry where network research has claimed that Silicon Valley, as a collaborative network, has advantages over the large chip producers (Saxenian, 1990a).

This paper argues that it is important to distinguish between different types of 'networks'. The term has been used widely, often confusingly, to describe virtually all intra- and inter-firm forms of collaboration. The network concept has been applied to focused technological partnerships among large firms (Mody, 1989; Hagedoorn, 1990) and the close technological user-producer linkages identified by Lundvall (1988). In addition, it has been used to analyze Japanese intra-firm *keiretsu* (societies of businesses) organizational structures and methods (Imai and Baba, 1989; Aoki, 1986, 1988). Sometimes the term has been applied to the regional clusters of firms identified by Porter (1990). These organizational forms differ substantially in terms of structure, duration, aims and motivations.

To avoid further confusion, this paper limits itself to the 'dynamic network' identified by Miles and Snow (1986). However, the idea that 'new', more efficient, flexible, industrial forms now exist has been put forward by a variety of other well-known writers on organizational theory and management (e.g. Piore and Sabel, 1984; Peters, 1987; Handy, 1989).

This chapter contends that the Silicon Valley dynamic network is not a viable production form at all, but a specialized system of innovation. While useful for generating new product innovations and carrying out specialist technical tasks, the network cannot capture the rewards from its innovations. The network lacks what Teece (1986) calls 'complementary assets' – the large-scale production, marketing, distribution and financial resources necessary for exploiting mass market innovations. These are usually embodied in very large 'Chandlerian' firms.[1] This explains why the US lost market share to Japan during the 1980s, despite the 'boom' in Silicon Valley.

While Silicon Valley functions well as an innovation network, many of the rewards for its innovations in the past have been transferred across national boundaries to *keiretsu*. However, in 1991, after several years of relative decline, the US regained its lead over Japan. This led many industry observers to speak of a US revival not only in chips but in electronics in general (e.g *Fortune*, 22 March 1993; *Business Week*, 11 January 1993; *Financial Times*, 9 February 1993). The conclusion suggests that recent events have more to do with the resurgence of large American corporations, such as Intel, Motorola and AMD, than networks. Whether or not the US will maintain its new found lead over Japan will depend on the prowess of its Chandlerian corporations, rather than on Silicon Valley and its network of innovators.

Networks and Silicon Valley

The network idea encompasses many organizational forms, motives, objectives and durations. Many network arrangements (e.g. research consortia, user-producer links and joint ventures) are not new. However, during the 1980s networks do appear to have increased in importance, incidence and variety.

A radically new version of the network is the idea of the dynamic network, first put forward by Miles and Snow (1986) and later used to describe the Silicon Valley region (Saxenian 1990a; 1990b; Angel 1990). The dynamic network is a vision of a new industrial form substantially different from previous forms. The argument goes as follows: Best practice organizational form evolved from the owner-manager of the 18th and early 19th centuries, to the vertical organization of the mid-19th century. During the mid-20th century divisionalized and matrix organizations emerged, suited to the mass production of industrial goods. Finally, it is held that the dynamic network became the suitable form for high technology production.

Its proponents argue that the dynamic network constitutes a break from the past. In contrast with 'conventional wisdom' on industrial efficiency and competitiveness (e.g. Chandler 1990; Porter 1990), corporate scale and size is often a positive disadvantage in the marketplace. Large corporations can lead to bureaucratic inertia, the stifling of innovation, risk averse behaviour and poor response to customer needs (Gilder, 1988; Peters, 1987; Handy, 1989).

It is held that large and small firms work in collaboration in the network, responding rapidly to fast-changing market needs, pooling resources, and coping with uncertainty and risk. Compared with the large vertically integrated firm, dynamic networks are vertically disaggregated industrial structures. Key business functions, including product design, R&D, manufacturing and distribution are performed by independent firms cooperating together. In Miles and Snow's version (1986), 'brokers' link partners, providing information to network members and coordinating overall operations. We are told that networks benefit from low levels of bureaucracy and flat pyramid structures.

Economically, the network allows firms to exploit their distinctive competences – so it is argued. It displays the technological specialization of the functional structure, the market responsiveness of the divisional structure and the balanced organizational characteristics of the matrix. The result, it is claimed, enables tasks to be carried out with low investment overheads when compared with the vertically integrated organizational hierarchy. The changing network is held together by market mechanisms through contracts for services and payments for results.

According to Miles and Snow (1986, p. 64) many US companies adopted this organizational mode during the 1980s, leading the economy onto the verge of a new breakthrough in organizational form. Examples of dynamic networks range from Nike athletics shoes, to software, bicycles, toys and semiconductors (*Business Week*, 3 March 1986). In many respects the dynamic network corresponds to the idea of flexible specialization first put forward by Piore and Sabel (1984). They argue that underlying a new flexible organizational form are 'common principles of organisation – principles that constitute a viable alternative to the survival strategies of the mass producers' (Piore and Sabel 1984, p. 195).

One of the strongest empirical sources of support for a new industrial form arises from case studies of Silicon Valley and high technology industry in Southern California (Saxenian, 1990a, 1990b; Angel, 1989; Scott, 1991). Saxenian (1990a) shows how chip firms collaborate with each other and downstream computer producers. As chip technology became more complex during the 1980s, more specialist activities began to be undertaken jointly by networked firms working on chip design, capital goods' development, test automation and new materials.

During the 1980s Silicon Valley underwent a boom. More than eighty-five new start-up firms entered the industry and the network model emerged. Within Silicon Valley some 25,000 jobs were created (Saxenian, 1990a). Many new linkages were forged between chip makers and electronics systems companies.

According to the above authors, Silicon Valley firms pioneered the new flexible model of production. Firms such as Mips Computer System and Cypress developed state-of-the-art RISC-based microprocessors and computer systems with computer makers including Sun, Hewlett-Packard and Apple. Often directors of the small firms originated from within the larger US chip companies. The larger firms became rigid and inflexible and, we are told, 'saw little need for the ongoing interaction with customers, suppliers, and competitors which had characterised specialty production' (Saxenian, 1990).

Despite the growth in Silicon Valley, US chip firms lost considerable ground to Japanese firms during the 1980s. In 1986, Japan overtook the US in traded semiconductors, a key indicator of competitive strength. From controlling around 80 per cent of traded chip sales in the early 1970s, by 1990 the US accounted for only 34 per cent of sales, compared with 46 per cent for Japan (Dataquest, cited in *Business Week*, 5 February 1990, p.37). During the 1980s, Japanese firms including NEC, Toshiba and Hitachi took leading positions in the industry. In 1989, Japanese chip firms occupied four of the top five positions worldwide (Dataquest, cited in *Electronic Business*, 16 April 1990). In dynamic random access memories (DRAMs) by 1989 four of the five market leaders were Japanese and one Korean. The US semiconductor equipment industry also suffered a deterioration in relation to Japan.[2]

Recently, US firms have staged a resurgence in semiconductors and related equipment. In 1992 American firms gained a larger share of the traded chip market than Japan. Intel of the US became the largest chip producer, overtaking NEC of Japan. Many industry observers have taken this as evidence that US restructuring has promoted competitiveness and that the US will maintain its lead over Japan in chips and other areas of electronics. It is sometimes said that Japanese firms now suffer from the industrial inertia which US firms previously suffered from.[3] While the merits of these arguments cannot be dealt with in detail in this chapter, the conclusion argues that US gains are the result of the new strategies of the large American corporations, rather than networks, as noted in the introduction. Whether or not the US will maintain its new-found lead will depend on its Chandlerian corporations, rather than on Silicon Valley innovators.

At least two important 'network' questions are relevant to this chapter. First, why did US industry perform so poorly during the 1980s, despite a booming dynamic network in Silicon Valley? Second, how does Silicon Valley contribute to the overall competitive position of US industry in semiconductors? To help answer these questions the next section provides a framework for understanding the limits of Silicon Valley.

Product Life Cycles and Technology Networks

Some evolutionary theories of technical change have related product life cycles (PLCs) to likely configurations of product and process technologies.

Utterback and Abernathy (1975) and Abernathy et al. (1983) argue that at the early stage of a new product, the rate of innovation is high, stimulated by changing market needs. Product markets are ill-defined and products non-standard. Process technology will be relatively uncoordinated and user-supplier relations critical. As the product is adopted, a dominant design is selected by the market, sales increase and market uncertainty diminishes. Eventually, a mass-produced product will reach a stage where competition is based on price and cost minimization, driven by incremental process improvements.

PLC theory says little about how firms might secure the rewards from innovation. To do this, firms must have access to the complementary assets needed to exploit the technology in the marketplace. As Teece (1986) points out, firms and developers of intellectual property often fail to obtain significant economic returns from their innovations. Customers, imitators and other industry participants frequently reap most of the rewards. Teece argues that innovators may be so badly positioned in the market that they will *necessarily* fail to gain the profits.

Although applied to the firm, Teece's analysis has direct relevance to rewards accruing to the dynamic network and to the national economy. To exploit a new product in large volume, the technology embodied in the innovation must be combined with complementary assets. These include large-scale marketing and distribution channels, competitive manufacturing facilities, after-sales support and specialist interconnected technologies. Very large-scale financial resources should also be added to Teece's list of complementary assets. In global markets such as semiconductors, complementary assets need to be applied quickly to bring the innovation to the market place in sufficient quantity and at an acceptable price.

Complementary assets are relatively unimportant during the early, low volume stage of a new design. Later on, when output increases, complementary assets become of overriding importance to competitive advantage. To explain the implications of complementary assets for the dynamic network, Table 11.1 puts forward a simple, three-stage PLC scheme.[4] During Stage 1 uncertainty and poor information act as barriers to the acceptance of the product – even if the innovation has superior features. During this slow adoption phase, firms engage in pre-investment learning, with innovation suppliers working closely with early adoptors. Information on capital costs, market prices and potential demand will be sparse and unreliable.

The market acts as a selection mechanism, adopting some innovations, rejecting others. Demand interacts closely with technology supply in order to select the most suitable chip innovations. Complementary assets may not yet be critical to competition. Suppliers compete by developing useful new designs for users. Production volumes tend to be low; prices are inelastic and less important than functionality.

Table 11.1 Stages of the semiconductor PLC and the network*

	Stage 1	Stage 2	Stage 3
Diffusion Stage	Selection Introduction Slow adoption Multiple niches	Imitation Rapid take-off Niche growth	Maturity Saturation Expansion Mass market
Investment Focus	Product innovation Pre-production	Capital goods Process technology Heavy investment	Incremental process/product Cost minimization Scale/scope economies
Complementary Assets	Least critical Technology-based	Growing importance Financial Marketing	Critical Global marketing and management
Organizational Form	Small firms Networks Large firms	Large firms High growth firms	Very large firms (e.g. *Keiretsu*) Vertical/horizontal integration
Learning	Pre-investment Trial and error Uncertain	Imitative Cumulative	Predictable Incremental
User-producer Linkages	Intense Changing Product design	Systematic Process focus Capital goods	Formalized Predictable Less critical

Note: *These stages roughly correspond to the first three stages of the semiconductor PLC scheme described below.

At this stage, the network form may offer advantages to suppliers and users. It is suited to rapid trial and error learning, prototype development and coping with uncertainty and risk. The network provides a focus for technology accumulation, collective learning, rapid skill deployment and risk sharing. The flow of key individuals between firms supplies the network with vital skills and information.

Long before the network writers of the 1980s, research carried out by Hall (1959), Lichtenberg (1960) and Vernon (1960) on agglomerations of industry in the New York region showed that with new products, producers are confronted with critical choices concerning the non-standard nature of the product and its processes, the need to change inputs rapidly, as well as the need for swift and effective communications. By locating closely together, firms in sectors such as apparel, printing and electronics benefited from external economies and from overcoming uncertainty:

> Rubbing elbows with others of their kind and with ancillary firms that exist to serve them, they can satisfy their variable wants by drawing upon common pools of space, labor, materials, and services. In more concise language, they can take advantage of external economies (Hall, 1959).

These externalities are among those frequently cited by modern network theorists. However, such factors are clearly not new to industrial development.

During the Stage 2 take-off the emphasis shifts to setting up capital goods and the expansion of production capacity. Selected innovations are adopted and used. There may be a shift away from intense producer-user collaboration as suppliers organize production facilities to meet the growing demand from customers. Some firms may emerge as market leaders in growing niche markets. These firms will grow rapidly and compete not only on the basis of design excellence but also on cost, manufacturing capability and market price. High rates of profit may attract large firms from related industries. New entrants will enter the industry via reverse engineering, improving and adapting the innovation and attracting key individuals from the market leaders.

Complementary assets become increasingly important in Stage 2. Volumes of output increase, scale economies come into play, costs per unit fall and price becomes a key competitive factor. Leading firms invest heavily in mass production capabilities and acquire any specialized technological assets required for volume manufacture. Non-technology complementary assets are needed to finance, manufacture, market and distribute the innovation. Fast movers benefit from their lead in building up core in-house technological and marketing competences.

During Stage 3 and the latter part of Stage 2 the main rewards from innovation are generated. Sales increase internationally and the product becomes a commodity item of very large scale and revenue. Demand becomes relatively predictable and new generations of the product can be planned for with a fair degree of certainty. Learning shifts away from user-producer interaction to product design enhancement and traditional production learning curves. Incremental process improvements become the key to cost minimization.

Complementary assets become of paramount importance during Stage 3. Firms compete on the basis of cost, price, mass production capabilities as well as global marketing and distribution channels. At this mature phase, leading firms rely less on the network and small firms. Incremental process and product innovations are achieved through in-house experience and accumulated competences. In order to gain the maximum rewards from innovation, firms must ensure that they assimilate sufficient in-house capability to bring new generations of the product to the market on a regular basis.

During Stage 3, Chandlerian firms with strong complementary assets from related industries may acquire the core technology and enter the market. For instance, the large *chaebol* in Korea successfully entered the volume DRAM market despite their lack of semiconductor experience. At Stage 3 the disadvantages of the network are the most obvious. Market leaders cannot afford the risk of distributing core activities within a dynamic network. Niche players may confront limits to growth due to their weak financial and marketing resources. Inevitably, only a few new firms are able to address international market niches and grow to become big league players.

From the individual firm's perspective, operating within the network at the early diffusion stage may be very profitable. However, at the national economic level, the network alone cannot realize the majority of the rewards from its innovations. Large innovating firms must be located within the economy. During the 1980s, in semiconductors, these firms were increasingly located in Japan. As the next section shows, the large Japanese *keiretsu* out-invested US firms, both in terms of R&D and capacity expansion in the growth phase of successive PLCs, thereby gaining the rewards from US innovations.

Semiconductor Technology and the Rewards from Innovation

Almost all mainstream semiconductor devices (such as DRAMs) began life as specialized, design-intensive products, often pioneered by small US firms in Silicon Valley. The four kilobit programmable read only memory (PROM) was one among many specialist memory devices pioneered by Intel, then a small firm. This was followed by further generations of PROMs and electrically erasable PROMs (EEPROMs). The first microprocessor (MPU) was introduced in 1971 for use in calculators. During the 1970s the MPU underwent a succession of incremental improvements and design enhancements. Between 1971 and 1981, twenty-two chip manufacturers introduced some 203 separate MPUs based on Intel's original device including sixty-nine original designs and 134 second sourced products (Swann, 1985).

With each new product design, sales increased substantially. Each new vintage required very large further investments in research, development and design. Life cycles were often extremely short. For instance, the 16K DRAM took off in the late 1970s and reached the decline stage by 1984. In 1981–82 the 64K DRAM took off and reached its peak in the boom of 1984–85. By 1986–87 sales of the 256K DRAM had overtaken the 64K DRAM. Only large US and Japanese firms with strong complementary assets were able to profit from second, third and fourth generation mass market products.

Individual products follow distinctive patterns of diffusion. The process of acceptance is neither automatic nor predictable and the industry is notorious for underestimating the time it takes for users to accept new products. Sometimes the introductory phase can be extremely long, as in the case of the gate array, a semicustomized chip. An early version of the gate array (the uncommitted logic array) was pioneered during the early 1970s by the British firm Ferranti. Later, US firms developed new versions of the product. Although experimental niche markets developed during the 1970s, only in the late-1980s did the gate array become a mass market product. By this time Japanese firms gained a majority share of the world market. Despite the strong US design performance, Japanese firms' complementary assets enabled them to secure the rewards from innovation.

A large proportion of chip revenues and profits accrue during the growth and maturity stages of the PLC, rather than the introduction stage. This is because output volumes increase substantially and shortages tend to force up prices during the upswing of each industry cycle. According to the consultancy firm ICE (McClean, 1987) the introduction stage accounts for around 7 per cent of total revenues. The vast majority of revenues (roughly 70 per cent) is generated during the growth and maturity stages.

Large firms tend to dominate the growth and maturity stages of semiconductor PLCs. Oligopolistic rivalry forces large firms to invest in production capacity, often ahead of demand. Complementary assets assume critical importance to competitive success. Economies of scale reduce the cost per unit of output. Economies of scope enable some high performance market niches to be serviced by the same large volume fabrication lines used for standard products.[5]

In the case of new versions of existing products, large firms often dominate the introduction stage as well as the growth and maturity stages (e.g. the 256K and 1 megabit DRAM). In these cases, the revenues and profits accrue almost entirely to the large firms which have built up effective marketing channels, product processes and experienced design teams.

Huge windfall profits can be made during market upswings (e.g. 1984 and 1988) when demand outstrips capacity and prices are forced upwards. During these periods of shortage, the agile and well-positioned large firm stands to reap the rewards from innovation. For instance, Toshiba (of Japan) invested ahead of most US and other Japanese firms in 1 megabit DRAMs. Due to shortages in 1988, profit margins on this device reached an estimated 300 per cent to 400 per cent (*Financial Times*, 25 July 1988). Rising overall chip demand enabled Toshiba to raise roughly one half of its overall corporate profits from its chip division in the first half of 1988. Prices of 1 megabit DRAMs rose to around ¥2,000 (roughly £9.00) each while production costs were in the region of ¥500 (£2.25) each (*Financial Times*, 10 May 1988). Toshiba's heavy forward investment planning enabled the company to capture more than one third of the world's demand for the 1 megabit DRAM during the first quarter of 1988 (ibid). Other large Japanese firms consistently out-invested US firms during the 1980s.[6]

The well-positioned large firm can quickly gain market share as new design-intensive products (e.g. application specific integrated circuits, ASICs) are transformed into mass-market products. Despite the importance of Silicon Valley small firms to ASIC innovations, their market share turned out to be small when the products took off in the late 1980s. In 1988, for instance, more than 62 per cent of ASIC sales were supplied by the ten market leaders (compared with 57 per cent for the total chip business worldwide) (ICE data, cited in *Electronic Times*, 8 June 1989, p. 2). Industrial concentration in the ASIC supply business was actually more intense than in the chip market overall. Large companies invested to gain ASIC market share, leaving small firms to niche, design-intensive markets. By 1988 the Japanese *keiretsu* accounted for almost half of the ASIC sales of the ten largest world suppliers (ICE data cited in *Electronic Times*, 8 June 1989, p. 2).

The semiconductor industry appears to follow an unusual pattern of rapid innovation along fairly predictable lines. This is in contrast with, say, automobiles where technological stability lasted for decades before product 'de-maturity' occurred (Abernathy et al., 1983). The life cycles of major new products such as the 256 kilobit DRAM are extremely short, with the introduction, growth and maturity stages lasting as little as four or five years. As yet, the chip industry has not reached a position where long-run, established technological trajectories define the boundaries of competition. Indeed, the fact that the industry overall refuses to mature is one of its major distinguishing features.

The rapid pace of innovation in chips has led some observers to argue, incorrectly, that small firms and networks are a more appropriate production form than large vertically integrated firms (Saxenian 1990a; Gilder 1988). The shortening of PLCs and their increasing capital intensity means that firms have to constantly *increase* their financial commitment to the technology base to accelerate the relevant intra-firm learning. The next generation of wafer fabrication plants will cost an estimated $800 million to $1 billion per factory (*Financial Times*, 9 February 1992). Firms have to repeat these massive process investments every three to four years, often under conditions of extreme market uncertainty. Therefore large firms are the appropriate organizational form except in small, niche markets.

The Silicon Valley network will continue to play a valuable innovation role in support of the large firms within and outside the US. However, large firms are likely to limit their involvements in multi-firm innovation networks for three sets of reasons. First, large firms will need to build up competences in-house to exploit economies of scale to reduce unit costs, as per Chandler (1990). Equally, large firms will seek to gain economies of scope by utilizing many of the same raw material inputs and production processes to make a variety of different chips. Firms which lead investment in product-specific capabilities stand to gain first mover advantages. For the economic reasons of scale and scope large firms can be expected to severely restrict their participation in shared networks.

Second, there are compelling technological reasons for the large firm to protect and nurture core competences within the firms' boundaries. As Pavitt argues in Chapter 29, successful firms rely on the accumulation of in-house assets and capabilities. Knowhow is often firm-specific, tacit and embodied in human beings as opposed to capital equipment or computers. Large-scale technology assets (e.g. megafab lines and DRAM design teams) are highly firm-specific, involving continuous, extensive interaction among functionally specialized groups within the firm. In turn, this requires fairly stable employment relations and intra-firm mobility among workers.[7] By contrast, the high employment turnover in the dynamic network mitigates against long-term human capital development. While the network system may be suited to fast innovation, it is unsuitable for building corporate competences over the long term.

Third, technological and complementary capabilities are the key assets which determine competitive advantage in the marketplace. Therefore, for strategic reasons, companies will seek to retain these core capabilities within the boundaries of the firm in order to maintain their competitive edge.

Large firms can gain advantage from network collaborations at the early phase of the PLC and in specialist and experimental niche markets. They will also continue to collaborate with other large firms in strategic partnerships to exchange technology either for market access or capital (Steinmueller, 1988). However, as noted earlier, strategic partnerships are a focused form of collaboration, quite distinct from the dynamic network. The distribution of core competences within a multi-firm dynamic network would expose a large firm to predatory behaviour on the part of other large firms. It could also diffuse the rewards from accumulated investments in core assets. Therefore, as an organizational form the dynamic network is severely limited within the competitive dynamics of the chip industry.

Conclusion

When discussing industrial collaboration it is vital to distinguish between the many different types of network. The 1980s witnessed an increase in inter-corporate technology agreements, R&D consortia and new small-large firm relationships. Intra-corporate *keiretsu* networks also received a great deal of attention. Given the wide variety of organizational forms bundled together under 'network', left unqualified, the concept is devoid of any analytical significance.

Rather than a new form of flexible production, the dynamic network in Silicon Valley is an innovation network best suited to the early stage of the product cycle. The network is useful for carrying out specialist technical activities and for supplying high technology niche markets, but it cannot meet the needs of large markets. Also, the growth of this type of network is no reason for assuming that 'the United States is on the verge of another breakthrough in organisational form' (Miles and Snow, 1986). Indeed, earlier research by Vernon (1960) and others, shows that firms often locate closely together to gain the benefits of shared resources and information.

Most importantly, small firms in the network and the network as a whole lack the complementary assets needed to exploit new mass-market innovations. Like the badly positioned first-mover firms (Teece, 1986), the network cannot realize the rewards from its innovations. Instead, large integrated Chandlerian firms gain the majority of the profits from the network's innovations. This explains why large Japanese firms gained market share during the 1980s, despite the thriving innovation network in Silicon Valley.

Large firms are unlikely to distribute their core capabilities within a network for economic, technological and strategic reasons. To do so would expose them to predatory behaviour from other large firms and risk their long-term investments in human and physical capital. Where large firms do participate in dynamic networks, the boundaries of its participation are likely to end where its core assets and advantages begin.

In the case of semiconductors, American industry has recently regained its position as world leader. Increasing demand for American computers, and the proprietary US chips used in them, has enabled US firms to regain the lead over Japan. In 1992, for the first time in six years, the US invested more than Japan in plant and equipment. The Chandlerian corporations of the US – Intel, AMD, Texas Instruments, National Semiconductor and Motorola – all embarked upon large investment projects. In 1993 the US chip industry will spend an estimated $5.2 billion on plant and equipment, compared with $4.6bn for Japan (VLSI Research, cited in *Business Week*, 11 January 1993, p. 50). The market reversal is also due to the price reductions in DRAMs caused by over-investment by Japanese and Korean firms (*Fortune*, 22 March 1993 p. 20). Continued US leadership will depend principally on the capabilities of its large firms, rather than on the Silicon Valley network.

One cannot generalize from the case of semiconductors to other sectors. However, the sources of disadvantage of the network may well apply to other global industries. Where competitiveness depends on cumulative long-term financial investments, process technology and global marketing, the dynamic network form is likely to be inferior to the large integrated firm.

This includes large segments of the computer, consumer electronics, chemicals, automobiles, steel and telecommunication industries. While the dynamic network may have some merits, there is little hope of its forming the basis of success in semiconductors or many other large-scale global industries.

Notes

1. Although large firms engage in strategic partnerships they are highly unlikely to distribute their core assets in a dynamic network for the economic, technological and strategic reasons discussed below. Strategic partnerships are quite different from the dynamic network arrangement. This underlines the need to carefully distinguish between the different 'network' types. See Hamel et al. (1986) for an analysis of strategic partnerships.
2. The reasons for the US decline and Japanese success are varied and controversial. See, for example, Ferguson (1988), Borrus (1988), Prestowitz (1988), NACS (1989), Dertouzos et al. (1989) and Langlois et al. (1988).
3. For example, see the special survey on Japan in *Fortune* (22 March 1993). See also *Electronics* (April, 1992) for US gains in semiconductor equipment production, and *International Business Week* (11 January 1993) and *Financial Times* (9 February 1992) for analyses of the chip industry.
4. Although most PLCs include a fourth, decline stage, for simplicity this is not included here. For PLC evidence see Kotler (1976) and Utterback and Abernathy (1975). As Kotler (1976) points out, PLC theory is based upon research into the diffusion of innovations. One of the major findings in fields such as microeconomics, sociology, education and public health is the S-curve (or 'sigmoid') curve by which many successful innovations diffuse (e.g. Rogers 1962; Rogers and Shoemaker 1971; Griliches 1957; Mansfield 1961). PLCs can be seen as a sub-set of diffusion analysis, dealing with industrial products. PLCs usually follow a normal, bell-shaped curve when frequency of adoption is plotted over time. If cumulative adoption is plotted over time the result is the standard S-shaped diffusion curve.
5. Other economies of scope are also gained. These include common material inputs, shared computer design facilities and shared management, planning, marketing and distribution channels. See Chandler (1990) for the importance of large-firm scale and scope economies in a wide range of industries.
6. For detailed comparisons of capital and R&D expenditures of US and Japanese chip companies through from 1976 to 1986 see Ferguson (1988). For details of the huge industrial scale of the six major Japanese *keiretsu* (societies of businesses) which supply chips and other electronics, see Ferguson (1990) and Anchordoguy (1990).
7. Aoki (1986) and Fransman in this volume discuss how Japanese firms benefit from employment stability; large US firms such as IBM and Hewlett-Packard also gain the advantages of stable intra-firm labour markets.

Bibliography

Abernathy, W.J., Clark, K.B. and Kantrow, A.M. (1983) *Industrial Renaissance: Producing a Competitive Future for America*, Basic Books, New York.
Anchordoguy, M. (1990) 'A Brief History of Japan's Keiretsu', in Ferguson, C.H. 'Computers and the Coming of the US Keiretsu' *Harvard Business Review*, July–August, pp. 55–70.
Angel, D.P. (1989) 'The Labour Market for Engineers in the US Semiconductor Industry',

Economic Geography, Vol. 65, No. 2, April, pp. 99–114.

Angel, D.P. (1990) 'New Firm Foundation in the Semiconductor Industry: Elements of a Flexible Manufacturing System', *Regional Studies*, Vol. 24, No. 3, p.211.

Aoki, M. (1986) 'Horizontal vs. Vertical Information Structure of the Firm', *American Economic Review*, Vol. 76, December, pp. 971–83.

Aoki, M. (1988) *Information, Incentives, and Bargaining in the Japanese Economy*, Cambridge University Press, Cambridge.

Borrus, M.G. (1988) *Competing for Control: America's Stake in Microelectronics*, Ballinger, Cambridge Massachusetts.

Chandler, A.D. (1990) *Scale and Scope: the Dynamics of Industrial Capitalism*, Belknap Press, Cambridge Massachusetts.

Dertouzos, M.L., Lester, R.K. and Solow, R.M. (1989) *Made in America: Regaining the Productive Edge*, MIT Press, Cambridge Massachusetts.

Ferguson, C.H. (1988) 'From the People who Brought You Voodoo Economics: Beyond Entrepreneuralism to U.S. Competitiveness', *Harvard Business Review*, May–June, pp. 55–62.

Ferguson, C.H. (1990) 'Computers and the Coming of the US Keiretsu', *Harvard Business Review*, July–August, pp. 55–70.

Gilder, G. (1988) 'The Revitalisation of Everything: the Law of the Microcosm', *Harvard Business Review*, March–April, pp. 49–61.

Griliches, Z. (1957) 'Hybrid Corn: an Exploration in the Economics of Technological Change', *Econometrica*, Vol. 4, No. 4, pp. 278–86.

Hagedoorn, J. (1990) 'Organisational Modes of Inter-firm Cooperation and Technology Transfer', *Technovation*, Vol. 10, No. 1, pp. 17–30.

Hall, M. (ed.) (1959) *Made in New York: Case Studies in Metropolitan Manufacturing*, Harvard University Press, Cambridge, Massachusetts.

Hamel, G., Doz, Y. and Prahalad, C.K. (1986) *Strategic Partnerships: Success or Surrender? The Challenge of Competitive Collaboration*, Working Paper Series, No. 24, Centre for Business Strategy, London Business School.

Handy, C. (1989) *The Age of Unreason*, Business Books, London.

Imai, K.I. and Baba, Y. (1989) *Systemic Innovation and Cross-Border Networks: Transcending Markets and Hierarchies to Create a New Techno-Economic System*, paper prepared for the International Seminar on the Contributions of Science and Technology to Economic Growth at the Organisation for Economic Cooperation and Development, Paris, June.

Kotler, S. (1976) *Marketing Management: Analysis, Planning and Control*, third ed. Prentice Hall International, London.

Langlois, R.N., Pugel, T.A., Hacklisch, C.S., Nelson, R.N. and Egelhoff W.G. (1988) *Microelectronics: An Industry in Transition*, Unwin Hyman, Boston.

Lichtenberg, R.M. (1960) *One-Tenth of a Nation: National Forces in the Economic Growth of the New York Region*, Harvard University Press, Cambridge Massachusetts.

Lundvall, B. (1988) 'Innovation as an Interactive Process: from User-Producer Interaction to the National System of Innovation' in Dosi, G., Freeman, C., Nelson, R., Silverberg, G. and Soete, L. (eds), *Technical Change and Economic Theory*, Frances Pinter, London.

Mansfield, E. (1961) 'Technical Change and the Rate of Imitation', *Econometrica*, Vol. 29, No. 4, pp. 741–66.

McClean, W.J. (1987) *Status 1987: a Report on the Integrated Circuit Industry*, Integrated Circuit Engineering Corporation (ICE), Scottsdale, Arizona.

Miles, R.E. and Snow, C.C. (1986) 'Organisations: New Concepts for New Forms',

California Management Review, Volume XXVIII No. 3, Spring.

Mody, A. (1989) *Changing Firm Boundaries: Analysis of Technology-Sharing Agreements*, Industry and Energy Department Working Paper, Industry Series Paper No. 3, The World Bank Industry and Energy Department, PPR.

NACS (1989) *Semiconductors: a Strategic Industry at Risk*, a Report to the President and the Congress from the National Advisory Committee on Semiconductors, Arlington, Virginia.

Peters, T.J. (1987) *Thriving on Chaos: Handbook for a Management Revolution*, Knopf, New York.

Piore, M.J. and Sabel, C.F. (1984) *The Second Industrial Divide*, Basic Books, New York.

Porter, M. (1990) *The Competitive Advantage of Nations*, Macmillan, London.

Prestowitz, C.V. (1988) *Trading Places: How We Allowed Japan to Take the Lead*, Basic Books, New York.

Rogers, E.M. (1962) *Diffusion of Innovations*, Free Press, Ontario.

Rogers, E.M. and Shoemaker, F.F. (1971) *Communication of Innovations: A Cross-Cultural Approach*, Free Press, New York.

Saxenian, A. (1990a) 'Regional Networks and the Resurgence of Silicon Valley', *Californian Management Review*, Fall, pp. 89–112.

Saxenian, A. (1990b) *The Origins and Dynamics of Production Networks in Silicon Valley*, Working Paper 516, Institute of Urban and Regional Development, University of California at Berkeley.

Scott, A.J. (1991) *The Technopoles of Southern California*, UCLA Research Papers in Economic and Urban Geography, No. 1, University of California, Los Angeles.

Steinmueller, W.E. (1988) 'International Joint Ventures in the Integrated Circuit Industry' in Mowery, D.C. (ed.) *International Collaborative Ventures in US Manufacturing*, Ballinger, Cambridge Massachusetts

Swann, G.M.P. (1985) 'Product Competition in Microprocessors', *The Journal of Industrial Economics*, Volume XXXIV, September 1985.

Teece, D.J. (1986) 'Profiting From Technological Innovation: Implications for Integration, Collaboration, Licensing and Public Policy', *Research Policy*, 15, pp. 285–305.

Utterback, J.M. and Abernathy, W.J. (1975) 'A Dynamic Model of Process and Product Innovation', *OMEGA*, Vol. 3, No. 6, pp. 639–56.

Vernon, R. (1960) *Metropolis, 1985: An Interpretation of the Findings of the New York Metropolitan Region Study*, Harvard University Press, Cambridge, Massachusetts.

12. Innovation in the Chemicals Industry

Margaret Sharp

The chemicals industry is a large and heterogeneous industry, notoriously difficult to define. The definition adopted in this study is a broad one, derived from its scientific base – the understanding and manipulation of molecules. It comprehends at one extreme the low value-added bulk chemicals in the organic and inorganic sectors, and at the other the speciality products such as dyes and paints, food additives and photography, as well as the production of highly sophisticated chemicals used as ingredients for pharmaceuticals and agrochemicals, requiring many manufacturing steps and selling for thousands of dollars a gramme.

The chemicals industry is often referred to as the first science-based industry. The development of inorganic chemicals – sulphuric acid and soda lime used for making bleach – was closely tied to the textile industry, but its methods were, like much else in the Industrial Revolution in Britain, the product of astute minds and tinkering technology. Although it was a British researcher, Perkin, who made the chance discovery in 1856 of aniline dyes – which marked the beginnings of organic chemistry – it was to be in Germany (where chemistry had been recognized as a subject for study at universities since the 1830s), and in the United States, that the major discoveries in organic chemistry were made: first the coal tar derivatives, and then, from the mid-1920s onwards, the important developments in petrochemicals. The fast pace of change between 1840 and 1960 is strikingly illustrated by Figure 12.1. (For a good general account of developments in industrial chemistry see Duncan (1982) and Brock (1992) chapter 16.)

Organic Chemicals and the Large Chemical Conglomerates

Organic chemicals are those obtained from coal, oil, gas, vegetable or animal products. Since the Second World War this sector of the industry has been dominated by petrochemicals and the whole range of new products – plastics, artificial fibres, detergents, etc. – which have been developed from oil and gas as feedstocks.

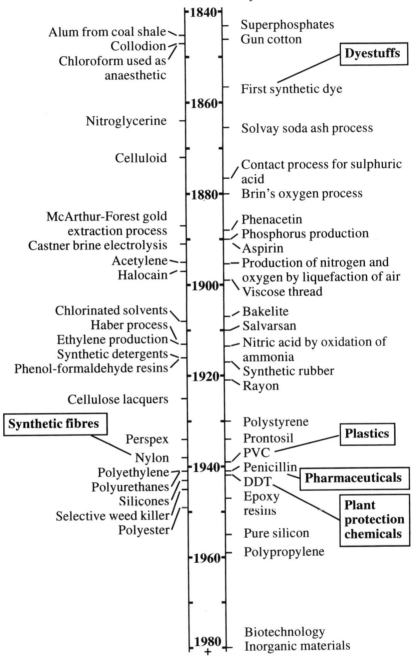

Figure 12.1 Major chemical innovations 1840–1960
Source: Duncan, 1982.

The production processes in the petrochemicals sector are complex and interlinked. Figure 12.2 illustrates the pathways from the basic feedstocks – natural gas and crude oil – through intermediate to final products. This shows very clearly how the three major intermediates – ethylene, propylene and benzene – each fosters a family of products downstream. It also illustrates how the chemicals industry is its own best customer – the upstream sector of the industry feeds the downstream sector – and, in turn, why there is much interdependence with many vertical and horizontal linkages.

The major breakthroughs in hydrocarbon chemistry were made in the 1920s and 1930s. Following on from basic research on macro-molecular

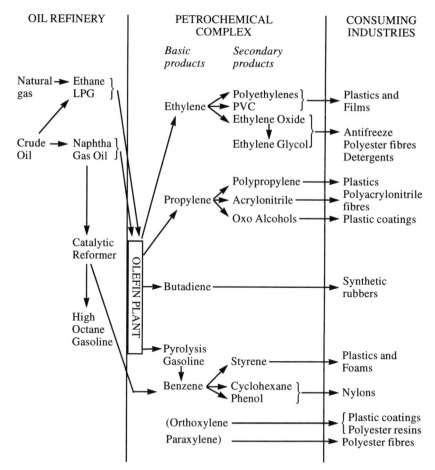

Figure 12.2 Petrochemicals: the production pathway from basic feedstock to final product
Source: OECD, 1979, xxvii.

structures, innovations came thick and fast: polystyrene, perspex, PVC, polyethylene, synthetic rubbers and nylon and all the artificial fibres. It is notable that all the major innovations were developed in the laboratories of large chemicals companies, and that most of the companies responsible for them still exist today. IG Farben (which was broken up after 1945 into Bayer, Hoechst and BASF), ICI and Du Pont were the most influential, but Union Carbide, Shell, Standard Oil and Dow all made major contributions.

Table 12.1 lists the major companies by sales and R&D expenditures. The continuing dominance of these large firms is largely explained by developments in technology. Product development is in general followed by process development, which may be based upon some significant innovation, but mainly takes the form of incremental change stemming from learning and experience in the application of new technologies. Over time there has been a very great increase in capital intensity and in the importance of economies of scale. This in turn has limited entry in the upstream sector of the industry where the only major entrants were the oil refiners who had ample funds and privileged access to feedstocks (gas and oil).

Table 12.1 Principal chemical manufacturers by sales and R&D, 1991

	Sales	R&D	R&D as % sales
Hoechst	31147	1894	6.1
BASF	30778	1362	4.4
Bayer	27989	1985	7.1
ICI	23346	1294	5.5
Dow	18807	1159	6.2
Rhône Poulenc	18111	1107	6.1
Du Pont	17941	948	5.3
Ciba-Geigy	15538	1611	10.3
Elf Acquitaine*	14035	607	4.3
Enichem	11699	356	3.0
Shell	11208	366	3.3
Sandoz	9922	979	9.9
Akzo	9871	525	5.3
Exxon	9171	185	2.0
Mitsubishi Kasei	9161	402	4.3

*Includes Sanofi
Source: *Chemical Insight,* September 1992.

NB: Montedison (which does not appear in this table because of its divesting itself of bulk chemicals and fertilisers to Enimont in 1990) spent 2.7 per cent of turnover on R&D in 1988 (OECD, 1992).

The seminal study of the large, in-house corporate R&D laboratory in the chemicals industry is that by Hounsell and Smith (1988) of the development of Du Pont's research laboratories. They describe the ups and downs of the company's early research strategy, and the perennial struggle between the notion of the central research laboratory with freedom to pursue 'blue sky' projects and the decentralized research laboratory, functionally organized and responsible to divisional managers. Nevertheless, the leaders of the company recognized early that the key to success lay with generous support for industrial research through cyclical swings. They thus established a corporate tradition which gave Du Pont such market successes as cellophane, neoprene, nylon, teflon, orlon and dacron – successive generations of products nurtured through the research laboratories and into the market place.

Companies such as Du Pont and its European counterparts played a major role in the development of Schumpeter's ideas on innovation. In his early writings on the subject, entrepreneurship was the key element and the small innovative firm the key player, 'swarming' around new innovations and overwhelming established enterprises in a wave of 'creative destruction' (Schumpeter, 1912). By 1929 the growth of the large monopolistic firm led him to revise his ideas, and he identified the professional in-house R&D laboratory as the key player in the dynamics of innovation (Schumpeter, 1939). He failed, however, to go on to examine the relationship between R&D and other functions within the firm (Freeman, 1982).

Further empirical work has shown that successful innovation requires in-house technical capabilities to be linked to *external* sources of scientific and technological information and ideas, and especially to basic research (National Science Foundation, 1973; Gibbons and Johnston, 1974). Indeed, in-house R&D is seen to be an essential complement to exploiting these external linkages (Freeman et al. 1963). In their classic study, *The Sources of Invention,* Jewkes et al. (1958) argued that the chemical industry was a major exception to their finding that most important new product inventions had come from universities or small firms rather than big firms.

Project Sappho, undertaken at the Science Policy Research Unit (SPRU) in the 1970s attempted to identify the factors which are important for success in innovation (Rothwell et al. 1974; Rothwell, 1985). Some interesting differences emerged between the chemical and other industries. One was the degree to which basic research was carried out within the leading firms in the industry. *Product* innovation came from the in-house laboratories, with the most important external links being with universities and design-engineering contractors. *Process* innovations often required expensive plant as well as laboratory research and were frequently undertaken in-house by specialist designers and chemical engineers, often working in conjunction with outside plant contractors.

Achilladelis et al. (1990), have carried forward the Sappho work to a comprehensive study of the process of innovation in two important subsectors of the industry, pesticides and organic chemical intermediates over the years 1900–1980. Their findings confirmed the importance of in-house expertise as a 'driver' of innovation. They also found that the success of an innovation is linked to previous experience in the field and/or to research at the forefront of the relevant science, which in turn suggests that it is possible to identify 'corporate technology traditions' (Achilladelis et al., 1987) where a company, once established in a particular area, succeeds in introducing a disproportionate number of innovations in that field over a period of anything up to thirty to forty years.

The concept of the corporate technology tradition is recognizable in Du Pont, but also in other firms (see Table 12.2). Success of course breeds success, and traditions get embedded in firms. Such things as the promotion of successful managers involved with an innovation and the competitive spur from being first in the field and defending that position all serve to reinforce an innovative tradition within a company. Achilladelis et al. develop from this a four-stage model of the dynamics of the chemicals industry. In the first stage (effectively covering the period 1930–50 in their research) the industry was characterized by few highly important innovations, low patenting activity and low demand. The second stage (1950 to mid-1960s) is one of rapid growth of innovations, patents and sales as companies rush to take advantage of a proven technology. The third stage is one of maturity, when innovation, patent and sales curves flatten out (mid-1960s to early 1970s), companies cut back on risky research and limit experimentation. The fourth stage is effectively the stage at which the chemical companies currently find themselves. It is characterized by a falling rate of innovation, flat sales and intense competition as surplus capacity and new entrants erode profit margins. Alongside these developments, however, are what the authors describe as 'the first stage of a new cycle' with pharmaceuticals, agrochemicals, electronic chemicals, high performance materials and bio-engineering identified as promising new sectors.

To sum up, innovation in the organics sector of the chemicals industry has been dominated by the large conglomerate chemical company which *in itself* constitutes an important part of the dynamic of the system. The key driver has been the in-house R&D department which, with its antennae tuned to recognize both market and scientific opportunity, has in effect 'colonized' new areas of development, grown in-house the skills with which to exploit them and thus pulled the rest of the firm behind it. It is interesting to consider how far current developments in biotechnology are a continuation of the same dynamic. We shall return to this later in the chapter.

Inorganics, Speciality Chemicals and Contestable Markets

The heterogeneous nature of the industry means that competition in innovation takes place *not only* between large firms of similar size, but also

Table 12.2 Some examples of corporate technological traditions

No	Company	Technological tradition	Radical innovation	Year
1.	American Cyanamid	Aminoplasts	Urea melamine resins	1935
2.	American Cyanamid	Organophosphorus insecticides	Thimet	1956
3.	BASF	Organic chemical intermediates	Ammonia synthesis	1913
4.	BASF	Polystyrene plastics	Polystyrene	1928
5.	BASF	Magnetic recording tapes	First magnetic tape	1935
6.	Bayer	Organophosphorus insecticides	Parathion	1942
7.	Bayer	Synthetic rubber	First synthetic rubber	1910
8.	Bayer	Polyurethane plastics, foams	Polyurethane	1942
9.	B. F. Goodrich	PVC	PVC	1930
10.	Celanese	Synthetic fibers	Cellulose acetate	1924
11.	Celanese	Organic chemical intermediates	Acetic acid	1933
12.	Ciba-Geigy	Insecticides	DDT	1939
13.	Ciba-Geigy	Herbicides	Triazines	1957
14.	Ciba-Geigy	Vat dyestuffs	Ciba violet	1905
15.	Dow	Halogenated hydrocarbons	Chloroform	1903
16.	Dow	Polystyrene	Polystyrene	1932
17.	Dow	Pesticides	Pentachlorophenol	1930
18.	DuPont	Synthetic fibers	Nylon	1936
19.	DuPont	Fungicides	Nabam	1936
20.	ICI	Herbicides	MCPA	1942
21.	ICI	Reactive dyes	Procion dyes	1956
22.	Monsanto	Herbicides	Randox	1955
23.	Montedison	Organic chemical intermediates	Ammonia	1924
24.	Montedison	Polypropylene plastics, fibers	Polypropylene	1954
25.	Rohm & Hass	PMMA-acrylics	Polymethylmethacrylate	1932

Source: Achilladelis et al. 1990.

between firms of many different shapes and sizes and indeed between small firms and the divisions of the large chemical conglomerates. In the long run, given a high rate of innovation, a large number of firms are in potential competition with each other because, through innovation, markets are made contestable both by new substitute products and from lower costs resulting from new or improved processes.

Inorganic Chemicals are a highly mixed group of chemicals ranging from products such as salt and titanium dioxide, which are low value added, bulk commodities, to others which are high value added, low volume products. They are not linked (as are organic chemicals) by a common raw material base, or as by-products or joint products. As a result, firms in the sub-branch can, and often do, produce a limited range of products on a relatively small scale, many exploiting a specific technology related to a particular family of chemicals. Firms such as Bayer, Hoechst and BASF, ICI, Du Pont, Dow, are the industry leaders in inorganic as well as organic chemicals. But in inorganics the production lines are more self-contained, and there are other, medium-sized and smaller firms as competitors to the divisions of the big multinationals. Technical progress has been less dramatic than in the petrochemicals industry. Nevertheless, there has been continuing incremental change in process plant technology and consequential increases in both scale and capital intensity.

The speciality sector includes such areas as dyes and paints, and specialist products for industries ranging from food manufacturing to textiles, paper and printing to electronics and automobiles. It includes fast-growing areas such as special composites (i.e. much of the new materials field), but there is no clear line of demarcation between speciality chemicals and other sectors.

For many years the speciality chemicals sector has been the preserve of the small or medium-sized firm. Companies such as Cookson or Morgan Crucible have bought as their raw materials the intermediate products of the major companies, added value to them by processing and reworking, and sold them either as final products or as inputs into other final products. The large chemicals companies have always had some stake in this market, either directly via wholly owned subsidiaries or indirectly via close linkages with the specialist firms. For their part, too, the speciality firms knit for themselves a web of special relationships which link suppliers and customers.

The most marked feature of recent years in this area has been the degree to which the large chemicals firms have integrated forwards into the speciality chemicals area using their R&D expertise in chemistry to aid the development of new products. One result is that the speciality sector is now the sector of the industry experiencing the fastest rate of technological change. This has not only made the sector more R&D intensive, but has also often changed the character of the sector. *Paints and packaging* are good examples. What had been an old-fashioned, fragmented industry, buying-in raw materials from the major chemicals companies, gradually found itself taken over and is now a modern, technology-based, concentrated industry. Its product is considerably improved, and highly differentiated. (ICI, for example, has gone to considerable trouble to differentiate its product for different markets, working closely with customers such as automobile manufacturers or off-shore oil rig constructors.) But, except for highly specialist niche areas, entry is now virtually impossible, because small companies cannot match the breadth of R&D capabilities of the big companies.

Customer-user collaboration has become almost routine in some sectors of speciality chemicals. *Carbon Fibre* is a good example where hands-on experience in development counts. Because carbon fibre properties can be varied according to use, the chemist and the engineer must work closely together in development. Both upstream and downstream relationships are of considerable importance: upstream with those developing acrylic fibres and epoxy resins, downstream with the aeronautical and other engineers designing the products.

The speciality chemicals sector illustrates graphically the impact of rapid technical change on both the structure of the industry and on the nature of competition. The intense technological activity, the new products, the new applications and refinement of existing products, represent a continuous process. This requires a change in the scale of operation because so much more of the industry is subject to dynamic economies of scale, and this in turn requires large-scale R&D and financial and technical resources to open up new opportunities. Firms with the corporate, technological and entrepreneurial capacity to innovate are growing; those without these capacities are declining or being acquired. Old-fashioned, smaller firms are simply being squeezed out; but the wider application of more scientific chemistry is also opening up new niches, and there are *new* small firms emerging to exploit these niches.

It should be remembered, too, that rapid change offers opportunities to enter markets by innovation rather than by price. The major firms in the industry are so large and so diversified that they are often seen as monopolists. In the more fragmented speciality sectors, they are in reality powerful potential competitors. This makes many of these markets contestable – despite patents, close customer-supplier relationships and successful market and product differentiation. Innovation and growth can, in fact, ensure that many apparently strong and highly profitable monopoly positions are only temporary.

Pharmaceuticals and Biotechnology

There are many similarities between pharmaceuticals and speciality chemicals: both feature a market broken up into small specialist areas with intense competition within each area, and both look to R&D and innovation as the key to successful competition. However, unlike speciality chemicals, pharmaceuticals are not customized and downstream linkages are limited. Indeed, in many respects pharmaceuticals represent an almost classic case of the linear model, with R&D separated from (but feeding into) the production and marketing processes downstream. Safety requirements also create regulatory barriers and it is the cost and time required to satisfy these that make the industry the preserve of large rather than small firms.

Given this intense oligopolistic competition in each market segment, R&D has become essential both for the discovery and development of new drugs and to underpin a firm's ability to move rapidly into a competitor's market. For pharmaceuticals as a whole, R&D now averages 16 per cent of net output (1988–9 figures) ranging from 12 to 20 per cent. The proportion has been increasing steadily over the last thirty years reflecting both diminishing returns to the traditional routes of drug discovery based on the screening and testing of new chemical entities for therapeutic properties, and the increasing costs of regulation. Typically, it now takes twelve years to bring a new drug to market, with only one in every 10,000 tested successful. The average cost of developing any *single* successful chemical entity has recently been estimated to be $40 million in the US, rising to $114 million if allowance is made for the cost of failures, and to $240 million if the time element is also allowed for (Di Masi et al. 1991).

The strategies currently being adopted by the pharmaceutical industry (and common to both European and American multinationals), are a direct response to these trends. They involve:

(i)   *merger and acquisition* as companies expand in an attempt to spread the overheads of R&D across a wider base;

(ii)   *pressure to extend the effective patent life* on drugs and hence extend the period of premium prices and profits;

(iii) *a shift from ethical (prescription) drugs to over-the-counter business* since governments are simultaneously battling to contain health care costs via limited lists etc;

(iv)   *an attempt to contain R&D costs* by adopting a more targeted approach to drug discovery and development.

Biotechnology falls into the final category, although in this respect it fits directly into the tradition of 'biomedicine' pioneered in the 1960s by the British pharmacologist Sir James Black which was based on greater understanding of the body's natural chemistry and immune system. Initially biotechnology offered the opportunity of manufacturing, via genetic engineering and cell culture, the whole range of therapeutic proteins, such as insulin, interferon and the interleukins, produced by the body's immune system. In practice the products of this first generation of the 'new biotechnology' have proved costly and often ineffective. Nevertheless, it has effected a wholesale revolution in methods of drug discovery as techniques of modifying and synthesizing molecules targeted to specific sites have been developed enabling companies to look towards a new generation of 'designer drugs'. Biotechnology is now generally acknowledged by pharmaceutical companies to be an important and essential enabling technology for drug design, even though it is likely that chemical synthesis will remain the main production technology (Sharp, 1991).

Biotechnology affects another area of the chemical industry, namely agrochemicals, which like pharmaceuticals has been an important high value added growth sector in the 1970s and 1980s. The use of genetic engineering to produce transgenic plant species which fix their own nitrogen or incorporate resistance to climate, pests or a particular herbicide, means potentially huge changes for traditional sales of fertilisers, pesticides and herbicides. In addition there are opportunities for developing biologically based products. Developments are still experimental, and some firms remain sceptical as to how big the changes will be. Bayer, for example, has argued that its traditional expertise in synthetic organic agro-chemicals will still be needed (Galimberti, 1992). But other traditional chemical firms, for example, ICI, Rhône Poulenc and Ciba Geigy, are investing heavily in this area and buying up seed companies to provide outlets for the new transgenic plants they are developing (Sharp and Galimberti, 1993).

Biotechnology, however, poses challenges as well as opportunities to the older firms of the chemical/pharmaceutical industry. Their roots were traditionally in chemistry. Earlier sections of this paper have stressed the importance for the industry of its in-house R&D department and its external linkages in creating its innovation system for this industry. Biotechnology, with its roots in micro-biology and molecular genetics, does not fit with this system and demands, instead, the building of a whole new range of relationships.

The small, specialist dedicated biotechnology firm (DBF), which has been such a feature of the US biotechnology scene, precisely fills this gap. Frequently a spin-off from academic research laboratories, it provides a mechanism for pulling together the necessary cross-disciplinary research team in an environment conducive to creative thinking. For the larger firms working through research contracts or joint ventures, the DBF has provided a source of expertise and skills, and an important mechanism for hedging against the uncertainties inherent in the early stages of development of any new technology. What is surprising is the resilience of these small firms as the technology has matured, for while many have been bought up, taken over and absorbed within the in-house teams of the major multinationals, others have sprung into existence. Indeed, the total population of DBFs in the US has remained remarkably stable throughout the last decade (OTA, 1991).

Case studies reveal a complex pattern of relationships between the older giants of the chemical industry and these new small firms. Some large companies, such as ICI, shun tying themselves up with competitors and prefer to rely upon their traditional links with academic science. Others, such as Bayer, have preferred to buy up potential partners and incorporate the skills directly into the company. It is notable, however, that quite a number of companies, such as Monsanto, Du Pont and Ciba Geigy, having experimented with outside relationships for the first time in the early 1980s, continue to use research contracting and joint ventures as a major input to their research capabilities (Sharp and Galimberti, 1993; Barbanti et al. 1993).

Conclusions – Innovation in a Research-Based Industry

This brief sketch has shown the chemicals industry to be a complex industry in which many types of innovation are proceeding simultaneously. The dominant feature of the industry remains the large, multiproduct chemical firm, operating in many market segments and able when necessary to take long-term decisions and cross-subsidize emerging but promising new technologies from profits on existing operations. This essentially Schumpeterian model is characterized both by a rapid rate of technological change and by the longevity of the main firms involved. In this latter respect it could be seen to be a highly successful model of innovation. More detailed investigation reveals:

(i)   the key role played by the R&D department as the nucleus of the dynamic;

(ii)   the importance of external linkage into the R&D department, feeding it with information both from the market and from basic research;

(iii)   the growing importance of downstream linkages with customers as the industry moves into increasingly specialized market segments; and

(iv)   the growing importance also of upstream interaction with the research base as new academically based technologies such as biotechnology and new materials become prominent.

This last development prompts a questioning of the role of the small firm which traditionally in this industry has played a negligible role in innovation, dominating only the downstream speciality sectors where they have established niche markets. The large companies, searching for higher value added segments, are now ousting the small firm from this domain, professionalizing the research and effectively squeezing them out. By contrast the small firm dominates the leading edge of research in the emerging sector of biotechnology. Whereas half a century earlier the large firms had dominated innovations in petrochemicals, none to date have made major contributions to the knowledge base in biotechnology. Indeed, in spite of now substantial investments in-house in biotechnology, these large firms often still rely upon the small firms both for linkage into the research base and, increasingly, for new product and process ideas. Could it be that we are witnessing a radical change in relationships – and in the innovation process – taking place in this industry?

Bibliography

Achilladelis, B.G. et al. (1987) 'A Study of Innovation in the Pesticide Industry', *Research Policy,* 16 (2), pp. 175–212.

Achilladelis, B.G. et al. (1990) 'The Dynamics of Technological Innovation: The Case of the Chemical Industry', *Research Policy,* 19 (1), pp. 1–35.

Barbanti, P., Gambardella, A. and Orsenigo, L. (1993) *The Evolution of the Forms of Collaboration in Biotechnology.* Mimeo, Università Luigi Bocconi, Milan, Italy.

Brock, W.H. (1992) *The Fontana History of Chemistry,* Fontana, London.

DiMasi, J.A., Hansen, R.W., Grabowski, H.G. and Lasajna, L. (1991) 'The Cost of Innovation in the Pharmaceutical Industry: New Drug R&D Cost Estimates', *Journal of Health Economics,* June.

Duncan (1982) 'Lessons from the Past: Challenge and Opportunity' in Sharp, D.H. and West, T.F. (eds) *The Chemical Industry,* Ellis Horwood for the Society of the Chemical Industry.

Freeman, C. (1982) *The Economics of Industrial Innovation,* Pinter Publishers, London.

Freeman, C. et al. (1963) 'The Plastics Industry: A Comparative Study of Research and Innovation', *National Institute Economic Review,* 26, p. 22.

Galimberti, I. (1992) Case study of Bayer's interests in biotechnology, undertaken for Sharp and Galimberti (1993). Mimeo, obtainable from Science Policy Research Unit, University of Sussex, UK.

Gibbons, M. and Johnston, R. (1974) 'The Role of Science in Technological Innovation', *Research Policy,* 3 (3), pp. 220–42.

Hounsell, D.A. and Smith, J.K. (1988) *Science and Corporate Strategy,* Cambridge University Press, Cambridge, UK.

Jewkes, J., Sawers, D. and Stillerman, J. (1958) *The Sources of Invention,* Macmillan, London.

National Science Foundation (1973) *Interactions of Science and Technology in the Innovation Process,* NSF 667, Washington DC.

OECD (1979) *The Petrochemical Industry: Trends in Production and Investment,* Paris.

OECD (1992) *Globalisation of Industrial Activities: Four Case Studies,* Paris.

Office of Technology Assessment (OTA) (1991) *Biotechnology in a Global Economy,* Office of Technology Assessment, Congress of the United States, Washington DC.

Rothwell, R. (1985) 'Project SAPPHO: A Comparative Study of Success and Failure in Industrial Innovation', *Information Age,* 7 (4), pp. 215–19.

Rothwell, R. et al. (1974) 'SAPPHO updated', *Research Policy,* 3 (3), pp. 257–91.

Schumpeter, J.A. (1912) *Theorie der Wutschaftlichen Entwicklung,* Dunker & Humbolt, Leipzig (English translation, Harvard University Press, 1934).

Schumpeter, J.A. (1939) *Business Cycles,* two volumes, McGraw Hill, New York.

Sharp, M. (1991) 'Technological Trajectories and the Corporate Strategies in the Diffusion of Biotechnology', chapter 5 in Deiaco, E., Hornell, E. and Vickery, G. (eds) *Technology and Investment: Crucial Issues for the 1990s,* Pinter Publishers, London.

Sharp, M. and Galimberti, I. (1993) *Coherence and Diversity: Europe's Chemical Giants and the Assimilation of Biotechnology.* Case study undertaken for EC FAST Project: *Coherence and Diversity in Europe's Industrial System.* Mimeo, SPRU, University of Sussex.

13. Innovation in Energy Supply: The Case of Electricity

Gordon MacKerron

Introduction

Advances in energy technology have been at the heart of industrial innovation throughout the twentieth century. The opening up of oil and gas supplies, combined with the development of the internal combustion engine and the petrochemicals industry, have had huge economic and social impacts. Equally, the steam turbine and the electric motor were fundamental in opening a new range of inexpensive, clean and flexible industrial activities, and the availability of cheap and consistent electricity supplies are an indispensable element in the development and diffusion of information technologies. Technology has also played a major part in extending and cheapening fossil energy supplies: contrary to the expectations of the neo-Malthusians, fossil fuel prices have in general fallen throughout the century.

This chapter is concerned with the processes and directions of innovation within the energy sector.

In the supply of energy, the sector is relatively easily bounded. Four main supply-based activities may be identified:

- Extraction (mainly of fossil fuels and uranium);
- Conversion of primary forms of energy to secondary forms; characteristic activities are the refining of crude oil into products, and the transformation of fossil fuels into electricity;
- Distribution of energy to consumers, often by capital-intensive network systems, as in the case of electricity and gas grids;
- Disposal of residues of fuel, for instance ash and sulphur from coal, and the management of spent nuclear fuel.

In the domain of energy demand, boundaries are less easy to draw. Technologies in which consumers use energy are clearly important in the overall development of the energy sector. Such technologies include refrigerators, boilers, lighting systems and internal combustion engines.

Technology development in all these areas pays some attention to energy issues, but – especially in the case of cars – energy is by no means the most important dimension. For this reason it is inappropriate to think of innovation in the automobile industry as energy innovation, even though patterns of innovation in cars may have profound energy use consequences.

Because the energy sector is so pervasive, it is necessary to be selective in the treatment given to innovation within it. The approach taken here is to focus on the electricity industry, a vital conversion process. This choice is for a number of reasons: electricity raises issues in all the main energy activities outlined above; demand for electricity universally grows faster than for other energy forms; it is the essential underpinning for most innovative industrial technologies; it is an arena for major choice in technology (e.g. as between nuclear, fossil fuels and renewables); and it has been politically prominent. This is partly because of technology choice issues, but also because it has been the focus for radical structural changes and is deeply implicated in major environmental issues such as acid deposition, radioactive waste management and climate change.

History

Aside from those countries whose geography led them to the hydro route, the steam turbine became established as the dominant basic technology of the industry in the early years of the century (Byatt, 1979). It has remained the core of electricity production technology to the present. The rapid expansion of the electricity industry that took place from the early 1900s was achieved in conditions of continuously declining cost and delivered price that endured until the 1970s (de Oliveira and MacKerron, 1992).

There were four main causes of falling cost:

- Various kinds of economies of size, including classic engineering economies of scale, but also economies of number (batch and mass production);
- The development of network systems (a specialized form of economies of size). Isolated plants could only be used for limited periods, and different plants had different efficiencies. Linking plants in a grid allows better utilization of all plant, and permits the most efficient plant to be used most intensively.
- Better conversion efficiency. Early steam turbines only converted 10 per cent or so of the total energy content of fossil fuels into electricity (Hannah, 1979). By the 1960s, efficiencies had risen to over 35 per cent, due mainly to higher pressures and temperatures. The search for better efficiencies has been a major priority.
- Lower fuel prices. The opening up of new deposits of all the fossil

fuels, plus much improved extraction technology, have cheapened fossil fuels significantly over the last seventy or eighty years, and fossil fuels are generally the largest cost element of steam-based systems.

The characteristic forms of innovation for the period to about 1970 were therefore incremental in the technological sense. However, they had radical economic impacts. Electricity prices fell in real terms very rapidly. In the post-World War II period this cheapening process was assisted by falling oil prices, and oil became the fuel of choice for many countries' new plants by the 1960s.

Postwar Technology Efforts

Attempts at more radical technological change started in the late 1940s and early 1950s, and were essentially an offshoot of the development of nuclear weapons. The conversion process of steam to electricity via a steam turbine was to be essentially unchanged: the radicalism was in the attempt to use a controlled nuclear reaction to raise the steam (Foley, 1978).

For the major nuclear weapons states, civilian uses of nuclear power represented an apparently boundless prospect of cheap power plus competitive advantage through development of nuclear technology. Nuclear power was seen as the leading sector, able to spread beneficial effects throughout the industrial economy through its demonstration effect and exacting standards (Walker and Lonnroth, 1983).

The expenditures on nuclear R&D for electricity grew rapidly in the 1950s (Surrey and Walker, 1975). In the UK, France and the USSR the expenditures were overwhelmingly concentrated in the public sector. In the USA and later in Germany and Japan, huge state expenditures were complemented by significant R&D spending by private firms, mostly the large heavy electrical firms that had previously concentrated on steam turbine or boiler production (e.g. Westinghouse, General Electric, Babcock and Wilcox, Siemens, AEG and Mitsubishi).

While the private sector was involved to a variable but substantial degree in this development process, the potential users of the technology (the electric utilities) were hardly involved at all (Thomas, 1988). This was partly because it was widely believed that replacing a fossil-fired boiler with a nuclear reactor at the front of a power plant was a relatively simple process, which would involve few changes for utilities. It was also partly because the whole nuclear enterprise was seen as so strategically important that consultations with utilities seemed a very second-order issue; besides, nuclear power would so cheapen electricity supply that it was self-evidently the way forward.

These very large, mostly state-based technology efforts led to the competitive evolution of a number of different reactor designs for quasi-commercial installation in the late 1950s and early 1960s. Early European designs were mostly based on gas-cooling and natural uranium, while US designs – which soon became dominant – used water-cooling and enriched uranium. Canada used heavy water and natural uranium in the only design which did not derive from earlier military needs (Patterson, 1983). By the early 1970s nuclear power was the characteristic innovation in the electricity supply industry: the USA, Canada, the UK, the USSR, France, Germany, Italy, Spain, Sweden and Japan were all making significant investment in new nuclear plants.

Nuclear power represented a further extension of the trend in the industry towards ever larger unit sizes. But it was also complex and inflexible, driven by 'technology-push' rather than demand. It also had very high front-end capital costs. The expectation was that these high initial costs would be more than compensated for by very low running costs, due to the limited quantities of uranium fuel needed (Thomas, 1988).

In practice nuclear power has proved a major economic disappointment. It started costly, and has generally become substantially more expensive. The classic pattern of learning and economies of scale and series production has not worked to reduce costs: such effects have been present, but have been heavily outweighed by an enormous increase in the complexity and cost of reactors. This increase is itself partly a consequence of initial optimism and error in design, but has been sustained by the interaction between safety regulation and the design process (MacKerron, 1992).

Safety standards have become continuously more stringent while the fundamentals of reactor design are unchanged since the 1960s. The result is that to make old reactor designs consistent with new standards it has been necessary to add enormously to the volumes of pipes, cabling, concrete and so on for each kilowatt of capacity (Komanoff, 1981). Safety standards tend to be 'ratcheted' (they never become less stringent and frequently become more so) and reactor types can only be made cheap enough to compete effectively with alternative sources of power if fossil fuel prices rise considerably. Only Japan and Korea (each with specific reasons of its own) have recently ordered any nuclear power plant.

The nuclear industry has therefore sought to develop entirely new types of reactor design, incorporating more passive or 'inherent' safety, and it may well be that this is the only way in which nuclear power can be made acceptably safe as well as sufficiently inexpensive. The difficulty is that such a development effort is long term and hugely expensive, and governments have lost their appetite for large new long-term projects with uncertain outcomes, even in the nuclear field (Thomas, 1993). Given the uncertainties (which are political as well as technological) it is difficult to foresee private companies achieving this task alone. The long-term survival of the nuclear option is therefore in some doubt.

The Oil Shocks of the 1970s and Their Consequences

Until 1973, nuclear power was the only electricity supply technology significantly funded by governments. In the mid-1970s the range of such funding enormously increased, almost entirely as a reaction to the first oil 'shock' (the quadrupling of oil prices in 1973/74 and the equally important sense of insecurity of oil supply from OPEC). While the problem was seen to pervade the energy system, the solutions were seen almost entirely in terms of electricity: almost 90 per cent of public R&D funding has gone to electricity-based technologies (IEA, 1991).

The new policy was based on three fundamental axioms:

- It was essential to substitute other fuels for oil, which was scarce and insecure;
- It would be impossible to restrain significantly the rise in energy demand: enhanced supply was to be the cornerstone of policy (MacKerron, 1988);
- Given the first two axioms, there was a need to develop technologies which would transform the whole basis of the energy supply system.

Thus the OECD countries' energy R&D budgets almost doubled in real terms between 1975 and 1981, from some $6 billion to over $11.5 billion (IEA, 1991). Nuclear power, already heavily funded from public sources, was well placed to receive significant amounts of the new resources, and fitted well into the 'radical/transforming' model. The more radical end of the nuclear technology spectrum (fast breeders and fusion) was particularly well suited to the new opportunities.

Other technologies were also well supported. Chief among these were the 'synthetic' fuels (especially in the US), which mostly involved converting more plentiful fuels (mostly coal) to forms which imitated the scarcer fuels (gas and oil). To a lesser but still significant extent the various forms of renewable energy were also supported in this process. While private firms participated in this R&D effort as contractors, few spent significant amounts of their own money on these technologies.

The direct results of this very large public effort in technology development were disappointing. Hardly any of the technologies supported have emerged in a commercial form subsequently. The 'axioms' on which the expansion was based turn out simply to have been very inaccurate long-term forecasts (difficult as that was to judge at the time: MacKerron and Walker, 1986). The programme was heavily technology-driven, and the enthusiasms of the research community that benefited from the new resources were not countered by perspectives of private firms or potential users. Perhaps most surprising was the almost total lack of attention given to possibilities for incremental improvement to existing technologies: such was the revolutionary mood of the times. Long-termism has as many dangers as short-termism, around which current fears are more concentrated.

However, while the direct technological results of this large R&D expenditure were poor, there were wider political results which were more positive from the OECD countries' perspectives. As part of a large and visible effort to become less dependent on oil, this R&D undoubtedly had an effect on the political economy of oil: it helped weaken OPEC's bargaining position and contributed to the fall in oil prices of the later 1980s.

From the 1980s to the Present

The second wave of oil price rises in 1979/80 gave a further but short-lived impetus to the radical research directions undertaken from the mid-1970s. By the early 1980s it was becoming clear that synthetic fuels had few prospects, and that fusion was a distant dream. Perhaps even more important, governments, especially in the USA and the UK, were increasingly keen to cut public expenditure, and long-term energy R&D was a relatively soft target (MacKerron and Walker, 1986).

In the second half of the 1980s fossil fuel prices began to fall rapidly, and the conviction grew that fossil fuels were likely to be much less scarce (and more secure) than had been believed in the 1970s. Long-term energy planning went out of fashion, partly because of earlier mistakes but also because of changed market conditions. At the same time, and with growing force towards the end of the 1980s, the principal energy problem came to be seen not as one of prospective supply shortage, but rather of various and wide-ranging environmental side-effects, particularly deriving from fossil fuel combustion.

Public energy R&D effort therefore fell back in the early 1980s (to under $7 billion by 1988: IEA, 1991) and there were significant changes of direction. Programmes became smaller, and while there was still work on long-term nuclear technologies, their extent was reduced by as much as 50 per cent. The most interesting new programmes concerned energy and environment, and the largest of these was the US Clean Coal Technology Programme. This was an explicit partnership between the public and private sectors, and involved a 50/50 cost sharing principle (House of Commons, 1991). The emphasis in this and in other programmes was on less radical technological change, and special emphasis was given to improvements in existing technologies. Characteristic technologies were new forms of combustion, especially variants of fluidized beds, which offered more effective removal of pollutants as well as higher overall levels of efficiency.

In the private sector, data on R&D and technology development are notoriously incomplete, but certain recent trends are clear. The period from the 1970s to the present has been one in which the international electrical industry has become more and more concentrated. The structure of the industry is now very much one of oligopoly, and four or five major groups now dominate the world market: Asea Brown Boveri, Siemens, GEC Alsthom, Westinghouse/Mitsubishi, General Electric/Hitachi/Toshiba. All of these companies used to have a significant presence in the nuclear business but all have severely curtailed their nuclear efforts.

In non-nuclear fields, there has been some expansion of effort, and improved forms of fossil combustion (in both environmental and efficiency terms) have been important. Companies like Asea Brown Boveri have spent considerable sums on various forms of fluidized bed combustion (House of Commons 1991), and clearly hope that such technology will become fully commercial before the end of the century.

But the characteristic innovation of the early 1990s is the combined cycle gas turbine (CCGT). This is a system which combines two familiar and well-tried technologies – the steam turbine and the gas turbine. Fuel enters the gas turbine to make the first round of electricity and the hot exhaust gases then (via a waste heat boiler) drive a steam turbine to make a second round. The efficiency of the overall process, which was previously reaching thermodynamic limits at close to 40 per cent, is now at 50 per cent and will probably rise to 55 per cent in the near future (MacKerron, 1991). Capital costs are lower than for competing technologies.

The CCGT is unlike nuclear power in many respects. It comes in relatively small modular units, has low capital costs, and is quick to build. In operation it also seems likely to achieve very high operating reliability. The reason that it has become dominant as a new technology, however, owes less to major technical improvements than to radical changes in the economic environment in which the electricity supply industry operates.

This economic environment includes reductions in the price of the main fuel input to CCGTs, natural gas, and the advantage which relatively clean fuels like gas increasingly possess in the market place. However, the dominant change in economic environment has been the move away from electricity supply as a long-term, public service industry with relatively low profitability towards a liberalized industry exposed to normal commercial objectives and pressures (MacKerron, 1993). In some cases, of which the UK is the most extreme, privatization has been combined with dis-integration and the introduction of competition (Hunt, 1991).

In this new environment, time horizons have shortened and the cost of capital has risen (Barnes, 1990). Where mistakes in technology choices leading to higher costs can no longer be passed automatically to consumers, utilities are much more averse to technological and commercial risk. In such a context, CCGTs fit ideally: they have rapid paybacks and manufacturers are willing to give performance guarantees of a kind that would be impossible in nuclear technology. Thus the primacy of CCGTs owes much more to radical changes in economic environment than to technological change as such.

However, it would be misleading to concentrate, in describing innovation in electricity, solely on individual decisions about new power plant technologies. As in other industrial sectors, a major (arguably *the* major) change has been the influence – at many points besides new investment decisions – of various forms of information technology (Walker, 1986). Influences of IT include: improvements to the very complex process of designing new plants or transmission systems; radical changes in metering, allowing much more interactive relationships between utilities and consumers (confined to date to larger consumers); and, most important of all, allowing a much wider range of experimentation with the structure and organization of the whole industry.

For instance, the new arrangements in the UK, where electricity is now sold at forty-eight different spot prices per day, and a hugely complex web of transactions is set up between a large and growing number of buyers and sellers, could only be managed with the benefit of IT-based systems for tracking and financial settlement (National Grid Company, 1993).

Opponents of interference with the traditional public sector monopoly model of electricity supply used to find comfort in the argument that very large transactions costs would overwhelm any cost savings of a liberalized system (House of Commons, 1992). The idea that liberalized systems are effectively unworkable is now out of date, mostly because of rapid developments in IT. Further ways in which IT will affect the electricity system are not yet discernible, but they will almost certainly be profound, especially because of their capacity to reach the whole system, rather than impact only on new vintages of investment. However, what is not yet clear is whether or not the new systems, with their short-term priorities, can deliver effective innovation across the board.

Bibliography

Barnes, M. (1990) *The Hinkley Point Public Inquiries,* Report to the Secretaries of State for Energy and the Environment, HMSO.

Byatt, I. (1979) *The British Electricity Industry 1875–1914: the Economic Returns to a New Technology,* Clarendon, Oxford.

Foley, G. (1978) *The Energy Question,* Penguin, Harmondsworth.

Hannah, L. (1979) *Electricity before Nationalisation,* Macmillan, London.

House of Commons (1991) *Clean Coal Technology and the Coal Market After 1993,* Energy Committee HC-208, March.

House of Commons (1992) *Consequences of Electricity Privatisation,* Energy Committee, 2nd Report 1991/92, HC-113, 26 February.

Hunt, S. (1991) 'Competition in the Electricity Market: the England and Wales Privatisation', *NERA Topics* 2.

IEA (1991) *Energy Policies and Programmes of IEA Countries,* International Energy Agency, OECD, Paris.

Komanoff, C. (1981) 'Alternative Energy' in MacKay, L. and Thompson. M. (eds) *Something in the Wind: Politics after Chernobyl,* Pluto, London, pp. 161–179.

MacKerron, G. (1988) *Power Plant Cost Escalation: Nuclear and Coal Capital Costs, Regulation and Economics,* Komanoff Energy Associates, New York.

MacKerron, G. (1991) *The Economics and Sustainability of Gas Use for Power Generation in the UK,* Coalfield Communities Company, Special Report 13, September.

MacKerron, G. (1992) 'Nuclear Costs: Why Do They Keep Rising'?, *Energy Policy,* Vol. 20, No. 7, pp. 641–52, July.

MacKerron, G. (1993) 'Policy Debates in the Electricity Distribution Sector in Developing Countries' in Eberhard, A. and Theron, P. (eds) *International Experience in Energy Policy Research and Planning,* Elan Press, Cape Town, pp. 153–65.

MacKerron, G. and Walker, W. (1986) 'Energy Forecasting: Does it Have a Future?' in Gretton, J., Harrison, A. and MacKerron, G. (eds) *Energy UK 1986,* Policy Journals, Newbury.

National Grid Company (1993) *1993 Seven Year Statement for the Years 1993/4 to 1999/2000,* London.

de Oliveira, A. and MacKerron, G. (1992) 'Is the World Bank Approach to Structural Reform Supported by Experience of Electricity Prices in the UK?', *Energy Policy,* Vol. 20, No. 2, pp. 153–62, February.

Patterson, W. (1983) *Nuclear Power,* 2nd edition, Penguin, Harmondsworth.

Surrey, J. and Walker, W. (1975) 'Energy R&D: A UK Perspective', *Energy Policy,* Vol. 3, No. 2, pp. 90–115, June.

Thomas, S. (1988) *The Realities of Nuclear Power,* Cambridge Energy Studies, Cambridge University Press.

Thomas, S. (1993) 'Waning Appetites Hinder New Technology', *Power in Europe,* 18 June, Financial Times Business Information.

Thomas, S. and McGowan, F. (1990) *The World Market for Heavy Electrical Equipment,* Nuclear Engineering International Special Publications, Sutton.

Walker, W. (1986) 'Information Technology and Energy Supply', *Energy Policy,* Vol. 14, No. 6, December.

Walker, W. and Lonnroth, M. (1983) *Nuclear Power Struggles,* Allen and Unwin, London.

14. Military Technology

William Walker

Introduction

In most writings on industrial innovation there is an unstated assumption that technical change is 'a good thing'. The ultimate aim of study is to increase the rate of technological development and to encourage the diffusion of new techniques in the expectation that humanity will benefit as a result. The literature on military technology is much more equivocal. Hugely destructive wars and the advent of nuclear weapons have caused as much attention to be focused on the restraint of military innovation as on its enhancement. The stability of the international system, even the survival of the planet, have at times seemed to depend on bringing military technology to heel.

The literature on military technology is distinctive for another reason. Although firms are the main technology holders (in the capitalist West), states are the main financiers of military innovation, and the sole purchasers of advanced military equipment. They also have large political and economic stakes in the arms trade.

Much effort has thus gone into explaining why states have devoted so many public resources to military technology in recent times, how states reach decisions on the technologies that are developed and purchased, how they manage relations with suppliers, and how they compete in or jointly regulate the international market for military technology. One consequence is that the study of military technology embraces, at its best, several branches of the political sciences and economics; in addition, it requires knowledge of the technologies and industries in question. It is unashamedly interdisciplinary.

In this brief overview, three of the central issues that have concerned academics and policy-makers since World War II are addressed (the effects of technical change on warfare are not discussed):

- the causes of the Cold War and its associated arms race;
- the efficiency of military innovation and production, and their consequences for broad economic performance;
- the international regulation of military technology.

The Arms Race

During the half-century since the end of World War II, huge resources have been devoted by industrial nations to the development and deployment of weaponry, despite the absence of war between them. Arms races are not unique to the modern era, but this one was exceptional in its intensity and longevity (Gilpin, 1983; Kaldor, 1990).

Three kinds of explanation have been put forward. The first is that this arms race was largely demand-led. It was driven by the conflict between two blocs of states which were divided by ideology, economic praxis and geopolitical interest. In addition, the legacy of mistrust left by two world wars in which the total resources of nations had been pitched against each other, and the ambitions of both the USSR and US to dominate the post-war international order, encouraged both East and West to arm themselves to the teeth in case war broke out again. Against this background, the desire to achieve military supremacy, or at least parity where that was not possible, led to heavy investment in new military technology. This occurred particularly in the West where there was concern that the Warsaw Pact's greater quantities of manpower and equipment could only be matched by qualitative advantages in technology. Hence the concept of the 'force multiplier' whereby technology would make it possible to resist a massed attack from the East.

By this account, the arms race was mainly driven by fear and by hegemonic rivalry, exacerbated by the failure to establish 'normal' relations involving trade, investment and human discourse across the Iron Curtain. The East-West conflict was also permeated by often fantastic images of high technology warfare. The inherent difficulty of testing military strategies and technologies (especially where nuclear weapons were involved) in the absence of the total war for which they were designed, and the tendency of military planners to address themselves to worst-case scenarios, made it difficult to keep innovators' feet on the ground. The results were often bizarre (50,000 nuclear warheads, Star Wars ...) and always extravagantly expensive (Kaldor, 1982).

A second set of explanations concerns the role of military expenditure in regulating and promoting economic activity. At a macroeconomic level, one school of thought maintained that the arms race was for the capitalist West a Keynesian response to a persistent (or cyclical) shortfall in the demand for goods and services, and to increasing competition which drove down the rate of profit (Kidron, 1968; Smith, 1978; Mosley, 1985). This was consistent with the Leninist tradition of depicting politico-military actions by the West as reactions to imminent economic crisis. Blame for the arms race and, by extension, for the Cold War was firmly pinned on the West, and on the United States as the place where capitalism was most highly developed.

Another argument is that military investment allowed states to create industrial opportunities by driving technical change in new directions. Expenditures on R&D that could not be supported in private markets, and the use of procurement to drive down costs, created the platform upon which new civilian capabilities could be built (Gansler, 1980; Kuhn, 1984). Particularly in the United States with its government's traditional reluctance to intervene directly in civil markets, the financing of military technology came to be regarded as one of the primary means of establishing new areas of competitive advantage. The industries established in the 1940s, 1950s and 1960s (aerospace, nuclear power, computers, electronic components ...) seemed to bear this out. From this point of view, the arms race was given additional impetus by the increasingly aggressive competition between western industrial nations. In the 1980s, the Reagan administration's Strategic Defense Initiative (Star Wars) was in part a response to concerns about the challenge from Japan and other nations to the US's technological leadership.

The third explanation is that the arms race was supply-driven. In both East and West, powerful military industrial complexes took shape during World War II, were reinstated during the Korean War, and succeeded in diverting resources from other objectives by exploiting Cold War anxieties (Lapp, 1968; Rosen, 1973). These complexes embraced both suppliers and consumers (the armed services, industrial firms, R&D laboratories, trades unions and military bureaucracies), and their 'agents' within the body politic. They became skilled at manipulating parliamentary institutions so that their hold on public resources was maintained.

The end of the Cold War has brought large reductions in military budgets in East and West. This supports the view that political conflict (the first of the above explanations) was the most important factor sustaining the arms race. However, recent events have also shown that the second and third explanations carry some weight. The loss of Cold War demand has been one factor driving the world economy into recession, as the resources bound up in the military sector have tended to become redundant rather than applied elsewhere. And the power of military institutions has been evident in the ways in which they have averted more substantial cuts and have prevented cancellation of cherished weapon programmes (such as the European Fighter Aircraft). Above all, the extreme dependence of the Soviet economy on military production now stands revealed. Some estimate that as much as two-thirds of Soviet industry was directly or indirectly involved in providing the Red Army with its hardware. It was the communist economies, not the capitalist economies, that were sustained, if ultimately undermined, by international conflict (Cooper, 1991; Konovalov, 1992).

Today another arms race threatens, this time in East Asia. Spending on military technology has been increasing rapidly in Japan, Taiwan, the Koreas, China and elsewhere in the region. The same factors seem to be at play: political and territorial rivalry, the internal quest for new markets and technological opportunities (particularly in Japan), and the crystallization of military industrial complexes. As yet, the formidable innovative resources in the region have not been put in the service of a radical military technological agenda. But there are concerns that this may be just a matter of time.

Problems of Inefficiency

There is a paradox about military innovation. Military industries have historically been the sources of many technological developments which have had positive economic and social consequences. But they have also been bedevilled by problems of inefficiency, to the extent that the industries have gone through periods, including the present one, when they have appeared comparatively backward. These problems have emanated partly from the special character of producer-user relations (normally referred to as 'procurement relations' in this context), and partly from the relationships between civil and military activities within firms and within the wider economy.

Procurement relations

States are both users and producers of military technology. Even where they do not own the means of development and production, they finance most technological development. Due to the cost and complexity of modern weapon systems there is a natural tendency towards monopolistic supply structures, particularly in countries which lack large home markets. Producer-user relations are thus inherently troublesome, and are unusually prone to political and bureaucratic distortion (Peck and Scherer, 1962).

Concern over the costs of military equipment tends to wax and wane, depending on the state of public finances and on the failure-rate in equipment programmes. Governments have taken five broad approaches when trying to limit costs and exert pressure on industries to increase efficiency in R&D and production:

(i) *Contracts.* Typically, contracts for military equipment are based on 'cost-plus' formulae, allowing costs to be passed on to consumers (defence ministries) as they are incurred, with an additional fee providing suppliers with their profit margins. Where applicable, states have therefore borne the risks of failure. Increasingly, defence ministries have tried to negotiate 'fixed-price' contracts which place the onus for completing contracts on time and to cost on the suppliers (Moray Stewart, 1988). However, such contracts are difficult to implement when there is substantial technological risk, and where states have to negotiate with monopoly suppliers which they feel bound to support for reasons of national security or political expediency.

(ii) *The revolving door.* Defence companies have traditionally tried to increase their leverage over markets by hiring former employees of defence ministries or armed services. Attempts are periodically made to put a spanner in this 'revolving door', but usually to no avail. Where the movement of personnel between government and industry is strongly institutionalized, as in France, efforts instead concentrate on maintaining norms of behaviour that lead to the penalizing of ineffective managers and companies (Kolodziej, 1987).

(iii) *Industrial restructuring.* Overcapacity and duplication have been endemic in defence industries. Governments have often intervened to encourage industrial concentration, often at the cost of increasing their dependence on monopoly suppliers (Molas-Gallart, 1992). Where that dependence is particularly troublesome they have also attempted to increase competitive pressures by encouraging new entrants, by obstructing an excessive consolidation of ownership, and by opening their markets selectively to foreign suppliers. In the late 1980s, there was an attempt, to date largely ineffective, to establish an open European market in defence equipment so that concentration could be accompanied by an increase in competition (Walker and Gummett, 1993). Instead, concentration has happened at the expense of competition.

(iv) *International collaboration.* Collaborative projects have been mounted in Europe since the early 1960s with a view to spreading costs and risks, and extending production runs (Hartley, 1983; Matthews, 1992). While some have been successful, such collaborations have tended to increase product complexity and reinforce the positions of national champions. In the 1980s and 1990s there has been an increasing abundance of joint ventures, consortia and other cooperative arrangements negotiated by firms rather than by governments (Sköns, 1993). Their efficacy remains an open question, since they seem to be driven as much by the need to overcome protective barriers as to exploit complementary assets. Markets in the advanced countries still remain heavily protected: the international division of labour characteristic of civil markets is still far away in the defence sector.

(v) *Arms exports.* The most common if regrettable means of cost reduction resorted to by governments has been to encourage and facilitate arms exports, particularly to the Middle East, Asia and other regions of conflict. During the 1970s and 1980s there was a boom in the arms trade, fuelled in particular by regional conflicts, the windfall gains resulting from higher oil prices, and the willingness of suppliers to provide cheap finance (Anthony, 1992). However, most export markets are now in recession so that there is little alternative to internal restructuring if costs are to be reduced.

Civil-military relations

The 20th century began as it is ending, with military innovation playing a secondary part in the evolution of technology, taken in the round. In contrast, there were high civilian returns from military innovation in the middle decades of the century. Several new industries (including electronics, aerospace and nuclear energy) developed rapidly as a result of military R&D and purchasing. The integrated circuit, the Boeing 707 and the light-water reactor were just a few of the products that began life in the military sector, all in the US (Smith, 1987). New design and production processes, such as systems engineering, numerically-controlled machine-tools and computer-aided design, were also pioneered there.

The apparent long cycles in the economic potency of military innovation have not been satisfactorily explained. Perhaps the best explanation is that in periods of intense conflict, resources are focused on unusual technological requirements, without much concern over cost. In the 1940s and 1950s, for instance, the development of nuclear weapons, long-range delivery systems and associated communication systems (satellites, and so forth) created a raft of technological problems demanding solutions.

Nor have the economic benefits from military innovation been satisfactorily assessed. Measuring 'spin-off' has always been difficult (Kubbig, 1986). One reason is that military technology is so diverse: it encompasses unit, batch and mass production, and ranges across different industrial sectors. Thus a rifle is very different from a fighter aircraft, a satellite from a tank. The degree to which technology diffuses across the civil-military boundary, and the mechanisms by which it diffuses, vary enormously (Walker, Graham and Harbor, 1988).

It has been frequently argued that costs began to exceed benefits in the 1960s. The abilities of countries with large military commitments (the UK, the US and especially the USSR) to reap the advantages of the electronics revolution were damaged by the heavy orientation of high technology industries towards military production. Firms were too preoccupied with selling into safe defence markets and lacked the techniques required to compete in open civilian markets; and too much priority was given to expensive and over-sophisticated technologies with military applications, to the neglect of others which often had greater commercial impact (Melman, 1974; Kaldor, Sharp and Walker, 1986).

Today, the debate is rather different. Attention is focused on how to diversify and/or convert defence industries, especially in Eastern Europe and the former Soviet Union where whole economies were built upon military production (United Nations, 1991; Pauker and Richard, 1991); and how to reorganize defence R&D and production so that the lower demand for military equipment does not result in higher costs and the increasing marginalization of defence industries (Gansler, 1989; Weidenbaum, 1992). A new concern has surfaced in this last context. Dominance in civil high technology could in time translate into dominance in military technology. Japan and other East Asian countries, whose defence budgets are relatively buoyant, could begin to challenge US and European pre-eminence in military technology (Russia will probably be unable to maintain its former position).

The Gulf War showed how dependent the US and other armed forces had already become on the availability of Japanese components and sub-systems developed mainly for civil purposes. The greater scale and dynamism of civil technological activity, and its increasing globalization, imply that the military powers may no longer have the same degree of autonomy that they enjoyed in previous times (Vernon and Kapstein, 1992; Kapstein, 1992). The apparent ease with which Japan manages the relationship between civil and military production has also attracted attention recently (Friedman and Samuels, 1992).

Regulation of Military Technology

Although individual states have long attempted to constrain the diffusion and deployment of military technology, international efforts began only after World War I. The search for multilateral instruments for controlling military technology intensified in the period of détente in the 1960s, and have since followed four main approaches:

- *Arms control.* By and large, this involved bilateral agreements between US and the former Soviet Union (or NATO and the Warsaw Pact) to place limits on the quantities and kinds of weaponry being deployed. Prominent examples are the Strategic Arms Limitation (SALT), Anti-Ballistic Missile (ABM), Intermediate Nuclear Force (INF), Strategic Arms Reduction Talks (START) and Conventional Forces in Europe (CFE) treaties (SIPRI, 1992). Their main purpose was less to constrain technological development, which they generally failed to do, than to reduce the risk of war by bringing some stability to politico-military relations between East and West. The ABM Treaty, which outlawed the testing and deployment of anti-ballistic missile defences, was the one treaty that aimed to prevent the development of a field of technology.
- *Non-proliferation policy.* Throughout the postwar period, attempts have been made to limit the spread of weapons of mass destruction, or the capabilities and materials required to produce them. There are three special regimes: nuclear, chemical and biological, and missile. Under the Chemical Weapons Convention (CWC) of 1993, *all* parties pledge not to acquire and deploy chemical weapons, and to destroy existing stocks (Perry Robinson, 1993). In contrast, the Nuclear Non-Proliferation Treaty (NPT) of 1970 recognizes two categories of

countries – the nuclear and non-nuclear weapon states – and concentrates on preventing the latter becoming more numerous (Shaker, 1980; Goldschmidt, 1980; Quester, 1981; Simpson and Howlett, 1993). Both nuclear and chemical regimes contain elaborate verification (safeguards) measures, and constrain or prohibit trade in certain goods (Fischer and Szasz, 1985). The Missile Technology Control Regime (MTCR) is more limited. Founded as late as 1987, it is a suppliers' club which inhibits transfers of ballistic missiles and of some key technologies used in their assembly and manufacture (Center for International Security and Arms Control, 1991).

- *Controls on the arms trade.* Besides the Cocom agreements involving embargoes on arms sales across the Iron Curtain, efforts to constrain the arms trade have mostly been unsuccessful (Pierre, 1982). The main constraints have been applied unilaterally by countries with constitutional inhibitions (Japan and Germany) or in response to public protest (embargoes of South Africa, and so forth), or multilaterally against pariah states (Iraq and Serbia today). Failure to achieve more can be put down to the power of defence contractors, the enormous sums of money involved, and the temptation of states to use arms exports (or imports) as instruments of foreign policy. While increasing transparency and thus political accountability, the arms trade register which will soon be established by the United Nations is not expected to place significant new constraints on military exports, at least in the medium term.

- *Dual-use technology controls.* Transfers of technologies with both civil and military applications were long constrained in the East-West context (notably by observance of Cocom rules). Iraq's success in acquiring sophisticated technology to build up its weapon manufacturing capabilities has encouraged efforts to inhibit the diffusion of dual-use items to other parts of the world. Such technologies have now been incorporated in the 'trigger lists' applied in the nuclear, chemical and missile regimes. In practice, it is difficult to inhibit the diffusion of dual-use technologies since so many that are relevant to advanced military products are now widely used in the civil sector (Alic et al., 1992; Saferworld, 1992). The super-computer is a good example: developed to simulate nuclear explosions, it now has many other applications including weather forecasting and the mapping of oil deposits. These export controls are especially contentious because military constraint often involves economic constraint.

As a general rule, these regulatory systems have done little to slow down the development of new military technology, and have only bought time where states have been determined to acquire technological capabilities that are being denied to them. The Iraqi nuclear and chemical weapon programmes have also shown that countries with rather backward scientific and industrial infrastructures can accumulate substantial capabilities by focusing their limited supplies of skilled manpower, and by adopting clever tactics in acquiring foreign knowhow and equipment.

Many states have nevertheless pledged to forego weapons of mass destruction and capabilities associated with them. The main holders of these technologies, the US and Russia, have now committed themselves to substantial arms reductions, if not to complete disarmament. Dismantling the many thousands of redundant nuclear, chemical and conventional weapons, and dealing with their residues, is a formidable environmental, industrial and economic challenge. So, too, is the task of preventing the skilled labour, military equipment and sensitive technologies and materials from spilling over into new areas of conflict. Unfortunately, the parlous state of the former communist economies makes all these tasks difficult to achieve. The Russians and Americans will also have to undertake the substantial dismantling of the huge military industrial complexes that developed during the Cold War (Wulf, 1993). Armament processes are beginning to seem politically and institutionally straightforward compared to disarmament.

Bibliography

Alic, J., Branscomb, L., Brooks, H., Carter, A. and Epstein, G. (1992) *Beyond Spin-Off: Military and Commercial Technologies in a Changing World*, Harvard Business School Press, Boston.

Anthony, I. (1992) 'The Trade in Major Conventional Weapons', SIPRI Yearbook 1992, Oxford University Press, Oxford, 1992.

Center for International Security and Arms Control (1991) *Assessing Ballistic Missile Proliferation and its Control*, Stanford University, Stanford, California.

Cooper, J. (1991) *The Soviet Defence Industry*, Frances Pinter, London.

Fischer, D. and Szasz, P. (1985) *Safeguarding the Atom: a Critical Appraisal*, Taylor and Francis, London.

Friedman, D. and Samuels, R.J. (1992) *How to Succeed without Really Flying: the Japanese Aircraft Industry and Japan's Technology Ideology*, MIT-Japan Program Working Paper, MIT, Cambridge, Massachusetts.

Gansler, J.S. (1980) *The Defense Industry*, MIT Press, Cambridge, Massachusetts.

Gansler, J.S. (1989) *Affording Defense*, MIT Press, Cambridge, Massachusetts.

Gilpin, R. (1983) *War and Change in World Politics*, Cambridge University Press, Cambridge.

Goldschmidt, B. (1980) *Le Complexe Atomique: Histoire Politique de l'Énergie Nucléaire*, Fayard, Paris.

Hartley, K. (1983) *NATO Arms Co-operation: A Study in Economics and Politics*, Allen and Unwin, London.

Kaldor, M. (1982) *The Baroque Arsenal*, André Deutsch, London.

Kaldor, M. (1990) *The Imaginary War: Understanding the East-West Conflict*, Basil

Blackwell, London.

Kaldor, M., Sharp, M. and Walker, W. (1986) 'Military R&D and Industrial Competitiveness', *Lloyds Bank Review*, October, pp. 31–49.

Kapstein, E.B. (ed.) (1992) *Global Arms Production: Policy Dilemmas for the 1990s*, University Press of America, New York.

Kidron, M. (1968) *Western Capitalism since the War*, Weidenfeld, London.

Kolodziej, E.A. (1987) *Making and Marketing Arms: the French Experience and its Implications for the International System*, Princeton University Press, Princeton.

Konovalov, A. (1992) 'Specific Problems of the Conversion Problem in the Evolving Russia', in Brunn, A., Baehr, L. and Karpe, H.-J. (eds) *Conversion – Opportunities for Development and the Environment,* Springer-Verlag, Berlin.

Kubbig, B.W. (1986) 'Military-Civilian Spin-Off: Promises, Premises and Problems', *Development and Peace*, Vol. 7, Autumn, pp. 199–227.

Kuhn, R.L. (ed.) (1984) *Commercializing Defense Related Technology*, Praeger, New York.

Lapp, R.E. (1968) *The Weapons Culture*, W.W. Norton, New York.

Matthews, R. (1992) *European Armaments Collaboration: Policy Problems and Prospects*, Harwood Academic Publishers, Chur.

Melman, S. (1974) *The Permanent War Economy: American Capitalism in Decline*, Simon and Schuster, New York.

Molas-Gallart, J. (1992) *Military Production and Innovation in Spain*, Harwood Academic Publishers, Chur.

Moray Stewart, J. (1988) 'Defence Procurement in Britain', *RUSI Journal*, Royal United Services Institute, Winter, pp. 43–47.

Mosley, H.C. (1985) *The Arms Race: Economic and Social Consequences*, Lexington Books, Lexington.

Pauker, L. and Richard, P. (eds) (1991) *Defence Expenditure, Industrial Conversion and Local Employment*, International Labour Office, Geneva.

Peck, M.J. and Scherer, W. (1962) *The Weapons Acquisition Process*, Harvard University Press, Cambridge, Massachusetts.

Perry Robinson, J. (1993) 'Origins of the Chemical Weapons Convention', in Morel, B. and Olson, K. (eds) *Shadows and the Substance: The Chemical Convention*, Westview Press, Boulder, Colorado.

Pierre, A. (1982) *The Global Politics of Arms Sales*, Princeton University Press, Princeton.

Rosen, S. (ed.) (1973) *Testing the Theory of the Military Industrial Complex*, Lexington Books, Lexington.

Quester, G. (ed) (1981) *Nuclear Proliferation: Breaking the Chain*, Wisconsin University Press, Wisconsin.

Saferworld (1992) *Arms and Dual-Use Exports for the EC: A Common Policy for Regulation and Control*, Bristol.

Shaker, M. (1980) *The Nuclear Non-Proliferation Treaty: Origin and Implementation*, Oceana Publications, New York.

Simpson, J. and Howlett, D. (1993) *Briefing Book: Volume II, Treaties, Agreements and other Relevant Documents*, Programme for Promoting Nuclear Non-Proliferation, Mountbatten Centre for International Studies, Southampton University.

SIPRI (1992) Stockholm International Peace Research Institute, *SIPRI Yearbook: World Armament and Disarmament*, Part I: Weapons and technology; Part II: Military expenditure, the arms trade and armed conflicts; Part III: Developments in arms control; Oxford University Press, Oxford, published annually.

Sköns, E. (1993) 'Western Europe: Internationalization of the Arms Industry', in Wulf, H. (ed.) *Arms Industry Limited*, Oxford University Press, Oxford.

Smith, M.R. (ed.) (1987) *Military Enterprise and Technological Change*, MIT Press, Cambridge, Massachusetts.

Smith, R.E. (1978) 'Military Expenditure and Capitalism', *Cambridge Journal of Economics*, Vol. 2, September, pp. 293–98.

Vernon, R. and Kapstein, E.B. (1992) *Defense and Dependence in a Global Economy*, Congressional Quarterly Inc., Washington D.C.

United Nations Department for Disarmament Affairs (1991) *Conversion: Economic Adjustments in an Era of Arms Reduction*, UN, New York.

Walker, W., Graham, M. and Harbor, B. (1988) 'From Components to Integrated Systems: Technological Diversity and Interactions between Military and Civilian Sectors', in Gummett, P. and Reppy, J. (eds) *The Relations between Defence and Civil Technologies*, Kluwer, Dordrecht.

Walker, W. and Gummett, P. (1993) *Nationalism, Internationalism and the European Defence Market*, Chaillot Paper No. 9, Institute for Security Studies, Western European Union, Paris.

Weidenbaum, M. (1992), *Small Wars, Big Defense*, Oxford University Press, New York.

Wulf, H. (1993) 'The Soviet Union and the Successor Republics: Arms Exports and the Struggle with the Heritage of the Military-Industrial Complex' in Wulf, H. (ed.) *Arms Industry Limited*, Oxford University Press, Oxford.

15. Innovation in the Construction Sector

David M. Gann

Introduction

There have been few attempts to explain innovation in construction which is often regarded as a mature, slow to change sector. In what follows it is argued that this traditional view is incorrect and that a number of lessons about industrial innovation in general can be learnt from the way in which change occurs in the construction industries. Most studies of technological and organizational change focus on what are considered to be rapidly changing sectors of the economy, such as microelectronics, automobiles, aerospace, some manufacturing industries, the banking sector etc. But it is important to understand innovation in construction for three reasons:

1. Construction is of great economic significance, producing between 6 and 10 per cent of GDP in most advanced economies – the Japanese construction sector accounts for around 18 per cent of Japan's GDP. When construction-related goods and services, such as materials, components and equipment are included, the sector accounts for more than 12 per cent of GDP in advanced economies. Construction also employs a similar proportion of the workforce.
2. Construction produces half of Gross Fixed Capital Formation – the buildings, factories and infrastructure essential for other economic and social activities. Failure to produce new, modern buildings and structures or to develop new production techniques can have adverse consequences for users who face competition from firms abroad which may occupy higher quality, cheaper buildings.
3. The industry has a broad social responsibility to produce safe buildings and structures which have minimal impact on the natural environment.

Technological Change in Construction and Other Sectors

Construction has a longer history than most industries and it continues to rely upon some of the craft practices developed before industrialization began. It has remained more labour-intensive, and productivity growth has been slower, than in many other sectors. Furthermore, it is often presumed that because mechanization has affected other industries in specific ways the effects must be similar in construction, and if not, it is because the sector is backward (Russell, 1981). This view is consistent with many interpretations of industrial growth and technological change which see modern technology producing more, faster; and producing objects that could not have been produced by traditional craft methods: for example, Landes (1969) argues that 'the one ingredient of modernisation that is just about indispensable is technological maturity and the industrialization that goes with it'.

The notion of construction as a backward industry is partly a consequence of the way in which it has been examined as a *physical process*, rather than in terms of *social practices*. This leads to an analysis which focuses on construction activities on building sites. Construction processes are therefore seen as being fragmented because each site is in a different place. The labour intensive, 'handicraft' character of production is said to continue to exist because craftsmen work independently on geographically dispersed sites. But this notion ignores a much richer view based on the whole set of social relations including those associated with the materials and components used in the production of the built environment (Clarke, 1992). If we adopt this broader perspective, construction can be seen to involve a complex of activities (see chapter by Marceau in this volume) resulting in the production of sophisticated systems. The construction process can then be examined in terms of relationships between different actors in the sector as a whole, rather than being confined to analysis of the production of each unique product which is physically and spatially fixed.

Nevertheless, the physical nature of the constructed product and its relation to production cannot be ignored. Constructed products differ from others in several important respects and it should therefore not be surprising that the relationship between the type of product, production process and innovation differs between construction and other sectors. Five characteristics of constructed products stand out: immobility, complexity, durability, costliness and the need for a high degree of social responsibility (Nam and Tatum, 1988). These characteristics tend to limit the possibilities for technological change. But while construction may be unique because of the way in which these characteristics are combined, it is by no means the only sector attempting to produce complex, durable, costly and safe products – ships, aircraft and medical equipment spring to mind.

Immovability of the final product, which necessitates that it is finished at the point of consumption, sets construction apart from the manufacturing industries, in which finished products are transported to the market. Immobility constrains activities to the extent that the economics of labour, machinery and transport of parts have to be considered in a different light to that in manufacturing: hence the name 'construction' industry. Complexity may stultify innovation because architects and designers are often reluctant to specify new materials and components unless they have a proven track record. The risk of failure – as experienced in some of the systems used in 1960s' high-rise buildings in Britain – helps to perpetuate conservatism in design (McCutcheon, 1975). Longevity of many building components places pressures on suppliers to maintain stocks of spares. This may reduce incentives for manufacturers to change product ranges. Longevity and the need for durability create problems in the testing of new materials and components: it is often difficult and expensive to simulate the effects of weathering on a material designed for a 60-year life span. The costs involved may render innovation prohibitively expensive.

There is a danger of over-emphasizing the limits caused by physical characteristics of construction when considering technological change. Such emphasis places the analysis within a technologically determined framework which tends to ignore the importance of the social relations of production. Furthermore, physical characteristics do not necessarily relate to the sector's presumed backwardness and just as they may hinder the development of some new techniques they may also play a part in promoting change. For example, one of the reasons for the development of prefabricated, off-site production techniques was to lessen the unfavourable physical conditions found on sites.

Just as technical change can facilitate the production of commodities which it would not have been conceivable to produce by hand, there is also a tendency for such changes to transform other physical characteristics of production which previously appeared insurmountable. Technological change and the physical characteristics of construction therefore influence each other (Ball, 1988).

Many theories of technical change have been developed through the analysis of changes in mass-market, batch and flow-process sectors, but construction is a project-based activity, which produces bespoke, or very low volumes of similar products. Firms build their businesses on the provision of specialized management skills and resources which often rely upon expertise accumulated over many years. But learning processes are usually informal with many breaks and little feedback up and down stream or to other parts of the industry. Capital intensity is generally low. Professionalization, codes of practice, standard procedures and building regulations, together with traditional craft demarcation lines upheld by trade unions and employers create a 'locked system' (Nam and Tatum, 1988). Tasks often vary from project to project and site environments do not correspond to those found in factories: the need to combat adverse weather conditions and the seasonal nature of work are often cited as hindering the development of construction techniques.

Technical Change in Construction

Five areas of major technological innovation have resulted in considerable changes in construction products and processes, as well as industrial structure and competition, over the past twenty years. They are:

(a)   the use of information technology in the construction process
(b)   the use of information technology in buildings themselves – 'intelligent buildings'
(c)   mechanization of construction activities
(d)   prefabrication
(e)   new materials.

Small changes and adaptations in any one of these may have far reaching consequences for other parts of construction because of the interdependencies which exist between components in the large, complex systems which make up many buildings and structures – there are many thousands more component parts in a house compared with a motor vehicle. Rosenberg's (1982) concept of technological complementarities and interdependencies in large systems provides a useful way of conceptualizing the relationship between small component changes and their effects on the rest of the system. He stresses the importance of understanding how small innovations are made – sometimes by a number of firms acting together. The concept of *complementary technologies* arises from the effects of interrelated clusters of innovations, which may have a cumulative impact, leading to improvements in the performance of a system, but which on their own are of limited significance. Rosenberg cites innovations made in the development of electric light bulbs as an illustration: he could well have been arguing about the development of modern intelligent building systems.

Technical change has resulted in a trend towards engineering and assembly processes with the decline away from traditional craft methods. Nevertheless, the juxtaposition of new and old methods has often resulted in existing technologies being stretched beyond their known limits. This has led to an increase in building defects since the 1950s, which Groak (1992) attributes to a decline in 'robust technologies' – the reliable, tried and tested methods which set well understood technical precedents. These were relatively robust or insensitive to errors of design, manufacture, assembly or use, but robustness is being eroded by technological, social and economic changes inside and outside the construction sector. New technologies are changing other parts of the system in such a way that traditional techniques can no longer be relied upon. The failure of feedback mechanisms to transmit information about new techniques is resulting in less stable, 'fragile technologies'. In consequence, more and more construction projects involve the need to innovate.

Many changes to materials and components are made by direct component suppliers or indirect basic materials manufacturers with markets far broader than the construction sector. Materials innovations can be classified in two main groups: those which change the product and those which affect costs and availabilities of inputs (Bowley, 1960). Some are developed as substitutes, fulfilling similar functions to those of existing products. From the builders' perspective these represent new products, developed and used either because they are cheaper or because they are more readily available than alternatives; although from the users' viewpoint the building's performance and function remains unaltered.

Changes in demand for different types of buildings and structures stimulates innovation more than the need to erect better and cheaper buildings to accommodate existing functions (Bowley, 1966). For example, the need to accommodate new types of industrial processes or new styles of office work involving the use of information technology, create radical changes in construction techniques. Construction markets are segmented and they may be highly specialized. Large users with specialist requirements, for example, those in the power and water industries, airport and aviation authorities, retail chains, banking, or certain types of manufacturing firms, play a part in developing construction technologies to meet their needs. These users have their own teams of construction experts who work closely with others in the supply chain to develop particular solutions. User-producer relationships which have evolved through the need to meet specialized requirements involve the transfer of knowhow which places them at the forefront of technological change in the sector. Producers who work closely with users are likely to gain through the interactive learning processes which occur in the development of new technologies (Lundvall, 1992). Nevertheless, the contractual nature of construction work, which must usually precede orders, means that firms are to an extent unable to gain some of the benefits of centralized and planned production enjoyed by many large firms in manufacturing (Fleming, 1980). Furthermore, fluctuations in demand are a disincentive to substantial investment in new technologies by contractors. Most clients lack the expertise needed to interact with construction and its supply industries. They have to rely upon professional advice from an array of consultant design, engineering and construction organizations.

The level of innovation in construction is contingent on two important relationships: between innovation and industrial structure, and between innovation and types of market. For example, in the case of industrial structure, the ability to innovate has been a factor in the rise to dominance of a few main building materials firms which have been able to block access to new entrants. Lack of competition in parts of the materials sector results in a proliferation of product innovations rather than cost-reducing process innovations. Furthermore, innovation is impeded by the small size and fragmented nature of local markets. There has been an absence of competitive pressures on non-innovating firms owing to the protection afforded by transport costs and a lack of internal dynamics which necessitates a secular expansion in markets to increase the willingness to innovate. The scope for market-expanding innovation by contractors is limited by their inability to specify their products while their scope for cost-reducing innovation is limited by the variability of the type of work they obtain. The relationships between size and type of firm and size and type of market segment within the sector therefore influences the extent to which innovation is likely to occur. The rate of innovation may be retarded by the form of contract, cost of carrying out experiments, lack of information on costs relevant to the development of cost-reducing innovations, and obstacles created by bylaws and codes of practice which enshrine procedures based on past experience. The selection of construction technologies involves different levels of bureaucracy such as the need to comply with building regulations developed to govern the use of old technologies.

We have so far identified some of the driving forces for, and constraints against innovation in construction. We shall now turn to the two main processes through which innovation occurs: formal R&D activity, and informal processes of change.

Formal R&D Activity

Construction R&D is sponsored by a range of organizations associated with the sector, including indirect and direct component producers, construction and design firms, large users, and public sector organizations. Figure 15.1 illustrates the sources of R&D in the construction system and shows technology flows through to end-users of buildings and structures. Much of the formal R&D carried out in the construction supply industries is oriented towards developing better products for building end-users, rather than for improving techniques in the construction process itself. For example, in 1989, the UK construction supply industries carried out about £267 million of R&D of which around £214 million was 'embodied' in products which flowed through the construction process into buildings and structures, to benefit end-users. But lack of feedback and the distance between end-users and up-stream suppliers may result in the development of inappropriate technologies.

Most R&D is carried out by materials and component producers who develop products aimed at improving the performance of buildings and structures. The benefits of this investment in R&D are experienced by the users of buildings and supply firms rather than the construction industry itself. Construction firms spend little on R&D and the industry's technical competences are not organized in a coherent manner aimed at exploiting the

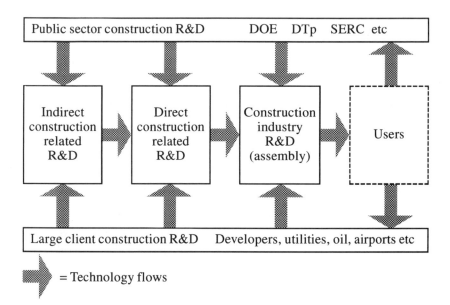

Figure 15.1 The construction R&D system
Source: Gann et al. 1992.

benefits of new technologies. Very little is spent on developing new processes aimed at reducing costs and improving the speed and quality of construction. Yet the industry's function of integrating an array of technology developed elsewhere places it in a pivotal position. Failure to develop new process technologies can cause bottlenecks in construction activities which result in an erosion of the benefits of R&D carried out upstream by supply firms.

In spite of the low level of investment in formal R&D, parts of the construction sector have been remarkably innovative. For example, during the 1980s many organizational changes were made in attempts to meet requirements of producing new types of buildings. Many new technologies were also adopted (Gann, 1991, 1992). Moreover, many design and construction organizations were involved in processes of incremental adaptation and improvement. Yet these activities hardly registered in the statistics on innovation. This is because analysis of industrial innovation often focuses on formal, measurable indicators of technological change such as input/output analysis of R&D, patenting statistics and bibliometrics.

These sources do not take adequate account of other types of technical innovation found in project-based activities such as small, informal incremental changes, information generated in design and engineering or in pre-project survey and feasibility studies.

Informal Innovation Processes

Construction has proven to be continually adaptable and innovative in spite of low levels of investment in formal R&D processes. Many new scientific and engineering methods have not yet diffused across the whole of the sector, and knowhow continues to be passed on by traditional methods of apprenticeships and on-the-job, peer group learning, or through the study of examples found in existing buildings. Construction technology is therefore less formalized than in many other sectors, having evolved through trial and error (Groak, 1992). But changes associated with minor incremental adaptations may be of critical importance in achieving successful outcomes. Small adaptive changes can be of such importance in complex project-based activities that without them many projects could not be successfully completed. These changes are often stimulated by the dynamics of the construction process itself, such as the need to compete by reducing tender prices, or to meet project deadlines. They may also involve the combination of existing technologies in new ways, resulting in the development of new systems. Kodama's (1992) concept of 'technology fusion' appropriately describes the type of 'systems integration' occurring in construction. Firms make use of existing technologies which come from different industries, often combining them and crossing traditional boundaries of knowhow in such a way as to provide significant improvements in products or processes.

While informal sources of change may play a significant role in the development of new technologies within construction, they are difficult to define, observe and measure, and the infrastructure in which development work takes place is less visible to conventional surveys because it is not documented in a structured manner. This will need to change if construction is to move from a 'management plus craft' framework, to become more engineering and technology led. Such a shift will result in new roles for designers who may become more involved *de facto* with R&D work on a regular basis.

Traditional approaches to the transfer of knowhow assume continuity of learning, technology, and theory and practice. This level of continuity ensures that for the most part, construction technologies evolve slowly through minor changes and adaptations. But continuity is thrown into question when radical technical change occurs such as was experienced with the need to install digital microelectronics technologies in buildings during the 1980s (Gann, 1992). New competences were required to exploit such opportunities, but construction and design firms were largely unable to respond through traditional informal processes of innovation. Firms from electronics and telecommunications sectors were able to move into the construction arena to fill the gap, sometimes in collaboration with traditional construction firms.

Conclusions

Project-based construction processes are similar to assembly-line production techniques in that they are both the final stages in long series of production activities. Buildings are constructed of hundreds of component parts which themselves are made of sub-systems. Construction is the integration and assembly phase in a process which involves a flow of products and services from up-stream extractive and manufacturing sectors through to the final point of consumption by end-users of the built environment. There is often a long supply chain in which much of the formal R&D activity is carried out. Technological interdependences and complementarities exist between clusters of components which are combined during sub-assembly, construction and installation. In consequence, the *flows of technology* within the construction system exhibit a more complex pattern than the *commodity flows* which result in final products. Construction processes involve 'systems integration' which include inter-sectoral flows of technology, when technical change occurs, boundaries between 'old' and 'new' construction activities and other industries shift. Construction firms therefore relate to many other industries in the supply chain, together with end-users and with government and industry organizations through particular technology and information flows. The analysis of technological change in construction requires an approach which takes account of chains of production (*filières*), complexes of industries as well as size, type, structure and relationships within and between firms (Marceau, 1992).

Processes of industrial innovation in a traditional sector have been explored in this chapter. Five general lessons can be drawn from the analysis:

1. It is important to study both formal and informal processes of change in order to understand the extent to which innovation is occurring. The construction sector itself carries out little formal R&D but firms are continually involved in small adaptations made through informal processes of change. Nevertheless, informal mechanisms of innovation may be inadequate to cope with radical technical change.
2. Many changes occur at boundaries between sectors or at interfaces between traditional trades. Too narrow a focus on a particular sector may result in a failure to recognize more important changes occurring at boundaries, where there may be greater fluidity in the transfer of

knowhow between one activity and another, or between several existing technologies which can be combined in new ways.

3. Small incremental changes can be of great significance in industries which produce large complex systems. These changes are often made at different points through long chains of production. These changes are cumulative and may eventually result in the decline of traditionally robust technologies.

4. There is often a tendency to overlook the importance of organizational change in industrial innovation. But many of the most important innovations developed from within the construction sector have been organizational rather than technical, for example, new 'fast-track' management techniques overlapping design and construction phases, which have subsequently been adopted in other sectors.

5. A comprehensive understanding of industrial innovation can only be acquired through an analysis of the different relationships occurring through the production chain. These include: relationships between producers and suppliers and between producers and users; the role played by government in setting standards, regulations and sponsoring R&D; and the way in which knowhow is acquired through different learning processes.

Bibliography

Ball, M. (1988) *Rebuilding Construction*, Routledge, London.

Bowley, M. (1960) *Innovation in Building Materials*, Gerald Duckworth, London.

Bowley, M. (1966) *The British Building Industry*, Cambridge University Press, Cambridge.

Clarke, L. (1992) *Building Capitalism*, Routledge, London.

Fleming, M.C. (1980) 'Construction' in Johnson, P.S. (ed.) *The Structure of British Industry*, Granada, London.

Gann, D.M. (1991) *Technical Change and Construction Skills in the 1990s*, Construction Industry Training Board.

Gann, D.M. (1992) *Intelligent Buildings: Producers and Users*, Science Policy Research Unit, University of Sussex, Brighton.

Gann, D.M., Matthews, M., Patel, P. and Simmonds, P. (1992) *Construction R&D: Analysis of Private and Public Sector Funding of Research and Development in the Construction Sector*, Department of the Environment/IPRA, Brighton.

Groak, S. (1992) *The Idea of Building*, E. & F.N. Spon, London.

Kodama, F. (1992) 'Beyond Breakthroughs: Harnessing the Power of Technology Fusion', *Harvard Business Review*, April 1992.

Landes, D.S. (1969) *The Unbound Prometheus*, Cambridge University Press, Cambridge.

Lundvall, B.A. (ed.) (1992) *National Systems of Innovation*, Pinter, London.

Marceau, J. (ed.) (1992) *Reworking the World*, Walter de Gruyter, Berlin.

McCutcheon, R. (1975) 'Technical Change and Social Need: The Case of High-Rise Flats', *Research Policy*, No. 4, pp. 262–89.

Nam, C.H. and Tatum, C.B. (1988) 'Major Characteristics of Constructed Products and

Resulting Limitations of Construction Technology', *Construction Management and Economics*, No. 6, pp. 133–48.

Rosenberg, N. (1982) *Inside the Black Box*, Cambridge University Press, Cambridge.

Russell, B. (1981) *Building Systems, Industrialisation and Architecture*, John Wiley and Sons, London.

16. Innovation in a Globalizing Industry: The Case of Automobiles

Andrew Graves

Introduction

The world automobile industry is a complex and ever-changing system of manufacturing, sub-contracting and alliances; together, assemblers, suppliers and distributors are a principal source of wealth and employment in the industrialized economies. It has been characterized as the 'industry of industries'[1] and its production techniques, in particular the mass-production assembly line, have had a profound influence on the organization and technology of other industries and services. The transformation, at the beginning of this century, from craft production to mass production, heralded an explosion of manufacturing capacity which has had a pervasive effect on all aspects of human activity. The industry's requirement for materials and components has spread far and wide throughout the mining, petrochemical, engineering and electronics sectors. Today's automobile, for example, contains over 12,000 separate parts sourced from a highly competitive and diverse range of suppliers. The automobile industry still remains an important and dynamic sector, even though it has now been displaced by the electronics industry as the largest and fastest growing major industrial sector.

Historical Overview

The historical development of the world automobile industry can be broken down into three distinct phases or transformations.[2] As can be seen from Table 16.1 the first transformation occurred in the US at the beginning of the century. This phase is generally associated with Henry Ford, who applied the rationale of 'scientific management' or 'Taylorism' to the production process. Taylor argued that management was required to 'gather together all the traditional knowledge which in the past has been processed by the workmen and then classifying, tabulating and reducing this knowledge to rules, laws and formulae' (Taylor, 1903, 1911).[3] To produce low-cost high-volume automobiles required basically two things: first, mass-production assembly work and specialized labour, with its ensuing economies of scale, and second, precision-made interchangeable components. Overall, the rationalization of models and mass-production techniques led to a huge increase in productivity and a subsequent reduction in the production cost of vehicles.

Table 16.1 Industrial transformations in automotive history

Transformation	Date	Production or product innovation	Geographic area of rapid market growth	National or regional industry responsible for shaping the world industry
I	1902 into 1920s	Standardized product, mass production systems	US	US
II	1950s into 1960s	Product differentiation, emphasis on product technology	Europe	Europe
III	late 1960s	Lean production 'just-in-time' high quality and corporate groups as a new system of production organization	Japan	Japan

Source: Adapted from Altshuler, A. et al. (1985) *The Future of the Automobile*, Table 2.1, p. 12.

Faced with a workforce, often immigrants from Europe, who could not easily communicate with each other, Henry Ford developed the moving assembly line which could be operated by relatively unskilled labour. Workers had access to stocks at all points during the assembly process. These buffer-stocks overcame both quality defects, through speedy substitution, and production down-time, but inevitably led to high inventory costs and the inefficient use of factory space. In 1903, prior to the introduction of the assembly line, Ford produced only 1,700 vehicles. However, by 1923 output rose to a staggering 1.9 million. In that year Ford, together with General Motors, produced over 2 million vehicles accounting for 91 per cent of world output (Altshuler et al. 1985, p. 15).

The second transformation occurred in Europe during the 1950s. It can be viewed as the challenge of the European producers to previous US domination, by the production of highly differentiated vehicles and a strong emphasis on product innovation. This new competitive phase was possible because of two main factors: first, the accumulated skills of European workers in product design and engineering, dating back to the 19th century, and second, the different geographical, economic and environmental conditions encountered in the various European manufacturing countries. The technical solutions to the problems posed by these different conditions varied from producer to producer. Often with unitized or monocoque body constructions, they encompassed front wheel drive water cooled engines (Fiat/Renault), air cooled rear engines driving the rear wheels (Volkswagen) and water cooled front engines driving the rear wheels (Volvo/Morris, and so forth). Instead of the standard straight six or V8 arrangement that dominated engine configuration in the US, the Europeans experimented with every conceivable alternative – from horizontally opposed air cooled twins to in-line four, five and six cylinders, through to V4s and V6s. Changes in other features such as body shape, suspension, brakes and transmissions also followed the same trend. This enabled the Europeans to exploit their comparative advantage in product-based innovation to such an extent that by 1960 they had managed to export more than eleven times the number of vehicles exported by the US, and by 1970 over twenty-five times. They also manufactured a total of 10.5 million units, compared with the 7.5 million produced by the US.

The third transformation occurred in the 1960s and 1970s in Japan and concentrated upon revolutionary changes in the organization of production rather than advances in technology. The existing US and European manufacturing techniques were viewed by the Japanese as wasteful of resources and a source of worker/management antagonism. They also regarded the management superstructure model developed by Alfred Sloan at General Motors in the 1920s as slow and cumbersome. Unlike Ford, Toyota had access to a highly homogeneous workforce that it was able to multi-skill and on whom Toyota imposed many existing management responsibilities.

To facilitate change, Toyota developed an alternative model of production known as 'lean production'.[4] The lean manufacturer 'combines the advantages of craft and mass production, while avoiding the high cost of the former and the rigidity of the latter'. In addition, lean manufacture requires 'half the human effort in the factory, half the manufacturing space, half the investment in tools, and half the engineering hours to develop a new product in half the time' (Womack, Jones and Roos, 1990, p. 13). In effect, lean production eliminates all activities that do not add value to the process or product. This concept will be explored further under 'Changes and Challenges Facing the Industry'.

Structure of the World Automobile Industry

Europe is the largest producer of automobiles in the world. Although production is slowly declining, a record 13.7 million units was being produced

Table 16.2 World automobile production (1950–1989)

	1960	1970	1978	1982	1986	1989	1950
N America	7001	7491	10315	5860	8890	7835	6950
W Europe	5120	10379	11321	10270	11805	13749	1110
Japan	165	3179	5748	6887	7810	9052	2
UK	1353	1641	1223	888	1091	1299	523
World	12985	22755	31226	27027	32848	35692	8168

Sources: Data for 1950–86 SMMT year books.
             Data for 1989 DRI World Automotive Forecast.

in 1989 compared with 7.8 million for North America and 9 million for Japan. The outstanding change in the world supply of automobiles, after the postwar recovery of European producers, was the enormous surge in Japanese production in the 1970s and 1980s. Table 16.2 indicates that by the mid-1980s Japanese production had caught up with US production.

It also shows that Japanese producers accounted for about a quarter of world car production. If Japanese car production from overseas transplants and trade barriers against Japanese imports are taken into account, Japan's share of automobile supply would have been even higher. By 1988 five Japanese manufacturers were amongst the top fifteen world producers of automobiles; this is shown in Table 16.3. Japanese car production in the US by 1989 was 2.2 million units and in Europe (EC) was 240,000. The latter is expected to rise to 1.2 million by the end of the 1990s.

Table 16.3 Leading world automobile production (million cars)

	1988
General Motors	5.7
Ford	4.2
Toyota	3.1
Volkswagen	2.7
Peugeot	2.2
Nissan	2.0
Fiat	1.8
Renault	1.8
Honda	1.5
Chrysler	1.2
Mazda	1.0
Vaz (Lada)	0.7
Mitsubishi	0.6
Hyundai	0.6
Daimler-Benz	0.6

Source: US Motor Vehicle Manufacturers Association.

The performance of Japanese automobile exports during the 1980s is even more extraordinary. Table 16.4 shows the value of Japanese foreign trade in automobiles with the rest of the world. Japanese penetration was greatest in the US domestic market, while the lower share of the European market was due in large part to the non-tariff barriers and trade agreements limiting imports into Europe. This is especially true in the cases of France and Italy, where Japanese penetration during this period was restricted to under 3 per cent of the market and to 2.5 thousand cars respectively.

Table 16.4 Value of Japanese trade in automobiles with rest of the world during the 1980s (millions of dollars)

Year	Export	Import	Auto Balance	Trade Balance
1981	18,445	326	18,119	+8,740
1982	18,017	347	17,669	+6,900
1983	19,535	400	19,134	+20,534
1984	21,899	461	21,438	33,611
1985	25,402	538	24,863	46,099
1986	32,945	1,069	31,875	72,743
1987	35,693	2,031	33,662	79,706

Source: White Paper on Science and Technology (1988).

Changes and Challenges Facing the World Automobile Industry

After a period of structural adjustment in the late 1970s and early 1980s (during which over 400,000 jobs were lost in the European industry alone) the automobile industry enjoyed rapid growth that seemed assured into the 1990s. However, producers now face a period of uncertainty brought about by various external and internal factors that may be the most serious and traumatic in their history.

A number of pressures are generating challenges for the Western automobile industry. These include:

- An inability to integrate 'lean production' techniques into existing assembler and supplier companies within a time scale which meets increasing competition from Japanese producers.
- Growing Japanese direct investment in Europe and the US, which is characterized by world best practice assembly plants and suppliers. In addition there is also increasing market penetration from 'new entrant' countries (for example, South Korea, Taiwan, Mexico).
- An inflexible cost structure and high overheads which reduce producers' abilities to cope with demand fluctuations.

- In Europe, a lack of a stable and dynamic economic and political environment as reflected in fluctuating EC currency and exchange rates. The failure to achieve a genuine Common Market with harmonized taxation levels, and the lack of a mobile, highly skilled technical and managerial labour force.
- The managerial, financial and political costs of investment in Eastern Europe.
- The need to rationalize automobile production on an international basis instead of within a national context, and to explore new possibilities for global expansion.
- The need to reduce waste and increase efficiency by implementing lean distribution and marketing systems.
- Failure to capitalize on existing strengths in the emerging areas of environmental technologies and Intelligent Vehicle and Highway Systems.

Space prevents consideration of all of these issues here, but a number of key challenges will now be examined.

The Challenge of Lean Production

The Toyota production system lies at the heart of lean manufacturing.[5] It was pioneered by Kiichiro Toyoda, founder of Toyota, and perfected by Taiichi Ohno, a Toyota engineer, over a twenty-year period to improve efficiency through a process of incremental improvement based upon the elimination of waste and the harmonization of production flows and communication. An essential element of this philosophy is the elimination of inventories and buffer stocks of components in the plant and the returning of some responsibility from management to supervisors and line-workers. A traditional mass-production Fordist plant is characterized by a hierarchical management structure where discipline is imposed through the speed of the production line and production targets set by management. In the Toyota production system, production workers and engineers are organized in multi-skilled teams and are directly responsible for quality, having the capacity to stop the line if necessary. Work is organized around the two guiding principals of 'just-in-time' (JIT) and 'total quality control', and workers and engineers are encouraged to initiate their own improvements to production efficiency. Crucial to the functioning of this system is not only an innovative internal management of workers and engineers within the factory but also new cooperative assembler-supplier relations.

The origins of the JIT concept are unclear. Cusumano (1985) has argued that Ohno credited Toyoda with developing JIT production and parts delivery stemming from the way he set up his Toyota factory in 1937 to receive materials for only one day's needs at a time, whilst the assembly plant built only the number of vehicles corresponding to the output of the machine shop.[6] Gradually Ohno and Toyoda worked together to eliminate bottlenecks and cut inventories through reversing the process-information and conveyance flows and by limiting production to small lots, so that previous stations would not have to wait for subsequent stations. This also involved educating suppliers to coordinate daily deliveries, thus eliminating warehousing and intermediate inspection.[7] It is also argued that JIT has cultural origins related to Japan's lack of resources and industry's need to optimize space and minimize waste. The importance of understanding the origins of and influences on JIT practices stems from the debate regarding their true transferability to other world regions and cultures. Mass production, on the other hand, was developed in the cultural context of the US where natural resources abound and land was not an impediment to plant design and construction.

One major difference between mass production and lean production relates to the management of time and workers' skills. In mass production one worker uses one machine and always performs the same task. This invariably leads to idle time for workers and irregularities in the flow of work. In the lean production system, production is rationalized through eliminating unnecessary buffer stocks and idle time by revising cycle times in direct relationship to production needs, running machines at full capacity and giving workers a range of tasks to perform. In Japan workers are also trained to maintain and repair their machines, thus minimizing down-time. This is in contrast to traditional job demarcation in the multi-union Western context of labour relations.

The lean production system, as described, highlights inefficiencies and exposes problems as and where they occur and concentrates management's and workers' efforts on immediate rectification of faults. This enables the maintenance of smooth-flowing and high quality production. The traditional mass-production 'buffered' system tends to conceal inefficiencies and reduces the input of ideas from management and workers. Built into the Japanese system of lean production is therefore a dynamic for continual improvement and change.

Product Development and Design: Challenges in the 1990s

As argued earlier, the growing Japanese competitiveness in automobiles was largely due to the development of a new manufacturing philosophy – lean production.[8] In the case of automobiles, the development of lean manufacturing has enabled leading Japanese producers not only to concentrate on high volumes but also to develop a high degree of flexibility in model runs, together with high productivity and high quality products.[9] As some Western producers close the productivity and quality gap with the Japanese and begin to implement some lean production techniques,

Japanese producers are driving the industry further forward through radical technological innovation and further organizational innovations.

Parallel to the organizational changes which are now sweeping the car industry in its attempts to meet world 'best practice' in productivity, is a technological transformation which is occurring through a combination of factors on both the supply and demand fronts. On the supply side a range of new technologies is being offered by traditional suppliers and new entrant companies especially in the areas of electronics and new materials. On the demand side several factors are combining to stimulate innovation: changing customer preferences regarding performance, style and fuel economies; and government policies on safety, environmental emissions and road traffic congestion. In addition, aggressive innovative marketing strategies on the part of some Japanese corporations have forced Western automobile companies to rethink radically their product development strategies.

Organizational Differences in Automobile R&D Systems

The Japanese and Western R&D systems are qualitatively different. This is best illustrated by comparing US and Japanese R&D organizations. As Figure 16.1 shows, the European and US systems are driven largely by perceived market opportunities. R&D is often only an appendage at the front end of the product development stage with few links, once the product development process gets going, between marketing and production.

Figure 16.1 Relationship between R&D, product development and production: European and US model
Source: Graves (1991), p. 111.

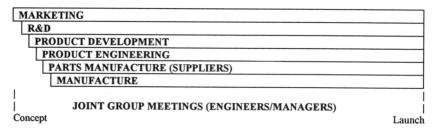

Figure 16.2 Relationship between R&D, product development and production: Japanese model
Source: Interviews with Nissan Motor Company (1986), cited in Graves (1991) p. 112.

Figure 16.2 shows the relationship between R&D, product development, marketing and production at Nissan. These relationships are more organic, with key engineers and managers maintaining a flow of information throughout the system.

In effect the US system of R&D is uni-directional while the Japanese process with its inbuilt feedback mechanism tends to be cyclical and dynamic.

Although there may be specific differences between how Japanese car companies organize their industrial R&D (Toyota differs considerably from Honda) certain organizational principles are shared.

A recent research study identifying world best practice in automotive R&D systems was conducted by Clark and Fujimoto of Harvard Business School.[10] Their study, which was undertaken between 1983-87, analyzed twenty-nine product development projects from automobile manufacturers in Japan, the US and Europe. Their primary unit of analysis was the 'product development organization', or that part of the firm concerned with major product development projects for passenger cars and new models.

Data for the study was collected at three levels – company, organization and project – and adjustments were made for variables such as project scope (parts carry over, supplier involvement, project content, and the size and number of body types). Findings of the study show that Japanese producers take forty-seven months to design a new vehicle compared with sixty months in the US and Europe. In addition, the Japanese producers use 1.7 million engineering man-hours whilst the US and European producers employ 3.1 million to develop a similar vehicle. Furthermore, they claim that US and European firms employ 903 engineers during the development process, as opposed to 485 by their Japanese counterparts. The efficient organization of product development not only requires fewer engineers over a shorter period of time to complete the same task but also results in a much lower staff turnover.

Clark and Fujimoto state:

> If the average European and Japanese firms began on the development of a comparable vehicle at the same time, the European product would enter the market over a year later... . A comparable vehicle would require almost twice the engineering hours of an average European producer. These differences in lead time, man-hours and design quality reflect underlying differences in engineering philosophy and the organisation and management of product development (Clark and Fujimoto, 1988a, p.1).

Leading Japanese producers are now not only challenging the Western European volume producers but, as previously mentioned, are investing heavily in new products and production lines for luxury and sports cars. The introduction of the Honda 'Legend', the Nissan 'Infinity' and Toyota 'Lexus' in the luxury car segment has heralded a significant competitive threat to leading European luxury car producers.

Since the 1950s the European manufacturers in particular have been able to offer different technical solutions to an expanding range of design requirements, related to a strongly diversified consumer demand. Design has been an integral part of their portfolios – it has been as important to the volume producers like Volkswagen, Fiat and Austin-Morris as it is to the specialized producers like Jaguar, Volvo and Mercedes-Benz. This battle for market domination through design originality has also been driven by an explosive growth in R&D activities by both producers and component suppliers – who are playing an increasing role in the design of new products.

The importance of combining the Japanese R&D system, with its superiority in engineering effort and 30 per cent reduction in development time, with the 'lean factory' system means that Japanese producers are able to make strategic choices regarding economies of scale. Average volumes per model, for example, are almost half that of US and European producers.[11] As the average age of each Japanese model is approximately two years, half that of their Western competitors, only 500,000 vehicles are produced, compared with almost four times that number in the US and Europe. This flexibility of model numbers and volumes enables the Japanese producers not only to exploit the increasingly fragmented markets of the world but also to generate their own niches in the market place. In an era characterized by rapidly changing technology, it is important for these innovations not only to be incorporated into the latest vehicles but also to be offered to customers in the shortest possible time.

The implications arising from this are two-fold. First, Western producers will be increasingly pushed to reduce their own product cycles to keep technological advance in step with consumer acceptance. Second, Western producers may well end up having to rely on the Japanese to bring consumers 'up to speed' on new styles and designs. By following trends set by the Japanese, they may well be more able to make greater steps in design change – but at the expense of losing their lead. Therefore, the Western automobile manufacturers may well become imitators rather than trendsetters in the realm of styling and design – as is occurring in the sphere of technology.

The European response to these challenges lies largely in its ability to introduce lean production techniques into its manufacturing base. However, some scepticism still exists regarding the effectiveness of these methods and their transferability to the European context.[12]

New Roles for Suppliers

Automobile assemblers throughout the world are requiring new and more demanding relationships with their suppliers and many component suppliers will not survive this restructuring. In response to the Japanese model, Western manufacturers now demand of their suppliers:[13]

- World class levels of productivity, quality, technology and design.
- Increased R&D from first-tier firms. (Many suppliers are now expected to supply complete systems.)
- The development of an 'organic' relationship with a single (often specialist) supplier, bringing the supplier into the product development programme at an early stage, and the building of stronger vertical relationships with assemblers.
- The supply (and manufacture if possible) in each region of assembly on a JIT basis and the servicing of global assembly plants, if required.
- Continual improvement in cost structure.
- Flexibility of supply in volatile market conditions.
- The attracting of new entrant suppliers who can address environmental and road traffic informatics concerns (for example, electric vehicles/information technology/new advanced materials for weight reductions and recyclability).

As the vehicle assemblers continue to divest themselves of in-house suppliers (from 50 per cent to as high as 70 per cent from outside sourcing) they will have to build less adversarial relationships with independent component manufacturers. In the European case, the arrival of the Japanese transplants will offer significant opportunities for suppliers, particularly those based in the UK. European suppliers who can successfully service the transplants will thus be capable of competing on a global basis. It will be of primary importance for their suppliers not only to increase their levels of productivity *and* quality to those achieved by their Japanese competitors but also to make significant cost reductions throughout their operations. In addition, there is a risk that if levels of technological ability are not increased across the supply base the transplants will be forced to source high value added parts from Japanese components transplants who will be encouraged to locate in Europe.

This strategy could have significant political and industrial implications for the indigenous components industry, undermining their core technological capability and resulting in a large part of the European industry being dedicated to supplying low value added components requiring little or no research and development input. Component suppliers in Europe also face two significant new challenges in the 1990s from both Eastern Europe and from the increasing concentration and globalization of the assemblers. In Eastern Europe, countries such as Poland, Czechoslovakia and Hungary are seeking investment through joint ventures, licensing agreements and transplants in order to build an export led industrial strategy.[14] In particular these countries offer low-wage and cost-effective production opportunities for Western European firms. In addition, they possess latent engineering, especially tooling capabilities vital to building a powerful component and assembler base.

In the automobile producing countries increasing resources are being invested in new products and new production technologies by both manufacturers and suppliers. The early fruits of the substantial increase in both R&D and patenting by the Japanese are now reaching the market place and will increasingly pose a threat to the one area where the European industry has been dominant.[15] As noted earlier, their market share doubled during this period at the expense of the US producers. This dominance was not just built on in-house capabilities but upon strategic alliances and cleverly managed subcontracting to suppliers, design firms and styling houses. The Japanese producers have recently challenged this dominance, building upon their existing advantages of high productivity with more efficient product development with shorter model cycles.[16]

Automotive suppliers also face a threat from the assemblers' increasing efforts to rationalize component costs and piece-part numbers. In particular, the growing number of alliances between the leading assemblers is being increasingly driven by their desire to reduce component costs through joint development projects and shared components. Suppliers will be confronted more and more with a greater interchange of both technology and purchasing information between their customers and will face a significant rationalization of parts across the industry. Attempts are already being made to develop common parts for differing makes and models in components that do not contribute to product differentiation.

In conclusion, the world automotive supplier base will continue to experience continuing structural change during the 1990s and suppliers will be forced to meet the Japanese challenge if they wish to survive. Those companies that can attune their organizations to these challenges will, for the first time, enjoy the certainty of a long-term relationship with their customer and will be able to utilize this new found efficiency to become truly global players. It is becoming increasingly clear that the key competitive region for automobile production in the next decade will be in Europe. An important role will be played in Europe by transplants.

Transplants

It is largely the arrival in the UK of the leading Japanese producers, Nissan, Toyota and Honda, that gives rise to optimism for the British automotive industry. However, not surprisingly it has led to uncertainty and concern amongst the rest of the European producers. As has happened in North America, the Japanese transplants are viewed not as creating new products to increase market opportunities but as replacing existing capacity at the expense of the least productive manufacturers. It is unclear which producers will suffer the largest cuts, but an analysis of US 'Big 3' plant closures clearly shows the effect the extra transplant capacity is likely to have in Europe (see Tables 16.5 and 16.6). Added to these concerns is the

Table 16.5 North America: Japanese transplants and US plant closures

Japanese Transplants	Location	1989 Production	Announced Capacity
Honda	Marysville, OH	351,670	360,000
	East Liberty, OH	–	150,000
	Alliston, ON	86,477	100,000
Nummi	Fremont, CA	192,235	100,000
Toyota	Georgetown, KY	151,150	240,000
	Cambridge, ON	20,859	50,000
Nissan	Smyrna, TN	216,200	480,000
Mazda	Flat Rock, MI	216,200	240,000
US Plant Closures	Location	Year Closed	Capacity
GM	Detroit, MI	1987	212,000
	Norwood, OH	1987	250,000
	Leeds, MA	1988	250,000
Chrysler	Kenosha, WI	1988	300,000
GM	Pontiac, MI	1988	100,000
	Framington, MA	1989	200,000
	Lakewood, GE	1990	200,000
Chrysler	Detroit, MI	1990	230,000
	St Louis, MS	1990	21,000
GM	Pontiac, MI	1990	54,000

Source: Author's interviews/company data.

Table 16.6 Europe: Japanese transplants and European plant closures

Company	Location	Capacity	European Closures
Nissan	Washington, UK	200,000	
	Barcelona	150,000	
Honda	Swindon	140,000	
Toyota	Burnaston, UK	200,000	None
	Hanover	15,000	to date
	Lisbon	15,000	
Isuzu	Luton, UK	80,000	
Suzuki	Linares	50,000	
	Esztergom	50,000	
Mazda	TBA	120,000	
Mitsubishi	Netherlands	200,000	
Total		**1,220,000**	

Source: Author's interviews/company data.

continuing falling sales and revenues from European luxury and sports vehicles worldwide as a result of tough competition from the Japanese in Europe's traditional export markets, particularly in the US. Luxury manufacturers who have tried to escape this challenge by driving their product range further upmarket have so far met with little success.[17]

This situation highlights two key issues for the European and North American industry with regard to the transplants. First, in order to compete, these producers must implement forms of lean production that will enhance their overall performance. Their inability, so far, to implement substantial changes (particularly in Europe) is of concern. Second, with the intensification of technological change in the industry in the 1990s the European producers need to regain their previous dominant position. Of considerable concern to the European manufacturers with regard to this issue is whether the Japanese manufacturing plants bring with them a fully supportive research, development and engineering capability. These fears are reinforced as a result of internal pressures on the Japanese manufacturers to maintain employment at home as their global trading position deteriorates. Nissan, for example, is now experiencing worldwide losses and Toyota saw its profits halved during the past year. In addition, Japanese domestic producers are now facing a severe labour shortage at the plant level and are having difficulty, particularly in the final assembly area of the factory, implementing lean production principles. Many Japanese assemblers are now being confronted with problems in maintaining the level of continuous improvement that they have achieved in the past. Finally, as historically the lean production system has been developed in an environment of annual market growth in Japan it will be interesting to observe how the Japanese transplants adapt to the cyclicality of the US and European markets. Many automotive analysts now believe that the most severe changes and challenges for the industry will be played out in Europe over the next decade. In particular, policy issues with regard to the role of government and industrial collaboration are again back on the agenda. At the present time, it is only the European producers who are not truly global in nature.

Environmental and Regulatory Issues: European Challenges

Notwithstanding the difficulties of Japanese entry into a post-1992 Europe, there are two other issues relating to technology development which will need to be addressed within a common policy framework. Moves in this direction are already under way. The first relates to environmental pollution and related concerns and regulations regarding vehicle emissions. Western companies and institutions are currently researching environmental pollution controls and advanced traffic management systems.[18] The PROMETHEUS research programme has already produced some intra-European cooperation between companies and research centres both inside and outside the automobile industry. Clearly the European Community must play a growing role in not only setting standards and goals but in fostering

R&D and technology commercialization on a pan-European basis. The time is now right for a global collaborative effort to target common environmental concerns.

The second issue concerns the need for improved traffic management systems, and in this area Europe is already making a determined attempt to spearhead advances with the development of 'smart cars' and 'Intelligent Highway Systems'. These powerful externalities of pollution control and road traffic congestion reinforce the need for the European producers to overcome the structural fragmentation of their current technological base. It is becoming clear that a greater concentration of resources needs to be invested in R&D on a pan-European basis to address these issues and that this will require closer collaboration between manufacturers, suppliers, research institutes and governments.

As the authority which owns (or controls) the traffic infrastructure, government plays a crucial role in deciding national policy options between public and private transportation. Government also acts as a coordinator of regulations and protocols between countries and trading partners. This is of crucial importance with regard to the development of Intelligent Vehicle and Highway System-type technologies to be fitted to export vehicles which will be operated across national and international boundaries. Government may also play a catalytic role by encouraging collaborative R&D programmes in order to foster industrial synergies and encourage innovation where firms lack the resources (or will) to invest in long-term projects. Whilst it is generally agreed in the industry (and by some governments) that government decision-makers, or their advisers, do not always possess the full competence to assess properly technological and market opportunities, it is clear that governments will (either by their actions, or inaction) play a major role in deciding the future trajectory of automotive R&D in the coming decade.

Conclusion

The Western automobile industry faces several severe challenges to its prosperity. In particular two key tasks face producers: the need to close the gap in productivity, quality and technology with both the Japanese transplants in the UK and the US; and the need to construct a strategy for a post-national automobile industry which is global in nature.

Both European and US manufacturers and suppliers need to adopt significant structural changes to meet these challenges since the global nature of the Japanese production system means they can no longer hide behind trade barriers and tariffs. The global strategy of Japanese car companies not only allows them to avoid the instability of exchange rates, but enables them to avoid the consequences of foreign protection.

Some Western manufacturers have, to some extent, developed strategies to bridge the gaps in performance. However, these strategies need to be based upon existing Western strengths, for merely to imitate the Japanese will leave producers lagging behind. The Western automobile manufacturers, suppliers and styling and design houses need to re-evaluate their strategies and interdependencies as the Japanese manufacturers move forward through growing investments in technology and design. However, as Japanese and South East Asian producers internationalize their production and R&D systems (and reduce reliance upon independent Western design and styling studios), they are developing a highly integrated and global design capability to compete in all automotive markets. This challenges the major comparative advantage of the most significant and successful automobile-producing region since the 1950s – Europe.

During the past decade, Japanese direct foreign investment has added to the global over-capacity problem. This is now being resolved through the substitution of inefficient mass-production capacity by lean production. This substitution clearly gives cause for concern in the US and Europe because of the implications for national competitiveness and employment as a result of the transplants.

The Western car industry clearly faces the most critical challenges in its history, not only from the arrival of the Japanese plants but through the global revolution in manufacturing, product design and supply – lean production. It now has the opportunity to restructure and expand its capabilities in order to build a world-class manufacturing and supply base. It is, for example, significant that BMW and Mercedes-Benz are prepared to risk investing in building their own transplants in North America thereby reversing the global perception of 'Fortress Europe'. Europe, in particular, has an industrial culture based upon engineering and design that is increasingly in demand in the modern world and has a desire and willingness to learn from the 'best practices' of its competitors. The immediate goal of the industry must be to establish mutual trust and understanding between the assemblers, suppliers and governments in order to re-establish the automotive sector as the main engine for economic growth and prosperity for the 21st century.

Notes

1. See Peter Drucker (1946) who first coined the phrase.
2. For an analysis of the major industrial transformations of the automobile industry over the last 100 years see Altshuler et al. (1985).
3. By detailing individual work tasks, management rewards workers in direct proportion to their levels of output. This has led to the practice, particularly in the car industry, of 'piecework' practices synonymous with mass production. For an interesting debate on the relationship between technology and social relations, see Kaplinsky (1984) Chapter 8, also Taylor (1903), Babbage (1832), Braverman (1974), Blauner (1964).
4. The term 'lean production' was first coined in 1987 by the author to describe this new

production paradigm. It is based upon the concept of 'lean design' as pioneered by racing car designers (practised and perfected in modern times by Colin Chapman of Lotus Cars) whose objective is to optimize material usage in order to effect the most efficient power to weight ratio. The term 'fragile production' is also used to denote the same concept. See Shimada (1986, 1989). The concept of lean production is fully analyzed in Womack et al. (1990).

5.   For an interesting analysis of the 'mechanics' of the Toyota production system see Monden (1983; 1993).
6.   Also see Voss (1987) who claims that JIT originated at Toyota. For a debate about the adoption of JIT techniques, particularly in the UK, see Voss and Robinson (1987a; 1987b).
7.   Similar techniques to JIT production have also been described in other sectors including Japanese shipbuilding. For example, Schonberger (1982) argues that during the 1960s Japanese shipbuilders cut their steel inventories from a month's supply to just a few days as a direct response to the over-capacity being experienced by the steel industry, so steel deliveries were received 'just-in-time'.
8.   See Womack, Jones and Roos (1990).
9.   For a debate regarding product variety see MacDuffie et al. (1992), MacDuffie and Krafcik (1989) and Krafcik (1988a).
10. For the findings of this study see Clark, Chew and Fujimoto (1987); Clark and Fujimoto (1987, 1988a; 1988b; 1988c); Clark (1988a; 1988b) and Fujimoto (1989).
11. See Sheriff (1988).
12. See, for example, Graves' chapter in Freeman, C. et al. (1991) *Technology and the Future of Europe*, pp. 261–80 on whether lean production is transferable to the European context.
13. For an interesting debate on restructuring in the automotive supply base, see Lamming (1993) who analyzes strategies for lean supply.
14. For an analysis of global strategic alliances in the automobile industry see Burgers et al. (1993).
15. For trends in European R&D, design and styling see Graves (1987; 1988).
16. For an analysis of the European model of product development see Clark and Fujimoto (1988a).
17. See Krafcik (1989) whose study of the luxury/speciality segment found a six-fold productivity and three-fold quality gap between the best (Japanese) and worst (British) plants. The primary explanation is, as with the volume producers, the type of production system employed. Product manufacturability also plays a key role in the pursuit of productivity and quality goals.
18. For a description of Intelligent Vehicle and Highway Systems and the PROMETHEUS programme, see Graves (1989) and Klein (1989).

Bibliography

Altshuler, A., Anderson, M., Jones, D.T., Roos, D. and Womack, J. (1985) *The Future of the Automobile: Report of MIT's International Automobile Programme*, George Allen and Unwin, London.

Babbage, C. (1832) *On the Economy of Machinery and Manufacture*, Charles Knight, London.

Blauner, P. (1964) *Alienation and Freedom: The Factory Worker and His Industry*, Chicago Press.

Braverman, H. (1974) *Labor and Monopoly Capital: The Degradation of Work in the Twentieth Century*, Monthly Review Press, New York.

Burgers, W.P., Hill, C.W.L. and Kim, W.C. (1993) 'The Theory of Global Strategic Alliances: The Case of the Global Auto Industry, *Strategic Management Journal*, Vol. 14, pp. 419–32.

Clark, K.B., Chew, W.B. and Fujimoto, T. (1987) 'Product Development in the World Auto Industry', *Brookings Papers on Economic Activity* 3, pp. 729–71

Clark, K.B. (1988a) 'Project Scope and Project Performance: The Effect of Parts Strategy and Supplier Involvement on Product Development', Harvard Business School Working Paper No. 88-069.

Clark, K.B. (1988b) 'Managing Technology in International Competition: The Case of Product Development in Response to Foreign Entry', in Spence, M. and Hazard, H.A. (eds) *International Competitiveness*, Ballinger, Cambridge, pp. 27–74.

Clark, K.B. and Fujimoto, T. (1987) 'Overlapping Problem-Solving in Product Development', Harvard Business School Working Paper No. 87-048. Also in Kasra, F. (ed.) *Managing International Manufacturing*, North-Holland, Amsterdam.

Clark, K.B. and Fujimoto, T. (1988a) 'The European Model of Product Development: Challenge and Opportunity', Working Paper for the International Motor Vehicle Programme, MIT, Cambridge, Massachusetts, USA (May).

Clark, K.B. and Fujimoto, T. (1988b) 'Lead-Time in Automobile Product Development: Explaining the Japanese Advantage', Harvard Business School Working Paper. Also in *Journal of Technology and Engineering Management* 1 (forthcoming).

Clark, K.B. and Fujimoto, T. (1988c) 'Shortening Product Development Lead-Time: The Case of the Global Automobile Industry', presented in Professional Program Session, Electronic Show and Convention, Boston, 10–12 May.

Cusumano, M.A. (1985) *The Japanese Automobile Industry: Technology and Management at Nissan and Toyota*, Harvard University Press, Cambridge, Massachusetts, USA.

Drucker, P. (1946) *The Concept of The Corporation*, John Day, New York.

Fujimoto, T. (1989) 'Organisations for Effective Product Development: The Case of the Global Automobile Industry', Doctor of Business Administration thesis, Harvard University, Graduate School of Business Administration.

Graves, A.P. (1987) *Comparative Trends in Automotive Research and Development*, Working Paper for the International Motor Vehicle Programme, MIT, Cambridge, Massachusetts, USA.

Graves, A.P. (1988) *European Design and Engineering Capabilities: A Continuing Strength*, Working Paper for the International Motor Vehicle Programme, MIT, Cambridge, Massachusetts, USA.

Graves, A.P. (1991) 'Globalisation of the Automobile Industry: The Challenge for Europe' in Freeman, C., Sharp, M. and Walker, W. (1991) *Technology and the Future of Europe*, Pinter, London, pp. 261–80.

Graves, A.P. (1989) *Prometheus: A New Departure in Automobile R&D?*, Working Paper for the International Motor Vehicle Programme, MIT, Cambridge, Massachusetts, USA (May).

Graves, A.P. (1991) *International Competitiveness and Technology Development in the World Automobile Industry*, Doctoral thesis, Science Policy Research Unit, University of Sussex, Brighton, East Sussex, UK.

Japan Science and Technology Agency (ed.) (1988) *White Paper on Science and Technology*, Japan Information Center of Science and Technology, Tokyo.

Kaplinsky, R. (1984) *Automation: The Technology and Society*, Chapter 8, Longman Group, Harlow, UK.

Klein, H. (1989) *Towards a US National Program in Intelligent Vehicle Highway Systems*, Working Paper for the International Motor Vehicle Programme, MIT, Cambridge, Massachusetts, USA (May).

Krafcik, J.H. (1988a) *The Effect of Design Manufacturing on Productivity and Quality:*

An Update of the IMVP Assembly Plant Survey, Working Paper for the International Motor Vehicle Programme, MIT, Cambridge, Massachusetts, USA (January).

Krafcik, J.H. (1988b) *Comparative Analysis of Performance Indicators on World Assembly Plants*, Working Paper for the International Motor Vehicle Programme, MIT, Cambridge, Massachusetts, USA (January).

Krafcik, J.H. (1989) *Assembly Plant Performance and Changing Market Structure in the Luxury Car Segment*, Working Paper for the International Motor Vehicle Programme, MIT, Cambridge, Massachusetts, USA (May).

Lamming, R. (1993) *Beyond Partnership: Strategies for Innovation and Lean Supply*, Prentice Hall, Hemel Hempstead, UK.

MacDuffie, J.P. and Krafcik, J. (1989) 'The Team Concept: Models for Change', *The Jama Forum*, Vol. 7, No. 3, Working Paper for the International Motor Vehicle Programme, MIT, Cambridge, Massachusetts, USA (February).

MacDuffie, J.P. et al. (1992) *Product Variety and Manufacturing Performance: Evidence from the International Automobile Assembly Plant Study*, Working Paper for the International Motor Vehicle Programme, MIT, Cambridge, Massachusetts, USA (May).

Monden, Y. (1983) *Toyota Production System*, Industrial Engineering and Management Press, Atlanta.

Monden, Y. (1993) *Toyota Production System: An Integrated Approach to Just-in-Time*, Industrial Engineering and Management Press, Atlanta.

Schonberger, R.J. (1982) *Japanese Manufacturing Techniques*, Free Press, New York.

Sheriff, A. (1988) *The Comparative Product Position of Automobile Manufacturers: Performance and Strategies*, Working Paper for the International Motor Vehicle Programme, MIT, Cambridge, Massachusetts, USA (May).

Shimada, H. (1986) with MacDuffie, J.P., *Industrial Relations and 'Humanware': Japanese Investments in Automobile Manufacturing in the United States*, Working Paper for the International Motor Vehicle Programme, MIT, Cambridge, Massachusetts, USA

Shimada, H. (1989) *The Economics of Humanware*, Working Paper for the International Motor Vehicle Programme, MIT, Cambridge, Massachusetts, USA.

Taylor, F.W. (1903) *Shop Management*, New York, reprinted in Taylor, F.W. (1947) *Scientific Management*, Harper and Brothers, New York.

Taylor, F.W. (1911) *The Principles of Scientific Management*, New York, reprinted in Taylor, F.W. (1947) *Scientific Management*, Harper and Brothers, New York.

Voss, C. (1987) *Just-in-Time Manufacture*, IFS, London.

Voss, C. and Robinson, S. (1987a) *Just-in-Time in the UK*, Paper presented at the 2nd Annual Conference of the Operations Managers Association.

Voss, C. and Robinson, S. (1987b) 'The Application of Just-in-Time Techniques', *The International Journal of Operations and Production Management*, Vol. 7, No. 4, pp. 46–52.

Womack, J.P., Jones, D.T. and Roos, D. (1990) *The Machine that Changed the World*, Rawson Associates, New York.

17. Innovation in Telecommunication: Bridging the Supplier-User Interface

Robin Mansell

Introduction

The liberalization of the telecommunication sector began as early as the 1950s in the United States. It gathered momentum in the 1980s and by the end of the decade virtually all countries were experiencing a restructuring of the telecommunication equipment and service supply industry (Mansell, 1989; Trebing, 1969). In part liberalization was a reflection of changes in the costs of supplying equipment and services that are increasingly dependent upon microelectronics-based digital products and software systems. It was also a reflection of the expansion of mobile and data communication services. In 1990 the European Community equipment market was valued at 26 billion ECU with an annual growth rate of about 7 to 8 per cent. The European equipment market represented one half a per cent of the Community's GDP and nearly a quarter of the world market valued at approximately 110 billion ECU in the same year. The equipment market was being driven by the telecommunication service sector whose turnover reached 90 billion ECU in 1990 (Commission of the European Communities, 1992).

The advantages and disadvantages of the introduction of competition, the privatization of state monopolies and the implementation of new forms of regulation had become the subjects of vigorous debate especially in the United States, the European Community and Japan (Noam, 1992a). Developing countries and the Central and East European states also began to respond to pressures to introduce competition and to consider the privatization of telecommunication suppliers.

The restructuring of the telecommunication industry involved a shift away from the presumed superiority of monopoly and quasi-vertical integration as modes of industrial organization most likely to stimulate innovation in the sector. Instead, competition came to be regarded as the harbinger of greater efficiency and flexibility in the design and implementation of advanced communication technologies and services (Antonelli, 1992). In the 1990s nationally-based public telecommunication monopolies are giving way to a complex pattern of public and private supply. Telecommunication network operators, globally operating telecommunication and computer equipment manufacturers and niche market suppliers are contending for a share of local, national, regional and international markets.

Telecommunication service and equipment suppliers are becoming rivals in each others' markets. Their competitive prospects and the success of their strategies toward establishing cooperative and competitive relationships have been closely linked with the so-called *globalization* of economic activity (Ohmae, 1990; Soete, 1991).

These trends have been complemented by increasing heterogeneity on the demand side of the industry. The strategic goals of globally operating firms have become increasingly enmeshed with applications of voice, data, text and imaging services. These services support a wide range of internal and external information requirements related to R&D, production and marketing activities (Commission of the European Communities, 1990). Smaller and medium-sized firms have also been incorporated into multiple, often exclusive, electronic communication networks in order to participate as customers and suppliers of larger firms (Antonelli, 1988; Jouet, Flichy and Beaud, 1991).

Two fields of research bear on the implications of the transformations in the telecommunication industry. The first has focused upon telecommunication as a distinct sector and it has been concerned primarily with supply side issues. The second has emerged within the strategic management literature and it has been preoccupied with demand side issues and perspectives. The first section of this chapter considers the extent to which these fields of research have been able to shed light on the implications of innovations in the telecommunication sector. The second section considers the results of research on innovations in telecommunication networking where the explicit aim has been to consider the *interface* between supplier-user activities in the telecommunication field.

Perspectives on Innovation in Telecommunication

During the 1980s two largely incommensurate strands of research considered the implications of technical and institutional change in the telecommunication industry. The *telecommunication policy* literature was concerned mainly with the dynamics of innovation in digital microelectronics-based technologies and the adjustment of institutional and market structures to the implementation of these technologies. The effects of the digitalization of networks, the introduction of optical fibre transmission and optical switching techniques, and the incorporation of software-based information processing within public and private networks were the main focus of attention. These developments were examined in terms of their impact on economies of scale and scope in equipment and service supply and on the future structure of the supply side of the industry (Mansell, 1990; Snow, 1988). This perspective considered whether competition in the supply of services or the privatization of public telecommunication operators would result in greater efficiencies in the provision of basic voice and data transmission services and advanced communication services such as voice messaging, videoconferencing, electronic data interchange services, etc. (Bernard, 1991).

Some analysts claimed that competition in all or most segments of the industry was inevitable, or at very least sustainable, in the face of technical change. Competitive entry in markets in which 'national champions' had prevailed for decades was expected to stimulate innovation and bring flexibility and choice of services especially for large globally operating firms (Beesley, 1981; Mueller and Foreman-Peck, 1988). Others claimed that the liberalization of the sector would threaten the long-established role of the public telecommunication operators in providing universal public services (Mulgan, 1991; Noam, 1992b). Competition might also threaten the financial viability of the public telecommunication operators and the technical integrity of their public networks. The empirical evidence generated mixed signals as to the viability competitive telecommunication markets. Nevertheless, pressures mounted to permit new entry in service markets and to prise open the procurement practices of public telecommunication operators (Ungerer and Costello, 1988).

A major contributing factor in the pressures for change in the telecommunication industry was the growing conviction that the monopolistic public telecommunication operators had failed to respond to the complex information service requirements of multinational firms. This conviction was articulated in the second major strand of research on innovations in telecommunication markets. The *strategic management* literature emphasized the role of telecommunication as a crucial factor contributing to the competitiveness of firms and industrial sectors (Teece, 1989). Research focused particularly on the inter- and intra-organizational use of advanced information and communication services (Ciborra, 1992). This literature focused upon issues such as the productivity gains associated with the introduction of electronic information systems within and external to the firm, large user service requirements, and the contribution of telecommunication to the locational, production and marketing strategies especially of globally operating firms (Porter, 1992).

Analysts frequently championed the need for market liberalization, de-regulation and greater competition (Porter, 1992). There was considerable interest in the organizational and structural innovations needed to enable firms to benefit from the productivity gains that were expected to arise with the introduction of advanced communication technologies (Hagstrom, 1990). Case studies examined the ways in which firms 'learned' to apply network technologies and services such as on-line information processing, computer-aided design and manufacturing, electronic data interchange and high speed data services (Commission of the European Communities, 1990; Mansell and Sayers, 1992). Generally, the results showed a failure to fully integrate and exploit new electronic service applications. Such failures were variously ascribed to the unresponsiveness of the supply side of the industry or to the uneven availability of the competencies needed to blend technical and organizational innovations within larger and smaller telecommunication using firms.

Both perspectives have tended to assume that the predominant trend in the telecommunication industry is toward a permeable global telecommunication fabric that supports the requirements of multinational firms as well as those of smaller businesses. Technical and organizational innovations in the supply and use of telecommunication are expected to result in multiple interconnected private and public networks which mingle together under the control of multiple suppliers and users (Noam, 1988). *Open* network access and a multi-vendor equipment supply environment are the expected long-term outcomes of the processes of innovation on the supplier and user sides of the telecommunication industry.

The segmentation of supply and demand side perspectives has contributed to a failure to deepen investigation into the underlying determinants of innovation in this sector. As in other sectors of the economy, there are tensions at the interface between supply and demand that shape the design of telecommunication networks. In some cases the resolution of these contributes to the evolution of open networks. However, in others, it creates pressures network closure, fragmentation and uneven patterns of telecommunication development (Mansell and Jenkins, 1992b). The supplier-user interface in the telecommunication sector is a site where the negotiation of technical and organizational design alternatives for future telecommunication networks is particularly visible (Mansell and Jenkins, 1992b). Innovations in the technical and organizational domains have resulted in the development of Electronic Trading Networks (ETN). These new forms of networks show the extent to which conflicting trends toward open networks and network closure are present in the telecommunication innovation process.

Electronic Trading Networks (ETN)

ETN depend upon a complex mix of traditional and advanced telecommunication equipment, network operators and communities of users. These networks are the product of considerable innovative activity in technical design and they generally involve the establishment of new competitive and co-operative relationships on both the supply and demand side of the telecommunication industry.

ETN are electronic communication systems that combine the *collaborative* aspects of electronic trading schemes which bring members of a scheme together with network operators and the *competitive* advantages of network-based markets such as the reduction of costs associated with geographical distance and the advantages of speed and accuracy of transactions. The technical design and membership criteria for participation in these networks can be open or closed (Mansell and Jenkins, 1992b). ETN are closely associated with the emergence of electronic network marketplaces and the internationalization of markets. For example,

> Network information services connect the needs and resources of users to the capabilities and services of producers and facilitate transactions between them. All the usual services of a marketplace can be offered within a large information network.... Indeed, the delivery of products and services for business, industry, the consumer, and government can be perceived as a marketplace in the emerging information society – a marketplace on a communications network or the *network marketplace* (Dordick et al. 1981: 1).

The establishment of ETN requires considerable innovation on the part of telecommunication and computer equipment suppliers, network operators in the public and private sectors and users in different sectors of the economy. Analysis of the development of these networks in, for example, the financial services sector points to the underlying trends in the evolution of telecommunication networks (Mansell and Jenkins, 1992a).

In the financial services sector network-based trading is highly sophisticated. Users of electronic markets in this sector are generally urban professional companies with access to advanced telecommunication networks. These companies tend to trade high value items which enables them to bear the substantial costs of technological innovation.

In an environment in which market confidence is easily shaken and where there are pressures for the liberalization of the movement of international capital, new rules and procedures have been needed to buffer industrial sectors, nations and regions from ephemeral swings in the market. NORDEX and GLOBEX are examples of strategic and technical responses to these developments.

NORDEX began operating in 1990 as a London-based, cross-border electronic marketplace for professional investors who traded in shares of companies based in the Nordic countries. NORDEX was owned and operated by Transvik, a subsidiary of Kinnevik (a privately controlled Swedish holding company) which has national and international interests in the information distribution industry. NORDEX was based on the Transvik Market System and was withdrawn at the end of 1992.

GLOBEX was introduced in 1992 to offer 'after hours' global trading of Futures and Options Financial Instruments using the Chicago Mercantile Exchange and the Chicago Board of Trade. Global telecommunication networking and facilities management are provided by Reuters. The impetus for the creation of this 'after hours' trading network was an investigation by the United States courts into corruption in the Chicago Exchanges. The investigation revealed the need to migrate financial trading into a more secure environment. Reuters expressed an interest in becoming involved. The market for its core business, e.g. placing information terminals on every dealing room desk, was becoming saturated and the company already operated one of the largest global private telecommunication networks.

In each of these examples of an Electronic Trading Network, the user firms, network operators and the suppliers of the telecommunication and computing equipment have broken with tradition in the technical and organizational elements of network design.

NORDEX

In the case of NORDEX the network users were familiar with screen-based trading. They were involved in the design phase by the market operator – Transvik. Prior to implementation users participated in the identification of weaknesses in the network software and in the institutional arrangements for clearing and settlement. The challenge for most users was to integrate an additional service with existing electronic services. In order to establish the electronic marketplace, the network operator, Transvik, arranged for Citibank to provide a central counterparty to ensure user confidence in the system. This was essential to the utilization of the system. Citibank also provided a local presence for activity. The bank ensured conformance with financial service regulations in each country where the system operated.

NORDEX obtained the telecommunication and software components for its electronic network from other members of its parent group, from national public telecommunication operators and from a third party network operator, GE Information Services (GEIS Co.). The development of the Transvik Market System required GEIS Co. to reconfigure its network to meet the communication specifications for the electronic market.

NORDEX users ranged from nationally-based investors to the largest transnational corporate investor. Membership was not determined by geographical location, but was restricted to institutions deemed by Citibank to meet traditional criteria established with respect to contractual obligations intended to ensure that trade execution is assured, timely and reasonably risk free. In order to enable the market system to work, the network operator, Transvik, was required to operate NORDEX within the regulatory conditions of each national market, e.g. the UK.

NORDEX membership was open to users who were professional brokers and not to institutional investors. Users were provided with a dedicated telephone line which connected a workstation to the Transvik Market System's central computer in London. From the perspective of the telecommunication equipment and network suppliers, innovations were required to meet the technical requirements of the network operators. These took the form of an interoperable cross-border network based on proprietary standards and protocols.

NORDEX was launched when the Swedish market ceased its paper-based trading in 1990. The reaction of brokers to the technical aspects of the system was positive but there was reluctance to accept the risk of trading on an anonymous system. The absence of a known counterparty had stalled the launch for six months. Citibank agreed to solve this problem by acting as the universal central counterparty. The main organizational problem was the need to ensure that each participating broker in the Transvik Market System agreed to contractual obligations.

NORDEX was withdrawn as a result of the falling volume of non-domestic trading in the Scandinavian equities market as a whole. However, the intention was always to implement similar electronic markets in different countries. As a result of the experience gained in operating Europe's only automated cross-border equities market, Transvik is now concentrating its efforts on selling the Transvik Market System as a generic platform for emerging and existing exchanges in Eastern and Western Europe and South America.

GLOBEX

In the case of GLOBEX, users were not involved as partners in the design phase. GLOBEX is an instance of collaboration though a joint venture. The United States partners provided knowledge of the domestic market for Futures and Options Financial Instruments. Reuters provided the expertise in the design, operation and management of a global telecommunication network. Reuters was willing to carry substantial up-front development costs. The company took responsibility for developing a new generation of software products and for configuring the global telecommunication network to meet stringent specifications for speed, reliability and cost.

GLOBEX involves medium-sized and large investors as well as multinational corporations based in North America, Asia and Europe. A global network operator was needed to function as a network operator. The network was required to connect Reuters' subscribers and to hub traffic in Hong Kong, London and New York. In order to meet requirements for security, speed and reliability coordination and investment was necessary.

The main organizational challenge to GLOBEX was to attract major exchanges onto the system. For example, early agreements have enabled the French stock exchange (MATIF) contracts to be listed on GLOBEX. The American Commodity Futures Trade Commission adopted a rule limiting the liability of parties involved in GLOBEX. This rule disclaims the Chicago Mercantile Exchange from liability related to the development of GLOBEX and losses arising from failures and malfunctions in the system. The total liability in a single day for all claims has been limited to

US $100,000. This ruling has required that member firms supply clients with customer information and risk disclosure statements.

In each of the case studies, the stimulus for investment has come, not from the cost/effectiveness of new developments in telecommunication, computing or software technologies, but from the initiatives of actors in the policy arena or in the marketplace. In-depth analysis of these and other examples of ETN has shown that the innovation process has involved compromises which favour some network participants over others. Trends toward the introduction of closed ETN are strong, even when there has been economic justification for their extension to new members to build critical mass. Countervailing pressures have arisen when communities of traders in the financial services and other sectors have considered the risk of admitting outsiders to a once club-like market. The result has been a trend toward fragmented and sectoral-based ETN such as NORDEX and GLOBEX.

In the case of NORDEX, users were involved from the outset in the development of the electronic trading initiative. If Transvik is successful in marketing the underlying trading system to other exchanges and market operators it will have gained from this experience and transferred to other cross-border trading environments. In contrast, GLOBEX has been designed from the 'top down' and in response to the concerns of regulators mainly in the United States that the systemic risks associated with electronic trading be reduced. Since this ETN has been operational only since mid-1992 it is too early to assess whether sufficient protection of investors has been incorporated within the technical aspects of the system to make it attractive to investors in the regions of the Triad of the United States, Europe and Japan.

Innovations in policy
The innovative activity required to establish ETN raises policy issues for public and private sector institutions. Public agencies are examining the policy and regulatory implications of these networks. There is little evidence that national government organizations in Europe or the European Commission have moved to establish innovative policies to counter the trends toward network closure.

In the European Commission the Directorates responsible for information technology and telecommunication (DG-XIII) and competition policy (DG-IV) have only begun to address the implications of ETN although attention has been given separately to electronic data interchange, information market and telecommunication issues.

With the wider diffusion of ETN, policy makers will need to consider how existing and new institutions can mediate between network providers and the regulatory regimes maintained by national and regional governments. It will be some time before ETN become as pervasive as today's public telecommunication networks which support conventional voice and data services. As they diffuse throughout the economy, they will do so unevenly. The negotiation of tensions in the relationships between suppliers and users is likely to continue to favour the design of closed proprietary telecommunication networks.

The advent of 'footloose' electronic trading hubs could have distorting effects on the structure of national economies. ETN are already stretching the capacity of the international policy community to monitor developments. These innovations in networking are challenging conventional wisdom as to how advanced telecommunication services contribute to sustainable competitive advantage in marketplaces that exist increasingly in electronic space.

In summary, recent evidence suggests that trends toward closed ETN are strong – despite economic justification to extend membership to new users. In the absence of policy intervention, whether at national, regional or international levels, the trend will continue toward fragmented sectorally oriented ETN. The strategic management literature tends to regard innovations in telecommunication infrastructure and service supply as simply providing the 'nervous system' for industrial activity in 1990s. At best this is an over simplification of the technical and institutional forces that are shaping the supply and use of telecommunication. The telecommunication policy perspective has found it difficult to integrate its supply oriented concerns with the information and communication requirements of disparate user communities.

Corporate strategies and public policies are more likely to achieve the goal of encouraging the design of advanced open telecommunication networks if they take account of the pressures toward network closure. These pressures are created by the interaction of disparate political and economic interests at the interface between technical and organizational design in the telecommunication field. From the perspective of management, all types of trade-related information with respect to trade possibilities and options, the movement of goods and services, trade execution, clearing and settlement and regulations have a strategic role to play in contributing to the competitiveness of firms. The relative scarcity and timeliness of such information can often contribute to the competitive prospects of firms and this in turn creates pressures toward network closure. These aspects of electronic trading combined with the advantages created by disparate policy and regulatory regimes are important factors which shape the growth potential of local, national and regional economies.

Bibliography

Antonelli, C. (1988) *New Information Technology and Industrial Change: The Italian Case*, Kluwer Academic Publishers, Dordrecht.

Antonelli, C. (ed.) (1992) *The Economics of Information Networks*, Elsevier Science Publishers, Amsterdam.

Beesley, M. (1981) *Liberalisation of the use of the British Telecommunications Network*, Report to the Secretary of State, Department of Industry, HMSO, London.

Bernard, J. (1991) *In-depth Analysis of Intelligent Networks: Perspectives on Advanced Communications for Europe*, PACE'90, Technology Investment Partners – Commission of the European Communities Brussels, February.

Ciborra, C.U. (1992) 'Innovation, Networks and Organizational Learning' in Antonelli C. (ed.) *The Economics of Information Networks*, Elsevier Science Publishers, Amsterdam.

Commission of the European Communities (1990) *Perspectives for Advanced Communications in Europe – PACE '90, Vol. 1*, Commission of the European Communities, Brussels, December.

Commission of the European Communities (1992) *The European Telecommunications Equipment Industry, The State of Play, Issues at Stake and Proposals for Action*, Commission of the European Communities, Brussels, 25 June.

Dordick H. et al. (1981) *The Emerging Network Marketplace*, Ablex Publishing Company, Norwood, New Jersey.

Hagstrom, P. (1990) 'New Information Systems and the Changing Structure of MNCs' in Bartlett C.A., Doz Y.L. and Hedlund G. (eds) *Managing the Global Firm*, Routledge, London.

Jouet, J., Flichy, P. and Beaud, P. (eds) (1991) *European Telematics: The Emerging Economy of Words*, North Holland, Amsterdam.

Mansell, R. (1989) *ICCP OECD Report No. 18 Telecommunication Network-based Services: Policy Implications*, OECD, Paris.

Mansell, R. (1990) 'Rethinking the Telecommunications Infrastructure: The New "Black Box"', *Research Policy*, 19, pp. 501–15.

Mansell, R. and Jenkins, M. (1992a) *Electronic Trading Networks and Interactivity: The Route to Competitive Advantage? Case Study Report*, Science Policy Research Unit, University of Sussex, April.

Mansell, R. and Jenkins, M. (1992b) 'Electronic Trading Networks and Interactivity: The Route Toward Competitive Advantage?' *Communications and Strategies*, 6 (deuxième trimestre), pp. 63–85.

Mansell, R. and Sayers, D. (1992) *European Cross-border Telecommunication: The Large Business User's View*, Science Policy Research Unit, University of Sussex, Brighton, October.

Mueller, J. and Foreman-Peck, J. (1988) *Liberalising European Telecommunications*, Blackwell, Cambridge.

Mulgan, G. J. (1991) *Communication and Control: Network and the New Economies of Communication*, Guildford Press, London.

Noam, E. (1988) 'The Next Steps in Telecommunications Evolution: The Pluralistic Network', Pacific Telecommunications Conference, Honolulu, Hawaii, October.

Noam, E. (1992a) *Telecommunications in Europe*, Oxford University Press, New York.

Noam, E.M. (1992b) 'Beyond the Golden Age of the Public Network', in Sapolsky, H., Crane, R., Neuman, W. and Noam, E. (eds) *The Telecommunications Revolution*, Routledge, London.

Ohmae, K. (1990) *The Borderless World*, Collins, London.

Porter, M.E. (1992) 'On Thinking about Deregulation and Competition', in Sapolsky, H., Crane, R., Neuman, W. and Noam, E. (eds) *The Telecommunications Revolution*, Routledge, London.

Snow, M.S. (1988) 'Telecommunications Literature: A Critical Review of the Economic, Technological and Public Policy Issues,' *Telecommunications Policy*, Vol. 12, No. 2, pp. 153–83.

Soete, L. (1991) *Technology in a Changing World, OECD Technology Economy Programme – Policy Synthesis*, MERIT, University of Limburg, The Netherlands, January.

Teece, D.J. (1989) 'Innovation, Cooperation and Antitrust: Balancing Competition and Cooperation', *High Technology Law Journal*, Vol. 4, No. 1, pp. 1–131.

Trebing, H.M. (1969) 'Common Carrier Regulation – The Silent Crisis', *Law and Contemporary Problems*, 34, pp. 299–329.

Ungerer, H. and Costello, N. (1988) *Telecommunications in Europe*, Commission of the European Communities, Brussels.

18. Innovation in Services

Ian Miles

The Service Sector

Services form the third of the three great sectors described by economists.[1] *The primary sector extracts raw materials (and sometimes goods) from the environment via activities such as mining and agriculture; the secondary sector transforms raw materials into goods, buildings, infrastructure, and physical utilities like water and electricity supplies.* For early commentators, the third great sector was often discounted as an unproductive residuum, but now this sector is by far the largest in terms of employment and output in most advanced industrial societies, and producer services are contributing substantially to economic activity in general (around 40 per cent of UK marketed services are sold as intermediate products, for example, according to input-output data). A more positive definition of services, then, might be: *the tertiary sector transforms the state of material goods, people themselves, or symbolic material (information).*[2]

A number of characteristics have traditionally been shared by many services. Table 18.1 lists the characteristics that are often seen as typical, or even as defining features, of services. (It also sets out material we shall return to later: how these features pose challenges and opportunities to innovation.) There are many exceptions to the specificities indicated in Table 18.1, but one or other 'peculiarity' applies to practically every service activity.

Services as Lagging

Theorists of *post-industrial society* suggested that with growing affluence people's expenditure shifts to services (perhaps because these are 'superior products', perhaps because people become satiated with material consumption). This leads to a shift in the overall pattern of demand in the economy away from goods (in relative terms) and toward services, and employment becomes additionally centred on services because of the automation of manufacturing. As societies evolve from agricultural to industrial to service economies, an upgrading of the labour force was expected to result from this process, with more white-collar and

Table 18.1 Characteristics of services

Aspect of Services	Characteristics often attributed to services	Innovation Strategies
SERVICE PRODUCTION		
Technology and Plant	Low levels of capital equipment; heavy investment in buildings.	Seek to reduce costs of buildings by use of *teleservices*, *toll-free phone numbers*, etc.
Labour	Some services highly professional (esp. requiring interpersonal skills); others relatively unskilled, often involving casual or part-time labour. Specialist knowledge may be important, but rarely technological skills.	Seek to reduce reliance on expensive and scarce skills by use of *expert systems* and related innovations; relocation of key operations to areas of low labour costs (using *telecommunications* to maintain coordination).
Organization of Labour Process	Workforce often engaged in craft-like production with limited management control of details of work.	Use IT to monitor workforce (e.g. tachometers and mobile communications for transport staff; aim for 'flatter' organizational structures, with data from field and front-office workers directly entering databases and thence Management Information Systems.
Features of Production	Production is often non-continuous and economies of scale are limited.	Standardize production (e.g. 'fast-food' chains), reorganize in more assembly-line-like feature with more standard components and higher division of labour.
Organization of Industry	Some services state-run public services; others often small-scale with high preponderance of family firms and self-employed.	Externalization and privatization of public services; combination of small firms using *network* technologies; IT-based *service management systems*.

244

SERVICE PRODUCT		
Nature of Product	Immaterial, often information-intensive. Hard to store or transport. Process and product hard to distinguish.	Add material components (e.g. client cards, membership cards). Use telematics for ordering, reservation and, if possible, delivery. Maintain elements of familiar 'user-interfaces'.
Features of Product	Often customized to consumer requirements.	Use of *Electronic Data Interchange* for remote input of client details. In general use of software by client or service provider to record client requirements and match to service product.
SERVICE CONSUMPTION		
Delivery of Product	Production and consumption coterminous in time and space; often client or supplier has to move to meet the other party.	*Telematics; Automated Teller Machines* and equivalent information services.
Role of Consumer	Services are 'consumer-intensive', requiring inputs from consumer into design/production process.	Consumer use of standardized 'menus' and new modes of delivering orders (EDI, fax, etc).
Organization of Consumption	Often hard to separate production from consumption. Self-service in formal and informal economies commonplace.	Increased use of self-service, utilizing existing consumer (or intermediate producer) technology – e.g. telephones, PCs – and user-friendly software interfaces.
SERVICE MARKETS		
Organization of Markets	Some services delivered via public sector bureaucratic provision. Some costs are invisibly bundled with goods (e.g. retail sector).	New modes of charging ('pay per' society), new reservation systems; more volatility in pricing using features of *EPOS* and related systems.
Regulation	Professional regulation common in some services.	Use of *databases* by regulatory institutions and service providers to supply and examine performance indicators and diagnostic evidence.
Marketing	Difficult to demonstrate products in advance.	Guarantees; demonstration packages (e.g. 'demo' software, shareware, trial periods of use).

245

professional workers (since service jobs were typically seen as skilled interpersonal work, if not as professional jobs).[3]

A contrary line of analysis notes that econometric analyses yield little evidence for a shift in consumer demand from goods to services – the elasticities of demand for goods and services seem roughly equivalent. Rather, the growth of the services sector reflects low productivity growth in services – as both services and manufacturing industries expand their output, services' share of employment grows. Low productivity growth is related to the relatively low level of the workforce in terms of training, etc.; and for those writers in the UK and USA who see the growth of services as constituting a burden on the manufacturing economy, the analysis becomes one of *deindustrialization*.[4]

While services are described in divergent terms in the two analyses (e.g. professionals versus unskilled workers), neither account places much faith on innovation in the services sector, which is assumed to lag behind manufacturing in productivity. This assumption is carried over in a more recent line of analysis articulated by Skolka (1976) and Gershuny (1978). They noted that differences in productivity growth between the sectors imply that the *price* of services will increase relative to that of goods – as can be seen in statistics for most advanced countries.[5] A consequence of this shift in relative prices is a shift of demand *from* services *to* goods (where these are substitutable). Gershuny demonstrated such shifts in consumer expenditure: within a category of expenditure like entertainment, the share allocated to goods has been rising. He described many of these innovations as involving 'self-services', with the final service being produced by the consumer's own efforts using new equipment, rather than being purchased.[6] Classic examples – the shifts from public to private transport, from cinemas to home entertainment, from laundries to home washing machines – suggest that technological innovation is important in terms of generating *new consumer products* (motor cars, TVs, washing machines) as well as in the productivity of manufacturing processes. This account does give some scope for the emergence of innovative new services to complement the new consumer goods – for example, the broadcasting industry, garages, etc.

Another recent account places more emphasis on technological innovation within services. Barras sees innovation in services as triggered to a large extent by innovation in manufacturing, but as taking on its own momentum. In contrast to the description of services in Table 18.1, he notes that many private services' capital expenditure is shifting away from plant and toward equipment, rather as happened in manufacturing at the time of the early industrial revolution.[7] Particularly important are new information technologies (IT), where over three-quarters of UK and US investment expenditure derives from services.[8]

Barras describes service industries' innovation process as a 'reverse product cycle', with process innovation preceding product innovation. A first stage in service innovation consists of process innovation, using new technologies generated in other sectors to increase efficiency of production/delivery of existing services. In a second stage, the new production systems are applied to increase the quality of the service – for example, in the frequency and volume of information provided to clients, in the availability of the service outside of normal office hours (automatic bank telling machines – ATMs – are a case in point). A third stage involves new services generated on the back of the new technology – for instance, as data being processed by IT can be put to other applications (e.g. online data services) or reworked in various ways (e.g. to provide a more flexible service).

This account fits the experiences of financial services in particular. It also sheds light on the emergence of new services from the internal IT departments of firms – for example, the emergence of online databases and similar services from publishing and automobile companies, among others.[9] But the implication that services are passive recipients of innovation from other sectors, at least until they become proficient with new IT, has never been entirely true. Transport and telecommunications services, for example, have long engaged in R&D. Though services appear to engage in very little R&D, on the whole, according to official statistics, these data fail to capture much of the software and organizational innovative activities of services as R&D. Batelle estimates for the USA that, in terms of total R&D spend, four of the top ten sectors are services; and of the ten largest sectors in terms of total sales, the highest R&D to sales ratio is that of 'other business and professional services', the tenth largest sector (Batelle, 1986).[10]

Diversity among Services

The sharply contrasting accounts of services reflect the wide variety of activities encompassed. Services serve different markets – most basically, *consumer* markets, *intermediate (producer)* markets, and *state or public service* allocative mechanisms – and involve different production processes – transforming the state of *physical objects, people* or *codified information*. Table 18.2 classifies services in terms of these two dimensions. (This is strictly an impressionistic picture of a situation which is in flux, especially as the structure of markets is changing.)

This typology helps us understand the sorts of process described by Gershuny and other authors. The specific features of the *service process and product* can then be related to the prospects for technological change in services. Briefly, *physical services* – transport, domestic services, etc. – have been subject to competition from new consumer goods such as the motor car and household appliances. While these goods have been associated with some new services (garages, repairs), the impulse has very

Table 18.2 A classification of services

Market Type	Production Type		
	PHYSICAL SERVICE	PERSON-CENTRED	INFORMATION SERVICE
STATE		Welfare Hospitals Health, medical Education	General government Broadcasting
CONSUMER	Domestic service Catering Retail trade Post	Barbers etc.	Entertainment
MIXED	Laundries Hotels Laundry Repairs		Real estate Telecommunication Banking Insurance Legal services
PRODUCER	Wholesale trade Physical distribution & storage		Engineering & architectural services Accountancy Miscellaneous professional services

much been from manufacturing industry competing with traditional services. In contrast, *information services* – entertainment in particular – have been subject to competition from a combination of new consumer goods such as TV and hi-fi, together with new services such as broadcasting and the recording industries. This indicates the importance of 'software' in association with electronic and microelectronic innovations, as compared to those based on cheap motor power. *Human services*, typically being produced together with and highly 'tailored' to, individual clients, are quite different. This is not to say that there has been no innovation – a notable case is health services, where pharmaceutical, radiological, and surgical technology have played very important roles. But in general cheap motor power and mass information delivery have not been very applicable to the core tasks of human services (peripheral functions, such as ambulance services and large-scale payment and invoicing systems are another matter). Processing highly specific data about individuals has been a task for service workers.

However, new IT, based upon microelectronic's ability to deliver cheap information-processing power, may change this. Until recently, computerization was applied only to the most large-scale, basic and routine administrative tasks, and their equivalents in financial and other information services. 'Automation' in service industries mainly involved application of machinery to extremely limited physical storage and cash transactions (e.g. vending machines, automatic tellers). But the availability of cheap personal computers with sophisticated and user-friendly software, and growing access to mobile communications and data networks, look set to bring automation to a much greater range of service functions.[11]

In *physical services*, computers have long been applied to the back office accounting and exchange tasks that surround their core functions. In a 'reverse product cycle'-like manner, these applications may set the scene for innovations bearing more on the core functions. Thus now that electronic cash registers and scanners have been widely introduced into supermarkets, they are being linked to the office systems being used for stocktaking and, in some cases, to automated warehouses and much wider systems of supermarket automation.[12] New systems of 'transport informatics' go beyond simple accounting of the timetables and whereabouts of vehicles, providing advanced routing and tariffing procedures backed up by mobile communications, 'smart cards' and other innovations.[13]

The large-scale *human services* have long been major computer users for large-scale administrative data processing applications (payroll, pensions, passports, driving licences, and the like), and for planning (for example, managing housing systems and waste disposal services, monitoring epidemiological and environmental statistics). The availability of cheap microcomputers enables some integration of services as service workers can access information from different databases on the same client (privacy rules permitting). More advanced information systems are being employed to assist decision-making when confronted by the complex details of individual clients – for example, expert systems to aid medical diagnosis and prescription, and to speed up the task of assessing individual entitlement to welfare benefits. Other applications involve the client's own use of equipment: public access terminals displaying information on library or other service provisions; interactive teaching aids based on microcomputers and related systems; and in several countries citizens are directly able to interrogate databases on the availability of jobs or their eligibility for benefits.[14]

Information services are major users of IT (and appear as major contributors to the large part played by services in IT investment, cited earlier). Sectors like telecommunications and financial services have used new technology to limit labour costs as well as to provide improved or new services, so that their levels of output growth are much higher than their employment growth (if any). As in the previous cases, the traditional IT applications involved large-scale electronic systems for massive number-crunching operations, together with specialized applications in broadcasting and other media. New IT is enormously important – and often very visible – in these industries, with innovations like automated teller machines and smart cards, new telephone and telematics services, and shifts from broadcasting to 'narrowcasting', all the focus of considerable activity. Some of the service firms involved play a prominent role in guiding the innovations, as in the case of banks that are heavily involved in defining the characteristics of new teller machines. The pace of innovation in these industries is quickened by the shift in regulatory policy in many countries, which has led to new entrants and increased international competition confronting many firms.

We have stressed the relation of service innovation to the specificities of service products and processes, but other characteristics of services cited in Table 18.1 may also be significant. For instance, those services based on low-quality (and thus low-pay) labour may have little incentive to invest in expensive equipment, while those employing large numbers of professionals such as doctors or teachers might find that these professional groups are empowered to resist technological changes which they perceive as against their interests. Small firms and self-employed people are usually late adopters of new technologies, public sector organizations are not noted for their dynamism, and so on. Table 18.1 suggests some ways in which the characteristic features of services lead to particular types of innovation.[15] The *industrialization of services*, a tendency apparent in several of the specific innovations, involves efforts to standardize services, to yield service products of predictable characteristics and quality, with improved economies of scale and delivery times.[16] It typically involves high levels of division of labour, and the use of pre-packaged and automated elements (such as pre-prepared meals, word processed templates for form letters, and the like).

Organizational and Technological Innovation in Services

The role of *organizational innovation* in services is very apparent – with supermarkets and similar facilities proving extremely significant in the development of modern service industries. Such organizational innovations will often have a technological dimension, whether this be very basic (e.g. shopping trolleys), or relatively high-tech (electronic point of sale equipment or ATM networks). As implied here, one important trajectory of organizational change has been towards *self-servicing* in the service establishment (there has only been slow development toward teleshopping and telebanking, with consumers at home using terminals), saving on labour costs and often increasing user satisfaction.

Other types of organizational change are being forced upon many service firms as new government philosophies have reshaped the regulatory structures governing sectors like banking and telecommunications, and privatized or externalized many public services. Ending monopolistic organization of a market may well spur innovation through competitive pressures. It can also stimulate innovations to cope with the new complexities – for example, competition in telecommunication services leads to new requirements as to how directories are established, accessed and maintained.

Another direction of organizational innovation is the search for *quality assurance and improvement*.[17] Recent developments in quality standards (e.g. BS 5750 and ISO 9000) have been taken up by services as well as manufacturing firms.[18] Measurement is an important feature of most quality programmes, and the role of *performance indicators* has been growing, often as a direct result of government policies which create regulatory bodies and set performance standards for public sector or newly privatized institutions. Indicator systems and the associated databases can be used to identify components of the service process suffering bottlenecks and inefficiencies, and such information will frequently lead to innovations being made; and the very act of monitoring will often also involve technological change.

Detailed charting, costing and monitoring of the service production process may also be associated with strategies aimed at charging clients for the full costs incurred in the course of producing services. New IT makes it possible to monitor the use of certain services in far more detail than was previously feasible, and the emergence of *pay-per* regimes is underway in various types of service which were financially supported in indirect ways in the past. For example, cable TV systems may charge viewers by the volume of programmes consumed (or, at least, displayed on their TV sets or downloaded to their videorecorders); the use of roads or of passenger information services (and other new services riding on the back of 'transport informatics') may likewise be charged to users via techniques ranging from the classical tollbooth to new methods employing 'smart cards' and mobile communications.[19]

Drawing on a range of examples spanning physical, human and information services, Quinn and his co-authors conclude that IT is being used by forward-looking firms to achieve both efficient and customized services.[20] This typically involves 'empowering' employees by enabling them to carry out sophisticated tasks without long learning curves. Software and planning staff assume a key responsibility for guiding the innovation process so that the technologies that are in use support the decisions required of the front-office staff. More decisions about product configurations are made at the local level, within these new frames of reference. And this decentralization is accompanied by a 'flattening' of firm structures, so that information on operations is rapidly processed and fed to senior levels of management, rather than proceeding through a long management chain of many layers.[21] These new organizational forms have implications for urban areas where many service jobs are currently concentrated – which will create new challenges for research on the spatial location of producer services.[22]

In discussing organizational innovation in services, van der Aa and Elfring (1991) identify a further three directions of development (which may have implications for technological innovation). First is *new combinations of services*, whereby service companies expand their portfolio (e.g. combining auditing and management consultancy). As well as representing a familiar diversification strategy, there may be economies of scope associated with the new combinations (e.g. some data about clients can be re-used). Second is the involvement of *clients as co-producers* which is an extension of the self-service model, discussed above, to knowledge-intensive business services, with the emphasis being laid upon client's role in advancing the expertise of service suppliers, and identifying new avenues for its application. Third is *multi-unit service firms*, a development that has been prominent as service suppliers have increased their geographic scope – especially as they have established bases in different countries in the wake of their transnational clients.

Recent studies have pointed out the role of technological innovation in the internationalization of services. IT, making it easier to separate the location and timing of service production from its delivery, is being used to alter the '*mode of presence*' of service organizations in foreign markets, hence transforming patterns of service trade.[23] Thus, 'offshore office services' carry out tasks such as data entry in countries with low labour costs.[24] As well as making some services more exportable, new technology can be used to alter management control systems, allowing for rapid appraisal and monitoring of local operations and circumstances through telematics networks. Such systems may also be used for maintenance activities, and telematics are already used in remote computer diagnostics and for environmental monitoring in several industrial countries.

Conclusions

Some services are at the forefront of innovation. Indeed, new IT-based services, such as software and telematics, are triggers to innovation across the economy, rather than passive recipients of innovation from manufacturing industry. If services are becoming more R&D- and technology-intensive, the traditional demarcations between services and manufacturing may be eroding – especially as manufacturing industry itself is becoming more service-like, with the shift to shorter and more customized production runs, and other features of 'flexible specialization'. With the growth of producer services, and the externalization of some service functions by firms in other sectors, manufacturing and services are becoming more intertwined. Notions of 'post-industrialism' or 'deindustrialization' become suspect – the real issue will be the mutual reinforcement of diverse economic activities, and the scope for innovation in all economic sectors.[25]

As has been noted, innovation in services often has high reliance on software, and frequently involves complementary organizational and technological innovation. These are not unique features of services, but bring to the fore aspects of innovation that have tended to be neglected in the R&D management and related literatures. Such features – together with other neglected aspects of work activities such as those that are at the focus of 'computer-supported cooperative work' and 'groupware' – may become prominent across the whole economy. Research into innovation in services may well carry important lessons for everyone involved in innovation studies.

Notes

1. Clark (1940); Fisher (1935).
2. This definition, inspired by the discussions of Hill (1977), Illeris (1989) and Riddle (1986), is used extensively in Miles et al. (1988) in a discussion of the applications of new IT.
3. The classic exposition of post-industrial theory is Bell (1973). See also Kuznets (1972).
4. Fuchs (1968); more recently Kravis et al. (1983) find little evidence for a preference for services emerging as countries get wealthier.
5. Gershuny (1978), Skolka (1976).
6. The term 'services' can be used to describe industries, commodities, forms of labour, and even the final functions which are obtained from purchases from the formal economy. Gershuny and Miles (1983) seek to clarify and demonstrate the relations between these aspects.
7. Barras (1984) discusses investment trends in services; other papers drawn on here include Barras (1986a, b).
8. Miles and Matthews (1992), Roach (1987).
9. Thomas and Miles (1989). Howell (1988) presents a stage model, based on his analysis of the emergence of information services like software from firms in other sectors, in which internal services are later marketed and finally spun-off; Baven and Elfring (1992) critically examine this thesis in case studies of services used in the auto industry.
10. Useful discussions of statistical issues in US services are carried in the newsletter *The Service Economy*, published by the Coalition of Service Industries.
11. See the various statistical overviews and case studies presented in Guile and Quinn (1988a, b) and Faulhaber et al. (1986).
12. Bar-code scanners require the cooperation of manufacturers in bar-coding their products. Similarly, financial service innovations like credit and debit cards require the cooperation of retailers in accepting these cards and using validation systems.
13. See Hepworth and Ducatel (1992).
14. For analyses of the *strategies* being pursued in the public sector, see Snellen and Frissen (1990), and the journal *Informatization in the Public Sector*.
15. This builds on the work of van der Aa and Elfring (1991) and Heuer (1990).
16. Levitt (1976) presents a classic study of services industrialization.
17. cf. Scheuling and Little (1991), and several chapters of Teare (1990).
18. About half of the companies applying for support for quality consultancy in the Department

of Trade and Industry's Enterprise Scheme are service companies, especially distribution, hotel and catering firms and professional services, and a substantial number of service firms participate in such schemes (Barker, 1992).

19. Pioneering formulations of 'pay-per' innovations are in Mosco (1988); for the transport case see Hepworth and Ducatel (1992).

20. E.g. Quinn and Pacquette (1990); Quinn, Doorley and Paquette (1990).

21. Quinn op cit. goes on to discuss several types of firm organization and strategic issue that arise from these developments.

22. E.g. Daniels and Moulaert (1991); Marshall et al. (1988).

23. Vandermerwe and Chadwick (1989); see also Dunning (1989).

24. Posthuma (1987).

25. On 'convergence' between manufacturing and services see Miles (1987), Postner (1991); on interpenetration and interdependence of the sectors, Miles (1989).

Bibliography

Barker, B. (1992) 'Quality in Services' presented at PREST seminar, November 1992 (mimeo: PREST, University of Manchester).

Barras, R. (1984) *Growth and Technical Change in the UK Service Sector,* Technical Change Centre, London.

Barras, R. (1986a) 'Towards a Theory of Innovation in Services', *Research Policy,* 15 (4), pp. 161–73.

Barras, R. (1986b) 'New Technologies and the New Services', *Futures,* 18 (6), pp. 748–72.

Batelle Institute (1986) *R&D Forecast and Analysis,* Batelle, Columbus, Ohio.

Baven, G. and Elfring, T. (1992) 'New Challenges for Management in the Make or Buy Decision: Knowledge-Intensive Services in the Car Industry'. Paper presented at 19th Annual Conference of European Association for Research in Industrial Economics, Stuttgart-Hohenheim (mimeo: Rotterdam School of Management).

Bell, D. (1973) *The Coming of Post-Industrial Society,* Heinemann, London.

Clark, C. (1940) *The Conditions of Economic Progress,* Macmillan, London.

Daniels, P.W. and Moulaert, F. (eds) (1991) *The Changing Geography of Advanced Producer Services,* Belhaven, London.

Dunning, J.H. (1989) 'Multinational Enterprises and the Growth of Services', *Services Industry Journal,* Vol. 9, No. 1, pp. 5–39.

Faulhaber, G., Noam, E. and Tasley, R. (eds) (1986) *Services in Transition: The Impact of Information Technology on the Service Sector,* Ballinger, Cambridge, Massachusetts.

Fisher, A.G.B. (1935) *The Clash of Progress and Security,* Macmillan, London.

Fuchs, V. (1968) *The Service Economy,* National Bureau of Economic Research, New York.

Gershuny, J.I. (1978) *After Industrial Society?,* Macmillan, London.

Gershuny, J.I. and Miles, I.D. (1983) *The New Service Economy,* Frances Pinter, London.

Guile, B.R. and Quinn, J.B. (eds) (1988a) *Managing Innovation: Cases from the Services Industries,* National Academy Press, Washington DC.

Guile, B.R. and Quinn, J.B. (eds) (1988b) *Technology in Services,* National Academy Press, Washington DC.

Hepworth, M. and Ducatel, K. (1992) *Transport in the Information Age,* Belhaven, London.

Heuer, F.J.P. (1990) 'Objectives and Instruments of Innovation Policy for Services', presented at the Six Countries Programme Workshop of Technological Innovation and the Services Sector, Vienna, October 1990.

Hill, T.P. (1977) 'On Goods and Services', *Review of Income and Wealth,* 23, pp. 315–38.

Howell, J. (1988) *Economic, Technological and Locational Trends in European Services,* Avebury, Aldershot.

Illeris, S. (1989) *Services and Regions in Europe,* Avebury, Aldershot.

Kravis, I., Heston, A. and Sommers, R. (1983) *World Product and Income,* John Hopkins University Press, Baltimore.

Kuznets, S. (1972) *Modern Economic Growth,* Yale University Press, New Haven.

Levitt, T. (1976) 'The Industrialisation of Service', *Harvard Business Review,* 54 (5), pp. 63–74.

Marshall, J.N., Wood, P., Daniels, P.W., McKinnon, A., Bachtler, J., Damesick, P., Thrift, N., Gillespie, A., Green, A., and Leyshon, A. (1988) *Services and Uneven Development,* Oxford University Press, Oxford.

Miles, I. (1987) *The Convergent Economy* (Papers in Science, Technology and Public Policy No. 14), Imperial College, London; and Science Policy Research Unit, University of Sussex.

Miles, I. (1989) 'Services and the New Industrial Economy' in Holst, E., Preissl, B. and Ring, P.O. (eds) *Dienstleistungen – Neue Chancen für Wirtschaft und Gesellschaft,* VISTAS Verlag, Berlin.

Miles, I. and Matthews, M. (1992) 'Information Technology and the Information Economy' in Robins, K (ed.) *Understanding Information,* Belhaven, London.

Miles, I., Rush, H., Turner, K. and Bessant, J. (1988) *Information Horizons,* Edward Elgar, Aldershot.

Mosco, V. (1988) 'Information in the Pay-Per Society' in Mosco, V. and Wasco, J. (eds) *The Political Economy of Information,* University of Wisconsin Press.

Neubauer, H. and Voithofer, P. (1992) *Innovation and the Services Sector* (report of a workshop in Vienna), TNO Policy Research, Delft.

Posthuma, A. (1987) *The Emergence of Offshore Office Services,* Occasional Paper No. 24, Science Policy Research Unit, University of Sussex, Brighton.

Postner, H.H. (1991) *The Goods/Services Convergence Hypothesis,* Economic Council of Canada (Working Paper No. 21) Ottawa.

Quinn, J.B. and Paquette, P.C. (1990) 'Technology in Services: Creating Organisational Revolutions', *Sloan Management Review,* Vol. 11, No. 2, pp. 67–78.

Quinn, J.B., Doorley, T.L. and Paquette, P.C. (1990) 'Technology in Services: Rethinking Strategic Focus', *Sloan Management Review,* Vol. 11, No. 2, pp. 79–88.

Riddle, D. (1986) *Service-Led Growth,* Praeger, New York.

Roach, S.S. (1987) *America's Technology Dilemma: A Profile of the Information Economy,* Morgan Stanley (Special Economic Studies), New York.

Scheuling, E.E. and Little, C.H. (1991) 'Service Quality in the 1990s: Panel Session' *Futures Research Quarterly,* Vol. 7, No. 1, pp. 37–65.

Skolka, J. (1976) 'Long Term Effects of Unbalanced Labour Productivity Growth' in Szalai, J. and du Pasquier, N. (eds) *Private and Enlarged Consumption,* North Holland, Amsterdam.

Snellen, I.T. and Frissen, P.H.A. (1990) *Informatisation Strategies in Public Administration,* Elsevier, Amsterdam.

Teare, R. (1990) *Managing and Marketing Services in the 1990s,* Cassell, London.

Thomas, G. and Miles, I. (1989) *Telematics in Transition,* Longmans, Harrow.

van der Aa, W. and Elfring, T. (1991) 'Innovation and Strategy in Service Firms', paper presented at 11th Annual Strategic Management Society Conference, Toronto (mimeo: Rotterdam School of Management).

Vandermerwe, S. and Chadwick, M. (1989) 'The Internationalisation of Services', *Services Industries Journal,* Vol. 9, No. 1, pp. 79–93.

PART 3

Key Issues Affecting Innovation

19. Financial Systems and Innovation

Andrew Tylecote

Introduction

We define a financial system as the network of institutions which connects the owners of financial capital to that which ultimately gives them value. Perhaps the most important division within any financial system is between that capital which confers the right to control industrial management – equity, ordinary shares or more precisely *voting* shares – and the rest. This is related to the distinction between two functions which the financial system performs: that of a market for capital, and that of a market for corporate control. Voting shares are involved in both; the rest, only in the market for capital. Financial systems affect innovation through the character of both markets.

The key characteristic of innovation in this context is its requirement for finance, since it involves a number of different categories of investment – broadly defined as a sacrifice of cash flow in the present or near future with a view to improved cash flow later:

- Physical capital
- Research and development
- Training
- Production: pre-launch diversion of resources; post-launch 'teething troubles'
- Marketing: market research; market testing; advertising and promotional expenses; building a distribution and after-sales service network; under-pricing to build market share

Product innovations may incur expenses in all five main categories; a 'pure' process innovation will not involve marketing expenses.

Any firm's willingness to invest, and thus to innovate, will be affected by the time rate of discount (TR of D) which it explicitly or implicitly applies. One might define an 'economically-rational' firm as one which applies a single TR of D (apart from allowance for risk) to all projects and all categories of expenditure within them, that rate being equal to its cost of capital. To the extent that such a firm requires external capital, the TR of D will be determined by the financial system through the rate of interest charged on fixed-interest debt (or implied on share capital through its price) and through any quantity limits. If it is entirely self-financing through retained profits, its TR of D will be its opportunity cost of capital – the (lower) rate of interest it could earn by lending out its own funds.

Innovation may involve not only expense but also change in organizational structures, power relationships and routines. Such change may provoke resistance, and vigorous resistance from those individuals and groups who in some sense will be adversely affected. Thus the rate and success of innovation will be affected by the nature of organizational power structures and the objectives of those in power; these in turn are affected by the operation of the financial system as an engine of corporate control.

A financial system can inhibit innovation in four ways, the first two relating to the capital market and the last two to the market for corporate control:

1. By having high interest rates generally, through high base rates or high margins for financial intermediaries: *dear money*.

The general level of interest rates is mainly a question of national and international monetary policy. We may note that real and nominal interest rates were generally low from the 1930s to the early 70s, particularly in the US and UK; that during the 1970s nominal interest rates were generally high but real rates very low, because of high inflation; and that during the 1980s, with inflation falling, real rates were, by historical standards, very high, particularly in the UK and US.

2. By setting the effective cost of capital for innovation well above the general level of interest rates: *discrimination against innovation*.

Such discrimination is most likely to be suffered by small firms heavily dependent on loan capital from banks, where the latter feel unable to judge the prospects of success for a specific project, or of survival for the firm as a whole, and cannot find enough collateral for their loans. Large firms may also suffer from it, at the hands either of banks or of stock markets, when confidence is low and/or information flows are defective. This is most likely

(a) in a recession;
(b) with a system of transactional as opposed to relational banking (see below);
(c) where small firms lack close relationships with one or more large firms which could guarantee loans or at least improve the information available to lenders (see Japan, below).

3. By inducing 'short-termism' within firms, i.e. a time rate of discount above the effective cost of capital: *short-termism*.

This will take place where both of two conditions hold: (a) Owners give more weight, in valuing the firm or assessing management's performance, to indicators of current or past profitability than to information bearing on long term prospects. We argue below that this is generally due not to *indifference* to long term prospects but to lack of the necessary information, or incapacity to evaluate it. (b) Managers are sensitive to owners' views. This may be due to *direct* owner-control, through votes in the AGM, or *indirect*, through a fall in the share price which would make equity funds more expensive and expose the firm to the danger of a hostile takeover bid.

4. By inducing or tolerating managerial inability or unwillingness to overcome resistance to change which would be in the interests of shareholders: *conservatism*.

Clearly much will depend on the extent of organizational trauma which the required innovation would involve, and on cultural factors. The role of shareholders is likely to be unhelpful if:

(a) They are personally sympathetic to the 'conservative' forces – as, for example, family shareholders in a family firm may be;
(b) They are ignorant or apathetic and leave management to its own devices.

Equally, a financial system could positively encourage innovation by low interest rates and/or preferential rates for innovation, by inducing 'long-termism', or by supporting management inclined to innovate even beyond what was in shareholders' interests (see Japan, below).

Bank-Based Versus Stock Exchange-Based Financial Systems

Existing financial systems in the developed world can broadly be assigned to one of two categories: bank-based and stock-exchange based, which we shall describe first in their extreme forms. In the bank-based system, only a small number of large firms are public companies quoted on the Stock Exchange and even these companies do not rely on it heavily as a source of funds, nor do they concern themselves much with it as a market for corporate control – either fearing takeover bids or seeking to make them. Instead they – and *a fortiori* the other, private companies – look to banks as their main source of external funding. Firms' relationship with banks is accordingly close, and lending is *relational*, that is each loan is seen as part of a long-term relationship in which the firm is bound to inform the bank fully as to its position and prospects, and the bank is committed to support the firm through bad times, in return for influence over its policy and personnel. Much lending is long-term. Where a large firm borrows from more than one bank, one of them is normally recognised as 'lead' or 'house' bank and maintains oversight of the firm's financial position (see Henderson, 1993).

The continental European countries, together with Japan, Korea and Taiwan, have long had essentially bank-based systems, although most of them are now moving in the other direction. The more southerly European countries (France, Italy, Spain, Portugal, Greece and Austria) form a sub-category in which the state plays a dominant role, mainly through ownership of banks, and/or direct ownership of industry. (Even in Japan and Germany state finance of various kinds plays a significant role.)

In a stock exchange-based financial system, a stock exchange quotation is the norm for any firm large enough to bear the transactions costs involved – and those too small may seek the nearest equivalent, such as the Unlisted Securities Market in London. Firms look to the Stock Market as a major source of equity and other finance, and also as a market for corporate control – seeking to establish a good reputation and correspondingly high share price so that they can take over others rather than be taken over themselves. Banks are not used as a major source of risk capital, since their lending is *transactional* rather than relational: each loan is seen as one-off and to be secured against collateral, against the 'carcass value' of the firm, rather than as part of a continuing relationship in which the bank's risk is reduced by thorough knowledge of the firm's prospects.

The Anglo-Saxon economies are stock exchange-based, although the role of banks varies considerably and has changed over time. For example, in the UK in the 1960s and 70s, while the system of lending in the UK was formally very short-term – on overdraft – and against collateral, in practice many companies, large and small, built up a close relationship with one bank and at certain times depended heavily on it for support. This only gave way to generally-transactional relationships in the 1980s, after financial deregulation. There was a similar evolution in the United States (see Mayer and Alexander, 1990; Jacobs, 1991).

The real differences between the two systems – and the variations within them – cannot be understood without taking account of the role of shareholders. The continental European countries have in common a tendency among founding families to insist on retaining control. While in the last century banks may have been effectively the only source of external capital, more recently they have been preferred as an alternative to the dilution of dominant shareholdings. The distinction between voting and non-voting (or lower-voting) shares was also exploited for the same purpose, depending on the regulations in each country (Rydqvist, 1992). There is a corresponding insistence on the obligations of ownership, including the exercise of control. This has been exploited by the German banks, which have not only acquired substantial industrial shareholdings on their own account, but have also developed a system by which they wield the proxies of small shareholders: as a result, many large firms – least dependent on bank lending – have in effect fallen under bank control or at least substantial influence. (On Germany see Cable, 1985 and Schneider-Lenne, 1992; on Sweden and Germany, Kester, 1992.)

The role of family shareholders in Japanese industry is less, first because culturally there is a tendency to regard firms as communities over which control by outsiders is illegitimate, and secondly because the great *zaibatsu* holding companies were largely purged of family ownership after the war. Precisely because of the distrust of outside control, a network of reciprocal shareholdings has grown up among companies – with banks and other financial institutions participating – so that 'stable' shareholdings are now dominant and hostile takeovers impossible. Decreasing reliance by large companies on bank lending has not, in Japan, been accompanied by any move towards a market for corporate control (Kester, 1992; Prowse, 1992; Watanabe and Yamamoto, 1992).

In the Anglo-Saxon economies, with their liberal traditions, wealth has been seen essentially as a commodity rather than enmeshed with rights and obligations, and accordingly family shareholders have been more ready than elsewhere to give up control – particularly in the UK, with its aristocratic anti-industrial tradition. Stock exchange flotation has provided a means of exit from owner-control; this led first to fragmented individual shareholdings and more recently to increasing concentration in the hands of financial institutions, now mainly pension funds – such institutions now hold over two-thirds of UK shares but less than half in the US. These institutions, particularly the pension funds, have sought to avoid any control relationship with management, acting as traders rather than investors, with highly diversified portfolios (Tylecote and Demirag, 1992; Porter, 1992 and 1993).

Influence on Innovation

The superior performance of the continental European and East Asian economies over the last 40 years has drawn attention to the merits of bank-based financial systems. They appear to derive largely from the superior quality of the relationship between firm and outside source of capital, where the latter is a bank with intimate knowledge of the business (Cable, 1985). We recall (in Table 19.1) the categories of expenditure required for innovation, arranged in order of the degree to which they are, in effect, *visible* from outside the firm.

The lower these categories are in the list, the greater the difficulty the outsider will have in distinguishing between expenses incurred for the sake

Table 19.1 Elements of innovation and their external visibility

HIGH		
V	Physical capital	
I	Research & Development	
S		
I	Training	
B	Marketing:	market research
I		market testing
L		advertising and promotional expenses
I		distribution and after-sales service networks
T		under-pricing to build market share
Y		
	Production:	pre-launch diversion of resources
LOW		post-launch 'teething troubles'

of innovation and future profit, and excess costs due to sheer inefficiency. (Only those at the top – physical capital and some elements of R&D – can be capitalized; the rest will lead immediately to a reduction in the profits shown in the firm's accounts.) Visibility will also be lower to the extent that the activity is carried on in a decentralized manner in a divisionalized firm.

The less visible the activity, the more *perceptive* the outsider must be in order to evaluate, *ex ante*, the firm's fitness to make good use of external capital in it, and to monitor progress while using it. In general, the banks in bank-based systems can be taken to have this quality, with the exception of the southern European state-dominated economies. In these economies the nature of state control tends to taint the relationship with firms; moreover it was in many cases precisely the unsupportive behaviour of private banks which was largely responsible for state involvement in the first place – and banking traditions die hard (Cox, ed., 1986). Elsewhere, the bank-based system will be a good backer of innovation – providing capital in sufficient quantity and at modest interest rates – where this has a particular emphasis on less visible activities. (Mechanical engineering fits this description well, and most of the (private) bank-based countries have a good record in it.)

The stock exchange-based economies will clearly suffer from a lack of *perceptiveness* due to the distant relation between the firm and all sources of finance, whether banks or stock markets. On the other hand they can be expected to have an advantage in coping with innovation involving high *risk* – which tends to be associated with high technology. In industries like mechanical engineering which are medium technology, where the emphasis in innovation is on less visible activities, and these tend to be decentralised, the position will clearly be worst. The problem of invisibility has been exacerbated by diversification through acquisition: in a recently-acquired business in which the main responsibility for innovation is several tiers down from group head office, the activities involved may be largely invisible to top management, let alone outsiders (Hitt et al., 1991). The Anglo-Saxon forte is in sectors like pharmaceuticals where the key innovative activity is (centralized) R&D and risk is high (Tylecote and Demirag, 1992; Porter, 1990, 1992, 1993). The US stock exchange also provides intelligent support for the electronics industry, whose major firms have kept a clear focus which facilitates visibility; in UK electronics by contrast there has been much more acquisition and less focus, and the rapport with the Stock Exchange is poor (NEDC, 1989).

Stock exchange-based economies may also have an advantage in some high-technology areas where major start-ups are appropriate – for example, electronics, instruments, bio-technology – since banks have no pre-existing relationship to build on and risk is high. For stock exchange capital, too, the difficulty of assessment is daunting; the problem has largely been solved in some areas of the US by *venture capitalists* with expertise in a particular technological area who take an equity stake and provide or find management expertise: they help the company to reach a suitable size for stock exchange flotation and provide some warranty of quality for investors who come in then (Perry, 1986). Venture capital has developed later and less in the UK but less still in the bank-based economies (Speirs, 1991). The state-dominated bank-based economies provide strong support in areas of high visibility which are targeted by the state (see, for example, Salais (1988) on France).

The argument above relates both to the capital market and to corporate control: the stock exchange economies suffer from discrimination against innovation and from short-termism, in those industries where visibility is poor. The state-dominated bank-based economies also tend to discriminate against innovation where visibility is poor. The private bank economies tend to discriminate against innovation in high-risk and major start-up areas. All the bank economies are virtually immune from short-termism since whatever the relationship between management and the owners of capital there, it does not involve power in the hands of outsiders who give priority to profit but are unable to assess long-term prospects for it.

What cannot be easily deduced is the effect on conservatism. The divorce of ownership from control, most common in the stock exchange economy, may create a situation where little outside pressure of any kind is exerted on management, encouraging conservatism – common in the UK in the 1950s and 60s. Once the market for corporate control becomes lively, as in both UK and US from the 1970s, there will be outside performance pressure of some kind. If this is only for short-termism, it may not force radical organizational change, even where this is in shareholders' long term interests. State ownership and control may also, of course, encourage conservatism. Family ownership removes the divorce of ownership from control but – depending on cultural factors – may provide another source of conservatism even though in this case 'economically irrational'. In large Japanese companies the lifetime employment system in large companies effectively makes the core employees shareholders, in varying degrees depending on their status, and thus largely internalizes ownership, to the advantage of employee motivation. The career prospects of these core employees depend heavily on organic growth and they therefore have, collectively, strong motives for resisting conservatism (Kono, 1984).

Bibliography

Cable, J. (1985) 'Capital Market Information and Industrial Performance: The Role of West German Banks', *Economic Journal*, Vol. 95, Issue 377, March, pp. 118–32.

Cox, A. (ed.) (1986) *State, Finance and Industry: A Comparative Analysis of Six Economies*, Wheatsheaf, Brighton.

Dosi, G. (1990) 'Finance, Innovation and Industrial Change', *Journal of Economic Behaviour and Organisation*, Vol. 13, No. 3, pp. 299–319.

Henderson, R. (1993) *European Finance*, McGraw Hill, London.

Hitt, M.A., Hoskisson, R.E., Ireland, R.D. and Harrison, J.S. (1991) 'Effects of Acquisitions on R&D Inputs and Outputs', *Academy of Management Journal*, Vol. 34, No. 3, pp. 693–703.

Jacobs, M.T. (1991) *Short Term America: The Causes and Cures of our Business Myopia*, Harvard Business School Press, Cambridge, Massachusetts.

Jenkinson, T. and Mayer, C. (1992) 'The Assessment: Corporate Governance and Corporate Control', *Oxford Review of Economic Policy*, Vol. 8, No. 3, pp. 1–10.

Kamin, J.Y., Bijaoui, I. and Horesh, R. (1982) 'Some Determinants of Cost Distributions in the Process of Technological Innovation', *Research Policy*, 11, pp. 83–94.

Kester, W.C. (1992) 'Industrial Groups as Systems of Contractual Governance', *Oxford Review of Economic Policy*, Vol. 8, No. 3, pp. 25–44.

Kono, T. (1984) *Strategy and Structure of Japanese Enterprises*, Macmillan, London.

Marsh, P. (1990) *Short-termism on Trial*, Institutional Fund Managers Association, London.

Mayer, C. and Alexander, I. (1990) 'Banks and Securities: Corporate Financing in Germany and the UK', *Journal of the Japanese and International Economies*, Vol. 4, No. 4, pp. 450–75.

National Economic Development Council (NEDC) (1989) *Performance and Competitive Success: Strengthening Competitiveness in UK Electronics*, McKinsey and Co. Inc. for the NEDC's Electronics Industry Sector Group, NEDO, London.

Perry, W.J. (1986) 'Cultivating Technological Innovation' in Landau, R. and Rosenberg, N. (eds) *The Positive Sum Strategy*, National Academy Press, Washington DC.

Porter, M. (1990) *The Competitive Advantage of Nations*, Macmillan, New York.

Porter, M. (1992) 'Capital Disadvantage: America's Failing Capital Investment System', *Harvard Business Review*, September/October, pp. 65–82.

Porter, M. (1993) *Corporate Investment and the Time Horizons of American Industry*, Harvard Business School Press for the Council on Competitiveness.

Prowse, S.D. (1992) 'The Structure of Corporate Ownership in Japan', *Journal of Finance*, Vol. 47, No. 3, pp. 1121–40.

Rydqvist, K. (1992) 'Dual-Class Shares: A Review', *Oxford Review of Economic Policy*, Vol. 8, No. 3, pp. 45–57.

Salais, R. (1988) 'Les stratégies de modernisation de 1983 à 1986: le marché, l'organisation, le financement', *Economie et Statistique,* No. 213, September.

Schneider-Lenne, E.R. (1992) 'Corporate Control in Germany', *Oxford Review of Economic Policy,* Vol. 8, No. 3, pp. 11–23.

Speirs, A. (1991) 'Trends in European Venture Capital: The Future isn't What it Was', *European Business Journal,* Vol. 3, No. 1, pp. 19–25.

Tylecote, A. (1987) 'Time Horizons of Management Decisions: Causes and Effects', *Journal of Economic Studies,* Vol. 14, No. 4, pp. 51–64.

Tylecote, A. and Demirag, I. (1992) 'Short-termism: Culture and Structures as Factors in Technological Innovation', pp.201–225 in Coombs, R., Walsh, V. and Saviotti, P. (eds) *Technological Change and Company Strategies,* Academic Press, London.

Watanabe, S. and Yamamoto, I. (1992) 'Corporate Governance in Japan: Ways to Improve Low Profitability', *NRI Quarterly,* Winter, pp. 29–45.

20. Supplier Relationships and Innovation

Mari Sako

Introduction

The link between supplier relationships and innovation may be explored by posing the following questions:

1. Is a vertically integrated firm more or less innovative than a disintegrated firm?
2. What is the nature of supplier relationships which is most conducive to innovative activities?

The two questions are analytically separate but they must be answered jointly. The kind of external links a firm can forge with other firms affects its decision over the degree of vertical integration. This article firstly defines the scope of supplier relationships and then proceeds to a discussion of existing theories and research findings which address the link between supplier relationships and innovation.

Supplier Relationships Defined

Subcontracting is the outsourcing of manufacturing or service by a firm to another firm. The term 'subcontracting' derives from its usage in projects requiring the signing of contracts between a party commissioning the project and those undertaking it. Public procurement, defence and construction projects are common examples. In manufacturing, all suppliers of inputs are sometimes called subcontractors, suppliers or vendors. But a distinction is often made between suppliers of standardized products and subcontractors of customized products, and between suppliers of simple operations (e.g. assembly) and suppliers of strategically sensitive parts. In this article, the supplier relationship is interpreted to include all types of relations in industry involving a firm and its suppliers of raw materials, components, equipment, and services.

In relation to innovation, the outsourcing of manufacturing processes may be distinguished from the subcontracting of R&D. Much attention has been focused on the subcontracting of manufacturing because of the excellence of Japanese auto and electronics firms in this area. The extent to which suppliers are asked to contribute to the design and development of products, combined with how the product is priced, is a crucial dimension affecting the scope for innovation. Whether in manufacturing or R&D, a firm's decision over what activities to organize in-house and what to subcontract out depends on a combination of criteria involving costs, value added, access to new technology, and the time horizon for achieving the firm's strategic goals.

From the viewpoint of purchasing policy, subcontracting is one possible form in the 'make or buy' decision continuum. There are two contrasting strands of thinking on supplier relationships today. On the one hand, subcontracting may be regarded as a temporary overspill due to internal capacity constraints, or as outsourcing of peripheral non-core activities at a cost lower than can be achieved in-house (Atkinson and Meager, 1986). On the other hand, supplier relationships may involve suppliers of strategically important components, with a view to forging long-lasting 'partnerships' or 'strategic alliances'. Both aim at enhancing competitiveness by taking account of cost and flexibility. But they have different implications for innovation.

Explanations

The review here concentrates on how various theories predict whether subcontracting promotes or hinders innovation.

Cost-based explanations

If the firm is regarded as a technological black box and if only production costs are taken into account, as in neoclassical economic theory, opportunities for subcontracting arise from at least two factors. First, if a firm's internal demand is relatively small, economies of scale in component production can only be exploited by buying rather than making the components in-house. Second, buying may be cheaper than making if suppliers face lower costs due to lower wages or overheads. Here, suppliers are regarded merely as a source of low cost production.

Transaction cost economics modifies the above analysis. In a condition of uncertainty, mutual suspicion in opportunistic behaviour would discourage suppliers from investing in customer-specific assets, such as specialized machinery. Williamson (1975) initially argued that vertical integration would be a solution to this problem. By implication, the more uncertain the environment (for R&D more so than for manufacturing), the more incentive there would be to integrate vertically. Later, quasi-vertical integration (the buyer's ownership of specialized assets) and relational contracting were put forward as superior alternatives to full vertical integration (Williamson, 1985). They can avoid the cost of vertical integration in terms of bureaucratic rigidity, and benefit from the flexibility of smaller firms.

A trade-off between the short run and the long run

Cost-based explanations are deficient particularly when they are applied to innovation. This is because they remain part of a theory of efficient allocation, defined in relation to known opportunities. But innovative activity is conducted in an environment in which firms are uncertain about some of the opportunities available to them.

Even without the above problem, firms may not behave according to the principle of minimizing transaction costs. They may incur high transaction costs (e.g. in haggling) so as to extract low prices from their suppliers. This is worthwhile as long as the savings on input costs are greater than the increase in transaction costs. A hard bargain is struck by retaining maximum in-house control over product design specification, which is a major source of bargaining power. A commercial bargain with a minimum disclosure of information to suppliers hinders technological diffusion and innovation. Thus, there is a trade-off between the short-term cost consideration and the long-term benefit of technological innovation. Helper (1990) analyzes the US auto industry in these terms, and argues that the US auto assemblers pursued the goal of competitive component prices at the expense of not tapping into the innovative capability of suppliers. This analysis differs from the Marxist analysis of subcontracting, which focuses on the exploitative nature of the relationship between large firms (monopoly capital) and small firms. According to the theory of exploitation, large firms squeeze the profit of small firms which are left with little to invest, but may remain themselves resourceful and innovative.

Suppliers' incentives to innovate

Instead of minimizing suppliers' innovative capability, the buyer can enhance their incentive to contribute to product and process innovation by relying on a number of mechanisms. A central mechanism is related to a clear reward for suppliers' innovative contributions in the form of a share of the benefit or a growing order level. Product and process innovation are dealt with separately below.

In the case of process innovation, suppliers would have an incentive to innovate as long as they can capture all, or part, of the gain from innovation. For instance, in Japanese manufacturing, one established mechanism is for the buyer firm to specify price reduction targets, or a time path of price reduction targets which remain unchanged whether suppliers enhance their efficiency or not. Suppliers can then capture 100 per cent of the gain from increasing their operating efficiency (McMillan, 1990). Another method is the joint analysis of costs using the value analysis (VA) and value engineering (VE) techniques, with arrangements for sharing benefits (Asanuma, 1985). The buyer may also rank suppliers according to their performance in quality, delivery and other aspects, and give more profitable orders to better performing suppliers. Making incremental improvements in the production and quality control capability, often initially with the help of assemblers, is a common part of supplier relationships in Japanese manufacturing. Toyota Motor Corporation, and other Japanese auto assemblers, perfected just-in-time (JIT) production and delivery with primary and secondary subcontractors in this way (Monden, 1983; Schoenberger, 1982).

As for product innovation, the buyer would be willing to involve suppliers in the design and development process only if he trusts the suppliers. Trust may be placed on the technical competence of the supplier, the supplier's moral norm not to disclose confidential information, and the supplier's disposition to enter into a loose reciprocity of give and take over the long run without taking advantage in the short run (Sako, 1992). Trust in these senses is a necessary prerequisite for supplier relations which involve joint product development. Clark and Fujimoto (1992), in their study of product development in the car industry, classified parts into supplier proprietary, black box, and detail controlled types. They found that the ratios of the three types were 8:62:30 in Japan, 3:16:81 in the US and 7:39:54 in Europe. A relatively large proportion of black box (i.e. jointly developed) parts in Japan is an indication of a high level of trust prevailing in supplier relations. By contrast, a high proportion of detail controlled parts in the US reflects low trust and a high degree of vertical integration. Once a supplier relationship gets stuck in low trust, it may be difficult to establish trust. But trust in business is not a mere cultural norm; rather it is built deliberately over time through a careful selection and close communication between trading partners. Firms are better disposed to take risk, a concomitant of innovative activities, when high trust supplier relations are present than when they are absent.

Product market and manufacturing strategy

In management, the choice between vertical integration and supplier relationships is discussed in the context of business strategy. In the established Harvard Business School tradition, the central problem is how the Strategic Business Unit (SBU) can earn profits above the industry average. Porter (1980) prescribes a solution by focusing on the 'value-added chain' starting with end products sold to consumers. Managers must decide, firstly, on a distinct product market strategy – either low cost, differentiation or focus – and, secondly, whether to make or buy by looking upstream to the efficiency of the supply chain. Potential benefits and costs of vertical integration are assessed by taking account of various factors, including production costs, transaction costs, capital investment requirements, access to technology, entry barriers, and flexibility of responses to market incentives. Ultimately, however, Porter views vertical integration (hence the use of suppliers) as a strategic response to the five forces of suppliers, buyers, potential entrants, substitutes, and industry competitors. The industrial structure dictated by these five factors determines the relative bargaining power of companies, which in turn plays a major role in determining the degree of vertical integration. Hayes and Wheelwright (1984), though more interested in manufacturing strategy, follow a similar line of reasoning to Porter.

The logic of the value-added chain ultimately implies keeping processes which create high value added in-house and subcontracting out all operations with low value-added. This appears to be biased towards niche marketing rather than differentiation or low cost strategies, and towards designing rather than manufacturing products. Rappaport and Halevi (1991) argue that a model of success for the future is the 'computerless computer company', such as the 'fabless' semiconductor companies in Silicon Valley, which design and sell semiconductors but do not manufacture them. These companies retain high profits by focusing on highly differentiated chips for niche markets. Their manufacturing subcontractors need only be reliable and adequate because chips are designed so as not to require state-of-the-art manufacturing processes. In the computer industry, companies with software-based technologies would be the engine of product innovation, defining new markets such as in multimedia. They can create and retain value by subcontracting hardware manufacturing. Product design and manufacturing are regarded as separable activities, and companies may specialize in one or the other according to their comparative advantage.

Core competence

No one disputes the wisdom of a business strategy which favours retaining the source of value creation in-house, but there is debate over how that source ought to be defined. The product market-based theory identifies the source in niche marketing, and regards in-house manufacturing as not critical to maintaining competitiveness. A more recent resource-based theory, based on the concept of core competence, argues that in-house manufacturing is crucial if the technology contains embedded skills that give rise to the next generation of competitive products (Prahalad and Hamel, 1990). A firm's core competence is a source for value creation, and is similar to market niche in that it should be difficult for competitors to imitate, but different in that it provides potential access to a wide variety of markets. Thinking in terms of core competence rather than products encourages firms to cross-fertilize innovation across SBUs. More generally, the theory focuses on the process of learning and skill development within the organization.

The implications of the core competence theory for supplier relationships and innovation are as follows: First, the assessment of the long-term potential of core competence (internal knowledge and skills) must inform what processes to subcontract out. A shorter-term evaluation of costs and profits only would lead to incremental outsourcing decisions in response to decreased competitiveness. This would erode core competence and would therefore be self-destructive in the long run. Second, firms can engage in subcontracting which is conducive to innovation only if the parties to the contract have an internal organization, both formal and informal, capable of taking advantage of learning opportunities. Taking these two aspects together, the core competence theory provides a logic for vertical integration, but also a logic for a measured use of subcontracting. The theory indicates that there are no easy short cuts to accumulating the technological capability of the firm.

Summary

The theories reviewed above indicate that supplier relationships may be structured to enhance or discourage innovation. Every firm has an incentive to retain the source of value creation in-house. The possible range of sources is identified to include cost minimization, product market strategy and core competence. The guiding principles for the use of subcontracting is clear, namely subcontract out processes for which costs can be saved, which add little value to the SBU's profitability, and which do not undermine the development of the firm's core competence. These principles may protect the innovative capability of the buyer firm, but it may be protected because of, at the expense of, or regardless of, the innovative capability of the supplier firm.

For example, the buyer may save on costs by bargaining hard with the supplier. But the buyer's tight control over design, which is necessary in order to engage in a hard bargain, undermines the scope for innovation by the supplier. Subcontracting is therefore a zero-sum game in the short run, and trades off a short-term cost saving for a long-term gain in technological innovation. Next, firms which focus on product markets and examine the efficiency of the value-added chain may fall into the danger of subcontracting out processes which erode the in-house knowhow in a strategically sensitive area. In order to retain the innovative capability of the firm, it may either decide not to rely much on suppliers, or it may forge 'partnerships' and 'strategic alliances' with innovative suppliers. A firm is likely to opt for the latter in the presence of mutual trust, a capacity to learn, and a reward for innovative contribution. These are prerequisites for turning subcontracting into a positive sum game. But there remains some ambiguity in the 'make or buy' decision over strategically sensitive processes because the firm has to define and identify what competence is core and what is non-core in relation to future, sometimes unknown, marketing opportunities.

Bibliography

Asanuma, B. (1989) 'Manufacturer-Supplier Relationships in Japan and the Concept of Relation-Specific Skill', *Journal of the Japanese and International Economies,* No. 3, pp. 1–30.

Atkinson, J. and Meager, N. (1986) *Changing Working Patterns: How Companies Achieve Flexibility to Meet New Needs,* NEDO, London.

Clark, K. and Fujimoto, T. (1992) *Product Development Performance,* Harvard Business School Press, Harvard.

Hayes, R.H. and Wheelwright, S.C. (1984) *Restoring Our Competitive Edge,* John Wiley & Sons, New York.

Helper, S. (1990) 'Comparative Supplier Relations in the US and Japanese Auto Industries: An Exit/Voice Approach', *Business and Economic History,* Second series, No. 19, pp. 153–62.

Helper, S. (1991) 'How Much Has Really Changed Between US Automakers and Their Suppliers?', *Sloan Management Review,* Summer, pp. 15–28.

McMillan, J. (1990) 'Managing Suppliers: Incentive Systems in Japanese and US Industry', *California Management Review,* Vol. 32, No. 4, pp. 38–55.

Monden, Y. (1983) *Toyota Production System,* Institute of Industrial Engineers, Atlanta.

Porter, M. (1980) *Competitive Strategy: Techniques for Analyzing Industries and Competitors,* The Free Press, New York.

Prahalad, C.K. and Hamel, G. (1990) 'The Core Competence of the Corporation', *Harvard Business Review,* May–June, pp. 79–91.

Rappaport, A.S. and Halevi, S. (1991) 'The Computerless Computer Company', *Harvard Business Review,* July–August, pp. 69–80.

Sako, M. (1992) *Prices, Quality and Trust: Inter-firm Relations in Britain and Japan,* Cambridge University Press, Cambridge.

Shoenberger, R.J. (1982) *Japanese Manufacturing Techniques: Nine Hidden Lessons in Simplicity,* The Free Press, New York.

Sengenberger, W. et al. (1990) *The Re-emergence of Small Enterprises,* ILLS, Geneva.

Thorburn, J.T. and Takashima, M. (1992) *Industrial Subcontracting in the UK and Japan,* Avebury, Aldershot.

Williamson, O.E. (1975) *Markets and Hierarchies: Analysis and Antitrust Implications,* The Free Press, New York.

Williamson, O.E. (1985) *The Economic Institutions of Capitalism,* The Free Press, New York.

Womack, J.P. et al. (1990) *The Machine that Changed the World,* Rowson Associates, New York.

21. User/Supplier Links and Innovation

Brian Shaw

Introduction

The links between users and suppliers are vital to the effective management of the innovation process. These linkages are the crucial element in an innovation system which sees the actors as a network of institutions and individuals in both the public and private sectors creating product champions not only within the organizations but also outside them.

This system encompasses a learning process consisting of learning by doing, learning by using, learning by interaction and learning by diffusion, which results in the speed and flexibility of new product development being dependent on an overlapping approach and information sharing. The sharing of rich and intense information between users, suppliers and the other actors is developed through creating linkages within organizations, with the accumulated knowledge embedded in society and with research.

The need for companies to appropriate the innovation benefit for themselves necessitates the creation of a window on complementary assets especially linking with key market players and actively pursuing relationships with users at an early stage in the technology's development. This clarifies the benefits of the technology in the market by adopting and maintaining a clear market focus and investing heavily in credibility building activities.

The effective management of the innovation process ensures opportunities for sustained cost advantage and/or product differentiation thus creating the competitive advantage needed to fund continuous innovation, profitability and growth.

The Role of the User in the Innovation Chain

The analysis by Rothwell (1977) of nine innovation studies demonstrated that understanding user need and good internal and external communications were crucial to successful innovations. Von Hippel (1976, 1977, 1982, 1988) focused attention on the role of the user in the innovation process in part to determine how an innovating firm goes about acquiring an accurate understanding of user need. He found that typically the manufacturers of scientific instruments and process machinery for the manufacture of semiconductors and electronic subassemblies are not constrained to perceive accurately user need as such. Instead they have available to them a hardware solution (a user prototype) to a need which the user had, hopefully accurately, perceived himself as having. Von Hippel classified the innovation process as 'user-dominated' where the user:

1. Perceives the need for the innovative industrial good.
2. Conceives a solution.
3. Builds a prototype device.
4. Proves the value of this prototype by using it.

Only when all the above has transpired does the manufacturer become active by performing product engineering work, manufacturing and marketing the product or process. In the 'manufacturer-dominated' paradigm the user's role is a simple expression of need and the manufacturer conceives a responsive solution and then builds, tests, manufactures and markets the innovation. His further research in the computer industry for the PC-CAD sector identified 'lead users' who:

1. Face needs that will be general in a market place some months or years before the bulk of that market place encounters them.
2. Are positioned to benefit significantly by obtaining a solution to their needs.

Since lead users are familiar with conditions that lie in the future they can serve as a need forecasting laboratory for marketing research. Also, because they expect a high rent from a solution to a need under study they often attempt to fill this need and can, therefore, provide valuable new product concept and design data to inquiring manufacturers in addition to need data. Quinn (1985) found that large companies were relying less on early market research and more on interactive development with lead customers. Hewlett Packard, 3M, Sony and Raychem frequently introduce radically new products through small teams that work closely with lead customers. These teams learn from their customer needs and innovations, and rapidly modify designs and entry strategies based on this information.

Rothwell (1976), Rothwell, Gardiner and Schott (1983) and Parkinson (1982) recommended, as a result of their researches, that suppliers plug into innovative customers who are representative, demand high quality, and high reliability products that provide a stringent design stimulus. Gardiner and Rothwell (1985) contended that manufacturers have a great deal to gain from involving the user in the design and development process, both in its pre-launch phase (initial innovation) and in its post-launch (re-innovation).

Firstly, manufacturers can complement their own R&D efforts through plugging in to the technical strengths of their customers. Secondly, involving the user is a great aid to establishing the optimum performance/price combination which in turn establishes the optimum design specification. Thirdly, involved users undergo a learning process that enables them better to operate the new equipment when it is installed. Because of the accumulated experience they are able to maintain equipment and use it optimally, and this provides strong demonstration effects for other potential customers. They can, in turn, accelerate the acceptance process for major new designs. Finally, this good relationship, engendered through user involvement in the formulation of the initial brief, can result, if maintained, in a flow of user-initiated improvements, thus extending the equipment's life-cycle. In fact they suggested that of the three design processes (i.e. design for demonstration, design for make-ability and redesign for altered specifications) it is perhaps at this third stage that the role of the user is most strongly felt.

Townsend's research into the Anderton Shearer Loader, (NEDO, 1982), illustrated Gardiner and Rothwell's view. The initial design of the Loader originated from a small National Coal Board (NCB) engineering maintenance team who then worked closely with the supplier. Following its introduction the machine was continuously enhanced through a series of major and minor innovations totalling one thousand in all. The two parties concentrated on developing their strengths. The NCB developed control systems, for which it was equipped by virtue of its superior R&D facilities following the integration of research with design and development functions. The machinery suppliers concentrated on developing the mechanics and power source of the machine – areas of their traditional experience.

The development of the Fiberlase which applied the technique of laser application via the fibreoptic endoscope for diagnostic endoscopy (Macdivitt, 1982) was also carried out through a joint working party composed of Barr and Stroud management (part of the Pilkington Group) and senior surgeons at a major Glasgow hospital. This working party, the Laser Coagulator Working Party (LWCP) met regularly to resolve problems. The continuous feedback of information from the surgeons, the speedy response by the engineering staff to the suggestions made and problems raised, facilitated the smooth technical development of a viable pre-production prototype. The need for cross-fertilization of information and a multidisciplinary team was especially important in evaluating the various design options. Throughout the development phase market factors were monitored continuously with the results of the test market in 1980 confirming a worldwide market for this new technology-based product. The ultimate unique features of the Fiberlase which set it apart from its competitors was the result of the creative collaborative development.

One other role that users may play is that of the entrepreneur in product innovation. This role was demonstrated by British Aerospace in its deliberate strategy of exploiting internally generated process innovations (Foxall and Tierney, 1984; Foxall et al., 1985 and Foxall, 1986). This was accomplished through the establishment of a Business Development Group charged with identifying such innovations, protecting them by legal means, and by negotiating and administering licensing and agency agreements with external organizations.

Shaw (1985) studied a sample of 34 medical equipment innovations from 11 companies. One major element in the innovation process for medical equipment which tends to make this process unique is the requirement that any equipment that is to be potentially introduced into clinical use first needs clinical trial and assessment. A special relationship is therefore needed between the user on the one hand and the supplier on the other. The users here were the centres of excellence consisting of 21 undergraduate and postgraduate teaching and research hospitals and 20 universities with hospital schools in the UK having technicians, scientists, engineers and clinicians/physicians all working together to find new means of achieving better patient care through equipment innovations. Lotz (1991) found that, in the Danish medical equipment industry, science appears predominantly in the user environment and as a result, invention is fuelled by downstream sources both by specific requirements from research physicists and by new medical knowledge. This characteristic applied in the UK where in 18 of the 34 innovations studied the users created hand-built prototypes. In fact in the sample of 34, 26 (76 per cent) were developed through multiple and continuous interaction between the users and suppliers, resulting in 22 being successful, one being too early to judge and three being failures. In 17 of the 18 user-dominated innovations, the users continued joint prototype development, testing, evaluation and marketing and in 13 cases specified the final product. In eight of the 16 manufacturer-dominated innovations, the user tested and evaluated the manufacturers' prototypes and helped market the final product, one user helped develop the prototype, test, evaluate and market it, and one user helped develop the manufacturer's prototype and market the final product (Shaw, 1986). One user introduced the supplier to a new use for a neonatal probe that they had developed jointly, which resulted in the Venus Oxygen Probe, another new and successful innovation. As a result of this development, however, there was a major re-innovation of the original probe resulting in the further penetration of its market.

When innovation performance takes the form of participation in interaction, production of the knowledge obtained by both parties during the activity is inseparable from the consumption of this knowledge, and the users' participation in the innovation process is a pre-condition. Therefore, Kristensen (1991) suggested that the producer engaging in innovation interaction with a user can be conceptually seen as delivering 'pre-sale service of innovation', and the role of the prototype must be seen in relation to this service. As Shaw (1988) found, the creation of the 18 hand-built prototypes enabled the suppliers to delineate clearly the R&D needed and permitted the channelling of technological problems and the focusing of activities. Because of the user-dominated nature of these innovations, the wider set of alternative product specifications relative to those technologically feasible was perceived not to be present. This resulted in a reduction in development time and cost and the more effective translation of user need into technological form.

The dominance of the consultant clinician/physician in the process of effective use and purchase of medical equipment results from their perception of the effectiveness of the equipment in improving diagnostic skills or enhancing therapeutic ability. The prime basis for these judgements is the clinical results achieved by using the equipment. The acceptance of these results is a function of who carried out the trials and their degree of contact in the network. This 'peer group buyer behaviour' relayed high credibility for the equipment to the medical technology decision-makers, the Area Health Authorities, and was fully accepted. Evidence was present in 27 of the innovations of peer group buyer behaviour (Shaw, 1991). The peer group behaviour mirrored that found by Coleman et al. (1966) in the diffusion of the drug Gammanym. They found that doctors relied on the experience of their peers, conveyed in interpersonal networks for evaluative information about the innovation. Similarly Greer (1984) found that the collegium deferred to the judgement and preferences of a requesting physician. Biemans (1989) in his study of 17 medical equipment innovations also found that users were involved in testing developed prototypes in 75 per cent of the cases.

Appropriation of Innovation Benefits

The continuous championing of *all* stages in the innovation process by the users, identified by Shaw (1993), enabled the 'inside product champions' (Schon, 1967) to progress the innovations more sensitively and more quickly because of the parallel developments and the overall enhancement of the physical and human resources through the interaction with the users, 'the outside product champions'. These resources of prototype development, clinical trials, scientific and medical knowledge, peer group buyer behaviour are all examples of what Teece (1986) calls complementary assets which were found to be essential for the supplier to link into so that he could appropriate innovation benefit to himself, especially where there was a weak appropriability regime.

The appropriation by the supplier of complementary assets is illustrated by the development of the Exercise Test Monitor developed by PK Morgan Ltd., analyzed in Shaw (1986). The managing director of this company noted that Dr Cotes of the MRC Pneumoconiosis Research Unit had been writing papers on the 'Tripartite Test' which quantified the effects of exercise. He initiated a period of intensive collaboration with Dr Cotes to develop equipment that could plot the necessary data in the form required. The software programming for the system represented four years of high quality work. The basis of this work was the BASIC programming system developed by Dr Nelson Braslow, a cardiorespiratory physician of Massachusetts General Hospital, USA. The chief engineer of the company developed the MGH work by translating the BASIC into FORTRAN, COBOL and PASCAL programmes giving over 100 comparisons of data. Knowing the output requirements of the Exercise Test Monitor, due to his close contacts with potential users, the managing director was attracted by the unique method of mathematical analysis developed at the Respiratory Department of Guy's Hospital for use with microcomputers, which had been developed to measure information about Body Plethysmography. Having checked the acceptability of this programme to the system being developed by the company, an agreement was reached with Guy's to use the programme, to lock into their research in the respiratory field and to accept their consultancy help in incorporating the mathematical analysis into the company's equipment.

Overlapping and Information Sharing

The speed and flexibility of Japanese new product developments chiefly depends on an overlapping approach and information sharing (Imai, Nonaka and Takeuchi, 1985). The overlapping implies a method of phase management in which overlap occurs at the meeting of adjacent phases or extends across several phases. For example, the overlap may be between design, test and product phases or research, development and production phases (see Figure 21.1). The overlapping approach creates linkages between different phases or sections or between different firms through a commitment to overlapped development. These linkages make it possible for Japanese firms to perform dynamic adaptation when market conditions change. Also, information sharing becomes a method of group or shared learning (Imai, 1991).

The chain-linked model of innovation (Kline and Rosenberg, 1986; see Figure 21.2) emphasizes the informational links between market findings, design, production and distribution (Link C-C-O-I). The mechanism of these linkages is the information feedback from the market to each of the above phases (Links F and f), and informational relationships between such corporate activities, research and accumulated knowledge which are embedded in the society (Links K and R). The PK Morgan case study also illustrates the mechanism of these linkages.

The user-supplier linkages enable the overlapping of phases and their

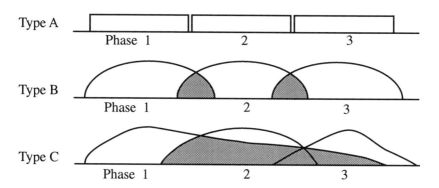

Figure 21.1 Sequential (A) vs. overlapping (B, C) phases of development
Source: Imai, K. et al., 1985.

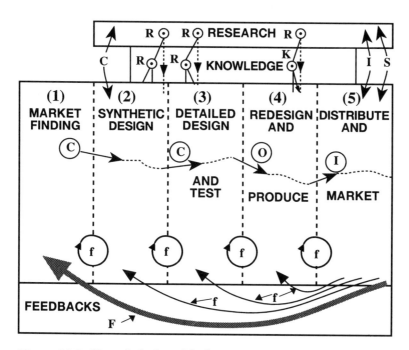

Figure 21.2 Chain-linked model of innovation
Source: Kline, S.J. and Rosenberg, N., 1986.

extension across several phases not only within the supplier firms but among firms, research institutes and public sector organizations such as universities, hospitals and research laboratories. For instance there was parallel testing of prototypes by users in the UK teaching hospitals, Medical Research Council (MRC) designated centres and foreign hospitals. The Multiple Detector Head Gamma Counter developed by Professor Chard, of St Bartholomew's Hospital's company, was tested in Glasgow, Cardiff, Birmingham, London, Amsterdam and Miami, thus reducing significantly the testing time for the company and at the same time increasing the number of hours of testing for the innovation to 1,000 hours. Not only did the parallel testing and evaluation of the prototype by the hospital consultants and MRC personnel create time reduction and resources for the company but, most importantly, ensured credibility for the equipment. Beard and Easingwood (1991), in their research on market launch strategies for high technology products, identified this need for adopting and maintaining a clear market focus and investing in credibility building activities.

The overlapping of idea generation, screening, concept identification, test and evaluation, preliminary technical and market assessment, prototype development and prototype testing and evaluation through user-generated prototypes being developed in collaboration with suppliers as identified by Shaw (1993), illustrates dramatically the benefit of such collaboration.

Conclusion

The research on the linking of users and suppliers in the innovation chain emphasizes and reinforces Giglierano's (1987) findings that a company start-up strategy which consciously stresses learning about customers is preferable to a strategy which initially focuses on other market activities. In addition, his emphasis on continuous learning from customers so that the product can be changed or a second product brought to the market in timely fashion, is endorsed fully. Based on the evidence from the 1987 research, Giglierano et al. (1989) proposed that new products in which value chains include activities and linkages intended to maintain flexibility will perform better than those which have no such activities or linkages. Thus it appears that user-supplier linkage is essential not only for start-up firms but for all firms especially those multinational firms, as studied by Quinn, whose flexibility and adaptability are becoming so crucial to performance in our present-day dynamic and discontinuous environment.

Bibliography

Beard, C.R. and Easingwood C.J. (1991) *Seven Market Launch Strategies for High Technology Products*, ISPIM 7th International Conference, Innovation Strategies, Israel.

Biemans, W.G. (1989) *Developing Innovations Within Networks*, Unpublished PhD Thesis, Technische Universiteit Eindhoven.

Coleman, J.S., Katz, E. and Menzel H. (1966) *Medical Innovation: A Diffusion Study*, Bobbs-Merrill, Indianapolis.

Foxall, G. and Tierney, J.D. (1984) 'From CAP1 to CAP2: User-Initiated Innovation from the Users' Point of View', *Management Decision*, Vol. 22, No. 5.

Foxall, G., Murphy, F.S. and Tierney, J.D. (1985) Market Development in Practice – a Case Study of the User Initiated Product Innovation, *Journal of Marketing Management*, Vol. No. 1.

Foxall, F. (1986) 'A Conceptual Extension of the Customer Active Paradigm', *Technovation* 4.

Gardiner, P. and Rothwell, R. (1985) 'Tough Customers: Good Designs', *Design Studies*, Vol. 6, No. 1.

Giglierano, J. (1987) *The Relationship Between Founders' Prior Experience, Strategy Making Style, Strategy and Third Year Performance in New Technical Firms*, Unpublished PhD Dissertation, Ohio State University.

Greer, A.L. (1984) 'Medical Technology and Professional Dominance Theory', *Soc. Sci. Med.*, Vol. 18, No. 10.

Imai, K., Nonaka I. and Takeuchi I. (1985) *Managing the New Product Development Process: How Japanese Companies Learn and Unlearn, The Uneasy Alliance – Managing the Productivity – Technology Dilemma*, in Clark, K.M., Hayes, R.H., Lorenz, C. (eds) Harvard Business School Press.

Imai, K. (1991) *Globalisation and Cross Border Networks of Japanese Firms*, 'Japan in a Global Economy Conference', Stockholm School of Economics, September.

Kline, S.J. and Rosenberg N. (1986) *An Overview of Innovation: The Positive Sum Strategy*, Landau, R. and Rosenberg, N. (eds) Washington DC, National Academy Press.

Kristensen, P.S. (1991) 'Production Departments' Direct Interaction with External Customers (Flying Prototypes)' *Third International Production Management and New Production Systems European Institute for Advanced Studies in Management* (EIASM), Brussels and University of Gothenberg, May.

Lotz, P. (1991) *Demand Side Effects on Product Innovation: The Case of Medical Devices*, Copenhagen Business School, Institute of Industrial Research.

Macdivitt, H. (1982) The Light of Recent Developments, *The Business Graduate*, Spring.

Parkinson, S.T. (1982) 'The Role of the User in Successful Product Development', *R&D Management*, Vol. 12, No. 3.

Quinn, J.B. (1985) 'Managing Innovation: Controlled Chaos', *Harvard Business Review*, May–June.

Rothwell, R. (1976) *Innovation in Textile Machinery. Some Significant Factors in Success and Failure*, Science Policy Research Unit, Occasional Paper Series No. 2.

Rothwell, R. (1977) 'The Characteristics of Successful Innovations and Technically Progressive Firms', *R&D Management*, Vol. 7, No. 3, June.

Rothwell, R., Gardiner, P. and Schott, A. (1983) *Design and the Economy*, Design Council, October, London.

Schon, D.A. (1976) *Technology and Change*, Delacouste Press.

Shaw, B. (1985) 'The Role of the Interaction Between the User and the Manufacturer in Medical Equipment Innovation', *R & D Management*, Vol. 15, No. 4.

Shaw, B. (1986) 'Appropriation and Transfer of Innovation Benefit in the UK Medical Equipment Industry', *Technovation* 4.

Shaw, B. (1986) *The Role of the Interaction Between the Manufacturer and the User in the Technological Innovation Process*, Unpublished D Phil Thesis, Science Policy Research Unit (SPRU) Sussex University.

Shaw, B. (1988) 'Gaining Added Value From Centres of Excellence in the UK Medical Equipment Industry', *R&D Management*, Vol. 18, No. 2.

Shaw, B. (1991) 'Developing Technological Innovations Within Networks', *Entrepreneurship and Regional Development*, 3.

Shaw, B. (1993) 'Formal and Informal Networks in the UK Medical Equipment Industry', *Technovation*, Vol. 13, No. 6.

Teece, D.J. (1986) 'Profiting from Technological Innovation: Implications for Integration, Collaboration, Licensing and Public Policy', *Research Policy*, Vol. 15, p. 285.

Townsend, P. (1982) *Innovation in the UK*, NEDO, London.

von Hippel, E. (1976) 'The Dominant Role of Users in the Scientific Instrument Innovation Process', *Research Policy* Vol. 5, No. 3.

von Hippel, E. (1977) 'The Dominant Role of the User in Semiconductor and Electronic Subassembly Process Innovation', IEEE Transactions in Engineering Management, *EM 24* No. 2.

von Hippel, E. (1982) 'Appropriability of Innovation Benefit as a Predictor of the Source of Innovation', *Research Policy*, Vol. 11.

von Hippel, E. (1988) *The Sources of Innovation*, Oxford University Press, New York, Oxford.

22. Technological Collaboration and Innovation

Mark Dodgson

Introduction

The sources and the process of innovation are rarely confined within the boundaries of individual firms. Innovation is such a complex and uncertain activity it commonly requires the combination of inputs from a multiplicity of sources; from higher education institutes and contract research organizations, and from other companies as suppliers, customers and competitors. In order to retain some element of management control over these inputs, firms' relationships with these external organizations are often formalized into 'collaborations'. Here a broad definition of collaboration is used which includes any activity where two or more partners contribute differential resources and knowhow to agreed complementary aims.

It is important to distinguish between *vertical* collaboration which occurs throughout the chain of production for particular products, from the provision of raw materials, through the manufacture and assembly of parts, components and systems, to their distribution and servicing, and *horizontal* collaboration which occurs between partners at the same level in the production process. As Shaw and other authors argue in this volume, vertical, user/supplier links are known to play a centrally important role in the innovation process. Horizontal links are also argued to assist the innovation process, although firms appear comparatively more reticent to form such collaborations as they may more often end in dispute over ownership of their outcomes, or in direct competition between collaborating firms.

Collaboration between firms can take a variety of forms. It may be a joint venture, formed by two or more partners as a separate company with shared equity investments. It could be a partnership linking firms on the basis of continuing commitment to shared business or technological objectives without equity sharing, often known as 'strategic alliances'. It may take the form of R&D contracts or technology exchange agreements whereby firms' shared objectives involve the interchange of research findings or technological knowhow. Where such relationships abound amongst groups of firms they are sometimes described as 'innovation networks'.

A wide variety of theoretical explanations are suggested for why firms collaborate. They include those which examine changing industrial structures and systems of production, and those focusing more particularly on the role technology and innovation play in this change. Others focus on economic explanations and the competitive relationships between firms, while others are less instrumental and focus on qualitative issues such as organizational learning (see Dodgson, 1993, for a discussion of these various approaches).

Although collaboration occurs in many different forms, and may reflect different motives, a number of generalizable assumptions underpin them. First is the belief that collaboration can lead to *positive sum gains* in internal activities. That is, partners can together obtain mutual benefits which they could not achieve independently. Such benefits may include:

Increased scale and scope of activities: The outcomes of collaboration may be applicable to all partners' markets, and thus may expand individual firm's customer bases. Synergies between firms' different technological competences may produce better, more widely applicable products.

Shared costs and risk: Collaboration can share the often very high costs, and therefore risk, of innovation (although it also, of course, shares future income streams).

Improved ability to deal with complexity: As Rothwell's chapter on the Fifth Generation Innovation Process shows, innovation is increasingly complicated, and closer strategic and technological integration between firms is a means for dealing with the complexity of multiple sources and forms of technology.

A second assumption regarding collaboration concerns the way it is believed to assist with *environmental uncertainty*. Increasingly sophisticated and demanding customers, growing competition in and internationalization of markets, and rapidly changing and disruptive technologies place pressures on firms to exist with, and attempt to control, these uncertainties confronting them. This is believed to be achieved more easily in collaboration than in isolation. A number of analyses of collaboration link it with uncertainties in the generation and early diffusion of new technologies (Freeman, 1991). The product life-cycle model of Abernathy and Utterback (1975), for example, implies a cyclical role for collaboration based on uncertainty. Thus in early stages of development there are periods of high interaction between organizations with numbers of new entrant companies possessing technological advantages over incumbent firms, and extensive collaboration between firms until a 'dominant design' emerges in a technology. As the technology matures, uncertainty declines and collaborative activity recedes. The high level of collaborative activity seen in the creation of technical standards is a means of reducing uncertainties by introducing interchangeable products and interfaces (Reddy and Cort, 1989).

A third set of assumptions underlying collaboration is one that considers it offers *flexibility* and *efficiencies* compared to its alternatives. For example, collaboration may be an alternative to direct foreign investment and mergers and acquisitions which are much less easily amended once entered into. It can allow firms to 'keep a handle' on external technological developments without having to invest heavily. Large firm/small firm interaction might be facilitated such that the resource advantages of the former are linked with the behavioural or creative advantages of the latter whilst maintaining their independence. Much technological knowledge is tacit – that is, it is difficult to codify in the form of blueprints, etc. – and firm specific (Pavitt, 1988). It is, therefore, difficult to transfer easily or quickly. Collaboration potentially provides a mechanism whereby close linkages among different organizations allow sympathetic systems, procedures and vocabulary to develop which may encourage the effective transfer of technology. It may also allow partners to 'unbundle' discrete technological assets for transfer (Mowery, 1988). Technological knowledge is also difficult to price; collaboration can provide a means of exchange without necessarily resorting to prices.

Potentially, therefore, there may be numerous advantages in innovation to be achieved through collaboration if these assumptions are correct. The efficacy of collaboration as an aid to innovation can perhaps best be adjudged by consideration of its current extent, and likely future use. However, examining whether the potentials of collaboration are in practice being realized is difficult as data on its extent and outcomes is often piecemeal and frequently contradictory. Furthermore, whereas the bulk of evidence suggests an increasing role for collaboration in industry, the majority of studies of its outcomes point to the very considerable difficulties in gaining mutually satisfactory outcomes amongst the partners.

Collaboration has a long history. Many leading companies around the world have collaborated extensively for over fifty years. Most major analyses of collaboration assume that it has, however, increased in its frequency over the past decade or so. Databases which record the number of collaborations being formed do generally, but not exclusively, suggest increasing activity. There are, nevertheless, major questions concerning the quality of these databases in their coverage and accuracy, and major uncertainties remain in important questions such as the trends of vertical as compared to horizontal collaborations. What is certain, however, is that the promotion of (primarily horizontal) collaboration has increasingly become the focus of attention of public policies. Policy initiatives promoting collaboration (which often underwrite half the cost of joint projects) such as the Japanese Fifth Generation Computer Programme, the European ESPRIT Programme, and the US Microelectronics and Computer Technology Corporation (one of many research consortia formed following the repeal of US Anti-Trust legislation specifically to encourage collaboration) are increasingly common.

Apart from the potential advantages for innovation, and the increased support for collaboration from public policies, two other reasons are suggested as to why collaboration may be increasing. These are the changing corporate strategies of firms, which are increasingly outward in their vision, and a perceived increase in the internationalization of technology. Thus collaboration may be seen as a strategic tool used by firms to assist their increasing technological diversification (Granstrand et al. 1992). An element of these corporate strategies is believed to be increased internationalization, or 'globalization', as firms attempt to link into, and exert influence over, the multinational sources of, and markets for, technology (Soete, 1991).

Discussions of the likely future increase in collaboration from both a corporate and public policy perspective emphasize its 'positive' aspects and often discount or underemphasize its 'negative' implications. These can be seen in the way in which collaboration can be used as a tool of corporate strategy or government policy to exclude competitors. Thus alliances between firms may be formed to isolate competitors or raise barriers to new entrants. The majority of international collaborations are within and between the 'Triad' of Western Europe, the USA and Japan, thereby excluding other nations. Many collaborative programmes within the Triad are also developed by one trading bloc in order to exclude the other two (Dodgson, 1992a).

Collaboration can be seen as a means by which large multinational firms can indirectly receive government assistance for R&D, thereby further distorting competition. Experience of a number of major national collaborative programmes has shown how the government's resources tend to be directed towards the large (and wealthy) corporations rather than the, perhaps more deserving, smaller companies. Furthermore, shared technological development might be argued to produce a technology to a standard of the lowest common denominator, rather than the objectively best achievable. Formal, legally-binding collaborative agreements between a limited number of firms may reduce the extensive and broad-based informal information exchange between managers, scientists and engineers shown by von Hippel (1988) to be so important to the innovation process. The extensive merger and acquisition activity in the USA and Europe during the 1980s may have reduced the potential number of partners with which to collaborate. It might additionally be speculated that if collaboration is associated with the early stages of a technology's development and diffusion – and many analyses point to the high number of collaborations in information technology – then the greater maturity of that technology (as arguably is being seen in information technology) might lead to reduced collaboration.

Another 'negative' aspect of collaboration is seen in the growing body of research which points to the difficulties firms encounter in trying to use it. Firms may have been encouraged to experiment with collaboration during the 1980s due in part to the considerable inexperience of many of them in partnerships of this kind, and their enthusiastic promotion within business schools. Many will have learnt the hard lessons of unrealistic expectations and will be much more cautious in their future use.

There are, therefore, a variety of reasons why the rate in increase in the *numbers* of collaborations being formed during the 1980s may slow in the future. At the same time, however, experience of collaboration may point to a corresponding increase in their *quality* inasmuch as relationships between partners may be closer and more intimate. A number of reasons can be suggested as to why this might be so:

Increased understanding of the real role of collaboration
Joint technological development cannot in any sustainable way be anything but a supplement rather than an alternative to firms' core method of technology development: internal R&D. Firms need differential proprietary competences with which to trade in collaborations. These can most effectively be achieved by means of internal R&D. Technology is such a key element of corporate competitiveness that there are obvious pressures to internalize it. Although some firms are increasing their external R&D expenditure, this remains a comparatively small element of their total efforts. Even the huge resources put into collaborative public policies are dwarfed by the expenditure of individual large firms. Collaboration is not an either/or option to internal R&D; it is a comparatively small-scale, but nevertheless important, adjunct for a number of reasons:

Shared cost
This may be seen as particularly important in the more expensive, speculative and risky projects in a firm's R&D portfolio.

The continuing complexity of science and technology
The heterogeneity of potential sources of technology, with the possibilities of specialist inputs and complementary knowledge from other firms, will ensure continuing uncertainty in industrial innovation. There will remain an enormous multiplicity of sources of technology. Internationally diverse research groups, and specialist firms of all sizes can continue to produce differential and advanced knowledge, perhaps unexpected knowledge, which will attract the interest of partners. The opportunities and threats of environment issues will, as Skea argues in chapter 34, further stimulate collaboration.

Enhanced learning abilities

With continuous and rapid market and technology change there are pressures on firms to improve their learning capacities so as to identify future opportunities and threats and to be able to respond effectively to them. At the same time firms face organizational pressures towards introspection and create strategies which favour existing ways of doing things. Collaboration can provide possibilities not only of learning about new technologies, but learning about methods of creating future technologies and of the ways those technologies might affect the existing business. It can teach companies new ways of doing things not only technologically, but organizationally and managerially, and can conceivably alter the nature of the business.

Two major factors which can be identified as a having a major bearing on the way collaboration is used to support innovation in the future are the use of information technology and the management skills utilized.

Whereas the innovation process has always involved close interaction between firms in clusters – and regional networks of customers and suppliers, and interacting competitors and collaborators – this is the first period in which information technology can cement and intensify these linkages. Speed to market will continue, as it is now, to be a fundamental driver of competitiveness. Intercorporate integration through electronic media such as CAD/CAM, and computerized purchasing and control systems, can facilitate the speedy development and production of new products.

The effective use of electronic media depends, of course, as with all aspects of successful collaboration, on its management. Research into the management of technological collaboration points to a number of important issues for its conduct. One issue of central significance is: what is success and failure? Technological success realized by all partners achieving their technological aims may not be translated into market success as resulting products may fail. Ostensible technological failure may, in fact, have successfully developed new skills and competences in a firm capable of valuable subsequent use. There may be advantages in taking the wider view of the contribution of collaboration, and instead of evaluating its success or failure in terms of *outputs* or readily identifiable products, it should examine *outcomes* more broadly defined. These include enhancements of the firm's knowledge base, and any technological or organizational learning the firm may have accumulated (including learning by failing, hopefully not to be replicated). The expectations of managers, in consequence, need not be too rigidly or restrictedly defined.

Given the many strategic reasons why firms enter collaboration (Dodgson, 1992b) – for example, to assist the innovation process and technological diversification so central to continuing competitiveness, and the lengthy periods of time it commonly takes for partners to develop effective means of communication – there are reasons why advantages might be achieved through partners being selected with a long-term perspective. Furthermore, firms often enter collaborations on the basis not of what technologies they currently possess, but of what they are capable of producing in the future. The management of collaboration needs, therefore, to exist within a strategic framework.

At a tactical or operational management level research has shown the advantages of utilizing particularly highly skilled project managers. Such skills are argued to be most appropriate in the context of flexible and adaptable project structures to allow projects to grow organically rather than restrict them through over prescription, and clear consideration of the ways in which the external search for technology through collaboration is to supplement and complement internal R&D projects and competences.

One of the most important aspects of the collaborative process is the nature of the relationship between partners. The strategic adhesion and complementarity of companies, the exchange of often valuable tech-nological knowhow, and the need for effective and open communications so as to equitably exchange resources, is often predicated on the existence of high-trust relationships. Partners trust one another to be honest, capable and committed to joint aims. Such high levels of trust can exist within the subcontractor relationships described by Sako in this volume, and underpins many user/supplier links. Perhaps the greatest challenge to management is to produce such trust-based relationships in firms' potentially more contentious horizontal collaborations.

If, in future, collaborations are characterized more widely by high-trust relationships this will have important implications not only for strategic management but also for our understanding of theories of the firm. The cooperative rather than universally competitive model of inter-firm relationships, in areas of such commercial importance as technological innovation, has implications for those theories that reduce all firm transactions to cost and price considerations without regard to the potentially mutually valuable synergies achievable through the sharing of competences and knowledge.

Bibliography

Abernathy, W. and Utterback, J. (1975) *Innovation and the Evolution of Technology in the Firm*, Harvard University, Cambridge, Massachusetts.

Arnold, E., Guy, K. and Dodgson, M. (1992) *Linking for Success: Making the Most of Collaborative R&D*, Institution of Electrical Engineers, London.

Contractor, F. and Lorange, P. (1988) *Cooperative Strategies in International Business*, Lexington Books, Lexington, Massachusetts.

Dodgson, M. (1991) *The Management of Technological Collaboration*, Centre for the

Exploitation of Science and Technology, London.

Dodgson, M. (1992a) 'The Future for Technological Collaboration', *Futures*, Vol. 25, No. 4, pp. 459–70.

Dodgson, M. (1992b) 'The Strategic Management of R&D Collaboration', *Technology Analysis and Strategic Management*, Vol. 4, No. 3, pp. 227–44.

Dodgson, M. (1993) *Technological Collaboration in Industry: Strategy, Policy and Internationalization in Innovation*, Routledge, London.

Freeman, C. (1991) 'Networks of Innovators: A Synthesis of Research Issues', *Research Policy*, Vol. 20, pp. 499–514.

Granstrand, O., Hakannson, L. and Sjolander, S. (1992) *Technology Management and International Business*, Wiley, Chichester.

Lundvall, B. (1988) 'Innovation as an Interactive Process: from User-Producer Interaction to the National System of Innovation' in Dosi, G., Freeman, C., Nelson, R., Silverberg, G. and Soete, L. (eds) *Technical Change and Economic Theory*, Pinter Publishers, London.

Macdonald, S. (1992) 'Formal Collaboration and Informal Information Flow', *International Journal of Technology Management*, Vol. 7, No. 1.

Mody, A. (1989) *Changing Firm Boundaries: Analysis of Technology Sharing Alliances*, Industry Series Paper No. 3, The World Bank, Washington.

Mowery, D. (1988) *International Collaborative Ventures in US Manufacturing*, Ballinger, Cambridge, Massachusetts.

Mytelka, L. (1991) *Strategic Partnerships and the World Economy*, Pinter Publishers, London.

Pavitt, K. (1988) 'International Patterns of Technological Accumulation' in Hood, N. and Vahlne, J.-E. (eds) *Strategies in Global Competition*, Croom Helm.

Porter, M. and Fuller, K. (1986) 'Coalitions and Corporate Strategy' in Porter, M. (ed.) *Competition in Global Industries*, Harvard Business School, Boston Press, Boston.

Reddy, N. and Cort, S. (1989) 'Industrywide Technical Product Standards', *R&D Management*, Vol. 19, No. 1, pp. 13–25.

Soete, L. (1991) *Technology in a Changing World: Policy Synthesis*, OECD Technology Economy Programme, MERIT, Maastricht.

von Hippel, E. (1988) *The Sources of Innovation*, Oxford University Press, Oxford.

23. Marketing and Innovation

Dale Littler

Introduction

It is widely recognized that marketing plays a vital role in establishing and sustaining a profitable competitive advantage because of its unique position at the interface of the business with its markets. Numerous reports and research studies have pointed to the importance of having a clear understanding of customer requirements, (Langrish et al., 1972; Rothwell, 1977; Cooper, 1980) of 'keeping close to customers' (Peters and Waterman, 1982) and of applying the full range of marketing techniques as significant factors in successful commercial ventures (Rothwell, 1976). Many reports have singled out marketing as a major influencer of commercial success. For example, NEDO concluded: 'Lack of expertise in marketing is the single most important cause of the disappointing performance of British companies in the last two decades'.

The aims of this chapter are to consider what is meant by marketing; to differentiate between marketing as a business function and as an overall philosophy of business; and to assess critically the manner in which marketing can contribute to effective industrial innovation.

The Nature of Marketing

Marketing can be considered from at least two perspectives: as a general business philosophy, 'the marketing orientation', whereby the major focus of the business production process is the generation of customer satisfaction; and as a functional activity of a business similar to R&D, and finance. It is clear that all aspects and all levels of a business must attempt to develop an insight into and empathy with the customer. In this sense, though, the marketing function may also have a key part in gathering, analyzing and disseminating throughout the organization intelligence on customer purchasing behaviour, satisfaction levels, attitudes towards the business and its competitors and such like, as well as contributing to the development of an overall corporate culture which not only acknowledges the central role of the existing and potential customers but also the manner in which the dynamics of the environment are continuously shaping demands, resulting in new customer priorities, with consequent implications for the development of new and existing products.

The marketing orientation can be formally defined as:

> The identification or anticipation of the requirements of specific group(s) of customers within a defined business scope, and the development of appropriate offerings with the aim of generating customer satisfaction, thereby attaining organisational objectives.

It is clear that given the rapidly changing nature of the environment within which businesses have to operate, they may need to *anticipate* and not merely react to changes which they are witnessing.

Second, the emphasis is not on generic needs, but rather the specific wants, or *requirements,* of selected groups of customers. In many cases, these wants may be latent or unclearly articulated, and it is how businesses interpret the specifications that customers may want and the effectiveness and efficiency with which businesses translate these into appropriate offerings that may be critical factors differentiating between the more and the less competitive.

Third, although demand for any particular product or service can be regarded as homogenous, individuals will have particular requirements and it may be possible to group customers with similar requirements so that inter cluster exceeds intra cluster variation. In this way, then, demand can be disaggregated and the market can be *segmented* (Wind and Cardozo, 1974; Bonoma and Shapiro, 1983; Hlavacek and Ames, 1986). By tailoring what is offered to particular segments, it may be possible to secure some form of competitive advantage.

Fourth, businesses tend to operate within some implicit or explicit business scope, defined in terms of products, technologies and customers. Thus, a business may regard itself as operating in the 'kitchen equipment' market with an appeal to discerning, design conscious customers. Or, its business scope may be defined in terms of fundamental needs, (Levitt, 1960) and it may view its business focus as being the transportation business, for example. History is a powerful influencer of the business scope; but as the environment changes, organizations may have to learn to shake off the grasp of the past and establish new directions, a process that in itself may demand a reassessment of traditional methodologies.

Finally, the business does not just market a product, but rather a collection of values such as the ability to perform a particular task, enhance appearance and augment or reinforce perceived self-image. In general, in many markets, particularly those which are maturing where there is an increasing commodification of technical product features, a greater proportion of the value added is derived from the 'softer' non-tangible aspects, such as service quality, distribution and technical support, so that the distinction between 'services' and 'products' is becoming increasingly indistinct: in many cases, each has a significant element of both.

Marketing has functional status in many businesses. Its role is seen to be concerned with commissioning and/or undertaking market research and analysis, and with having an active part in the development of all aspects of the offering that include pricing, advertising, promotion, service support, distribution, packaging, sales and design. Its prime purpose should be to ensure that the offering which emerges from the development process has significant appeal to the customer segments which it has identified as having the optimum potential for the business, whilst at the same time having a perceived differentiation from its competitors with regard to those values which its target customers regard as important. In a sense, marketing aims to facilitate the process of exchange with its customers. In many technologically new sectors, though, the focus is still on technology. This was evident in the mobile communications sectors.

> The focus of the mobile communications operators so far has been firmly on the technology and the product. Whilst this focus may have been appropriate to the cellular radio operators, facing an almost insatiable demand for their service, it is less appropriate to the present market situation. It is important that benefits sought by customers are increasingly taken into account by the operators. There is a need to consider whether or not each of the mobile communications technologies is offering appreciable customer values and to question some of the assumptions made about the mobile communications sector (Littler and Leverick, 1992).

In the case of new technology products, where experience suggests that technology and the product rather than the values perceived by customers are often given undue attention, marketing has an especially important role to play. It has to ensure the emerging innovation genuinely satisfies the basic criterion of presenting the customers with something which they regard as having some differentiating benefits, such as ease of use.

It is a truism that the rate of environmental change is somewhat frenetic; in particular, product innovation is observed as being at a high pace, with obvious implications for the life cycles of extant products and the need for short development times and rapid extensive marketing of new products in order to recover investments and ensure an adequate return whilst some form of quasi-monopoly position exists. There are also other implications: in an increasingly turbulent environment it is advisable to build customer loyalty that in effect means that the business is given some discretionary space when mistakes and misunderstandings arise; and in particular to forge durable links with customers in order to have direct knowledge of their changing requirements. It has been argued that the central thrust of marketing is relationship building and management (Gronroos, 1989; Hakansson, 1982), for the costs of losing a customer are significant, (Strong, 1990) both in terms of the adverse information which may be disseminated by that dissatisfied customer, and the effort and resources required in re-establishing or replacing that relationship.

Product Innovation

Although the deterministic nature of the product life cycle has been rightly questioned, (Dhalla and Yuspeh, 1976; Levitt, 1965) it highlights the need for businesses to assess constantly the competitiveness of their existing products and to adapt them as appropriate. Where diminishing marginal returns to effort from such investment are evident or there are significant switches in technologies and customer tastes and preferences, or it is aimed to have significant increases in the business' growth, the development of new products will have to be considered as part of the *product planning* process.

The major criticism that can be levelled at the traditional marketing strategy and management methodologies is that they are depicted as intrinsically logical and rational, involving a cool, intellectual and reflective analysis of the environment and the apparently unproblematic application of planning procedures (Kotler, 1988; Greenley, 1986). The subjectivity of the analysts, the bounded rationality of the decision-makers, the political context of organizations, the uncertainties surrounding any decision process, the manner in which the exigencies of the process can themselves affect outcomes and such like, are all evidently ignored (Littler and Leverick, 1993). Such issues must be of particular concern in the case of innovation, where even minor consequential changes can offer disruption to the parties involved.

Indeed, the risks and uncertainties of new product development have been repeatedly identified. Empirical research points to a high rate of attrition of product ideas throughout the product development process, with a large number of new product development projects being abandoned before they reach the commercial stage. Moreover, a high proportion of those that are actually launched are commercially unsuccessful. Booz, Allen and Hamilton (1982), for example, suggest that for every seven product ideas, only one will result in a successful product launch. A study of the US food manufacturing sector found that for every 1000 product ideas, only thirty-six led to marketable products on a continuing basis, (Buzzell and Nourse, 1967) whilst research (Mansfield et al. 1972) on the outcomes of R&D programmes in a variety of industrial sectors suggest a 'success' rate of between 12 and 20 per cent.

The second element of risk is the costs of failure. These embrace not only the investment in the development and launching of the new product that is tending to increase in many cases because of tighter regulations on health and safety, the inflation in R&D costs (Cox, 1989), more extensive marketing programmes in a highly competitive environment and the significant costs of communications campaigns, but also the potential damage to the status of the business with its distributors, suppliers and customers from any failure. The monetary costs can be extremely high, as the results of many unsuccessful ventures indicate (Hartley, 1992). Even product extensions can demand high advertising and promotional spends in the range of millions of pounds (*Financial Times*, 26 July 1990).

The uncertainties surrounding product innovation have been described by Freeman (1982) amongst others. They include market uncertainties, which stem from the difficulties in predicting the form and intensity of competition, the reactions of targeted customers and so on; and technological uncertainty because of unforeseen technological problems which in turn can affect the timing and costs of development. In addition, there is general business uncertainty which can arise from those random and difficult-to-forecast events which surround any business decision.

New Product Development Process

In the context of risk and uncertainty, it is surprising that received marketing theory presents the new product development process as a sequential series of stages, often representing the different functional activities of the business (Cannon, 1986; Scheuing, 1974). This is the 'relay' model in which one task is completed, such as the design of the final product, before being passed on to the next major activity, such as, for example, manufacture. It is based on a clear division of labour and a distinct separation of tasks: researchers research, designers design, marketers market and so on. This view of the innovation process assumes that each activity completes its task before handing the development to the next activity in the sequence. The ineffectiveness and inefficiency of this approach are obvious. It can mean that technologists can work in isolation from customers, so that products emerge that are, for instance, overelaborate and inconvenient to use. The lack of close contact between R&D, design and manufacture may mean that products are devised which are difficult to mass manufacture at a realistic cost, thereby involving in some instances significant product redefinition and redesign. The product may also, of course, not be aesthetically pleasing to the customer.

The problems resulting from such an approach are manifold and in an era of rapid change, intense competition and increasing product development costs, the need for efficiency and speed suggest that the appropriate model for new product development should be more a 'scrum' approach, with a high level of interaction between all the different activities. Not only will the chance that such difficulties highlighted above are likely to be reduced, but it also means that there will be a more rapid response to the problems which will inevitably arise during the development process. Thus, for example, problems emerging in customer tests can be analyzed with the involvement of R&D and design staff, and a solution is more likely to emerge quickly.

The focus throughout the process should be customer values. It has already been noted, though, that technology can have a powerful role in driving innovation. In addition, customer requirements can be latent, often deeply so, and technological development *per se* may be influential in stimulating and even creating demand. This suggests that the strict application of the marketing orientation may not, particularly in the case of radical innovation, be especially straightforward. Indeed, it could reasonably be argued that in such instances, it is leaps in imagination, creative insights and entrepreneurial flair that may be more relevant than the careful application of traditional marketing research methodologies which may only lead to pedestrian innovation, as some have suggested (Rosenbloom and Abernathy, 1982).

The problem with employing customer market research techniques as a basis for justifying particular product developments is that respondents may find it difficult to visualize the innovative product, and how things might be. Rather, they are more likely to extrapolate from what they have experienced. This suggests they should be employed circumspectly in such a way that they do not lead to product development being placed in the straitjacket of the extant.

Although freedom to experiment with new product ideas should be encouraged and facilitated, this should be within the context of evaluating the innovation constantly and rigorously at defined review stages (or 'milestones') against the criteria of the major customer values which the emerging innovation offers over those already available from existing products, and the price that the customer is prepared to pay to obtain these values. The danger is that the benefits perceived are those as seen by the developer and not by potential customers, and that even where extensive market research and testing are undertaken, the information is selectively ignored or interpreted in a way favourable to the innovation. It is as well to cultivate at least an awareness of such impediments to effective product innovation.

The contribution of marketing during the development in carrying out preliminary market and competitor analysis, ensuring constant appraisal of competitive position, undertaking continual customer testing and generally assessing the product as it evolves is evident. This often demands close liaison with customers which, *inter alia*, may involve *in situ* assessment of the innovation. Marketing must also assume responsibility for devizing a strategy that meets the business's objectives for the innovation. It has to formulate the total offering, including the brand where appropriate, and develop the market, involving the formulation of the launch campaign and a follow-on marketing campaign which stimulates adoption and an acceptable rate of diffusion of the product.

Diffusion and Adoption

The launch strategy will need to take into account *inter alia* the need to generate a favourable response amongst intermediaries, such as wholesalers and retailers; form commendatory attitudes in those who act as opinion formers, such as advisers and trade bodies; and create awareness, stimulate interest and provoke purchase by potential customers. Advertising, promotion and personal selling can all be critical to the adoption and rate of market penetration. Innovative offerings should have intrinsic values which command premium prices, and this in itself emphasizes the importance of securing rapid diffusion before competitors emerge.

There needs to be a detailed understanding of the factors that affect the rate of adoption, (Rogers and Shoemaker, 1971) so that these can be manipulated in favour of the offering, and whether or not there are categories of potential customers with a greater propensity to adopt innovations. There may, for example, be highly regarded businesses which others in the industry seek to emulate.

Conclusion

The marketing function's concern is to ensure that industrial innovations are conceived and developed with a careful regard to the differential customer benefits they offer. This involves constant close liaison with potential customers throughout the development process, from the formulation of the new product concept to testing in use the evolving product and the assessment of the proposed marketing strategy. This suggests that throughout the process of development marketing should be involved with other activities in the firm.

Bibliography

Bonoma, T.V. and Shapiro, B.P. (1983) *Segmenting the Industrial Market,* Lexington Books, Lexington, Massachusetts.

Booz, Allen and Hamilton (1982) *New Product Management for the 1980s,* Booz, Allen and Hamilton, New York.

Buzzell, R.D. and Nourse, R.E.M. (1967) *Product Innovation in Food Processing: 1954–1964,* Harvard University Press, Cambridge, Massachusetts.

Cannon, T. (1986) *Basic Marketing,* Second Edition, Holt, Rinehart and Winston, Eastbourne.

Cooper, R.G. (1980) 'How to Identify Potential New Product Winners', *Research Management,* September, pp. 10–19.

Cox, B. (1989) 'Strategies for Drug Discovery – Structuring Serendipity', *Pharmaceutical Journal,* September 16.

Dhalla, N.K. and Yuspeh, S. (1976) 'Forget the Product Life Cycle Concept' *Harvard Business Review,* January/February, pp. 102–12.

Freeman, C. (1982) *The Economics of Industrial Innovation,* Frances Pinter, London.

Greenley, G.E. (1986) *The Strategic and Operational Planning of Marketing,* McGraw Hill, London.

Gronroos, C. (1989) 'Defining Marketing: A Market-Oriented Approach', *European Journal of Marketing,* Vol. 23, No. 1, pp. 52–60.

Hakansson, H. (1982) *International Marketing and Purchasing of Industrial Good: An Interaction Approach,* John Wiley and Sons, Chichester.

Hartley, R.F. (1992) *Marketing Mistakes,* Fifth Edition, John Wiley and Sons, Chichester.

Hlavacek, J.D. and Ames, B.C. (1986) 'Segmenting Industrial and High-Tech Markets' *Journal of Business Strategy,* Fall, pp. 39–50.

Kotler, P. (1988) *Marketing Management: Analysis, Planning, Implementation and Control,* Sixth Edition, Prentice Hall International, Englewood Cliff, New Jersey.

Langrish, J., Gibbons, M., Evans, W. and Jevons, F.R. (1972) *Wealth from Knowledge,* Macmillan, London.

Levitt, T. (1960) 'Marketing Myopia', *Harvard Business Review,* July/August, pp. 45–56.

Levitt, T. (1965) 'Exploit the Product Life Cycle', *Harvard Business Review,* November/December.

Littler, D.A. and Leverick, F. (1992) *From Technology to Marketing: The Way Forward for Mobile Communications,* PICT Policy Paper No. 18, Economic and Social Research Council, PICT, Oxford.

Littler, D. and Leverick, F. (1993) 'Strategic Archetypes in Nascent Technology Sectors' in Baker, M.J. (ed.) *Perspectives on Marketing Management,* Vol. 3, John Wiley and Sons, Chichester.

Mansfield, E. et al. (1972) *Research and Innovation in the Modern Corporation,* Macmillan, London.

Peters, T. and Waterman, R.H. (1982) *In Search of Excellence,* Harper and Row, New York.

Rogers, E.M. and Shoemaker, F.F. (1971) *Communication of Innovations: A Cross-Cultural Approach,* Collier-Macmillan, London.

Rosenbloom, R.S. and Abernathy, W.J. (1982) 'The Climate for Innovation in Industry', *Research Policy,* 11, pp. 209–25.

Rothwell, R. (1976) 'Marketing: a Success Factor in Industrial Innovation', *Management Decision,* Vol. 14, No. 1.

Rothwell, R. (1977) 'The Characteristics of Successful Innovation and Technically Progressive Firms (with some comments on Innovation Research)', *R&D Management,* Vol. 7, No. 3, June.

Scheuing, E.E. (1974) *New Product Management,* The Dryden Press, Hinsdale, Illinois.

Strong, L. quoted in: Holberton, S. (1990) 'How BA Tries to Make Friends and Keep Them', *Financial Times,* 14 September, p. 16.

Wind, Y. and Cardozo, R. (1974) 'Industrial Market Segmentation', *Industrial Marketing Management,* III, pp. 153–66.

24. Innovation and Intellectual Property

Don Lamberton

Introduction

Intellectual property 'is a broad term that is used to describe the wide range of rights that are conferred by the legal system in relation to discrete items of information that have resulted from some form of human intellectual activity' (Ricketson, 1992), e.g. inventions, scientific discoveries, literary and artistic works, trade marks and industrial designs. It should therefore occasion no surprise that as economies have become more information-intensive, first, greater attention has perforce been given to these property rights; second, such traditional categories as patents and copyrights have become overloaded as new items such as integrated circuits, software, plant varieties and genetic materials have proliferated; and, third, the social and economic effects have been far-reaching, even if not as spectacular as either Utopians or Luddites would have had us believe.

In developed economies, traded information goods and services, i.e. those intrinsically conveying information, or directly useful in producing, processing or distributing information, are reported to account for as much as one third of GDP. Information occupations, i.e. those primarily concerned with the creation and handling of information *per se*, can represent more than 40 per cent of employment. Disaggregated data tell the same story: for example, wage and salary costs of the global operations of large Swedish manufacturing firms split 53 per cent for information production and use and 47 per cent for goods manufacturing (Eliasson et al., 1990). American purchases of information processing equipment as a percentage of all durable equipment bought by private enterprise (excluding farms) increased from little more than 10 per cent in 1970 to more than 50 per cent in 1989. In the course of this gorging, the US economy could be said to have reached a mature IT stage, with a significant cross-over in the late 1970s when investment per worker in 'high-tech' industries first exceeded that in basic industrial activities.

While these information goods and services are used predominantly by industry, commerce and government, they nevertheless figure both on the job and in the home; a growing variety of information consumption goods even blurs the distinction between workplace and home. Business and government make extensive use of a mix of telecommunications and computers and an information processing capability – a chip – is incorporated into many processes and products, e.g. household appliances, toys, traffic control, motor cars, manufacturing equipment, airplanes.

In this knowledge-based information economy, information processing in its most general sense has become the greatest claim on resources. All innovation uses information processing and much innovation is directed to changing the methods of information processing. Additionally, property rights are subjected to new and stronger pressures, both technological and economic.

Economic Theory of Intellectual Property

Many rationales are offered for the institution of intellectual property rights, e.g. the natural law doctrine by which the individual has property rights in the fruits of labour. As this brief paper on what is an enormously complex subject can be little more than the barest introduction, it will focus on the economics of these property rights and their role in the process of innovation.

In so doing, two basic propositions must be accepted. The first builds upon the statement: 'Inasmuch as research and invention are activities directed to producing *information*, an economic analysis of R&D activities must inevitably rest upon recognition of the peculiar characteristics of information viewed as an economic commodity' (Dasgupta and David, 1987). Even if a simple linear model were adequate in linking research and invention to production through innovation, the role of information in that linking would necessitate attention to those 'peculiar characteristics'. Such linear modelling is now widely accepted as inadequate and has been replaced by more complex conceptualizations of the research-production nexus, with their stages and feedbacks, which are still incomplete and misleading without explicit treatment of the information-theoretic aspects.

The second proposition is closely allied to the first: modelling of the role of intellectual property must be supported by knowledge of the information flows and patterns of information usage. This is no more than is taken for granted in the analysis of economic activity involving tangible goods that is depicted in an input-output framework. The Leontief tradition has yielded much detail on product flows and associated payments but has not mapped information activities in either their information or payments dimensions.

By taking account of the peculiar economic characteristics of information and the information flows involved, it becomes possible to modify the traditional economic theory of intellectual property, reaching conclusions that have analytical, managerial, and policy significance in the modern information economy. We turn therefore to brief consideration of the basic economics of patent protection and those peculiar characteristics.

Basic Economics of Patent Protection

The case of patents illustrates most of the basic features. Ignore the weaknesses in the protection offered by a patent and consider the basic economics of the right created. At a cost (which has two elements: an initial charge and a recurring payment), the patentee secures exclusive rights over the use of the information embodied in the patent for a lengthy period of time. From a policy point of view this is intended to provide an incentive for the production of useful information (i.e. technology) as a first step in the process of invention, innovation, and economic growth. The rights granted are subject to various limitations in the social interest; for example, there are limits on scope, term and geographical area. Further, the right not to use, to retard innovation or unduly restrict availability in order to enhance profits may be limited by provisions for compulsory licensing. However, for a variety of reasons this element of the system has not worked very effectively – a matter that will be touched upon again later.

While the rights granted are exclusive monopoly ones, there is no guarantee of profit. Assuming, however, that the new idea yields a 'manner of new manufacture' that becomes profitable, the inventor is rewarded; excess profits from the invention are held down and finally eroded when competitive supply becomes possible; and – a feature that is all too often neglected – the nature of the invention and some detailed information about it has been disclosed and can in turn help others with the ability to climb on the shoulders of giants in their search for new ideas (Scotchmer, 1992).

The basic model is that the possible reward induces the creation of useful information. The value of this information is assumed to be perceived and to provide investment targets. A resultant producer's surplus is eventually transformed into consumer's surplus on expiration of the patent. A static 'triangles' analysis supposedly enables determination of an optimal life of the patent, but recognition of the administrative costs that would be involved – along with the overriding uncertainty – ensures adoption of a standard life.

Interestingly, a major exception has developed: the German *Gebrauchsmuster* or petty patent has been introduced in a number of countries. Lower standards have to be met, the process is quicker, the costs lower, and the protection afforded is less. The intention was to facilitate the whole innovation process. Greater success might have attended these efforts if those seeking patents had had to choose between a standard and a petty patent; but in the event the petty patent has served as quick protection while awaiting issue of a standard patent.

Within this general framework, two characteristics of information are held to have considerable explanatory power: indivisibility and inappropriability. The indivisibility point can be presented in several ways: first, if one has a piece of information, there is no incentive to buy it a second time; alternatively, we can note that the cost of the information contained in a patent about a 'manner of new manufacture' is a sunk cost that is independent of the scale of application of that knowledge. From this viewpoint, a role of information is to introduce economies of scale and to foster the argument that the more information-intensive the economy, the greater the departure from the competitive model.

The second characteristic has been summed up as follows:

> Information is inappropriable because an individual who has some can never lose it by transmitting it. It is frequently noted in connection with the economics of research and development that information acquired by research at great cost may be transmitted much more cheaply. If the information is, therefore, transmitted to one buyer, he can in turn sell it very cheaply, so that the market price is well below the cost of production. But if the transmission costs are high, then it is also true that there is inappropriability, since the seller cannot realize the social value of the information (Arrow, 1984: 142).

A Major Reinterpretation

At this point, the stage has been set for a major reinterpretation. Information does not flow through individuals or organizations that lack capability, i.e. information and capability of transmitting or using that information are complementary. Remove such capability, and transmission costs will be high, so there is inappropriability on the part of the imitators, which can serve to strengthen the monopoly power of the original inventor/innovator.

The term capability has crept into general usage in economics, but it calls for care. Nussbaum (1992), for example, defines it as 'that condition in virtue of which one is *able* to do something'. The capability of using information is partly internal, e.g. the state of readiness of the individual, and partly external, e.g. institutional support.

The context in which the information was originally generated may ensure capability that will be lacking elsewhere in the imitation process. Modelling needs therefore to recognize this capability as an important component of organizational capital and a potential basis for monopoly power quite apart from but reinforced by any legal rights. It is important to note that this power is initially only potential, dependent upon the prospects of the invention.

In relation to such circumstances, dominated as they are by lack of information, uncertainty, and learning processes, it is difficult to give meaning to *optimal* choice; perhaps it is what economists treat as optimal, in view of their dislike for non-optimal or irrational behaviour! Nevertheless, short-run optimization may be in conflict with long-run interests. In the present context, decisions based on current perceptions may lead to organizational obsolescence:

> (T)he combination of uncertainty, indivisibility, and capital intensity associated with information channels and their use imply (a) that the actual structure and behavior of an

organization may depend heavily upon random events, in other words on history, and (b) the very pursuit of efficiency may lead to rigidity and unresponsiveness to further change (Arrow, 1974: 49).

There is therefore an economic rationale for a form of non-optimal behaviour. Successful invention may lead to profitable innovation, and the internalization of some parts of the process can create capability that will protect the rents from erosion by competitive supply. However, the information conditions and processes involved may well lead to rigidity, as the organization's decision-makers become locked into certain informational resources, just as they might be locked into a mix of physical assets. The economic analysis of these situations has erred by assuming, first, that the actors are well-informed and, second, that they make good use of the information.

The inadequacy of this traditional approach has, in this case of intellectual property, been reinforced by the other basic characteristic attributed to information, that of indivisibility. The lawyer's definition introduced in the opening paragraph of this chapter stressed the discrete nature of the information embodied in a grant of intellectual property and that discrete nature is compatible with the emphasis upon indivisibility.

An innovation process involving significant inputs from science, technology (Nelkin, 1982) and organization is not to be likened to the discovery of a rich lode that can then be worked – although such discovery was once the meaning of invention. (Kaufer (1988) points out that the medieval Latin *invenire* meant accidental discovery while *ars* meant technological knowhow.) Rather the information inputs are flows that have to be managed (Itami, 1987), perhaps mostly complementing one another but at times being substitutes.

The basic complementarity between information and this management capability then requires reinterpretation of the notion of indivisibility. There is no clear end to the process of producing an item of information. Costs continue to accumulate through later phases. Nor is there, in the case of a patent, a simple *copying* process akin to xeroxing; copying must include replication of at least some, and possibly a substantial part, of the informational and organizational costs of the pioneer. Clearly there are great differences in these respects between individual patents, between patents and copyrights (Patterson and Lindberg, 1991), and between these and other forms of intellectual property. For example, copying costs are low in the copyright case; and while the new developments in genetic information might seem to bear likeness to mining discovery, there are strong complementarities amongst basic research, researcher capability, and survey activity.

It becomes enormously difficult, given this view of the role of information in the innovation process, to attempt to separate the influence of the property right from these other protective elements. Of course, the advantages of the pioneering role have been noted before but it seems worthwhile, particularly in respect of information-intensive activities, to elucidate these informational/organizational aspects, as against the market structure considerations that have tended to receive the major emphasis in economic research.

International Dimension

The complex system of laws at national level relating to intellectual property long ago spilled over to the international scene. In the intermingling and interweaving of R&D, innovation, technology transfer, joint ventures, networking, marketing and trade, it has been held that intellectual property rights are an important instrument in promoting the production and dissemination of new ideas, technologies and creative endeavours needed for the innovation, modernization and competitiveness that might restore growth and prosperity (Luostarinen and Welch, 1990).

GATT negotiations now extend to TRIPS (trade-related aspects of intellectual property) but it is important to look to the real policies of the major countries as opposed to their articulated, ostensible policies. It has for a long time been recognized that the intellectual property system tends to favour those that have technology to sell rather than those who are basically buyers. To this must be added the role of the capability considerations discussed in the previous section of this chapter. Remove such capability and it may remain very difficult to escape from an adverse TRIPS balance of trade.

But the component capabilities are both internal and external; in either case they may assume even greater importance in an international as opposed to a domestic context. Herein lies the importance of information technology developments. On the one hand, the intangible goods of the information age are easily copied and have accordingly been difficult to accommodate within intellectual property systems (Katz, 1986). On the other hand, the difficulties besetting sustainable capability of using information in innovation imply high transmission costs. Quite clearly, there are enormous differences between the cases of intellectual property rights in a refinery process for a raw material to be produced in a developing country and a concert broadcast that can be relayed around the world. These differences may well force the abandonment of efforts to preserve common elements of protection in the legal arrangements and eventually bring greater diversity: the old bottles can only hold so much new wine (Ricketson, 1992).

When these considerations are combined with recognition of the real policies of the major nations, it is the more understandable when pleas for the weakening of the overall system of protection are voiced. *The Economist* (22 August 1992) has recently criticized America's zeal for extending intellectual property rights, arguing that it is not only confusing, but may also be stifling, rather than encouraging, innovation. Given the imprecision of key concepts such as scope and obviousness (Katz, 1986; Kingston, 1987; Merges and Nelson, 1992), it is possible to make a case for simplification. As it is, much of the benefits of intellectual property rights go to those best able to cope with or live off the legal system. 'Doing things with ideas is what makes innovation a reality, not charging rent on dreams. The doing merits the reward' (*The Economist,* 22 August 1992).

Research Agenda

The operation of intellectual property systems has always been a subject of controversy. Clearly, much remains that can be tackled on a theoretical basis, and equally there is a grave need for empirical research that explores the information flows and patterns of information use (Griliches, 1990). The special line of attack emerging from this chapter concerns information-handling capability as part of organizational capital.

A first step would be to replace the narrow R&D concept with a much wider notion of exploratory behaviour (Lamberton, 1992). A significant part of activity is always experimental so forms of exploratory behaviour can be identified and related to the actual information activities and their associated expenditures. Exploratory behaviour is characteristic of all parts of the firm's activities: internal management, organizational change, marketing, industrial intelligence, computing, employee training, risk assessment, competition and cooperation with other firms. It is convenient to use the term business intelligence to embrace these diverse exploratory activities.

A second step would be to examine closely the information stocks and flows involved in the firm's operations: the generation and acquisition of information; the learning processes by means of which the information is processed and utilized (Malerba, 1992).

A third step would be the study of the capability of using information, ranging from the perception of its value to the keeping open of channels of communication and subsequent evaluation of performance. Two indicators of importance might well be (a) concern in advance about ability to appropriate the benefits from particular flows of information (Rosegger, 1991), and (b) accounting for the costs of information.

At each step information protected by intellectual property rights would need to be identified and its path in the information matrix plotted. Only in the light of such research can there be any resolution of the doubts that continue to feature in the intellectual property debate. Perhaps the best illustration would be the failure of compulsory licensing, which is widely regarded as a possible alternative to abolition of the property system. The most likely explanation of this failure lies in the dual lack by licencees of (a) the capability of using the information contained in a patent, and (b) the knowhow information that necessarily complements what is made available under licence.

Bibliography

Arrow, K.J. (1974) *The Limits of Organization*, Norton, New York.

Arrow, K.J. (1984) *Collected Papers of K.J. Arrow: The Economics of Information*, Basil Blackwell, Oxford.

Besen, S.M. and Raskind, L.J. (1991), 'An Introduction to the Law and Economics of Intellectual Property', *Journal of Economic Perspectives*, Vol. 5, No. 1, pp. 3–27.

Braman S. (1990) 'Trade and Information Policy', *Media, Culture and Society*, Vol. 12, pp. 361–85.

Dasgupta, P. and David, P.A. (1987), 'Information Disclosure and the Economics of Science and Technology', in Feiwel G.R. (ed.) *Arrow and the Ascent of Modern Economic Theory*, Macmillan, London.

Economist, The (1992) 'The Harm of Patents', Vol. 324, No. 7773, 22 August, p. 15.

Eliasson, G., Folster, S., Lindberg, T., Pousette, T. and Taymaz, E. (1990) *The Knowledge Based Information Economy*, Industrial Institute for Economic and Social Research, Stockholm.

Friedman, D.D., Landes, W.M. and Posner, R.A. (1991) 'Some Economics of Trade Secret Law', *Journal of Economic Perspectives*, Vol. 5, No. 1, pp. 61–72.

Griliches, Z. (1990) 'Patent Statistics as Economic Indicators: A Survey', *Journal of Economic Literature*, Vol. 28, No. 4, pp. 1661–1707.

Griliches, Z. (ed.) (1984) *R&D, Patents and Productivity*, University of Chicago Press, Chicago.

Griliches, Z., Hall, B.H. and Pakes, A. (1991) 'R&D, Patents and Market Value Revisited: Is There a Second (Technological Opportunity) Factor?', *Economics of Innovation and New Technology*, Vol. 1, No. 3, pp. 183–201.

Itami, H. (1987) *Mobilizing Invisible Assets*, Harvard University Press, Cambridge, Massachusetts.

Jensen, R. (1992) 'Dynamic Patent Licensing', *International Journal of Industrial Organization*, Vol. 10, No. 3, pp. 349–68.

Jussawalla, M. (1992) *The Economics of Intellectual Property in a World without Frontiers: A Study of Computer Software*, Greenwood Press, New York.

Katz, M. (1986) 'The Role of the Legal System in Technological Innovation and Economic Growth', in Landau R. and Rosenberg N. (eds) *The Positive Sum Strategy: Harnessing Technology for Economic Growth*, National Academy Press, Washington, DC.

Kaufer, E. (1988) *The Economics of the Patent System*, Harwood Academic Publishers, London.

Kitch, E.W. (1977) 'The Nature and Function of the Patent System', *Journal of Law & Economics*, Vol. 20, pp. 265–90.

Kingston, W. (ed.) (1987) *Direct Protection of Innovation*, Kluwer Academic Publishers, Dordrecht.

Lamberton, D.M. (1992) 'Information, Exploratory Behaviour and the Design of Organizations', *Human Systems Management*, Vol. 11, No. 2, pp. 61–5.

Lamberton, D.M (1993) 'The Information Economy Revisited', in Babe R. (ed.) *Information and Communication in Economics*, Kluwer Academic Publishers, Dordrecht, pp. 1–33.

Lamberton, D.M. (ed.) (1971) *Economics of Information and Knowledge,* Penguin Books, Harmondsworth, Middlesex.

Luostarinen, R. and Welch, L. (1990) *International Business Operations,* Helsinki School of Economics, Helsinki.

Malerba, F. (1992) 'Learning by Firms and Incremental Technical Change', *Economic Journal,* Vol. 102, pp. 845–59.

Mandeville, T.D., Lamberton, D.M. and Bishop, E.J. (1982) *Economic Effects of the Australian Patent System,* Australian Government Publishing Service, Canberra.

Mandeville, T.D. and Macdonald, S. (1987) 'Innovation Protection Viewed from an Information Perspective', in Kingston, W. (ed.) *Direct Protection of Innovation,* Kluwer Academic Publishers, Dordrecht.

Merges, R.P. and Nelson, R.R. (1992) 'Market Structure and Technical Advance: The Role of Patent Scope Decisions', in Jorde, T.M. and Teece, D.J. (eds) *Antitrust, Innovation, and Competitiveness,* Oxford University Press, Oxford.

Nelkin, D. (1982) 'Intellectual Property: The Control of Scientific Information', *Science,* Vol. 216, No. 4547, 14 May, pp. 704–8.

Nussbaum, N. (1992) 'Justice for Women!', *New York Review of Books,* Vol. 39, No. 16, 8 October, pp. 43–8.

Oniki, H. (1992) 'Mathematical Appendix', in Jussawalla, M. (ed.) *The Economics of Intellectual Property in a World without Frontiers: A Study of Computer Software,* Greenwood Press, New York.

Ordover, J.A. (1992) 'A Patent System for Both Diffusion and Exclusion', *Journal of Economic Perspectives,* Vol. 5, No. 1, pp. 43–60.

Patterson, L.R. and Lindberg, S.W. (1991) *The Nature of Copyright: A Law of Users' Rights,* University of Georgia Press, London.

Ricketson, S. (1992) 'New Wine into Old Bottles: Technological Change and Intellectual Property Rights', *Prometheus,* Vol. 10, No. 1, pp. 53–82.

Rosegger, G. (1991) 'Advances in Information Technology and the Innovative Strategies of Firms', *Prometheus,* Vol. 9, No. 1, pp. 5–20.

Scotchmer, S. (1992) 'Standing on the Shoulders of Giants: Cumulative Research and the Patent Law', *Journal of Economic Perspectives,* Vol. 5, No. 1, pp. 29–41.

Silberston, A. (1967) 'The Patent System', *Lloyds Bank Review,* No. 84, pp. 32–44, as reprinted in Lamberton, D.M. (ed.) (1971), *Economics of Information and Knowledge,* Penguin Books, Harmondsworth, Middlesex, pp. 224–38.

25. Innovation and Size of Firm

Roy Rothwell and Mark Dodgson

Introduction

The debate over the relative roles that large and small firms play in industrial innovation has raged for many years. Some eminent economists such as J. K. Galbraith (1957) have argued for the importance of large size and monopoly power while others, perhaps most notably E. F. Schumacher (1973), have strongly argued that 'small is beautiful'. We will argue that the role played in innovation by small and medium-sized enterprises (SMEs – here taken to be firms employing under 500) is strongly sectorally influenced; that the relative innovatory roles of large and small firms can vary over the industry lifecycle; and that dynamic complementarities frequently exist between the technological change activities of large and small firms.

SMEs and Innovation[1]

Table 25.1 lists the advantages and disadvantages generally ascribed to small and large firms in innovation. It is clear from the various statements that innovatory advantage is unequivocally associated with neither large nor small firms. The innovatory advantages of large firms are in the main associated with their relatively greater financial and technological resources, i.e. they are *material* advantages; small firm advantages are those of entrepreneurial dynamism, internal flexibility and responsiveness to changing circumstances, i.e. they are *behavioural* advantages. Large firms that combine both material and behavioural advantages are, of course, in an extremely strong position and it is to this end that major US companies such as 3M have attempted (in most cases with only limited success) to establish internally small firm-type structures to enhance their innovativeness (Hlavacek, 1974; Roberts, 1977; Roberts and Berry, 1985).

Generally speaking, comprehensive databases showing nationally produced innovations by size of firm do not exist. One exception is the Science Policy Research Unit's innovation database which contains details on some 4,400 significant innovations introduced into commercial use by

Table 25.1 Advantages and disadvantages of small firms in innovation

Advantages	Disadvantages
Management	
Little bureaucracy; entrepreneurial management; rapid decision-making; risk-taking; organic style.	Entrepreneurial managers often lack formal-management skills.
Communication	
Rapid and effective *internal* communication; informal networks.	Lack of time and resources to forge suitable *external* S&T networks.
Marketing	
Fast reaction to changing market requirements; can dominate narrow market niches.	Market start-up abroad can be prohibitively costly.
Technical manpower	
Technical personnel well plugged in to other departments.	Often lack high-level technical skills. Full-time R&D can be too costly. (Need technical specialists for external links.) Can suffer diseconomies of scope in R&D.
Finance	
Innovation can be less costly in SMEs: SMEs can be more 'R&D efficient'.	Innovation represents a large financial risk; inability to spread risk; accessing external capital for innovation can be a problem. Cost of capital can be relatively high.
Growth	
Potential for growth through 'niche strategy' techno/market leadership (differentiation strategy).	Problems in accessing external capital for growth; entrepreneurs often unable to manage growth.
Regulations	
Regulations sometimes applied less stringently to SMEs.	Often cannot cope with complex regulations; unit costs of compliance can be high; often unable to cope with patenting system; high opportunity costs in defending patents.
Government schemes	
Many schemes have been established to assist innovation in SMEs.	Accessing government schemes can be difficult: high opportunity costs. Lack of awareness of available schemes. Difficulty in coping with collaborative schemes.
Learning ability	
Capable of 'fast learning', and adapting routines and strategies. If new, no 'unlearning' problems.	
Organization	
Generally simple and focused. 'Organic' form.	
Joint ventures/strategic alliance	
Can prove attractive partner if technological leader.	Little management experience; power imbalance if collaborating with large firms.
Supplier relations	
	Can exert little control over suppliers.

Table 25.1(cont) Advantages and disadvantages of large firms in innovation

Advantages	Disadvantages
Management	
Professional managers able to control complex organisations and establish corporate technology strategies.	Often controlled by risk-averse accountants; managers become bureaucrats and lack dynamism.
Communication	
Able to establish comprehensive external science and technology networks.	Internal communication can be cumbersome; long decision chains result in slow reaction times.
Marketing	
Comprehensive distribution and servicing facilities, high market power with existing products.	Can ignore emerging market niches with growth potential; see new technology as a threat to existing products and not as an opportunity in the marketplace.
Technical manpower	
Able to attract highly skilled specialists; can support the establishment of a large R&D laboratory: economies of scale and scope in R&D.	Technical manpower can become isolated from other corporate functions.
Finance	
Able to borrow; can spread risk over a portfolio of products; better able to fund diversification.	Shareholder pressures can force a focus on short-term profits. Can access external capital on favourable terms.
Growth	
Able to obtain scale and learning curve economies through investment in production; can fund growth via acquisition, can gain price leadership.	
Regulations	
Able to cope with government regulations; can fund R&D necessary for compliance; able to defend patents.	Regulations often applied more stringently to large companies.
Government schemes	
Can employ specialists to assist in accessing government schemes. Able to manage collaborative schemes.	Increasingly government innovation support has focused on SMEs.
Learning ability	
	Slow to learn; often locked in to well-established practices and routines.
Organization	
Potential synergies across divisions.	Generally complex: multidivisional, and increasingly multinational. Mechanistic organization.
Joint ventures/strategic alliances	
Possess strategic managerial resources to enable the selection of appropriate partners and the proper management of collaboration.	
Supplier relations	
Can encourage innovative suppliers.	

British companies between 1945 and 1983 (Townsend et al. 1981). Table 25.2, based on the SPRU data, lists for eight different time periods between 1945 and 1985 the share of innovations gained by firms in five size categories. Perhaps the most notable feature of the data is the increasing share of national innovations taken by small firms (employment 1–199). For SMEs (employment between 1–499), the innovation share increased from 22.6 per cent during 1965–69, to 29.2 per cent during 1975–79, to 38.3 per cent during 1980–83. The marked decrease in innovation share taken by firms in the 1,000–9,999 size category is the result partly of structural industrial shifts due to takeover and merger activity and partly of a decline in relative innovative efficiency.

As might be expected, the contribution of small firms to innovation varies considerably between sectors of industry. In areas such as aerospace, motor vehicles, dyes, pharmaceuticals and shipbuilding, small firms' innovation share has been only small. In areas such as scientific instruments and specialist machinery, small firms' innovations share has been significant and growing. In general, where capital and/or R&D requirements and other entry costs are high, small firms' share has been small, and vice versa.

The case of electronic computers is interesting since it illustrates clearly the necessity for adopting a *dynamic* approach to the question of firm size and innovation. For most of the period up to 1970, SMEs' share of innovations in this area was relatively small or zero. Between 1970 and 1983, however, SMEs' share increased dramatically from 36 per cent during 1970–74, to 47 per cent during 1975–79, to 64 per cent during 1980–83. During the 1950s and the 1960s UK production was composed almost entirely of mainframe computers with associated high R&D, manufacturing and servicing costs, which effectively debarred SME participation on an appreciable scale. With the introduction of the integrated circuit and more significantly of the microprocessor, entry by SMEs – particularly new technology based firms (NTBFs), those newly established on the basis of new technological possibilities – became entirely possible. They rapidly became involved in the production of mini- and micro-computers and peripherals to satisfy the many new market segments that emerged. Similarly the rapidly developing field of biotechnology is today opening up niche opportunities for SMEs in healthcare and agriculture. Thus, while one type of technology might effectively prevent significant participation by SMEs, another can present them with many new product-market opportunities.

Another major study, this time conducted in the US, utilised the Small Business Administration's listing of 8,000 innovations introduced in 1982 (Acs and Audretsch, 1991). The data were analyzed on the basis of the 'innovation rates' for large firms (at least 500 employees) and small firms (under 500 employees). The innovation rate is defined as the number of innovations divided by the number of employees. Using the aggregated data

Table 25.2 Innovation share by size of firm in the UK 1945–83

Time period	Size of firm							No. of innovations
	1–199	200–499	500–999	1000–9999	10000–29000	30000–99999	100000+	
1945–49	16.8	7.5	5.3	28.3	13.7	18.1	10.2	226
1950–54	14.2	9.5	4.5	32.2	18.4	12.0	9.2	359
1955–59	14.4	10.1	9.1	24.9	16.3	13.2	11.9	514
1960–64	13.6	9.2	6.0	27.8	16.2	14.5	12.7	684
1965–69	15.4	8.2	8.5	24.7	15.6	14.9	13.2	720
1970–74	17.5	9.0	6.3	20.7	17.1	15.4	14.0	656
1975–79	19.6	9.6	7.5	16.2	14.1	18.6	14.5	823
1980–83	26.3	12.1	4.3	14.9	14.6	12.1	15.2	396
Number of innovations	744	411	299	1004	690	660	670	4378
Average percentage	17.0	9.4	6.8	22.9	15.8	15.1	13.0	100

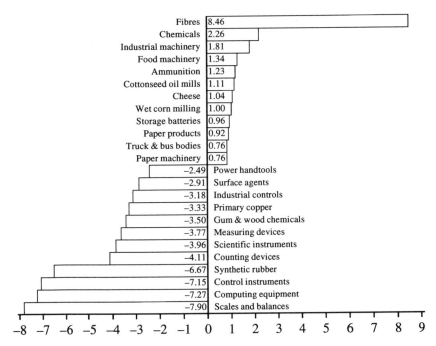

Figure 25.1   Industries with the largest differences between the large-firm and small-firm innovation rates (measured as the number of innovations divided by the total employment (thousands); the difference measured is the innovation rate of large firms minus that of small firms)

for manufacturing, the large firm innovation rate (LIE) was 0.225 while the small firm innovation rate was 0.322.

More disaggregated data are given in Figure 25.1 which shows industries in which the greatest differences between LIE and SIE occurred. The analysis also showed, looking at capital/output ratios, that for small firms the average value between the low- and high-innovative industries (0.300 and 0.260 respectively) is statistically significant. The small firm innovation advantage in general tended to occur in highly innovative industries where the use of skilled labour was relatively important.

Two further points are worth mentioning here. Both US and UK data suggest that there is an U-shaped relationship between innovative activity and firm size (Gellman Research Associates, 1976; Acs and Audretsch, 1981) and, in terms of innovations per unit of R&D expenditure, small firms can be considerably more efficient than their larger counterparts. The latter point is further addressed below.

Because a firm is very large, this does not necessarily mean that the unit producing the innovation is very large also. Table 25.3 gives UK time series data for innovation share not by size of firm, but by size of innovating unit, i.e. subsidiary, division, and so forth. This illustrates a marked shift in innovation share towards small and medium-sized units (SMUs), from 27.9 per cent during 1945–49 to 49.8 per cent during 1980–83. This change was associated with an increased share of innovations taken by subsidiary companies between about 1955 and 1975, following which independent companies – mainly SMEs – increased their share considerably. The share deriving from public sector institutions and firms' divisions declined significantly. To some extent at least, the above pattern might reflect attempts on the part of large companies to marry the resource-related advantages of large firms to the behavioural advantages of smaller firms. The SPRU data do indicate that large firms have tended to acquire smaller firms to facilitate their movement into new areas of activity. In other words, large firms have frequently diversified through a process of small-firm acquisition, a pattern seen particularly clearly in recent large Japanese firm investment in US and European small multimedia and biotechnology firms.

Simply counting innovation shares, of course, tells us nothing about the relatively innovative efficiency of firms of different sizes measured as innovations per unit of employment; nor does it provide any indication of relative R&D efficiency measured as innovations per unit of R&D expenditure. This issue has been dealt with in some detail by Wyatt (1984), whose results will be only briefly summarized here.

Utilizing the SPRU innovation data and employment statistics published by the UK Business Statistics Office, Wyatt derived time series data on the ratio, innovation share/employment share, for firms in five employment categories. This analysis, using aggregated data, showed:

- An increase over time in the relative innovative efficiency of firms with employment between 1 and 199.
- An increase over time in the relative innovative efficiency of firms with employment between 200 and 499.
- A decrease over time in relative innovative efficiency of firms with employment between 500 and 999.
- A more marked decrease over time in the relative innovative efficiency of firms with employment between 1,000 and 9,999.
- A consistently greater than unit relative innovative efficiency of firms with employment greater than 10,000.

On the basis of these data, Wyatt concludes that the fact that SMEs maintained their share of British innovations more successfully than firms with employment between 500 and 10,000 reflects not only structural industrial shifts, but also changing patterns of innovative efficiency. While

Table 25.3 *Innovation share by size of innovating unit in the UK 1945–83*

Time period	Size of Innovating Unit							No of innovations
	1–199	200–499	500–999	1000–9999	10000–29000	30000–99999	100000+	
1945–49	18.6	9.3	8.8	48.7	11.5	0.9	2.2	226
1950–54	20.1	13.6	6.1	46.8	9.2	2.8	1.4	359
1955–59	17.9	14.0	11.5	39.7	11.9	2.7	2.3	514
1960–64	17.4	12.7	10.2	41.8	11.7	3.4	2.8	684
1965–69	21.4	14.2	11.4	37.9	9.2	3.3	2.6	720
1970–74	24.5	14.0	12.2	34.0	10.1	2.9	2.3	656
1975–79	31.3	13.6	13.0	29.8	8.3	2.7	1.3	823
1980–83	32.1	17.7	10.1	29.3	6.8	2.8	1.3	396
Number of innovations	1025	605	480	1625	427	125	91	4378
Average percentage	23.4	13.8	11.0	37.1	9.8	2.9	2.1	100

the aggregate data indicate that it is firms in the largest size category that have attained the highest levels of relative innovative efficiency, the disaggregated data, as we might expect, indicate considerable variation between sectors, and small firms show relative innovative efficiency levels of greater than unity in plastics, textile machinery, mining machinery, radio, radar and electronics capital goods and scientific instruments.

Turning to relative R&D efficiency of innovation, Wyatt's data paint a rather different picture. In 1975, firms with employment between 100–499 enjoyed two per cent of total national manufacturing R&D expenditure; between 1969 and 1980, they produced 20.6 per cent of total innovations, yielding a relative R&D efficiency ratio of 10.3. The comparable figures for firms in the largest size category (employment greater than 10,000) are 80 per cent and 43.4 per cent respectively, yielding a relative R&D efficiency ratio of 0.54. Thus, on the basis of these data, R&D efficiency is very much higher in the smaller firms. A possible explanation of this, and one favoured by Wyatt, is that there is a lower degree of functional specialization in small firms with a higher proportion of innovative activities occurring outside of what is formally defined as R&D, a point emphasized by Segal, Quince and Wicksteed (1985) in their study of new small firms in Cambridge. This would imply, however, that the informal R&D performed in small firms is very considerable indeed. For example, even if we ascribe a 20 per cent share of total R&D to the smaller firms – a factor of ten increase – their relative R&D efficiency would still be almost double that of the largest firms. From the viewpoint of the importance of SMEs in national innovation systems the most interesting feature is the increasing innovative efficiency of SMEs; despite their relative lack of R&D resources. Data taken from a study of innovations produced by 620 firms in the USA in 1985 (NSF, 1987) also suggest a high relative R&D efficiency of innovation in small firms: the data also show a higher relative small firm innovation output per unit of sales (Figure 25.2).

SMEs and the Dynamics of New Technology-Based Sectors

The previous discussion was concerned with the role of SMEs in the production of specific innovations. Adopting a more dynamic view of industrial structural and technological change, it can be demonstrated that NTBFs in particular can play important (although sectorally specific) roles in the emergence of new technology-based sectors of industry. This is illustrated in Figures 25.3 and 25.4 which refer to the evolution respectively of the semiconductor/CAD and the 'new-wave' biotechnology industries in the US (Rothwell, 1989). In the first case, while the initial inventive and innovative activity occurred in large firms, semiconductor devices and CAD systems were diffused throughout the US economy largely through the

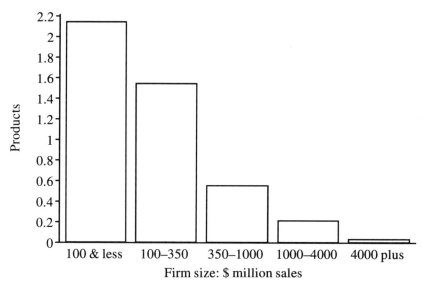

(a)   Per $m R&D

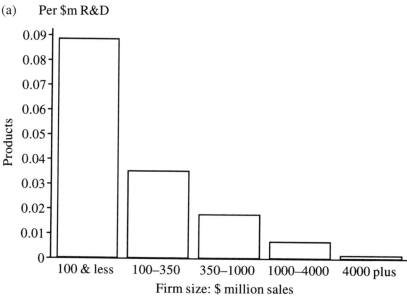

Number of firms: 620

(b)   Per $m Sales

Figure 25.2 New products first marketed in 1985 by size of firm
Source: National Science Foundation (1987), *Science and Technology Indicators*, Washington DC.

Industry origins	Rapid growth phase	Consolidation phase
Basic inventions and initial innovations produced in the R&D laboratories of large electronics companies	NTBFs formed as spin-offs from large companies	Some NTBFs grow to national and international importance
Innovations mainly directed towards 'own use'	Transfer of technological and manufacturing knowhow from large companies to NTBFs via movement of key personnel	Some NTBFs concentrate on marketing specialist market niches
Limited diffusion of innovations to other sectors	Financial flows to NTBFs from large companies and venture capital	Takeover activity
Diffusion of devices across many sectors of the US economy	Trend towards a mature oligopoly	
	Multiple spin-offs from fast growing NTBFs to form other NTBFs	Japanese and European companies established

Figure 25.3 The evolution of the US semiconductor and CAD industries

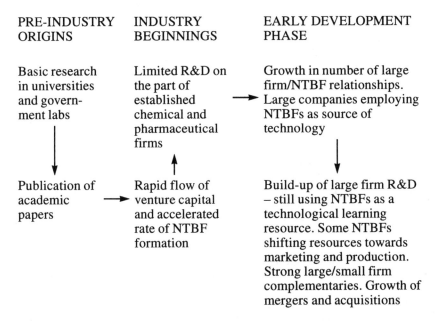

Figure 25.4 Evolution of the 'new wave' biotechnology industry

efforts of NTBFs, which were founded specifically to fulfil this role. In the case of biotechnology, in contrast, the bulk of the early inventive/innovative activity came about in NTBFs, while the commercialization of new products, and particularly ethical pharmaceuticals, will depend mainly on the efforts of established large firms (Dodgson, 1991).

The brief discussion above clearly illustrates the *dynamic complementarities* that can exist between large and small firms. Indeed, small firms are often a crucial component in large firms' technological change activities, and vice versa. Table 25.4 lists some of the many ways in which large and small firms interact to their mutual advantage.

If, as seems likely, inter-company relationships generally are intensifying, and innovation is becoming even more of a networking process (a move toward the fifth generation innovation process), the ability of firms of all sizes to forge mutually complementary relationships will be an increasingly important factor in the creation of competitive advantage through innovation. This is especially true in the case of SMEs which often lack not only large scale in, but also wide breadth of, technological and related resources making them vulnerable to technological diseconomies of scope, limiting their potential in finding synergies across technologies.

Table 25.4 Some modes of large/small firm interaction

Manufacturing subcontracting relationships
SMEs supply components and sub-assembly to large companies. As part of this process large companies frequently transfer technological, manufacturing and quality control knowhow to their small suppliers. Stable, trust-based relationships can develop which are mutually advantageous.

Producer/customer relationships
SMEs supply finished products to large companies. Large companies can transfer technological knowhow and supply suggestions for improvements to small suppliers based on user experience.

Licensing agreements
Large companies provide licences to small firms for innovative new developments. This frequently involves technology that the large company does not wish to exploit in-house but from which it wishes to gain a financial return. In some cases it can involve technology that the large company will subsequently purchase in the form of equipment for in-house use, for example large process companies transferring new process control technology to small instrument companies.

Contract-out R&D
Large companies fund targeted R&D in small specialist consultancy companies, e.g. automobile companies funding R&D in specialist engine developers; pharmaceutical companies funding R&D in small biotechnology companies.

Collaborative development
Large and small companies collaborate in the development of a new product for the large company, e.g. small software or design houses collaborating respectively with large computer and automobile manufacturers.

Large/small firm joint ventures
Large and small firms collaborate in the development of an innovative new product containing technology new to the large partner. The large firm provides financial, manufacturing and marketing resources; the small firm provides specialist technological knowhow and entrepreneurial dynamism. Generally the new products are complementary to the large firms' product range. They may be manufactured by the small partners.

Learning opportunities
Large companies acquire NTBFs to provide them with a window on new technology and an entrée to new business areas. Examples of this are fairly common in the biotechnology field. SMEs can learn about production and manufacturing.

Sponsored spin-outs
The large company offers financial backing for entrepreneurial employees to spin out to form a new small firm to exploit technology developed within the parent company which is deemed unsuitable for in-house exploitation.

Venture nurturing
The large company offers not only financial support to the sponsored spin-out, but also access to managerial, marketing and manufacturing expertise and, if appropriate, to channels of distribution.

Independent spin-out assistance
The large company offers technical assistance to an independent spin-out and sometimes acts as first customer for its products. Pre-payments can provide a crucial source of income to the new company.

Table 25.4 (cont) *Some modes of large/small firm interaction*

Personnel secondment
A number of large European companies have developed schemes to 'loan' experienced managers to assist new and existing SMEs in their locality.

Source: Rothwell, R. (1989) 'SMEs, Interfirm Relationships and Technological Change', *Entrepreneurship and Regional Development*, Vol. 1, pp. 275–91.

Summary

This brief chapter has highlighted a number of significant points concerning the issue of innovation and size of firm:

(i)   Innovatory advantage is unequivocally associated with neither large nor small firms. Small firm advantages are mainly behavioural while those of large firms are mainly material.

(ii)   Available data suggests that the firm size/innovation share relationship is U-shaped.

(iii)   Small firms' innovatory contribution varies significantly from sector to sector. In the main, SMEs' main contribution is in sectors where entry costs are not too high and niche markets exist.

(iv)   Small and large firms do not operate in isolation from each other and they enjoy a variety of complementary relationships in their technological change activities.

(v)   Any study of the roles of small and large firms in innovation should be dynamic; their relative roles can vary considerably over the industry cycle. In the case of the US semiconductor and CAD industries, and during the later emergence of the 'new-wave' biotechnology industry in the US and Europe, both large and small firms have played important but different roles in the dynamics of industrial evolution.

Notes

1.   This section is taken largely from Rothwell and Dodgson (1993) and Rothwell (1989).

Bibliography

Acs, Z.J. and Audretsch, D.B. (1981) 'Innovation, Market Structure and Firm Size', *Review of Economics and Statistics*, Vol. 69, pp. 567–75.

Acs, Z.J. and Audretsch, D.B. (1991) 'Innovation and Firm Size in Manufacturing',

Technovation, Vol. 7, pp. 197–210.

Dodgson, M. (1991) *The Management of Technological Learning: Lessons from a Biotechnology Company*, De Gruyter, Berlin.

Galbraith, J.K. (1957) *American Capitalism*, Hamilton, London.

Gellman Research Associates (1976) *Indicators of International Trends in Technological Innovation*, prepared for the National Science Foundation, Washington DC, April.

Hlavacek, J.D. (1974) 'Towards More Successful Venture Management', *Journal of Marketing*, Vol. 38, October, pp. 56–60.

National Science Foundation (1987), *Science and Technology Indicators*, Washington, DC.

Roberts, E.B. (1977) 'Creating Effective Corporate Innovation', *Technology Review*, October/November, pp. 27–33.

Roberts, E.B. and Berry, C.A. (1985) 'Entering New Businesses: Selecting Strategies for Success', *Sloan Management Review*, Spring, pp. 3–17.

Rothwell, R. (1989) 'Firm Size, Innovation and Industrial Change', *Small Business Economics*, Vol. 1, No. 1, pp. 51–64.

Rothwell, R. and Dodgson, M. (1993) 'Technology-Based SMEs: Their Role in Industrial and Economic Change', in Dodgson, M. and Rothwell, R. (eds) *International Journal of Technology Management*, special edition.

Segal Quince and Wicksteed (1985) *The Cambridge Phenomenon*, Segal Quince and Wicksteed, Cambridge.

Schumacher, E.F. (1973) *Small is Beautiful*, Harper and Row, London.

Townsend, J., Henwood, J. and Pavitt, K. (1981) *Innovation in Britain Since 1945*, Occasional Paper Series No. 16, SPRU, University of Sussex, Brighton, UK.

Wyatt, S. (1984) 'The Role of Small Firms in Innovative Activity', SPRU, University of Sussex, Brighton, UK, mimeo.

26. Innovation and Organization

Gerard Fairtlough

Introduction

Although Alfred Chandler (1962) said that in organizations, structure should follow strategy, it is essential that the structure, systems and human resources of an innovative organization should all interact with its strategy, both influencing and being influenced by it, and further, that its strategy formulation should be guided by a good understanding of the nature of innovation. This chapter starts with a brief typology of innovation, but other chapters in this book should be consulted for a more detailed or for an industry-specific picture.

When describing different types of innovation, the first distinction to be made is between radical (or revolutionary) innovation and incremental (or evolutionary) innovation. *Incremental* innovation is the kind which goes on continuously in any industry, much of it through learning-by-doing. Incremental innovation is often firm-specific and is always industry-specific. *Radical* innovation results from individual inventions and usually requires new production techniques and organizational changes, as well as the technical breakthrough, if it is to be industrially useful. An example might be the discovery of nylon, the first true synthetic fibre. Radical innovation can take place in a firm, or in a university, or elsewhere. It represents an obvious discontinuity, sometimes one which the organization concerned finds hard to handle (Rothwell, 1992; Tushman and Anderson, 1986).

Abernathy and Utterback (1978) show how the character of its innovation changes as a firm moves from the entrepreneurial stage of bringing a radical innovation to market, to the mature stage of efficient production, continuously improved through incremental innovation. Henderson and Clark (1990) add two further types: *modular* innovation, which represents a substantial step-change in the design of a component within a product or system, but where the new design of component fits comfortably into the previous configuration of the product, and *architectural* innovation, where the components are much the same but their technical interrelationship shows greatly enhanced sophistication. From the point of view of a battery maker, a car battery with a much longer life might be a radical innovation. For a car maker, it would be an example of modular innovation if the new battery were used in the traditional way, since the rest of the car's design could be unaffected. On the other hand, a battery-powered car, if it used well-established components but represented a major improvement in performance, would be an architectural innovation.

It is sometimes useful to distinguish between *product* innovation and *process* innovation, and between *pioneers* and *followers* in innovation, the latter relying on superior skills in incremental or architectural innovation to overtake the pioneers (Johne, 1984; Rothwell, 1986). Another useful concept, introduced by Abernathy and Clark (1985), is the *transilience* of an innovation, by which is meant the capacity of an innovation to influence established systems of production and marketing (i.e. to change the relevance of a firm's existing resources, knowledge and customer contacts). Rothwell, in chapter 4, categorizes innovation into *generations*, the most advanced of which is presently the fifth generation, a generation based on system integration and networking (see also Amara, 1990). Freeman and Perez (1988) add to the incremental/radical pair two further types of innovation: changes in technology *system* and changes in techno-economic *paradigm*, the first of these being a cluster of interrelated innovations in several industries, such as those necessary to bring about the widespread use of thermoplastics; the second being a change so far-reaching in its effects that the whole economy is transformed, something which happens only once or twice in a century. Finally, there is the associated concept of a *dominant design*, a formula which sets the pattern for a whole industry, such as the Ford Model T car or the Douglas DC 3 aircraft (Sahal, 1986; Anderson and Tushman, 1990).

Saren (1984) sees the need for a definitive model of innovation, which not only relates these various types of innovation to one another, but also describes in some detail the processes which take place within each type. However, after a survey of numerous different models of innovation, Forrest (1991) concludes that it is unlikely that a useful generalized model can be developed.

Types of Organization

The comprehensive study of innovative organizations owes much to the work of Burns and Stalker (1966). They described two ideal types of organization: *mechanistic*, which is hierarchical, prescribed and demanding of obedience, and *organismic* or *organic*, which avoids precise job-descriptions or channels of communication, seeks flexibility and initiative and encourages commitment to the overall goals of the organization, rather than the slavish following of orders. They suggested that, when a high degree of innovation was sought and when an organization's environment was changing so rapidly that adaptability was vital, the organic type was the best choice. Lansley et al. (1974) considered that this model was too simple to describe the types of organization encountered in practice. They reserved the term 'mechanistic' for those organizations which were undertaking technically-defined tasks, such as assembly-line production, and which therefore did not need much human interaction to coordinate these tasks, but which also had very strong control of the people involved, under the name of 'labour discipline'. This low-coordination, high-control type of organization was in contrast to the high-coordination, high-control type on the military or Weberian pattern, with its specialist staffs and masses of paper, which they called the *bureaucratic* type. The high-coordination, low-control type kept the 'organic' label, while the low-coordination, low-control type was classed as *anarchic*, which was, in its extreme form, little more than a collection of freelance workers.

Hull (1988) analyzed R&D organizations within manufacturing industry by considering organization size and technological complexity. He found that if complexity was low and size small, traditional craft innovation could be successful and as size, though not complexity, increased, bureaucratic methods worked well. However, if technological complexity was high, organic-professional types of R&D organization became essential. These worked best on the small scale and, in large organizations, technological complexity required decentralisation of R&D if it was to be successful.

During the 1960s and 70s, industrial firms often had a semi-anarchic (or professional) research component, modelled on curiosity-driven academic science and located in campus-like surroundings. These firms often organized development (the D of R&D) on bureaucratic lines, while organizing production mechanistically, in separately located factories. However, during this period there was an increasing shift towards organic types of organization, taking into account what McGregor called 'the human side of the enterprise' (1960) and the success of matrix organizations in space programmes and other areas of technological complexity (Knight, 1976). A key feature of this shift was the closer integration of R&D with the production and marketing and sometimes the financial functions of the firm. In the last twenty years, the shift in western industry to the organic type has continued, influenced particularly by the perception that Japanese industrial success owes much to this type of organization.

In summary:
- Innovation needs a flow of ideas, and this arises in a low-control organization, which encourages 'bottom-up' initiatives, the uninhibited expressions of opinions, and a high level of commitment to the success of the organization.
- Innovative people have to have a wide range of information and much interchange between different scientific disciplines and between different business functions. In particular, technological possibilities need to be linked to market opportunities and to production economics.

- The organic type of organization, with low control and high coordination, is therefore preferred for innovation.

The current practice of innovating organizations is now described, under the headings of structure, systems, planning, people, skills, culture and coordination.

Structure

The structure of an organization is its framework of formal roles and procedures, usually depicted in an organization chart with boxes for positions and lines for accountability. But this is only half the story. The willingness of people to follow procedures and to accept authority is what makes the structure a social reality, what makes it a meaningful part of an organization's life. Formal structure encourages people to accept authority, and the exercise of authority reinforces the structure. Restructuring is necessarily a political process, even if it is precipitated by events external to the organization. It is also a symbolic process, making explicit shifts of power and priorities in an organization (Ranson et al. 1980; Giddens, 1984). This is illustrated by the disputes which used to rage in large corporations about 'dotted lines' to staff departments and about responsibility for international operations.

Numerous studies, from Burns and Stalker onwards, have shown that creativity is elicited by a loose structure. But innovation does not simply require creativity. Rothwell's system integration and networking model suggests that extensive coordination and dense information flows are necessary, so structure must also support these. Hence the frequent advocacy for a 'loose-tight' structure (Peters and Waterman, 1982; Hampden-Turner, 1990) which provides both the freedom to create and the discipline to turn creativity into real innovation, into commercial success, and which means that neither mechanistic nor anarchic types of organization are likely to succeed. The organic type will, in this view, be favoured but with something of the bureaucratic type, to introduce a degree of control.

Chisholm (1989) points out that information flow and coordinated decision-taking are not necessarily enhanced by formal structure. Formality means that decisions become precedents and therefore engender much deliberation and consultation, while informality encourages quick, bilateral 'deals' between organization participants. An example of loose-tight structure is the kind of matrix organization in which people belong to 'skill pools' of engineers, marketeers, accountants, etc. from which they join project teams, formed only for the duration of a project. The project team is not subject to detailed control, but each of its members gains professional discipline from his or her skill pool. Another example is the 'flat' organization, in which a dozen or more people report to one manager. This wide span of control makes it hard for the manager to meddle in, rather than to empower, the work of those reporting to him or her. The same principle applies at the top of large organizations when fifty or more business units report to a corporate centre with no more than twenty people.

If a move to a still looser structure is desirable, then one can turn to Handy's (1989) recommendation of 'federal' organization, in which the drive and the power is at the periphery and the centre is a low-profile influencing force. This is an example of 'heterarchy' (Ogilvy, 1977), a term indicating that authority varies with the task being undertaken. Another heterarchical example, given by Michael (1983), is of a team, skilled in interpersonal process, in which the leader of the team changes as it moves to a tackle new task.

Systems

All organizations need systems, electronic or otherwise, for providing information and for organizing activities. There is little argument about the need for some of these; for example, most people like the idea of good systems in the library and certainly of a good payroll system. But others can be regarded as bureaucratic impositions, and then they usually do not work properly. Experience in innovative firms, like that described by Dodgson (1991) and by Fairtlough (1989), suggests that a limited number of well-chosen and well-designed systems (especially systems for project management) is the answer, with all systems being tested on a pilot scale before general use and developed with widespread consultation. This is a recommendation for a loose-tight approach to systems; tight in the limited number of areas in which there are systems, loose everywhere else.

Planning

Planning might seem to be the antithesis of innovation, since how can one plan for the new and unknown? Indeed, planning as analysis of strengths, weaknesses, opportunities and threats may well leave out all but incremental innovation. But planning can be politics, a process in which rival factions seek a vision of the future of the organization favouring their interests; planning can be image-building, a process of developing a coherent picture of the organization for internal and external presentation; planning can be ordered learning and ordered preparation for the future, an approach which is particularly suitable for an innovative organization, opening the collective mind of the organization to a wider range of possibilities (Michael, 1973; Argyris and Schon, 1978) and planning can be done through 'discovering' or 'enacting' (Daft and Weick, 1984). Discovering organizations assume their environments are analyzable and that a course of action should not be chosen until alternatives have been carefully compared. Enacting organizations try out an idea to see whether it works; if it does, they build on it, if not, they try again. A combination of discovering and enacting might be another example of a loose-tight approach.

Planning considers what are the right boundaries for an organization. If it is a business firm, should it try to extend its boundaries by acquiring other firms, or retract them by divestment? Harrigan (1985) sees businesses as 'reservoirs of capabilities' and that acquisition may be a way to obtain new capabilities. Another way to gain capabilities is by joint ventures or strategic alliances. Pisano (1990) shows how knowledgeable pharmaceutical companies can extend their areas of expertise by collaboration with smaller, specialist R&D companies. Dodgson (1992) thinks that technological collaboration is likely to remain an important option for the technology strategies of firms.

People

Roberts and Fusfeld (1981) see the need in innovative organizations for five types of role: idea generators, entrepreneurs or champions, project leaders, gatekeepers (who deal with the world outside the organization, and who need networking and boundary-spanning capabilities) and coach/sponsors, who are usually experienced and senior people. Some roles need to be filled by more than one individual (for instance, idea generating), some individuals can fill two or more roles at the same time, and people can, during their careers, change the roles they fill. An innovating organization must be able to attract, retain and motivate people to fill all these roles, rewarding them for success, but in a way which fairly recognizes that most innovations are a team achievement. It must keep an up-to-date inventory of peoples' skills, deploy them appropriately and help individuals to perform different roles as their careers develop (Mohrman et al. 1990).

Skills

Senge (1990) describes five skills which must be widely spread in a learning organization: systems thinking, personal proficiency in consistently getting results, ability to conceptualize and to communicate with others about concepts, ability to share a vision of the future with others and team-working skill. Most of these relate to what Habermas (1984) calls 'communicative competence', which is the ability to communicate objectively about factual matters, openly about ethical matters and sincerely about personal feelings. Technical skills are also essential for innovation; not only intellectual ones, but also the craft skills on which so much of incremental innovation depends and which makes German industry so successful (Piore and Sabel, 1984).

Culture

The culture of an organization, according to Hampden-Turner (1990), defines behaviour, bonds individuals and defines values. If an organization's culture values activities which are critically important to innovation, like openness or risk-taking, its members will feel supported when they act in these ways. The completely open sharing of almost all information, which is possible in a small organization, leads to high levels of mutual trust, which in turn encourages risk-taking entrepreneurship by individuals. It is mutual reinforcement between factors of this kind which builds a strongly innovative organizational culture. In a study of a firm whose innovation failed, Webb (1992) found that its organic-type structure was not effective, because a management style emphasizing short-term control resulted in distrust and defensiveness, and, in the end, in poor business performance.

Entrepreneurial ('intrapreneurial', if internal to a large organization) attitudes often involve individual championship of ideas or projects, usually vital for overcoming the difficulties which surround radical or architectural innovation. Howell and Higgins (1990) find that champions are innovative, risk-taking and good at influencing others, often appealing to the organization's goals and values to get their ideas accepted, and that organic types of organization encourage championing behaviour. The crystallization of such behaviour into organizational myths and symbols preserves an innovative culture.

Leadership has a key role in forming cultural attitudes. Since innovation does not happen by someone giving orders, leaders must influence by the example of their own behaviour, by networking within their organization, by coaching, and by articulating an inspiring vision (Mintzberg, 1973; Sveiby and Lloyd, 1987). This is not to say that successful leaders of innovative organizations do not seek power, because they do. But they have learnt that power comes from success and that success comes from building organizational values which favour mutual trust, commitment, openness and risk-taking (Clegg, 1990). Hart (1990) suggests that leadership is of various kinds: the motivator, the analyzer, the task-master and the vision-setter. For successful innovation, some combination of all of these must be provided by one or more individual leaders.

Coordination
The above list of organizational attributes is similar to the 'seven S's' model used by the consultants McKinsey and Co., in which three 'cold' attributes (structure, systems, strategy) and three 'warm' ones (staff, skills, style) are bound together through a seventh attribute, superordinate goals, which is a term describing the overall vision and values of the organization. The proper balance of warm and cold attributes seems necessary for an organization to be innovative. (The warm-cold, loose-tight, free-controlled, romantic-classical pairs are similar; Cooper, 1990). As well as the coordination of organizational attributes, business functions need to be coordinated too. R&D needs close links to manufacturing (Florida, 1991) and to marketing (Shanklin and Ryans, 1984). Maidique and Hayes (1984)

suggest that it may be useful to have a deliberate policy for alternating tighter and looser control in an organization, in which a couple of years of loose control is followed by a similar period in which 'cold' organizational features are emphasized.

Three Examples

In conclusion, three imagined organizations are described, all successfully using the methods of Rothwell's fifth generation of innovation: networking and systems integration.

Global Energy Corporation

Global is one of the world's largest companies, discovering fossil fuels (oil, gas, coal), extracting, transporting and processing them, and selling and advising on the use of derived products in most of countries of the world. It spends around $3 billion a year on R&D. Because its operations are on such a huge scale, improvements in operating efficiency of one or two percentage points, say in the cost of distillation of crude oil, translate into large annual savings, achieved mainly by incremental innovation. Sometimes modular innovation plays an important part, for example in new methods for imaging geological structures to aid oil exploration.

Global has a decentralized structure of several hundred operating companies which are bound together by extensive networking between them, with the head office departments and with the central laboratories of the corporation. There are strong financial reporting systems but the biggest effort in system design goes into systems for the capture and exchange of technical and commercial information on a very large scale and into excellent internal communication systems. Another force binding together the decentralized operations is strategic planning, which is done in a way which closely involves the operating managers and helps them prepare an uncertain future. People are cross-posted throughout the corporation, most have long-term careers with Global and there is extensive formal training. Skills in anticipating problems and finding answers to them, often by using the corporation's internal network and by teamwork, are highly valued.

Innovative Instruments Company (IIC)

IIC manufactures instruments, mainly electronic, for laboratories, hospitals, industrial measurement and control, and similar uses. The company sells these throughout the world and has a reputation for reliability, for frequent up-dating of its product range and for user-friendly software.

IIC is structured into a dozen or so business areas, each responsible for running its operations profitably and for maintaining the company's high reputation. New product development is a major emphasis and it is carried out by fairly autonomous project teams. Small head office departments coordinate skill pools of software writers, chip designers, product assembly experts etc. whose members spend much of their time working in the project teams. Everywhere there are sophisticated cost reporting systems and systems for the support of project teams. IIC has an 'enacting' strategy, with emphasis on quality, rapid development, prices at the high end of the market and state-of-the-art instruments. In certain fields, its products have set the dominant design for several decades. IIC rewards individuals for their innovative skills but also makes great use of rewards for project teams, publicizing their successes, having a 'team of the year' and so on.

Innovation is generally pioneering but sometimes follows the ideas of smaller companies, producing more reliable and user-friendly products. Its innovation is mostly architectural, through finding ways to put together standard components in highly original ways. Sometimes IIC makes a radical innovation and has learnt how to cope with the effects of high transilience innovation by creating new autonomous business areas to deal with innovations of this kind.

The Plant Research Institute

The Institute is located close to a leading research university and has over 500 researchers of its own. It undertakes basic research in plant science and, although it is not a commercial operation, it has a deep understanding of commercial crop breeding and gets a substantial income from licensing its discoveries. The rest of its funding comes from international and national agencies and from foundations. The Institute's strategy is to produce both scientific knowledge and radical innovations and to train excellent plant scientists.

Its structure is best described as organic with anarchic features, and its systems are simple, apart from extensive databases of botanical and agronomic information. The Institute's alumni are everywhere and great efforts are made to keep in touch with them and with other plant scientists worldwide, through the conferences, seminars and journals. It aims to have on its staff outstanding scientists, with good networking capabilities and broad vision. It prides itself on understanding the economic and social significance of its discoveries and in working with governments, industry and others to turn these discoveries to good use without delay.

Summary

Innovation in firms and other organizations depends on effective interconnection between many groups of people, both within the organization and externally. The highest priority for these connections varies with the type of innovation being pursued. For instance, incremental process innovation requires the closest possible links between people in production and research, while architectural product innovation needs similarly close links between researchers, marketeers and customers.

The loose-tight rule is the key one for organizing innovation. Organization structure should be loose, that is decentralized, but tight, in the sense that once there is a consensus on priorities everyone should respect them. There should be few systems, but those few should work superbly well. Strategy should be adaptable because a radical innovation may require it to change fundamentally, and it must be devised with great care and expertly communicated. People should be loosely managed, by empowering them and encouraging them to use initiative, but a lot should be expected of them. Skills should be constantly developed, but their use should be tightly planned. The culture in an innovative organization should be loose, in that it is open, trusting and non-controlling, but tight, in that everyone should be bound together by a deep understanding of and commitment to organization goals.

Bibliography

Abernathy, W. and Utterback, J. (1978) 'Patterns of Industrial Innovation' *Technology Review,* June/July, pp. 59–64.

Abernathy, W. and Clark, K. (1985) 'Innovation: Mapping the Winds of Creative Destruction', *Research Policy,* Vol. 14, pp. 3–22.

Amara, R. (1990) 'New Directions for Innovation', *Futures,* Vol. 22, No. 2, pp. 142–52.

Anderson, P. and Tushman, M. (1990) 'Technological Discontinuities and Dominant Design: A Cyclical Model of Technological Change', *Administrative Science Quarterly,* Vol. 35, pp. 604–33.

Argyris, C. and Schon, D. (1978) *Organisational Learning,* Addison-Wesley, Reading.

Burns, T. and Stalker, G. (1966) *The Management of Innovation,* Tavistock, London.

Chandler, A. (1962) *Strategy and Structure,* MIT Press, Cambridge.

Chisholm, D. (1989) *Coordination without Hierarchy: Informal Structures in Multiorganizational Systems,* University of California Press, Berkeley.

Clegg, S. (1990) *Modern Organizations: Organization Studies in a Postmodern World,* Sage, London.

Cooper, R. (1990) 'Organization/Disorganization' in Hassard, J. and Pym, D. (eds) *The Theory and Philosophy of Organizations: Critical Issues and New Perspectives,* Routledge, London.

Daft, R. and Weick, K. (1984) 'Toward a Model of Organizations as Interpretation Systems', *Academy of Management Review,* Vol. 9, No. 2, pp. 284–95.

Dodgson, M. (1991) *The Management of Technological Learning: Lessons from a Biotechnology Company,* De Gruyter, Berlin.

Dodgson, M. (1992) 'The Future for Technological Collaboration', *Futures,* Vol. 25, No. 5, pp. 459–70.

Fairtlough, G. (1989) 'Systems Practice from the Start: Some Experiences in a Biotechnology Company', *Systems Practice,* Vol. 2, No. 4, pp. 379–412.

Florida, R. (1991) 'The New Industrial Revolution', *Futures,* Vol. 23, No. 6, pp. 559–76.

Forrest, J. (1991) 'Models of the Process of Technological Innovation', *Technology Analysis & Strategic Management,* Vol. 3, No. 4, pp. 439–52.

Freeman, C. and Perez, C. (1988) 'Structural Crises of Adjustment, Business Cycles and

Investment Behaviour' in Dosi, G. et al. (eds), *Technical Change and Economic Theory,* Pinter, London, pp. 38–65.

Giddens, A. (1984) *The Constitution of Society: Outline of the Theory of Structuration,* Polity, Cambridge.

Habermas, J. (1984) Trans. McCarthy, T. *The Theory of Communicative Action,* Vol. 1: 100.

Hampden-Turner, C. (1990) *Corporate Culture: From Vicious to Virtuous Circles,* Economist Books, London.

Handy, C. (1989) *The Age of Unreason,* Random Century, London.

Harrigan, K. (1985) *Strategic Flexibility: A Management Guide for Changing Times,* D.C. Heath, Lexington.

Hart, S. (1990) 'Leadership and Performance in High Technology Firms' in Lawless, M. and Gomez-Mejia, L. (eds) *Strategic Leadership in High Technology Organizations: Proceedings of the Second International Conference on Managing the High Technology Firm,* University of Colorado, Boulder.

Henderson, R. and Clark, K. (1990) 'Architectural Innovation: The Reconfiguration of Existing Product Technologies and the Failure of Established Firms', *Administrative Science Quarterly,* Vol. 35, pp. 9–30.

Howell, J. and Higgins, C. (1990) 'Champions of Technological Innovation', *Administrative Science Quarterly,* Vol. 35, pp. 317–41.

Hull, F. (1988) 'Inventions from R&D: Organizational Designs for Efficient Research Performance', *Sociology,* Vol. 22, No. 3, pp. 393–415.

Johne, F. (1984) 'The Organisation of High-Technology Product Innovation', *European Journal of Marketing,* Vol. 18, No. 6/7, pp. 55–71.

Knight, K. (1976) 'Matrix Organisation: a Review', *Journal of Management Studies,* Vol. 13, No. 2, pp. 111–30.

Lansley, P., Sadler, P. and Webb, T. (1974) 'Organisation Structure, Management Style and Company Performance', *Omega,* Vol. 2, No. 4, pp. 467–85.

Maidique, M. and Hayes, R. (1984) 'The Art of High-Technology Management', *Sloan Management Review,* Winter 1984, pp.17–31.

McGregor, D. (1960) *The Human Side of the Enterprise,* McGraw-Hill, New York.

Michael, D. (1973) *On Learning to Plan – And Planning to Learn,* Jossey-Bass, San Francisco.

Michael, D. (1983) 'Neither Hierarchy nor Anarchy: Notes on Norms for Governance in a Systemic World' in Anderson, W. (ed.) *Rethinking Liberalism,* Avon, New York, pp. 251–67.

Mintzberg, H. (1973) *The Nature of Managerial Work,* Harper and Row, New York.

Mohrman, S., Mohrman, A. and Cohen, S. (1990) 'Achieving Integration in a High Technology Company: What Human Resources Practices are Required?' in Lawless, M. and Gomez-Mejia, L. (eds) *Strategic Leadership in High Technology Organizations: Proceedings of the Second International Conference on Managing the High Technology Firm,* University of Colorado, Boulder.

Ogilvy, J. (1977) *Many Dimensional Man,* Oxford, New York.

Peters, T. and Waterman, R. (1982) *In Search of Excellence,* Harper and Row, New York.

Piore, M. and Sabel, C. (1984) *The Second Industrial Divide: Possibilities for Prosperity,* Basic Books, New York, pp. 229–34.

Pisano, G. (1990) 'The R&D Boundaries of the Firm: An Empirical Analysis' *Administrative Science Quarterly,* Vol. 35, pp. 153–76.

Ranson, S., Hinings, B. and Greenwood, R. (1980) 'The Structuring of Organisation Structures', *Administrative Science Quarterly,* Vol. 25, pp. 1–17.

Roberts, E. and Fusfeld, A. (1981) 'Staffing the Innovative Technology-Based Organization', *Sloan Management Review,* Spring 1981, pp. 19–34.

Rothwell, R. (1986) 'The Role of Small Firms in the Emergence of New Technologies' in Freeman, C. (ed.) *Design, Innovation and Long Cycles in Economic Development,* Pinter, London, pp. 231–48.

Rothwell, R. (1992) 'Successful Industrial Innovation: Critical Factors for the 1990s', *R&D Management,* Vol. 22, No. 3, pp. 221–39.

Sahal, D. (1986) 'Technological Guideposts and Innovation Avenues', *Research Policy,* Vol. 14, pp. 61–82.

Saren, A. (1984) 'A Classification and Review of Models of the Intra-firm Innovation Process', *R&D Management,* Vol. 14, pp. 11–24.

Senge, P. (1990) *The Fifth Discipline,* Doubleday, New York.

Shanklin, W. and Ryans, J. (1984) 'Organizing for High-Tech Marketing', *Harvard Business Review,* Nov./Dec. 1984, pp. 164–71.

Sveiby, K. and Lloyd, T. (1987) *Managing Knowhow: Add Value...by Valuing Creativity,* Bloomsbury, London.

Tushman, M. and Anderson, P. (1986) 'Technological Discontinuities and Organisational Environments', *Administrative Science Quarterly,* Vol. 31, pp. 439–65.

Webb, J. (1992) 'The Mismanagement of Innovation', *Sociology,* Vol. 26, No. 3, pp. 471–92.

27. Innovation and Industrial Relations

Roderick Martin

Introduction

There is a close link between innovation and industrial relations. Industrial relations are seen as a major constraint on innovation in some countries (e.g. UK), whilst both product and especially process innovation impact on industrial relations (Williams, 1986, Piatier, 1984; for industrial relations specifically see Willman, 1986). This chapter examines firstly the ways in which industrial relations influence innovation and, secondly, the impact of innovation upon industrial relations. The focus is upon process innovation as this has the greatest significance for industrial relations.

Industrial relations refers to systems of job regulation, related terms and conditions of employment and the ways in which they are determined (Flanders, 1970). Such issues may be determined individually or collectively and, if the latter, at one or a combination of five major levels – national, sectoral, firm, establishment or work group, whose importance differs between countries and between issues. The national and sectoral levels may exercise direct and indirect effects on innovation, for example directly by mandating procedures for introducing new technologies; but the lower levels are the most significant (Ozaki et al., 1992; Batstone et al., 1987).

The chapter is organized in two sections, the first examining the effects of industrial relations upon innovation, the second the effects of innovation upon industrial relations.

Industrial Relations and Innovation

Conventionally, the major issue considered in discussing the link between industrial relations and innovation has been the inhibiting effects of industrial relations upon successful innovation (Bauer, 1993). However, a more rounded approach is needed. The system of industrial relations affects four elements in innovation: motive, content and process as well as outcome. The *motives* for innovation are likely to include reducing production costs through lowering the amount or quality of labour, increasing management control over labour or using labour more flexibly and creatively: these inevitably involve industrial relations issues. The *content* of innovation itself may necessitate changes in skill levels, and need to accommodate existing industrial relations structures. The *process* of innovation needs to take account of social organization, including work group and union organization as well as the physical form of the production process. Finally, the *outcome* of innovation is substantially affected by industrial relations, at both the individual and collective level.

Motive

Reducing labour costs may be necessary because the industrial relations system generates wage increases above the level of increase in productivity, 'excessive' levels of wage settlements. This is especially necessary where labour costs represent a high proportion of total costs and/or in mature product markets where differences in labour costs are a major source of competitive advantage (Kaplinsky, 1984). The incentive to concentrate innovation effort on the reduction of labour costs is due to features of the labour market (the scarcity of labour) and the ability of labour to organize to maximize rewards from a given level of labour supply. The classic example of labour shortage incentives to technological innovation was the US in the late nineteenth century, as a result of the scarcity of labour (Habbakuk, 1962). The focus may also be due to specific features of the product market, whether declining demand (as in mechanical engineering) or the need to restrain labour growth with expanding throughput, as in the banking sector in the 1980s in the UK (Ozaki et al., 1992). The structure of the industrial relations system itself may reinforce this concern with labour costs, which is especially likely to be strong where industrial relations systems are decentralized; centralized systems help to take labour costs out of the competition between firms (at least in relatively closed national economies) and in so doing reduce the incentive to reduce labour costs as a source of competitive advantage (Gospel, 1992). From a different perspective, it has been argued that the focus upon labour costs is a feature of the downswing of the Kondratieff wave (Freeman, 1984); however, the argument here is that other conditions are more directly relevant.

Labour costs may be reduced by lowering the quality as well as the quantity of labour: skilled labour is generally – but not universally – more expensive than unskilled labour (Braverman, 1974). Hence telephone exchange modernization strategies have been concerned both to reduce the number of technicians required for exchange maintenance and to replace senior with junior technicians (Clark et al., 1988). The higher price of skilled labour may itself be the result of the industrial relations system, since union organization and union involvement in training (whether formally as in apprenticeship systems or informally) are major influences on the supply of suitable labour. Moreover craft work involves employee autonomy and limitations on management control over work tasks: the requirement to use discretion in the task provides a lever in any argument with management. This individual capacity is reinforced by craft socialization and collective organization. However, changes in skill requirements with technological innovation have reduced the differences between skilled and unskilled labour in this respect (Martin, 1988).

The third motive for innovation is increasing management control. This is an especially strong imperative with skilled workers, although the motive is also relevant to other groups. Marxist writers, especially following the Braverman tradition, have argued that technological innovation is largely concerned with management control, whilst others have argued that control is subordinate to profit considerations which are more likely to be realized through reductions in labour costs (Wood, 1982). According to one view, the direction of innovation reflects technological choices, which have usually involved separating conception from execution and embedding responsibility for conception firmly in the managerial hierarchy (Braverman, 1974; Mumford, 1983). Others have stressed the possibility of 'responsible autonomy' as a means of reconciling management control with the exercise of legitimated autonomy by subordinates (Friedmann, 1977).

Work intensification associated with innovation may involve increasing labour flexibility (Pollert, 1991). This may be motivated by the desire to restructure work groups or to reduce job territory jurisdictions, often but not always associated with union demarcation lines. The most fundamental flexibility sought is the removal of the division between maintenance and production work, and the creation of production teams with responsibilities for preventive maintenance and urgent repairs (Cross, 1984). Achieving flexibility is a cyclical process: flexibility involves reducing demarcation lines and once demarcation lines are weakened further flexibility is more likely. The flexibility sought may be internal – reallocation of labour within the firm – or external – the use of variable terms and conditions of employment, for example over hours; in both cases trade union organization may be a major barrier (Atkinson and Meager, 1986).

Finally, technological innovation may be motivated by the desire to achieve other industrial relations objectives which are difficult to achieve in isolation. For example, reforms in work organization and in payments systems are more acceptable to employees if they are associated with technological innovation than if they occur alone (Daniel, 1987).

Content
The content of process innovation depends on motive, resources and capabilities, discussed elsewhere in this volume. The significance of industrial relations for the actual content of process innovation is limited. Trade unions or work groups are rarely involved in the initial conception or planning of innovation in Western Europe or the United States, although such involvement is common in Scandinavia (Hammerstrom, 1987).

However, in some circumstances industrial relations considerations may make it impossible to introduce innovations which would make a significant contribution to increasing productivity. For example, the actual technology introduced into Fleet Street in the late 1970s was determined by the need to preserve key stroking by compositors, although on other grounds the most effective form of new technology would have involved direct journalist input (Martin, 1981). However, such direct influence on the actual content of innovation is rare. Firms introducing micro-electronics in UK manufacturing in the 1980s regarded industrial relations as only an insignificant barrier against innovation (Northcott et al., 1985). More commonly, features of the technology may be introduced but not used through fear of the impact on industrial relations, for example the capability for increasingly sophisticated monitoring of individual performance. However, management sensitivities on this issue have declined with accompanying work intensification in the 1980s.

Process
The major impact of industrial relations is upon the process of implementing innovation. The conventional consultant approach to implementing innovation involves a rationalized process of systems planning, project definition and survey, preliminary systems design, systems installation and development of production systems support. This model requires adaptation in practice to reflect the structure of the organization, the conflicting interests of the groups introducing and affected by the innovation and the interests and attitudes of the employees involved. Industrial relations considerations are integral to the process of implementation. The eventual success of the innovation depends upon its acceptance by employees, which is heavily influenced by the way in which the process of implementation is handled (Martin, 1988; Davies, 1986; McLoughlin and Clark, 1988).

There are major international differences in the extent to which the process of implementing innovation is regulated at national level. In Sweden, Germany and France legislation has established the right of workers to participate in technological changes, whilst in Italy, the US and Japan, as well as the UK, worker participation is dependent upon collective agreement (Ozaki et al., 1992).

There are three major approaches to handling the relevant aspects of implementation: unilateral management imposition, consultation and bargaining.

The first approach views process innovation as an integral feature of work organization, and as such an essential part of management prerogatives. Project teams may involve representatives from the work groups affected, but the role of the group is to plan and carry the project through in the most efficient way from management's perspective. The introduction of automatic tellers in UK banking was carried through in this manner. Similarly, the introduction of electronic point of sale terminals in supermarkets was implemented without consultation with the union (Bamber and Willman, 1983). Of course, this procedure can only be carried out where there is no legislation mandating consultation with affected employees or where union organization is weak. The effectiveness of the approach is likely to depend on the extent to which the active commitment of employees is needed to make the innovation effective. However, even where limited commitment is required unilateral imposition may involve managements in ignoring important factors which might influence effectiveness. For example, the initial introduction of electronic security devices in clothes departments in department stores led to much customer frustration since staff were preoccupied with ensuring accurate data input.

There is consensus amongst academic experts on the importance of consultation. According to both management and union respondents in the Workplace Industrial Relations Survey consultation is widespread (Daniel, 1987). The process of consultation may occur at any stage of innovation, beginning with the initial conception of the project. However, in practice consultation is usually undertaken at the implementation stage, although unions complain that major issues have often been decided by the time that the implementation stage is reached (Davies, 1986). From the management perspective, early consultation may result in fostering unnecessary anxieties amongst employees and the disclosure of commercially confidential information to competitors.

The process of consultation has two objectives: the acquisition of inform- ation directly relevant to the workability of the project, and the satisfaction of employees' democratic rights to be consulted about changes affecting their work situation. The two considerations may require different forms of representation. For detailed understanding the input from the employees directly affected is required, since they have knowledge of relevant work processes. To achieve the second objective it may be more desirable to include union representatives, whether full time officials or shop stewards, since they are likely to have the representational and argumentational skills needed to defend employees' interests. The forms of representation chosen may affect the agenda and results of the process, since the interests of the workers directly affected and the interests of the union may differ, with the union being more concerned about the need to protect overall employment levels than the workers directly affected whose jobs are likely to be preserved. Surveys of managers show a preference for direct representation by employees, rather than outside union officials (Daniel, 1987). The process of consultation may be concerned with the content of the innovation itself, especially where the innovation raises anxieties over safety issues, or with the social issues surrounding the project, in particular employment levels. In practice consultation is primarily concerned with social issues, whether directly related to the innovation itself like health and safety or with wider issues such as employment levels. Union involvement in discussions on the technology itself is limited.

Consultation does not involve any infringement of managerial prerogatives; management is free to accept or reject the outcome of the consultation process. The process of consultation may occur with or without a simultaneous process of bargaining. In situations with high levels of union organization during periods of union strength or under government pressure managements may be forced to agree to bargain with unions over innovation (Willman and Winch, 1985).

Employers were reluctant to agree to bargain over new technology, since bargaining implied that unions had a legitimate standing on production issues and that responsibility for the production process was shared between management and labour. However, even in the UK some unions, especially in the public sector, were sufficiently strong to oblige some managements to negotiate over new technology in the early 1980s (Williams and Steward, 1983). Such negotiations were concerned with the price to be paid for introducing innovation, rather than with the principle of innovation itself. Bargaining on new technology in the private sector was normally carried on at the company or the plant level; only in very rare instances did negotiations involve employers' associations (for example both the national and the provincial press).

There is evidence to suggest that employers were anxious to avoid bargaining directly over the price for the acceptance of innovation, since this seemed to give an incentive for resistance to change (Daniel, 1987). Similarly, official union policy favoured acceptance of the principle of technological innovation (Dodgson and Martin, 1987). Management were therefore readier to accede to pressure for above average increases in the annual wage round than to agree to increased earnings for specific groups of workers affected, especially as granting increases to the employees directly affected created further divisions amongst employees, which was damaging both to employers and to unions.

In the early 1980s there was extensive discussion of collective agreements specifically concerned with new technology – new technology agreements – negotiated between managements and unions (Williams and Steward, 1983). Such agreements were especially common in white collar occupations, often relating to the introduction of office technology, especially in the public sector; the union most heavily involved was NALGO. The distribution of the agreements reflected the attitudes of employers as well as the relative strength of the union. Job security, pay and health and safety were the most common issues subject to negotiation. In some circumstances procedural as well as substantive issues were subject to negotiation, for example the formation of specific new technology committees; but such committees were rare (Daniel, 1987; Davies, 1986).

Outcomes

It has been argued that the industrial relations system is a major influence on the effectiveness of innovation, with familiar contrasts drawn between Japanese, North American, European and British experience (Williams, 1986). The impact of industrial relations on the outcome of innovation may operate in three ways: first, making it unlikely that innovations will be introduced at all; second, reducing the benefits of innovation by delay or by increasing the cost, so that competitive advantage is not realized; third, distorting the final form of the innovation so that its potential benefits are not obtained.

It is impossible to provide a comprehensive assessment of the significance of industrial relations considerations in the first sense. The factors affecting rates of innovation are so numerous and varied that it is impossible to attach great general significance to industrial relations. There are specific sectors in which innovations have occurred sooner in some countries than others, even where simultaneous developments might have been expected. Docks, iron and steel and newspapers are three sectors with different trajectories of change internationally. However, industrial relations considerations are likely to have played only a minor role. It has been suggested that the 'hassle' factor – the expectation of large numbers of small difficulties – may inhibit managers from attempting to introduce innovations (Williams, 1986). Yet the 'hassle factor' could be redefined as managerial timidity, the manager's role necessarily involving dealing with small difficulties – and managers themselves do not cite this as a major issue even in the UK (Northcott, 1984). More frequently, failure to keep to schedule in introducing new systems results in failure to meet targets and cost over-runs, including occasions on which industrial relations have been difficult, although over-optimism in project planning is more likely to be a source of difficulty than labour relations. Sub-optimal forms of technology and higher levels of manning than technically required also occur; but again issues of industrial relations and inadequate management planning merge.

The Impact of Innovation on Industrial Relations

Innovation affects five features directly relevant to industrial relations: work tasks, work organization, pay, employment levels and union organization.

The direct impact of innovation on work tasks is discussed elsewhere. Innovation increases the skill level involved in work tasks more often than it reduces it, although in the UK managers and workers' representatives disagree on the extent of the increase with representatives perceiving more enhancement (and therefore more need for increased pay) (Daniel, 1987). Innovation is also likely to lead to increased responsibility, if only because of the increased value of the equipment monitored (and the reduced manning levels which usually accompany innovation). Employees' skill repertoires are also likely to widen, especially with an expansion in 'intellectual' skills, partially balanced by some reduction in manual skills (McLoughlin and Clark, 1988). The overall effect of the changes is to increase the proportion of skilled workers in the labour force, especially in private manufacturing.

Work organization refers to the pattern of deployment of employees resulting from the technical requirements of the production system and employers' control strategies. Innovation may influence work organization directly, through requiring the reallocation of labour (characteristically from single person single station to group work multiple stations) or indirectly, through providing opportunities for adapting control strategies (more or less tight monitoring). Such changes affect work group cohesion, for example by increasing interaction between group members (by changing work stations or by reducing noise levels) or by increasing the distance between groups. These changes have an impact on union organization, frequency of interaction stimulating cohesion, increasing involvement in union affairs and the ability to exert pressure.

Innovation affects three aspects of pay: level, differentials and relativities and in some circumstances the principles governing pay systems. The most obvious effects occur when innovation is accompanied by direct payment to the employees affected, whether through increased rates, opportunities for increased bonuses or enhanced gradings. In the UK managers reported increased earnings for employees directly affected by new technology in twenty-four per cent of establishments (Daniel, 1987). However, innovation left pay unchanged in the majority of cases. Instead, above average increases in earnings were reported for all employees in establishments introducing new technology, especially advanced technology involving manual workers, demonstrating the high productivity/high earnings virtuous circle. Innovation may also change relativities (within establishments) and differentials (between establishments) especially where payments are directly related to the acceptance of change. Such 'productivity bargaining' was associated with inflationary wage pressures in the 1960s, but less so in the 1980s, probably reflecting the growth of job evaluation schemes in the intervening years, which provided an institutionalized mechanism for increasing pay in recognition of increased skills and responsibility (Millward and Stevens, 1986). Where innovation involves the expansion of group working it might be expected to involve group in place of individual incentive schemes.

The impact of innovation on employment levels is highly controversial (see Freeman and Soete, 1985, for an initial review). According to one view, the overall decline in employment levels is small because the jobs created in capital goods industries – as well as the growth in service industries – balance the jobs lost in manufacturing (Leontief and Duchin, 1986). According to other views, technological innovation is a major destroyer of jobs, especially in the long term (Jenkins and Sherman, 1979; Gill, 1985). Northcott's surveys of micro-electronics indicated that the introduction of micro-electronics resulted in gradual but cumulatively substantial job losses (Northcott, 1984; Northcott, 1986). For trade unions, the loss of jobs due to recession has been a far more pressing concern than the loss of jobs through new technology and unions have remained committed to the view that investment in new technology is necessary as a means of maintaining competitive position (Willman, 1986).

Finally, innovation affects union organization in five ways. First, changes in employment levels in specific sectors, where rationalization results in fewer employees, affect union recruitment arenas and thus potential membership levels. Second, changes in the distribution of employment between sectors and between occupations affect the scope for recruitment. Third, change may undermine the political influence of specific groups within unions, for example reducing the ability of elite groups to maintain their influence (as compositors lost their influence in the National Graphical Association with the introduction of computerized photo-composition). Fourth, earnings growth may affect the financial strength of unions, increased earnings making higher subscription levels possible, just as declining membership may lead to reduced revenues. Finally, changes in the distribution of work tasks may change demarcation lines between unions, resulting in one union gaining members at the expense of another, as the growth in electronics at the expense of traditional mechanical engineering affected the distribution of membership between the EETPU and the AEU.

Conclusion

Innovation is intimately linked to industrial relations. This chapter has examined the influence industrial relations has on innovation and the influence innovation has on industrial relations. It is not enough to be concerned solely with the issue of whether the industrial relations system increases or reduces the rate of innovation; it affects the whole process of innovation – motive, content, process and outcome. The major influence is exercised by the industrial relations system at establishment level, although national and sectoral level influences may also be important, for example in mandating consultation procedures (Batstone et al., 1987; Ozaki et al., 1992). Although the weaknesses of the industrial relations system have been cited as a major reason for the poor performance of countries such as the UK in innovation, more detailed consideration attributes a relatively minor role compared with capital shortage, lack of appropriate engineering skills and other wider factors. British trade unions have generally been major supporters of technological innovation, both in principle and to a large degree in practice; disagreement with management has been over the price to be paid for innovation, not the principle of innovation (Willman, 1986).

Bibliography

Atkinson, J. and Meager, N. (1986) *Changing Working Practices: How Companies Achieve Flexibility to Meet New Needs*, National Economic Development Office, London.

Bamber, G. and Willman, P. (1983) 'Technological Change and Industrial Relations in Britain', *Bulletin of Comparative Labour Relations*, No. 13, Kluwer, Deventer.

Batstone, E., Gourlay, S., Levie, H. and Moore, R. (1987) *New Technology and the Process of Labour Regulation*, Oxford University Press, Oxford.

Bauer, M. (1993) *Resistance to New Technology – Past and Present*, Conference April 1993, Science Museum, London.

Braverman, H. (1974) *Labour and Monopoly Capital: The Degradation of Work in the Twentieth Century*, Monthly Review Press, New York.

Clark, J., McLoughlin, I., Rose, H. and King, R., (1988) *The Process of Technological Change: New Technology and Social Change in the Workplace*, Cambridge University Press, Cambridge.

Cross, M. (1984) *Towards the Flexible Craftsman*, Technical Change Centre, London.

Daniel, W.W. (1987) *Workplace Industrial Relations and Technical Change*, Frances Pinter, London.

Davies, A. (1986) *New Technology and Industrial Relations*, Croom Helm, London.

Dodgson, M. and Martin, R. (1987) 'Trade Union Policies on New Technology: Facing the Challenges of the 1980s', *New Technology, Work and Employment*, Vol. 2.

Flanders, A. (1970) *Management and Unions*, Faber and Faber, London.

Freeman, C. (1984) *Long Waves in the World Economy*, Frances Pinter, London.

Freeman, C. and Soete, L. (1985) 'Information Technology and Employment', Science Policy Research Unit, University of Sussex, Brighton.

Friedmann, A. (1977) *Industry and Labour*, Macmillan, London.

Gill, C. (1985) *Work, Unemployment and New Technology*, Printing Press, Oxford.

Gospel, H. (1992) *Markets, Firms and the Management of Labour in Modern Britain*, Cambridge University Press, Cambridge.

Habbakuk, M.J. (1962) *American and British Technology in the Nineteenth Century: The Search for Labour Saving Inventions*, Cambridge University Press, Cambridge.

Hammerstrom, O. (1987) 'Sweden' in Bamber, G.J. and Lansbury, R. (eds) *International and Comparative Industrial Relations*, Allen and Unwin, London.

Jenkins, C. and Sherman, B. (1979) *The Collapse of Work*, Eyre Methuen, London.

Kaplinsky, R. (1984) *Automation: The Technology and Society*, Longmans, London.

Leontief, W. and Duchin, F. (1986) *The Future Impact of Automation on Workers*, Oxford University Press, New York.

Martin, R. (1981) *New Technology and Industrial Relations in Fleet Street*, Oxford University Press, Oxford.

Martin, R. (1988) 'Technical Change and Manual Work', in Gallie, D. (ed.) *Employment in Britain*, Blackwells, Oxford.

McLoughlin, I. and Clark, J. (1988) *Technological Change at Work*, Open University Press, Milton Keynes.

Millward, N. and Stevens, M. (1986) *British Workplace Industrial Relations 1980–84: The DE/ESRC/PSI/ACAS Surveys*, Gower, Aldershot.

Mumford, E. (1983) *Designing Human Systems*, Manchester Business School, Manchester.

Northcott, J. (1984) *Microelectronics in British Industry: The Pattern of Change*, Policy Studies Institute, London.

Northcott, J., Fogarty, M. and Trevor, M. (1985) *Changes and Jobs: Acceptance of New Technology at Work*, Policy Studies Institute, London.

Northcott, J. (1986) *Micro-electronics in Industry: Promise and Performance*, Policy Studies Institute, London.

Ozaki, M. et al. (1992) *Technological Change and Labour Relations*, International Labour Office, Geneva.

Piatier, A. (1984) *Barriers to Innovation*, Frances Pinter, London.

Pollert, A. (1991) *Farewell to Flexibility?*, Blackwells, Oxford.

Williams, B. (1986) *Attitudes to New Technologies and Economic Growth*, Technical Change Centre, London.

Williams, R. and Steward, F. (1983) 'Technology Agreements in Great Britain: A Survey 1977–83', *Industrial Relations Journal*, Vol. 16.

Willman, P. and Winch, G. (1985) *Innovation and Management Control*, Cambridge University Press, Cambridge.

Willman, P. (1986) *Technological Change, Collective Bargaining and Industrial Efficiency*, Oxford University Press, Oxford.

Willman, P. (1986) *New Technology and Industrial Relations: A Review of the Literature*, Department of Employment, London.

Wood, S. (1982) *The Degradation of Work? Skill, Deskilling and the Labour Process*, Hutchinsons, London.

28. Innovation and Training

Malcolm Warner

Introduction

Innovation and training in modern economies are inextricably linked. Their respective strengths are often as much a reflection of industrial performance as a cause of it. The connections are thus reciprocal and complex. We must therefore use a *holistic* approach to understand these relationships, rather than concentrate on just one factor to the detriment of another (Sorge et al., 1983). Industrial performance, in turn, hinges on the ability to combine flexibility in work methods with productivity-enhancing techniques. Both are dependent on the development of skills which result from training. Training not only requires micro-level investment in developing people, but also macro-level investment in creating a training infrastructure, so that external economies can be achieved. Innovation may, however, sometimes precede training. For example, technology transfer may make new machines or products available for production. A good illustration of this may be new computer-controlled production systems; these may well require training on-site after they are installed to achieve the best level of performance; or they may call for the recruitment of new personnel with the requisite skill-levels required to operate the new systems.

Economic Performance and Skills

The level of skills is normally a pre-condition for and often a determinant of economic performance and international competitiveness (Aldcroft, 1992). Today, the principal growth area in trade is increasingly high value-added, technologically sophisticated products among high-income economies. Innovation lies at the heart of such activities, with R&D central to the supply of new products. Inability to keep up innovation may mean a slide to a low wage, non-tradeable economy (Stoneman, 1984). Failure to innovate may ultimately be seen as a major cause of a country's relative economic decline, with Britain often seen as a prime example in the West European context. A nation which fails to develop skills risks the inability either to take advantage of innovations, or indeed to promote innovations in the first place by, for example, not investing enough in those able to carry out R&D.

In both instances, the lack of skills and training acts as a constraint.

When the economy begins to pick up in the trade cycle, such bottlenecks hamper growth. In boom periods, these skill shortages may become acute as in the upswings of the 1980s. Even in conditions of recession, employers such as those in the high-tech sectors complain they still cannot recruit enough qualified staff. Such skills are in particularly short supply at the intermediate skill level. Given the failure of domestic producers to service the home market, imports flow in to further worsen the trade gap. Conversely, the lack of innovation and training affects exports. The UK has fared particularly badly vis-à-vis technologically intensive exports. Its share of such a category in world trade was only 8.5 per cent, compared with 25.2 per cent for Japan and 14.5 per cent for West Germany in the 1980s (De Jonquières, 1987). It is thus clear that underlying patterns of innovation and training can help shape international competitiveness, and we shall offer examples illustrating this relationship comparing British with German, Japanese and US experience in recent years.

Technical Education and Training

In this context, British companies were reluctant to spend money on training, fearful of the 'poaching' of their employees at best, or 'wasting money' at worst (Campbell et al., 1989). Cuts in funding both education and training were a recurrent feature of government policy in the postwar period and continue in the 1990s. An endemic short-termism continues to persist at both macro- and micro-levels of the economy. The rationale is that investments must show a short-term improvement in performance. By contrast, in Germany the application of *Technik* (the knowledge and skill related to manufacturing) is long term and training is part and parcel of it. German technical education, particularly at intermediate levels, is extensive and well-funded. In the postwar period, the need for training has been central to the tripartite social partnership of employers, unions and government. External inputs in the dual system in Germany come from both the *Berufsschulen* (trade-schools) for craftsmen and the *Fachschulen* (technical institutes) for technicians and foremen.

In this context, 'technical work and training, organisation and industrial relations' are closely intertwined (Sorge et al., 1983). Firms train skilled workers for production as well as maintenance jobs. Apprenticeships are all-pervasive, with examination and certification of skills at all levels, unlike the British or US cases. The line hierarchy is more technical compared with other countries, with a closer liaison between line managers and technical expertise (Sorge and Warner, 1986). Would-be managers learn how to do their job after their formal education, and some during it, on an in-house basis and most big corporations run induction or traineeship programmes. In commerce, many entrants come in after the *Abitur* qualification, the equivalent of British 'A' levels or US style high-school graduation, although this is rarer for production or technical posts. Those destined for management would probably have already obtained their tertiary-level qualifications and/or taken part in an in-house programme. Sometimes trade associations offer preparatory training for future employment graduates in the industry, especially where they have had no former technical background.

The typical German manufacturing organization is distinctive for its tightly-knit technical staff superstructures closely linked with supervision and managerial tasks, which, given the highly trained workforce, combine to produce high levels of performance. The technical emphasis of the management, however, goes back to the mid-nineteenth century when the German industrial-technical tradition took root. Investment in human resources has supplemented that in the latest physical plant and technology, with industrialists taking a long-term perspective. Technical expertise is as closely linked to the workflow level as possible. High levels of competence are associated with wide spans of control. Compared with Britain and the US, there are much closer links between in-house training and external (public) technical education in the Federal Republic and Japan. As well as extensive apprentice arrangements, there is continuing technical education mid-career for German craftsmen and foremen, for instance. A step-by-step approach is general, whereby each stage must be completed before the next qualification is attempted – for example a fully qualified technician must have completed his or her technical apprenticeship first.

As Porter (1990) points out, companies can influence 'factor creation' by which innovation and competitive edge are advanced by the breadth and depth of their involvement in education and training, by sponsoring students or sending personnel to courses, by contacts with schools, colleges and universities, by creating new research institutes and so on.

> High levels of corporate participation in such activities are typical in Germany and Switzerland, an important reason why these nations have been able to upgrade factors and sustain innovation in industries for many decades. In Germany, for example, virtually every significant company participates in apprenticeship programs involving local technical schools (But) ... In Japan, advanced factor creation is mostly within firms ... (Porter, 1990: 595)

Innovation and Management Training

Training for managers is also an important variable. In countries where managers have a strong *functional* base to their management training, particularly where this has a technical underpinning, there appears to be a higher degree of innovation and competitive advantage. The cases of Germany and Japan clearly stand out in this respect where a high proportion of managers are university-trained engineers and technologists.

The linking of innovation and training is due to the different ways people are trained in Germany (as well as Austria and the German-speaking areas of Switzerland), compared with Britain and the US. Indeed, the entire education and training system needs to be encompassed, we have hypothesized elsewhere, to capture the essential ingredients which distinguish national forms and style from each other where work organizations and their members are considered (Maurice et al., 1980). In Germany, the majority of managers have been to either universities or to other tertiary-level institutions, such as *Fachhochschulen*. There is a clearer division of labour between these bodies than there is between British universities and the former polytechnics. The German universities offer an academic four-year *Diplom*, whereas the *Fachhochschulen* lay on a three-year vocational qualification. The former is more like a UK or US first degree; the latter, more resembling a Higher National Diploma (HND). Examples of German degrees include *Diplom-Ingenieur* (Engineer), *Diplom-Wirtschafts-Ingenieur* (combining engineering with business studies), *Diplom-Volkswirt* (Economist), *Diplom-Chemiker* (Chemist) and so on (Sorge, 1978).

In the *Fachhochschulen* vocational degrees abound: the qualification of *Betriebswirt* (*grad*) is, for example, geared to running commercial activities, as is the *Ing. grad* to looking after technical responsibilities. They can also be combined in a *Wirtschaftsingenieur* (*grad*) degree. Another kind of institution which trains for commercial management, other than the *Diplom-Kaufmann* (Commerce) degree courses in universities, are the *Handelshochschulen* (Colleges of Commercial Training) which are to be found in big cities and whose origins go back to the late nineteenth century.

In countries where a generalist tradition prevails, such as the UK or US, managers are said to lack a technical professional base: 'The classification of the hierarchy as management could only emerge to the extent that managerial functions were not inherent to specialist careers and forms of vocational education training' (Sorge and Warner, 1986). In France, Germany, the Netherlands, Sweden and Switzerland this was not the case, with advantages accruing providing a boost for innovation-based, technology-intensive exports.

Innovation and Hybrid Skills

A further dimension of training needed to promote innovation is the development of *hybrid skills*, increasingly common in the EC countries noted above, and in Japan. Training imparts formal knowledge, but informal knowledge is acquired on the job and enhances the individual's learning-curve. In this *post-training* phase, output-based development, as opposed to input (of knowledge-based) preparation for work, helps both managers and workers to find ways of making the enterprise more productive and profitable. A field-study argues that: 'the proposed system of mutual recognition (within Europe) will have to put emphasis on formal learning (inputs) as much on capabilities and experience developed at the workplace (outputs).' (Rajan, 1992)

The hybridization process calls for more workers trained with both function-specific and general skills. Three kinds of generic competencies are involved:

1. *Technical skills* – specific to the technology involved;
2. *Business skills* – specific to the company's products, markets, etc.
3. *Social skills* – based on interpersonal abilities, team working skills, etc. (Rajan, 1992).

Indeed...

> The development of hybrid skills and the motivation of knowledge workers (or *informaticiens*) require a new approach to training that is based on the concept of *continuous learning*. With rapid changes in technology, shorter product cycles and more solutions-orientation of user-needs, many knowledge workers need to update their work skills on a life-time basis. (Rajan, 1992: 29)

In Japan, as in Germany, Dore and Sako point out:

> (A) Japanese factory is more likely to be *a learning organization* (emphasis added) ... A recurring need for special training programmes is taken for granted. They do not have to be justified on the grounds that 'these boffins just keep coming up with something new and we jolly need to keep up' but are perfectly acceptable even when they are presented as getting people up to long established levels of satisfactory competence. (Dore and Sako, 1989: ix)

In innovation, the 'devil is in the details', as the old German phrase goes, and perhaps analogous to the Japanese concept of *Kaizen,* which means continuous improvement. The German influence on Japanese production methods over its formative years ensured a similar emphasis on technical and product quality, particularly in manufactured products. The German strength in contemporary product innovation rests on a distinct philosophy of what later was dubbed *Forschung durch Technik,* which may be broadly translated as innovative development through technological excellence.

Concluding Remarks

Societal differences in organizing and business strategies may be seen as reciprocally related (Sorge, 1991). Such a relationship implies that both economies and societies develop whatever Ricardian comparative advantages result from their organizational traits and human resource strengths respectively. This argument in turn holds for a wide variety of cases of innovation, be they the introduction of computer numerically controlled (CNC) machine-tools in Great Britain and West Germany (Sorge et al., 1983), similar developments in France and West Germany (Sorge, 1991), microelectronic product innovations in these countries (Campbell et al., 1989), as well as JIT/TQM applications in Japan and elsewhere (Conti and Warner, 1993). Another robust confirmation came from an international study of the automobile industry (Sorge and Streeck, 1985).

Such innovation strategies require companies to identify the appropriate competence requirements to achieve them. In Germany, product innovation and the rate of application of microelectronics in manufacturing was much higher than in other countries because of the skills and training infrastructures (Campbell and Warner, 1992). In Germany, as in Japan, the levels of skills competence reveal a greater human resource management investment in craft worker and technician training as well as linking this with the work of engineers in design and product development, compared with Britain and the US. The upshot of this analysis, we may conclude, is *a neo-contingency explanation*: namely that industries will thrive where comparative advantage reflects the societal profiles of 'corresponding organizational forms, human resources and business strategies' which are relevant to achieve their economic objectives (Sorge, 1991).

Bibliography

Aldcroft, D.H. (1992) *Education, Training and Economic Performance*, University of Manchester, Manchester.

Campbell, A., Sorge, A. and Warner M. (1989) *Microelectronic Product Applications in Great Britain and West Germany*, Gower, Aldershot.

Campbell, A. and Warner, M. (1992) *New Technology, Skills and Management*, Routledge, London.

Conti, R.F. and Warner, M. (1993) 'Taylorism, New Technology and Just-in-Time in Japanese Industry', *New Technology, Work and Employment*, Vol. 8, No. 1, pp. 31–42.

De Jonquières, G. (1987) 'Research and Development', *Financial Times Supplement*, 9 July.

Dore, R.P. and Sako, M. (1989) *How the Japanese Learn to Work*, Routledge, London.

Maurice, M., Sorge, A. and Warner, M. (1980) 'Societal Differences in Organizing: A Comparison of France, West Germany and Britain', *Organization Studies*, Vol. 1, No. 1, pp. 59–86.

Porter, M. (1990) *The Competitive Advantage of Nations*, Macmillan, Basingstoke.

Rajan, A. (1992) *Enterprise and People Aspects in the Information Technology Sector to the Year 2000: Special Issue of Social Europe,* Commission of the European Communities, Brussels.

Sorge, A. (1978) 'The Management Tradition: A Continental View', in Fores, M. and Glover, I. (eds) *Manufacture and Management,* HMSO, London.

Sorge, A., Hartmann, G., Nicholas, I. and Warner, M. (1983) *Microelectronics and Manpower in Manufacturing*, Gower, Aldershot.

Sorge, A. and Streeck, W. (1985) 'Industrial Relations and Technical Change', in Hyman, R. and Streeck, W. (eds) *New Technology and Industrial Relations*, Blackwell, Oxford.

Sorge, A. and Warner, M. (1986) *Comparative Factory Organization*, Gower, Aldershot.

Sorge, A. (1991) 'Strategic Fit and Societal Effect', *Organization Studies*, Vol. 12, No. 2, pp. 161–91.

Stoneman, P. (1984) 'Technological Change and Economic Performance', in *Out of Work: Perspectives of Mass Unemployment*, University of Warwick, Coventry.

PART 4

The Strategic Management of Innovation

29. Key Characteristics of Large Innovating Firms

Keith Pavitt

Introduction

In what follows, I shall identify and discuss the essential features of the large innovating firm. There are at least three reasons for doing this.

The first is that large firms are a major source of technology and innovations. Although formal R&D activities exaggerate the share of firms with more than 10,000 employees, their contribution is at least in proportion to their sales (Pavitt et al., 1987). They make particularly big contributions in the chemical, electrical and electronic, aerospace and automobile sectors, where their technological strategies can have a major impact on the performance of whole countries (Patel and Pavitt, 1991).

The second is that large innovating firms in the 20th century have shown remarkable resilience and longevity, in spite of successive waves of radical innovations that have called into question their established skills and procedures (Mowery, 1983). Such institutional continuity in the face of technological discontinuity cannot be explained simply by the rise and fall of either talented individual entrepreneurs, or groups with specific technical skills.

The third is that we have no satisfactory theory of the large innovating firm. Schumpeter observed that the locus of innovative activities has shifted from the talented individual entrepreneur to the organized R&D laboratory, but he had little to say about the organizational and other characteristics of innovating firms that succeed in maintaining their existence over long periods by continuously changing their products, processes, markets and operating procedures.

Key Characteristics of Innovative Activity

Past empirical research has helped to delineate the following key characteristics of technological activities in large firms.

(a) They are largely specific in nature, and show cumulative development over time. Most technological knowledge emerges from the development, testing, production and use of specific products. Tacit knowledge obtained through experience is of central importance. Although firms can buy in some technology and skills from the outside, what they have been able to do in the past strongly conditions what they can hope to do in the future.

(b)   They are highly differentiated. The range of feasible choice open to a firm is limited strongly by the extent to which its accumulated technology skills are proximate to other technologies: thus skills in the development of pharmaceutical products may be applicable in the development of pesticides, but they are not much use in design and building of automobiles.

(c)   Innovative activities involve continuous and intensive collaboration amongst professionally and functionally specialized groups. Knowledge inputs for any specific innovation normally draw on a wide variety of professional skills within both science and engineering. In nearly all innovating firms with more than 10,000 employees, these skills are organized into product divisions and functional departments (Pavitt et al., 1989).

(d)   Contrary to Schumpeter's prediction, innovative activities have remained highly uncertain in their commercial outcome (Freeman, 1982). In addition, both practitioners and theorists still have great difficulties predicting the rate and direction of radical technical change.

In the light of these characteristics, it is plainly misleading to assume – as in standard production theory in economics – that technological strategies in firms consist of easily implemented choices from amongst a large and easily accessible range of process technologies, on the basis of clear signals about relative factor costs. Given the specific, differentiated and cumulative nature of technological development, the range of possible choices about both product and process technologies depends on accumulated, firm-specific competence. Given functional and professional specialization, the implementation of technological choices requires organization and orchestration across disciplinary, functional and divisional boundaries. Given cumulative development and uncertainty, the improvement of these competencies requires continuous and collective learning. And in the light of all these characteristics, it is necessary to develop appropriate systems for evaluating progress and allocating resources.

Firm-Specific Competencies

Firms gain profitable innovative leads through firm-specific competencies that take time or are costly to imitate. Innovating firms can discourage imitation through secrecy and patent protection. But their competitive advantage essentially results from the ability to do useful and difficult things better than their competitors. The nature of these competencies, the rate and directions in which they can be developed, and their implications for management, vary greatly according to the firm's size and its core business activities. Table 29.1 summarises an attempt to map out this variety.

Innovating small firms are typically specialized in their technological strategies, concentrating on product innovation in specific producers goods, such as machine tools, scientific instruments, specialized chemicals or software. Their key strategic strengths are in the ability to match technology with specific customer requirements. The key strategic tasks are finding and maintaining a stable product niche, and benefiting systematically from user experience.

Large innovating firms, on the other hand, are typically broad front in their technological activities, and divisionalized in their organization. The key technological strengths can be based on R&D laboratories (typically in chemicals and electrical-electronic products), or in the design and operation of complex production technology (typically in mass production and continuous process industries), and – increasingly – in the design and operation of complex information processing technology (typically in finance and retailing).

In R&D based technologies, the key strategic opportunities are horizontal diversification into new product markets. The key strategic problems are those of mobilizing complementary assets to enter new product markets (e.g. obtaining marketing knowledge when a pharmaceutical firm moves into pesticides), and continuous organizational redesign to exploit emerging technological opportunities (e.g. personal computers cutting across previous responsibilities in computers, office machinery, and even consumer electronics. See below.)

In production-based and information-based technologies, the key strategic opportunities are in the progressive integration of radical technological advances into products and production systems, and in diversification vertically upstream into potentially pervasive production inputs (e.g. CAD-CAM, robots, and software). The key strategic tasks are ensuring diffusion of best practice technology within the firm, and choices about the degree of appropriation (i.e. internalization) of production technology.

Organising Firm-Specific Competencies

Firm-specific competencies are based on skills and knowledge that are functionally and organizationally specialized. An essential dimension of a firm's competence is the ability to combine these competencies into unique and effective units for developing innovations.

Considerable progress has been made in understanding the importance

Table 29.1 A technology-based classification of business firms

Characteristics	Category of firm				
	Supplier dominated	Scale intensive	Information Intensive	Science based	Specialized supplier
Typical core sector	Agriculture Housing Private services Traditional manufacturing	Bulk materials (steel, glass) Consumer durables Automobiles Civil Engineering	Finance Retailing Publishing Travel	Electrical-electronics Chemicals	Capital goods Instruments Software
Size of Firm	Small	Large	Large	Large	Small
Type of User	Price sensitive	Mixed	Mixed	Mixed	Performance sensitive
Main Focus of Technological Activities	Cost reduction	Mixed	Mixed	Mixed	Product improvement
Main Sources of Techn. Accumulation	*Suppliers Production learning Advisory services*	*Production engineering Production learning Suppliers Design*	*Corporate software and systems eng.* Equipment and software suppliers	*Corporate R & D Basic research Production engineering Design*	*Design and development Advanced users*

360

Main Direction of Techn. Accumulation	Process technology and related equipment (*upstream*)	Process technology and related equipment (*upstream*)	Process technology and related software (*mixed*)	Technology-related products (*concentric*)	Product improvement (*concentric*)
Main Channels of Imitation and Techn. Transfer	Purchase of equipment and related services	Purchase of equipment Know-how licensing and related training Reverse engineering	Purchase of equipment and software Reverse engineering	Reverse engineering R & D Hiring experienced engineers and scientists	Reverse engineering Learning from advanced users
Main Strategic Management Tasks	Use technology generated elsewhere to reinforce other competitive advantages	Incremental integration of new technology in complex systems Improvement and diffusion of best practice Exploit process technology advantages	Design and operation of complex information-processing systems. Development of related products	Develop related products Exploit basic science Obtain complementary assets Reconfiguring divisional responsibilities	Monitor advanced users needs Integrate new technology in products

for the successful implementation of innovation of inter-functional integration. Horizontal communications across functional boundaries, flexibility in the definition of tasks, links with outside sources of expertise and with users, and the authority and experience of responsible managers, are all factors that influence a successful implementation, in addition to the quality and competence of R&D and related technological activities (Rothwell et al., 1975; Rothwell, 1977; Cooper, 1983; Maidique and Zirger, 1984; Burgelman, 1985; Shrivastava and Souder, 1987). However, we know much less about the problems posed by the divisional form of organization, which Chandler (1977) identifies as a key element in the managerial revolution and the emergence of large firms. There are at least three problems that innovative activities pose for the 'pure' M-form organization, and that deserve further research.

The first is the exploitation of synergies across divisions or, alternatively, of core competencies that pervade the technologies of all product divisions. As we can see in Table 29.1, these are of central importance in all types of large innovating firms. At the very least, they require central (i.e. corporate-wide) coordination, and interdivisional exchanges of personnel and experience (Aoki, 1986). They may also require strong direction from central R&D or production engineering activities.

Second, the development of technological opportunities and competencies do not necessarily fit tidily into established divisional structures. Rigid definition of divisional markets and missions can result in missed opportunities that cut across existing organizational structures: for example, PABX (small telephone exchanges) probably requires competencies from divisions in telecommunications, office machinery, computers and components. In addition, existing firm-specific technological competencies may not be sufficient to exploit new opportunities, and may require the purchase of what Teece (1986) has called 'co-specific assets': for example, marketing competence for pharmaceutical firms moving into pesticides, or for computing firms moving into telecommunications.

The third organizational problem is the inevitable tension and balance between corporate centralization and decentralization. On the one hand, the strategic exploitation of technology at the corporate level requires a strong technological and managerial input at the centre, in order to exploit synergies and to redesign organizational missions and competencies in the light of emerging opportunities (for example, see Reader, 1975, on the emergence of plastics in Imperial Chemicals Industry). On the other hand, we have seen that effective transformation of technology into commercial advantage requires decentralization, with effective horizontal communications and rapid decision-taking. Thus, too much centralization is likely to result in ambitious, radical and ill-conceived innovations. Too much decentralization is likely to result in incremental and safe innovations in established businesses, with consequent diminishing returns and decline.

Firm-Specific Learning

In an activity as complicated and unpredictable as innovation, it is misleading to represent innovative activities in large firms as once-for-all decisions on the content of strategies or policies which, when taken, are easily and predictably implemented. In fact, firms develop what Nelson and Winter (1982) call 'routines', or rules of thumb, to help them cope with a murky, messy and ever-changing world. In the terminology of this paper, 'routines' embody 'firm-specific competencies'; and their adaptation and change in the light of experience and further information is 'learning'. Sources of learning are very diverse, and their relative importance will vary according to the nature of the core competencies of the firm:

- 'learning by doing' (in production and information intensive firms);
- 'learning by using' in specialized suppliers of capital and intermediate goods;
- 'learning by failing' in product innovations;
- 'learning by studying' and 'learning by hiring' in pervasive technologies and radical discoveries;
- 'learning from competitors' (in all innovating firms).

R&D laboratories and other technical functions in the firm are necessary and centrally important components in nearly all the dimensions of learning described above. In particular, they are the means to learn about, evaluate and – if necessary – assimilate major technological discontinuities. Examples include the assimilation of computing and solid state physics into the core competencies of electro-mechanical firms (like IBM) in the 1950s and 1960s; and the present process of evaluation and assimilation of biotechnology in firms in chemicals, pharmaceuticals and food products (Orsenigo, 1989). Few (if any) technological discontinuities are now 'competence destroying' in that they make completely obsolete the whole range of existing competencies in large innovating firms with strong technical functions (Tushman and Anderson, 1986). Cumulative assimilation and adaptation appear to be the norm.

Allocating Resources

The allocation of resources by firms to create firm-specific competencies poses unusual and difficult problems. Since these involve processes with considerable uncertainties, methods of resource allocation tend to be incremental and closely coupled to the learning processes described above, with constant feedback from improved knowledge and experience to evaluation (Freeman, 1982).

In addition, the choice of appropriate criteria and procedures for allocating resources to the creation of firm-specific competencies still poses important and unresolved problems for theory and practice. Myers (1984) points out that conventional techniques of resource allocation are inappropriate when there are strong links between today's investment and tomorrow's opportunities, which is precisely the case for the cumulative and path-dependent learning that augments firm-specific competencies. Here, investment projects do not necessarily produce additions to the net present value of the firm now, but have an 'option value' for further investments in some time in the future. Since it cannot deal with option values: 'DCF is no help at all for pure research and development. The value of R&D is almost all option value. Intangible asset's value is usually option value'. (Myers, 1984: 135).

Thus, coping with option values is an important challenge to the developments in financial theory (see Mitchell and Hamilton, 1988). In the meantime, large innovating firms have developed (more or less effective) 'routines' to deal with learning and option values, and these are often observable in the qualitative checklists commonly used by large innovating firms to evaluate R&D related programmes and projects. Again, the technico-economic expertise at the centre of the corporation is particularly important for the formation of corporate expectations about future developments in technology and their implications for future investment opportunities. Evidence shows that such engineering expertise is stronger in German and Japanese firms than those in British and American companies (Pavitt and Patel, 1988).

Conclusions

Given the characteristics of the innovation process described above, much of the conventional wisdom from business schools and management consultants is irrelevant and even misleading for its management.

First, it is not useful for a firm's management to begin by asking whether it should be a technological leader or follower, broad or narrow front, product or process. These characteristics will be determined largely by the firm's size and the nature of its accumulated competencies. There are no easy and generalizable recipes for success.

Second, the implementation of technology strategy is just as important as its definition, and an integral part of it. Given firm-specific competencies and the inevitable uncertainties surrounding innovative activities, the capacity for in-house learning from experience will be essential for success.

Third, conventional methods of project appraisal and divisional organization will result in myopic technological strategies that both neglect the effects of technological choices today on the innovative opportunities of tomorrow, and hinder the exploitation of product opportunities that do not slot tidily into established divisional markets or missions.

Fourth, the central technical function in the large firm should involve more than being a major actor in the implementation of innovation. It also involves inputs into the definition of appropriate divisional boundaries, into the exploration of radical new technologies and other forms of corporate learning, and into the formation of technological expectations that influence the corporate allocation of resources to R&D and investment opportunities.

Bibliography

Aoki, M. (1986) 'Horizontal vs. Vertical Information Structure of the Firm', *American Economic Review*, Vol. 76, (December) pp. 971–83.

Burgelman, R. (1985) 'Managing the New Venture Division: Research Findings and Implications for Strategic Management', *Strategic Management Journal*, Vol. 6, pp. 39–54.

Chandler, A. (1977) *The Visible Hand: the Managerial Revolution in American Business*, Harvard University Press, Cambridge, Massachusetts.

Cooper, R. (1983) 'A Process Model For Industrial New Product Development', *IEEE Transactions in Engineering Management*, Vol. EM-30, (1), pp. 2–11.

Freeman, C. (1982) *The Economics of Industrial Innovation*, Frances Pinter, London.

Maidique, M. and Zirger, B. (1984), 'A Study of Success and Failure in Product Innovation: The Case of the US Electronics Industry', *IEEE Transactions on Engineering Management*, Vol. EM-31, (4), pp. 192–203.

Mitchell, G. and Hamilton, W. (1988) 'Managing R & D as a Strategic Option', *Research Technology Management*, May/June, pp. 15–22.

Mowery, D. (1983) 'Industrial Research and Firm Size, Survival and Growth in American Manufacturing, 1921–1946: An Assessment', *Journal of Economic History*, Vol. 43, pp. 953–80.

Myers, S. (1984) 'Finance Theory and Finance Strategy', *Interfaces*, Vol. 14, No. 1, pp. 126–37.

Nelson, R. and Winter, S. (1982) *An Evolutionary Theory of Economic Change*, Belknap, Cambridge, Massachusetts.

Orsenigo, L. (1989) *The Emergence of Biotechnology*, Pinter, London.

Patel, P. and Pavitt, K. (1991) 'Large Firms in the Production of the World's Technology: an Important Case of Non-Globalisation', *Journal of International Business Studies*, Vol. 22, No 1, pp. 1–22.

Pavitt, K. and Patel, P. (1988) 'The International Distribution and Determinants of Technological Activities', *Oxford Review of Economic Policy*, Vol. 4, No. 4, pp. 35–55.

Pavitt, K., Robson, M. and Townsend, J. (1987) 'The Size Distribution of Innovating Firms in the UK: 1945–83', *The Journal of Industrial Economics*, Vol. XXXV, No. 3, pp. 297–316.

Pavitt, K., Robson, M. and Townsend, J. (1989) 'Technological Accumulation, Diversification and Organisation in UK Companies, 1945–1983', *Management Science*, Vol. 35, No. 1, pp. 81–99.

Reader, W. (1975) *Imperial Chemical Industries: A History*, Oxford University Press.

Rothwell, R. (1977) 'The Characteristics of Successful Innovations and Technically Progressive Firms', *R&D Management*, Vol. 7, No. 3, pp. 191–206.

Rothwell, R., Freeman, C., Jervis, P., Robertson, A. and Townsend, J. (1975) 'SAPPHO

Updated – Project SAPPHO Phase II', *Research Policy*, Vol. 3, No. 3, pp. 258–91.

Shrivastava, P. and Souder, W. (1987) 'The Strategic Management of Technological Innovation: a Review and a Model', *Journal of Management Studies*, Vol. 24, No. 1, pp. 25–41.

Teece, D. (1986) 'Profiting from Technological Innovation: Implications for Integration, Elaboration, Licensing and Public Policy', *Research Policy*, Vol. 15, No. 6, pp. 285–305.

Tushman, M. and Anderson, M. (1986) 'Technological Discontinuities and Organisation Environments', *Administrative Science Quarterly*, Vol. 31, pp. 439–65.

30. Managing Innovation in Multi-Technology Corporations

Ove Granstrand and Sören Sjölander

Introduction

This chapter introduces the concept of a multi-technology corporation (MTC), gives an empirical and theoretical rationale for it and elaborates upon some critical problems in managing innovation in such a context. Two empirical case illustrations are given. One case analyzes how the Swedish telecommunications company Ericsson managed its successful technological transition from old, electro-mechanical switching technology to new telephone exchanges based on stored program control (SPC) and digital signal processing. The other case analyzes how the Swedish auto and aerospace company Saab-Scania has attempted to manage technology transfer internally. The chapter ends with an exposition of strategic management problems in 'mul-tech' firms in general.

The Concept of a Multi-Technology Corporation (MTC)

By MTC, or a 'mul-tech firm' (Granstrand and Oskarsson, 1993) for short, we mean a corporation that operates in at least three different technologies. Technology in this context is defined roughly at the level of coherent textbooks, chairs in academic departments or specialization of scientists and engineers. Our purpose in this paper is to focus mainly on some qualitative aspects of managing R&D and innovation in typical MTCs. Thus it is not critical here to have a precise measure of degree of 'multi-technologicalness' or degree of *technology diversification* of a company. (This is possible using expert panels or indicators based, for example, on the number of professional categories represented by R&D personnel or patent statistics.) However, it must be kept in mind, even in a qualitative analysis, that the number of technologies (and relations among them such as convergence or fusion) is highly dependent on the level of abstraction used. Also the concept of a technology changes continually as more knowledge is generated and technologies split and merge as specialization goes on and terminology changes.

Moreover, technological diversification has to be distinguished from *product diversification*, just as an MTC has to be distinguished from a *multi-product firm*. On the latter there is a certain amount of literature (Laitinen, 1980; Teece, 1982) while to our knowledge nothing has been written on MTCs. The development, production and use of a product usually involve several technologies and each technology can usually be applied in several products. In fact, the couplings between different technologies, products, functions, applications, market segments and business areas are typically numerous in complex industrial organizations. The present prevailing mode of organizing large companies into decentralized divisions, oriented by product families or business areas, usually underexploits technological commonalities between the divisions (see Coombs in Chapter 31). This is one major rationale for elaborating upon the concept of MTCs. There are other rationales as well, both empirical and theoretical, as will be described next.

Empirical Studies of MTCs

An astoundingly strong association between a rough measure of technology diversification and sales growth was found in a study of twenty-five large Swedish multinational corporations, reported by Granstrand and Sjölander (1990a). The prevalence of large MTCs and the propensity for technology diversification in Japan and the US had been observed by Granstrand and Alänge (1989) and by Granstrand et al. (1990). Subsequent studies by these and other authors investigated the central role of technology diversification as a causal factor behind not only growth of sales but also growth of R&D expenditures and degree of external acquisition of technology. This causal relation appears both at corporate level and at product area level, which raises the strategic issue of technology-based product diversification as a way to economize on a set of related technologies without taking the risk of a high reliance on external technology acquisition. These empirical findings are based on interview and questionnaire studies of approximately fifty large technology-based corporations in Europe, Japan and the US, plus a set of product and company case studies. The importance of technology diversification has also been observed in other contexts, for example in realizing the growth potential of small, technology-based firms after being acquired by large ones (see Granstrand and Sjölander, 1990b).

Thus, technology diversification and the emergence of MTCs has been observed to improve economic performance. However, this causal relation is clearly not automatically guaranteed, but is realized through management, or more specifically multi-technology management.

Theoretical Rationale for MTCs

On theoretical grounds, technology diversification may lead to increased sales in a number of ways. There are static economies of scale to the extent that the same or similar technologies may be used in several products. Because knowledge application is characterized by small variable costs in relation to the fixed cost of generating the knowledge, the static economies of scale are significant when a technology has a wide applicability to many product areas in the firm. This is the case for generic technologies almost by definition. But not only is knowledge not consumed or worn out when applied many times, it is typically improved through learning processes, which give a kind of dynamic economy of scale. Furthermore, different technologies have a potential for cross-fertilization, yielding new functionalities and increased product and/or process performances, regardless of whether they have a wide applicability or not. This then may be called true *technological economies of scope*, not the kind that arises from shared inputs, and is thus a special case of economies of scale. These economies potentially associated with technology diversification depend on the specific technologies that may be combined or integrated, and also vary over time, depending upon the intra-technology advances.

In addition, technology diversification tends to lead to increasing R&D costs, because the more technologies are involved, the more co-ordination and integration work is needed, and the more difficulties arise in connection with conducting multi-disciplinary R&D. These difficulties are widely reported and typically involve conflicts between professional subcultures in science and technology, NIH-effects (Not Invented Here) and other innovation barriers (Granstrand, 1982). If N is the number of important technologies, all with mutual relations, the R&D expenditures could specifically be hypothesized to vary according to R&D $= a + bN + cN^2$. If all possible interdependence relations among the N technologies are assumed to contribute roughly equally to R&D costs, these would hypothetically grow exponentially, i.e. R&D $= a * \exp(bN)$, as a result of technology diversification. The often observed progressive rise in R&D in a product area over time or over successive product generations can then be explained, at least partially, by technology diversification.

Given both empirical support and theoretical rationales for economic performance in MTCs deriving from technology diversification, the question then is – what managerial abilities are needed to realize multi-technology-based economic performance? There are several managerial issues and challenges involved. Two generic ones will be illustrated next through two company cases – how to manage technological transitions involving new technologies temporarily coexisting with old ones in the corporate technology base, and how to manage technology transfer in an MTC in order to realize economies of scope.

Managing Technological Transitions in Ericsson

A telecommunication network for speech, text, data and images consists of subscriber equipment (telephone, data terminal, etc.), transmission equipment (cable, radio, satellite) and switching equipment, which connects subscribers locally, regionally and internationally to 'the world's largest machine'. Technological changes in these three types of equipment occur at a different pace in different periods. A core technology is switching technology. Figure 30.1 shows the main technological transitions or substitutions in this field. (A substitution between two technologies at some level in a hierarchical classification of technologies may correspond to substitutions at a higher level in the classification scheme. Each number indicates substitutions that correspond accordingly. For example, a substitution from crossbar to analogue switching also means a substitution from indirect electromechanical control to electronic stored program control.) In contrast to many other industries, technological changes have been absorbed by the industry without disrupting it too much, even when the major sources of innovation were largely outside the industry as with stored program control (SPC).

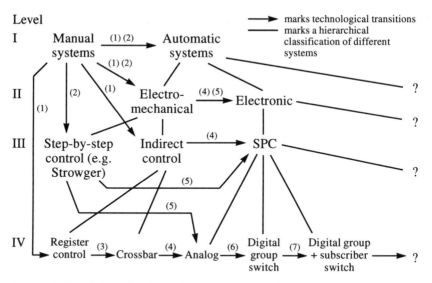

Figure 30.1 Main technological transitions in telephone switching

In the early 1960s pre-studies of new telephone exchanges were initiated by Ericsson, with the primary focus on computerization. The computer people in the 1960s had little understanding of the special application of computers in telecommunications and the Ericsson engineering people, consisting of 'telephone people' (a special professional subculture, just like computer engineers) and newly graduated engineers, had but minor contact with the established computer world. At the same time the top management in Ericsson were not acquainted with electronics and computer technology. A centralized computer could provide all the necessary 'brainpower' for a telephone exchange and would additionally yield the lowest hardware cost. The alternative was to distribute the computer power throughout the exchange, which would result in higher costs given the fairly expensive circuitry of the computers of the time. (The dramatic reduction in circuitry costs during the 1970s could hardly have been foreseen at this time, but nevertheless significantly favoured the Ericsson approach.) The second approach, though more costly, would facilitate the design of the system. The AXE system was built on the second approach and this is attributed to a few engineers who advocated that electronic exchanges should in certain ways be patterned on electro-mechanical exchanges. This favoured the

Table 30.1 Generations of telephone exchanges

Technology	Ericsson's product generation	First large installation	Last large installation	R&D time till market introduction	R&D cost[a] (man-years)
Manual switching	Ericsson's manual	1880	1930	?	10–20
Automatic, indirect control, electro-mechanical	500-switch	1923	ca. 1960	ca. 1918–23	50–100
Crossbar technology	Crossbar switch (Code-switch)	ca 1950	Still supplied	ca. 1945–50	200–500
SPC and digital signal processing, electronic	AKE and later AXE	1968[b] (AKE) 1976 1978[d] (AXE)	Still supplied (AKE) Still supplied (AXE)	1961–71 (AKE) 1970–78 (AXE)	1000–2000[c] (AKE) 5000–10000[c] (AXE)

Notes:
(a) R&D cost until market introduction
(b) Experimental station in Tumba, Sweden. First export order to Rotterdam
(c) Basic development
(d) First installation with digital group switch in Åbo 1978

decentralized computer power approach. In a way one could argue that the fact that Ericsson was not in mainline computer development made it much easier to follow the pragmatic approach of not making too bold design innovations. Furthermore, the Ericsson approach followed a step-by-step electronification of the exchanges in contrast to several of the competing companies, which went immediately to fully electronic exchanges.

Thus most of Ericsson's work on computerization was self-development, often along unconventional lines. Competence in computer technology was built up internally during the 1960s, especially in computer architecture, systems reliability, multi-processing and structured programming. The latter experience then paved the way for systems modularization, an important feature of the AXE system. The transition of an old application into a new technology was therefore achieved through self-development, creating design concepts which were novel also to the new technology.

Around 1970 there were many internal discussions on whether to continue development along the lines of a centralized telephone exchange (AKE), or develop a new system (AXE), based on modularized software and reed selectors. For a few years AXE and AKE were developed in parallel, although the AKE development became more geared towards market adaptation. A strategic decision was taken in the early 1970s about full-scale development of AXE. At that time Ellemtel had been created, a company jointly (50/50) owned by Ericsson and its Swedish customer, the governmental telecom administration (PTT) Televerket. This company was to be responsible for the development work of the new telephone exchange. Economic calculations for AKE and AXE were presented, giving estimates of some 100 man-years for AKE, and some 1000 man-years for AXE, with several years longer R&D time. However, there was almost a tie between AKE and AXE. The managing director of Ericsson then asked Ellemtel which way they believed the economically viable technology would go in general. Their answer was in favour of the technically more advanced system, AXE – a likely choice by development people.

The first AXE pilot plant was ready in 1976. Then things happened rapidly. Technologically the system was updated in several stages. An important step was to digitalize the system, which represented a second AXE generation. The coming transition from analogue to digital voice transmission was recognized and decided upon in 1973–74 and a fully digitalized version was introduced in 1978–79. The subsequent market development of AXE will not be described here, but is a major success story, involving some spectacular events.

Managing Technology Transfer in Saab-Scania

Saab-Scania Combitech, the business-oriented 'high-tech' group, formed through a merger between the Swedish-based auto and aerospace company

Saab and the truck company Scania, provides an interesting example of how to manage internal technology transfer. One of the major divisions of Saab-Scania was its Aircraft Division with a series of well-known fighter jets. The culture of the aircraft division was very much technology-oriented and very little business-oriented.

At the end of 1982 a strategic decision was made by the Saab-Scania management to pick out a number of projects, internal ventures and 'skunk works' from the Aircraft Division to form a business-oriented high-tech group, called Saab-Scania Combitech, with its own dedicated management. The companies contained a wide range of products based on a spectrum of technologies (see Table 30.2).

The idea behind the Saab-Scania Combitech group was to provide the companies with dedicated management at company as well as at group level, and to orient the companies towards specific well-defined businesses, using the common base of technology and culture to do so. With such a broad range of technologies these small companies could not be expected to maintain a competitive technological position on their own in all key technological areas. For financial reasons (R&D effectiveness) the technological resources of these companies had to be combined in some way or other. This was the core of the Combitech organizational principle: to combine technological economies of scope with (joint) economies of scale.

At the outset it was clear to the management that the slim group management, staffed with business men and 'bean counters', had to be equipped with a technology transfer function and a manager to facilitate technology transfer and develop a policy and routines for technology transfer. It was not clear (conceptually) at the outset which technologies were contained in the group or how these influenced the competitive position of the various companies. Nor was it clear which companies should combine their technological resources and how this should be done to the benefit of the Combitech and the Saab-Scania group.

In order to develop the Combitech organizational principle the group management tried to spot similar examples of organizational principles in other companies but did not find any. In 1984 a research group at Chalmers University of Technology was engaged and the project partially reported here was initiated.

Together with group management a series of key questions was formulated. What were the technologies? What were their competitive impacts? Which were the key technologies with the power to substantially affect product performance and quality? How could the technology transfer function be organized, implemented and performed? What would the effects be? What technology transfer mechanisms were there and what technology transfer activities should be performed? Parallel to these questions a series of research questions was elaborated.

Here we shall focus on one: Can the base of technology in an MTC be monitored and affected by specific technology transfer activities, policies and routines?

The technology base was outlined through a series of interviews with group and company management and key technologists in the Saab-Scania Combitech Group and was finally defined in a joint workshop with these people. The technology-company matrix of key technologies is presented in Table 30.2.

Table 30.2 The technology-company matrix, showing key technologies in the various companies of the Saab-Scania Combitech Group

Technology	C1	C2	C3	C4	C5	C6	C7	C8	C9	C10
Electronic hardware	X	X	X	X	X	X	X	X	X	X
Man/machine communication		X	X	X	X	X	X			
Electronic packaging	X	X				X				
Micro-mechanical design		X	X	X	X	X	X			
Software		X	X	X			X			X
Computer communication		X		X		X				
Electrooptics		X	X			X	X	X		
Infra-red technology	X	X				X		X		
Microwave technology				X	X		X			
Laser technology		X					X			
Hydroacoustics		X		X						
Image processing				X	X		X			
Artificial intelligence		X	X	X	X	X	X			
Systems technology		X	X	X	X	X	X	X		X

A spectrum of technology transfer activities, policies and routines was implemented during late 1984, 1985 and 1986. Among these were:

- formulating and retaining a technology transfer policy;
- appointing lead houses[1] in prioritized key technological areas;
- appointing lead engineers[2] in prioritized key technological areas;
- formulating, communicating and implementing the technology transfer routines;
- implementing incentive schemes for group and company management as well as for lead engineers;
- creating a strategic intra-company joint technology development fund managed by the CEO and the technology transfer manager – the CEO fund;
- organizing focused seminars in key technological areas with internal and external experts;
- creating internal technology consultation networks and policies;
- establishing payment routines for internal consultation and the transfer of key technologists between companies in the group;
- establishing joint technology development projects (funded by lead houses and the CEO fund);
- creating and communicating 'The Combitech Way', an internal policy guide aimed at facilitating a common language and culture.

In the aggregated communication networks from early 1985 and late 1986, i.e. before and after implementation of the technology transfer activities, policies and routines, the number of reciprocal interpersonal, intercompany links had increased, in some instances drastically (Granstrand and Sjölander, 1990a).

In Figure 30.2[3] we can see the technology interdependence map showing the technology interdependence need structure created in the diagnosis step and changes in the number of reciprocal interpersonal and intercompany links. Figure 30.2 shows that there has been a significant increase in the number of interpersonal links between technology source companies and technology need companies for various dependence dyads. Eight out of eleven links were strengthened.

Of course this simple 'tip of the iceberg' analysis does not prove that the implemented technology transfer activities, policies and routines are the only explanation of the fact that in most dependence dyads there has been an increase in the number of links. We do not know what the pattern would have been if no activities had been implemented. What the example indicates is that:

- it is possible to define the base of technology for an MTC;
- it is possible to monitor the intercompany (intra-group) flow of

technology in an MTC;
- it is possible to draw meaningful conclusions from the diagnosis;
- it is likely that carefully applied technology transfer activities will actually affect the flow of technology in the anticipated direction (from technology source companies to companies that need technological support in key technological fields);
- it is indicated that MTCs within a group can share a common base of technology.

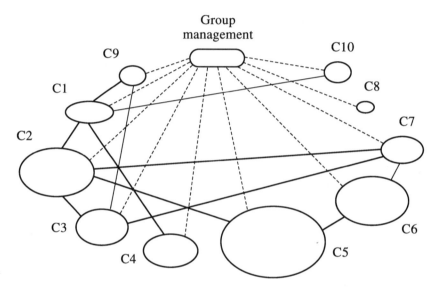

Figure 30.2 The technology interdependence need structure and changes in number of reciprocal intercompany communication links

___   indicates a significant (5% level) increase in number of interpersonal and intercompany links
___   indicates that two companies are technologically dependent on each other but that the number of communication links did not increase between 1985 and 1986
----   denotes links to group management

However, it is *not* shown that the Combitech structure is prosperous in the long run and that it is the single best structure to fulfil the needs of a corporate technology house and the need to business-orient a portfolio of engineering ventures. It is not clear that the group does not harvest investments made earlier when the projects and later companies were included in the Aircraft Division.

The development process of the Saab-Scania Combitech organizational principle has led to the decision to change the technology transfer function from a staff function to a staff/line function, and from a technology transfer manager with tactical and operational responsibilities towards a vice president of technology also responsible for strategically important inter-company technology development projects and technology-based ventures. The development process has also generated a redesign of the incentive schemes for group and company management. They are now based on a combination of incentives in proportion to company *and* group profits. This has been done to facilitate the prosperous combination of technologies and to create a force for exchange of managerial knowledge among group and company management. It is also worth pointing out here that a multi-company MTC rests heavily on a joint corporate culture. Seven of the ten companies in this study have their roots in the Saab Aircraft Division but three of them were acquired from outside Saab-Scania. Subcultures stemming from different professional foci inhibit the communication among people in different professional areas if the corporate culture also differs.

Some Critical Managerial Abilities in Management of MTCs

As mentioned earlier, the cases have been chosen in order to illustrate two different situations in MTCs rather than to allow systematic comparisons. The two questions to be raised in this section are what critical managerial abilities could be identified in the cases and whether any improvement (learning) has taken place with respect to these abilities.

Managing technological transitions in MTCs

In the Ericsson case of managing technological transitions, a number of key managerial abilities could be identified. First is the ability to perform environmental scanning (including technology scanning and competitor scanning) and to produce technological, industrial and market forecasts. It is doubtful whether the precision in forecasts of technological developments and their impacts has improved over the years, but certainly the awareness that the sources of innovations and competition are often outside the company's industry (as traditionally defined) has improved, as well as the responsiveness to signals about emerging technologies and potential competitors (or joint venture partners).

Second, the ability to make investments with the proper rate, direction and form of strategic competence building is critical. There is a long process, perhaps 20–30 years, from the first signals of an emerging technology (e.g. discovery of semiconductivity) to the commercial success of a new product generation based on it. All the time the technology develops, technological options proliferate and the competitors' technological approaches and positions change. Several general strategies or responses are feasible in a situation with an emerging technology, such as:

1. Improving the old technology in the existing product generation (producing what is sometimes called the 'sailing effect');
2. Developing a new generation based on some version of the new technology;
3. Developing a hybrid generation, based in part on both the old and the new technology, as a 'gap-filler';
4. Introducing the new technology in an evolutionary manner in the existing generation (e.g. piecemeal replacement of transistors with integrated circuits);
5. Skipping the emerging technology and jumping to the next technology (this has been attempted unsuccessfully in the telecom sector); or finally
6. Doing nothing (wait and see).

When and how to introduce the new technology (if at all) and when and how to exit the old technology are crucial timing decisions. The experience in Ericsson suggests that the building of competence for these decisions ought to be made at the outset in an experimental manner without a precise plan and involving good technologists, young and old. (The latter may be difficult if the product with the old technology is simultaneously successful on the market.)

Again it is doubtful whether this second critical ability has improved, but the awareness that no technology lasts forever has certainly increased. However, the tendency to cling too long to an old technology is always present if it is successful on the market, producing a kind of success-breeds-failure syndrome. On the other hand, technological transitions take place at an increasing rate, while the mandate times for technology managers last long enough for them to experience an increasing number of transitions. The technical director who makes his corporate career in connection with a major technological transition in the company, and then delays the next transition because he was unaware of his emerging technological obsolescence is possibly a (slowly?) vanishing breed.

A third critical ability in connection with technological transitions is the ability to handle conflicts. It is almost axiomatic that such transitions involve conflicts. This should be recognized as natural rather than pathological in the organization. Some conflicts derive from confrontations between different professional subcultures associated with different scientific and technological disciplines involved in a transition (see the Saab case). Sometimes, as in the Ericsson case, these conflicts could be mitigated by a strong corporate culture (Granstrand, 1982). Some conflicts are associated with power struggles among managers, whose power is based on knowledge in a certain technology. Some conflicts have good effects, for example increasing motivation as in some 'guerrilla' development work ('skunk work') in a large company, but conflicts may be disastrous. The ability of managers (and board members) to handle conflicts has probably not developed very much, if at all. For several reasons, managers often avoid dealing with conflicts until it is too late.

Fourth, organizational ability is important in connection with technological transitions. The scale of the old has to shrink eventually, while the scale of the new has to grow. Thus, major shifts and renewals of resources, personnel, power, attention and so on have to be made. At the same time the new always runs a risk of being killed by the old. To organize the work on the new technology separately from that on the old in a semi-autonomous organization has often proved to be a viable organizational solution (Sjölander, 1985). It is not only a way of separating the new from the old but also makes it possible to combine the advantages of large and small organizations. In the Ericsson case, the formation of Ellemtel proved to be highly successful and, in retrospect, timely. The special connection to the Swedish (PTT) 'Televerket' as a qualified user gave Ellemtel advantages in addition to those of separation and small/large combination. Although there are also problems and drawbacks associated with this kind of organizational solution, it seems on the whole that managerial ability in this respect has improved over the years. Furthermore, the employment of divisionalized organizational forms (M forms) represents a managerial improvement in general.

A fifth ability concerns how to work with parallel approaches in R&D and when to concentrate R&D resources on a major design direction for a new product generation (cf. the question whether management or markets provide the most efficient selection environment in the terms of Nelson and Winter, 1977). It is doubtful whether the managerial ability to diverge and converge R&D work has improved. At the same time rising R&D costs, greater possibilities of combining different technological options (due to a general accumulation of S&T) and rather constant R&D times (as in the Ericsson case) increase the importance of this ability.

Managing technology transfer in MTCs

Now let us turn to some critical managerial abilities in managing inter-company technology transfer as they have become evident in the Saab case.

Combining technologies in R&D work – technology fusion and diver-sification (Kodama, 1986a and b) – always involves the problem of how to manage professional subcultures. It is of fundamental importance that these subcultures rest on a common way of interaction, problem solving, etc. for the benefit of the company's business, that is, a common corporate culture. Facilitating the growth and maintenance of a *common corporate culture* are common historical roots and *coherence in vision, goals and explicit strategies*. If these are not fulfilled to a certain degree, the combination of technologies in a *multi-company* structure probably has poor chances of success. This is even more true in a multinational setting in which there are national culture differences. Thus, multi-technology management in multinational companies (MNCs) is compounded by cultural differences in two dimensions, differences that have to be suppressed by an even stronger corporate culture. (For case presentations of problems and approaches in managing multinational R&D, see Granstrand and Fernlund, 1978; Håkansson and Zander, 1986; Granstrand and Sjölander, 1992.)

Also of fundamental importance is the existence of a well-thought-through *technology transfer policy* backed by the business leaders of the various companies. This is not sufficient, however. Without a common corporate culture and coherence in vision, goals and strategies it is likely that a technology transfer policy will have no effect (cf. the isolated, acquired companies C8 and C10 in Figure 30.2).

The experience of Saab-Scania Combitech also points to the need for *incorporating strategic perspectives and responsibilities into the technology transfer function*. The *technology transfer function* probably operates more effectively if it incorporates *operative, tactical as well as strategic activities and responsibilities*. The development should be from a technology transfer manager (staff function) to a vice president of technology (staff/line function) with direct executive responsibilities for group strategic projects, ventures and new technology-based firms, as well as staff responsibility – together with the CEO and the various company managements – for the strategy development process.

The *process of developing the management ability* of an MTC such as Combitech requires time and much experimentation. This can hardly be done if the group profitability is low or poor. It needs healthy companies, projects and ventures at the outset to develop this knowledge.

To sum up, among key managerial abilities that have to be developed in order to manage internal technology transfer in MTCs are:

1. The *ability to manage subcultures* and to resolve conflicts;
2. The *ability to identify and exploit* commercially sound technological possibilities often triggered by technology fusion (combining technologies);
3. The *ability to spot, monitor and take strategic actions* on internal and external changes in competition and technological development;
4. The *ability to experiment with new managerial routines and policies*, to evaluate the effects and to act according to the analysis.

Technologists often consider the growth of scientific knowledge and its industrial application to be the basis of human progress. Business management, on the other hand, sometimes seems to hold a less positive view of the role of S&T in the creation of human welfare. The general management cadre, strongly influenced by financial and marketing knowledge, tends to consider S&T as one among several factors contributing to successful business. In this top-down view, technologists are there to implement business strategy. Companies behaving this way will most probably have difficulty in creating balanced functional strategies that are coherent with business strategies. To integrate the technologist perspective more thoroughly into the process of strategic development – to create balanced business and functional strategies – and to facilitate the managerial learning process of the top management level, MTCs need to incorporate technologists in their top management ranks to the same extent as large Japanese MTCs. Companies do not, however, need more technical staff directors. In order to bridge the managerial knowledge gap between businessmen and technologists and to balance the influence of finance and marketing, business-oriented technologists are often needed in the position of executive vice president of technology.

General Strategic Management Problems in MTCs

The preceding sections have illustrated two generic or strategic management problems in mul-tech firms, each in turn related to further problems, such as managing technology scanning or managing professional subcultures. (These problems can be called tactical if one wants to distinguish between strategic, tactical and operative management of technology. However, this hierarchical view of management, although useful, often leads to oversimplification.)

Other strategic problem areas will be briefly mentioned in conclusion. Essentially, they relate to the theoretical rationales for MTCs. One such problem area concerns how to manage the process of *technology-based product diversification* in order to reap economies of both scale and scope among the technologies in the technology base of an MTC. This involves realigning corporate strategies in many Western companies, which have not only rested on past successes of product specialization but have also been reluctant to diversify because of past failures with diversification. Japanese MTCs have managed this process quite well and several features of Japanese corporate culture and society facilitate the development and operation of MTCs (Granstrand et al., 1989).

Another problem area concerns how to reap dynamic economies of scope through using old as well as new technologies in new applications. An important factor is what can be called *application vision*, that is, the ability to see new combinations of technologies and applications. This requires a certain creativity, perhaps not as highly esteemed as scientific creativity but nevertheless of considerable economic importance. A recognition of the work of application engineers and their efforts in application engineering in general is significant. As often reported in literature, the first application of a new technology is usually not the one that subsequently becomes the most important one commercially (e.g. computers at first for mostly scientific and later for mostly administrative applications). The application of Ericsson's

AXE technology to mobile telephony was never envisaged at the beginning, but later quite luckily turned out to be very successful commercially. Managing the whole process of application diversification for new technologies requires application, vision and the flexibility to move the technological and commercial emphasis from one application to another. Companies may easily get 'locked in' with an initial application. Finally, an efficient feedback of ideas for technological improvements from each application must be secured in order to reap the dynamic economies of scope; that is, the whole learning process must be managed rather than allowed to be spontaneous.

Another strategic problem concerns how to manage external acquisition of technology and blend it with in-house R&D (Granstrand et al., 1992). This involves not only managing technology scanning but managing all the various means by which new technologies may be acquired, e.g. acquisition and integration of small innovative firms, conducting cooperative R&D and alliances with customers, suppliers, competitors, universities etc., using contract R&D and engineering services and licensing in. The blending process involves transferring technology externally and internally, combining innovation and imitation (not easy for companies used to being technology leaders), overcoming NIH-effects, and integrating external technologists in the organization and external technologies in the products of the MTC. For this process to work, a significant amount of communication and coordination is needed; nor should business skills and technological competence in buying and accessing externally available technology be forgotten.

Finally, there is the problem of how to manage in-house R&D for reaping economies of scope across technologies and scientific disciplines. This is well recognized in traditional R&D management, involving, for instance, the setting-up of small multi-technology project teams and mitigating conflicts (for example by avoiding overlapping competencies in the project teams), and will not be elaborated on here. Needless to say, these aspects of R&D management acquire greater importance in MTCs.

Notes

1. A company with responsibility (and group funding) to develop knowledge and skills in a key technological area for the benefit of all companies in the group.
2 . A senior engineer with responsibility for information gathering and dissemination along with internal consulting to the benefit of all companies in the group.
3 . Owing to the military secrecy act, the explicit couplings of technologies and companies have been withheld. C1-C10 are abbreviations for company names.

Bibliography

Biggadike, R. (1979) 'The Risky Business of Diversification', *Harvard Business Review*, May.

Granstrand, O. and Fernlund, I. (1978) 'Coordination of Multinational R&D: A Swedish Case Study', *R&D Management,* pp. 1–7.

Granstrand, O. (1982) *Technology, Management and Markets,* Frances Pinter, London.

Granstrand, O., Jacobsson, S., Sjölander, S. and Alänge, S. (1989) 'Strategic Technology Issues in US Manufacturing Industries – A Critical Analysis,' *CIM-Working Papers,* WP 03, Department of Industrial Management and Economics, Chalmers University of Technology, Göteborg.

Granstrand, O., Sjölander, S. and Alänge, S. (1989) 'Strategic Technology Issues in Japanese Manufacturing Industry', *Technology Analysis & Strategic Management,* Vol. 1, No. 3, pp. 259–72.

Granstrand, O., Oskarsson, C., Sjöberg, N. and Sjölander, S. (1990) 'Business Strategies for New Technologies' in Deiaco, Hörnell and Vickery, *Technology and Investment,* Pinter Publishers, London.

Granstrand, O. and Sjölander, S. (1990a) 'Managing Innovation in Multi-Technology Corporations', *Research Policy,* Vol. 19, No. 1, pp. 35–60.

Granstrand, O. and Sjölander, S. (1990b) 'The Acquisition of Technology and Small Firms by Large Firms', *Journal of Economic Behavior and Organization,* 13, pp. 367–86.

Granstrand, O., Bohlin, E., Oskarsson, C. and Sjöberg, N. (1992) 'External Technology Acquisition in Large Multi-Technology Corporations', *R&D Management,* Vol. 22, No. 2, pp. 111–33.

Granstrand, O. and Sjölander, S. (1992) 'Internationalization and Diversification of Multi-Technology Corporations' in Granstrand, O., Håkanson, L. and Sjölander, S. (eds), *Technology Management and International Business,* John Wiley & Sons, London.

Granstrand, O. and Oskarsson, C. (1993) 'Technology Management in "Mul-Tech" Corporations', Department of Industrial Management and Economics, Chalmers University of Technology, paper presented at the Portland International Conference on Management of Engineering and Technology – PICMET, 27–31 October 1991, forthcoming in IEEE Transactions on Engineering Management.

Håkansson, L. and Zander, U. (1986) *Managing International Research and Development,* Sveriges Mekanförbund, Stockholm.

Kodama, F. (1986a) 'Japanese Innovation in Mechatronics Technology – Fumio Kodama Studies Technological Fusion', *Science and Public Policy,* 13 (1), pp. 44–51.

Kodama, F. (1986b) 'Technological Diversification of Japanese Industry', *Science* 233, pp. 291–6.

Laitinen, K. (1980) *A Theory of the Multiproduct Firm,* North-Holland, Amsterdam.

Lindholm, Å. (1993) 'Acquisition and Growth of Technology-Based Firms', forthcoming in *Strategic Management Journal.*

Nelson, R. and Winter, S. (1977) 'In Search of Useful Theory of Innovation', *Research Policy,* 6, pp. 36–7.

Sjölander, S. (1985) *Management of Innovation,* PhD dissertation, Department of Industrial Management, Chalmers University of Technology, Göteborg.

Teece, D.J. (1982) 'Towards an Economic Theory of the Multiproduct Firm', *Journal of Economic Behavior & Organization,* 3 (1), pp. 39–63.

31. Technology and Business Strategy

Rod Coombs

Introduction

Until the mid-70s the study of industrial innovation was mainly conducted within a framework which took the individual instance of innovation as the unit of analysis. Studies were concerned with such issues as the relative importance of technology-push and market-pull influences on particular innovations, the role of product champions, and the management of the innovation process. This was a necessary phase in the evolution of the study of innovation because these were issues on which there was a genuine lack of data and understanding.

Gradually however, the focus of research shifted towards taking larger samples of innovations and looking for distinctive patterns of firm behaviour which characterized successful innovation. The Sappho project perhaps best captures the essence of this stage in the evolution of the field. Indeed, as early as 1974 Freeman was beginning to identify innovation 'strategies' which could be discerned almost as 'ideal types' in firm behaviour. But he was careful to qualify his taxonomy of innovation strategies by saying that it was not yet an adequate basis for any alternative approach to what economists call the 'theory of the firm'.

Since then, a number of factors have added to the trend to see the firm as the unit of analysis for the study of innovation rather than the individual innovation. Two factors are particularly worth noting:

1. Beginning with the early work of Nelson and Winter (1977), and developing through the work of many authors since, there has been a realization that innovations are often incremental steps along a *technological trajectory*. These trajectories are rooted in learned competencies within the firms that produce the innovations. Therefore the innovative actions of the firm, and indeed its actions more broadly, are *path-dependent*, and thus constrained to some extent by these acquired competencies.
2. There has been a dramatic growth in literature on firm strategy, quite independently of research on innovation, which has produced a bewildering variety of theoretical and practical frameworks for the

analysis and construction of strategies for firms. (See Johnson and Scholes (1984) for a widely used guide to this literature.)

The combination of these two factors has led to an important emerging synthesis which can be expressed as follows: Past innovative activity within a given firm results in a process of *specialization of the technological assets* within that firm. This gives rise to competitive advantage in the form of superior ability to use that particular specialized set of competencies, but it also gives rise to possible weaknesses in the firm's ability to acquire other specialized skills. At the same time however, products and processes are becoming more 'system-like' in their properties and tend to draw on a wider and wider variety of technologies.

Thus there is a continuing tension for firms between the tendency to focus on proprietary technologies which give competitive advantage (and which may therefore increase specialization), and the need to widen their technological portfolio, both for reasons of maintaining a position in existing product markets, as well as for reasons of product diversification. This tension between technological convergence and divergence has to be continually managed by putting it at the centre of a rolling process of assessment of future technical requirements, followed by practical steps to *re-balance the technology portfolio.*

But such assessments of technological needs and possibilities can only be properly conducted if they are *related to the overall business plan* for the firm in question, covering such things as which markets are prioritized, what product strategies are to be followed, whether acquisitions or mergers are likely, etc. In other words, *the evolution of the technological resources of the firm becomes an item in the 'strategy agenda' of the firm.* The concept of 'Strategic Technology Management' has therefore become established as a component part of the broader field of business strategy, and the term finds its way into the titles of articles, courses and books (see, for example, Dussauge et al., 1992).

Levels of Strategy

There is then, an established view that technology and strategy issues in a firm are closely linked. But the task of relating technology to strategy within a firm presents itself differently depending on whether the context is the strategy of an *individual business unit*; or of a *business division* comprising a number of related business units; or of a *corporate* entity comprising a larger number of business units and/or divisions. In the interests of brevity, and to draw out some important points starkly, we will caricature the way in which these issues might be treated at the two extremes, namely the relatively autonomous business unit, and the large diversified corporation.

Technology and business strategy

At the business unit level, the strategic issues essentially revolve around how that unit chooses to compete within its particular markets – its *competitive strategy*. In this field the work of Porter (1980) has been very influential through the concept of 'generic' competitive strategies such as *cost leadership, differentiation,* and *focus*.

Business units, especially in established markets, tend to develop an understandable obsession with financial success within those markets, and are not usually willing to spend too much money on technology which cannot be shown to be fairly directly relevant to the current markets and concerns of the business. This means that at business unit level the process of strategic alignment between technology and business strategy tends to be dominated by the business strategy, with the technology portfolio having to be structured to hit the 'targets' derived from the business strategy. This has consequences for some of the most obvious aspects of R&D portfolio management such as short-term versus long-term balance; product/process balance. To take an example, the relative importance and balance between process innovation and product innovation will be different for a firm which chooses cost leadership than for a firm which chooses product differentiation as a strategy.

Put simply, it is normal to find technology issues at business unit level being managed in a way which owes a lot to the view that technology should be 'market-driven' in order for innovation to be successful. The main factor which can sometimes moderate this market-driven approach to R&D is the circumstance of an industry which is being affected by a particularly vibrant area of scientific or technical change which is advancing rapidly. In these circumstances, where the firm is more genuinely 'technology-driven', the firm has to place great emphasis on maintaining a delicate balance between technology-push and market-pull forces in its overall strategy. A classical current example of stand-alone firms which face this situation in stark terms are the so-called 'dedicated biotechnology firms'.

But genuinely technology-driven firms are the exception rather than the rule. For most business units, R&D is conducted in a market-pull context. R&D budgets are therefore often drawn directly from the operating budgets of the business unit itself, with little input from the corporate parent, and the managerial control of R&D is characterized by a strong involvement of non-R&D staff, including personnel from marketing, operations, and from the business leadership team.

Technology and corporate strategy

How does this contrast with the role of technology in strategic discussions at the corporate level? Corporate strategy is largely concerned with the issues raised by the portfolio of businesses which are owned or operated by the corporate parent. Some of the dimensions along which that portfolio of business can be analysed include the following:

- the degree of diversity of the business units in terms of products, markets, and technologies;
- the profitability, market maturity, and competitive position of the units ('Boston Consultancy Group Matrix'-type issues);
- the opportunities for synergies between the business units in terms of shared marketing and distribution, production facilities, and product and process technologies;
- the opportunities for divisional groupings of business units to exploit such synergies.

The main features of the corporate strategy agenda arise from the analysis of this range of issues and the need to modify the shape of the business portfolio by divestment, acquisition, selective investment, or re-organization of divisional structures. The aspect of this agenda which we are concerned with is the role of technology in these decisions.

At one extreme, there can sometimes be no substantive role for technology at all. If the corporation is a conglomerate and/or it is characterized by what Goold and Campbell (1987) call a 'financial control' style of strategic management, then there will be little detailed consideration of technology issues at the corporate centre. In such organizations there is often a low level of synergy between divisions or business units, and business unit management teams have a relatively high degree of discretion concerning competitive strategy. Their relationship to the corporate centre is focused around agreeing upon, and then reaching, key financial performance targets. The consequence for technology is that there is usually a strong business unit control over R&D as described earlier, and relatively little interaction with other business units on technology, or on other issues for that matter.

However, if there are strong overlaps or synergies between businesses within a corporation, and if the 'strategic style' falls into either of Goold and Campbell's other two categories of 'strategic planning' or 'strategic control', then the picture with respect to technology can be quite different. These companies are more likely to have (or to have had at some time in the past) a central corporate R&D facility which serves more than one division in the corporate structure. The corporate laboratories may not be heavily involved in close-to-the-market product development for business units (although they contribute in some circumstances); but they will probably have an important role in developing underlying competence in generic technology areas that have relevance across a number of business in which the company has a long-term position. They may also have a role in generating or acquiring new technologies which are 'option-opening' for the corporation in terms of creating new business opportunities. Such companies are also more likely to be at the higher end of the R&D intensity spectrum (that is, they will spend higher proportions of turnover on R&D) and, in the terms of Pavitt (1984) they will probably be 'science-intensive' firms or 'specialised supplier' firms. They may possibly be 'scale-intensive' firms, but they are unlikely to be 'supplier dominated' firms.

Although corporations of this general type (with strong technology or market relationships between their component businesses), have good reasons to take a corporate view of technology, this has not always been the case. In the past two decades the desire to make innovation more effective by making R&D more market-driven has been a deep-running trend. Many companies have pursued decentralization of R&D funding and control even though they are not conglomerates, and are not examples of pure financial control in their corporate strategic styles. Thus we see the following trends in recent years:[1]

- Where firms have corporate R&D laboratories, the balance of their funding has shifted from corporate sources to business unit sources, which are more closely monitored through customer–contractor relationships.
- Many corporate laboratories have either shrunk absolutely, or have reduced in relative importance within the total R&D effort of a company. This is reflected in the growth of decentralized R&D at division or business unit level. This tendency has been fuelled by mergers and acquisitions which have brought previously separate R&D facilities under one corporate parent.
- This decentralization of R&D has permitted new and more intimate arrangements to develop which bring technical, commercial and operations staff together at business unit level in effective teams for product and process innovation. *This is a major historical gain and should not be underestimated.*

However, there are also a number of negative consequences which have arisen from this decentralization of R&D, which have been aggravated by other contextual features:

- Business unit 'ownership' of R&D is very effective at consolidating strength *within the existing technological regime* (or set of technological trajectories) applying in that company at that time. If that regime is a competitive one, all well and good. If the technological regime of the company becomes less competitive, the business unit ownership of R&D could run the risk of digging a deeper hole for the company.
- If new 'generic' technologies emerge which are 'competence-destroying' for such business units, their R&D infrastructure may not be able to cope. This has been a feature of the 80s and the 90s.

The natural place to look for a compensating source of technical competence in these circumstances is the corporate parent and its R&D capacity, which will generally be oriented to longer-term strategic research. But, for a significant proportion of UK companies, this corporate competence is weak. The weakness at corporate level arises from two major sources:

- Firstly, the process of decentralization, within a flat or slow-growing total R&D-funding regime, has weakened both the competencies and the organizational influence of corporate R&D.
- Secondly, there is an Anglo-Saxon bias toward corporate management styles which are *financially* oriented, rather than oriented toward strategic coordination of the activities of a portfolio of businesses.

The combination of these two factors has meant that the overall technology and skill portfolio of a diversified corporate structure can often become simply *invisible* to the company. There is frequently no responsible individual or structure to 'own' this problem. Consequently there can be serious deficiencies in transferring relevant technical expertise between member divisions of a large corporate structure, and there can be further deficiencies in assuring sponsorship for new technologies which might be relevant to more than one division.

What these points add up to is a significant shift in the organizational focus of UK R&D organization towards *products* and markets, and away from *technologies*. This shift is wholly appropriate at the business unit level, but wholly inappropriate at the level of a collection of businesses within a corporate structure. It has led to a relative under-performance of some firms in identifying, adapting to, and commercializing newer technologies which fall outside the established competencies of individual businesses.

Fortunately, however, there is evidence of some R&D managers and chief executives trying to correct this problem (Coombs and Richards, 1992). The most favoured method for this is the creation of a corporate unit for strategic management of technology with the following functions:

- to analyze the structure of the overall technology portfolio;
- to ensure that a technological competence in one business is known to and available to other potential user businesses in the group;
- to identify technical competencies which straddle businesses and to take steps to strengthen them through 'horizontal' organizational links and through small special budgets;
- to consider the overall technology portfolio and inject an appreciation of this portfolio into the broader strategic management processes of the company.

These principles amount to maintaining a market-driven focus for R&D at business unit level, but treating the sum of the technological competencies in all the business units as a key corporate resource, which needs to be actively managed. There is evidence that the UK companies turning to these policies in the early 90s are in step with the practice of large R&D performing corporations globally, and in step with current thinking in the management literature (see, for example, Roussel et al., 1991).

Tools for Strategic Management of Technology

We have established that for large R&D performing firms, one of the biggest problems in linking technology to strategy is the problem of coordination across diverse businesses. The other major problem is that of actually analyzing the dynamics of technologies and assessing their significance for the businesses in the corporation. To put the problem another way, how can one set targets for R&D and control it in such a way as to maintain its relevance to business and corporate strategies?

For many years the main concepts which R&D managers used in a systematic way to analyze their R&D portfolios were concepts based on the *type of R&D activity*. Thus in the early days the discussions were about concepts such as 'basic', 'blue-sky', 'applied', 'strategic', 'development', 'technical support', etc. Later, particularly following discussion within such bodies as the European Industrial Research Management Association (EIRMA), there has been a shift towards concepts which focus on the *target of the R&D activity*. This has introduced concepts such as R&D for *existing* businesses (subdivided into improved products and new products for existing businesses); and R&D for *new* businesses.

Contemporary approaches to strategic management of technology use yet another set of concepts which do not derive from reclassifying the R&D activity itself, but start from the other end by inserting an appreciation of technological competencies into received techniques for business planning and corporate strategy-making. The central feature of these approaches is as follows: The traditional methods for strategic planning proposed by consultants (often underpinned by the writings of business school academics), tend to focus attention on *the growth potential of particular markets*, and on the *competitive position of the firm in these markets*. The Boston Consulting Group Matrix is the best known of these schemes, but there are many other variants. This two-dimensional approach can be expanded to a three-dimensional one if an explicit analysis of relevant technologies is incorporated. This analysis can deal both with the 'external-to-the-firm' features of the technology such as its 'maturity'; and with internal features such as the firm's competence in the technology; the appropriability of the technology; the extent to which the technology is a major or a minor contributor to the firm's competitive position in a given market; and the extent to which the firm is relevant to a small or a large number of the markets and businesses in the corporate portfolio.

These approaches, (which are well exemplified in the range of techniques described in Dussauge et al., 1992) all depend to a considerable extent on the revitalization of the concept of a *technology audit*. This concept was originally aimed at auditing technology competencies in terms of fitness for purpose and effectiveness (see Twiss, 1980). The newer approaches to audit expand the idea to include the notion of the technology portfolio a set of assets which *create new options* as well as serving existing goals. Clearly, this is an exercise which has to be done at the corporate level as well as at the business unit level, and hence will probably be best coordinated by a corporate technology management unit such as that described earlier.

Conclusion

The main factors which have been shown to shape the interaction between technology and strategy are the following:

1. The extent to which particular product markets are being 'driven' by scientific or technical change, or are based on 'mature' technology.
2. The structure of the firm; in terms of the number and diversity of business units.
3. The corporate 'strategic style' and its emphasis on financial control or more direct intervention in business unit strategy.
4. The presence or absence of a corporate group charged with owning and managing corporate technological assets and promoting their mobility between businesses.
5. The involvement of such a technology group in business strategy and corporate strategy making.
6. The degree of development and use of analytical tools for auditing and assessing technologies, and using that information as an integral part of business strategy formulation.

Note

1. The analysis of trends conducted here is based on research carried out on firms operating in the UK (although many of these firms are multinational and also conduct R&D outside the UK). Other research (see Roussel et al., 1991) suggests that the trends are fairly widespread.

Bibliography

Coombs, R. and Richards, A. (1992) 'Strategic Control of Technology in Diversified Companies with De-Centralised R&D', Manchester School of Management, UMIST,

Working Paper 9215.

Dussauge, P., Hart, S. and Ramanantsoa, B. (1992) *Strategic Technology Management*, Wiley, Chichester.

Freeman, C. (1974) *The Economics of Industrial Innovation*, Penguin, Harmondsworth.

Goold, M. and Campbell, A. (1987) *Strategies and Styles*, Blackwell, Oxford.

Johnson, G. and Scholes, K. (1984) *Exploring Corporate Strategy*, Prentice Hall.

Nelson, R. and Winter, S. (1977) 'In Search of a Useful Theory of Innovation', *Research Policy*, Vol. 6, pp. 36–76.

Pavitt, K. (1984) 'Sectoral Patterns of Technical Change: Towards a Taxonomy and a Theory', *Research Policy*, Vol. 13, pp. 343–74.

Porter, M. (1980) *Competitive Strategy*, Free Press.

Roussell, P., Saad, K. and Erickson, T. (1991) *Third Generation R&D: Managing the Link to Corporate Strategy*, HBS for AD Little.

Twiss, B. (1980) *The Management of Technological Innovation*, Longman, Harlow.

32. Innovation and Manufacturing Strategy

John Bessant

Introduction

One of the key managerial capabilities required in the successful innovating firm is the ability to align the various decisions and actions taken about technological changes so that they support the broader objectives of the business. Thus new products need to be developed in response to a clear understanding of market needs, technological opportunities and internal technological capabilities; as Johne and Snelson (1988) point out, successful product innovation is not a matter of luck but of strategy. By the same token, process innovation – the set of radical changes and incremental improvements which a firm makes to the ways in which it produces its outputs – requires a strategic framework to focus and direct such activity. Manufacturing strategy represents such an organized response to the development of technological competence in the operations and processes of the firm. It is '... a long term plan for developing consistent operations policies and structures and providing focused facilities to achieve limited but absolutely key corporate strategic objectives...' (Skinner, 1983a).

The Strategic Role of Manufacturing

The strategic management literature of the 1970s and 1980s essentially ignored manufacturing and most emphasis was on market and product development strategies. Manufacturing was often cast in a subservient role, expected to follow where marketing or R&D led. For many firms manufacturing was primarily an operational issue, something to be thought about once the overall strategic directions for the business had been set. One indicator of this in some countries (such as the UK) was the relatively low level of participation at board level of manufacturing managers; whereas it would be unthinkable not to have directors responsible for marketing, finance and (usually) R&D, it was common to find the manufacturing function missing. Skinner (1983b) wryly comments on this situation '... to many executives, manufacturing and the production function is a necessary nuisance – it soaks up capital in facilities and inventories, it resists changes in products and schedules, its quality is never as good as it could be and its people are unsophisticated, tedious, detail-oriented and unexciting...'

Yet manufacturing does have a strategic role to play. Ever since the Industrial Revolution changes in the way in which things are made have been a powerful force for economic and social change. Industrial structure is not determined solely by the rise of new industries based on exploiting new products or markets but also by the changes in both price and non-price factors associated with their manufacture. This interplay between product and process innovation has been widely discussed elsewhere (see, for example, Abernathy and Utterback, 1978); although there may be periods in which one form of innovation dominates over the other, they are both of considerable strategic importance. Industry studies bear this out; for example, the car industry began with a product innovation but its real breakthrough as a major industrial force arose out of Ford's development of a new manufacturing system which enabled mass production. Subsequently the history of that industry has involved a series of structural transitions triggered by both product and process change (Altschuler et al., 1984). Similar patterns can be found in electronics (Braun and Macdonald, 1980), chemicals and textiles (Freeman, 1982).

At a national level the same pattern can be discerned; the most powerful recent illustration of the strategic role which manufacturing can play is the Japanese case. From a weak and resource-constrained economic base in the postwar years, Japan has advanced to become the premier industrial power in the world. Although some of this growth has come through product innovation (especially in key targeted market segments) the early foundations were laid in industries like steelmaking and shipbuilding which were essentially 'commodity' products with little scope for major product innovations. Success in these industries was largely due to well-managed and strategically planned manufacturing innovation; the basic principles behind such process innovation were then applied with considerable success in the newer industries such as electronics and motor vehicles. Even the revaluing of the Yen in the 1980s failed to halt Japanese growth; although costs effectively rose the system for manufacturing innovation was able to reduce overall manufacturing costs to retain a competitive advantage.

Given the global nature of manufacturing today, whereby it is possible to buy Japanese cars, German machinery, Swedish hi-fi systems and American computers anywhere in the world, it becomes critically important to develop such manufacturing capability to a level which can compete at a 'world class' level of performance. Protection (via trade and tariff barriers) is at best a short-term option and throughout the world countries are revising their policies towards becoming increasingly open to competition; this has serious long-term strategic implications for the development of manufacturing capability. Government support for manufacturing has increasingly focused on promoting innovation in processes as a way of building national competitive strengths.

Manufacturing is also a strategic issue because of the nature of many of the decisions it involves. Major commitments in terms of location, type and capacity of facilities and characteristics of capital equipment essentially lock a firm in for many years; they cannot be rescinded or changed quickly without severe financial and social penalties. Thus getting the right set of decisions – and right not just for the current conditions but aligned with those anticipated in the future – is a critical long-term strategic issue.

Problems Arising from the Lack of Manufacturing Strategy

The importance of taking a strategic perspective on process innovation within manufacturing is highlighted when we examine cases where it is absent. Whilst process innovation is commonplace, progress can be erratic; improvements across a broad front or occurring randomly may not be sufficient to enable a firm to remain competitive. Simply improving things – or adopting improvements developed elsewhere – is no guarantee that they will develop technological competence or help achieve overall business objectives. In order to contribute, process innovation must be focused and managed towards clear strategic ends.

Examples abound of firms which have adopted expensive and complex innovations to upgrade their processes but which have failed to obtain competitive advantage from this. For example, in recent studies of the adoption of advanced manufacturing technology (AMT) a disturbingly high incidence of failure has been reported in a variety of studies (Bessant, 1991). The consultants A.T. Kearney surveyed 1200 firms in the UK where it is estimated that spending in 1989 on AMT amounted to around £2 billion or twenty per cent of all manufacturing investment; their study concluded that '... benefits on the whole were disappointing, with an achievement of only 70% of planned gains ...' The report goes on to identify the lack of a strategic framework as the most significant factor to account for such failure.

Similar findings emerge from other studies; for example, in chapter 33 Voss comments on the problem of narrow performance measures. Fleck (1988) highlights the problems of firms adopting robots, many of whom treated this technology rather as a fashion accessory; his studies reveal a disturbing lack of planning or foresight in developing suitable skills or adapting work organization to exploit the opportunities offered. Other research on flexible manufacturing systems (FMS) suggests that many firms are preoccupied with the short-term application of such technology and fail to plan adequately for its integration into future manufacturing systems; the result is that they are left with costly 'islands of automation' which cannot exploit the potential benefits of integration with other systems.

Another common issue highlighted by a lack of strategic planning is the failure to take a broad view of technology and to focus solely on the physical components. AMT, by its nature, is a radical technology and its successful implementation requires considerable adaptation and adjustment in the organizational context – in skills, working patterns, organizational structure and coordination, etc. As Dempsey (1982) put it, commenting on the case of flexible manufacturing systems, '... FMS requires a whole new way of thinking...' Thus there is a need for careful consideration of issues of organizational design and development in parallel with the technological component; many reported failures of AMT innovation can be traced back to this gap in strategic thinking.

Problems also occur when major process change is handled in a non-strategic fashion – for example, without the support and commitment of senior management and/or without adequate preparation of the organizational ground before the innovation is introduced. Much interest has been shown by Western firms in adopting innovations such as 'total quality management' which involve a significant change in the underlying philosophy and values of the firm, accompanied by far-reaching changes in structure and operation (Atkinson, 1990). Where such programmes fail (and the incidence of failure is high) it is very often the consequence of viewing this as another operational innovation rather than a major strategic realignment of the manufacturing business.

Whilst these problems may be embarrassing and expensive for the larger firm, they can be a matter of survival for the smaller enterprise. Without a clear strategic framework such firms risk making decisions which, if inappropriate, may tie up scarce capital and production resources and endanger the future of the company. Developing technological competence through process innovation is much more than a shopping expedition for new equipment; it requires the systematic assessment, exploration and development of capabilities so that they support the broader business objectives.

Emerging Importance of Manufacturing Strategy

Partially as a reaction to these problems there has been a growing recognition of the importance of manufacturing and the need to take a strategic approach to decisions about process innovation to ensure a coherent development of relevant technological competence. A number of writers have been influential in this process including Skinner, Hayes, Wheelwright, Clark and Abernathy in the USA, Samson in Australia and Hill and Voss in the UK. Their theories and concepts have been translated into useful methodological frameworks and tools through a number of activities.

Government policy has also shifted to embrace the concept strongly; whereas emphasis in the early 1980s was on providing subsidies for process innovation investments, it now highlights the importance of a strategic framework and provides consultancy support and advice to firms wishing to develop one.

Content of Manufacturing Strategy

Given such interest, it will be useful to explore the typical content of a manufacturing strategy. It usually consists of two key elements – a policy framework which provides a clear context within which decisions about process innovation can be taken, and a set of decisions which lead to actions involving the development of technological competence in manufacturing. The content of such decisions involves the auditing and development of a wide range of resources; an important distinction should be made between what Hayes et al. (1988) call 'structural' and 'infrastructural' elements in manufacturing. Structural elements include the basic building blocks of manufacturing capability – what to make and what to buy-in from outside, the number, location, size, quality, etc. of facilities, the type and capacity of equipment, the basic choice of manufacturing process, the range and extent of support services (power, water, drainage, etc.) and the nature and range of the external supply and distribution networks. Infrastructural elements are, on the other hand, less tangible but by no means less important; they include things like the systems for controlling production, for managing quality, for introducing new products, for maintaining plant and equipment and the overall information flow management system in the factory. They also include the human resource dimensions – the quality, age, experience, flexibility, etc. of the workforce, the way in which work is organized, the ways in which different functions contribution is coordinated, the communication patterns within the factory and the overall command and control infrastructure. Finally the underlying culture – the set of shared beliefs and values which shape the behaviour of people working in the factory – represents a key element in the infrastructure.

Manufacturing strategy involves auditing the relative strengths or weaknesses in each of these areas and then exploring and deciding upon options for their development. Traditionally emphasis has been given to structural decisions – for example, shifting locations to take advantage of lower factor costs, building bigger plants to exploit economies of scale, or upgrading equipment through new investment. However, recent years have seen a marked shift in emphasis as manufacturers have realized the potential in infrastructural innovations; much of the Japanese success in manufacturing appears to have been due to infrastructural change in areas like quality and inventory management rather than in major structural investments.

Links Between Manufacturing and Other Strategic Plans

In order to develop the framework for such decisions it is necessary to have a close understanding of the overall competitive strategy of the business. Which products are being targeted at which markets? What is the pattern of competition and what influences competitiveness? Is the firm to compete on the basis of cost leadership, differentiation or focus? Effective manufacturing strategy requires a clear understanding of these competitive determinants; in this context the concept of 'focused factories' is of critical importance. The focused factory is a term originally developed by Wickham Skinner which involves identifying a clear business segment which manufacturing can then support in a coherent fashion. For example, a business which requires great flexibility and rapid response will require streamlined and flexible manufacturing systems which have the necessary agility; by contrast one which requires low costs may involve a very different configuration.

The important contribution of the focus principle is that it moves away from the idea of the general purpose factory, in which manufacturing would attempt to make whatever marketing requested and to be competitive along several dimensions simultaneously. Different businesses (products/markets) require different kinds of factory performance characteristics and it is unlikely that one factory could meet these different needs. Instead some degree of focus – either by dedicating factories to particular businesses or by grouping resources within a factory into areas or cells dedicated to particular businesses – is advocated. With such focus it becomes possible to align all the operations involved in manufacturing behind the achievement of a clear market objective – and to guide their development and improvement in a coherent fashion.

It is important to note, however, that such focus and targeting need not be static; successful firms develop flexibility within their operations such that they can be refocused quickly to meet different challenges emerging in a turbulent and uncertain environment.

A Process for Strategy Development

The basic process for developing manufacturing strategy is essentially the same as for any other strategic aspect of the business; there are various prescriptions and methodologies available but all share three common elements. Strategy involves auditing current strengths and weaknesses (where are we now?), articulating a future vision (where do we want to get to?) and then developing a staged set of actions which will enable progress towards this vision (how do we get there?).

A typical process is that given below, which is based on Hill (1985) and Gregory and Platts (1988).

(i)   Identify targets for competing (where do we want to get to?)
The beginning of the process is the development of an understanding of the basis of competitiveness with regard to the chosen product or market. In a multi-product or multi-market company it will be necessary to explore the overall portfolio of products and markets and to group these into separate businesses or product families.

Having separated the different product/market families it is necessary to explore systematically what the determinants of competitiveness are in that segment of the market. Hill makes a useful distinction between what he terms 'order qualifying' and 'order winning' factors; the former refer to those factors which must be offered by a manufacturer just to be able to participate in a particular market. Price is the obvious order qualifier – unless a firm is selling at prices more or less in line with the rest of the industry for a particular product, it will be unable to compete. However, an increasing number of other factors – notably quality – are now becoming essential order qualifiers. Order winning factors are then those which determine whether a customer buys from one firm or another – and here the emphasis is shifting away from price and towards a range of non-price factors such as design, customization, delivery speed and delivery reliability.

An indicator of the importance of non-price factors in manufacturing competitiveness can be seen in the results of the regular 'Manufacturing Futures' survey. This explores the concerns and priorities of manufacturers in the USA, Japan and Europe; for the past decade non-price factors have been the major preoccupation. Table 32.1 lists these for 1991.

Table 32.1   Competitive priorities in manufacturing, 1991

Europe	Japan	USA
Conformance quality	Product reliability	Conformance quality
On-time delivery	On-time delivery	On-time delivery
Product reliability	Design change	Product reliability
Performance quality	Conformance quality	Performance quality
Delivery speed	Product customization	Price
'the borderless factory'	'the design factory'	'the value factory'

Source: Miller et al., 1992.

In order to develop competitive manufacturing capabilities, firms need to know what levels of performance the market requires along these dimensions, and what levels are currently being offered by their major competitors. Manufacturing is increasingly a globalized activity – it is possible for a consumer to buy products from anywhere in the world rather than just from a domestic industry – and so the basis of assessing this relative performance must be against the best in the world. In recent years there has been an upsurge of interest in what is termed 'benchmarking' – measuring performance against world class competition as an aid to identifying what areas of manufacturing need upgrading and improving.

(ii) Audit current manufacturing performance

Having established the basis of world class competitiveness the next stage is to assess the contribution of current various manufacturing resources – structure and infrastructure – to achieving this. Such an internal audit requires a careful examination of the ways in which different aspects of manufacturing help or hinder world class performance and an indication of the priorities for change. A key issue here is the question of process choice; as Hayes and Wheelwright (1984) point out, different stages in the evolution of markets require different types of process capability, and getting a good match is an important element in manufacturing strategy. At an early stage in the product life cycle the requirement is for low volume high flexibility arrangements to accommodate the high rate of product innovation and to respond to a market in which non-price factor competition is likely to predominate. As the product matures so emphasis shifts to volume manufacturing and price competition – which requires different process arrangements.

The process of exploring and assessing internal capability, especially in the infrastructural areas, is one which can provide valuable opportunities for learning and development. There is a danger that manufacturing strategy becomes synonymous with the replacement of equipment and facilities; this is to ignore the many intangible elements in the manufacturing system and the considerable levels of tacit and accumulated knowhow which are present in the infrastructure.

(iii) Explore options for innovation

This next stage involves an extensive search process, trying to find appropriate mechanisms for developing the manufacturing capability by enhancing areas of strength and improving areas of weakness. Success here is associated with wide-ranging exploration of opportunities; although the natural tendency is to view manufacturing innovation in terms of investment in new plant and equipment, much can be achieved through reorganization and through sustained incremental innovation.

Wide search also includes looking at alternative options for reaching the same goal; for example, flexibility is a key strategic objective and can be achieved through investments in various forms of advanced manufacturing technology, such as flexible manufacturing systems. However, flexibility can also be achieved through reorganization, changes in work organization, redeployment of machinery and people, etc. and such innovations may represent less expensive and more organizationally acceptable solutions. By the same token, change need not always be radical; although rapid improvements in key performance areas are important the potential of sustained incremental improvement in areas like quality and flexibility should not be underestimated.

(iv) Forecasting
Developing strategy is difficult because it does not take place in a static context but in one which is rapidly changing along several dimensions. Thus it is important to include some form of forecasting, scanning the future for emerging threats and opportunities in technological, economic, political, social and other spheres which may affect some of the assumptions or decisions being considered. For example, the emergence of new markets, competitors or technologies could all have a major impact on the shape and relevance of the manufacturing strategy being developed.

(v) Implementation
Effective strategy needs to include careful consideration of the question of implementation of change. As Voss points out in chapter 33, implementation is often neglected in innovation studies yet it is often the site of the most serious difficulties. Part of the implementation problem arises from a lack of attention at the strategic planning stage to dimensions of the proposed change – for example, ensuring suitable development of both infrastructure and structural elements. Since many process innovations represent major changes in 'the way we do things round here' the question of managing cultural change and overcoming resistance to innovation needs to be addressed, and planning for such organizational development is an important element in manufacturing strategy formulation. To some extent implementation difficulties can be reduced through involving those likely to be affected by the change in some of the strategy formulation and debate.

(vi) Review and repeat as the critical stage in the process
To be effective, strategy must be seen as a process of learning and development. The most important outcome is not the plan itself but the improved awareness and understanding of the context in which the firm is operating and the relative state of its technological competence in process terms. Thus it is important to institutionalize the process of strategy review and development, and to diffuse this widely within the organization. Even where strategic decisions turn out to be wrong it is also important to capture

the learning from this (rather than try and bury the evidence of past mistakes) to enable improved decision-making in the future. For this reason the practice of post-innovation auditing is recommended (although rarely practised in most firms).

Strategy as Competence Building

The fundamental point of manufacturing strategy, in common with other elements of corporate strategy, is the need to take a systematic and coherent approach to auditing and developing technological competence to support the way in which the operations of the business are carried out. There is a need to undertake the development and improvement of technological competence within the context of a clearly articulated strategic framework, if the benefits of the innovations introduced are to be fully captured and exploited.

This raises the issue of managerial as well as technological capabilities. According to Nelson and Winter (1982), successful innovation is associated with organization-specific routines – behaviour patterns around searching, decision-making, etc. which the firm learns over time and through trial and error. It is thus of considerable interest to try and identify those routines which appear to be associated with successful performance and which may be transferred to or learned by other firms. One such routine is likely to be the ability to recognize, assess and develop technological competence in an organized and coherent fashion – that is, a process of manufacturing strategy development.

Such a capability may enable firms even with limited internal resources to maintain a high level of successful process innovation, whilst its absence may mean that well-resourced large firms consistently fail in their process innovation behaviour. The transferability of this routine will depend on a better understanding of not only the process of strategy formulation but also that of the underlying 'technical progressiveness' of managers responsible for its development and implementation.

As Pavitt points out, in chapter 29, technological competence is a cumulative process which develops over many years and is often highly firm-specific. Much of what confers an advantage is in tacit form and represents the product of an extended learning process; arguably developing, implementing and reviewing manufacturing strategy along the lines described above represents an important mechanism for such learning to take place.

Bibliography

Abernathy, W. (1977) *The Productivity Dilemma: Roadblock to Innovation in the Automobile Industry*, Johns Hopkins, University Press, Baltimore.

Abernathy, W. and Utterback, J. (1978) 'Patterns of Industrial Innovation', *Technology Review*, June/July, pp. 40–47.

Altschuler, D. et al. (1984) *The Future of the Automobile*, MIT Press, Cambridge, Massachusetts.

Atkinson, P. (1990) *Total Quality Management: Creating Culture Change*, IFS Publications, Kempston.

Bessant, J. (1991) *Managing Advanced Manufacturing Technology: The Challenge of the Fifth Wave*, NCC-Blackwell, Oxford/Manchester.

Bessant, J. and Rush, H. (1993) 'Government Support of Manufacturing Innovations: Two Country Level Case Studies', *I.E.E.E. Transactions on Engineering Management*, Vol. 40, Issue 1, pp. 79–91.

Bolwijn, P. (1990) 'Manufacturing in the 1990s – Productivity, Flexibility and Innovation', *Long Range Planning*, Vol. 23, No. 4, pp. 69–76.

Braun, E. and Macdonald, S. (1980) *Revolution in Miniature*, Cambridge University Press, Cambridge.

Dempsey, P. (1982) 'New Corporate Perspectives on FMS', 2nd International Conference on Flexible Manufacturing Systems, IFS Publications, London

Ettlie, J. (1988) *Taking Charge of Manufacturing*, Jossey-Bass, San Francisco.

Fleck, J. (1988) 'Innofusion or diffusation?', Working Paper, Department of Business Studies, University of Edinburgh.

Freeman, C. (1982) *The Economics of Industrial Innovation*, 2nd ed., Frances Pinter, London.

Gregory, M. and Platts, K. (1988) *Competitive Manufacturing*, Department of Trade and Industry, London.

Hayes, R. and Wheelwright, S. (1984) *Restoring Our Competitive Edge: Competing Through Manufacturing*, John Wiley, New York.

Hayes, R., Wheelwright, S. and Clark, K. (1988) *Dynamic Manufacturing: Creating the Learning Organization*, Free Press, New York.

Hill, T. (1985) *Manufacturing Strategy*, Macmillan, London.

Jantsch, E. (1980) *Technological Forecasting in Perspective*, OECD, Paris.

Johne, A. and Snelson, P. (1988) 'Successful New Product Development', Blackwell, Oxford.

Kearney, A.T. (1989) *Computer-Integrated Manufacturing – Competitive Advantage or Technological Dead-End?*, ATK Consultants, London.

Macbeth, D. (1989) *Strategic Manufacturing*, IFS Publications Report.

Miller, J. et al. (1992) *Benchmarking Global Operations*, Irwin, Homewood, Ill.

Nelson, R. and Winter, S. (1982) *An Evolutionary Theory of Economic Change*, Harvard University Press, Cambridge, Massachusetts.

P.A. Consultants (1989) *Manufacturing into the Late 1990s*, Department of Trade and Industry Report, London.

Samson, D. (1991) *Manufacturing and Operations Strategy*, Prentice-Hall, Sydney.

Schroeder, D. and Robinson, A. (1991) 'America's Most Successful Export to Japan – Continuous Improvement Programmes', *Sloan Management Review*, Vol. 32, No. 3, pp. 67–81.

Skinner, W. (1974) 'The Focused Factory', *Harvard Business Review*, May/June, pp. 113–21.

Skinner, W. (1978) *Manufacturing in the Corporate Strategy*, John Wiley, New York.

Skinner, W. (1983a) 'Operations Strategy: Past Perspective and Future Opportunity', 1st Annual Winter Conference of the Operations Management Association, Operations Management Association, San Francisco.

Skinner, W. (1983b) *Operations Technology: Blind Spot in Strategic Management*, Harvard Business School, Cambridge, Massachusetts.

Slack, N. (1992) *The Manufacturing Advantage: Achieving Competitive Manufacturing Operations*, Mercury, London.

Smith, S. and Tranfield, D. (1990) *Managing Change*, IFS Publications, Kempston.

Vickery, G. and Blau, E. (1989) *Government Policies and the Diffusion of Microelectronics*, Organisation for Economic Cooperation and Development, Paris.

Voss, C. (1986) 'Implementation of Advanced Manufacturing Technology', in Voss C. (ed.) *Managing Advanced Manufacturing Technology*, IFS Publications, Kempston.

33. Implementation of Manufacturing Innovations

C.A. Voss

Implementation of new technology in manufacturing has long been recognized as problematical. An innovation is often considered successful if it reaches the point of being sold. However, in many cases success in use is not guaranteed; it requires successful implementation for the innovation to be truly valuable. Indeed, for many innovations one person's product is another person's process. For the adopting firm, the successful implementation of innovation can be critical to obtaining commercial benefits. It is an underlying proposition of this chapter that successful implementation of innovation is a major contributory factor to the competitiveness of firms and thus nations.

Defining Implementation

It has been argued (Voss, 1988a) that the study and literature of innovation and the diffusion of technological innovation has generally split into two separate areas. On the one hand has been the study of the process of innovation. In the definition of innovation given by Utterback (1971), the innovation process is complete when the innovation has been successfully developed. The second area is the study of the diffusion and adoption of innovations. The process of diffusion starts with the first adoption of an innovation, and examines the subsequent spread.

Though this separation of research traditions naturally arises from the different processes being studied there are reasons for examining the interface further. If we examine the adoption of *process* innovations we find that many issues fall between these two traditions. There is much evidence that a *process* innovation can succeed in one attempt at adoption and fail in another. Once a new process technology has completed the innovation process (that is, first successful use), success or failure in subsequent applications can be considered as *implementation* success or failure. Unlike innovation success, many of the activities and conditions that influence implementation success take place in the *adopting* organization rather than the innovating organization. Indeed the study of implementation might be called more precisely the study of the process of adoption of innovations.

Success and Failure of Implementation

A study of the literature on process innovations and implementation will reveal that success (or failure), when not defined in purely subjective terms, is stated in *technical* terms: it works, it meets specification, productivity has been improved, uptime is increased. Even when there are *business* objectives, rarely is success measured in terms of meeting these objectives. Organizations (and researchers) would seem to believe that they have successfully implemented new operating technology when two conditions are met. First, when all the bugs have been ironed out and it is working technically. Second, when the operation is working reliably and there is little downtime, and/or the new technology has a high utilization rate. One can put forward the proposition that in getting the technology to work only half the battle has been won. If we take the example of Advanced Manufacturing Technology (AMT), the prime motivation for installing AMT must be to increase the competitiveness of the organization (see, for example, Hayes and Wheelwright, 1984; and Rosenbloom and Vossaghi, 1983). The improvements in competitiveness promised by advanced manufacturing technology come not just from increased labour and machine productivity, but increased responsiveness, quality, flexibility and reduced inventories, lead time, etc.

Full success can only be considered to have been realized if the benefits being looked for are realized, and ideally so in the market place through increased competitiveness. Technical success is a necessary but not sufficient condition for realizing the full benefits of advanced manufacturing technology. We can propose two levels of success in implementation:

(1)   technical success;
(2)   realization of benefits (business success).

Both measures of success can be seen both in absolute terms and in terms of a company's prior objectives or expectations. Tyre and Orlikowski (1992) have examined the fit between technical success and expectation, prior to implementation. They found that expectations were often adjusted to fit actual experience.

There is considerable empirical evidence that product and process innovation does not necessarily lead to success in use, Voss (1984), Tidd (1991), Chew et al. (1991). Of greater importance are the findings of various studies that, although implemented to the point of technical success, many process innovations fail to reach business success Voss (1988b), Jaikumar (1986).

Jaikumar (1986) studied thirty-five flexible manufacturing systems (FMS) in the US, and sixty in Japan. FMS are installed to deliver flexibility. Success can therefore be seen, at least in part, as the ability to realize flexibility. He found that US systems 'show an astonishing lack of flexibility, and in may cases perform worse than the technology that they replace'.

In conclusion, process innovations are not always successful in conventional, technical terms, and even when successful on this basis, often fail to achieve the capability and wider ranging benefits required of them, 'business' success.

The Process of Implementation – a Model

Implementation of innovations can be defined as 'the process that leads to the successful adoption of an innovation of new technology'. A commonly held view of implementation is that it encompasses the actions from purchase and installation to the successful use of the technology. This is a narrow view of the process of implementation. For example, it can be argued that many important determinants of implementation success are actions and conditions prior to purchase or installation, for example strategic planning, technical planning, workforce consultation. In addition one can postulate that the antecedents – for example, the context of the firm, its skills, existing technology, managerial attitudes, etc. – will have a significant impact on the process of implementation. The process of implementation starts has its roots in the firm's background and history, and includes both pre-installation and post-installation factors.

Voss (1988b) has proposed a simple life-cycle model of the process of implementation of process technology in terms of a sequential process consisting of three phases. The first phase includes those factors prior to installation that may have a positive or negative impact on the final outcome. This phase can be called pre-installation. It finishes with the evaluation and go ahead. The second phase is that of installation and commissioning. This can be said to be complete when the process is working successfully; that is, when the technical and utilization targets are being met consistently. The third phase takes place post-commissioning and can be called consolidation. In this phase further technical improvement is likely to take place as will further activities needed to move beyond technical success to business success. The dividing line between phases 2 and 3 is diffuse, as is the end of phase 3. It could be argued that phase 3 should not end as an effective company but should be continually seeking ways of improving its process. This model is represented diagrammatically in Figure 33.1.

Implementation can be considered a process and there is much to be learned from research into various aspects of that process. In the technology management area Pavitt (1990) has stated:

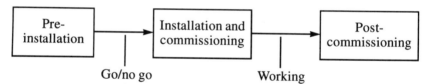

Figure 33.1 Life-cycle model of the process of implementation

A major criticism of 'content' view of technological strategy is that it neglects the context within which – and the process whereby – technological strategies are generated, chosen and implemented. These processes are bound to involve more than the technical function.

The last point is a theme repeated in many reviews of process-based approaches. Processes cross both functional and disciplinary boundaries.

Pre-Installation Phase

This phase takes place prior to the decision to purchase. It includes many activities that can be considered crucial to the subsequent success of the implementation process. Bessant in chapter 32 points to the importance of a strategic approach to manufacturing. The impact of different strategies in implementation can be illustrated by the work of Tidd (1991). He studied the adoption of assembly robots in Japan and the UK (see Table 33.1). He found, in contrast to prior expectations about Japan and technology, that the robots installed in the UK were more complex and technically sophisticated than those in Japan. However, despite this seeming technical advantage, the performance of robot assembly lines was far superior in Japan than in the UK. He proposed that the reasons for this are the differences in strategies between firms in the two countries.

   This is a remarkably similar set of conclusions to those of Jaikumar (1986). He too found that the technology choice in the West was more sophisticated but less effective. US process innovations were highly sophisticated but because of their complexity were very difficult to implement effectively. In addition the pressure to start up the systems on time resulted in the systems not using their potential capability. In contrast, the Japanese systems were designed more simply and as a result were more reliable and more highly utilized. Despite their relative simplicity they were managed more flexibly. Indeed, their simplicity gave greater reliability, and enabled the maximum potential of the systems to be realized. Strategy is clearly an important factor in subsequent implementation performance.

Table 33.1 Assembly robots in UK and Japan

	UK	Japan
Primary motives for development and adoption	To increase productivity and improve quality through the elimination of direct labour	To improve flexibility of production but continue to reduce costs through the elimination of waste
Technological trajectory pursued	Complex, sophisticated technology consistent with long-term goal of 'CIM', a computer systems approach	Relatively simple proven technology with continued reliance on operators, essentially a production engineering approach
Manufacturing	Reduction in diversity of production to facilitate further automation and computer integration	Flexible, but low cost production
Source of most significant developments	Specialist suppliers essentially 'technology push'	Major uses essentially 'demand pull'

Source: Tidd, 1991.

Evaluation

The evaluation stage as part of the implementation process has been studied by Winch and Voss (1991). They examined a set of manufacturing innovations. They found that despite common technology across cases, applicability and ease of use of new processes was very context dependent, with these dependencies not being known to the firms at the time of evaluation. Evaluation was being undertaken in a complex technical environment, both with much choice and with a rapidly changing technical capability, which resulted in many of the initial choices becoming obsolete during the implementation and/or early use of the technology implementation process. In most cases, even at this early stage, there was an 'implementation champion' who could be credited with pushing the implementation through. The early adopters tended to evaluate on a narrow basis such as drawing office productivity. However, later adopters used a much wider, more business-driven set of criteria. One of the things that emerged through the longitudinal nature of this study was the existence of both strong industry and firm dynamics at the evaluation stage of the implementation process, reflecting technological development and diffusion of information and organizational learning.

Installation and Commissioning Phase

A wide range of factors have been found to be associated with effective installation and commissioning. Table 33.2 shows some factors identified by Horte and Lindberg (1991), in Sweden and from work elsewhere.

Table 33.2   Factors   associated   with   successful   installation   and   commissioning

Incremental stepwise installation
Workforce engagement
Relations to technology vendors
Operator training
Few technology vendors
Project management
Workforce participation
Project champion
Start-up management
Cross-functional implementation teams

These factors have been found in many studies of implementation, including those mentioned previously.

Training
As Warner argues in chapter 28, comparative empirical research has demonstrated the importance of employee training for the effective exploitation of technology.

Organization
The use of cross-functional teams has been seen as a particular requirement for successful installation (and implementation in general). Many innovations involve a number of different technologies. They have to be implemented in an existing production environment and draw upon the expertise of various equipment suppliers.

Many other organizational aspects have been identified with successful implementation at the installation phase (and throughout the process). Leonard-Barton (1992), identifies the presence of champions, and the high status of the project team.

Relationships with suppliers
The importance of good user/supplier links discussed by Shaw in chapter 21 for product innovation applies equally to process innovation. There is evidence that the implementation of CAD/CAM in UK companies has been adversely affected by poorly managed relationships with technology suppliers.

Consolidation Phase

The consolidation phase encompasses all activities that take place after the new process is installed and operating to specification. In characterizing the implementation strategies of Japanese companies in comparison with US installers of FMS, Jaikumar (1986) found many of the major differences took place post-installation. In US companies, once the system was up and running, the installation team was disbanded and left to work on other projects. In Japanese companies, they remained in place and *after* installation. Even after installation, they continually made changes and as a result learning was maximized. This learning was translated into mastery of processes and productivity enhancement. It can be argued that the post-installation phase is too often neglected, yet it is a vital part of the innovation and implementation process.

Leonard-Barton (1988) has developed a model that brings together the organization and technical changes that take place during implementation, and the processes by which they occur. She views implementation as a process of mutual adaptation of technology and organization. When an innovation is first used, there are likely to be a number of misalignments between organization and technology and between both of these and the objectives of the innovation. To overcome these there should be a series of cycles of adaptation of both the technology and the user environment. Implementation thus becomes a continuous process of mutual adaptation.

In a study of implementation of processes, Voss (1988b) observed that those companies that had made some form of matching organizational change had achieved some element of business success, and those that had not done so had not move beyond technical success.

The neglect of organizational issues in the implementation process has been identified as one reason for under-achievement of the anticipated benefits from such technologies. This finding is perhaps not surprising, given that managers are often faced with short deadlines in which to prove satisfactorily the investment in technologies. However, unlike many technologies that are isolated in their operation (what Kaplinsky (1984) terms 'intra-activity technologies'), the new integrated technologies have, if benefits are to be realized, a more widespread effect on the organization and management of the technology. Figure 33.2 reflects this need; typically, technologies are implemented with a disproportional emphasis placed on technical integration (along line A–T). However, attention should now be directed towards organization issues (a shift to the right).

Managerial Control

Kaplan (1983) has argued that management control systems no longer recognize the priorities and needs of manufacturing systems. This is

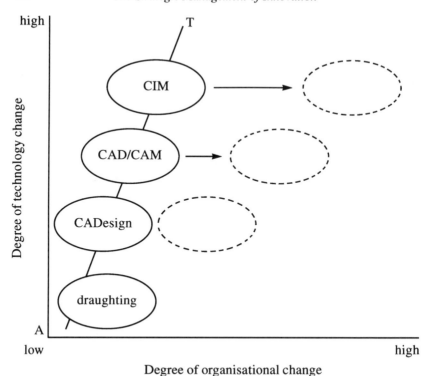

Figure 33.2 Effect of new integrated technologies

particularly true as we move from innovations whose sole objectives are cost reduction and maximization of output to those innovations in processes whose objectives include flexibility, cycle time reduction and quality.

Winch and Voss (1991) found that the performance of CAD/CAM systems tended to be bound up in the departments that used it. Usually these were cost centres. This led to a tension between manufacturing and engineering, and extra effort was needed in engineering to gain benefits in manufacturing without reward for engineering. This could be a barrier to achievement of business benefits across the company. The environment of the company was found to play an important role in this phase with activities such as collaborative ventures and takeovers changing policies and objectives during implementation. In addition, increasing pressures for reduced product lead times and smaller batch sizes also changed the requirements for the systems during their implementation.

Jaikumar's (1984) research on FMS identified a mismatch between the objectives of the technology and the managerial control systems as a major reason behind the problems with gaining effective innovation.

Although the evidence in this chapter has been derived from technological innovation in processes, much process innovation is procedural and involves new management processes. A good example is the approach of just-in-time (JIT) or 'lean' production. It has been found that lean production implementation is highly sensitive to performance measurement. Lean production approaches emphasize linked production and group production, where it is essential to produce in exact sequence. However, individual incentive schemes put pressure on the workforce to do what is easiest and pays the biggest bonus. They thus conflict with the procedures of lean production and this leads to poor implementation.

Technology Change

The dynamic nature of technology change can be found as much in implementation of innovations as it is with the innovation process itself. As stated in Leonard-Barton's framework, we should expect to see both large cycles of change and small cycles of technology adaptation during implementation. The latter are consistent with incremental innovations – a phenomenon well documented in the innovation literature. There is growing evidence of the former happening as part of the innovation and implementation process (Lindberg, 1990; Winch and Voss, 1991).

Implementation, the Model Revisited

An increasingly important view of management is that from a learning perspective (Senge, 1991). Pavitt (1990) states that 'the ability to learn from experience – whether internally (learning by doing) or from suppliers, customers, and competitors (learning by using, learning by failing, reverse engineering) – is of major importance in the management of innovation'. Chew et al. (1991) puts forward the management of learning as one of the key ways in which implementation problems can be overcome. He proposes that companies should learn in many ways at once including vicarious learning (from others), simulation, prototyping and on-line learning. He sees learning as being embodied in the know-how and know-why of technical knowledge and organizational knowledge. Dodgson sees learning as dissolving the sharp distinction between the 'content' and 'process' schools of strategy.

Leonard-Barton (1991) reports on a case study of a factory that has a very successful implementation record through, in great part, effective learning, and develops the concept of the factory as a learning laboratory. It can be argued that improvement in an organization's ability to learn will greatly increase its ability to implement process innovation successfully.

Rothwell's Fifth Generation Innovation Process described in chapter 4 analyzes the iterative nature of new product development. The importance

Table 33.3   Factors influencing success and failure in implementing process technology

Implementation Phase	Pre-Installation	Installation and Commissioning	Consolidation
Success Measure		Technical	Business
Factors influencing success and failure of process implementation	Identifying and forecasting capabilities of the technology	Broadly based project teams	Keeping teams in place after commissioning
	Strategy – Business *and* technical objectives for process technology	Effective support from the supplier	Mutual adaptation of organization and technology
	Broadly based evaluation team and implementation champion	Implementation champion	Appropriate managerial control
	Matching complexity of technology to the firm's ability to handle it	Managing industrial relations	
		Training and availability of skills	
	Long-term evaluation of the full system, not short-term evaluation of parts of it		

Source: Voss (1992).

414

of learning, the complexity of many innovations particularly in manufacturing, the importance of cycles of adaptation all lead to a view that models of implementation should also be iterative (Ettlie, 1980).

Conclusions, Towards Successful Processes

This chapter has set out to develop a framework for looking at innovation and implementation of processes. It has illustrated this with data from a number of sources which are summarized in Table 33.3. Any such framework has limited use if it cannot be used to help companies manage new process technology. Part of the research described above has been adapted for use by practitioners through a workbook on managing organization integration (Twigg and Voss, 1991). In reviewing the above, Voss (1992) identified a number of guidelines and practical steps emerge. As above, these are listed in the sequence of the three-stage model used earlier.

Pre-installation
Important considerations at the installation phase are as follows:

- Innovation of processes should not just be technically led, but to be most effective should support both the organization's strategic direction and the characteristics of the products to be produced.
- The complexity, uncertainty etc. of the technology should match the knowledge and capability for the firm to handle it, as well as the business needs.
- Evaluation should be based on the full system to be developed, not on parts of it.

Installation and commissioning
Installation requirements include:

- effective interaction with suppliers;
- the use of appropriately composed cross-functional teams;
- appropriate labour skills and availability.

Consolidation
Innovation and implementation do not stop at installation. Effective management of the post-installation consolidation phase can be crucial in obtaining success.

- Technical and user environment adaptations and modifications should be actively sought out.
- The implementation team should stay with the innovation until the main adaptations and learning have taken place.

- Appropriate organizational change should be actively sought out. Change should reflect the impact of the innovation on roles, communications flows and tasks.
- Performance measurements for those implementing and managing processes should match the objectives of the innovation.

The successful innovation of new processes is critical for the continued success of companies. Even when process technology is available off the shelf, the ability to implement that process well, to get the best out of it, to continually learn and improve, and above all to realize the full business benefits will gain competitive advantage for a company. Managing the innovation and implementation of new processes is increasingly a key task for companies.

Acknowledgements

We acknowledge the support of the SERC and the ESRC/SERC joint committee who funded the LBS research quoted in this chapter.

Bibliography

Chakravarthy and Doz, Y. (1992) 'Strategy Process Research: Focusing on Corporate Self-Renewal', *Strategic Management Journal*, Vol. 13, pp. 5–24.

Chew, W. et al. (1991) 'Beating Murphy's Law', *Sloan Management Review*, Spring 1991, Vol. 32, No. 3.

Ettlie, J.E. (1980) 'Adequacy of Stage Models for Decisions on Adoption of Innovation', *Administrative Science Quarterly*, Vol. 46.

Ettlie, J. (1982) *The Implementation of Programmable Manufacturing Technology*, Working Paper, De Paul University, March.

Hage, J. (1980), *Theories of Organisations*, New York, Wiley.

Hill, T. (1993) *Manufacturing Strategy*, London, Macmillan.

Hayes, R. and Wheelwright, S.C. (1984) *Restoring Our Competitive Edge, Competing through Manufacturing*, New York, Wiley.

Horte, S.A. and Lindberg, P. (1991) 'Implementation of Advanced Manufacturing Technologies, Swedish FMS Experience', *International Journal of Human Factors in Manufacturing*, Vol. 1, No. 1.

Hrebiniak, L.G. and Joyce, W.F. (1984) *Implementing Strategy*, Harlow, Longman.

Jaikumar, R. (1984) *Flexible Manufacturing Systems: a Managerial Perspective*, Working Paper, Harvard Business School, January.

Jaikumar, R. (1986) 'Postindustrial Manufacturing', *Harvard Business Review*, Nov./Dec., pp. 69–76.

Kaplan, R.S. (1983) 'Measuring Manufacturing Performance: A New Challenge for Accounting Research', *The Accounting Review*, LVII (4).

Kaplinsky, R. (1984) *Automation*, Harlow, Longman.

Leonard-Barton, D. (1988) 'Implementation as Mutual Adaptation of Technology and Organisation', *Research Policy*, Vol. 17, pp. 251–67.

Leonard-Barton, D. (1991) *The Factory as a Learning Laboratory,* Harvard Business School Working Paper, No. 92-023.

Leonard-Barton, D. (1992) 'Core Capabilities and Core Rigidities', *Strategic Management Journal,* Vol. 13, pp. 111–25.

Lindberg, P. (1990) 'Strategic Manufacturing, a Pro-Active Approach', *International Journal of Operations and Production Management,* Vol. 10, No. 2, pp. 94–106.

Pavitt, K. (1990) 'What We Know About the Strategic Management of Technology', *California Management Review,* Vol. 32, No. 3, Spring 1990, pp. 17–26.

Pavitt, K. (1991) 'Key Characteristics of the Large Innovating Firm', *British Journal of Management,* Vol. 2, pp. 41–50.

Rosenbloom, S.R. and Vossaghi, H. (1983) *Factory Automation in the US,* Research Report Series, Manufacturing Roundtable, Boston University School of Management, March.

Russell, V. (1991) unpublished research documents, London Business School.

Senge, P. (1991) *The Fifth Discipline,* New York, Doubleday.

Tidd, J. (1991) *Flexible Manufacturing Technologies and International Competitiveness,* London, Pinter.

Twigg, D. and Voss, C.A. (1991) *Managing Integration, a Workbook for Implementing Organisational Change in CAD/CAM and Simultaneous Engineering,* London, Chapman and Hall.

Tyre, M.J. and Orlikowski, W.J. (1992) *Windows of Opportunity,* Working Paper No. 3309, Sloan School for Management, MIT.

Utterback, J.M. (1971) 'The Process of Technological Innovations Within the Firm', *Academy of Management Journal,* March, pp. 75–88.

Voss, C.A. (1984) 'Multiple Independent Invention and the Process of Technological Innovations', *Technovation 2,* pp. 169–84.

Voss, C.A. (1986) 'Implementing Manufacturing Technology, a Manufacturing Strategy Approach', *International Journal for Operations and Production Management,* Vol. 6, No. 4, pp. 16–26.

Voss, C.A. (1988a) 'Implementing, a Key Issue in Manufacturing Technology, the Need for a Field of Study', *Research Policy,* Vol. 17, pp. 53–63.

Voss, C.A. (1988b) 'Success and Failure in Advanced Manufacturing Technology', *International Journal of Technology Management,* Vol. 3, No. 3, pp. 285–97.

Voss, C.A. (1992) 'Successful Innovation and Implementation of New Processes', *Business Strategy Review.*

Winch, G. and Twigg D. (1989) 'The Implementation of Integrating Innovations: The Case of CAD/CAM', paper presented at British Academy of Management Conference, Manchester, September.

Winch, G. and Voss, C.A. (1991) *The Process of Implementation, the Evaluation Stage,* Operations Management Working Paper, London Business School.

Womack, J.P., Jones, D. and Roos, D. (1990) *The Machine That Changed the World,* Macmillan.

PART 5

Future Challenges of Innovation in a Global
Perspective

34. Environmental Issues and Innovation

Jim Skea

Introduction

Since the latter part of the 1980s, environmental issues have become a major concern for many industries. Consumer preferences have shifted in favour of 'environmentally friendly' goods while the need for compliance with new environmental regulations eats into capital budgets. Both product and process innovation are an inevitable component of the industrial response.

An earlier proliferation of environmental controls and incentives in the 1970s was viewed with concern by many segments of industry. While government and environmentalists could talk of the benefits of 'technology-forcing', it became a received wisdom in the business community that 'over-regulation' slowed down productivity growth and diverted R&D from profitable business innovations.

The current interest in environmental issues is marked by a more sophisticated view of the interplay between regulation, economic activity and technical change. Companies with strong R&D capabilities and the capacity to bring innovative products and processes to the market have realized that environmental performance can enhance market performance if tighter regulatory standards are anticipated.

Companies are playing a less passive role with respect to the regulatory process, recognizing that the precise form of environmental controls can shape market advantage. Equally, regulators are keen to forge informal alliances with industry in order to facilitate the introduction of new controls.

The internationalization of environmental issues continues apace. Whereas past environmental problems have been experienced at the local or perhaps regional levels, more recent problems such as acid rain and climate change have impacts on a continental or even global scale. At the same time, regulatory solutions developed at the national level have created differential cost structures and have become a factor influencing international trade. The resulting motivation for harmonized environmental controls has been a particularly important driving force for greater regulation within the European Community.

The UN Conference on Environment and Development (UNCED) held in Rio de Janeiro in June 1992 symbolizes this growing internationalization of environmental issues. This intergovernmental conference, attended also by business groups and environmental organizations, considered how environmentally sustainable economic development could be promoted. One of the principal outputs was *Agenda 21,* a detailed action programme addressing problems such as technological development, technology transfer from North to South and the vital role which business, particularly transnational corporations, has to play.

A final theme which marks recent environmental developments is the growing interest in instruments other than administrative standards (sometimes known as 'command and control' regulation). Among the 'market-based instruments' currently being considered are a carbon/energy tax proposed by the European Commission and a tradeable sulphur dioxide emission permits scheme in the United States. At the same time there is a growing use of non-coercive administrative procedures such as eco-labelling and eco-auditing. These provide for independent certification procedures for products and company operations.

The remainder of this chapter addresses in more detail the impact which these trends are having on innovative activity. First, however, the lessons from environmental controls already in place are reviewed.

Experience with Environmental Controls

There is widespread evidence that government regulation is probably the single most important factor leading to improvements in the environmental performance of companies (Good, 1991; Rothwell, 1992). However, regulation is the source of intrinsic tensions between government and industry. The 1970s drive towards higher standards of environmental protection was substantially weakened by assertions that regulations had reduced economic growth, slowed productivity improvements and diverted R&D resources away from business innovation. Although systematic research has shown that these assertions were exaggerated (Rothwell and Zegveld, 1981; Rothwell, 1992), they have proved politically potent during periods of slow economic growth.

Nevertheless, the way in which specific regulations have been developed and specified has created problems stemming from:

- unrealistic objectives;
- lack of clarity in the specification of requirements;
- unrealistic compliance schedules;
- lack of a clear scientific basis for regulations;

- inadequate consultation between regulators and industry; and
- conflicts between the activities of different regulatory agencies.

These lessons have now been learned. Most sections of industry accept the need for environmental regulation (though still opposing vigorously some specific measures) while governments and international bodies acknowledge the need for strong industry participation in the formulation of environmental controls (Commission of the European Communities, 1992).

Business, the Environment and Trade: *Agenda 21*

There is a growing realization in the business community that high standards of environmental performance are not inconsistent with economic performance. At the same time, government and regulators began to appreciate that industry, while the source of pollution and waste, is also the agent through which cleaner production technologies could be applied and diffused. *Agenda 21*, one of the main outputs of the UNCED, crystallizes many of the strands of emerging thinking about the relationship between governments and industry with respect to environmental performance.

Agenda 21 proposes two programmes relating to business and industry – one on cleaner production, the other on responsible entrepreneurship. The cleaner production programme aims to increase the efficiency with which natural resources are utilized, by moving towards processes which generate less waste and increasing the recycling and re-use of process wastes. Cleaner production technologies are viewed as being distinct from 'clean-up' processes which are applied end-of-pipe and simply transfer pollution from one environmental medium to another.

While industry must play a central role, governments can encourage technological cooperation between different companies as well as stimulate education, training and awareness activities. Several international organizations also conduct relevant activities. For example, the International Chamber of Commerce (ICC) has produced a Business Charter on Sustainable Development to which companies are invited to subscribe.

Within the responsible entrepreneurship programme, *Agenda 21* advocates: responsible and ethical management of products and processes from the point of view of health, safety and environmental aspects; increased self-regulation through codes, charter and initiatives; increased R&D in environmentally-sound technology; the development of environmental management systems; and, for transnational corporations, the establishment of worldwide corporate policies on sustainable development and arrangements for access to environmentally sound technologies, at no extra charge to affiliates operating in developing countries.

There are obstacles to the take-up of these practices by small and medium-sized enterprises (SMEs) which have limited financial resources and little operational flexibility. Most SMEs operate in a reactive mode with respect to environmental pressures. Acknowledging this, *Agenda 21* suggests that larger business should 'consider partnership schemes ... to help facilitate the exchange of experience in managerial skills, market development and technological knowhow'. *Agenda 21* also notes that regulatory measures and economic incentives have a key role to play in encouraging the establishment and operation of sustainably managed enterprises.

A cynical view would be that *Agenda 21* contains many laudable aspirations but has little to offer in the way of practical measures. Nevertheless, the process by which *Agenda 21* was negotiated and agreed has stimulated awareness in the business community and has fostered links between industry, governments and international organizations.

Trade questions are central to the internationalization of the environmental debate. Differential environmental standards can be viewed as a non-tariff barrier to trade. Consequently, there are strong incentives for the harmonization of standards, notably in the European Community in the context of the Single Market. In some countries, particularly those in the Mediterranean region, harmonization may have been a more powerful force for higher environmental standards than domestic political concerns. The question of environmental regulation has also surfaced in negotiations on GATT and the North America Free Trade Association.

The harmonization process has led to the concept of *first mover advantage*. Countries which pre-emptively set high environmental standards can establish strong domestic markets for new technologies which may be used as a springboard for international trade when the standards are taken up elsewhere. Business in Germany and Japan has certainly benefited from this phenomenon.

The Role of Regulation

Regulatory culture varies from one country to another, and from one agency to another within specific countries, while environmental regulations can take many forms (Weale, O'Riordan and Kramme, 1991). The relationship between regulation and innovation is complex and is influenced by: the type of regulatory instrument employed; the process by which regulations are developed; and implementation procedures.

Regulatory instruments
A broad distinction may be drawn between administrative regulation ('command and control') and market-based regulatory instruments. Most past regulation has involved standard setting by public authorities though

interest in market instruments has been growing (Department of the Environment, 1990).

Administrative standards may specify either the technology to be used or emissions performance. Technology-based regulations specify the design characteristics of the equipment to be used while performance standards leave the choice of technology to the plant operator. It is now widely acknowledged that technology-based standards may inhibit technical change because they provide no incentive for industry to generate innovative solutions (OECD, 1985). With a performance standard, industry has an incentive to develop new processes which can comply at lower cost. In the US, regulators have specified performance standards which could not be met by technologies commercially available. This 'technology-forcing' certainly led to a rapid improvement of pollution abatement technology, but exacerbated industry-regulator tensions.

In practice, the line between technology and performance standards is blurred. Most actual regulations, including those issued under the new system of Integrated Pollution Control (IPC) in the UK, contain elements of both approaches. Although concepts such as 'best available technology' (BAT) are embodied in legislation, detailed regulations often specify performance standards such as emission limits. The use of umbrella concepts such as BAT introduces a dynamic element into the regulatory process. Performance standards can easily be revised from time to time to take account of improvements in control technology.

Many economists (e.g. Pearce et al., 1989) have criticized the use of administrative controls. It is argued that industry will have no incentives to seek innovative technologies once a performance standard has been attained. Equally, industry is better placed than regulators to assess cost-effective levels of pollution abatement as part of its normal commercial decisions. For these reasons, the greater use of market-based instruments has been advocated.

The two main types of market instruments are taxes and tradeable emission permits. Taxes applied to residual emissions coming from a process are relatively easy to administer and provide a continuing incentive to cut pollution. An example is the carbon/energy tax recently proposed by the European Commission.

With taxes, the regulator sets the 'cost' of emissions and industry through its investment and operational decisions, determines the resulting overall level of pollution. With a tradeable emission permit, the regulator distributes permits for a fixed amount of pollution to plant operators. Those with low abatement costs may find it cost-effective to sell their emission permits and install control technology. Those with high abatement costs can buy permits and continue to pollute. In principle, this should result in the lowest overall compliance cost. Tradeable permits are appropriate only for ubiquitous pollutants or for sources in a limited geographical area. A recent example is the comprehensive national trading programme for sulphur dioxide established under the US Clean Air Act Amendments 1990 (Lock et al., 1991).

Tradeable permits may encourage the application of existing technology to existing sources in a cost-effective way, but they do not offer strong incentives for innovation. Once the emissions quota is attained, there are no further incentives to develop new technology. There is also a need to ensure that existing firms do not use tradeable permits as a device for controlling entry to a market, and that large emitters do not use their market power to manipulate prices.

Regulatory processes

The means by which regulatory instruments are developed is at least as important as the form which they take. Experience has shown that industry should be involved in the regulatory process from the earliest possible stage. From the regulators' point of view, early consultation will minimize delays in introducing new controls. From industry's point of view, participation promises realistic targets and compliance deadlines.

The European Community, which has been particularly susceptible to regulatory delay, is explicitly moving towards a participatory approach rather than the use of proscriptive measures (Commission of the European Communities, 1992). In the UK, all new regulations developed under the 1990 Environmental Protection Act by HM Inspectorate of Pollution (HMIP) and local authorities involve consultation with individual companies and trade associations.

The consultative process has risks as well as advantages. 'Cosy' relationships between industry and the regulator may develop. Equally, dominant firms may be able to influence market structure and ease of entry, thus using the regulatory process to reinforce their technological capabilities and competitive advantage. In the long term this may not favour the introduction of more innovative technological solutions.

Implementation

A well-designed regulation is futile unless there is an effective compliance regime. Technology is having a profound effect on the implementation of environmental regulation. In the past, compliance has often been checked on a hit-or-miss basis by inspectors making infrequent visits to check on pollution levels.

Improvements in technology for monitoring, measuring and recording emissions, coupled with significant reductions in unit costs, have opened up a range of new possibilities. It is now possible to install automatic continuous monitoring equipment, while information technology enables the storage of enormous amount of data. In some more sophisticated regulatory contexts it is possible to transmit emission data to the regulatory agency in real time, enabling instant compliance checks to be made.

Under European Community law and under the UK's 1990 Environmental Protection Act it is now obligatory to place monitoring information on public registers. This enables environmental groups such as Greenpeace to monitor the performance of companies and initiate private prosecutions. As a result of changes in technology and attitude, symbolized by the willingness of courts to impose high fines, compliance pressures on companies are now higher than ever.

Voluntary Action: Means and Incentives

Apart from regulation, a wider range of social forces, notably 'green consumerism', is now bearing down on industry. Consumer pressure has forced companies operating in sensitive markets, such as the manufacture of soap powders, to ensure that actual environmental performance bears out the claims which are made in advertising copy.

The need to substantiate advertising claims has led to pressures for the introduction of eco-labelling schemes which will provide independent verification of the environmental virtues of any particular product. Germany has run a 'Blue Angel' labelling scheme for some time, while the European Community is on the point of introducing an eco-labelling scheme which will harmonize procedures across all member states. Washing machines are an early candidate for inclusion in the new scheme with certification to be based on consumption of water, detergent and electricity. The eco-labelling scheme will be voluntary but, nevertheless, is likely to encourage further innovation in processes and products. Companies with established standards of environmental performance have been instrumental in getting the new scheme launched, seeing competitive advantage in the process.

Related to eco-labelling are environmental auditing and environmental management systems. Generally, an audit may be regarded as a once-off check on performance based on physical criteria (e.g. emissions, waste disposal). An environmental management system is a set of management procedures designed to ensure that environmental performance is satisfactory and that it can be maintained or improved.

A new British Standard on environmental management systems (BS 7750), the first of its kind in the world, is now undergoing a set of sector by sector tests. It is anticipated that companies will use the new standard as an element of their marketing strategy. Downstream companies may demand that their suppliers be certificated to BS 7750 in order to justify environmental claims made to their own customers. The combination of these various voluntary procedures – eco-labelling and environmental management systems – could provide a complex web of incentives for companies to maintain and improve their environmental performance. The threat that voluntary certification procedures might some day become compulsory provides an added political uncertainty which firms may wish to address.

In addition to certification procedures, other voluntary devices are under discussion. Debates about climate change in the European Community have led to the idea of industrial sectors entering into 'voluntary' agreements about the rate at which carbon dioxide emissions might be reduced. These are perhaps less voluntary than might at first appear since they could be used as conditions for exemption for the application of a carbon/energy tax. Nevertheless, they demonstrate the growing importance of regulator-industry discussions as a way of advancing environmental policy.

The Environmental Protection Industry

One company's cost is another's business opportunity. The environmental protection industry comprises a wide range of activities, including the manufacture of:

- measuring and monitoring equipment;
- end-of-pipe and effluent treatment technologies;
- cleaner or integrated production technologies;
- recycling technology; and
- waste disposal technology.

In addition to manufacturing activity, a wide range of environmental consultancy and technical services are available to companies wishing to achieve regulatory compliance or improve their environmental management practices.

It has been estimated that the highly fragmented market for environmental technology in the UK accounts for between 1 and 2 per cent of GDP (ACOST, 1992). Cleaner process technologies are highly specific to the industry in which they will be used. Competences are usually located in traditional suppliers of equipment, though new market leaders are emerging in specific areas such as air pollution control.

The demand side of the environmental protection market depends almost entirely on the intensity of regulatory activity which is subject to great political uncertainty. While there may be a substantial market for new processes in the years immediately following a new regulation, demand quickly falls back to replacement levels. This instability in the environmental protection market makes it unattractive to many companies.

Governments therefore need to adopt an integrated approach to industrial and environmental policy if a continued improvement in environmental quality and a healthy environmental protection industry is to be maintained. A smooth, incremental approach to environmental regulation, involving consultations with both directly affected industry and equipment suppliers, coupled with well understood compliance schedules, has several benefits. Not only does it reduce uncertainties for regulated industries, but it establishes a more secure market in which equipment manufacturers and consultants can market their services.

Government can also influence the *supply* side of the market through the promotion of cleaner technologies. At the national level, this activity is important in order to: (a) prevent markets created by new environmental regulations from being dominated by foreign suppliers; and (b) create export opportunities.

The means by which environmental technologies may be promoted are illustrated by the activities of the Environment Unit of the UK Department of Trade and Industry. A combination of R&D support, funding for demonstration projects and more general information and dissemination activities makes up its portfolio of activities. The Environmental Technology Innovation Scheme (ETIS) supports collaborative research projects in four areas: cleaner technologies; recycling; effluent treatment and disposal; and environmental monitoring. The Department's Environmental Management Options Scheme (DEMOS) provides capital supports for projects which will demonstrate available technology to a wider range of companies. The more general activities include the organization of regional seminars in collaboration with the Confederation of British Industry (CBI).

Future Developments

Although there are signs that political interest in environmental issues may be waning following UNCED in June 1992, a wide range of environmental regulation in the pipeline holds implications for industrial activity throughout the 1990s. New regulatory initiatives are still likely, driven by a combination of regulatory momentum, a desire on the part of some companies to derive competitive advantage from the environment, and a drive towards harmonization at the international level.

Consequently, companies need to take account of environmental concerns in developing their technological strategies. Those who adopt a wait-and-see attitude could be forced to implement expensive clean-up technologies which push up their costs and erode their competitive position. Meanwhile, governments have the challenge of establishing industrial and environmental policies which are mutually reinforcing. They must aim to protect both the global commons and the environment at the national level, while fostering strong domestic capabilities in the environmental protection field. The perceived risks of *not* meeting these challenges are sufficient by themselves to ensure further developments in the standards and techniques of environmental protection.

Bibliography

Advisory Committee on Science and Technology (ACOST) (1992) *Cleaner Technology*, Cabinet Office, HMSO, London.

Ausubel, J.H. and Sladovich, H.E. (eds) (1989) *Technology and Environment*, National Academy Press, Washington DC.

British Standards Institution (1992) *BS 7550: Specification for Environmental Management Systems*, Milton Keynes.

Commission of the European Communities (1992) *Towards Sustainability: A European Community Programme of Policy and Action in Relation to the Environment and Sustainable Development*, COM(92) 23 final, Vol. II, Brussels, 27 March.

Cramer, J. and Zegveld, W.C.L. (1991) 'The Future Role of Technology in Environmental Management', *Futures*, June, pp. 451–68.

Department of the Environment (1990) *This Common Inheritance: Britain's Environmental Strategy*, Cm 322, HMSO, London, September.

ECOTEC Research and Consulting (1991) *The Impact of Environmental Management on Skills and Jobs*, Birmingham.

Elkington, J. (1990) *The Green Wave: A Report on the 1990 Greenworld Survey*, SustainAbility/British Gas, London.

Good, B. (1991) *Industry and the Environment: A Strategic Overview*, Centre for the Exploitation of Science and Technology, London.

Groenewegen, P. and Vergragt, P. (1991) 'Environmental Issues as Threats and Opportunities for Technological Innovation', *Technology Analysis and Strategic Management*, Vol. 3, No. 1, pp. 43–55.

International Chamber of Commerce (1991) *Business Charter on Sustainable Development*, Geneva.

Irwin, A. and Vergragt, P. (1989) 'Re-thinking the Relationship between Environmental Regulation and Industrial Innovation', *Technology Analysis and Strategic Management*, Vol. 1, No. 1, pp. 57–70.

Kemp, R. and Soete, L. (1992) 'The Greening of Technological Progress: An Evolutionary Perspective', *Futures*, Vol. 24, No. 5, June, pp. 437–57.

Lock, T. et al. (eds) (1991) *The New Clean Air Act: Compliance and Opportunity*, Public Utility Reports Inc., Arlington, VA.

National Audit Office, (1991) *Control and Monitoring of Pollution: Review of the Pollution Inspectorate*, Cm 637, HMSO, London, July.

Organisation for Economic Cooperation and Development (1985) *Environmental Policy and Technical Change*, OECD, Paris.

Organisation for Economic Cooperation and Development (1989) *Economic Instruments for Environmental Protection*, OECD, Paris.

PA Consulting Group (1991) *Cleaner Technology in the UK*, Department of Trade and Industry, HMSO.

Pearce, D., Markandya, A. and Barbier, E.B. (1989) *Blueprint for a Green Economy*, Earthscan, London.

Recherche Développement International (1990) 'The Environmental Services Industry', in *Panorama of EC Industry 1990*, Commission of the European Communities, Brussels.

Rothwell, R. (1992) 'Industrial Innovation and Government Environmental Regulation: Some Lessons from the Past', *Technovation*, Vol. 12, No. 7, pp. 447–58.

Rothwell, R. and Zegveld, W. (1981) *Industrial Innovation and Public Policy*, Pinter, London.

Sema Group Management Industries (1990) 'Industrial Competitiveness and the

Environment', in *Panorama of EC Industry 1990*, Commission of the European Communities, Brussels.

Weale, A., O'Riordan, T. and Kramme, L. (1991) *Controlling Pollution in the Round: Change and Choice in Environmental Regulation in Britain and Germany*, Anglo-German Foundation, London.

W.S. Atkins Management Consultants (1991) *Markets for Environmental Monitoring Instrumentation*, Department of Trade and Industry, HMSO, London.

35. The Global Innovatory Challenge Across the Twenty-First Century

Thomas G. Whiston

Introduction

This chapter outlines the innovatory challenges to be faced in the 21st century. Comparatively early in that century the global population will have increased by more than 3,000 million individuals. Much of this pressure will be in the underdeveloped regions of the world. Ancillary demographic factors (life expectancy, heightened expectations regarding standards of living) accentuate the total resource demand/needs. Meanwhile north-south economic gaps continue to grow; science and technology (S&T) knowledge, experience and major directions of S&T trajectories are concentrated in OECD nations.

The global consequences (environmental, social, world security and stability) of maintaining such a gap could be tragic. Alternatively a universal homogenization of the dominant life style of the north across the whole world population poses its own threats and difficulties. Resolution of this dilemma or paradox demands the most creative social, political, economic and S&T innovations in all sectors. S&T has to be viewed in that wider context.

The innovatory challenge is twofold: to introduce, *in a global setting,* new institutional arrangements regarding S&T transfer, knowledge transfer and wider distribution, whilst also commonly seeking alternative socially and environmentally sustainable systems and organizational structures. Eighty percent of the world has yet to fully develop its physical and human resource infrastructure to levels compatible with adequate provision levels of the basic necessities of life. This provides both opportunity and room for manoeuvre. Successful achievement offers the possibility of population equilibrium and intergenerational sustainability.

The Innovatory Challenge

The challenges of industrial innovation throughout the next century are fourfold:

(i)   To provide the *basic* necessities of life to *all* members of the planet;
(ii)   To seek, encourage, and further, social and environmentally *sustainable* methods of organization, production, manufacture and usage of materials, resources and services;
(iii)   To develop organizational, socio-economic and political structures which encourage *full* and *meaningful employment* for all individuals commensurate with capability and potential;
(iv)   To develop the most effective and efficient methods of *education*, training and human resource development, accessible to all.

These four fundamental requirements need to be viewed within a global context. They are dynamic, interdependent, interactive in both nature and requirement. They go beyond present perspectives of national, inter-national or inter-regional competitiveness. They will demand the most fundamental innovations with regard to economic ideology, socio-economic frameworks, institutional structures, technology and knowledge transfer mechanisms and procedures, governmental-industry relationships and legislative frameworks, social and environmental accountability, international collaborative research, technology policies and environmental assessment procedures.

The requirements set an agenda for government, industry, consumers, academia, research institutes – in every walk of life, but most especially in areas of

- Agricultural systems and food production
- Water usage
- Energy systems
- Transport systems
- Shelter, housing and urban development and design
- Health delivery
- Communication systems
- Consumer durable design and usage
- Educational delivery systems
- Land-use, desert reclamation, oceanic-bed use, afforestation programmes

In many of these areas the dominant concern in relation to the need to provide the basic necessities to all members of the planet whilst simul-taneously satisfying within a planetary (as well as local) context sustainable means of production and usage, implies that within such areas as agricul-ture, water, energy, transport, shelter, communication, consumer durables, health, education and land-use, (a) entirely new, alternative systems design will be required; (b) as knowledge develops it will be transferred and communicated as widely as possible; (c) local indigenous infrastructures will be encouraged as rapidly as possible in order to modify, adapt, absorb, utilize this universal or generic knowledge-bed of information toward local need, special circumstance and the wider global equation; (d) every area under consideration addresses as fully as possible a wide fabric of so-called 'externalities' – i.e. all the wider social, public, environmental and ecological costs so often ignored by the normal economic equation.

Dependent upon how robust and meaningful is our planetary concept of the term 'sustainability', a full addressing of the 'externalities' which derive from any systems-usage will ultimately imply not only that the first-order 'physical' or environmental downside effects are constantly considered but that our analytic mode of thinking concerning design, usage, production, will have to extend into a much wider and deeper 'externality framework': namely, social, socio-economic, ecological, human, attitudinal, inter-generational effects and consequences.

The above requirements are extremely radical in nature. They imply the most enormous changes in the way that the world conducts its mode of living; its present values and dominant trajectories; and its contemporary patterns of geo-economic structures, international dependencies, economic frameworks and socio-political systems. Why is such a radical agenda called for? Is it either necessary, appropriate or viable? What conditions might we expect across the 21st century if contemporary patterns of life, manufacturing systems, international trade (and underpinning economic structures) are continued unattenuated? Is there detailed quantitative data (and analytical accompaniment) available by which to judge the call for change? How quickly must all this be done? What intermediate stepping-stones might be envisaged, what institutional innovations, what new research agenda, what immediate tasks for industry, government and trading-blocs need to be considered? Which major national and international bodies need to encourage further debate, analysis, monitoring, evaluation, assessment, co-ordination and stimulatory actions? Also, in an increasingly market-oriented society, with deregulation, the decline of state interventionism and a reduced faith in the value of centralized planning, must one consider a more dominant force: namely, the increasing power of the private sector, of multinational conglomerates with their marketing, economic and consumer ethic?

Thus, if government, the public sector, is not the most powerful agency; if in historical terms to the accompaniment of a return to socio-liberalism, the private sector in all its manifestations of international concentration and transregional unaccountability is the most powerful agency, then what counter-balance of innovations will be necessary in terms of regulatory frameworks, legislative enforcement, socio-economic incentives, in order to better synergize private and public interest?

It is to some of these questions that we now turn. The primary task, however, concerns the need to justify radical change in the next century.

Why Is This Challenge So Necessary?

At present we live in a world with a population of approximately 5½ billion inhabitants. Over the past couple of centuries enormous, marvellous, economic progress has been achieved. This is in no small measure due to scientific and technological advance, increases in productivity (by several orders of magnitude in some sectors), innovatory development and partial diffusion of the same.

At the same time, however, the fruits of that advance have, to a large degree, been restricted to about 20 per cent of the world's population – variously categorized as the 'north', OECD nations or industrially advanced nations. To some extent other nations (the 'four tigers' of S.E. Asia, Mexico, Brazil, India) have made impressive strides; the former USSR achieved, though it is presently compromised, much economic might; China would appear to be making good economic progress. The older terms of 'First', 'Second' and 'Third' Worlds leave much to be desired, and are partly discredited. 'Energy-rich' nations gain temporary respite against debilitating debt burden and can, if wise, finance the development of infrastructure. It is still true to say, therefore, that we live in a divided world.

The underlying reasons for this division are economic, political, cultural and historical. The untying of the historical Gordian knot which has led to this state of affairs is a major global task. Whether this can be achieved quickly and effectively through reliance upon market forces, or requires the most careful interventionist and socially purposive, directive policies, is a continuing dilemma. This dilemma, if unresolved, contains the seeds of historical tragedy on a scale almost too awful to contemplate. The perspective taken here is that because of the immediacy and scale of this 'global dilemma', the urgent need is for interventionist, purposive policies. To await the beginnings of tragedy – with its attendant human and social upheaval and loss; the possibility of military instability; the continuation of global as well as regional environmental degradation possibly beyond the point of return – is not a robust strategy for providing the basis of a new global response. Thus, the innovatory task is with us now. The 21st century is merely the stage upon which the various acts have to be explored; the social and technical creativity encouraged; a new political and economic framework elaborated; a new agenda for industry and commerce laid down; a new academia institutionalized.

The planetary division takes two major forms but possesses numerous dimensions. How do these compromise the planet, its people and its future? The essence is as follows: 20 per cent of the world's population in the richer industrialized nations consume perhaps 80 per cent of the world's physical and energy resources. These same nations carry out approximately 95 per cent of the world's R&D; they encapsulate much of the world's tacit technical and organizational knowledge and capability; in many ways they set and control the present global economic agenda, of which IMF and World Bank perspectives, GATT and commodity-pricing are only some of the facets. In many ways they both set the dominant trajectories of what we might call the S&T agenda and establish dominant life-styles to be sought after. Setting the S&T agenda implies that such forefront areas as biotechnology, information technology, new materials, advances in transport and energy-systems, pharmaceuticals, and communications technology attend to the rich industrialized regions' needs. All of that, and much more, is the first form of division.

The second form of division occurs *within* the so-called less developed nations. It is characterized by the term 'dualism'. A minority of individuals (5, 10, perhaps 20 per cent in some nations) are in the 'formal' economy. To a large degree they are urbanized, industrialized, in part 'Westernized'. The vast remainder may be characterized as a rural and disenfranchised population. Even when not living in absolute squalor their circumstances are unenviable. Sixty-four per cent of the world's population – 80 per cent of 80 per cent – may be so characterized. In several ways these two forms of division – inter- and intra-national – create a form of global social poverty trap.

Many would go no further and argue from a moral standpoint that the agenda for the 21st century is therefore established: to alleviate suffering; to remove institutional obstacles which militate against change on a world setting; to introduce programmes whereby science, technology, managerial and organizational skills lead to vastly improved circumstances for the impoverished majority. But such a 'remedy', were it available, is most probably insufficient in itself. Even if it were sufficient, several other component factors need to be recognized which increase the urgency of the global innovatory challenge for the 21st century, challenges which include:

(i) *Population increase and demographic factors:* As noted earlier, by the year 2010 it is expected that the world population will have increased by three thousand million people over the present five and a half billion, leading to an *increased* planetary demand in terms of food, resources and environment. Even if this were to take longer, in a progressively culturally-shrinking planet, an individual's enhanced *expectations and demands* reinforce the overall problem.

(ii) *Lifestyle and environment:* Most nations and communities increasingly and understandably seek the material standards enjoyed by the West. At present the 20 per cent minority accounts for an enormous material and energy-intensive 'appetite'. Contemporary fears regarding global warming and ozone-layer depletion, for example, thus become accentuated as such a life-style becomes ever more universal. In addition, if poorer economies cannot afford so-called 'best practice' technology; or if local infrastructure compromises the development of less material and energy-intensive systems, then ultimately the local despoilation extends into a wider global environmental dilemma. Technology transfer and knowledge transfer limitations, economic and trade barriers, 'enforced' reliance on the part of many poorer nations upon essentially single-crop commodity provision systems – all interweave into this 'global dilemma'. This forces us, therefore, to examine in more detail the third debilitating component factor in a global setting, namely the 'Integration-Exclusion' factor.

(iii) *The integration-exclusion factor:* There is much talk of a developing 'global economy': an economic society which stretches across the planet. In some senses this now exists in terms of economic interdependency, of industries that cross national borders, of multinational corporations seeking global markets, and in more sophisticated terms with respect to so-called 'glocalisation'. But there are fundamental distortions in the overall pattern.

On the one hand we may speak, more meaningfully, of a partly-integrated world (OECD or Triadic, for example) which concentrates knowledge, power and expertise, which controls R&D and dominates in defining technological pathways; and on the other hand a technically and informationally much excluded larger world community. The current economic framework, terms of trade, socio-economic conditions, barriers to knowledge and technical transfer *maintain* that division.

More recently, new patterns of international comparative advantage have only served to amplify the problem. Patterns of economic debt, concentration of production of high value added products, reduced commodity-prices further maintain the structure.

For the 'excluded', demographic pressure only offsets the economic growth gains which have been so hard won. In particular, this leads to economic limitations with respect to significant expansion of human-resource programmes and thereby ensures a lack of development of human skills commensurate with need. Integration and exclusion are therefore maintained in both an intra- and inter-national sense.

Under such conditions the present or nascent 'global economy' is neither equitable nor environmentally friendly. Most certainly, as presently structured, it does not satisfy the wider planetary need. Such a division and structure is not conducive to global sustainable development, nor the satisfaction of the needs of the vast majority of the planet's present, let alone future, population.

If we attempt to combine all of the above into a coherent picture what does it suggest for the 21st century? We see an increasing population, of thousands of millions, in just those nations who can least afford it. We see an interlinked global environmental dilemma as material, energy, food and basic human living demands increase. We see that those nations most needful of scientific and technological advance are compromised, 'locked out' by the lack of economic and institutional knowledge, S&T concentration, and inappropriate S&T trajectories which are not of their own making. We see lack of local infrastructure in poorer nations as a limiting rate-determining step with regard to the absorption and modification of existent and future knowledge. We see, in short, a global communication gap, a transmission problem, a coding and decoding problem (see Figure 35.1) at both ends of the north-south divide.

What Is To Be Done?

The need, in local, regional and global terms is to improve transmission in S&T communication and infrastructural development and also, through international collaboration to seek new S&T trajectories in all the sectors referred to earlier. Most especially these would include new energy and transport systems, improved food production and agricultural systems, greatly improved urban structures, adequate provision of fresh water, pollution minimization, widest diffusion of low cost best practice communication and control systems, and much more accessible, efficient and relevant education and training systems and new patterns of employment in a world of 8–10 billion as the 21st century progresses.

Without such international *mutuality* of concern and involvement the very concept of a globally sustainable, environmentally friendly planet becomes an empty dream, mere rhetoric. This is because, ultimately, it must be recognized that global environmental sustainability is predicated upon global social stability and global economic equitability. A divided, partially integrated much excluded world does not permit or encourage such global social stability: war and environmental degradation are its inheritance. An informationally and scientifically partitioned world does not allow sufficient technological or innovatory response to the local regional or ultimately wider global need. Problems of global warming, acid rain, ozone depletion, oceanic despoilation, nuclear accident and ecological losses know no international boundaries. Local inadequacy therefore has global consequences.

The prime innovatory need, therefore, if our earlier four fundamental requirements are to be addressed, is for removal of the Integration-Exclusion barrier in order to provide a basis for the innovatory technological tasks themselves. But there is one other requirement: we are not saying here that it is merely a matter of improved 'diffusion mechanisms', of 'learning about tacit knowledge', of poorer nations 'absorbing' or having better access to all that the richer industrialized nations now know. Much of that, certainly, where needed. But the global need across the 21st century is more fundamental. The global innovatory task is for *all* regions, rich and poor, developed and underdeveloped, to seek, collaboratively a new, 'green' techno-economic paradigm that permits sustainability. This is not just a technical requirement. It is social, economic and cultural in form. Its

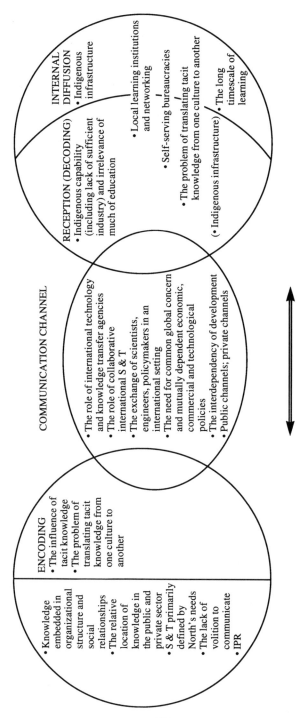

NORTH

SOUTH

COMMUNICATION CHANNEL

ENCODING
• The influence of tacit knowledge
• The problem of translating tacit knowledge from one culture to another

• Knowledge embedded in organizational structure and social relationships
• The relative location of knowledge in the public and private sector
• S & T primarily defined by North's needs
• The lack of volition to communicate
• IPR

• The role of international technology and knowledge transfer agencies
• The role of collaborative international S & T
• The exchange of scientists, engineers, policymakers in an international setting
• The need for common global concern and mutually dependent economic, commercial and technological policies
• The interdependency of development
• Public channels; private channels

RECEPTION (DECODING)
• Indigenous capability (including lack of sufficient industry) and irrelevance of much of education

INTERNAL DIFFUSION
• Indigenous infrastructure

• Local learning institutions and networking
• Self-serving bureaucracies
• The problem of translating tacit knowledge from one culture to another
• The long timescale of learning

(• Indigenous infrastructure)

2 WAY COMMUNICATION

Figure 35.1 Global communication for sustainable development: factors influencing knowledge and technology transfer

tentacles stretch across all facets of life: educational, leisure, social, commercial. It is not just about saving forests and oceans, porpoises and whales – it is about understanding the complex socio-ecological equation where there is no such thing as an 'externality'. Thus there is a task for the north to change; for the south to move toward alternative socially and environmentally sustainable systems and organizational structures; and, indeed, for the very terms 'north' and 'south' to become obsolete. That is the real task of the 21st century. It is not a challenge, but a necessity.

With its achievement comes the possibility of population equilibrium; best use of land, sea and air; energy, transport and communication always viewed as interdependent social and environmental *systems*. It is to be suspicious of single-factor solutions, and requires a new environmental accountancy which goes well beyond our present economic calculus – a total systems costing which forever seeks the 'next externality'.

Can all this be expected, or achieved, by reliance upon so called 'free-market economics'? The trick will be to see that there is no such thing as a 'free' market, no such thing as a free global dinner; no future in paternalistic aid programmes predicated upon distorted economic injustice and environmental insult. The outstanding requirement is to search for a new dialogue, a new era, the recognition of past failure as well as success. Some of the ingredients of such a recipe are briefly indicated below.

In institutional and organizational terms this implies the development of massive international collaborative S&T programmes; mutual involvement of 'north' and 'south'; greatly enhanced international technology transfer agencies and procedures; new frameworks for environmental assessment; enormous resources allocated to a search for environmentally friendly energy, transport, urban development, agricultural systems; massive commitment to enhanced human-resource development programmes, more socially relevant training programmes; an international search for a new global economic framework – a new, workable, equitable 'Bretton Woods'; and the removal of institutional barriers to knowledge exchange.

Within a framework of such *institutional* innovation the specific technical, scientific innovations can then occur that must reach not a selective but a universal audience. Out of that 'sustainability', planetary hope, a less morally-bankrupt society may emerge. Technology, innovation, efficiency, scientific understanding are not ends in themselves; they are to serve the global society at large and permit the foundation of intergenerational progress.

Bibliography

Barnett, A. (1992) *Knowledge Transfer and Developing Countries,* report to the EC-
    FAST on Global Perspective 2010, Science Policy Research Unit, University of

Sussex, Brighton.

Bookchin, M. (1982) *The Ecology of Freedom: The Emergence and Dissolution of Hierarchy,* Cheshire Books, Palo Alto, California.

The Brandt Commission (1983) *Common Crisis – North-South: Cooperation for World Recovery,* The Brandt Commission, Pan Books, London.

Brotchie, J., Batty, M., Hall, P. and Newton, P. (eds) (1991) *Cities of the 21st Century: New Technologies and Spatial Systems,* Longman, Cheshire, Harlow.

Brown, L.R. (1992) *State of the World: 1992,* A Worldwatch Institute Report on Progress Toward a Sustainable Society, Norton, New York.

Burrows, B., Mayne, A. and Newburg, P. (1991) *Into the 21st Century: A Handbook for a Sustainable Future,* Adamantine Press, Twickenham.

Cassiolato, J.E. (1992) *High Technologies and Developing Countries: Trade Related Problems and Specificities of their Diffusion to the Third World,* report to EC-FAST on Global Perspective 2010, SPRU, University of Sussex, Brighton.

Chase-Dunn, C. (1990) *Global Formation: Structures of the World Economy,* Basil Blackwell, Oxford.

Freeman, C. and Hagedoorn, J. (1992) *Globalisation of Technology,* MERIT, Maastricht, The Netherlands, report to EC-FAST on Global Perspective 2010.

Freeman, C. and Jahoda, M. (eds) (1979) *World Futures: The Great Debate,* Martin Robertson, Oxford.

Garrett, M., Barney, G.O., Hommel, J.M. and Barney, K.R. (eds) (1991) *Studies for the 21st Century,* Institute for 21st Century Studies 'Future-Oriented Studies' Programme, UNESCO.

Gaudin, T. (1990) *2100 Récit du Prochain Siècle,* Editions Payot, Paris.

Hirsch, F. (1977) *Social Limits to Growth,* Routledge and Kegan Paul, London.

Leggett, J. (ed.) (1990) *Global Warming: the Greenpeace Report,* Oxford University Press, Oxford.

Meadows, D.H., Meadows, D.L. and Randers, J. (1992) *Beyond The Limits: Global Collapse or a Sustainable Future,* Earthscan, London.

MITI (1988) *Trends and Future Tasks in Industrial Technology: Developing Innovative Technologies to Support the 21st Century and Contributing to the International Community,* Summary of the White Paper on Technology, Ministry of International Trade and Industry, Japan.

Pearce, D. (ed.) (1991) *Blueprint 2: Greening the World Economy,* Earthscan, London.

Reich, R.B. (1991) *The Work of Nations: Preparing Ourselves For 21st-Century Capitalism,* Alfred A Knopf, New York.

The Research and Development Society (1987) *R&D for the 21st Century: An Analysis of Trends Affecting Strategies for Industrial Innovation,* Cranfield Press, Cranfield, Bedford.

Salam, M.A. (1991) *Science, Technology and Science Education in the Development of the South,* Third World Academy of Sciences, May 1991, prepared for the last meeting of the South Commission and for the meeting of the UN Economic and Social Council (ECOSOC) Geneva, July 1991.

Wenk, E. (1979) *Margins for Survival: Overcoming Political Limits in Steering Technology,* Pergamon, Oxford.

Whiston, T.G. (1992) *Global Perspective 2010: Tasks for Science and Technology – A Synthesis Report on the EC-Fast Programme,* SPRU, University of Sussex, Brighton.

Whiston, T.G. (1990) *The Global Environment: Technical Fix or Radical Change?* Social Audit Paper No. 2., ENED, University of Sussex, Brighton.

Whiston, T.G. (1988) 'The Coordination of Education Policies and Plans with those for

Science and Technology: Western Europe and Developing Countries', *Bulletin of the International Bureau of Education*, No. 247, pp. 1–144 (Complete Issue).

Whiston, T.G. (1987) *The Training and Circumstances of the Engineer on the Twenty First Century*, report to the Fellowship of Engineering, March 1987, SPRU, University of Sussex, Brighton.

Whiston, T.G. (1991) 'Forecasting the World's Problems. The Last Empire: The Corporatisation of Society and the Diminution of Self', *Futures*, Vol. 23, No. 2, pp. 163–78.

Whiston, T.G. (ed.) (1979) *The Uses and Abuses of Forecasting*, Macmillan, London.

World Bank, *World Development Report 1990: Poverty*, Oxford University Press, Oxford.

World Bank, *World Development Report 1991: The Challenge of Development*, Oxford University Press, Oxford.

Index